DIMENSIONS OF NORMATIVITY

Dimensions of Normativity

NEW ESSAYS ON METAETHICS AND JURISPRUDENCE

Edited by David Plunkett
Scott J. Shapiro
and Kevin Toh

OXFORD
UNIVERSITY PRESS

OXFORD
UNIVERSITY PRESS

Oxford University Press is a department of the University of Oxford. It furthers the University's objective of excellence in research, scholarship, and education by publishing worldwide. Oxford is a registered trademark of Oxford University Press in the UK and certain other countries.

Published in the United States of America by Oxford University Press
198 Madison Avenue, New York, NY 10016, United States of America.

Library of Congress Cataloging-in-Publication Data
Names: Plunkett, David, editor. | Shapiro, Scott J., editor. | Toh, Kevin, editor.
Title: Dimensions of normativity: new essays on metaethics and jurisprudence / edited by David Plunkett, Scott J. Shapiro, Kevin Toh.
Description: New York: Oxford University Press, 2019. | Includes bibliographical references and index.
Identifiers: LCCN 2018031202 | ISBN 9780190640408 ((hardback): alk. paper)
Subjects: LCSH: Law—Philosophy. | Jurisprudence. | Normativity (Ethics) | Law—Moral and ethical aspects. | Metaethics.
Classification: LCC K235 .D53 2018 | DDC 340/.112—dc23
LC record available at https://lccn.loc.gov/2018031202

Note to Readers
This publication is designed to provide accurate and authoritative information in regard to the subject matter covered. It is based upon sources believed to be accurate and reliable and is intended to be current as of the time it was written. It is sold with the understanding that the publisher is not engaged in rendering legal, accounting, or other professional services. If legal advice or other expert assistance is required, the services of a competent professional person should be sought. Also, to confirm that the information has not been affected or changed by recent developments, traditional legal research techniques should be used, including checking primary sources where appropriate.

(Based on the Declaration of Principles jointly adopted by a Committee of the American Bar Association and a Committee of Publishers and Associations.)

Contents

Acknowledgments

EDITING THIS VOLUME has been a rewarding experience, and we would like to thank everyone who has helped to make it a success. First, we would like to thank all of our contributors for signing on to this project, and for writing excellent papers. Second, we would like to thank Yale Law School for funding a workshop on metaethics and legal philosophy in April 2015, where earlier drafts of many of the papers for this volume were presented. Thanks also to all the participants in that workshop, as well as to Lise Cavallaro for her help in organizing it. Third, we would like to thank Sona Lim for help in going over the index of this volume. Finally, we are grateful to everyone at OUP for their help in putting this volume together.

List of Contributors

Mitchell N. Berman is the Leon Meltzer Professor of Law and Professor of Philosophy at the University of Pennsylvania

David Copp is a Distinguished Professor of Philosophy at the University of California, Davis

Luís Duarte d'Almeida is a Professor of Jurisprudence at the University of Edinburgh

David Enoch is the Rodney Blackman Chair in the Philosophy of Law, The Faculty of Law and the Philosophy Department at the Hebrew University of Jerusalem

Stephen Finlay is a Professor of Philosophy at the University of Southern California

Brian Leiter is the Karl N. Llewellyn Professor of Jurisprudence at the University of Chicago Law School

George Letsas is a Professor of the Philosophy of Law at the University College London Faculty of Laws

Kathryn Lindeman is an Assistant Professor of Philosophy at Saint Louis University

Teresa Marques is a Researcher at the LOGOS Group, Philosophy Faculty, University of Barcelona

Katharina Nieswandt is an Assistant Professor of Philosophy at Concordia University

David Plunkett is an Associate Professor of Philosophy at Dartmouth College

Peter Railton is the Gregory S. Kavka Distinguished University Professor, John Stephenson Perrin Professor, and Arthur F. Thurnau Professor at the University of Michigan

Connie S. Rosati is a Professor of Philosophy at the University of Arizona

Scott J. Shapiro is the Charles F. Southmayd Professor of Law and Professor of Philosophy at Yale University

Sam Shpall is a Lecturer in Philosophy at the University of Sydney

Alex Silk is a Lecturer in Philosophy at University of Birmingham

Nicholas Southwood is an Associate Professor and ARC Future Fellow in the School of Philosophy at the Research School of Social Sciences, Australian National University

Kevin Toh is an Associate Professor at the Faculty of Laws, University College London

Introduction

David Plunkett, Scott J. Shapiro, and Kevin Toh

THERE IS A conspicuous gulf in contemporary philosophy between metaethical theorizing on the one hand, and debates in general jurisprudence on the other. To be sure, there has been important and innovative work done in both areas in recent years. But, for the most part, there has been little sustained engagement between those working in the two areas, respectively. Things need not be or remain thus, we believe. These essays are aimed at bridging this gulf and establishing a new rapprochement between metaethics and general jurisprudence.

There is always room, and arguably *need*, for increased engagement between philosophers working in different areas. So why focus on the relation between metaethics and general jurisprudence in particular? We believe that certain connections between these two areas are tight, and surprisingly under-scrutinized. We have previously made separate attempts to explore, and in some ways exploit, these connections (see, e.g., Toh 2013; Plunkett and Shapiro 2017). Here, we neither repeat the full cases we previously set out, nor canvas the varied cases that the contributors to this volume make. But what we deem one compelling way of motivating a rapprochement between these two areas of philosophy can be summed up as follows. Understood one way, metaethics concerns certain second-order questions about ethics—questions not *in* ethics, but rather ones *about* our thought and talk about ethics, and how the ethical facts (insofar as there are any) fit into reality. Analogously, general jurisprudence deals with certain second-order questions about law: questions not *in* the law, but rather ones about our thought and talk about the law, and how legal facts (insofar as there are any) fit into reality. Put somewhat more roughly (and using an alternative spatial metaphor), metaethics concerns a range of foundational questions about ethics, whereas general jurisprudence concerns analogous foundational questions about law.

As these ways of putting things are meant to underscore, there is a striking similarity between metaethics and general jurisprudence. The similarity becomes even more pronounced when we focus on the following, related considerations. First, both ethics and law concern what are (or are at least meant to be) systems (or perhaps "schemas," to borrow a term Peter Railton uses in the opening chapter of this volume) of action-guiding norms. Second, substantial parts of both legal and ethical thought and talk invoke deontic concepts and terminology such as "rights," "obligations," and "permissions." Third, philosophers in both areas are concerned with and intrigued by different *kinds* of value and normativity, some of which are (or at least appear to be) more normatively weighty or important than others. (For example, notice the differing importance that many people attribute to the demands of morality, prudence, and epistemic justification, on the one hand, and etiquette, laws, and game rules, on the other.) Based on these and similar considerations, we think that philosophers specializing in the two subfields could learn much from widening their gaze. In short, we think that the connections between metaethics and general jurisprudence are deep and likely to provide fertile grounds for innovative new work.

With the goal of fostering and prompting work that shares this vision, we bring together here work by metaethicists and legal philosophers that deal with some questions of common interest. Some of the chapters deal with questions that show up in both subfields, but which are often pursued in relative isolation from each other—for example, how to understand the nature of normativity, as well as the different varieties of it. Some chapters draw on work from one of the subfields to make progress in the other—for example, how resources developed by metaethicists for thinking about realism in ethics might help legal philosophers in developing a theory of the nature of constitutional law. Other chapters focus on a debate in one of the subfields that touches on issues of general interest to philosophers in both subfields—for example, how best to understand the nature of deep and persistent disagreements.

Many chapters in this volume bring out connections not only between general jurisprudence and metaethics, but also between general jurisprudence and other areas of philosophy—e.g., philosophy of language, aesthetics, moral psychology, and political philosophy. This aspect of the volume is tied to a second goal we have. We wish to highlight the ways in which both metaethics and general jurisprudence are deeply connected to—i.e., motivated and disciplined by—*many* other parts of philosophy. This is a familiar theme in much recent work in metaethics, which increasingly draws on wide-ranging ideas and resources from other areas of philosophy, as well as from related empirical disciplines such as linguistics, psychology, and biology. Our thinking about the nature of law too is susceptible to such interdisciplinary thinking. But our impression is that general jurisprudence has been more prone to philosophical autarchy than metaethics for much of the last several decades, and more tightly bound to discussion and interpretation of canonical works in the subfield itself. One of our aims in putting together this volume is to help encourage those working in general jurisprudence to engage more often and directly with the work in other areas of contemporary philosophy and contiguous empirical disciplines. Our hope is that, by promoting that sort of engagement, we can help foster new directions for research in general jurisprudence, both on the core questions that already are at the heart of it, and also on new ones that are on the cusp of emerging. More generally, we aim to foster new directions of research not only in general jurisprudence (as we have glossed it above), but in legal philosophy more broadly understood.

References

Plunkett, David, and Scott Shapiro. 2017. "Law, Morality, and Everything Else: General Jurisprudence as a Branch of Metanormative Inquiry", *Ethics* 128: 37–68.

Toh, Kevin. 2013. "Jurisprudential Theories and First-Order Legal Judgments", *Philosophy Compass* 8: 457–471.

1 "We'll see you in court!"

THE RULE OF LAW AS AN EXPLANATORY AND NORMATIVE KIND

Peter Railton*

WHAT MIGHT METANORMATIVE theory contribute to our understanding of law? That depends in part upon how narrowly or broadly one construes meta-theory. On a narrow approach, the metatheory of a domain is primarily concerned with giving an account of the core *concepts* in that domain. Such an approach to the metatheory of law might, for example, draw upon a century's work in metaethics, developing an *analytic* framework for interpreting the meaning of normative thoughts and language. On a broader approach, the metatheory of a domain is additionally concerned with a wide array of foundational questions about the nature of the domain, the distinctive role it plays in thought and practice, its epistemic status, the kind of normativity (if any) it possesses or reasons it gives rise to, its origin and dynamics, the psychological infrastructure that sustains it, and so on.[1] The answers to these questions are likely to be *synthetic*, and to be justified in light of how well they describe or explain aspects of the domain. The broader approach can hardly ignore questions about meaning—it will resort at many points to facts about how we interpret discourse in the domain. But answering some of the broader questions might be a preliminary to, rather than consequence

* I would like to thank co-participants in the workshop on law and metaethics for very helpful comments and criticisms. And I am especially grateful to David Plunkett and Kevin Toh for thoughtful written comments that have led me to rethink a number of issues in the current chapter, and helped me be aware of relevant literature in the philosophy of law and meta-normative theory—though I have only myself to thank for the fact that I remain much less aware than I should be.

[1] This "broader conception" bears many similarities with the project of meta-normative inquiry as outlined by Plunkett and Shapiro (2017), who write of the "explanatory task: how a certain part of thought, talk, and reality fit into reality."

Dimensions of Normativity. David Plunkett, Scott J. Shapiro, and Kevin Toh.

of, an interpretive theory of content. For example, Charles Stevenson argued for a form of emotivism about moral discourse by developing a picture of the social function of normative language, and asking what theory of meaning might enable moral discourse to fulfill this role (1937). Here, then, we will be focusing on broad questions about the nature and functions of legal discourse—questions any satisfactory interpretive theory of legal discourse would presumably seek to explain—without presupposing any particular theory of the meaning of legal statements.

In particular we will be asking about what light might be cast upon law by treating it as a *normative* domain. It might seem obvious that law is a normative domain, since it is full of requirements and permissions. The metanormative challenge would then be to say what kind of normative force, if any, these requirements and permissions have—is there, say, a distinctive kind of legal normativity? However, according to an influential tradition in the philosophy of law, it *is* a mistake to view law as a normative domain—one should give a descriptive or positive theory of law. According to (what we will call) the "*in foro externo* Hobbesian" view of law, *a law is a command of a sovereign power backed by force*—where "sovereign power" is understood not in terms of a normative notion such as legitimacy, but in Weberian terms as an effective monopoly of fundamental coercive force over a territory.[2] Law in this sense would be a distinctive kind of social practice or institution, in which the primary form of social regulation comes via such commands and the means by which they are enforced. If this were in fact the appropriate way of understanding law, then treating law as obviously a normative scheme would involve a certain kind of *naiveté*—taking the nominal character of law as its real nature.

One could, however, approach this question by asking, first, about the *general* features of normative schemes of social regulation, and then consider whether or when law has the characteristics necessary to constitute such a scheme. This approach might throw into relief some features of law that are less visible when we study established institutions of law at close range.

Asking whether law is a normative scheme is not the same question as asking whether the fact that something is a law gives us a pro tanto reason for acting in accord with it—it is a substantive question about the kind of thing law might be, whether good or bad. To be sure, one way of understanding the notion of a normative conception of law would be that only law that is good or genuinely reason-giving *is* law. But we are after something different. For example, morality is typically thought of as a paradigm case of a normative scheme of social regulation, but there is a broad conception of "morality" in which Kantians, Utilitarians, and virtue theorists take themselves to be offering accounts of a common subject matter, and so they concede that there is a perfectly legitimate sense of "morality" in which views they do not endorse on normative grounds are nonetheless moralities. For there to be such a common subject matter all sides must agree that there are certain features that distinguish moralities from other schemes of individual or social regulation—moralities, for example, involve standards or evaluations of personal and interpersonal conduct that are taken to be

[2] See Hobbes (1651/1994) (hereinafter abbreviated in the text as "*Lev.* Part:Chapter"; Weber (1922/1978, 40–41). To forestall the thought that this is Hobbes's complete view of law, I should mention that we will be considering his account of *in foro interno* law, below.

objective, impartial, general, non-hypothetical, etc. One of these features is *normativity*—the moral standards and evaluations *purport* to give reasons for thought and action with significant normative weight. A metaethicist might be engaged in trying to understand morality as a distinctive kind of normative scheme, without taking a stand on whether any candidate moral theories live up to their normative purport.[3]

Characterizing morality thus involves saying something informative about what this notion of a normative scheme amounts to—and that is the task that will first occupy us here. We will start, therefore, by giving the beginnings of an account of what is distinctive about a regulative social scheme that is normative for those taking part in it: Can we meaningfully distinguish this from a scheme that regulates society via threat of punishment alone (e.g., a curfew imposed by a conquering army upon a defeated populace)? Central to our answer will be an account of the nature and working of *normative guidance.* We will then go on to ask whether this account might help us to understand the nature of law as we find it in contemporary or historical societies, and to say something about the notions of *rule by law* and *rule of law.*[4] Might these notions correspond to normative schemes in the sense under discussion here? Might they at the same time have some *explanatory* value in theorizing about societies and their dynamics—akin to the explanatory value of such notions as *exchange currency, language,* or *nation-state*? Might *rule by law* and *rule of law* constitute both normative kinds (in the sense in which *morality* is a normative kind) and explanatory kinds (in the sense in which *exchange currency*, etc., are explanatory kinds).

This also raises an interesting prospect—a way in which we can do more than ask how metanormative inquiry can contribute to our understanding of law. We can also ask how the study of law can contribute to metanormative inquiry. For example, it is sometimes complained that metaethics has focused excessively upon the nature of moral *judgments* or moral *motivation*, without paying sufficient attention to morality as a social phenomenon within which such judgments or motivations are typically embedded. Law is an outstanding example of a scheme of social regulation, and understanding its nature and operation might enable us to redress somewhat the imbalance in metanormative theorizing and look at morality in novel ways.

---

[3] There is a parallel, I believe, between this way of distinguishing the study of regulative social schemes that are normative in character from questions about whether to endorse any such scheme, and David Plunkett's distinction between the "Moral Aim Thesis" versus the "Represented-as-Moral Thesis" in the metatheory of law (see Plunkett 2013).

[4] "Rule by law" and "rule of law" are expressions I am using as something like terms of art, so I will follow the practice of putting them in italics—as *rule by law* and *rule of law*—below. I hope that my usage will be linked sufficiently to our normal understanding of these words to be able to draw upon our commonsense ideas. The difference between the two notions won't be clear until later in this chapter, though a rough characterization can be given here: in *rule by law* the fundamental order in a society is based upon a fairly unified de facto authority that promulgates and enforces a scheme of publicly recognized rules or procedures (though not necessarily explicitly codified, e.g., English common law), typically using such institutions as police and courts; in a *rule of law*, the ruling authority in question is *itself* subject to this same scheme of laws, and the members of society have some share in the making and enforcing of the laws. Intuitively, under a *rule of law*, members of the society who are not members of the ruling group have a reasonable chance of challenging and defeating actions of that authority, or of changing the laws, through means provided for *within* the scheme of law, using police and courts.

Since I am a neophyte in approaching questions of law, I may be to some extent repeating what is already well known (if my muddling along is on track) or replicating well-known mistakes (if it is not). For this I apologize in advance, and offer what follows as a somewhat elaborate invitation to help sort me out.

First we will need some background.

1. Background: Social construction. It is common ground among the views of law we will be discussing here that law is in some sense a "social construction." While no clear definition of "social construction" is available, some distinguishing features are readily noted.

First, while a given form of social construction—e.g., *exchange currency, language, national state*—might be an explanatory kind for the study of society, it is not a "natural kind" in the sense of corresponding to some underlying physical substance or process. Second, this does not preclude the possibility that social constructions can be in distinctive states that are not simply reducible to the attitudes of the individuals who compose them. Consider an academic recruitment committee that has deliberated and agreed to send to the department a rank-ordered list of the top candidates for a position. Let us say that four candidates are ranked—candidates A, B, C, and D, with B at the top of the list. Now it could be that no members of the committee identified B as the top choice in their individual ballots. Still, it is the view of the committee that B is the top choice.[5] Moreover, even if all members of the committee *did* individually rank B first, *this* fact alone would not make it the case that this is the view of the committee as such. For that, certain procedures must be followed, e.g., a vote taken in accord with the rules for this committee. So "the view of the committee" is an *emergent* fact, but just as real as the first-order facts about individual attitudes and actions upon which this emergent fact supervenes. Social constructs thus can occupy states with semantic *content*—such as a rating of candidates, a verdict of a jury, or an enacted law—that is significantly different from the contents of the mental states of the individuals whose collective activity has brought them into being. Likewise, social constructs can persist over time and extend in space beyond the lives of the actual humans composing them.

Third, social constructs can exhibit robust, counterfactual- and explanation-supporting *dynamic* features that are quite distinct from any individual ideas or intentions. The existence of a common currency or medium of exchange, for example, is widely recognized as a "socially constructed fact," since the value of a currency depends fundamentally upon the willingness of enough people to accept the currency in exchange for non-monetary goods and services. Such a medium can emerge and become stable, however, even if no individual exchanges ever initially aimed at this—as cigarettes are said to have more or less spontaneously become an exchange currency in some areas of Europe immediately after World War II. And once a common medium of exchange has come into existence, it will tend to exhibit dynamic properties not congruent with people's conception of the currency or aspirations in using it. Inflation or deflation, for example, can arise unwanted from individual decisions about consumption or saving.

Of course, we must not *reify* socially constructs—they cannot subsist entirely on their own and their continuing existence depends upon the thoughts, feelings, and behaviors

[5] Margaret Gilbert makes effective use of such examples in her book (1992), though the view of social constructs here does not presuppose her view of "social facts."

of individuals and groups. Social constructs always exist *through* the attitudes and actions of actual humans. For example, the "monetary forces" at work in contemporary economic theory might appear to have the character of laws lying outside our power. But even as robust a social construct as an exchange currency must still be "brought to life" and kept alive day by day by the actual dispositions, thoughts, feelings, and behaviors of living agents. Thus, while a monetary system and its principles may confront the individual as an external reality resistant to her will and yet deeply shaping her life, still, the monetary system must at the same time have an *internal* reality in the willingness of a sufficiently widely distributed array of individuals to accept the currency in exchange for goods and services. Should these individuals lose confidence in it and refuse to accept it in exchange, preferring instead to barter for what they need, its "power to command goods and services" or "drive the economy" will evaporate altogether.

2. Background: normative guidance. What would be the characteristics of a social construct that is *normative* in nature? It would not be enough if the individuals involved simply exhibited certain behavioral *regularities*, since such regularities could have any one of a number of origins. Some might be natural features of the human animal and its condition, in the way that reflexes, instincts, or restrictions on human capacities and resources can yield widespread regularities in behavior in a manner that does not depend upon any social construct. Others might depend upon social constructions, but in a way that hardly seems normative. Thus, the effective enforcement of Hobbesian *in foro externo* law could induce social order (consider the example of a curfew imposed upon an unwilling populace by a conquering army), but unless we want to say that a dog who obeys her master to escape punishment is exhibiting normative behavior, we are unlikely to think that such social order has a normative origin. The question, then, is: What kind of origin should we be looking for?

The argument here will be that we should be looking for *normative guidance* as a distinctive way in which individual and group behavior can give rise to social regularities. While reflex, instinct, physical limitations, and external force may play a role in any aspect of human behavior, the behaviors attributable to normative guidance are *underdetermined* by these. Humans need nutrients in order to survive, for example, but notions of which forms of potential nutrition constitute *food* or are *appropriate to eat* is not wholly determined by physical need—indeed, humans may starve even in situations where nutrients are available if those nutrients are not seen by them as appropriate to eat. To be guided in choice of nutrients by a sense of what is appropriate to eat is an example of normative guidance.

A distinguishing feature of normative guidance is that it involves the *self-imposition* by individuals or groups of requirements or aims. This principally involves two elements. First, individuals who are normatively guided must *mentally represent* certain requirements or aims, and these mental representations must play a role in *mediating* thought and behavior. Such representations can be tacit rather than explicit, while still functioning in this way. For example, when one is new to speaking a second language, one often consciously consults the grammatical rules one learned, e.g., for the conjugation of verbs. By contrast, a native speaker's usage is typically fluent, guided by a tacit competency with the language's grammar. This tacit competency is not a mere summary of past experience or matter of habit—it is projective and generative, permitting the formation and understanding of novel sentences in novel contexts. There is an active debate over how native language competence is represented in the brain, but what is essential for our purposes is that native speakers acquire an internally represented model of rules or constraints that plays an active role in shaping the speech of the individual and in her interpretation of the speech of others. This kind of tacit mediation by a projective, generative model is suggested, for example, by the phenomenon of over-regularization in infant's speech, in which an infant might spontaneously use the word *go-ed* rather than *went*, even though she has always previously heard and used *went* as the past tense of *to go* (cf. Cox 1989).

Second, because such rules or constraints are normative, they can be violated, and violations are not treated as "disconfirming" the rules or constraints, but as errors that call for correction. Normative guidance thus exhibits itself not only in regular patterns of behavior, but also in dispositions to respond to violations of those patterns, whether one's own speech or others'. For example, a native speaker of a language is disposed to "hear" violations of verb agreement spontaneously, whether they occur in his own speech or that of others, and to take them as errors to be corrected. Such dispositions to notice and respond to violations are said to be "intuitive"—most of us would be unable to articulate all of the grammatical and semantic constraints we can hear being violated. And in practice the "felt need" to correct may not show itself in overt behavior, but only in a kind of mental recognition. But the point is that violations are not experienced as mere surprises (as they would be if the internal representation were of a descriptive behavioral regularity), but as faults. Often one becomes aware that one has acquired a linguistic certain rule or constraint only when a violation occurs, and one senses there is something wrong and spontaneously imagines how to correct it, without need of any external incentive to do so.[6]

3. **Background: the structure of normative concepts and attitudes.** Normative guidance, then, involves a connected set of psychological representations, attitudes, and processes in the generation, monitoring, and interpretation of behavior. But the account given thus far is incomplete, for reasons that perhaps aren't apparent until we look more closely at the *structure* of the normative concepts and attitudes that figure in normative guidance.

Within the normative realm, we can distinguish three broad families of concepts and three corresponding kinds of mental states or processes, which operate jointly in normative guidance of the kind that interests us here:

(a) **Regulatives:** *norm, rule, right, wrong, correct, incorrect, regulation, canon, orthodox, criterion*

(b) **Evaluatives:** *good, bad, value, worth, virtue, vice, fairness, equity, truth, trustworthy, credible, knowledge, desirable, important, strong, weak, poor, healthy, flourishing, diseased, skilled, effective, inefficient, admirable, based, beautiful, sublime, lovable, great, noble, hateful*

(c) **Deliberatives:** *ought, reason, must, may, rational, reasonable, deserved, fitting, proportional, warrant, merit, obligation, due, justified, acceptable, weigh, deliberate, decide, conclude, obligation, legitimate, responsible*

---

[6] For fuller discussions of normative guidance, see Gibbard (1990, ch. 4), Railton (2006).

Intriguingly, while the words in these families come into English through multiple languages, the historical root meanings cluster in telling ways:

(a) **Regulatives:** *norm* (from *norma*, a carpenter's square), *rule* and *regulation* (from *regulus,* a straight edge), *right* (straight or perpendicular), *wrong* (twisted or bent), *correct* (co-aligned), *standard* (to stand upright), *canon* (a straight measuring line), *criterion* (sieve).

(b) **Evaluatives:** *good* (unified, fitting together), *bad* (ill), *value* (strength), *virtue* (virility), *vice* (defect, failing), *trust* and *true* (firm, steady), *important* (having causal power), *health* (whole), *useful* (useable), *credible* (of the heart), *noble* (knowing), *fine* (end-like, goal), *poor* (little or few), *disease* (discomfort), *beauty* (favored), *fair* (pleasing).

(c) **Deliberatives:** *must* (taking appropriate measure), *rational* and *proportional* (calculation, ratio), *deliberate* (to put in scale, to weigh), *merit* (to get a share), *reason* (to fit together), *ought* (to be master of, to own), *decide* (to cut off), *conclude* (to close off), *justify* (to fit with the law), *due* (to give or take), *obligation* (to be tied to), *responsible* (to engage oneself, to spend), *legitimate* (to gather together, to pronounce or speak).[7]

Reflecting on these origins, we can see a division of labor within the normative realm, and understand why each of these families is needed for a complete picture. Imagine that we are building a house together. As each of us works laying foundations, cutting lumber, or nailing it home, we face the challenge of making our several contributions compatible, capable of fitting together in a sound and weathertight structure. To do so, we need not only tools like trowels, saws, and hammers, but also a special class of tools that provide shared standards for our work to meet. If I am cutting planks to make a floor and you are nailing them in, then if I use a ruler to test the straightness of the wood by assessing co-alignment, and thereby rule out twisted wood, you will be in a position to nail the floor flat. Similarly if I use a right-angled carpenter's square to guide my cuts, then you will be able to join the planks tightly with one another and the walls. And if you and I both use rulers marked with standard units of measurement, then you can determine the lengths I need to cut to fill in the remaining gaps. If you need aggregate of the right size to make a smooth wall, then I must use a finer sieve (*criterion*) than if you need aggregate of the right size for a strong foundation. And so on. What is, in the natural world, continuously varying in shape or size can be bifurcated into "right" and "wrong" for our purposes by using shareable instruments that can be applied to an open-ended array of materials.

If we impose the use of these tools upon ourselves, and hold our work to the standards they set, then we can say that they are *regulative* of our practice. This distributed self-discipline to common standards underwrites the *mutual expectations* and *default reliance* upon which our joint enterprise depends. By regulating our practice and relying upon one another in these ways, we reduce the number of *degrees of freedom* in our work and social setting, but at the same time create *opportunity paths* that would not otherwise have been available, e.g., for a coordinated division of labor in realizing a common project that predictably will satisfy

[7] These word origins are largely derived from (Watkins 1985).

certain specifications or desiderata. In philosophical terms, these tools are, thanks to our disciplining our behavior to them, functioning as *shared a priori regulative standards*, which permit the emergence and maintenance of a shared productive practice.

Similarly, the generative rules or constraints of a natural language—phonetic, syntactic, or semantic—can function as shared a priori regulative standards, making it possible to communicate reliably in an open-ended way across a wide community of individuals. But they can do so only if we all in some way represent these rules or constraints internally, tacitly or explicitly, and discipline our behavior to them. Relative to our individual speech, these rules or constraints are a priori regulative—they are not up to us as individuals, and our words and sentences are to fit them, not the other way around. And there must be sufficient overlap across the rules or constraints we represent internally that we can communicate by relying upon them—enabling us to interpret and understand each other, even when among strangers and even in the face of substantive disagreements.

We know from information theory that a scheme in which all sounds occur with equal frequency constitutes *noise*, and thus we owe the ability of a language to communicate information to the fact that it pares down the space of permissible sounds and sequences of sounds, reducing the number of degrees of freedom in our utterances and creating projectable regularities in usage that can sustain shared expectations. Part of this is the capacity of language to introduce discontinuities where, in the natural world, there is continuous variation. Language learning is possible for prelinguistic infants because the sounds speakers make have been regimented enough that regularities can be extracted from overheard speech that enable infants to form the expectations that are the basis for segmenting speech into identifiable, repeatable units, providing an entry point for the association of meanings with words (Aslin et al. 1998; Kidd et al. 2012). As with the builders' tools, these characteristics of language can be inferred from the conditions for creating and sustaining a successful joint project—in this case, a shared, learnable medium of mutual intelligibility and informativeness. And as with the builders themselves, speakers' distributed self-discipline to standards adequate for such a joint project creates opportunity paths—in this case, for communication and coordination—that would not otherwise exist. Members of a linguistic community are able to enter into verbal exchanges with a rich body of *default conversational expectations* about how their words will be understood and how they will be able to understand the words of others.

This background structure of self-discipline and mutual correction includes more than phonetic, syntactic, and semantic elements. It also includes the informal conversational norms that serve to further constrain the space of possibilities away from randomness so that our speech will be useful to others, and a high enough level of mutual trust can be sustained to keep communication afloat.

Afloat and worthwhile. For there is more to normative guidance than the discipline of rules and constraints. There is an indefinite number of rules and constraints we *might* follow, and they cannot enforce themselves—why do some, but not others, have an important role in our lives? Consider first *evaluative* questions. Thus far, we have simply assumed that the builders would have some motive to constrain their work by shared standards. But unless it were worthwhile to work together and to construct houses that are sound and weathertight, these standards would have no interest for us—yet notions of worthwhileness or interest take us beyond the realm of regulatives and into the realm of evaluatives. For some purposes, a square structure would be inappropriate, and so simply following the standard rectilinear tools would be a poor idea. And language is found wherever humans are found because it serves such a range of vital interests, and makes possible such a range of worthwhile activities, but language is subject to constant change in response to social, cultural, political, and technological changes. These changes in language are not matters of "following rules" that are already in place, but of the more or less successful evolution of human practices, language included, to meet changing demands, needs, purposes, and goals—an evaluative rather than merely regulative enterprise.

At times, we find ourselves having "internalized" a scheme of rules or constraints that we no longer see as worthwhile, or have begun to see as actively harmful. Social norms or linguistic conventions can be oppressive, failing to afford opportunity paths adequate to our needs or aspirations. In such cases, while these rules or constraints often continue to exert some form of guidance in shaping how we feel and act, they will tend to lose their normative character as we become alienated from them.[8] Kant himself realized that the subjective condition for receptiveness to duty *as* duty is not a mere matter of following a rule—one must see some point, purpose, or value in doing so, lest duty confront one as an alien demand or mere "legalism" (1797/1996). Evaluatives thus enter in the attitudes that initiate, motivate, and sanction the following of rules—including the self-directed favorable or unfavorable feelings as one meets or violates the rules, or observes such conduct in others, and the restorative or dissociative feelings that motivate behavior in the wake of violations.

Evaluatives thus play a foundational role in normative guidance—rules will tend to lose normative force if they cease to be associated with any worthwhile purpose, and doubts will arise about whether they *deserve* or *merit* our allegiance, or *ought* to be followed. To raise such questions is to pass beyond the regulative and evaluative domains into the *deliberative*. Or consider a case in which following either of two rules would advance a valuable purpose, but in which both cannot be followed at the same time. Which to obey? Here we need a capacity for decision and action—for "cutting off" one option and "owning" the other—that is not simply a matter of rule-following or evaluation. Yet we must be equipped with such a capacity—as individuals and groups—if we are to be successfully normatively regulated in a scheme of mutual coordination and cooperation. More generally, the full equipment for normative guidance must include the ability to bring together multiple kinds of constraints upon or reasons for action—rules, values, uncertainties, resources, abilities, etc.—and then on that basis to elect, initiate, and guide action.

We draw upon deliberative concepts to give voice to such questions, but deliberation is not restricted to the level of conscious thought any more than is rule-following or evaluation. Most speakers don't know, except implicitly, the rules of their native language or the norms of conversation. And many of us have, and are deeply shaped by, values of which we are not fully aware and have never articulated. The weighing of alternatives is a process that occurs in all intelligent animals, as does decision-making based upon such weighing. We inherit these capacities to bring together and compare diverse decision weights without self-conscious deliberation, and our capacity for conscious deliberation draws regularly upon them—lest we be lost in endless deliberation about how much to deliberate about how much to deliberate . . . , or what to consider in thinking about what to consider in thinking about what to

[8] Compare Gibbard's notion of being "in the grip" of a norm versus norm-acceptance (1990, ch. 4).

consider, . . . and so on, for all of the elements of deliberation. It is thanks to tacit assessments of urgency, degree of uncertainty, relative importance, seriousness of violation, etc., that we are able to deliberate and decide at all (Railton 2006). Any given tacit assessment can of course be given conscious scrutiny, but not all tacit assessments at once.

4. Background: the elements of a normative social scheme. Normative guidance, then, is to be distinguished from other ways in which an individual's behavior might exhibit patterns congruent with a norm—e.g., an external threat of punishment might induce individual compliance with a rule that is not functioning normatively for the individual at all, such that violation will seem to that individual a risk rather than a fault. Even by age three or four, children in cross-cultural studies exhibit a tacit mastery of the distinction between morality and rules that are simply how people around them act, or are enforced by authorities, taking a different view of violations of morality as opposed to violating mere conventions or authority-imposed rules. If a substitute preschool teacher says to the class, "While I'm here, you are to raise your hand before talking," children at this age typically have the social understanding needed to recognize and adapt to this new rule. But if the teacher says instead, "While I'm here, you are to poke your neighbor with a sharp pencil when you wish to speak," children will balk (Turiel 2002). Moreover, if pressed to explain why they fail to comply, they will point to morally-relevant features of the act being required, e.g., the harm that it would inflict. In such cases, children advert to the value (or disvalue) that is at stake in violating a moral constraint—indicating that their thinking is not merely a matter of "following rules enforced by authority," but involves a fundamentally evaluative sense of why the rules matter, how rules can be bad, and why one ought not to obey bad rules, even if this brings criticism or punishment from the person in power in the situation. In this way, the child's developing social competence involves as well a developing *normative* competence, with a structure that reflects the structure of the normative realm in much the same way as a tacit linguistic competence reflects the structure of a language or of conversational settings.

The structure of the normative realm is reflected as well at the social level, when we consider normative schemes that are functioning regulatively in a society. Such schemes depend upon shared patterns of normative guidance. To improvise somewhat upon a framework developed in a tradition in sociology that descends from Durkheim and includes Michel Foucault, we can think of a normative social scheme with a distinctive, interdependent structure (cf. Durkheim 1912, 298; Foucault 1974), which is brought to life as social construction by thoughts, attitudes, and actions of individuals:

(1) The *content of the normative scheme*. A set more or less explicit of *constraints, requirements*, or *ideals* concerning: how one should think, feel, or act; what relations one should form; who is to count as a full member of the normative community; who has authority concerning norms or ideals; and so on.

(2) *Processes of acquisition and enforcement*. Social practices by means of which these norms and ideals are acquired or taught, and by which compliance is determined and enforcement exercised.

(3) *Mechanisms of normative guidance*. How does the content of this normative scheme play a role in shaping the decisions, feelings, and actions of individuals or groups? How do they regard it, and what force does it have in shaping their lives?

(4) *The motivating grounds (sometimes, the telos) of the normative scheme.* What goals, aims, purposes, or values does the scheme purport to achieve or protect, and what functions does it in fact serve? Why are these important to people? How is participation in the scheme related to one's identity, and how does the scheme recruit and maintain the allegiance of participants?

We should think of all four elements as part of a normative scheme in that their presence is essential for such a scheme to be a real, persistent social "fact" with potential explanatory value. Content is necessary for the scheme to have a definite set of relations to thought and action, acquisition and enforcement are necessary for the scheme to persist over time, normative guidance is necessary if the way in which the scheme shapes behavior is to have a genuinely normative character, and some evaluative motivating grounds are vital if the scheme is to generate motivation for normative guidance by the scheme, and to attract and retain sufficient commitment to sustain it in the face of competing interests.

Such a structure might be found in a hunter-gatherer band, where, anthropologists have argued, (1) strong norms and ideals of egalitarianism typically prevail; (2) these seem to be acquired through acculturation and ritual practices, and adjudication and enforcement is via group-based attitudes and sanctions; (3) these norms play an internal role in regulating attitudes and behaviors, so that both those who are successful in hunting and those who are not spontaneously share the catch; and (4) these norms and ideals contribute to group solidarity in and to meeting of needs in the face of scarcity and chance over the course of whole lives in which everyone will spend time as dependent (Boehm 2012)—a sufficiently effective and efficient normative scheme that humans appear to have spent by far the longest period of their history living in such bands, and during that period come to dominate other hominid species and colonize some of the most remote and inhospitable regions of the world.

Such a structure can also be found in a language community, with (1) shared linguistic and conversational norms and standards; (2) acquisition of language as a central part of psychological development, and distributed forms of mutual correction in use; (3) normative guidance by internal representations of the norms and standards; and (4) the motivating ground of (inter alia) effective and efficient communication. The spontaneous emergence and spread of pidgins and creoles as the result of contact between diverse linguistic groups, and of a lingua franca such as English in the contemporary, electronically linked world, make it clear that institutional imposition of norms or coercive force is not needed for a robust normative social scheme to exist and flourish—a sufficiently salient and robust motivating ground of participating in a communicative community can suffice to motivate the complex task of learning a new language.

5. Rule by law as a normative social scheme: Hobbes. Finally, we come to law, and to the question whether *rule by law* is to be understood as more than a social scheme in which a set of tacit or express rules are successfully imposed upon a population. Is there more to a stable, effective "government of laws, not men" than Hobbesian *in foro externo* enforcement? Or, might even the Hobbesian *in foro externo* conception, if it is to be a "government of laws, not men," rely upon a broader underlying normative scheme?

It is notable that Hobbes himself was among those who have recognized the importance of answering this question, and argued for the position that stable, effective *rule by law* requires an *in foro interno*, normative underpinning. He uses the starting point of a hypothetical state of nature to make this evident, by asking how a scheme of civil law could come into existence and function effectively, given that it cannot be presupposed from the outset. Hobbes thereby reveals the *dependency* of *rule by law* on such a scheme upon normative elements it neither includes nor, by itself, produces.

Hobbes's account of the transition from a state of nature to civil society is usually represented as depending upon the normative force of *contract.* But Hobbes himself would seem to block this route. Quite apart from the fact that, as Hobbes recognizes, there is no such social contract to point to by way of legitimating civil society, there is a more serious problem of circularity in explaining how the force of contract could sustain the transition. Contracts for future behavior, Hobbes argues, even when mutual, do not have binding force unless they are backed up by a threat of reliable coercion should either party fail to perform—they are "void . . . under any reasonable suspicion" of nonperformance by the other (*Lev.* 1:14). However, a reliable coercive force of this kind could exist only exist through a combination of men working together over time to undertake the often burdensome and risky tasks of policing and enforcing contracts. And a combination of men who can be relied upon to cooperate in this way is just what we are missing in a state of nature. Hobbes concludes that, when two parties make a contract in a "mere state of nature" for some future behavior, if one party performs his part without any *in foro externo* guarantee that the other will likewise do so, "he does but betray himself to his enemy; contrary to the right (he can never abandon) of defending his life" (*Lev.* I:14). Thus we seem to be led into a dead end, and *in foro externo* law cannot get off the ground.[9]

What, then, is the real machinery that could drive a transition from a state of nature to civil society, or succeed in beginning the "confederation" we need if there is to be a combination of sufficient force and reliability to sustain *in foro externo* enforcement of contracts or a scheme of civil law? Hobbes invokes the "laws of nature," which are *normative* principles, "precept[s] or general rule[s] of reason" (*Lev.* I:14) that "oblige *in foro interno*" (*Lev.* I:15). These laws "bind" us through our rationality and understanding, relying not upon "natural necessity" or "threat of force," but upon a mechanism of *self-imposition* through voluntary acts, which can operate in the absence of external force. As a result, "whatsoever laws bind *in foro interno* may be broken," but such violation is construed as a "breach," contrary to reason (*Lev.* I:15).

Consider the primary law of nature, which has two clauses: (1) "*every man ought to endeavor peace, as far as he has hope of obtaining it,*" and (2) that "*when he cannot obtain it, that he may seek and use all helps and advantages of war*" (*Lev.* I:14). (2) has rational force only conditionally, if (1) cannot be met. Therefore our *default* obligation is to "endeavor peace," where "endeavor" cannot be a mere show, but is a "duty" of "unfeigned and constant" effort (*Lev.* 1:15).

---

[9] The seeming exception Hobbes notes, "commonwealth by acquisition," occurs when an invading force establishes a monopoly of power and issues commands over a submissive population (*Lev.* I:20). Here no contract is required to establish the commonwealth. But what of the invading force itself? In the last analysis, it is but one more form of combination, dependent upon the continuing obedience of its members, and that in turn presupposes an overawing power to hold would-be defectors in check. Even the family as a unit of sovereign power—founded upon "natural lust" (*Lev.* 1:13)—is no proof against loss of willingness to obey the patriarch, as English history and the wayward lusts of royal families would have made painfully clear to Hobbes.

Since there is no hope for peace except through "the help of confederates," then *if* I perceive an opportunity to come together with you "to gain friendship, or service," thereby improving the chances for confederation and peace between us (*Lev.* I:15), I am *obliged in foro interno* to seize this opportunity and pursue it in an "unfeigned and constant" way.

What would such an opportunity look like? Suppose that you perform an act of friendship or service toward me as a "free gift." Doesn't Hobbes himself say that this would be contrary to reason—a way of opening oneself to the predation of the other—in the absence of any *in foro externo* security that it will be returned in kind? Here Hobbes makes a surprising move, anticipatory of a mechanism in contemporary evolutionary theory—your act, because it makes you vulnerable to my exploitation, constitutes an "expensive" and therefore credible signal of your cooperativeness. Contrast the case if you had instead tried to extract a promise from me to reciprocate, as a condition of your friendship or service:

> Words alone, if they be of the time to come and contain a bare promise, are an insufficient sign of a free gift, and therefore not obligatory. [*Lev.* 1:14]

But if your friendship or service is actually *performed* first, as a "free gift," then the very insecurity of the state of nature makes your act a "sufficient sign" that there is some "hope" of peace between us, engaging part (1) of the primary law of nature and creating an obligation on my part to respond constructively to further this friendship or reciprocate this service. All voluntary acts, Hobbes argues, are done by someone with an eye to their potential benefit. Your "free gift" of cooperation must therefore be understood, not as a foolish mistake, but as serving the rational purpose of creating an opportunity for peace that could not otherwise exist. If, instead of responding in kind, I were to take advantage of you, I would have squandered the "hope." Given the most credible sign I could reasonably expect to receive from another, I would destroy by my own hand the prospect of peace between us. We will remain trapped in the state of nature.

> . . . if men [in giving this "free gift" of cooperation] see they shall be frustrated, there will be no beginning of benevolence or trust nor consequently of mutual help nor of reconciliation of one man to another; and therefore they are to remain still in the condition of *war*, which is contrary to the first and fundamental law of nature, which commands men to *seek peace*. [*Lev.* I:15]

This becomes the basis for Hobbes's derivation of the fourth law of nature, "GRATITUDE":

> *That a man which receives benefit from another of mere grace endeavor that he which gives it have no reasonable cause to repent him of his good will.* [*Lev.* I.15]

"Free gift" as an unsecured performance of a "good will" or "grace" does in a state of nature what first performance does for contract in civil society, namely, creates an obligation on the part of the other to perform in turn, as a matter of "justice" or what is "*due*" (*Lev.* I:14): "The breach of this [fourth] law is called *ingratitude*, and has the same relation to grace that injustice has to obligation by covenant" (*Lev.* I:15).

Such a process of signaling cooperativeness and seizing opportunities for peace could proceed, in principle, iteratively—from individual to individual, group to group—creating the kind of confederation of trust needed to create capacity for exerting *in foro externo* enforcement of contract and law. Civil society and *rule by law* become possible. But the role of the *in foro interno* normative scheme of the laws of nature does not end at this point. Hobbes argues that an enduring, effective, and prosperous civil society depends upon people's willingness to "accommodate themselves" to one another, and to reciprocate the benefits of civil society, reserving to oneself only what one is willing to accord to others. This normative underpinning figures in Hobbes's answer to "the Foole"—who fails to realize that *in foro interno* reason lies with returning the benefit he receives from the peaceableness and civil behavior of others, even in those instances where no *in foro externo* enforcement is poised to stop a deceitful failure to reciprocate in kind. Just as it figures in Hobbes's account of how to escape the vicious circle of distrust that would hold us in a state of nature, so, in civil society, does this normative underpinning figure in Hobbes's account of how to respond to "the Foole". And it figures in the answer Hobbes would give to the worry about a potentially vicious regress of enforcement: Laws are not self-enforcing, and if enforcement is needed to hold people in line, then who holds the enforcers in line? What holds the enforcers in line is what holds all of us in line—"that restraint upon themselves in which we see [men] live in commonwealths" (*Lev.* II.17), a restraint whose origin is ultimately normative and *in foro interno*, not positive and *in foro externo*.

Hobbes gives an extensive account of the elements of this underlying normative scheme, as he "derives" the other laws of nature:

(2) "That a man be willing, when others are so too, as far-forth, as for Peace, and defence of himself he shall think it necessary, to lay down this right to all things; and be contented with so much liberty against other men, as he would allow other men against himself."
(3) "that men perform their covenants made"
(5) "*that every man strive to accommodate himself to the rest*";
(6) "*that upon caution of the future time, a man ought to pardon the offenses past of them that, repenting, desire it*";
(7) "*that in revenges*—that is, retribution of evil for evil—*men look not at the greatness of the evil past, but the greatness of the good to follow*";
(8) "*that no man by deed, word, countenance, or gesture declare hatred or contempt of another*";
(9) "*that every man acknowledge another for his equal by nature*";
(10) "*that at the entrance into conditions of peace, no man require to reserve to himself any right which he is not content should be reserved to every one of the rest*";
(11) "if *a man be trusted to judge between man and man,* it is a precept of the law of nature *that he deal equally between them*";
(12) "*that such things as cannot be divided be enjoyed in common, if it can be*";
(16) "*that they that are at controversy submit their right to the judgment of an arbitrator*";
(17) that "no man is a fit arbitrator of his own cause";

(18) that "no man in any cause ought to be received for arbitrator to whom greater profit or honor or pleasure apparently arises out of the victory of one party than of the other". [*Lev.* I:14-15]

These laws of nature hold *in foro interno*, within as well as without civil society. They are "precepts" of reason that we represent to ourselves, and that mediate our behavior toward one another via normative guidance—the sovereign included (who is outside the scope of *in foro externo* civil force)—as rational obligations of prudence. Given Hobbes's life experience of civil unrest, one can see how he would be sensitive to the inadequacy of system of rules, however well-conceived, to secure the persistent peace of *rule by law* in the face of challenges if there is little or no underlying presence of the attitudes captured in the "laws of nature" detailed above.

What makes a successful scheme of *rule by law* possible, according to Hobbes, is the existence of an underlying normative scheme that (1) has a distinctive set of constraints and aims; (2) can be acquired through reason and mutual accommodation, and can support a system of (3) individual and mutual *in foro interno* restraint that makes possible a stable, reliable regime of *in foro externo* enforcement; and (4) enables people to avoid or overcome the conflict and insecurity that exists where civil law fails, and sustain the many benefits of peaceful existence when civil law succeeds.

Hobbes, then, can be understood as articulating precepts of *in foro interno* reason that also provide a *recipe* for a society that is effectively guided by an *in foro externo* scheme of law—a normative recipe to underwrite a regime of positive law. Bundling the normative foundation and the positive law together, then, we get the "restraint upon themselves" of a normative social scheme of *rule by law*, a restraint that includes the formation of, and default willingness to obey and support the enforcement of, the *in foro externo* civil law.[10]

---

[10] What is the relation of this idea to Hart's notion of the "internal point of view" of law (1961, 55–57)? As I understand him, Hart sees law as a hierarchy of rules, and those taking the internal point of view have "accepted" these rules as regulative for their behavior. This is an important advance over views of law that are entirely *in foro externo*. However, it isn't Hart's ambition, I believe, to look behind this rule-acceptance for the values and motives that might explain it or make it rational, or to say how the character or structure of these values or motives are linked to questions about the nature or efficacy of *rule by law* or the *rule of law*. The notion of *normative guidance* at work in the present chapter is an attempt to give an account of when and why, the kind of acceptance of rules Hart discusses could have a genuinely normative character for the individuals concerned, and thus help us to understand *rule by law* and *rule of law* as normative social schemes. In *The Concept of Law*, Hart writes of the centrality of rules and rule-following in order to "understand the whole distinctive style of human thought, speech, and action which is involved in the existence of rules and which constitutes the normative structure of society" (1961, 86). Here I am arguing that understanding "the whole distinctive style of human thought, speech, and action" involved in a normative social scheme must look at the attitudes, values, and deliberative capacities that underlie rules and rule-following, and that are important in providing the motivational force and meaning such rules have. For example, among the motives Hart considers as compatible with rule-following as a "normative structure of society" is "the mere wish to do as others do" (Hart, 1994, 203), yet such a wish would not seem to constitute regarding the rule as legitimate, rational, intelligible, meaningful, or worthy. By contrast, Hobbes's account of the *in foro interno* normative scheme that underwrites an effective *rule by law* provides for the rule-follower an available appreciation of *rule by law* as legitimate, rational, etc.—even in those cases where he is in substantive moral disagreement with the content of a particular law, or when he sees the kind of short-term personal advantage in violating the law that misleads "the Foole." (I am indebted

To be sure, Hobbes's account *rule by law* is an idealization, but it is not a merely hypothetical scheme—it is an explanatory claim about the *kinds* of normative attitudes that underlie and enable successful civil societies, whether on the part of subjects or sovereigns, or subjects *as* sovereigns. We might dispute any element of his list, and want to add some of our own. And certainly it is not necessary for everyone in civil society to have these attitudes, or to have them to the same extent or degree. Neither is it necessary that individuals share a view about the motivating grounds the civil law ideally or actually serves. The law can serve the essential function of reducing the number of degrees of freedom of social interactions in ways that also create opportunity paths for constructive individual and shared action over time thanks to widespread default obedience with publicly known, prescriptive principles and reasonably reliable enforcement, without such commonality in fundamental value or aim. But Hobbes's *structural* point is independent of these questions: *rule by law* must be more than a set of *in foro externo* rules and procedures—even a set of rules and procedures that is prospective, general, open, clear, stable, etc. (Raz 1979)—if it is it is to have any hope of effectively and securely serving this essential function. *Rule by law* in this sense is both a normative and an explanatory notion: other things equal, the lower the profile of a society in terms of the dispositions and attitudes contained with the laws of nature, the more likely it is to suffer such detrimental consequences as loss of trust, poor economic performance, corruption, arbitrariness, and instability, and the higher the profile of a society in terms of these dispositions and attitudes, the more likely it will be able to resist such dysfunctions of civil society. This is a predictive, potentially explanatory hypothesis. It might or might not hold. But it suggests how normative and explanatory kinds might work together.

In Hobbes's account we are still in an *instrumental* realm: on his view, the *in foro interno* normative dispositions and attitudes reflect nothing but the principles of rational self-interest as qualified by an understanding of human nature and social dynamics. There is no claim that these virtues are grounded in an *intrinsic* value or normativity in law. Nonetheless, they create dispositions and attitudes that lead to default obedience to law—and thus that *treat* law and mutual accommodation as having a kind of *prima facie evaluative* standing, even apart from other interests and the threat of enforcement:

> . . . all men agree on this: that peace is good, and therefore also that the way or means of peace, which, as I have showed before, are *justice* [the keeping of covenants], *gratitude, modesty, equity, mercy*, and the rest of the laws of nature, are good . . . [*Lev.* I:15]

To move beyond this—which Hobbes himself sees as enough, even for "*moral virtue*" (*Lev.* 1:15)—we must introduce the idea of distinctly legal *value* or *virtue* that is embodied in *rule of law*.

6. The rule of law as a distinctive normative kind. If Hobbes's laws of nature were to have been enacted as principles of civil law, this would capture many features that have been associated with the *rule of law*. It would still leave open, however, a feature of law that history itself left open for several millennia after systems of settled law and enforcement emerged: Is

to Kevin Toh, David Plunkett, and Scott Shapiro for drawing my attention to Hart's notion of "the internal view" of law. For discussion, see Toh 2005; Shapiro 2006; and Plunkett 2013.)

there a distinguished class of those at the top of the social hierarchy, who, by birth or by role, promulgate and enforce the law, but who are not themselves accountable to the law? Hammurabi and many kings and chiefs and emperors who followed him did not see the need.[11]

The *rule of law*, as that expression will be used here, adds to *rule by law* two provisions. First, that the law apply—and not merely nominally, but in actual practice—to those exercising governance and their subjects alike: no one is above the law, and no one is below it.[12] Second, those who are subject to the law have some claim—and not merely nominally, but in actual practice—to participate in the making of law and in its *in foro externo* enforcement upon them. At least in post-medieval Europe, forms of governance with these features did not come into prominence until the peoples of Europe had passed through long and painful experience of the deficiencies of societies in which these features are absent—Hobbesian rational incentives in fact proved insufficient to induce reasonable and equitable rule. And it was not until the eighteenth century that there emerged a compelling answer to the charge of incoherence if subject and sovereign are combined in the notion of a people co-participating in the making and enforcing of its own law: *autonomy* as a form of self-imposition of constraint that is independent of one's particular will, and makes one *subject* to regulation, but *sovereign* in so doing (Rousseau 1762/1968).[13] If the civic virtue of *rule by law* is constituted by mutual accommodation, seeing others as "equal by nature," and default law-abidingness, the civic virtue of *rule of law* is constituted by autonomy, seeing others as "equal as persons," and default willingness to participate in lawmaking and law enforcement.

But might *rule of law* be more than an ideal of civic virtue, or (to use Kant's phrase, 1785/1996) a "high-flown fantasticality"? Might the kinds of social practices, attitudes, and institutions that conduce to realizing such an ideal—even if in practice they often fall regrettably short of it—constitute a practicable, functionally coherent social kind? Might social constructions with this character be capable of generating their own support and being resilient in the face of challenges, and thus a reasonable aim for political activism and institutional design? Just as Hobbes thought he had devised the best recipe for effective, prosperous *rule by law*, might Lord Bingham have been right in saying that the *rule of law* is "the best recipe" of those yet devised "for peace, order, cooperation and sound governance"?[14] If so, this might help us understand why societies or countries approximating a *rule of law* have, in the wake of a long, conflictual history, come to flourish and persist in the ways they have—and also why things have tended to go disastrously badly for peace, order, cooperation, and sound governance in such countries when the *rule of law* has been lost or destroyed.

Since *rule of law* involves *rule by law* (understood in our broad, normative sense) as a necessary but insufficient condition, we would need to ask whether the distinguishing features

---

[11] Similar questions arise about whether there are any who are *below* the law, e.g., slaves, who in some slaveholding societies lacked "juridical personality."

[12] It might be argued that one could use Hobbes's laws of nature to reach the conclusion that no one should be above or below the law, though this might invest more substantive normative content into conditions such as treating others as "equal by nature" than Hobbes, certainly, intended.

[13] For further discussion of autonomy in connection with normative guidance, see Railton (2006).

[14] See Bingham (2011). Bingham's characterization of the "rule of law" is somewhat different from the characterization given here.

of rule of law could be a difference that makes a difference, such that societies regulated by a *rule of law* have distinctive dynamics and potentialities, such that *rule of law* is a worthwhile category for social and political analysis and explanation. The question is complicated by the fact that extant polities, while often embodying some degree *rule by law* (including the widespread, self-imposed default obedience to the law within the populace), only very imperfectly approximate a condition in which there is genuine equality in the formation and enforcement of codified law. The Rousseauvian idea of a self-constraining *moi commun* constituted by the General Will that is in all of us (1762/1968), might have some application in mutualist, small-scale communities, but for large-scale societies with advanced divisions of labor and substantial differentials in power and wealth, indirect and representative means must be found if *rule of law* is to have any reality. Here, too, Rousseau had a point: the most promising solution lies in *multiplying* and *diversifying* the forms of governance. Hence, the institutional *fracturing* of power, authority, and process, for example, by development or creation of a constitution that provides for an independent judiciary, universal suffrage, and countervailing powers and levels of power accountable to somewhat different norms and constituencies, with a variety of processes for deciding who will occupy what role, operating on different timescales. This is not a design for finding a *moi commun* or making rapid change via centralized decision-making and implementation, but it might accomplish as much as institutional design can toward realizing a *functional rule of law* by lessening certain distinctive risks of ways in which *rule of law* can fail: the rise of personalist politics, excessive partisanship, the use of the power of appointment to undermine the relative independence of the courts or investigative bodies, the corruption of electoral processes or civil service by ruling parties or special interests, and so on.

Our question then becomes whether societies with such operative constitutional structures and institutions display interestingly different trajectories over time from those with legal schemes that may approximate *rule by law*, but where lawmaking and enforcement are not constrained or constituted in these further ways. This turns out to be a domain of lively debate within the social sciences, where attempts have been made to develop quantitative measures of the approximation of countries to the "rule of law," and to ask how this correlates with—and perhaps might contribute to—various social, economic, and political features. The World Justice Project (2016) has developed a set of indicators of the extent to which a given society embodies the "rule of law" as they understand it, which includes 9 factors and 47 subfactors, including constraints on government, independence of judiciary, openness of government, regulatory enforcement, and absence of corruption, among others. Call this a measure of "functional rule of law." Any such survey is of course liable to a host of conceptual and methodological problems, and yields correlations rather than causal relationships. A recent version of the Survey found Denmark, Norway, Finland, Sweden, Netherlands, Germany, Austria, New Zealand, Singapore, the United Kingdom, Australia, and Canada in the top range, with scores over .8 on a 1.0 scale.[15,16] Socially, these societies

[15] Uganda, Pakistan, Ethiopia, Zimbabwe, Cambodia, Egypt, Afghanistan, Cambodia, and Venezuela were at the bottom with scores under .4.

[16] Although a number of these countries are nominally monarchies (United Kingdom, Netherlands, Norway, Sweden, etc.), the monarch does not really exercise power outside a constitutional framework.

are among those independently measured to have the highest average subjective well-being (Jorm and Ryan 2014), and, among relatively prosperous countries, the relationship between such political indicators and subjective well-being does *not* show the diminishing returns characteristic of rising per capita GDP (Veenhoven 2000). Moreover, these countries also (with a few exceptions) rank relatively high in terms of income inequality (Gini coefficient, World Bank, 2015) as well as GDP per capita (IMF 2016).

Such correlations could mask the underlying explanatory relations, so that "functional rule of law" shares common causes with such factors as subjective well-being, income equality, and prosperity, and in itself has merely an epiphenomenal role in the real social dynamics. Looking at societies where functional rule of law has broken down, however, it seems likely that the re-emergence of unaccountable rulers and loss of judicial independence, for example, have more than an epiphenomenal relation to the population's subsequent well-being, or to their economic flourishing and equality.

Perhaps, then, Hobbes's recipe can be improved, and the instrumental motivating ground of Hobbesian *rule by law*—long-term rational self-interest—can be more reliably attained under a functional rule of law. It would then be of interest to ask whether this corresponds to an interesting *normative* improvement as well. Might there be, for example, an identifiable civic ideal that is not simply a moral ideal, but something distinctively "legal"? Under the normative scheme of Hobbesian *rule by law*, we have a form of *legal or civil solidarity* in the form of the subject's willingness to abide by the law in his dealing with others and to ask for himself no legal rights he would not accord to other subjects as well. Under *rule of law* as understood here, the individual sees herself as both subject and sovereign, and is willing not only to obey the law in her dealings with others, but willing to play her part in the making and enforcing the law. Similarly, she not only does not ask for legal rights she won't allow to others, she is unwilling to rest content if *her* rights are respected but others' are not—as participant in sovereignty, protecting their rights is within her remit. This is a distinctive kind of *legal or civil solidarity* that extends beyond *rule by law*. It is expressed in Martin Luther King Jr.'s "Letter from the Birmingham Jail" (1963):

> Injustice anywhere is a threat to justice everywhere. We are caught in an inescapable network of mutuality, tied in a single garment of destiny.

Can this picture of the legal or civic ideal of a *rule of law* be helpful in finding a principled way to begin to answer the vexed question whether some forms of basic human rights should be thought of as included in the rule of law (cf. Bingham 2011)? A compromise offers itself. Some human rights, including some of the most important ones, can gain the status of (almost) indispensable means if those subject to law are really to have any meaningful role in determining its content and enforcement: *protection of personal security and privacy, equality before the law, non-discrimination, freedom of thought and expression, freedom of association and movement, right to vote and hold office, right to a trial by peers, right to appear in court and call witnesses,* and *right to education* might be among the clearest cases.

These rights could be thought of as (almost) indispensable building-blocks of the role of being a genuine participant in one's own right in a normative scheme of shared creation and enforcement of law. Such reductions in the degrees of freedom with which law can weigh upon individuals have the effect of creating opportunity paths necessary if individuals are to live up to their responsibility to participate in the making and enforcing of laws. In the end, it might be of no interest whether one *defines* "rule of law" to include such rights—what matters is whether there is a natural basis for these rights in the social ideal that motivates, and makes normatively intelligible, the *rule of law*—element (4) in a normative scheme incorporating the *rule of law.* In all these cases, moreover, it is not a question of *legal forms* alone, element (1) of the normative scheme, but of the actual practices and attitudes that might give such legal forms a genuine life in society, elements (2) and (3).

But we need not go into these questions for our present purpose, which was to see if we could find a way to raise and discuss the question whether *rule by law* and *rule of law* might be both normative social schemes and worthwhile explanatory categories. And perhaps we have made a start. This brings us back to the evaluative question broached at the outset, only to set it aside as separate from the idea of law as a normative scheme: Do we have a pro tanto non-prudential reason to play our part in *rule by law* or a *rule of law*, e.g., by default obedience to the law, or, by taking part in shared responsibility for its content and enforcement?

Put in the framework of law as a normative social scheme, *rule by law* and *rule of law* are in fact complex sets of interdependent social relations and expectations expressing and promoting a range of important values. Would the existence of such forms of legal or civil solidarity, for example, give us reason to take part in that solidarity—even if it incorporates some forms of injustice, and even as we seek to change it to remove those injustices? If so, is this a *moral* reason? It would be a reason heavily mediated by the ways in which our fates connect through social schemes that are largely independent of our particular wills. But perhaps what we should say is that moral reasons are often like this. Moral purists might find that compromising—must we be *implicated* in social schemes we did not create and cannot, on our own, control? The trouble is that our *lives* are already implicated in social schemes, just as they typically are in family schemes—and many find it unpalatable to imagine that moral agents have no "special responsibility" to family. Autonomy can't be a matter of self-definition. Whatever we do is "defining" more than our selves—e.g., partially defining what kind of society we live in, or what kind of family one's family is. And the terms we use for self-definition cannot be freely stipulated. The nonviolent civil disobedience of the Civil Rights Movement could not help but be at the same time a form of *obedience* to the prevailing, unjust legal regime. But in accepting *rule by law* in order to change it, following an opportunity path brought into existence by *rule by law* itself, civil disobedience can also be understood as something more: enacting one's responsibility in a yet-to-be-realized *rule of law* and inviting others to do so as well. One is, in effect, treating members of the community as something other than a "social context" one rejects—rather, one is manifesting one's own autonomy in accepting the penalties of an unjust law voluntarily, and expressing a form of respect for others as autonomous as well, in refusing to give up hope that they will be able to see for themselves the injustice to which one's act draws attention, and to accept for themselves the shared task of overcoming it. According to legend, Thoreau, jailed for his civil disobedience in refusing to pay a poll tax, received a visit from Emerson. When Emerson asked, "Henry, what are you doing in there?", Thoreau replied, "Waldo, what are you doing out there?", inviting Emerson to take up just this kind of shared responsibility.

To be sure, what's at issue is only a pro tanto reason—there could be circumstances in which treating the *rule of law* as a nonnegotiable ideal would be catastrophic: "The Constitution is not a suicide pact," as we have often been reminded. Roosevelt's and

Churchill's self-exemption from certain restraints on their power during World War II—*without* handing themselves over for the penalties this might incur—is a possible example: in Roosevelt's case, to deliver desperately needed supplies to an ally and to issue unprecedented commands to industry for wartime production, or, in Churchill's case, to protect the secrecy of breaking the German code by allowing the destruction of civilian targets by German bombing. These are decisions lovers of the *rule of law* might need to concede.

Still, unrealized ideals—for surely that is the case for the *rule of law* in the United States or United Kingdom today—are not idle things. The ideal of the *rule of law* is intelligible and powerful, and we will take to the streets to defend it. But more tellingly—since people have been known to take to the streets even when there is no hope for a *rule of law*—we will also take to the courts. There may be no more reliable sign that the ideal of the *rule of law* has some life in the contemporary United States than the commitment—and faith—expressed by the cover of the ACLU newsletter that appeared immediately after the 2016 election. Featuring a close-up image of the new president, it read, simply—and, as it turned out, accurately—"We'll see you in court!"

References

Aslin, R. N., et al. 1998. "Computation of Conditional Probability Statistics by 8-Month-Old Infants." *Psychological Science*, 9:321–324.

Bingham, T. 2011. *Rule of Law*. London: Penguin.

Boehm, C. 2012. *Moral Origins: The Evolution of Virtue, Altruism, and Shame*. New York: Basic Books.

Cox, M. V. 1989. "Children's Over-Regularization of Nouns and Verbs." *Journal of Child Language*, 16:203–206.

Durkheim, E. 1912. *Les Formes elementaires de la vie religieuse.* Paris: Alcan.

Foucault, M. 1974. *The Order of Things: An Archaeology of the Human Sciences*. A. Sheridan, trans. London: Tavistock.

Gibbard, A. 1990. *Wise Choices, Apt Feelings.* Cambridge, MA: Harvard University Press.

Gilbert, M. 1992. *On Social Facts*. Princeton, NJ: Princeton University Press.

Hart, H. L. A. 1961. *The Concept of Law*. Oxford: Clarendon.

_____. 1994. *The Concept of Law*, 2nd ed. Oxford: Clarendon.

Hobbes, T. 1651/1994. *Leviathan*. E. M. Curley, ed. Indianapolis: Hackett.

International Monetary Fund. 2016. http://www.imf.org/external/pubs/ft/weo/2016/02/weodata/index.aspx.

Jorm, A. F. and Ryan, S. M. 2014. "Cross-National and Historical Differences in Subjective Well-Being." *International Journal of Epidemiology*, 24:330–340.

Kant, I. 1785/1996. *Groundwork of the Metaphysics of Morals.* M. J. Gregor, ed. and trans. Cambridge: Cambridge University Press.

_____. 1797/1996. *Metaphysics of Morals.* M. J. Gregor, ed. and trans. Cambridge: Cambridge University Press.

Kidd, C. et al. 2012. "The Goldilocks Effect: Human Infants Allocate Attention to Sequences That Are Neither Too Simple or Too Complex." *PLOS-One*, 7:e36399.

King, Martin Luther Jr. 1963/1986. "Letter from a Birmingham Jail." In J. M. Washington, ed. *Testament of Hope: The Essential Writings of Martin Luther King, Jr.* New York: Harper Collins.

Plunkett, D. 2013. "Legal Positivism and the Moral Aim Thesis." *Oxford Journal of Legal Studies*, 3: 563–605.

Plunkett, D., and Shapiro, S. 2017 "Law, Morality, and Everything Else: General Jurisprudence as a Branch of Metanormative Inquiry." *Ethics* 128, no. 1: 37–68.

Railton, P. 2006. "Normative Guidance." *Oxford Studies in Metaethics*, 1:3–33.

Raz, Joseph. 1975. *Practical Reason and Norms*. Oxford: Oxford University Press.

Rousseau, J.-J. 1762/1968. *The Social Contact*. M. Cranston, trans. London: Penguin.

Shapiro, S. J. 2006. "What Is the Internal Point of View?" *Fordham Law Review* 75: 1157–1170.

Stevenson, C. L. 1937. "The Emotive Meaning of Ethical Terms." *Mind*, 46:14–31.

Turiel, E. 2002. *The Culture of Morality*. Cambridge: Cambridge University Press.

Toh, K. 2005. "Hart's Expressivism and His Benthamite Project." *Legal Theory*, 75:75–123.

Veenhoven, R. 2000. "Freedom and Happiness: A Comparative Study in Forty-Four Nations in the Early 1990s." In E. Diener and E. M. Suh, eds. *Culture and Subjective Well-Being*. Cambridge, MA: MIT Press.

Watkins, C., ed. 1985. *The American Heritage Dictionary of Indo-European Roots*. Boston: Houghton-Mifflin.

Weber, M. 1922/1978. *Economy and Society*. In *Weber: Selections in Translation*. W.G. Runciman, ed., E. Matthews, trans. Cambridge: Cambridge University Press.

World Bank 2015. *GINI Index (World Bank Estimate)*. https://data.worldbank.org/indicator/SI.POV.GINI?view=map.

World Justice Project 2016. *Rule of Law Index*. https://worldjusticeproject.org/our-work/publications/rule-law-index-reports/wjp-rule-law-index%C2%AE-2016-report.

2 Laws as Conventional Norms

Nicholas Southwood*

SOME NORMATIVE PHENOMENA—ETIQUETTE, dress codes, rules of a game—seem to be straightforwardly conventional. Others—morality, rationality, epistemic normativity—don't.[1] How about law? What I shall call the *Conventional Thesis* holds that law too is somehow to be explicated in conventional terms. The Conventional Thesis represents an important research program in general jurisprudence.[2] It is not hard to see why. At least on the face of it, legal and conventional phenomena have much in common. The Conventional Thesis might seem to be particularly well placed to vindicate a naturalistic account of law without the apparent costs of rival positivistic accounts.

Yet, in spite of its popularity and promise, a persistent worry concerning the Conventional Thesis is that it is ill equipped to account for the *normativity* of law. The problem is that

* I am grateful to Jeffrey Kaplan and David Plunkett for detailed and helpful written comments on an earlier version of this chapter; to Bob Goodin, Jeff Howard, George Letsas, Scott Shapiro, Kevin Toh, and Daniel Wodak for stimulating discussion; and to Bill Edmundson and Stephen Galoob and Adam Hill for independently raising the question of what my account of conventional normativity might imply for the issue of the normativity of law. Research for the chapter was supported by DP120101507 and DP140102468.

1 This is not to deny that there are conventionalist accounts of these phenomena (e.g. Mackie 1977, Harman 1975; Wong 2006); or even that such accounts might well turn out to be true. The point is just that morality, rationality, and epistemic normativity, unlike norm of etiquette, dress codes, and the rules of a game, do not *seem* to be conventional. I take it that this is common ground between conventionalists and anti-conventionalists—and part of what makes conventionalist accounts of these phenomena especially philosophically interesting.

2 Canonical statements of the Conventional Thesis include (Hart 1994); (Gans 1981); (Postema 1982); (Lagerspetz 1989); (Marmor 1998, 2001).

Dimensions of Normativity. David Plunkett, Scott J. Shapiro, and Kevin Toh.

law seems to have a special normative character that genuinely conventional phenomena seem to lack. Call this the *Normativity Objection*. It is hardly surprising that those with *antipositivistic* sympathies should be impressed by the Normativity Objection (Dworkin 1978; Letsas 2014). Antipositivists hold that the normativity of law derives, in part, from the normativity of *morality*. Assuming, plausibly, that the normativity of morality cannot be explicated in conventional terms, it follows straightforwardly that the Conventional Thesis cannot account for the normativity of law. Yet the view that the Conventional Thesis falls foul of the Normativity Objection also transcends jurisprudential party lines. Many card-carrying *positivists* have also rejected the Conventional Thesis on precisely these grounds (see Raz 1999; Green 1990; 1999; Dickson 2007).

To appreciate the force of the Normativity Objection, consider what sorts of conventional phenomena might potentially be thought to be constitutive of law. One possibility is that laws are taken to be explicable in terms of *conventions*—understood as solutions to coordination problems (Lewis 1969). Call this *the Conventions Thesis* (Gans 1981; Postema 1982; Lagerspetz 1989; cf. Marmor 1998; 2001). While the Conventions Thesis had a brief heyday, it has now been virtually universally abandoned—and for good reason. While the precise normative character of law is, of course, a matter of controversy, no one doubts that law is normative in the sense that it is constituted by *rules* or *requirements*. But conventions are not necessarily normative in even this *minimal* sense; some indeed are necessarily non-normative (Southwood 2010; Southwood and Eriksson 2011).[3]

A second possibility is that laws are taken to be explicable in terms of *positive norms*. Call this the *Positive Norms Thesis*. Positive norms are rules that are in some sense "recognized" or "accepted" or "established" in particular groups or communities and that may or may not be valid. They are to be distinguished from so-called *critical norms*, namely *valid rules* that may or may not be recognized or accepted or established in any groups or communities.[4] The problem is that positive norms needn't be *conventional*. Examples of *non-conventional* positive norms include the norms that compose the moral codes that exist within particular societies: say, the norm that one not engage in gratuitous violence towards others. The Positive Norms Thesis is therefore compatible with it being true that laws are to be explicated in terms of norms that are not genuinely conventional. It is therefore not really a version of the Conventional Thesis at all.

A third possibility—the most promising—is that laws are taken to be explicable in terms of *conventional norms* (Hart 1994; Marmor 1998; 2001). Call this the *Conventional Norms Thesis*. H. L. A. Hart is often interpreted as endorsing the Conventional Norms Thesis—an interpretation that Hart himself appeared to confirm in the Postscript to the Second Edition of *The Concept of Law* (Hart 1994). According to this interpretation, a legal system is a system of rules founded on a conventional "rule of recognition" that specifies the conditions that rules must satisfy in order to count as laws of the system.[5] Unfortunately, as we shall see, Hart

[3] Another problem is that the Conventions Thesis appears to lack sufficient generality. While *some* laws certainly serve a coordination-facilitating function, it is highly implausible to suppose that this is true either of laws *in general*, or of those norms that purport to confer legal validity on putative laws (Green 1990, 1999).

[4] The distinction between "positive" norms and "critical" norms is based on Hart's (1994) well-known distinction between norms of "positive morality" and norms of "critical morality." Morality is, of course, just one domain where this distinction is at play.

[5] While Hart is *often* interpreted this way, such an interpretation is not universally accepted. For important dissenting voices, see (Dickson 2007) and (Green 1999, 39–41).

himself does not provide a remotely plausible account of conventional norms. The theory he offers—the so-called "practice theory"—is subject to fatal shortcomings.

My aim in what follows is to explore a way of interpreting the Conventional Norms Thesis that is very much in the spirit of Hart's practice theory but that avoids its problems. This is based on the *practice-dependent* account of conventional norms that I have offered elsewhere (Southwood 2011; Southwood and Eriksson 2011; Brennan, Eriksson, Goodin, and Southwood 2013). I shall begin by rehearsing the practice-dependent account (Section I) and considering what an interpretation of the Conventional Norms Thesis based on the practice-dependent account might look like (Section II). I shall then consider whether this interpretation of the Conventional Norms Thesis is vulnerable to the Normativity Objection (Section III). To anticipate, I shall argue that it *isn't*. For it can account for all the ways in which law can justly claim to be normative. While there are ways of being normative that it cannot account for, it is an error to suppose that law is normative in any of those ways. Or so I shall argue.

I. Conventional Norms

Paradigmatic examples of conventional norms include norms of etiquette (e.g., the requirement not to talk with one's mouth full of food), dress codes (e.g., the requirement to wear a suit in certain workplaces), and the rules of games (e.g., the requirement not to tackle below the waist in Australian Rules Football). How should we understand norms of this kind? What unifies them? And what distinguishes them from other related phenomena?[6]

A. Positive Norms

Conventional norms are special kinds of positive norms. As noted above, positive norms are social facts: rules or normative principles that are in some sense "recognized" or "accepted" or "established" in particular groups or communities, and that may or may not be valid. Take the norm that existed among the pre-twentieth century Han Chinese that upper-class girls must have their feet bound (see Mackie 1996). This was obviously an absurd norm. Yet it existed for more than 700 years and exerted profound effects. By the nineteenth century virtually all upper-class girls and women had bound feet.[7]

---

[6] The issue of how to understand conventional norms has received little systematic attention to date from meta-ethicists, who have tended to focus more or less exclusively on *moral* norms, or, more recently, *robustly normative* norms, and to mention conventional norms only in order to note that they are *not* moral and/or *not* robustly normative. For some interesting recent work that bucks the trend see (Wodak 2017) and (Woods 2018).

[7] It is important to distinguish positive norms from two other types of norms. The first distinction is the one mentioned above between positive norms and critical norms. As noted above, critical norms are not social facts. Rather, they are *valid* normative principles that may or may not be recognized or accepted or established in any groups or communities. Take a moral norm according to which affluent individuals must give up most of their discretionary income to assist the destitute. This norm might well be valid. Hence, there may very well be such a critical norm of morality to that effect. However, it is certainly not sufficiently widely recognized, accepted, or established within our own societies for us to be able to say that there is a positive norm to the effect that affluent individuals must give up most of their discretionary income to assist the destitute.

How should we understand the nature of positive norms? Some philosophers hold that norms are (special) kinds of *conventions* (see Young 2003, 390; Posner 2000, ch. 1; Verbeek 2002; cf. Ullmann-Margalit 1977; Lewis 1969). The problem with the norms-as-conventions view is that the existence of a convention seems to be neither sufficient nor necessary for the existence of a positive norm (Eriksson and Southwood 2011). It is not sufficient because it seems possible for social practices not to be normative in any sense. (Think of a driving-on-the-left convention in a society of normative nihilists.) It is not necessary because it is possible for positive norms to be virtually universally breached. (Think of a society with an anti-adultery norm—for example, there is strong disapproval whenever one discovers that others are committing adultery—but where adultery is, as a matter of fact, rampant.)

Another view is that positive norms are clusters of *non-normative attitudes* such as (non-normative) beliefs and desires. For example, Cristina Bicchieri (2006, 11) holds that a normative principle[8] P is a positive norm of group G if a significant proportion of the members of G prefer to comply with P on condition that a) a significant proportion of the members of G comply with P, and b) either i) a significant proportion of the members of G expect her to comply with P; or ii) a significant proportion of the members of G expect her to comply with P, prefer her to comply with P, and may sanction her for not complying with P. Again, I am skeptical that any such cluster of desires is either sufficient or necessary for a positive norm (Brennan, Eriksson, Goodin, and Southwood 2013, ch. 2).[9] It is not sufficient since it would seem to be possible for the members of a population to have (secret) desires to behave in a way that is diametrically opposed to the positive norms that actually exist in their society conditional on others also behaving in that way and expecting an individual member to act in that way. (Think of a highly repressive society where the entire population strongly desires to behave in accordance with libertine principles on condition that others behave in a libertine fashion and expect each member to act in that way too.) It is not necessary since it also seems possible for the positive norms of a society to be dramatically at odds with members' desires. (Think of norms that individuals have absolutely no desire to comply with—and yet continue to do so because they have internalized the norms.)

A better view, I believe, is that positive norms are clusters of *normative attitudes* plus widespread knowledge of those clusters (Brennan, Eriksson, Goodin, and Southwood 2013, 29; cf. Hart 1994, 55–56). Call this the *norms-as-normative attitudes view*. More precisely, a normative principle P is a positive norm in a particular group G iff a) a significant proportion of the members of G have normative attitudes that reflect P and b) a significant proportion of the members of G know that a significant proportion of the members of G have normative attitudes that reflect P. Take the norm of etiquette in Zealand that holds that one must not talk with one's mouth full of food. The norms-as-normative attitudes view implies that this

It is also important to distinguish positive norms from what we can call *statistical norms*. Statistical norms are simply true generalizations. They do not involve normative principles in any way. Consider the claim that giving birth to 4–18 pups is the "norm" among female Mako sharks. That is just to say that most female Mako sharks give birth to 4–18 pups. It certainly does mean that there is any kind of normative principle that would be violated if a female Mako shark were to give birth to more or less than that.

[8] Notice that by a "normative principle" in this context I mean a *minimally normative* (as opposed to a *robustly normative*) principle. See below, Section III.

[9] Notice that Bicchieri does not say that it is necessary, only that it is sufficient.

is a norm in New Zealand just in case two conditions are met. First, a significant proportion of New Zealanders must have normative attitudes that reflect the requirement that one must not talk with one's mouth full. For example, they must *believe* that one must not talk with one's mouth full, or have *expectations* of those who talk with their mouths full, or be disposed to *disapprove* of those who talk with their mouths full. Second, a significant proportion of New Zealanders must *know* that a significant proportion of New Zealanders have such normative attitudes toward talking with one's mouth full.

The norms-as-normative attitudes view easily avoids the problems with the norms-as-conventions view and the norms-as-non-normative attitudes view. However, it might seem to face other problems. Consider, for example, a long forgotten rule of chess that permits a player to convert a rook to a bishop when the player's pieces are configured in some specific way. Given that the rook-conversion rule is long forgotten it is not the case that chess players have normative attitudes that reflect the rook-conversion rule, still less know that others have such attitudes. Yet for all that it might still potentially remain a rule of chess. Suppose that there is some document that details the rules of chess that is generally accepted as authoritative by chess players and that the rook-conversion rule is contained in the document. Plausibly this is enough in order for the rook-conversion rule to be a rule of chess.

This objection is based on a mistake. Normative attitudes may "reflect" a normative principle in two very different ways (Brennan, Eriksson, Goodin, and Southwood 2013, ch. 3). First, the conduct covered by the principle may *directly* reflect the principle inasmuch as the principle figures explicitly in the content of the attitudes, as when a New Zealander believes that one must not talk with one's mouth full or has expectations of those who talk with their mouths full. But, second, the normative attitudes may *indirectly* reflect the principle by directly reflecting some secondary rule (say, a rule of recognition) that is appropriately connected to the principle. This is the sense in which our chess players might potentially have normative attitudes that reflect the rook-conversion rule. That is, the chess players are disposed to criticize other players insofar as the other players are seen to violate the rules that are contained in the authoritative document. Since the rook-conversion rule is contained in the authoritative document, chess players are disposed to criticize players insofar as they are seen to violate the rook conversion rule (say, by converting the rook to a bishop when a pawn is at C6 rather than C7). To be sure, the normative disposition is never *activated* because, being ignorant of the rook-conversion rule, chess players are not in a position to "see" what would amount to obeying or violating it. But this does not mean that chess players lack normative attitudes that reflect the rook-conversion rule.

B. Practice-Dependence

Conventional norms, then, are positive norms, which I shall take to be clusters of normative attitudes plus widespread knowledge of those clusters. But, clearly, this cannot be the whole story. As noted above, there are also *non-conventional* positive norms. Take the moral, rational, and epistemic *codes* that exist within different groups. The norms that comprise these codes are clearly also positive norms and, hence (again, assuming that the norms-as-normative attitudes view is correct), clusters of normative attitudes plus widespread knowledge of those clusters. Nonetheless, positive norms of etiquette, dress codes, and the rules of games are (or at least seem to be) crucially different from positive moral, rational, and epistemic norms. For example, the positive norm of etiquette according to which one must not spit one's food onto the floor in a restaurant seems to be crucially different from the positive rational norm according to which one must not believe that p and believe that not-p. In virtue of what are conventional norms distinctive?

Conventional norms are distinctive, I suggest, inasmuch as they involve what I shall call *practice-dependent* normative attitudes (Brennan, Eriksson, Goodin, and Southwood 2013, ch. 4). Here is a rough test for whether a normative attitude counts as practice-dependent in the sense I have in mind: the agent is disposed to adduce a presumed practice in response to a certain kind of "why" question. Consider a paradigmatic conventional norm such as the norm in an Oxbridge college that one must pass the port to the left. Suppose that one asks a member of the college, "But why are you are disposed to disapprove of those who fail to pass the port to the left?" Insofar as her normative attitudes involving passing the port to the left are practice-dependent, we might reasonably expect her to answer by adducing the port-passing practice. "Because passing the port to the left is just what we do." "Because passing the port to the left is what we do around here." Compare this to a paradigmatic non-conventional norm such as the norm that one must not torture innocents for fun. Suppose that one asks someone who judges that it is wrong to torture innocents for fun, "But why (do you think that) it is wrong to torture innocents for fun?" We would certainly not expect her to answer, "Because refraining from torturing innocents for fun is just what we do around here."

Can we say something about what it means for a normative attitude to be practice-dependent in the particular sense I have in mind? I suggest that it means that the attitude is *grounded*, in part, in a presumed *social practice* (Southwood 2011). A social practice is a behavioral regularity that is explained, in part, by the presence of pro-attitudes or beliefs about the presence of pro-attitudes that are a matter of common knowledge (Southwood 2011, 775). Consider again the social practice of passing the port to the left. This is a social practice in some Oxbridge college just in case some significant proportion of the members of the college engage in the activity of passing the port to the left and their doing so is explained, in part, by the presence of pro-attitudes (or beliefs about the presence of pro-attitudes) involving passing the port to the left, where this is a matter of common knowledge among a significant proportion of the members of the college.

The other important idea is that of the *grounds* of a normative attitude. To say that normative attitudes are grounded in a presumed practice in the sense I have in mind is to say that the presumed practice constitutes some non-derivative part of the justification, in the mind of the agent who holds the attitude, for the content of the attitude: the justification for the requirement to act in a certain way, or for disapproval insofar as individuals fail to act that way, or for an expectation that individuals act in that way. So, for example, to say that the judgment of a member of an Oxford college that one must pass the port to the left is grounded in the presumed social practice of passing the port to the left is to say that the port-pass practice constitutes some non-derivative part of the justification, in her mind, for the requirement to pass the port to the left.

It is worth emphasizing several features of this account of conventional norms. First, social practices are playing a *justificatory* role with respect to the attitudes that are constitutive of conventional norms. This is by no means the only way that practices might interact with our normative attitudes. They might simply *explain why* we came to hold certain normative attitudes (or perhaps why we maintain them). Practices might also figure in the *content* of our normative attitudes. Suppose that a visitor to Britain judges that she (morally) ought to obey the British practice of orderly queuing. This is not a practice-dependent normative attitude in the sense I have in mind. For the queuing practice needn't be playing any kind of justificatory role in the visitor's attitude. Rather, it is simply figuring in the content of her attitude.

Second, practices are playing a *subjective* justificatory role. To say that a normative attitude is grounded in a presumed social practice is to say that the practice is playing a role in justifying the content of the attitude *in the mind* of the possessor of the attitude. It is entirely possible that the content of the attitude is, in fact, objectively wholly *un*justified, or objectively justified in a way that has nothing to do with any social practice. Indeed, the presumed practice may not even exist. Recall the case of an anti-adultery norm in a society that, unbeknownst to members of the society, is in fact widely violated. In this case, the justification for refraining from adultery may come from a presumed practice of refraining from adultery, even though there is no such practice.

Third, presumed practices must be playing a *non-derivative* justificatory role. Suppose that a Western woman judges that she ought to wear a head scarf when she is in Saudi Arabia. Plausibly the practice of wearing a head scarf is playing a role in justifying the requirement in her mind to wear a head scarf. But its role may be wholly derivative. The justification, in her mind, for wearing a head scarf may be simply that she ought to avoid attracting unwelcome attention, and that contravening certain social practices associated with how she dresses may result in attracting unwelcome attention. By contrast, practice-dependent normative attitudes are attitudes where the justificatory role of the practice is not purely derivative in this way. Rather, part of the justification for the content of the attitudes comes from the practice itself.

Fourth, practice-dependent attitudes are attitudes that are grounded *in part* in social practices. They need not be—and typically are not—grounded wholly in practices. Rather, practice-independent considerations may also very well figure in their grounds. Thus, for example, someone who judges that one mustn't commit adultery at least in part because of a presumed practice of refraining from committing adultery might very well also do so in part because she judges that adultery tends to be hurtful, to violate trust, and so on. The point is just that such practice-independent considerations must not *exhaust* the grounds of the attitudes. Practices must also figure.

Finally, it might be wondered how this practice-dependent account is supposed to be different from the so-called "practice theory" of conventional norms associated particularly with H. L. A. Hart. According to Hart's version of the practice theory, "rules are conventional . . . if general conformity to them is part of the reasons which its individual members have for acceptance" (Hart 1994, 255). According to Marmor, "a necessary *reason* for following a [conventional] rule . . . consists in the fact that others follow it too" (Marmor 2001, 5). Why think that the practice-dependent account is anything more than a *version* of the practice theory?

Clearly, there are important similarities between the practice-dependent account and the practice theory. Nonetheless, there are also two key differences. First, whereas the practice-dependent account holds that conventional norms only entail *presumed* practices, the practice theory entails that corresponding practices actually exist. This means that, unlike our practice-dependent account, the practice theory is inconsistent with the existence of conventional norms that are generally violated, such as the anti-adultery norm mentioned above.

Second, whereas the practice-dependent account holds that presumed practices are part of the *grounds* of the normative attitudes that constitute conventional norms, the practice theory holds that practices play a *reason-providing* role. Hart and Marmor disagree about the precise character of this role. For Hart, practices constitute reasons for *accepting* the relevant rules. Accepting a rule presumably does not entail *complying* with it, though plausibly it does entail being disposed to comply with it. For Marmor, practices constitute reasons for *following* the relevant rules. Following a rule *does* involve at least complying with it—and arguably also accepting it (and complying with it *because* one accepts it).

Either way, the practice theory has a fatal defect. For notice that, typically, the mere fact that there is a practice of behaving in a certain way is *not reason-providing*. As Green aptly notes, "[t]he fact that most people X and expect others to do likewise does not generally give one a reason for Xing. Typically, one should do likewise only if there is a reason for conformity" (Green 1999 38). Green himself takes this to show that the practice theory cannot explain the normativity of law. As we shall see, I think this is a mistake. Rather, there is a more obvious and serious defect with the practice theory. Since the practice theory makes the *existence* of conventional norms turn on whether a certain practice provides its members with reasons—either reasons to accept or reasons to follow relevant rules—and the fact that there is a certain practice does *not* typically provide its members with reasons, this means that the practice theory simply cannot accommodate the vast majority of conventional norms. It implies that any norm with which we do not have reasons to conform is *not a conventional norm*. Such an implication is absurd. By contrast, the practice-dependent account does not have this absurd implication. That's because it holds that the contribution that presumed practices make to the normative attitudes that constitute conventional norms is simply to constitute part of the justification *in the minds* of those who hold the attitudes for acting accordingly. Clearly it does not follow that the practices *in fact* give individuals reason to do anything. So, unlike the practice theory, the practice-dependent account is perfectly consistent with the existence of non-reason-providing conventional norms.[10]

II. The Conventional Norms Thesis

The Conventional Norms Thesis holds that laws are to be explicated in terms of conventional norms. I have suggested that conventional norms are to be understood in terms of practice-dependent normative attitudes. So, if the practice-dependent account of conventional norms is right, this suggests that we should interpret the Conventional Norms Thesis as the thesis that laws are to be explicated in terms of practice-dependent normative attitudes (plus knowledge of these practice-dependent normative attitudes).[11] Take any law—say, the law in a small nation Legislavia—that forbids driving with a blood alcohol reading of more than .05. This is to be explicated as follows: Some significant proportion

[10] Of course, this assumes that by "reasons" Hart and Marmor mean something other than merely considerations that play a subjective justificatory role. For relevant discussion see Kaplan 2017.

[11] I shall generally omit the knowledge condition in what follows.

of Legislavians (or relevant subset of them) have normative attitudes that are connected in the right way to the requirement not to drive with a blood alcohol reading of more than .05 and that are grounded, at least in part, in a presumed relevant Legislavian social practice. However, this is vague in at least three important respects. First, what exactly is the relation between the attitudes and law? Second, whose attitudes are relevant? Third, what is the relevant practice (and why think the attitudes are grounded in it)? Let us briefly consider some ways in which we might potentially make a start on answering each question in turn.

A. The Connection between Normative Attitudes and Law

The first important interpretative issue concerns the character of the connection between the practice-dependent attitudes that are supposed to be capable of explicating laws and the rules that constitute the laws that they are supposed to be capable of explicating. One possibility is that the normative attitudes are supposed to *directly reflect* the rules that constitute the laws they purport to explicate such that the acts covered by the laws figure explicitly in the normative attitudes. On this view, the drunk driving law in Legislavia is to be explicated directly in terms of practice-dependent normative attitudes toward the act of driving with a blood alcohol in excess of .05. That is, a significant proportion of relevant Legislavians judge that one mustn't drive with a blood alcohol in excess of .05, or expect others not to drive with a blood alcohol in excess of .05, or are disposed to disapprove of anyone who drives with a blood alcohol in excess of .05, at least in part because, or so they assume, there is a social practice of refraining from driving with a blood alcohol in excess of .05.

While a *direct* view of this kind is plausible in the case of *informal* conventional norms, such as norms of etiquette and dress, I take it that it is a nonstarter in the case of *formal* norms, of which laws are a paradigmatic instance. Consider laws that are known to be generally violated, such as the law in India mandating wearing a seat belt. Given the extent to which this law is violated, it is not plausible that there is a social practice of wearing a seat belt in India. Moreover, let's suppose that this is a matter of common knowledge. In consequence, even if there is a significant proportion of Indians (or some relevant subset of them) who judge that one should wear a seat belt, it is not plausible to suppose that these attitudes are practice-dependent: that a presumed practice of wearing a seat belt constitutes any part of the *grounds* of the attitudes. (There simply is no presumed practice.) So, the seat-belt-wearing law cannot be explicated in terms of practice-dependent attitudes that directly reflect the requirement to wear a seat belt.

The alternative is that laws are supposed to be explicated in terms of practice-dependent normative attitudes that are *indirectly* connected to the requirements that constitute the laws. For ease of exposition I shall focus here on the Hartian view according to which laws are rules that accord with a relevant "rule of recognition"—understood as a "duty-imposing" norm (Shapiro 2009). Suppose that Legislavia contains a very simple rule of recognition according to which laws are those rules that are enacted by the Legislavian legislature. This is to be understood as follows: there is some significant proportion of Legislavians (or some relevant subset of them) who have normative attitudes that reflect the requirement on officials to apply and enforce all and only those rules that are enacted by the Legislavian legislature—normative attitudes that are grounded, at least in part, in a presumed practice of applying and enforcing all and only those rules enacted by the Legislavian legislature. Laws—such as the Legislavian drunk-driving law—are to be explicated in terms of these attitudes. The attitudes indirectly reflect the content of the drunk-driving law inasmuch as the relevant Legislavians have normative attitudes, not toward drunk driving, but toward the act of applying and enforcing certain rules, of which the rule not to drive with a blood alcohol of more than .05 is an instance.

Unlike the direct view, an *indirect* view of this kind can readily accommodate laws that are known to be generally violated. Consider again the law in India mandating wearing a seat belt. According to the indirect view, it does not matter whether there is a social practice in India of wearing a seat belt. The relevant practice-dependent attitudes are instead ones connected to the act of applying and enforcing laws that satisfy certain conditions.[12] So long as the seat-belt-wearing law satisfies these conditions, this is enough for it to count as a law in India.

B. *Whose Attitudes?*

A second important interpretative issue concerns the set of individuals whose attitudes are supposed to be capable of explicating laws. One possibility is that the relevant set includes *all* (sane, adult) members of the relevant community. So, for example, the Legislavian law is to be explicated in terms of the practice-dependent normative attitudes of all (sane, adult) Legislavians concerning the application and enforcement of rules that are enacted by the Legislavian legislature. In the imaginary case of Legislavia, an *inclusive* view of this kind has some plausibility. That's because the imaginary Legislavian rule of recognition is extremely simple—simple enough that it is plausible to suppose that a significant proportion of all Legislavians could potentially have normative attitudes that directly reflect it. It is plausible to suppose, in other words, that a significant proportion of all Legislavians have normative attitudes concerning the act of applying and enforcing all and only those rules that are enacted by the Legislavian legislature.

But when we turn to *actual* legal systems, it might seem that an inclusive view is hopeless. The problem is that the rules of recognition that characterize actual legal systems may be much more complex. There may simply be no way that ordinary citizens who lack legal training and expertise can be expected to have the requisite understanding of these complexities. In consequence, there is simply no way that they can have the requisite normative attitudes—attitudes concerning the application and enforcement of those rules that have the right kind of complex profile.

What is the alternative? It might seem that the only alternative is some kind of *exclusive* view according to which the relevant set includes some special *subset* of the (sane, adult) members of the relevant community: say, the legal officials of the community (Hart 1994). The main advantage of an exclusive view of this kind is that it is better equipped to accommodate the complex rules of recognition that often exist within actual legal systems. For, in virtue of their special training and expertise, a society's legal officials are clearly better

[12] Of course, there are different views about precisely what these conditions are. I shall touch on some of the relevant issues in the following subsections.

equipped than ordinary citizens to appreciate and be sensitive to the complexities of the legal system's rule of recognition.

But there is also a different kind of inclusive view that is worth mentioning. Return again to the obscure rook-conversion rule in chess. We saw that a chess player who is unaware of the rook-conversion rule might nonetheless have normative attitudes that are connected (albeit indirectly) to it—say, if she judges that chess players must obey all and only those rules that are written down in the authoritative Rule Book. Now consider a modification of this case. Suppose that the player is unaware, not merely of the rook-conversion rule, but of the rule of recognition itself. She might still retain normative attitudes that are connected—albeit even more indirectly—to the rook-conversion rule. To see this, suppose that her reliable chess partner, who is one of the Special Few who knows what the rule of recognition is and who also possesses a copy of the authoritative Rule Book, informs her that he has discovered the existence of the rook-conversion rule, but does not tell her how he has discovered it. This might very well lead her to employ the rook-conversion rule in her subsequent chess playing. But it is hard to see how this could be so unless she has normative attitudes connected to the rule of recognition in spite of being ignorant of what it is. That is, she is disposed to judge that chess players must abide by all and only those rules that satisfy the chess rule of recognition—whatever it is.

This suggests the possibility of a different kind of inclusive view of the law. On this view, it is not enough that the rule of recognition is enshrined within the normative attitudes of a significant proportion of legal officials. In addition, what matters is that a significant proportion of the population at large have practice-dependent normative attitudes that are indirectly connected to this rule of recognition—whatever it is. One possibility is that a significant proportion of the population must judge that citizens must *obey* those rules that accord with the society's rule of recognition. A second possibility is that a significant proportion of the population must judge that legal officials are entitled to apply and enforce those rules that accord with the society's rule of recognition. Or perhaps both are required.

C. Practices

A third important interpretative issue concerns the presumed practices that ground the normative attitudes that are supposed to be capable of explicating laws. One question is simply: What *are* these practices? Consider, first, the presumed practice that grounds the (rule of recognition-constituting) normative attitudes of *legal officials* concerning the application and enforcement of certain rules. The obvious thing to say here is that the presumed practice is one of applying and enforcing certain rules and not others. Thus, for example, in the case of Legislavia, we might reasonably expect a significant proportion of legal officials to be disposed, if asked why they judge that legal officials must apply and enforce all and only those rules that are enacted by the Legislavian legislature, to adduce a presumed practice of applying and enforcing all and only those rules that are enacted by the Legislavian legislature. This does not necessarily mean that there *is* any such practice. It could very well be that, as a matter of fact, the rules that legal officials tend to apply and enforce come apart from the rules that are enacted by the Legislavian legislature (in either or both directions).

Next, what kind of presumed practices might ground ordinary citizens' normative attitudes? This will depend on what we think these attitudes are. Suppose that we think that a significant proportion of ordinary citizens must judge that there is a *duty to obey* those laws that accord with their society's rule of recognition. In that case, presumably the attitudes must be grounded in a presumed practice of obeying those rules that accord with the society's rule of recognition. This needn't mean a presumption of universal obedience for any such rule, or even a presumption of general obedience for all such rules. It is enough that there is a presumed practice of obeying such rules in general. And, again, even the weaker presumption may very well be mistaken. Or suppose instead that we think that a significant proportion of ordinary citizens must judge that legal officials are entitled to apply and enforce all and only those laws that accord with their society's rule of recognition. In that case, the presumed practice will presumably be of the same kind as the legal officials' practice mentioned above.

A further question is why we should think that these sorts of presumed practices should be capable of grounding the normative attitudes of legal officials and/or ordinary citizens in the first place. Even if we are happy to grant that presumed practices are capable of grounding the normative attitudes that are constitutive of, say, norms of *etiquette*, law might seem importantly different. What exactly is the *mechanism* by which these practices are supposed to take on a "normative life of their own?"

One possible mechanism is what I have called elsewhere *identification* (Southwood 2011, 779). That is to say that particular presumed practices come for us to represent aspects of a valued identity; they come to be part of what it means for us to see ourselves as members of groups to which we belong. This is surely part of the story. The normative attitudes of *some* legal officials and ordinary citizens surely *sometimes* reflect a sense of identification with the group and its practices. It is less clear, however, that recourse to identification has sufficient generality for this to be a credible general account. As William Edmundson nicely puts it, it doesn't seem plausible to suppose that "legal insiders" always or even typically "identify so strongly and stickily with legal practice" (Edmundson 2012).

A second possible mechanism is simple *habituation* (Southwood 2011, 780). That is to say that through force of habit, some ways of doing things come to strike us as especially valuable or important. Again, this is surely an important part of the story in the case of law. It may well be the primary mechanism in the case of ordinary citizens who tend to be relatively unreflective about the law and its putative normative credentials. But, again, it is doubtful that it is the whole story. Consider, in particular, the normative attitudes of legal officials. Even if habituation can explain the normative attitudes of those legal officials who have been living and breathing the relevant legal practice for years, this seems less plausible in the case of newcomers. Moreover, whereas habituation seems to be a potent force in relatively unreflective contexts, contexts of legal application, interpretation, and enforcement at least sometimes require being highly explicit and reflective about the rules and practices that are being evoked.

It seems likely, then, that further mechanisms will also have to be at play—mechanisms beyond identification and habituation. One interesting candidate mechanism is some kind of *pretense* (Toh 2018; Wodak 2017). The idea would be that legal officials engage in a kind of *fiction* or *make-believe* according to which certain practices have a special kind of normative significance that is not reducible to practice-independent features and that makes it appropriate to "take one's cue" from these practices.[13]

This is all I am going to say here about how we might go about filling in the details of the Conventional Norms Thesis, interpreted in light of the practice-dependent account of conventional norms. Obviously I have only scratched the surface. Let us now turn to the key question of whether the Conventional Norms Thesis, thus interpreted, is vulnerable to the Normativity Objection.

III. The Normativity of Law

The Normativity Objection holds that law possesses a certain kind of normative character and that conventional phenomena lack the right kind of normative character for law to be explicable in conventional terms. Is our interpretation of the Conventional Norms Thesis vulnerable to the Normativity Objection?

A. Minimal Normativity

Let's start with the idea that law is *minimally normative*.[14] Call this the *Minimal Normativity Thesis*. A phenomenon is minimally normative inasmuch as it involves *rules* or *requirements* that permit, forbid, and require certain actions and attitudes. The Minimal Normativity Thesis is relatively weak. To say that law is minimally normative is merely to say that it possesses the kind of normativity that is possessed by children's games such as Tiddlywinks and Snakes and Ladders. Tiddlywinks and Snakes and Ladders are also normative in the minimal sense inasmuch as there are moves that are permissible, impermissible, and obligatory insofar as one is playing these games. At the same time, this certainly doesn't mean that the Minimal Normativity Thesis is entirely toothless. Recall that I relied upon the Minimal Normativity Thesis above when I argued against the Conventions Thesis. To recap: the argument was that the Conventions Thesis is false because whereas a) law is necessarily minimally normative, b) conventions—understood as solutions to coordination problems—are not necessarily minimally normative.

Might a critic seek to deploy the Minimal Normativity Thesis to argue against our interpretation of the Conventional Norms Thesis in the same fashion? The idea would be that our interpretation is false because whereas a) law is necessarily minimally normative, b) conventional norms—understood as practice-dependent normative attitudes—are not necessarily minimally normative.

Perhaps. But notice that there is a significant difference between our account of conventional norms and the Lewisian account of conventions. The Lewisian account holds that

---

[13] I am not committing myself to a fictionalist proposal of this kind. But it strikes me as a promising and intriguing subject for further inquiry. I am grateful to Daniel Wodak and Kevin Toh for helpful discussion here.

[14] The idea that that we must distinguish between *minimal* (or *formal*) normativity, on the one hand, and *robust* (or *substantive*) normativity, on the other, has come to be an important theme in the contemporary philosophy of normativity (see, e.g., Parfit 2011; Broome 2013; McPherson 2011; McPherson and Plunkett 2017: Plunkett and Shapiro 2017).

the attitudes that partially constitute conventions are *non-normative* attitudes: desires and non-normative beliefs (Lewis 1969). So the Conventions Thesis, thus interpreted, is perfectly consistent with there being no minimally normative talk and thought whatsoever associated with law. It is enough that legal officials and/or ordinary citizens have *desires* to behave in certain ways conditional on others also behaving in those ways and *beliefs* that others will do so. In contrast, our account of conventional norms holds that conventional norms are clusters of special *normative* attitudes. There simply cannot be law unless legal officials and/or ordinary citizens possess practice-dependent normative attitudes that are appropriately connected to relevant rules.

A natural response is that, at most, this shows that conventional norms are *taken* to be minimally normative, not that they really *are* minimally normative. Thus, it might be argued, it does not follow from the fact that a significant proportion of the legal officials and/or ordinary citizens of Legislavia *judge* that Legislavians must not drive with a blood alcohol level of more than .05 that there is a *genuine rule* that requires Legislavians not to drive with a blood alcohol level of more than .05—any more than it follows from the fact that a significant proportion of the citizens of Saudi Arabia judge that women who commit adultery should be stoned to death that there is a genuine rule that requires that women who commit adultery be stoned to death.

This is based on a simple confusion. Of course, if we interpret "a genuine rule" to mean "a robustly normative rule"—that is, a genuinely reason-providing rule—then it is obviously right that believing falsely doesn't make it so. But we are not interested here in robust normativity. Rather, we are interested in whether a cluster of normative attitudes plus knowledge of that cluster is *minimally* normative. So, the question is whether a cluster of normative attitudes plus knowledge of the cluster is sufficient for there to be a positive norm that permits, forbids, or requires individuals to act in certain ways. It seems clear that it *is* sufficient. Thus, for example, if a significant proportion of the citizens of Saudi Arabia judge that women who commit adultery should be stoned to death and this is a matter of common knowledge among Saudi Arabians, then this *is* sufficient for there to be a genuine rule in Saudi Arabia that requires that women who commit adultery be stoned to death. A truly awful rule, obviously. But a genuine rule nonetheless.

B. Robust Normativity

Next, what about the idea that the normativity of law is somehow to be understood, not merely in terms of minimal normativity, but in terms of *robust* normativity? Call this the *Robust Normativity Thesis*. Robust normativity as I shall understand it here is a matter of entailing claims about what we *ought* or *have reason* all-things-considered to do.[15] The "all-things-considered" is critical in order for there to be a meaningful distinction between robust and minimal normativity. There is a sense in which we might say that the rules of Tiddlywinks tell us what we "ought" (or "have reason") to do. But the "ought" here is certainly not the all-things-considered

[15] Notice that this is nonetheless neutral regarding the issue of whether reasons (or something else, such as, say, value) is the *most fundamental* normative notion.

ought.[16] Rather, it is simply, as we might put it, the "ought of Tiddlywinks." But the claim that we ought$_{\text{tiddlywinks}}$ to refrain from playing a "sqopped" piece certainly does not entail that we ought$_{\text{all-things-considered}}$ to refrain from playing a sqopped piece. (Suppose that the only way to avert a nuclear war is to annoy one's opponent by illegitimately playing a sqopped piece.) Nor does it entail the weaker claim that one has *reason* to refrain from playing a sqopped piece. Reasons for action are considerations that *contribute* to positive verdicts about what we ought all-things-considered to do.[17] It will *often* be the case that one has some reason to refrain from playing a piece that has been sqopped. But it doesn't take much imagination to devise scenarios where this isn't so: say, where one ought not to be playing Tiddlywinks in the first place, where one's opponents are notorious cheats, where there is much to be gained and nothing to be lost by flouting the rules, and so on.

How might we seek to capture the normativity of law in terms of robust normativity? The simplest idea is to insist that law *is* robustly normative. Morality and prudence are commonly (though not universally) thought to be robustly normative. That is to say that, necessarily, if morality or prudence requires one to perform some act then one ought or has reason to perform it. Similarly, we might hold that, necessarily, if there is a *law* that requires one to perform an act, then one ought or has reason to do so. If this is right, then it spells doom for our interpretation of the Conventional Norms Thesis. For it is demonstrably false that conventional norms, understood as clusters of practice-dependent attitudes, *entail* corresponding claims about what we ought or have reason to do.[18] Consider a ghastly conventional norm that exists among the male students of a prestigious university of hall of residence, that prescribes that freshmen must upload naked photographs of their sexual partners to the internet without their partners' consent. Suppose that a significant proportion of the students judge that freshmen "must" do this—at least in part because they judge that this is "just the done thing." Yet it is manifestly false that freshmen ought or have reason to act in this way.[19]

16 I have argued elsewhere that, rather than a *single* all-things-considered ought, there is in fact a *plurality* of all-things-considered oughts (Southwood 2016). However, this is not relevant in the current context, so I shall set it aside.

17 This isn't supposed to be an *analysis* of the notion of a reason. Some philosophers hold that reasons are somehow to be analyzed in terms of the notion of ought (Broome 2013; Schroeter and Schroeter 2011). Others hold that reasons are to be analyzed in some other way, say in terms of actual or hypothetical desires (Smith 1994; Schroeder 2007). Still others hold that the notion of a reason should be treated as a primitive and hence as unanalyzable (Scanlon 1998; Parfit 2011). I shall remain neutral on these difficult questions here.

18 This version of the Normativity Objection is particularly associated with Ronald Dworkin (1978, 46–80; see also Shapiro 2009). Dworkin famously took Hart to task for confusing "social" and "normative" rules. By a "normative" rule Dworkin means precisely a robustly normative rule: that is, a rule that necessarily provides agents with reasons for action. As Dworkin correctly notes, the fact that the members of a group have certain (practice-dependent) normative attitudes does not necessarily provide agents with reason to act accordingly. Given that law involves "normative" (i.e., robustly normative) rules, explicating law in terms of "social" (or conventional) norms is plainly incapable of accounting for the normativity of law. As a matter of fact, Dworkin's claim is even stronger than the claim that law is robustly normative as I have been interpreting it, since he holds, not merely that law *entails* that we have corresponding reasons for action, but that law *provides* us with (i.e., is a *source* of) corresponding reasons for action.

19 To be sure, we may *often* have reason to comply with conventional norms. The point is just that this is not *necessarily* so. Whether we ought or have reason to comply with conventional norms depends, inter alia, on their particular content and the particular circumstances in which agents find themselves.

The crucial question, I take it, is whether law is indeed robustly normative. I see absolutely no reason to think that it is (Enoch 2011). Just as there are ghastly conventional norms with which we have no reason to comply, so too there are ghastly *laws* with which we have absolutely no reason to comply. Until 1997 when the Tasmanian Criminal Code was revised in the aftermath of *Croome v Tasmania*, homosexuality was a criminal offense. It does not follow that until 1997 homosexual men necessarily had reason to refrain from homosexual activities.

However, it is worth briefly mentioning an important argument due to Leslie Green that might be thought otherwise. The argument centers on "the way that rules figure in practical reasoning." According to Green,

> [t]he fact that a valid rule exists may be cited as a *reason* for action. To the novice's question, "why must I move my rook diagonally?" a complete response is "It is required by the rules." Of course, . . . there may be cases in which the fact that a rule exists does not provide a conclusive reason for acting one way or another. But *as far as this question goes*, the citation of the rule is an answer, and any plausible theory of rules needs to explain how that could be so. . . . The fact that most people X and expect others to do likewise does not generally give one a reason for Xing. (Green 1999, 37–38)

Green's thought appears to be as follows: Laws are rules that can be (and often are) appealed to in practical reasoning. But rules can only be appealed to in practical reasoning insofar as they entail reasons for action. So it follows that laws must entail reasons for action—something that the Conventional Norms Thesis manifestly cannot explain.

Suppose we grant Green's claim that laws are rules that can be appealed to in practical reasoning. Nonetheless, we should reject his claim that rules can only be appealed to in practical reasoning insofar as they entail reasons for action. Return again to the case of the awful conventional norm that prescribes that freshmen must upload naked photographs of their sexual partners to the internet without the partners' consent. Suppose that a newly arrived freshman asks the question, "Why must I upload the photos?" Here, too, a "complete" response is "Because it is required by the rules." Of course, to say that the response is "complete" is not to say that it is a good response. On the contrary, the response is utterly awful. But surely Green cannot think that the only rules to which we can appeal in practical reasoning are nice rules. If he does think that, then we obviously shouldn't grant his claim that all *laws* are rules that can be appealed to in practical reasoning.

To be sure, there is a *different* interpretation of Green's argument. According to this alternative interpretation, the "reasons" needn't be all-things-considered ones. In the case of chess, they may be "reasons of chess." In the case of the law, they may be "legal reasons." And so on. We can grant Green's claim that rules can only be appealed to in practical reasoning insofar as they entail reasons, thus construed. But, of course, that's because we are now simply talking about minimal normativity. And, as we saw, there is no reason to think that conventional norms lack this kind of normativity. Either way, we do not yet have any reason to suppose that law possesses a kind of normativity that the Conventional Norms Thesis is incapable of capturing.

I have argued that the idea that law is robustly normative cannot plausibly be maintained. But this is not the only way to understand the Robust Normativity Thesis. A promising alternative is that law *claims* to be robustly normative (Raz 1979; 1999; Shapiro 2011; Plunkett and Shapiro 2017). For example, David Plunkett and Scott Shapiro (2017, 50) write: "The law, in other words, claims or invokes the same kind of fully loaded normativity that is a core focus of metaethical concern. When the law obligates adults to pay taxes, it claims that, all things considered, adults should pay their taxes. Tax evaders are punished precisely because they fail to respect the normative claims of the law." If this is right, then plausibly it suffices to explain how the normativity of law differs from, say, the normativity of the rules of Tiddlywinks. While both are minimally normative, it seems a considerable stretch to hold that the rules of Tiddlywinks claim to be robustly normative. It also avoids the objectionable implication that, necessarily, agents ought, or have reason, to comply with abhorrent laws. Recall the Tasmanian anti-homosexuality laws. The idea that law claims to be robustly normative implies that, before 1997, Tasmanian law claimed that, necessarily, homosexual men had all-things-considered reason to refrain from homosexual intercourse. But it does *not* imply that they in fact had reason to do so.

What does it mean to say that law "claims" to entail reasons? On one view, it means that a significant proportion of legal officials and/or ordinary citizens *take* it to entail reasons. This implies that a significant proportion of legal officials and/or ordinary citizens are in the grip of a serious error. It also suggests a way of rendering a law legally invalid: get enough legal officials and/or ordinary citizens to see the error for what it is. Finally, it means that, insofar as we think law is a valuable institution that we have reason to preserve, it is important to take steps to ensure that the error remains intact. These implications are not credible, or so it seems to me.

On a different proposal, it means that *from a certain point of view* one has reasons to comply with law (Raz 1979; 1999; Shapiro 2009). As Scott Shapiro (2009, 258) puts it, "To say that one has a legal obligation, for example, is simply to assert that *from the legal point of view*, one has an obligation. Statements of legal obligation, on this interpretation, are perspectival assertions." On the face of it, talk of what we ought or have reason to do "from a point of view" sounds awfully like we are back within the domain of minimal normativity.[20] However, Shapiro means something quite specific by "the legal point of view," namely "the perspective of a certain normative theory. . . . The legal point of view of a certain system, in other words, is a theory that holds that the norms of that system are morally legitimate and obligating" (Shapiro 2009, 258). So the idea is that where there is a law requiring us to X, this means that there is a normative theory that claims (or entails the claim) that one has reason to X. This is supposed to explain how law is different from Tiddlywinks since, whereas we need to postulate such a normative theory to make sense of law, we do not need to postulate a normative theory that makes claims about what moves we ought or have reason to take in order to make sense of Tiddlywinks. Moreover, it needn't entail that legal officials and ordinary citizens are in the grip of an error. That's because judging that a certain normative

[20] Thus, it is not obvious how this is supposed to capture something special about the normativity of law—something that makes it qualitatively normatively different from, say, the rules of Tiddlywinks. (That is, to say that one has an obligation of Tiddlywinks (say, to refrain from playing a sqopped piece) is to simply to assert that *from the Tiddlywinkish point of view*, one has an obligation to refrain from doing so.) And, as we have seen, the Conventional Norms Thesis is perfectly compatible with the Minimal Normativity Thesis.

theory *claims* that, say, homosexuals have reason to refrain from homosexual intercourse clearly doesn't entail judging that in fact homosexuals have reason to refrain from homosexual intercourse.

While this isn't the place to evaluate Shapiro's important proposal in depth, it also seems to have some unwelcome implications. For one, if I have understood the proposal correctly, it is possible that not a single member of a society (not a single legal official or ordinary citizen) *accepts* the normative theory that claims that we have reason to perform the various acts that law prescribes. But then it is hard to see why we are entitled to privilege *this theory* in particular. There is presumably a different theory that says that one ought or has reason *not to perform* the acts that the law of one's own society prescribes. Why privilege the former over the latter? For another, while it is true that Shapiro's proposal does not entail that legal officials and ordinary citizens are in the grip of an error, it entails something that, if anything, seems even worse: namely, that the entire edifice of law rests on an error. Since it's false that, necessarily, we have reason to obey the laws, the legal point of view consists in the perspective of a theory that is straightforwardly mistaken. Theories aim at truth, and the theories that constitute the legal point of view fall spectacularly short. That being so, it is tempting to say, "so much the worse for the legal point of view."

C. *Authority*

Next, consider the idea that law is an *authoritative* institution (Raz 1979; 1999). Call this the *Authority Thesis*. The notion of authority is often understood in terms of special (all-things-considered) *reasons*. For example, on the popular Razian view, law is authoritative in the sense that it provides or claims to provide *exclusionary reasons* (Raz 1979). That it is to say that law necessarily "offers a reason for acting as it requires and a reason for not acting on certain valid reasons against acting as it requires" (Green 1999, 44). I shall set aside this view. If I'm right that we should reject the Robust Normativity Thesis, then it follows, a fortiori, that we should also reject the Authority Thesis, thus construed. If law does not entail reasons or claims about reasons, then, *a fortiori*, it does not entail or claim to entail special kinds of reasons or claims about exclusionary reasons.

How else might we understand the authority of law if not in terms of reasons? One possibility is to avail ourselves of the Hartian idea that law encompasses certain kinds of secondary rules: in particular, rules of enforcement and change (in addition to rules of recognition). The fact that law encompasses rules of enforcement means that there is a recognized power to enforce many laws. This is plausibly part of what makes law authoritative in a way that is different from, say, the rules of Tiddlywinks.[21] The fact that law encompasses rules of change means that there is a recognized power to create new (minimally normative) obligations. We might think that this is part of what makes law authoritative in a way that is different from, say, the norms of etiquette.[22] Clearly, there is no reason to think that this kind of "authority"

---

[21] At the same time, this does not distinguish law from games as such. Australian Rules Football also encompasses rules of enforcement.

[22] Alternatively, it might be said that while this makes law *different* from etiquette, it does not make it any more *authoritative*. I am grateful to David Plunkett for this observation.

poses any difficulty for the Conventional Norms Thesis. The Conventional Norms Thesis is perfectly capable of accounting for both rules of enforcement and rules of change.

But, more interestingly, we might also go further and hold that even if law does not entail, or claim to entail, exclusionary reasons, it nonetheless has, as it were, an *exclusionary structure*. What might this exclusionary structure look like? Here is one idea: Suppose that we understand the obligations of law as (minimally normative) demands to treat the relevant rules *as if* they are exclusionary reasons. This might be thought to be enough to make problems for our interpretation of the Conventional Norms Thesis. As Leslie Green has pointed out, "it is obvious not all [conventional norms] impose obligations. It is a [conventional norm] in my society that men do not wear skirts, but there is no obligation to refrain from doing so." That's because conventional practices do not generally have an exclusionary structure. Rather, as Green puts it, "it is the ordinary process of balancing all reasons against each other, taking into account all the available information, which itself recommends these practices" (Green 1999, 44).

My response is that there are special conventional norms that *do* have the requisite exclusionary structure. Consider the rules of chess. These plausibly involve requirements to treat the rules as if they are exclusionary reasons. Thus, the rule that forbids moving a rook diagonally seems to involve a requirement to set aside the strategic advantage one might achieve by moving one's rook from A1 to E5, the fact that this would make one's opponent laugh, and so on. According to the Conventional Norms Thesis, this rule can be explained in terms of the fact that a significant proportion of chess players, say, judge that one must exclude such considerations at least in part because, in their minds, there is a practice of excluding such considerations.

Returning now to the law: Suppose that we hold that law has a special kind of exclusionary structure. This can be explained by the Conventional Norms Thesis as follows: a significant proportion of legal officials and/or ordinary citizens judge that we must exclude certain considerations (say, the fact that other social authorities issue conflicting directives) at least in part because there is a presumed corresponding exclusionary practice. While conventional norms do not necessarily have this exclusionary structure, the particular conventional norms that are constitutive of law do. Or so it might be argued.

D. Categoricity

Finally, consider the idea that laws are categorical imperatives. Call this the *Categoricity Thesis*. Once again, we had better not understand this as the claim that law entails *categorical reasons*. But this is consistent with the idea that law nonetheless has a *categorical structure*. That is to say that many laws make *unconditional demands*. In this respect, laws are quite different from those norms that make *conditional* demands. Consider norms of fair play. Plausibly, these entail that we must perform certain acts so long as—but only so long as—others generally do so.

It might seem that our interpretation of the Conventional Norms Thesis is straightforwardly inconsistent with the Categoricity Thesis. That's because the normative attitudes that constitute conventional norms might seem to be straightforwardly conditional rather than unconditional. Consider my judgment that one must hold a fork in one's left hand. If this is a practice-dependent attitude, then it must be grounded, in part, in a presumed social practice of people holding their forks in their left hand. If I become aware that individuals no longer behave in the relevant way (they no longer hold their forks in their left hand), this will necessarily undercut part of the justificatory support that is required in order for it to be a practice-dependent normative attitude. So my judgment would seem to involve a principle that makes a demand that is conditional on the way people generally behave.

This objection involves a mistake. It does not follow from a normative attitude being practice-dependent that it makes demands that are conditional on the practice. The easiest way to see this is to consider cases where practice-dependent attitudes involve *rigidification* with respect to the relevant practices (see Southwood 2011, 793–794). Take my judgment that one must hold one's fork in one's left hand. As we have seen, if this is a practice-dependent attitude, then it follows that the practice of people holding their forks in their left hand must constitute part of the justification, in my mind, for the requirement to hold one's fork in one's left hand. But this does not mean that, in my mind, were there not to be such a practice, one would not be required to hold one's fork in one's left hand. Even if the justification in my mind for the requirement comes, in part, from a practice, which does not exist necessarily, given that there is such a practice, I may believe that one must hold one's fork in one's left hand even in the absence of such a practice. It may be that I would not judge that one must hold one's fork in one's left hand if I took there to be no such practice. Still, right now, I do presume there to be such a practice; and the practice justifies a requirement that has application, in my mind, to cases where there is no such practice. So, it is simply false that the normative attitudes that constitute conventional norms must be conditional rather than unconditional. Our interpretation of the Conventional Norms Thesis is perfectly capable of capturing law's categorical structure after all.

IV. Conclusion

I have offered a particular interpretation of the Conventional Norms Thesis and considered its capacity to account for the normativity of law. I have argued that we have reason to be optimistic—and certainly more optimistic than many critics have assumed.

Suppose I'm right. This provides us with some reason to believe that the Conventional Norms Thesis, thus interpreted, is true. Only some reason, to be sure. Law is complex and multifaceted. There are many other things that an account of law, to be plausible, will also have to account for. A thoroughgoing defense of the Conventional Norms Thesis would have to consider in depth many topics that I have not even touched upon here.

Suppose instead that I am wrong. Our interpretation of the Conventional Norms Thesis fails to account for the normativity of law. Suppose that my account of conventional normativity is correct (or that we have very good reason to believe that it is correct). In that case, the failure of our interpretation of the Conventional Norms Thesis would give us very good reason to believe that the Conventional Norms Thesis is false.

Alternatively, suppose that we have good independent reason to believe that the Conventional Norms Thesis is correct. (I'm not quite sure what those reasons would be, but never mind.) In that case, the failure of my interpretation of the Conventional Norms Thesis would give us very good reason to reject my account of conventional normativity.

I retain the (pious) hope that the first of these three possibilities is the correct one. But each of them is interesting. Either way, we will have learned something about legal and/or conventional normativity.

References

Bicchieri, Cristina. 2006. *The Grammar of Society: The Nature and Dynamics of Social Norms*. New York: Cambridge University Press.

Brennan, Geoffrey, Lina Eriksson, Robert E. Goodin, and Nicholas Southwood. 2013. *Explaining Norms*. Oxford: Oxford University Press.

Broome, John. 2013. *Rationality through Reasoning*. Oxford: Blackwell.

Dickson, Julie. 2007. "Is the Rule of Recognition Really a Conventional Norm?" *Oxford Journal of Legal Studies*, 27:373–402.

Dworkin, Ronald. 1978. *Taking Rights Seriously*. Cambridge, MA: Harvard University Press.

Edmundson, William. 2012. "Law in the Neighborhood of Morality and Convention," *JOTWELL* (January 20, 2012), http://juris.jotwell.com/law-in-the-neighborhood-of-morality-and-convention/.

Enoch, David. 2011. "Reason-Giving and the Law," In *Oxford Studies in Philosophy of Law*, 1, edited by Brian Leiter and Leslie Green.

Galoob, Stephen and Adam Hill. 2014. "Norms, Attitudes, and Compliance," *Tulsa Law Review*, 50: 614–636.

Gans, Chaim. 1981. "The Normativity of Law and Its Coordinative Function," *Israel Law Review*, 16:333–349.

Green, Leslie. 1990. *The Authority of the State*. Oxford: Clarendon Press.

______. 1999. "Positivism and Conventionalism," *Canadian Journal of Law and Jurisprudence*, 12:35–52.

Harman, Gilbert. 1975. "Moral Relativism Defended," *Philosophical Review*, 84:3–22.

Hart, H. L. A. 1994. *The Concept of Law*, 2nd ed., revised and edited by P.A. Bulloch and J. Raz. Oxford: Clarendon Press.

Kaplan, Jeffrey. 2017. "Attitude and the Normativity of Law," *Law and Philosophy*, 36:469–493.

Lagerspetz, Eerik. 1989. *A Conventionalist Theory of Institutions*. Helsinki: Societas Philosophica Fennica.

Letsas, George. 2014. "The DNA of Conventions," *Law and Philosophy*, 33:535–571.

Lewis, David. 1969. *Convention: A Philosophical Study*. Cambridge, MA: Harvard University Press.

Mackie, Gerry. 1996. "Ending Footbinding and Infibulation: A Convention Account," *American Sociological Review*, 61:999–1017.

Mackie, J. L. 1977. *Ethics: Inventing Right and Wrong*. Harmondsworth, UK: Penguin.

McPherson, Tristram. 2011. "Against Quietist Normative Realism," *Philosophical Studies*, 154:223–240.

McPherson, Tristram and David Plunkett. 2017. "The Nature and Explanatory Ambition of Metaethics." In *The Routledge Handbook of Metaethics*, edited by Tristram McPherson and David Plunkett. New York, NY: Routledge.

Marmor, Andrei. 1998. "Legal Conventionalism," *Legal Theory*, 4:509–531.

_____. 2001. *Positive Law and Objective Values*. Oxford: Oxford University Press.
Parfit, Derek. 2011. *On What Matters*. Oxford: Oxford University Press.
Plunkett, David and Scott Shapiro. 2017. "Law, Morality, and Everything Else: General Jurisprudence as a Branch of Metanormative Theory," *Ethics*, 128:37–68.
Posner, Eric. 2000. *Law and Social Norms*. Cambridge, MA: Harvard University Press.
Postema, Gerald. 1982. "Coordination and Convention at the Foundations of Law," *Legal Studies*, 11:165–203.
Raz, Joseph. 1979. *The Authority of Law*. Oxford: Oxford University Press.
_____. 1999. *Practical Reason and Norms*. Princeton, NJ: Princeton University Press.
Scanlon, T. M. 1998. *What We Owe to Each Other*. Cambridge, M.A.: Bellknap Press of Harvard University Press.
Schroeder, Mark. 2007. *Slaves of the Passions*. Oxford; New York: Oxford University Press.
Schroeter, Laura and Francois Schroeter. 2011. "Reasons as Rightmakers," *Philosophical Explorations*, 12:279–296.
Shapiro, Scott. 2009. "What Is the Rule of Recognition (and Does It Exist)?." In *The Rule of Recognition and the US Constitution*, edited by Matthew Adler and Kenneth Einar Himma. Oxford: Oxford University Press.
_____. 2011. *Legality*. Cambridge, MA: Harvard University Press.
Smith, Michael. 1994. *The Moral Problem*. Oxford: Blackwell.
Southwood, Nicholas. 2010. "The Authority of Social Norms." In *New Waves in Metaethics*, edited by Michael Brady. Aldershot: Palgrave MacMillan: 234–248.
Southwood, Nicholas. 2011. "The Moral/Conventional Distinction," *Mind*, 120:761–802.
_____. 2016. "Does 'Ought' Imply 'Feasible'?" *Philosophy & Public Affairs*, 44:7–45.
Southwood, Nicholas and Lina Eriksson. 2011. "Norms and Conventions," *Philosophical Explorations*, 14:195–217.
Toh, Kevin. 2018. "Law, Morality, Art, the Works." In *Law as an Artifact*, edited by Luka Burazin, Kenneth Himma, and Corrado Roversi. Oxford: Oxford University Press.
Ullmann-Margalit, Edna. 1977. *The Emergence of Norms*. Oxford: Clarendon Press. 1977.
Verbeek, Bruno. 2002. *Instrumental Rationality and Moral philosophy: An Essay on the Virtues of Cooperation*. Dordrecht; Boston: Kluwer Academic.
Wodak, Daniel. 2017. "Mere Formalities: Normative Fictions and Normative Authority," *Canadian Journal of Philosophy*, 37:231–262.
Wong, David 2006. *Naturalistic Moralities: A Defence of Pluralistic Relativism*. Oxford: Oxford University Press.
Woods, Jack. 2018. "The Authority of Formality," *Oxford Studies in Metaethics*, 13: 207–229.
Young, Peyton. 2003. "The Power of Norms." In *Genetic and Cultural Evolution of Cooperation*, edited by P. Hammerstein. Cambridge, MA: MIT Press: 389–399.

3 Legal Teleology

A NATURALIST ACCOUNT OF THE NORMATIVITY OF LAW

David Copp*

PLURALIST-TELEOLOGY IS THE naturalist account of normativity that I have proposed in other work (Copp 2009). Legal Teleology is an account of the normativity (or authority) of law that is implied by pluralist-teleology. Legal Teleology is compatible with the positivist view that law consists at root in a social practice of a certain kind. Yet Legal Teleology also can accommodate at least some claims about the relation between law and morality that were advocated by twentieth century opponents of positivism, including natural law theorists. Insofar as law is normative, it sees the law as having a "purpose," and it says that law is defective insofar as it does not further that purpose. It agrees that jurists can sometimes help law better to serve its purpose when they invoke moral principles in interpreting law. Legal Teleology therefore represents a kind of intermarriage between legal positivism and natural law theory.

There are five propositions about law that I will use to frame the argument. Each of these propositions is plausible in its own right, or so it seems to me, yet the five form what seems to be an incoherent set. I call this the "Five Theses Problem." Two of the theses are characteristic of legal positivism while three are characteristically accepted by natural law theorists and other opponents of positivism. As I shall explain in Section IV of this chapter, Legal Teleology can accommodate all of these theses. Each of the other theories I shall discuss rejects one or more of them or else lacks the machinery to accommodate one or more. For my purposes, the most important is the thesis that law is "robustly normative"—law is a source of

* My thinking about pluralist-teleology has been helped by many people over the years. I am grateful to all of them. I am especially grateful to George Letsas, Kevin Toh, and the members of DaGERS who discussed the original version of this chapter at a meeting in 2015.

Dimensions of Normativity. David Plunkett, Scott J. Shapiro, and Kevin Toh.

genuine reasons in a way that mere games are not. Games such as pick-up sticks have a formal or internal normativity since their rules specify what is to be done in certain circumstances, but their rules are not robustly normative (Copp 2009, 30). I will say more about this in Section I. I contend that law *is* robustly normative. Standard forms of legal positivism cannot account for this, but if I am correct, the central doctrines of positivism are compatible with the robust normativity of law. At least, Legal Teleology is compatible with the robust normativity of law.

In Section I, I explain the intuitive distinction between merely formal normativity and robust normativity. In Section II, I introduce the basic ideas of pluralist-teleology. In Section III, I introduce Legal Teleology. In Section IV, I turn to the Five Theses Problem and explain how Legal Teleology accounts for all five theses. Sections V through VIII briefly discuss the theories of H. L. A. Hart, Joseph Raz, Ronald Dworkin, and John Finnis and show that each of them fails to accommodate one or more of the theses. Section IX is a brief conclusion. Legal Teleology does not set itself in opposition either to legal positivism or to natural law theory. It is an ecumenical position that seeks to embrace and to ground the most plausible tenets of both.

I. Formal and Robust Normativity

Pluralist-teleology is intended to provide an account of the nature of robustly normative facts—facts about how we ought to act or live, and facts about how we have reason to act and live. It is intended to explain the nature of these facts in a way that is compatible with the realist view that there are normative properties, such as the property an action can have of being morally required. And it is also intended to be compatible with the naturalist view that sees normative facts as metaphysically on a par with ordinary non-normative natural facts such as the facts of economics or psychology.[1] My aim in this chapter is to use pluralist-teleology to explain the robust normativity of law.

Robust normativity contrasts with the merely formal normativity of a game. The rules of typical games require certain things or prohibit certain things, and, in light of this, there is a "reason" in the game for players to do these things. Intuitively, however, these reasons have no genuine normative significance. In pick-up sticks, for instance, the goal is to pick up sticks from a jumbled pile, and a player is required in each move to pick up a stick without moving any other stick. Given the rules, there is a reason in the game to try to pick up a stick without moving any other stick, but this reason has merely an "internal" or "formal" status. Of course a player might have moral or prudential reasons to follow the rules, and a player who violates a rule might be guilty of cheating and deserve moral criticism. But the mere fact that she broke a rule would not in itself be a mistake for which she would deserve criticism other than the merely formal criticism that she violated a rule. To make this completely obvious, consider a made-up game, *hat-or-scratch*, which requires everyone to wear a hat at all times when outdoors or else to scratch her scalp every hour on the hour. Many of us break this rule, but

[1] So understood, normative naturalism is compatible both with "natural law theory" in jurisprudence and the denial of natural law theory. Say that natural law holds that there are moral constraints on what can count as law, or on what can count as a legal system. Normative naturalism can agree with this.

merely in doing this we intuitively make no mistake for which we deserve criticism. There is not a genuine reason to follow this rule. In themselves, the rules of games have a merely "internal" or "formal" normativity, I shall say.[2]

The merely formal status of the requirements and reasons of a game contrasts with the status of the requirements and reasons of prudential rationality and morality, which intuitively are "genuinely" or "robustly" "normative" or "binding" or "authoritative." These terms are in scare quotes because it is not clear how to explain what is meant, but I think the idea is intuitive. Intuitively, the reasons and requirements of morality and prudential rationality are binding or authoritative in a way that the rules of pick-up sticks are not. Morality for instance is no game. Its requirements are "robustly normative," as I will say. There is a reason, a moral reason, to act as morally required. Intuitively, a person who violates a moral requirement thereby makes a mistake for which she deserves criticism unless she has a relevant excuse.

Some philosophers are skeptical about robust normativity in general, and some might deny that morality is robustly normative. Some might contend, for example, that moral reasons and requirements are merely "internal" to morality just as the hat-or-scratch reason to wear a hat or scratch is merely internal to hat-or-scratch. I maintain, however, that these skeptical views about robust normativity fly in the face of the strong intuition that moral violations are normatively significant in a way that violations of the rules of a game are not, at least not in themselves. Intuitively, a person who breaks the hat-or-scratch rule does not *deserve* criticism on that basis alone, nor need she have acted contrary to any *genuine* reason. Intuitively, she need not have made a mistake, nor need she be at fault. So I think there is an intuitively plausible distinction between the merely formal normativity of a game and robust normativity.

It is not within the purview of this chapter to attempt to respond to those who are skeptical of robust normativity, or to those who deny that morality is robustly normative. I am going to assume that morality is genuinely binding and authoritative or robustly normative in a way that the rules of a game are not. I aim to show that the requirements of law are similarly normative.

I agree with positivists that facts about the existence and content of law are ordinary facts about institutionalized social practices. Such practices create formal requirements that are laid down by their rules or standards, just as games do. One might therefore think that law has merely the formal normativity of a game. The challenge I face is to explain how it can be that the requirements of law are robustly normative—with qualifications—despite their merely social pedigree, and how it can be that their relationship to moral obligations and requirements is more than merely coincidental. To meet this challenge, I turn to pluralist-teleology.

---

[2] In "Hard Cases," Ronald Dworkin uses an analogy with chess to illustrate his view about law (Dworkin 1975a, 1079–1082). As Kevin Toh pointed out to me (in correspondence), one might think on this basis that Dworkin views the normativity of chess as relevantly similar to the normativity of law. Dworkin points out that chess officials might appeal to ideal conceptions of the game in adjudicating difficult disputes about the rules just as, in his view, judges can appeal to principles in adjudicating difficult legal disputes. But even if there is this similarity, it does not follow that the law and the rules of chess are both robustly normative. It also does not follow that they are both merely formally normative.

II. Pluralist-Teleology

There are two basic intuitions lying behind pluralist-teleology.[3] One is that the realm of the normative is diverse or plural. There are different kinds of reasons and different kinds of requirements, including moral requirements, requirements of practical reason, epistemological requirements, and so on. Among these, I shall be arguing, are legal reasons and requirements. The second basic intuition is that the realm of the normative is unified, despite its plurality, by the fact that the different kinds of reasons and requirements answer to different kinds of generic problems that people face and that are (or would be) ameliorated by their subscribing to appropriate standards or norms. Since these are problems that we can better cope with when we subscribe to appropriate systems of norms, I call them *problems of normative governance*. Since there are more than one problem of this kind, the theory is pluralist. It implies that the different kinds of reasons and different kinds of normative consideration correspond to different problems of normative governance. Let me explain what I mean by a problem of normative governance, first in general terms, and then by means of some examples.

There is a problem of normative governance just in case there is a state of affairs or set of facts such that, first, these are general facts about the circumstances of human life and about human beings' biological and psychological nature that, other things being equal, interfere with or hinder humans' ability to meet their basic needs and to serve their values—no matter what they value, within a wide range of possible things to value—or would so hinder them if they did not subscribe to appropriate norms.[4] Second, people's ability to cope with this state of affairs is affected by their actions and choices. Third, the state of affairs is ameliorated or better coped with when people subscribe to and comply with an appropriate system of standards or norms than would otherwise be the case.[5] Situations of this kind are what I call problems of normative governance. These are *generic* problems. They are problems for human beings as they are in general, given the kinds of things that people tend to value, for a very wide range of things to value. The idea is that normativity is to be understood and explained in relation to such problems.

One example is the *problem of autonomy*. To be self-governing, we need to govern our lives in accord with our values, but we have a tendency to seek short-term or shortsighted advantages at variance with our values. The problem is that whatever we value, within a wide range of things that we might value, this tendency makes us less likely to achieve what we value than would otherwise be the case. We are susceptible to temptations. This problem can be mitigated if we subscribe to a standard of prudential rationality that calls roughly for behavior that serves our values and meets our needs (Copp 2007, ch. 10). To *subscribe* to a norm in the sense I have in mind is to have an intention to conform to it, and it is also to be

[3] This section follows (Copp 2015, 63–67), and (Copp 2009, 27–28).

[4] Take it that something is needed by human beings just in case, given the circumstances of human life and the physical and psychological nature of humans, humans must have this thing in order to achieve what they value, no matter what they value, within a wide range of possible things to value.

[5] Systems of norms in the sense I have in mind are abstract systems of rules.

disposed to experience a negative emotional response if one fails to conform. Hence, subscription to the standard of prudential rationality, other things equal, would enhance and reinforce any tendency a person already had to serve her values and meet her needs. On this view, there is a requirement of rationality so to behave. There is reason so to behave. This requirement and this reason are grounded in the problem of autonomy.

A second example is the *problem of sociality*. People need to live in societies in order to meet many of their basic needs and to be in a position to achieve the things they value, but there are a variety of familiar causes of discord and conflict that can undermine cooperation and make a society less successful than it otherwise could be at enabling people to pursue what they value with a reasonable prospect of success. This is the problem of sociality. Unless it is mitigated in some way, members of the society are less able than would otherwise be the case to achieve what they value. Moreover, our ability to cope with the situation is affected by our actions and choices. And our ability to cope with the situation would be enhanced if enough of us subscribed to an appropriate system of standards. Plainly, widespread subscription to a moral code can help to ameliorate the problem, provided that the code calls for people to be willing to cooperate, and generally to avoid discord and conflict. Of course, some moral codes would do better than others at ameliorating the situation. Simplifying, say that the *ideal moral code* is the one the currency of which—its being embedded in the culture—would do most to ameliorate the problem of sociality. On this view, moral requirements are the requirements set out in the ideal moral code, and moral reasons are, similarly, considerations the ideal moral code counts in favor of acting in various ways. These requirements and reasons are grounded in the problem of sociality.

I have been simplifying in various ways. First, I have been assuming that there is a *single* code the currency of which would do *most* to ameliorate the problem of sociality. There could however be cases in which there is a tie, or at least a rough tie. That is, it could be that several codes are such that their currency would do (roughly) equally well, and at least as well as the currency of any other codes, at addressing the problem of sociality. In such cases, we could perhaps say that an act is morally required if and only if failing to do it would be disallowed by all of the codes tied as "equal best."[6] Second, I am ignoring the fact that the moral culture of any actual society almost certainly is not ideal. Given this fact, a person's compliance with the ideal code might not *actually* do as much to ameliorate the problem of sociality as compliance with some other code that is designed to take into account how other people actually are likely to act.[7] There are other complications as well, but for present purposes, it is best to ignore them.[8]

The theory says, in effect, that morality is the solution to the problem of equipping people to live comfortably and successfully together in societies.[9] The basic idea was proposed by J. L. Mackie, who remarked that morality is best understood as a "device" needed to solve a

[6] Here I use an approach suggested by T.M. Scanlon (1998, 153). I have discussed this issue elsewhere (Copp 1995, 198–199; 2007, 17, 243).

[7] I have discussed this issue elsewhere (Copp 1995, 199–200).

[8] See (Copp 1995, 213–245) and (Copp 2007, 25–26, 55–150, 203–283).

[9] For details, see (Copp 2007), especially the introduction, and (Copp 1995).

"problem" faced by humans because of "certain contingent features of the human condition" (1977, 121).

It will be useful to mention a third example, the *problem of politeness*. To achieve what we value, at least within a wide range of things we might value, we need to be attractive to others as potential collaborators, to be able to interact with others in ways that others will find pleasing and comfortable. Societies have complex norms that call for behaviors that are not required in the abstract to enable us to cooperate with others, but that are required to facilitate our ability to interact cooperatively only because they are called for by the culture. These complex norms are standards of etiquette, such as the one requiring people not to belch during a meal. If we do not comply with these norms, and do not otherwise interact with others in ways they find pleasing and comfortable, we will be less able to achieve what we value than otherwise might be the case. The standard of politeness answers to this problem by requiring us to comply with the local standards of etiquette (Copp 2007, ch. 10, 343).[10]

One might raise many questions about this account of normativity. Most important, perhaps, one might doubt that the reasons and requirements that pluralist-teleology implies to exist are robustly normative. I contend, however, that they have the marks of robust normativity. On my account, for instance, moral requirements are categorically binding under a reasonable understanding of what this consists in (Copp 2015). They are not simply the requirements of games. The ideal moral, epistemic, and other normative systems postulated by pluralist-teleology answer to very real problems of normative governance.

According to pluralist-teleology, the normative truth in a given context, where a specific normative question has been raised, is a function, roughly, of the content of the system of norms the currency of which would do most to ameliorate the relevant problem of normative governance. On this view, the moral truth depends on the content of the ideal moral code.

Wrongness is the property (roughly) of being ruled out or prohibited by the ideal moral code. Of course, I do not hold that this is a conceptual truth (see Copp 2009). Accordingly, pluralist-teleology is a version of non-analytic normative naturalism since it sees normative facts or truths as metaphysically on a par with ordinary non-normative natural facts such as the facts of economics or psychology.

III. Pluralist-Teleology and Legal Teleology

There are obvious differences between law and etiquette on the one hand and morality on the other. Law and etiquette are actual social practices or institutions whereas morality, at least as I and other moral realists think of it, is a body of truths about (inter alia) how we ought to treat one another. This body of truths need not be reflected in actual social practices. In my view, as I explained, the moral truth is a function of the content of the *ideal* moral code.[11] In real-world situations, unfortunately, the moral view embraced by the actual moral culture of a society—its positive morality—is not the same as the ideal moral code for

---

[10] Note that it does not follow, on this picture, that there is a *moral* requirement to comply with the local standards of etiquette. Whether this is so, in my view, depends on the content of the ideal moral code.

[11] Of course our moral duties can refer to social practices or their rules. Because of this, the duties implied by the ideal moral code may depend on the nature of local social practices. There might be, for instance, a moral

that society. The requirements of this ideal code—the requirements of the *true, correct*, or "*critical*" morality—are not guaranteed to be the same as the requirements of the local moral culture. In the case of law, however, there is not intuitively a similar contrast between our legal duties and what is called for by the local legal institutions, nor, in the case of etiquette, is there intuitively a contrast between the duties of etiquette and what is called for by the local code of etiquette. Intuitively, our legal duties are grounded in the local legal institutions.[12] If this is correct, the account pluralist-teleology gives of morality would not be a good model for an account of the normativity of law.

Three models of the normativity of law are compatible with pluralist-teleology. According to the first, law is merely formally normative. According to the second, the normativity of law is comparable to the normativity of etiquette. The third model, which I see as most plausible, postulates a close relation between law and morality.

A) *The Internal Normativity Model.* We should note, to begin, that law is "formally" normative in the sense that it requires certain actions and prohibits others. For instance, traffic laws establish a legal requirement not to exceed certain speed limits. Games have a similar formal normativity, for the rules of a game count things we may do as permissible or impermissible. Law has this kind of formal normativity even in the case of corrupt or unjust legal systems. Hence we may say that people are required in law to do certain things, intending merely to assign to these acts the status of being required by the local legal system. The normativity here is internal to the local system.[13]

One might take the position that formal normativity of this kind is all that there is to the normativity of law. Call this the "Internal Normativity Model." On this model, the reason in law not to exceed the speed limit has a similar status as, for example, the reason in pick-up sticks to avoid moving an unintended stick. Of course, we often have robustly normative reasons to act in accord with law, such as moral and prudential reasons, but according to the Internal Normativity Model, considered in themselves and apart from any moral or prudential evaluation, the reasons provided by law are not robustly normative.

B) *The Autonomous Normativity Model.* It seems to me that the normativity of law is not merely the formal normativity of a game. And this is not merely because its requirements are typically backed up by threatened sanctions. Rather the law plays an important role in society and deserves our respect because of this, at least on the assumption that it is not unjust or problematic in other ways. I will express this idea by saying that there are genuinely or robustly normative reasons to do what the law requires, other things being equal. As John Finnis says, "law establishes reasons for action" (2014, 1).

To explain this from the perspective of pluralist-teleology, we need to show that law is (as it were) a device needed to ameliorate a problem of normative governance. I will argue that there is such a problem, which I will call the "problem of security." The relation between law

---

requirement to avoid rudeness. I thank Kevin Toh for suggesting (in correspondence) that I should make this point.

12 In this and the preceding sentence, I attempt to be neutral among the views of positivists, natural law theorists, and others regarding what determines the content of law.

13 "Positive morality" has a similar formal normativity. We can assess people's actions in relation to the standards of the local positive morality.

and the problem of security is similar to the relation between etiquette and the problem of politeness. Beyond this, I will argue, the problem of security is an aspect of the problem of sociality. The normativity of law is akin to the normativity of etiquette, but law is closely related to morality in a way I will explain. In this way, Legal Teleology is friendly to natural law theory.

What, then, is the *problem of security*? What general facts about the circumstances of human life interfere, other things being equal, with humans' ability to meet their basic needs and to serve their values, such that the existence of a legal system and the subscription of relevant people to relevant legal norms would tend to ameliorate this problem, other things being equal?

The problem of security is in part the risk of conflict and discord. For a variety of reasons, there is a tendency among humans to discord and conflict, and in the absence of law, the risk of conflict would be nontrivial, at least in large diverse societies. The problem is also, in part, the risk of missed opportunities for productive activity, including cooperative activity, due to an inability to protect property and enforce agreements. These problems are related. People could use threats and coercion to protect property and enforce agreements, but in the absence of law, this could exacerbate the risk of conflict. Agreements to cooperate could in principle deal with the grounds of conflict, but in the absence of law there would not be a way to enforce agreements without risking further conflict. Law can provide ways to resolve conflicts that at least do not make them worse, and it can provide a system of sanctions that can deter the worst kinds of conflict. It can provide a way of protecting property and enforcing agreements.

H. L. A. Hart cast light on the problem in his discussion of what he called the "minimum content of Natural Law." He outlined certain "obvious generalizations" concerning "human nature and the world in which men live" (1994, 192–193). These include the facts that human beings are vulnerable to violence, that they are approximately equal in their vulnerabilities, and that they have limited altruism, limited resources, limited understanding, and limited strength of will (194–198). These facts underlie the problem of security and the need for law. As Hart said, an understanding of these generalizations is "of vital importance for the understanding of law and morals" (199). Indeed, he maintained that reflection on these generalizations "show[s] that as long as [they] hold good, there are certain rules of conduct which any social organization must contain if it is to be viable." These rules are the "minimum content of Natural Law" (192–193). They include rules restricting the use of violence, rules creating an institution of property and providing for exchanges of goods, and rules providing sanctions for those who violate the other rules (194–198). Hart said that there is a "*natural necessity*" that such rules exist, given "the setting of natural facts and aims" that make the existence of such rules "both possible and necessary in a municipal [legal] system" (199).[14]

Of course, it is not metaphysically or conceptually necessary that a legal system will ameliorate the problem of security. It could be that the laws perversely exacerbate the causes of

[14] Hart adds that "for the adequate description" of law and "many other social institutions," we need to recognize that there are truths of natural necessity in addition to ordinary claims of fact and conceptual claims (1994, 199).

conflict and discord by, for instance, favoring the welfare of a small group over the welfare of the society as a whole. It could be that the laws do not include some of the rules that Hart had in mind as the minimum content of natural law. It could be that not enough people in positions of responsibility have a policy of doing what the law requires, or that the law is not effectively enforced. Or it could be that most ordinary citizens reject doing what the law requires, with the result that the laws are unenforceable. In order for a legal system to function effectively, enough people, and especially enough of the people in positions of responsibility, would need to subscribe to a norm calling on them to comply with law. There are many ways for law to fail in addressing the problem of security.

One might object that, in principle, people could ameliorate the problem of security, or even avoid it completely, without creating a legal system. Hart discusses the possibility of a society that has "rules of obligation" governing people's behavior, such as rules restricting "the free use of violence," but that lacks a legal system (1994, 91). He concedes that a small society in a stable environment could live successfully with such "a regime of unofficial rules." But in other circumstances, he contends, such a regime would be defective in several ways (92–94). First, there would be no rule determining what the rules are. Second, there would be no rule concerning how to change the rules or how to add a new rule. And third, the rules would only be enforced, inefficiently, by social pressure. For there would be no rule specifying how to settle whether a rule has been violated, or providing for a sanction in case a rule has been violated. More could be done to ameliorate the problem of security if these defects were remedied. To remedy the defects, Hart says, the rules of obligation would need to be supplemented by "secondary rules," including a rule of recognition, rules of change, and rules of adjudication (94). But once secondary rules of these kinds were added to the primary rules of obligation, we would have a rudimentary legal system.

A second objection might be suggested by John Finnis's remark that "Natural law theories all understand law as a remedy against the great evils of, on the one side anarchy (lawlessness), and on the other side tyranny" (2014, 4). In light of this remark, one might wonder whether a lawless tyranny would offer an alternative to law as a way of ameliorating the problem of security. Perhaps a lawless tyrant who had the power to enforce her will could ameliorate the problem of security. The tyrant could enforce her own preferences regarding conflict resolution, property, contracts, and so on, and this would not amount to creating a legal system. As I will explain, however, more would be done to ameliorate the problem of security if a legal system existed.

Why is this? Consider Lon Fuller's views about the "rule of law." In a legal system with the rule of law, laws are promulgated, which ideally at least gives people notice of what is expected of them. Further, in a legal system with the rule of law, the rules are not simply promulgated, but they are also adhered to by legal officials in their dealings with people (Finnis 2014, 6). These two factors taken together presumably would tend to increase the likelihood, other things being equal, that people will actually follow the rules, so that, other things being equal, the enforcement of a given set of rules *as law* under the rule of law would be expected to do more to ameliorate the problem of security than would be the case if the same rules were enforced by a tyrant simply as a matter of preference.

The Autonomous Normativity Model makes the following two claims. First, the problem of security is among the problems of normative governance. Second, the existence of a legal system that includes Hart's minimum content of natural law would tend to ameliorate this problem, other things being equal, provided that enough of the relevant people subscribe to a standard or a norm calling on them to comply with the law. Given these claims, pluralist-teleology implies that there is a robustly normative but autonomous requirement to comply with the laws of a legal system that includes Hart's minimum content of natural law. Call this the requirement of lawfulness. On this model, the requirement of lawfulness has the same kind of status as the standard of politeness. It has the robust normativity possessed by morality and by the requirements of rationality.

C) *The Moral Model.* The Moral Model agrees that law has a formal normativity, and it agrees that law has an autonomous normativity, since the requirement of lawfulness answers to the problem of security. The Moral Model adds that the problem of security is an aspect of the problem of sociality. I think that we can see that this is so by inspection—by considering closely what the problem of sociality is, as I described it. If I am right about this, it then turns out that there may be (defeasible) moral reason to act lawfully. This is the "Moral Model."

The problem of sociality is that, unless people subscribe to an appropriate moral code, discord and conflict can undermine cooperation and make a society less successful than it otherwise could be at enabling people to pursue what they value with a reasonable prospect of success. The problem of security is that, in the absence of a legal system, or if enough people do not subscribe to a norm calling on them to act lawfully, there is a risk of conflict and discord and a risk of missed opportunities for productive activity due to an inability to protect property and enforce agreements. These problems are obviously closely related, and they are rooted in similar facts about human beings and the circumstances in which they live. Indeed, one might claim that there is in fact only the one problem, the problem of sociality, and one might see morality and law as two ways to address that problem. The important point is that a well-functioning legal system that includes Hart's minimum content of natural law can help to ameliorate the problem of sociality by reducing the risk of discord and conflict and by facilitating cooperation.

If this is correct, as seems plausible, then the ideal moral code for a society would contain, inter alia, a norm calling on us to comply with the law—provided the law is not unjust.

In more familiar terms, I am suggesting, the most plausible view is that there is a pro tanto moral obligation to do what is required by laws that are not unjust (Copp 2009, 33).[15] That is, if a legal requirement R could be retained in a legal system even once the system is reformed as needed so that it is fully just, then there is a pro tanto moral obligation to act in conformity with R.[16]

It is important to understand how the Moral Model differs from the Autonomous Normativity Model. Both are compatible with there being a moral requirement to comply with laws that are not unjust. Both say that there is such a requirement just in case the ideal moral code includes a norm calling on us to obey laws that are not unjust. But the Moral

[15] Similarly, compliance with the local rules of etiquette can make for more pleasing and comfortable social interaction, which can in turn contribute to our addressing successfully the problem of sociality by helping to reduce the risk of discord and conflict. If this is correct, then, it seems plausible, the ideal moral code would contain a norm creating a defeasible requirement to comply with the local code of etiquette.

[16] I make no claim as to how stringent this obligation is, or as to how strong is the reason for obedience to law that it supports.

Model adds to the Autonomous Normativity Model the claim that there is an intimate connection between law and morality. As far as the Autonomous Normativity Model goes, law and morality are two normative systems that operate in parallel, where morality may or may not require us to act lawfully, and where law may or may not contain reference to moral considerations. According to the Moral Model, however, the problem of security is an aspect of the problem of sociality, and this means that law and morality ideally work in tandem to address the problem of sociality. On this view, we might say, there is a "design connection," or a "problem based" connection, between law and morality, and not merely an accidental one.

My claim is that there is a design connection between law and *ideal* morality. The problem of security might actually be exacerbated by moral disagreements between people. One reason societies need law is, arguably, to deal with such disagreements in a peaceful way.[17] But disagreements of this kind are due to differences between people's actual moral commitments, not to glitches in the content of ideal morality. Ideal morality speaks with one voice and, ideally, law works in tandem with it to address the problem of sociality.

The Moral Model seems to me to offer the most plausible way to apply pluralist-teleology to the case of law. Hence, in what follows, I shall sometimes speak of "Legal Teleology" without mentioning that I have in mind the Moral Model.

According to Legal Teleology, then, we can say that law ideally works in league with morality. Morality and law ideally enlist each other to help address the problem of sociality. Law and morality share a purpose in the sense explained by pluralist-teleology. That is, there is a "design connection" between law and morality, or a "justificatory connection," since both are properly held to a standard of evaluation that is defined as a function of the problem of sociality.

IV. The Five Theses Problem

The following five propositions about the law are individually plausible yet seem to form an incoherent set. Much of the debate in general jurisprudence can be framed as one driven by the apparent tension among these propositions. Different theories disagree as to which of the five they reject. A major advantage of Legal Teleology is that it allows us to accept all five propositions.

First is the thesis that the content of law in a given legal system depends only on the social customs and practices among those who are subject to the law of that legal system, or at least among those who are officials of the system. Call this the "positivist thesis."

Second is the thesis that there can be unjust law and unjust legal systems. Call this the "justice-not-guaranteed thesis."

Third is the thesis that law is robustly normative in itself, that the normativity of law is not merely the formal or internal normativity of a game. There are genuinely normative reasons to do what the law requires. Call this the "robust normativity thesis."

Fourth is the thesis that there is a nontrivial moral duty or obligation to obey the law. (I will use the terms "duty" and "obligation" interchangeably.) Even if this duty is conditional

[17] I am grateful to Kevin Toh for drawing this to my attention (in correspondence).

and defeasible, it is more than merely a trivial requirement to obey the law insofar as doing so is required. Call this the "moral duty thesis."

Fifth is the thesis that law is intimately linked to morality through its purpose, that the connection between law and morality is not merely contingent and extrinsic. Call this the "natural law thesis."

These five theses seem to form an incoherent set. This is the Five Theses Problem that I mentioned in the introduction. The positivist thesis seems to imply the justice-not-guaranteed thesis, and the two taken together seem to make trouble for the others. Most obviously, the robust normativity thesis seems incompatible with the positivist thesis. If the content of law depends only on the nature of existing social customs and practices, there would seem no guarantee that law would be normative in any robust way. Its normativity would seem akin to the normativity of a game. If the positivist thesis is true, there would of course be the trivial moral duty to obey the law when doing so is morally required, but no stronger general duty to obey the law would be plausible. For if the positivist thesis is true there would seem to be no guarantee that the law is just, and if the law is unjust, there surely is no moral duty to obey it.

Moreover, the positivist thesis seems to undermine the natural law thesis for it seems to mean there is no guarantee that the connection between law and morality is not merely adventitious. It would seem that law in itself has no purpose if at bottom it consists merely in a social practice.

It may seem that the positivist thesis is the main source of difficulty, for the positivist thesis seems to conflict with each of the robust normativity theses, the moral duty thesis, and the natural law thesis. As we will see, the positivist thesis is rejected by natural law theorists and others who reject positivism, including Ronald Dworkin. Yet the positivist thesis is difficult to deny. Legal systems are social institutions, and the nature of such a system would seem very obviously to be a sociological matter, dependent among other things on the practice of legal officials. Even John Finnis, whose view seems in the end to force him to deny the positivist thesis, does not deny it forthrightly. Indeed, he claims that natural law theorists do not deny the positivist thesis. He says that their central claims are about issues that positivists do not address, and that these claims are compatible with the positivist thesis (Finnis 2014, 1).

The justice-not-guaranteed thesis is also of course highly plausible and difficult to deny. History shows that there can be unjust legal systems. Any legal theory that implies otherwise must surely be rejected.

If we accept the positivist thesis, however, as well as the justice-not-guaranteed thesis, we must somehow grapple with the remaining three theses. The positivists Joseph Raz and H. L. A. Hart each deny at least one of these theses. As we will see, Raz denies the robust normativity thesis because he thinks there is no guarantee that there are genuinely normative reasons to do what the law requires (Raz 1986, 74). For Raz, law is not as such robustly normative or authoritative. Hart rejects the moral duty thesis (Hart 1994, 203) and he does not accept the natural law thesis (1994, 248). Furthermore, I do not believe his theory gives him the resources to account for the robust normativity of law.

As I have already said, I find the robust normativity thesis to be very plausible. The law is not merely a game; its normativity is not the merely formal normativity of a game. Plausibly, it seems to me, where the law requires someone to do A, she has a pro tanto moral reason to do A unless doing A would be wrong on independent grounds.[18] To have a moral reason to do A in such a case, there does not need to be a moral reason independent of law to do A. We could also put the point in terms of duty or obligation. We could say that there seems plausibly to be a moral duty to obey the law even though this duty is conditional and defeasible. The connection between law and morality is not merely contingent and extrinsic. The trick, however, is to explain how these seemingly plausible ideas can be compatible with the positivist thesis.

Legal Teleology attempts to explain this. Let me briefly summarize the main points. As I shall explain more fully in what follows, Legal Teleology is fully compatible with the positivist thesis and with the justice-not-guaranteed thesis. Given that people's subscription to a standard that calls for compliance with law would tend (other things being equal) to ameliorate the problem of security, it holds that there is an autonomous and robustly normative reason to comply with law (other things being equal). So Legal Teleology is compatible with the robust normativity thesis. Given the close relation between the problem of security and the problem of sociality, it holds, in addition, that the connection between law and morality is not merely contingent and extrinsic. And it holds that, in the circumstances faced by most complex societies, the ideal moral code would contain a norm calling for compliance with laws that are not unjust, other things being equal. So it holds that there is a moral duty to comply with laws that are not unjust, other things being equal. Legal Teleology can accept all five theses.

In what follows, I will look in more detail at the competing views and explain their responses to the Five Theses Problem.

V. Legal Teleology and Legal Positivism

H. L. A. Hart presented his important account of the nature of law in *The Concept of Law* (1994). Legal Teleology is compatible with all of Hart's central claims. It is compatible with his views regarding the "rule of recognition" (246), and it is compatible with his "practice conception" of customary rules, such as the rule of recognition (256).

Hart holds that a sophisticated municipal legal system is characterized by a rule of recognition that specifies the "ultimate criteria of legal validity" for the system. This rule, Hart says, is "a form of judicial customary rule existing only if it is accepted and practised" among legal officials in relevant contexts (256). The content of this rule is determined by the nature of the relevant practice. As Hart explains, the rule of recognition, so understood, supplies criteria of legal validity that "most often" refer "not to the content of the law but to the manner and form in which the laws are created or adopted." He adds, however, that a rule of recognition may also specify criteria relating to "substantive moral values or principles" (258).

In Hart's view, although the existence of a rule of recognition consists merely in the existence of a relevant social practice among legal officials, the rule of recognition is "normative" (257). The question to ask is how the existence of such a practice can have normative significance beyond the mere formal normativity of the rules of a game. Imagine an arbitrary

[18] Again, I make no claim as to how strong this reason is.

system of rules regarding, say, what color of clothes are to be worn, and imagine a group of people who, according to the rules, determine what the precise rules about clothing are to be. Imagine now that these people endorse these rules. There is a social practice of the relevant kind among these people. The mere existence of such a practice clearly would not mean that the rules are a source of genuine reasons for acting one way or another. So I conclude that Hart's practice conception cannot explain the robust normativity of law. I see no reason why Hart would need to disagree.

Legal Teleology says, in effect, that law has "a point" or a "purpose," that law should be understood as a response to the problem of security. Hart says, however, that his theory, "like other forms of positivism, . . . makes no claim to identify the point or purpose of law and legal practices as such" (248). Yet there is no tension between Hart's central claims about the law and the thesis that law has a purpose or a point when this thesis is explained in accord with Legal Teleology. Legal Teleology claims only that, to the extent that the law of a given legal system is robustly normative—to the extent that it is a source of genuine reasons for action—this is because the law helps to ameliorate the problem of security. And to the extent that the law has a moral claim on its subjects, this is because it helps to ameliorate the problem of sociality. We can express these points by saying that the "purpose" of law is to ameliorate the problems of security and sociality. I see nothing in positivism as such that is incompatible with these ideas.

Legal Teleology holds that, in the circumstances faced by most complex societies, there is a pro tanto moral obligation to do what is required by laws that are not unjust. Presumably, for example, there is a pro tanto moral duty to abide by legally established highway speed limits. Hart makes no such claim, yet I see no reason that Hart would need to disagree. Hart says that there is not *necessarily* a moral obligation or even a moral permission to do what the law requires (1994, 203). Legal Teleology agrees with Hart about this.

Hart says it is "central" to his view that "there is no important necessary or conceptual connection between law and morality" (259). Legal Teleology does not claim otherwise, yet it holds that there is an important *justificatory* connection between law and morality. I think that the kind of justificatory connection postulated by Legal Teleology is compatible with Hart's basic position. As we saw, Hart maintained that "reflection on some very obvious generalizations . . . concerning human nature and the world in which men live, show[s] that as long as these hold good, there are certain rules of conduct which any social organization must contain if it is to be viable." These rules are, he said, the "minimum content of Natural Law" (192–193). Hart said that there is a "*natural necessity*" that such rules exist (199). Legal Teleology argues that the generalizations Hart had in mind underlie the problem of security. And it adds that the normativity of law is ultimately grounded in the fact that law can ameliorate this problem. As far as I can see, there is nothing in positivism as such that is incompatible with this view. In fact, Hart's views about the minimum content of natural law greatly influenced the thinking that led me to pluralist-teleology and ultimately to Legal Teleology.

To summarize, Legal Teleology offers an account of the normativity of law that is not found in Hart's positivism. The account is nevertheless compatible with Hart's views.

VI. Raz on the Authority of Law

Unlike Hart, Joseph Raz does offer an account of the authority of law. But as I will explain, his account commits him to denying three of the five theses in the Five Theses Problem.

Raz holds that law has a legitimate authority, in making demands of citizens, only if law is a source of reasons for action. And, he holds, the fact that a legitimate authority requires something is a reason to act accordingly (Raz 1986, 46).[19] Raz holds that the law "claims unlimited authority," for it claims there is an obligation to obey the law regardless of its content (77). Raz contends, however, that there is no such general obligation to obey the law (70).[20] At most, the law has limited authority; certain citizens may have reason to obey certain laws but other citizens may have no such reason (77).

Raz argues for these claims on the basis of his "Normal Justification Thesis" (NJT). According to the NJT, in "normal" cases, a person A has authority over B only if it is likely that B will "better comply" with the basic authority-independent reasons that apply to her—reasons other than any reasons that may consist simply in the fact that A has directed her to do something—if she accepts A's directives "as authoritatively binding" and attempts to act as A directs rather than attempting to act on these basic reasons (53). The NJT reflects a "service conception of authority"—"the point" of having authorities is that they help their subjects to comply with the reasons that would exist anyway, even if the authority did not (67).

The NJT yields a case-by-case account of authority. It suggests that the authority a government has over a person depends in part on how good she is at acting on the basic reasons she has for doing things, and this can vary from person to person (74). A person who is very good at determining what she has basic reason to do may have no reason to comply with the law if it ever requires her to do something that she thinks is less well supported by basic reasons than an alternative. Raz does allow that some people may have reasons of different kinds for complying with the law—reasons other than the fact that compliance with law promises to increase the likelihood that they will comply with their pre-legal reasons (98–100). But these are not reasons for people in general to obey the law. So the existence of other kinds of reasons to obey the law still leaves us with a case-by-case account of the authority of law. In Raz's view, the authority of law is gappy (104).

Raz accordingly is committed to denying the robust normativity thesis. He thinks there is no guarantee that there are genuinely normative reasons to do what the law requires. Law is not *as such* robustly normative. Raz also seems to deny the moral duty thesis. He seems to deny that there is in general a nontrivial moral duty to obey the law. He also denies the natural law thesis. But he does think that the law has a purpose, at least insofar as it is genuinely normative. For he accepts the service conception of authority, which says that the purpose of

---

[19] It is not a reason *in addition to* all other reasons to do the thing, but a reason that "should exclude and take the place of" some of these other reasons (1986, 46).

[20] In discussing authority, Raz shifts from talking about whether there is a *reason* to obey to talking about whether there is an *obligation* to obey. It seems to me that there could be a reason to obey the law even if there is not a general obligation to obey, but I ignore this in the text.

authoritative law is to increase the likelihood that people will act in accord with their basic pre-legal reasons.

In Raz's view, the NJT gives the fundamental ground for the authority of law (67, 47). I think, however, that the NJT provides a poor explanation of the circumstances under which citizens have reason to obey the law, and I think that the service conception of authority needs to be reconsidered. Much of law is appropriately *not* designed to help citizens comply with underlying pre-legal reasons. Rather, in some cases, a person who conforms successfully with the balance of her pre-legal reasons may act in socially problematic ways. The law may be designed to change people's behavior in cases of this kind. It can do this by changing people's incentives so that they have reason to behave differently than they otherwise would, or by giving them opportunities they otherwise would lack, or by setting up systems that enable people to coordinate in ways that are beneficial, or by giving people assurance of how others will behave, and so on. In such cases, the law can give us new reasons.

Raz is, of course, aware of this objection and provides an answer. First, a state might act "quite properly" in deciding among otherwise acceptable options (1986, 49).[21] Second, where there is a coordination problem, we might all have reason to want there to be a convention, and reason to comply with one if one exists. In such a case, Raz says, it is compatible with the NJT for the state to issue a directive that establishes a convention, and such a directive would give citizens reasons they did not have before (49). Third, in Prisoner's Dilemma situations, Raz says, the state might properly issue a directive that changes the situation so that people have reason to act differently from the way they had reason to act before the directive was issued (51–52). In all of these ways, the law can make a difference to what citizens ought to do (48).

Raz's response may be successful in cases where everyone has pre-legal reason to want there to be a convention and to comply with any convention that comes to exist. But there are other kinds of case. We want to have a safe community, and this is a good reason to establish a speed limit. But according to the NJT, this is not enough to give the state authority to establish any specific speed limit since it does not show that establishing this particular speed limit will make it more likely that we will drive at speeds that accord with our *pre-legal* reasons. Similar worries undermine Raz's reasoning about Prisoner's-Dilemma-type cases. Everyone may have sufficient pre-legal reason to want the state to change people's incentives in a Prisoner's Dilemma situation. But, for example, the pre-legal reason a fisherman has to maximize her catch does not go away when the government sets a quota. This reason is still in place and it is a reason for the fisherman to try to exceed her quota if she can get away it. According to the NJT, the fact that it would be for the public good to change people's incentives is not enough to show that the state has the authority do so (71). For it does not show that doing so will make it more likely that people will act in accord with their *pre-legal* reasons.

Of course, Raz might respond that these objections merely show that the authority of law must be assessed on a case-by-case basis. Yet it seems to me that an adequate theory must at least account for the authority of the state in setting speed limits in residential

[21] Raz's example along these lines is the state's making a decision among antecedently acceptable schedules for the payment of a tax (49).

neighborhoods or in addressing Prisoner's Dilemma situations. So it seems to me that Raz's account is inadequate.

VII. Dworkin, the Content of Law, and the Duties of Judges

Ronald Dworkin has argued trenchantly against most of the central claims that characterize positivism. Hart has responded at length to Dworkin's arguments in the "Postscript" to *The Concept of Law* (1994). Since I agree with Hart on most of the issues, I will here focus on Dworkin's denial of the positivist thesis.

Dworkin insists, as against Hart, that the proper judicial interpretation of a given legal text always depends on a moral judgment. In general, he holds, a proposition to the effect that such and such is law in a given legal system is true if and only if, roughly, it follows from facts about the legal system's institutional history together with legal principles that pass a twofold test of fit and justification. First, the principles must fit sufficiently well with the legal system's institutional history. They must pass a "threshold test." And second, the principles must show the system as a whole "in a better light from the standpoint of political morality" than any other principles that pass the threshold test (Dworkin 1986, 255–256). Dworkin views his theory as defining law in terms of a "fraternal attitude," which aims, he says, "to lay principle over practice to show the best route to a better future, keeping the right faith with the past" (413).

This view has difficulty accounting for the interpretation of law in unjust legal systems. If a legal system is acutely unjust, no moral principles would justify it, and any putative moral principles that pass the threshold test of fit would show the system in a very bad light. "From the standpoint of political morality," it could be that none of the putative principles that would pass the threshold test of fit have any normative standing whatsoever since they could be unjust and unfair, racist, or morally arbitrary in other ways. In cases of this kind, a properly "fraternal attitude" would endorse fidelity to principles of political morality rather than keeping faith with past practice. In an acutely unjust legal system, fidelity to principles of political morality and fidelity to law would lead in different directions.

Dworkin might agree. He says at one point that a proper interpretation of law must invoke principles or putative principles that show the institutional history in the best *available* light (Dworkin 1982, section C). Perhaps he would say that, even in an acutely unjust legal system, the putative principles that pass the test of fit would include principles that show the system in the *least bad light* from the standpoint of political morality. These are the putative principles, he might say, that would fix the content of law in that legal system. Yet the putative principles that pass the test of fit with an evil system might only show that the system is evil in a "principled" way. This hardly recommends them from the standpoint of political morality.

The dispute between Hart's positivism and Dworkin's approach concerns whether the principles that pass the test of fit and that show a legal system's institutional history in the best available moral light are in every case *legal* principles. Hart agrees that there may be legal systems in which the rule of recognition treats certain moral principles as part of law. In such cases, legal officials might be authorized to use something similar to Dworkin's interpretive method in arguing for propositions of law. But there presumably could be legal systems in which the rule of recognition—or the practice of legal officials—at least seems *not* to permit reference to moral principles in legal reasoning. In such cases, Dworkin faces a dilemma. On the one hand, he could insist that, even in such cases, the truth of a legal proposition would depend on whether, inter alia, it followed from putative principles that would show the system in the best available moral light. On this horn of the dilemma, he would be saying in effect that the system's rule of recognition *would* treat as law the putative principles that show the system in the best light. If the practice of legal officials was not to treat such principles as principles of law, these officials would be mistaken. This is difficult to accept. On the other hand, Dworkin could say that, in such cases, if the practice of legal officials ruled out reference to moral principles in legal reasoning, then fit with institutional history would become the sole criterion of the correct interpretation of the law. On this horn of the dilemma, it would be unclear whether there is any interesting disagreement between Hart and Dworkin.[22]

One might wonder whether Dworkin's approach does actually commit him to denying the positivist thesis.[23] He once wrote, "the law of a community consists not simply in the discrete statutes and rules that its officials enact but in the general principles of justice and fairness that these statutes and rules, taken together, *presuppose* by way of implicit justification" (Dworkin 1975b, 1437, emphasis added). On a standard, *strict*, account of presupposition, a positivist could agree that the principles that a legal system's explicit statutes and rules presuppose play the same role in determining the content of the law as does the *meaning* of these statutes and rules. It seems clear, however, that Dworkin has something different in mind.[24] The principles that are "presupposed" in his sense are those the inclusion of which as legal principles would show the overall system in the best available moral light. Dworkin thinks that such principles *are* legal principles, which is not something a positivist could accept.

The trouble is that the positivist thesis is highly plausible. Legal systems are social institutions, and the nature of such a system would seem very obviously to be a sociological matter, dependent on the practice of legal officials. It seems to me, then, that Hart has the best approach on these matters. The truth of a proposition of law depends on the content (perhaps including any strict presuppositions) of the rule of recognition and this depends, in turn, on the practice of legal officials.

We could describe Dworkin as holding that judges are bound *in law* to interpret the law, given its institutional history, in a way that minimizes the degree to which it is morally unjustifiable. I am denying that they are bound *in law* to do this. But I agree they are *morally* bound to do this. This is not a trivial claim. It would be denied by people who see law as a morally sanctioned morality-free sphere of normative requirements. On a view of this kind, setting aside extreme situations, legal officials are *morally* bound not to let their moral

[22] Dworkin denies that the practice of legal officials can be captured by any *rule*, so he claims that there is not (in general) such a thing as the rule of recognition of a legal system. Yet he cannot avoid the dilemma by invoking this claim. He cannot deny that the practice of legal officials either does or does not rule out reference to moral principles in legal reasoning.

[23] Kevin Toh suggested this point and pointed me in the direction of (Dworkin 1975b).

[24] In the strict sense, for example, the claim that the king of France is bald presupposes that there is a king of France. Dworkin has a looser sense of presupposition in mind.

opinions intrude into their *legal* reasoning, except when authorized to do so by the local rule of recognition. I reject this view, and Dworkin and Hart surely would agree in rejecting it.

VIII. Natural Law

Although I agree with the basic tenets of Hart's theory, I find many of the views defended in the natural law tradition to be highly attractive. I believe that these views are compatible with Hart's positivism. John Finnis would seem to agree, for according to him, natural law theorists aim to answer questions that positivist theories do not address, so their theories need not conflict with positivism. The most important of these questions from my perspective is, in Finnis's words, "How and why can law, . . . in legislation, judicial decisions, and customs, give its subjects sound reason for acting in accordance with it?" (Finnis 2014, 2). Finnis says that law should be considered as an institutional system of the kind Hart described but that it should also be recognized as providing citizens with "a set of reasons for action" that are genuinely "normative for reasonable people" (Finnis 2014, 1). How can this be so?

Finnis's answer emerges in his discussion of the Nuremberg trial. Finnis here seems to say that although "the social fact sources" of law are "normally [the] dominant and quasi-exclusive source of law," in some cases—such as the case of Nazi Germany—they provide "inadequate and insufficient guides to fulfilling obligations such as the judicial obligation to do justice according to law." When this is so, he says, "moral rules" are an additional source of law since these are "rules of the 'higher law applicable in all times and places"; they are "rules *of law*" (Finnis 2014, 10). This view is of course *not* compatible with Hart's positivism according to which all law ultimately has its source in "social facts."

Finnis's view seems to be that the normativity of law is grounded in the normativity of morality. When the laws established by "social facts" provide adequate guides to fulfilling moral obligations, they are a source of reasons, but when they are inadequate guides, they are not normative, and in such cases they are replaced or modified by moral rules "applicable in all times and places." In Finnis's view, such rules are *rules of law*.

In my view, Finnis's mistake is to claim that moral rules are *just as such* rules of law. A symptom of the problem is that his view implies, against all common sense and the evidence of history, that no legal system can be unjust. In a case in which the putative legal rules that are revealed by the usual social sources are unjust, these rules are superseded by or replaced by moral rules. The moral rules disqualify as law any social rules that are unjust. This at least seems to be Finnis's view.[25] If so, then Finnis is committed to denying both the positivist thesis and the justice-not-guaranteed thesis. He is so committed by his apparent answer to the question of how and why law can be a source of reasons. His answer seems to be that law is a source of reasons because and to the extent that it is an adequate and sufficient guide to fulfilling moral obligations.

[25] Finnis might hold, as Kevin Toh suggested in correspondence, that a legal system that contains unjust statues and judicial decisions is *defective* even if it is not strictly speaking *unjust*. Only a defective legal system would need correction by moral rules that, as Finnis says, are "rules of law" over and above "the social fact sources" of law (Finnis 2014, 10).

IX. Conclusion

Legal Teleology is compatible with legal positivism yet it goes beyond legal positivism to provide a theory of the robust normativity of law. It is friendly to natural law theory because it affirms the robust normativity thesis as well as the moral duty thesis and the natural law thesis. Indeed, it is the only one of the views I have discussed that can accept all five propositions of the Five Theses Problem. This speaks in its favor. As an account of the normativity of law, Legal Teleology is an application to law of the teleological view that I take of normativity in general. This also speaks in its favor since it allows us to affirm the normativity of law while taking a unified view of normativity.

Legal Teleology is a form of legal positivism. It accepts the metaphysical positivist view that law consists simply in a social practice, a cluster of conventions. It also accepts the moral positivist view since it allows that there is not necessarily a moral requirement to act lawfully. Yet Legal Teleology is also a form of natural law theory. It holds that law is robustly normative. For, given our nature and the circumstances in which we live, we face the problem of security. And this problem is best addressed, I claim, by a norm that requires compliance with the law, at least in legal systems that meet Hart's minimal content of natural law. Moreover, given our nature and the circumstances in which we live, we face the related but more general problem of sociality. And this problem is best addressed, I think, by the currency of a moral code that, inter alia, requires compliance with laws that are not unjust, other things being equal. Given the importance law can have in addressing the problem of sociality, law is ideally in league with morality. Morality ideally enlists law to help address the problem of sociality.

References

Copp, David. 1995. *Morality, Normativity, and Society*. New York: Oxford University Press.

_____. 2007. *Morality in a Natural World*. Cambridge: Cambridge University Press.

_____. 2009. "Toward a Pluralist and Teleological Theory of Normativity." *Philosophical Issues* 19: 21–37.

_____. 2015. "Explaining Normativity." *Proceedings and Addresses of the APA* 89: 48–73.

Dworkin, Ronald. 1975a. "Hard Cases." *Harvard Law Review* 88:1057–1109.

_____. 1975b. "The Law of the Slave Catchers." *Times Literary Supplement* (December 5, 1975):1437.

_____. 1982. "Natural Law Revisited." *University of Florida Law Review* 34:165–188.

_____. 1986. *Law's Empire*. Cambridge, MA: Harvard University Press.

Finnis, John. 2014. "Natural Law Theories," *The Stanford Encyclopedia of Philosophy* (Fall 2014 Edition), Edward N. Zalta (ed.), http://plato.stanford.edu/archives/fall2014/entries/natural-law-theories/.

Hart, H. L. A. 1994. *The Concept of Law*, 2nd ed. Oxford: Oxford University Press.

Mackie, J. L. 1977. *Morality: Inventing Right and Wrong*. Harmondsworth: Penguin.

Raz, Joseph. 1986. *The Morality of Freedom*. Oxford: Oxford University Press.

Scanlon, T. M. 1998. *What We Owe to Each Other* (Cambridge, MA: Harvard University Press).

4 Is General Jurisprudence Interesting?

David Enoch*

I. Introduction; Or: Is *Interesting* an Interesting Philosophical Category?

I have to confess I find it hard to get excited over general jurisprudence. I don't find it hard to get excited about many philosophical topics. Abstractness does not turn me off. And yet when it comes to general jurisprudence—questions about the nature of law, the necessary and sufficient conditions of legal validity in general (as opposed to legal validity within a jurisdiction), obviously the wars over legal positivism, and so on—I always get the feeling that if there is a *point*, I'm missing it. It's not general impatience with metadiscourses: If anything, I'm even less a lawyer than I am a jurisprude. And though I sometimes share the sentiment of many that philosophers—certainly, moral, political, and legal philosophers—should make more of an effort to engage the real world rather than just reflect about it from afar, in other areas I'll go meta as happily as the next guy. Not so in jurisprudence, though. I think that by now I've been around the jurisprudence circles for long enough to be reasonably confident that it's not just about me, and to try to explain my doubts. This is what I try to do in this chapter.

A provocative way of putting my conclusion is that general jurisprudence is not that interesting. As things will develop, it will be clear that this is too strong and general a way of

* In thinking and writing about these issues, I found David Plunkett and Scott Shapiro's "Law, Morality, and Everything Else: General Jurisprudence as a Branch of Metanormative Theory" (2017) extremely helpful. For comments on earlier versions I thank Charles Barzun, Omri Ben-Zvi, Mitch Berman, Haonch Dagan, Adam Kolber, Pau Luque, Joseph Raz, Kevin Toh, William Twining, and audiences at the Yale workshop on metaethics and jurisprudence and at the Oxford Jurisprudence Discussion Group.

Dimensions of Normativity. David Plunkett, Scott J. Shapiro, and Kevin Toh.

making my point, but it's a good start. Of course, it immediately raises the question—how does one argue that a topic is or is not interesting? One is tempted to go Millian,[1] and say that a topic is interesting if people—certainly, intelligent, well-informed, virtuous people—find interest in it. And judging by this standard, it cannot be denied that general jurisprudence is fascinating. I will not go Millian here, though, because I believe that even intelligent, well-informed, and virtuous philosophers may be mistaken in what they take an interest in. It's not impossible for many such philosophers to take interest in something that doesn't merit interest, that is not genuinely interesting. In order to establish such a claim, then, it would be helpful to have some criteria of what is and what is not interesting, and then to apply them to general jurisprudence. But I do not have such criteria, and I'm not sure such criteria can be had.[2] So I'm going to pursue a different route. For the most part, I will compare general jurisprudence to *metaethics*, a discourse that has two relevant advantages here—metaethics is, I take it, *paradigmatically* interesting, and it is a philosophical discourse that I have a good feel of. And—comparing general jurisprudence to metaethics—I will explain why the former is nowhere nearly as interesting as the latter.

This methodology renders me vulnerable to two objections right off the bat: First, it may be denied that metaethics is interesting. This will render my argument here inadequate. But of course, such a move will not—by itself—save the interest of general jurisprudence. Also, I think that the comparison between metaethics and general jurisprudence is itself interesting, and dialectically, that the premise about metaethics being interesting is one many of my interlocutors will happily accept. Second, and more worryingly, even if general jurisprudence is not interesting in the way and for the reasons that metaethics is interesting, it may be interesting in *other* ways, and for *other* reasons. This is a point I want to accept without reservation—all I will argue for in this chapter is that the comparison between metaethics and general jurisprudence does not reflect well on the philosophical interest of the latter. I want to remain entirely open-minded about the possibility that jurisprudence is interesting—philosophically and otherwise—in some other ways. Indeed, a possible conclusion of my discussion (to which I return in the concluding section) is precisely that philosophers interested in the law should stop obsessing about the parts of jurisprudence that seem to be the pale shadows of metaethics, and focus on other things instead. And if I'm right in what I say in Section VII, it's not just that these parts of jurisprudence are not themselves of much interest; rather, they also fail to have any implications to other, obviously interesting (and usually normative) parts of the project of thinking about the law. If so, general jurisprudence is not even vindicated, as it were, by proxy.

I don't think that in order to get the discussion going we need a *definition* of "general jurisprudence" (which from now on I'll just call jurisprudence). Here as often elsewhere too, we know what we are talking about, and definitions are of little philosophical interest.

---

[1] See Mill's (1863, ch. 4) infamous proof of the principle of utility.

[2] I once heard it said that *interesting* is not an interesting philosophical category. I think that this assertion is strictly speaking false, but that in most contexts, it can serve to convey a right message. Usually, there's something frustrating, unhelpful, and perhaps also unpleasant (and potentially objectionably hierarchical) in proclaiming certain parts of the discipline uninteresting. I hope to avoid these dangers here, utilizing the methodology I explain in the text.

What I'll be talking about here are the kinds of jurisprudential discussions—in the analytic tradition—that if you're reading this chapter, you probably know well. The controversy over legal positivism—how best to understand it, whether it's true, the distinction between different kinds thereof, and so on—is of course central to these discussions, but does not exhaust them. Further relevant questions are those about the nature of law, what grounds legal status (in general, in a way that is presumably constant across jurisdictions), the constitutive relations (if there are any) between law and morality and other normative systems, the semantics of legal statements, their epistemology, and so on. For my purposes here, this rough characterization will do.[3]

In the following section, I note one feature of moral discourse that seems to ground (partly, at least) the interest in metaethics. It may be thought—it *has* been thought—that this general feature is shared by legal discourse—legal discourse is, it is often said, *normative*. I comment on such common thoughts, also distinguishing between two families of things that may be meant by such claims—that legal discourse involves real, genuine, full-blooded normativity (in the same way that moral discourse does, at least if moral rationalists are right), and that it involves normativity in a thinner, merely formal sense. In Section III I discuss full-blooded normativity, arguing that while it is an interesting question whether morality is normative in this way, legal discourse is clearly not. In Section IV I concede that legal discourse is weakly, formally normative, but argue that while formal normativity is certainly an interesting topic for philosophical inquiry, the role of the law (and so of jurisprudence) within that inquiry is going to be rather minimal. In Section V I note another important difference between metaethics and general jurisprudence: In the former, response-dependence is a highly controversial, problematic view; in the latter, it's the obvious way to go. And in Section VI I note another, related way in which I think that metaethics is interesting, but that jurisprudence is not—by having non-neutral implications within the target discourse (morality, or the law). In a short concluding section I point out the kind of investigation in which I think people with a philosophical interest in the law should engage.

II. The Normativity of Law

Moral discourse is paradigmatically normative. This much is clear—indeed, that this is so seems clearer even than what exactly this means[4]. But here are some of the things people mean when they say such things as that moral discourse is normative: Many moral statements

[3] William Twining suggested to me that perhaps I should say explicitly that I'm talking about "Oxford jurisprudence." Twining himself thinks that it may be important to develop theoretical concepts—such as general jurisprudence, perhaps—that better fit as tools with which to understand the contemporary, heavily international legal order. Regardless of terminology, none of what I say in this chapter is meant to apply to anything but the kind of jurisprudence loosely characterized in the text.

[4] The discussion is here made trickier by the phenomenon Korsgaard (1996, 42) diagnosed a long time ago—different thinkers use different words as the "normatively loaded" terms—roughly, those for which it's analytic that they are normative. So for each term, someone will agree that morality is related *to it*, but question *its* normativity ("sure, you *ought* to act morally, but why care about what you ought to do?." etc.). The attempt in the text to list some normativity-indicators in a way that's not too theory-laden is an expression of a hope to overcome this difficulty.

fall on the ought side of the is/ought distinction, or on the value side of the fact/value distinction, or on similar sides of similar distinctions (however exactly such distinctions themselves are understood); moral judgments seem to have the world-to-mind direction of fit; there are very close connections (the nature of which is of course controversial) between sincerely uttering moral judgments and such things as recommending, requiring, encouraging, blaming, praising; moral terms seem to have "to-be-done-ness" woven into them; motivations—the speaker's, perhaps, or the agent's, or both—seem to be engaged in moral discourse in ways that are not common in descriptive discourses; moral judgments are in an important sense about the reasons we have—specifically, our reasons for action; the language used in ethics is of the normative kind—we talk of rights and duties, of good and bad, right and wrong, of justified actions, of reasons; and the thought that moral discourse can be reduced without remainder to descriptive, or naturalist discourse—while still very much a contender on the scene—is at least far from obvious.

Another way of getting at the same idea is to compare morality to other normative domains. Many of the normativity-indicators just mentioned can also be found (with some minor revisions, perhaps) in the normative part of epistemology, or sometimes in talk of prudence. It's harder to find them, though, in paradigmatic non-normative discourse (mathematics, say, or basic physics).[5]

The marks of normativity mentioned above are, of course, controversial, and nothing here is obvious. I want to remain as neutral as I can on the relevant controversies. But I think it is safe to note that many of the puzzles that render metaethics interesting are due to morality's normativity. For instance, morality's normativity seems to tie it closely to motivation, in ways that are—given some other seeming commitments of moral discourse (to objectivity, perhaps) perplexing; the epistemology of the normative seems different in important ways, and perhaps more mysterious, than that of descriptive discourses. Even the semantic theory of morality becomes much more interesting because it has to account for morality's normativity. And of course—if there is a principled reason to resist a naturalist reduction of morality (and this is a big "if"), this reason is grounded in the normativity of moral discourse.[6]

We can now proceed in the opposite direction. We can—as many do—take it as a given that morality is normative (or that moral discourse is normative discourse), and use that in order to show that *some other* discourse is normative, by showing that it is sufficiently like moral discourse in the relevant ways.

Enter the law. For it does seem that the law is like morality in some of these normativity-indicators ways. Legal statements—at least from the mouths of the insiders—often do have "to-be-done-ness" built into them, they are closely related with recommendations and requirements, and so on. Certainly, much of the language we use when we make legal statements looks normative through and through—we speak of legal requirements, of legally acceptable reasons, of oughts and shoulds, of rights and duties, and the like. And when we

---

[5] Indeed, metaethics is now often regarded as a particular instance of metanormativity more generally. See, for instance, my *Taking Morality Seriously (TMS)* (2011a, 2–3).

[6] Something along these lines is, I think, the grain of truth in Moore's now-infamous (and conclusively refuted) open question argument. See (Ridge 2014, section 2).

look at the philosophical discussion over legal positivism, we see that something like a naturalist reduction has been at the heart of the discussion here as well.[7]

Now, it's not at all clear what people have in mind when they talk about the normativity of law—and I suspect that different people mean different things by that obscure phrase.[8] But I think that what we've been discussing—the fact that the law seems to exhibit many of the characteristics of normative discourses (for instance, of morality) is a major part of "the problem" of the normativity of law. And so we get the how-jurisprudence-is-like-metaethics line of thought: Moral discourse is normative, and this is a part of what makes metaethics (that is, philosophizing *about* morality and not just within it) interesting. Legal discourse—though perhaps importantly different from moral discourse in numerous ways—is also normative. And this is what makes jurisprudence (that is, philosophizing about the law in roughly the ways metaethics amounts to philosophizing about morality) interesting.

The rest of the chapter is my attempt at rejecting this line of thought.[9]

III. Formal and Full-Blooded Normativity: A Distinction

Formal normativity[10] can be had for relatively cheap. This kind of normativity is present whenever there are any relevant criteria of correctness at all. Set up a game—no one is allowed to step on the lines—and immediately some actions are correct (stepping between the lines) and some aren't (stepping on the lines). And this suffices for some normative-sounding language ("No, you shouldn't step on the lines!", "Yeah, you're okay, you didn't step on any line", and so on). This kind of normativity is very, very common[11]—whenever people talk of any kind of rule or standard, whenever they engage in games, or practices, or take part in institutions, there are some correctness conditions.

But when we say that morality is normative, we seem to want more. We're not merely highlighting a feature that morality has in common with any other area in which there are correctness conditions. At the very least, the claim that morality is normative only in this very common, formal kind of way will be highly nontrivial, and indeed, a surprising (and implausible) metaethical thesis. We need, then, a stronger kind of normativity to capture what

---

[7] Yes, I know that there are controversies over how to understand the positivism debate. I hope—I *really, really* hope—that I can avoid entering them here. The point in the text—with the "something like" qualifier—is hopefully weak enough to allow me to do that.

[8] I've already complained about this in "Reason-Giving and the Law" (2011b, 2). See also (Marmor 2011, section 2).

[9] To anticipate: to the extent that this is the kind of reasoning that motivates much interest in jurisprudence, it rests on an equivocation. There is *a* sense in which the law is normative, and there is *a* sense in which being normative calls for a certain kind of philosophical investigation. But these are not the same sense of "normative." I thank Pau Luque for suggesting to me this way of putting things.

[10] I take the term from McPherson (2011). Parfit (2011) uses "normativity in the rule-implying sense" for the same phenomenon.

[11] I'm not sure Hershovitz (2015, 1168) has formal normativity in mind, but if he does, he seems to disagree, citing nothing less than Hume's rejection of inferences from an is to an ought as a problem for accounts of such normativity. As the example in the text shows conclusively, though, no serious problem of this kind arises for formal normativity.

it is that we're after when we say that morality is normative (if only to then defend the surprising thesis that morality is not normative in this stronger sense, but merely in the formal sense it shares with so many other phenomena). Unfortunately, it's not easy to characterize this other kind of normativity—but let's start with a name, a placeholder. Let's call it, then, *full-blooded* normativity.[12]

One is tempted to draw the distinction in the following way: Morality is *really* normative, in the sense that morality connects—as a matter of necessity, perhaps by its very nature—with the genuine reasons that apply to us, or with what it makes sense to do, or with whatever else is the normatively-loaded set of words.[13] That is, when you have a moral reason to ϕ, you *thereby* have a reason to ϕ—a *real* reason to ϕ, a reason *sans phrase* to ϕ, the kind of reason that genuinely counts in favor of ϕ-ing. This is not so for many cases of formal normativity. It may very well be the case that you have a fashion-reason to never wear white after Labor Day. That is, it may very well be a result generated by the subtle and complicated rules of fashion-discourse and practice that wearing white after Labor Day is incorrect.[14] But this leaves it entirely open whether you have any reason to avoid wearing white after Labor Day, whether there's anything to be said for that policy, whether it makes sense to endorse it. One is tempted to say—this rule is a part of the fashion game, but it is of course entirely open whether you have a reason—a real, *sans-phrase*, counting-in-favor-of reason—to play the fashion game at all. Fashion-discourse is normative, all right, but not in a way that (necessarily) merits your allegiance. Perhaps, then, this is the distinction we are after between formal and full-blooded normativity—the latter implies reasons, and the former does not.[15]

But problems arise. First, we do not want the normativity of a moral statement to depend on its truth value.[16] Presumably, normativity is a feature of moral statements that remains constant across the truth-falsehood divide. If "You shouldn't cause pain for no good reason" is normative, presumably "You shouldn't care about the pain of dogs" is also normative. But because this last moral judgment is false, it does not imply anything about real reasons in the way that the former one presumably does. Similarly, one can presumably know that "One

[12] I follow Plunkett and Shapiro (2017) here. Parfit calls this "normativity in the reason-implying sense," a problematic term, as we're about to see.

[13] Again, see (Korsgaard 1996, 42).

[14] See? I just made my point without saying anything about reasons. This suffices to show that we shouldn't worry about the question whether *there are* fashion-reasons, or whether "reason" is a term that functions in a more unified way, so that there are no different kinds of reasons in this sense. In our context this may be important, because sometimes people write as if it's clear that there are legal reasons, that reasons are reasons are reasons, and therefore, that the law is normative also in a reason-implying sense. But no such linguistic moves can succeed, of course. See my "Reason-Giving and the Law (2011b, 17, and the references there).

Also, as the text also shows, there is really no room for ontological worries about the fashion-duties or fashion-reasons or fashion-normativity—though the sociology of them is complex, the metaphysics of fashion correctness conditions is clear enough (a point I return to below). A non-factualist or eliminativist view of them (as in Hershovitz (2015), if I understand him correctly) is thus left entirely unmotivated.

[15] I think that the point in the text is the one implied by Plunkett and Shapiro's talk of enjoying *full authority* (a term that I believe is best reserved for other phenomena).

One is tempted to say that formal normativity is no real normativity at all. But of course, we are interested in the substance here, not in who gets to wear what badge of linguistic legislation.

[16] A point emphasized by Plunkett and Shapiro (2017).

ought not to kill an innocent threat in self-defense" is a moral judgment, and so normative, even without still making up one's mind whether it's true. False moral judgments, we seem to want to say, while they do not imply anything about real reasons, are at least *in the business of* claiming such authority or power. But talk of claiming authority—when applied to discourses or judgments—seems especially unclear and unhelpful.[17] Perhaps the way out of this difficulty—an attempt to make good on the thought that even false moral judgments are *in the business of* achieving normativity—is to say that what's needed for full-blooded normativity of a judgment is that the judgment *belong to a kind* other members of which, if true,[18] have full authority, or entail real reasons, or some such.

Another problem with this way of understanding full-blooded normativity is that claiming that moral discourse is full-bloodedly normative in this sense seems to presuppose something like moral rationalism—roughly, the claim that morality is necessarily tied to rationality, perhaps so that there's always a reason to act morally.[19] But this thesis is anything but obvious or uncontroversial.[20] And though I do think a suitably weak version of it is true,[21] I do not want to assume anything like this here. Perhaps we can say that those who reject even moderate versions of moral rationalism are best understood as rejecting the full-blooded normativity of morality, of allowing morality to have only formal normativity. I'm not sure about this (or that it matters, other than for terminological clarity).

Perhaps for our purposes, though, we don't need much more. We can say that full-blooded normativity is the kind of normativity morality has according to moral rationalists, the kind that often (when all goes well, perhaps) entails or implies something about real, genuine reasons, reasons *sans phrase,* the kind that merits our allegiance. It's the kind of normativity that prudence seems to have, perhaps, and (some part of) epistemology, and—arguably, but not uncontroversially—morality too. It's being normative in the way that many other formally normative discourses are not normative. And it is the kind of normativity about which controversies of a specific kind seem to make sense—asking whether morality is normative doesn't make much sense, it seems, if we're asking whether it's formally normative, for quite obviously, it is. Asking about its full-blooded normativity may be more interesting. Similarly for other discourses—that fashion-discourse is formally normative should be a starting point of discussion, but that is entirely consistent with it not being full-bloodedly normative. And

[17] Perhaps the idea is either what the relevant judgments *entail,* or what they *presuppose*—or perhaps it's about the felicity conditions of such locutions, in something like the sense Darwall (for instance, (2006, 24) borrows in related contexts from Austin.

[18] This "if true" may be needed in order to accommodate error theories. One way of going error-theoretic regarding morality is to acknowledge that a commitment to moral rationalism is central to it, and then to argue that it cannot be made good on. Such an error theory seems to say about morality as a whole roughly what I've said in the text about false specific moral judgments (assuming that some other moral judgments are true).

[19] See TMS 96-7, and the references there.

[20] See, for instance, (Brink 1989) (though the kind of thesis I call rationalism in the text Brink calls internalism about reasons; (Brink 1989, 39)), and Copp (for instance, 2007, 280 and the references there, though Copp is more interested in rejecting the thought that moral considerations are *overriding* than the thought that they always supply *some* genuine, counting-in-favor reason).

[21] Again see TMS, 96-7.

similarly for religious discourse (of many different kinds), for talk of the normativity of meaning, and, of course, for talk of the normativity of law, to which we shortly return.

One last preliminary: Morality is normative (if indeed it is) as a matter of *necessity*. Indeed, we may want to say something stronger than that—it is *of morality's very nature* that it is normative. Much weaker claims—like, that morality is *sometimes* or *often* normative, that *often* when you have a moral reason to ϕ you also have a real reason to ϕ, but that this is not necessarily so—are of no interest in our context. For similarly weak claims are true of almost any other systems that are merely formally normative: Clearly, *sometimes* when the rules of fashion render a certain action incorrect, you have a real reason to avoid it. Indeed, you may have that reason partly *in virtue of* the proclamation of the fashion rules (together with some other, contingent circumstances). But we were trying to capture the special way in which morality is normative and fashion-discourse presumably is not. For a discourse to be normative in this stronger sense, then, it must be *necessarily* related to real reasons, it must have good normative credentials *in virtue of its very nature*, it must be such that correctness and incorrectness according to the rules of that discourse *guarantee* reasons for and against (respectively).

IV. Law Is Not Full-Bloodedly Normative

Recall the how-jurisprudence-is-like-metaethics line of thought: Morality's normativity renders metaethics philosophically interesting; the law is also normative; therefore, jurisprudence is philosophically interesting (in roughly the way metaethics is). It is now time—in this and the following section—to examine this line of thought, now equipped with the distinction between formal and full-blooded normativity.

Is the law, then, full-bloodedly normative? Granted, it's normative in the same way that many game-discourses are, and in the way fashion-discourse obviously is. Is it, though, normative in something like the way morality is normative (at least according to moral rationalists)? If you have a legal reason to do something, does it follow that you have a *real* reason to do it? In showing that a move is incorrect according to the rules of the legal game (in a given jurisdiction), have we *thereby* shown that it's also an irrational move, or a move against which there is at least some reason (*sans phrase*)? Or is it still open to us to respond in a way analogous to that we used regarding the Labor Day rule of the fashion game?

Once questions about the full-blooded normativity of the law are clearly stated, there shouldn't even be a temptation to answer them in the positive.[22] Obviously, sometimes when the law requires that you ϕ, it thereby succeeds in giving you a reason to ϕ. But just as obviously, sometimes this is not the case—think about exceptionally stupid or corrupt laws, perhaps in exceptionally stupid or corrupt legal systems. Remember, we are now dealing with a thesis about what is *necessarily* true of law. But then all that has to be shown to establish the falsehood of the suggestion that law is full-bloodedly normative is one (metaphysically, perhaps even conceptually) possible case where the law—*any* law—requires that you ϕ and

[22] I borrow some text here from my "Reason-Giving and the Law" (2011b).

yet you do not have a reason to ϕ. And I don't see how it can seriously be doubted that there are such possible cases.

Here is another way of seeing the same point: If you tell me "This would be wrong. You ought not to do it!," and I respond with "Sure, I can see that it's *morally* wrong, but what is it to me? Why should I care about morality, or play the morality game?," my answer is at the very least nonstandard.[23] Moral rationalists would say that I have already betrayed some confusion, because by conceding that the action would be wrong, I *have already* conceded that there is a reason, indeed that I have a reason, not to perform it. To repeat, not everyone agrees—not everyone is a moral rationalist. But the oddity of this response is what drives the discussion—it's the phenomenon rationalists sometimes rely on, and the one that non-rationalists try to explain away. No such oddity arises in legal cases—or more carefully, in *some* legal cases. Suppose we live under a stupid, inefficient, often morally corrupt legal system (surely, it's at least possible that there are such systems), and that I'm about to perform an action that violates some stupid, inefficient, morally corrupt but legally valid rule (surely, the existence of this too is possible[24]). You then tell me "Don't do *that!* It's illegal!," and I respond with "I see that it's illegal, but what is it to me? Why should I play the legal game (within this jurisdiction, at least)?" This response doesn't sound to me even initially odd. It doesn't sound at all more problematic then "Sure, I see that fashion requires that I don't wear white after Labor Day, but what is *that* to me? Why should I play the fashion game?"[25]

It's important not to confuse the question at hand—whether the law is full-bloodedly normative—with other, related ones.

One such family of questions is about a privileged subset of legal statements—perhaps those by officials, or by a subset of officials, or some such. Perhaps not all legal statements, as a matter of necessity, entail real reasons; but all *internal* ones do, or anyway, all those making them *are committed* to their full-blooded normative credentials. Perhaps we can restrict our philosophical attention to just this subset, and ask about *its* full-blooded normativity. Now, much more needs to be said—and has been said—about how to understand and accommodate such internal legal statements, or statements from the internal point of view, or some

---

[23] Notice that the point in the text is not about the why-be-moral challenge. You can be a rationalist, and think that that challenge is one it is important to meet. Your being rationalist will then guarantee that it *can* be met, but will not, on such a view, immediately show how to meet it. I think, for instance, that this characterization is true of Korsgaard in *The Sources of Normativity* (1996).

Myself, I do think that the why-be-moral challenge is by and large confused. See TMS 242-7.

[24] In case you're not sure about these "surely"s, I briefly revisit them below.

[25] I'm not sure what exactly Greenberg (2014, 1288) has in mind when talking of "the commonsense idea that a legal obligation is a kind of obligation." It *seems* like he's suggesting that the obvious point in the text here is not just *false*, but contra common sense. I have no idea what makes him think that.

Similarly, Hershovitz (2015) seems to be committed to the extremely implausible claim that it's never the case, say, that you have a legal obligation to ϕ, but no moral obligation to ϕ. But when he discusses this problem, he settles for talking about why it may be a good idea to say, and perhaps also to think, that this is so. He doesn't say in a more straightforward matter what the truth value of the sentence (for some morally bad law) "Your legal duty is to ϕ, but you do not have a moral duty to ϕ." is. I'm pretty sure on his theory it comes out false, and this suffices, it seems to me, to refute that theory as a theory of the relevant parts of our natural language. (I also think none of this matters much. See Section VII.)

such. What I have to say about this I said elsewhere.[26] For our purposes, though, we can settle for just noting that this much is true of many other discourses, discourses we would not want to attribute full-blooded normativity to. Think of fashion again. Perhaps, though *I* can say something such as "Sure, fashion requires that so-and-so, but what's it to me?" without mistake or confusion, still there's a subset of fashion judgments—perhaps those by the fashion-czars—that have a full-blooded normative commitment built right into them.[27] This doesn't sound that implausible to me—at least, not more implausible than saying something similar about the law. But this shows that the presence of a subset of internal judgments that are plausibly considered normatively committed (in a sense yet to be made fully precise) does not suffice for full-blooded normativity—the kind of normativity that morality has, and that fashion-discourse presumably does not. Notice that this is so even if, as I speculate elsewhere,[28] the interesting thesis in the vicinity of legal statements from the internal point of view is one about *explanatory priority*—namely, that this subset has a special, privileged role to play in understanding and explaining legal discourse and practice. Even if it's true not just that internal legal statements are normatively committed, but also that understanding the law requires first understanding such committed statements, we still don't have a vindication of the full-blooded normativity of the law—for with fashion too, arguably, committed statements enjoy a similar kind of explanatory priority. (Let me remind you, though, that fashion is merely an example here. If you think I don't take fashion sufficiently seriously, as it too is full-bloodedly normative, or that I take it too seriously, as internal judgments do not enjoy explanatory priority when it comes to fashion, feel free to replace the fashion example with other more suitable ones.)

Another set of questions with which the question of the full-blooded normativity of the law may be confused is about whether and how the law is ever *normatively relevant*. To be normatively relevant, the law must be such that its directives (and the like) sometime make a normative difference. For instance, if there is some agent A, and some action ϕ, and some set of circumstances C, such that independently of the law (or of a specific valid legal norm) A does not have a reason to ϕ in C, but given the law, A does have a reason to ϕ in C, then the law makes a normative difference in this case. Similarly if the law made something into a reason, or into a weightier reason, or rebutted or undermined a reason, and so on. That the law makes a normative difference—that sometimes what the law says matters rationally—is,

[26] See my "Reason-Giving and the Law" (2011b, 20–26), and our "Legal as a Thick Concept" (Enoch and Toh, 2013, 268–270), and the references there.

[27] A lot depends here on the details. If we understand the nature of internal fashion statements as statements that involve a commitment to everyone always having a reason to play the fashion game—if fashion-czars have to be understood as fashion-rationalists—then their discourse is infused with systematic error, and we should go error theoretic about fashion-discourse, or at least its central, internal part. I don't know of anyone taking the analogous kind of view with regard to internal legal statements—though perhaps some anarchists could. If, however, we read the commitments of fashion-czars expressivistically—so that we merely assert that the mental states they are expressing with such statements are, say, more desire-like than belief-like—we get a different view of fashion-discourse, perhaps one analogous to the one that Kevin Toh has been developing (mostly as an interpretation of Hart) about the law. See Toh (2005).

[28] See my (2011b, footnote 35), to an extent following Raz. And in the context of tying the discussion in the text here to that of thick concepts, see (Enoch and Toh 2013, 271).

I take it, entirely uncontroversial. It is also entirely uninteresting, because *this* much is true of pretty much everything else. Though fashion is not (we're assuming) full-bloodedly normative, it's still sometimes normatively relevant (if looking nice and fashionable for an interview will help you land a job you have a reason to want, and if it's after Labor Day, . . .). That cats can feel pain is (it seems) a non-normative fact, but it is of course normatively relevant, it explains why it's morally wrong to kick cats. Indeed, even *formal* normativity is not needed for normative relevance. The weather is normatively relevant (the weight of the reason you have to stay indoors strongly depends on the weather), whether you have a headache is normatively relevant (vis-à-vis your reason to take a pain-relief), whether I'm in front of you is normatively relevant (vis-à-vis your reason not to move your fisted hand rapidly forward), and so on. So *of course* the law is normatively relevant—in many different circumstances it affects what it makes sense for you to do. Perhaps it can even be said that the law is more *systematically* normatively relevant: Perhaps it affects not just what it makes sense for you or me to do, but what it makes sense for *all of us* (for some "us") to do. And perhaps it affects what we have reason to do not in some anecdotal way but a more holistic way (within a specified domain). But still, there's nothing unique to the law here (think of the weather's normative significance, again), and so nothing interesting that can be learned from this about the law, and in particular, about the thought that it's full-bloodedly normative.[29]

Let me make three final points before leaving full-blooded normativity behind. First, you may have noticed that I avoided all talk of the law's *claiming authority*. You may think this is relevant, for you may think that *morality* claims authority, and indeed that its claim to authority is a part of its being full-bloodedly normative.[30] And you may think that this distinguishes the law from many other discourses, including my toy example of fashion—fashion-discourse, you may think, does not (in *any* relevant sense) claim authority, in the way that morality and perhaps the law do. Still, I think we can avoid talk of claiming authority—and given its ambiguity and unclarity,[31] I think we should. To see this, think of the community of the *fashion Nazis*—like many of us (I guess), they think that fashion requires that you not wear white after Labor Day. But they also take fashion *very* seriously. Indeed, in their community, fashion-discourse claims authority in whatever sense you may want to say that morality or the law do. Still—the fashion-Nazis' beliefs and practices to the contrary notwithstanding—it's very clear that their fashion-discourse too is not full-bloodedly normative. After all, when told not to wear white after Labor Day, my response ("Sure, that's what the fashion rules say, but what is it to me?") still makes perfect sense. Claiming authority may be important in many contexts, but not, I think, in ours.

Second, as you may recall, I assumed that it's not impossible for a legally valid norm to be stupid or morally wrong, and indeed that it's possible for a legal system to be stupid or wrong. You may be worried about this—you may think, perhaps because you still have in mind a *lex-injusta-non-est-lex* conception of non-positivism, that I've begged the question against the non-positivist. But I don't think that this is so. *Law* (and its cognates) is a natural-language

[29] In "Reason-Giving and the Law" (2011b) I argue that this is one, fairly trivial, sense in which the law gives reasons for action, and that it may also be the only sense in which this is so.

[30] I think that Plunkett and Shapiro (2017) think so.

[31] See my (2013b, 34–35).

word, and we have linguistic and other intuitions about it. Presumably, it captures the concept *law*, about which we are asking questions when we're doing general jurisprudence. And pre-theoretically, when I tell you that this-or-that law—while valid—is morally corrupt, you don't hear a contradiction. When I describe a historical or counterfactual example of a stupid legal system, you are happy to think of it as a legal system, though a stupid one. So does everyone else. Therefore, such a legal norm and such a legal system are conceptually possible. It's not clear, of course, what conditions *are* needed for a system to qualify as legal (perhaps it has to be the union of primary and secondary rules; perhaps it has to be enforced by an Austinian sovereign; . . . .) but not being stupid or wrong—sufficiently stupid or wrong so that its correctness conditions do not match real, counting-in-favor-of reasons—are not so needed.[32] Of course, we could engage in linguistic legislation, forbidding the application of the word *legal* to any systems that do not guarantee full-blooded normativity. But it is hard to see how such linguistic legislation can help, or be the source of philosophical interest.[33]

Finally, perhaps all of this is wrong. Perhaps law is after all full-bloodedly normative. Perhaps this is so because the law *just is* a part of morality, or some such.[34] Even on this assumption, though, it's really hard to see why jurisprudence should be interesting. Because then, it's not as if the normativity of law makes jurisprudence interesting in the way that morality's normativity makes metaethics interesting. Rather, it's that jurisprudence is, on this theory, *a particular instance* of metaethics. And then, it's not clear why we should be especially interested in jurisprudence, or in the part of metaethics that applies to the law, compared to other particular instances of metaethics (say, that part of metaethics that applies specifically to the wrongness of actions performed with the agent's left arm). It's not impossible, I guess, that some way of filling in the details can be found that will render this part of metaethics more interesting than others. But it's hard to see how this can be done.

Thoughts about full-blooded normativity, then, will not render jurisprudence interesting—most probably, because the law is *not* full-bloodedly normative, and even if it is, it's not clear how this helps.

---

[32] Joseph Raz suggested the following condition: Perhaps the conceptual necessity of a connection between law and normativity operates more holistically, in something like the following way: It's conceptually necessary that [If in a legal system you have a legal reason to $\phi 1$, a legal reason to $\phi 2$, a legal reason to ϕn, then you have a real reason either to $\phi 1$ or to $\phi 2$, or . . . to ϕn]. It's not obvious to me that law is full-bloodedly normative in even this weaker sense, but let me note that if it is, this too calls for explanation, one that may be of genuine interest.

[33] A point seriously underestimated by Greenberg (2014, 1288), who claims—to an extent, rightly—that linguistic intuitions are not conclusive evidence here. But first, though not conclusive evidence, they do constitute evidence. On points related to the one in the text, Greenberg's theory obviously loses many plausibility points. Second, this is where the discussion in Section VII below comes in—if jurisprudential theories do not have explanatory or other normative payoffs elsewhere, where will Greenberg get plausibility points to compensate for the bad loss here? It's not clear he can give us any reason to change the way we talk and think with these natural language terms.

[34] A possible reading of Greenberg (2014), and maybe also of Hershovitz (2015) and of Dworkin's most recent view.

V. Law *Is* Formally Normative. But so What?

So much, then, for full-blooded normativity. Still, it cannot be denied that the law is formally normative—it includes, and generates, criteria of correctness. Formal normativity too is interesting, it is natural to think, even if not quite as exciting as full-blooded normativity. And so, the law's formal normativity can suffice for the interest of general jurisprudence.

One could question, I guess, the depth of the phenomenon of formal normativity. Sure, many things are formally normative, and many aren't, but it's not obvious that this way of cutting up the world is of genuine theoretical interest. Perhaps, it may be thought, formal normativity is in this sense not a *philosophical kind*. Such thoughts can be strengthened by observing the multiplicity and variety of things that can manifest formal normativity, and how little they have in common (except, that is, for manifesting formal normativity). In particular, when one thinks of the epistemological, metaphysical, and maybe also psychological issues that metaethicists spend their time worrying about, it's really not clear that they apply in anything remotely resembling a unified way to all the things that manifest formal normativity. Arguably, there is no metaphysics of correctness conditions as such, or epistemology of correctness conditions as such. In these respects, it seems, formal normativity does not capture a kind.

But this would be too quick, I think. For it does seem like a plausible hypothesis to me that there is something that *makes* all formally normative systems formally normative, that there is something—plausibly, *one* thing—in virtue of which formally normative systems are formally normative. And while I agree that there is no plausibility to the idea of a metaphysics or epistemology of correctness conditions as such, metaphysics and epistemology do not exhaust philosophy, or even metaethics. Perhaps, for instance, while there is no informative general metaphysical account of formal normativity, there *is* such a general account of the semantics of formal normativity. And perhaps, while there is no informative general epistemological account of correctness conditions as such, there is quite a lot by way of such a general account that can be given of their psychology (the kind of mental states involved in ascriptions of formal normativity). So I am going to proceed on the assumption that formal normativity is, at least for some philosophical purposes, sufficiently interesting.

This will not suffice, though, in order to save jurisprudence. The reason is simple. If we're interested in the study of formal normativity, there is a whole host of phenomena we can use for our research. We can study fashion-discourse. We can study talk of any game whatsoever. We can study the rules of any social institutions (even those we would not be tempted to call legal). We can study etiquette. (Etiquette, in fact, is a *much* more interesting case, I think. I return to it below.) And yes, we can observe and think about the law as well. If it's formal normativity you're interested in, the law is not inferior as an example compared to many others. But it is not superior either. And this, really, is *all* that it is—it is merely *an example* of a much wider phenomenon.

But this means that there is nothing special about the law that can be learned from studying its formal normativity. It also means that jurisprudence is not more philosophically interesting than meta-fashion, the somewhat underdeveloped philosophical inquiry into the nature of fashion-discourse. There are no, as far as I know, international conferences devoted to meta-fashion. There are no scientific journals whose main order of business is to do meta-etiquette. Indeed, I don't think there are many philosophers whose main professional endeavor is within these domains. And while there certainly is serious philosophical interest in games, and indeed in sports, it is typically not the kind of philosophical interest that focuses on formal normativity, and asks about, say, baseball discourse the analogous questions to those metaethicists ask about moral discourse.[35] If what is supposed to render jurisprudence interesting is law's formal normativity, and if all these other things also exhibit formal normativity, it becomes puzzling why we do—and whether we should—have these asymmetries between the study of jurisprudence and the study of meta-fashion, meta-etiquette, and meta-baseball. Jurisprudence, on this picture, may just be meta-fashion with larger research funds.

The defender of jurisprudence can agree that formal normativity only allows the law to be one example among many of the studied phenomenon, but insist that it's a *special* particular instance of that wider phenomenon. Law, it may be thought, is more interesting than fashion, or interesting in other ways. And the law is more important than etiquette, or perhaps important in other ways. Perhaps this is why jurisprudence is interesting: it's interesting because it studies an especially significant particular instance of formal normativity.

I agree that the law is especially important in many ways. I also agree—a point I return to below—that the law's importance merits interest in it, philosophical among others. But the law is not special or significant *in ways that are relevant to its formal normativity.* If the law is special, that is because it is powerful; or because it's an especially powerful part of a Marxist superstructure; or because it affects people's lives in deep ways and structures the ways many of us think; or because it penetrates almost any other social practice—things of this sort. None of these is related in an interesting way to the law's having correctness conditions. Vis-à-vis its formal normativity, the law is not special. Focusing attention on the law's formal normativity as if it's special, just because the law is special in some *other* ways, would be like focusing your study of the common cold on my daughter's common cold, simply because she's so charming (and so special in some other, unrelated way).

Here is another way of making what I think is the same point. I've been arguing that if we're studying formal normativity, the law is merely a non-special particular instance, and so not very interesting. Perhaps one can respond: But our main area of interest here is not formal normativity. What we are primarily interested in studying is *the law*. We're not starting, as it were, interested in formal normativity, then looking for interesting examples thereof. Rather, we're starting with an interest in the law, then noting its formal normativity, and trying to come up with a theory of the law that accounts for that as well. True enough. And I agree that the law is a worthy topic for philosophical inquiry. But then what we should study are primarily those features of the law that make it worthy of inquiry—namely, its ability to create false consciousness, its role in promoting worthy causes, and so on. Not its formal normativity.

Law *is* formally normative, then. But this simply doesn't suffice to render jurisprudence interesting—at least not more interesting than meta-fashion.

---

[35] Perhaps the main exception here is some work by Mitch Berman. See, for instance, his (2011), and his contribution to this volume.

VI. Response-Dependence

Some properties and facts are *response-dependent*. Perhaps traditional secondary qualities are like this—though, of course, any specific case is potentially controversial.[36] Perhaps, if beauty truly is in the eye of the beholder, aesthetic properties and facts are response-dependent. Perhaps the property of being disgusting is of this sort—perhaps there's no more to being disgusting than eliciting a feeling of disgust (perhaps among a suitably qualified set of people, perhaps in some suitably defined hypothetical conditions). Other properties and facts are *response-independent*—they do not constitutively depend, as a part of their nature, on the response of observers or judgers. Perhaps traditional primary qualities are of this kind—though, of course, any specific case is potentially controversial.[37]

One central dividing line in metaethics is between theories that see moral properties and facts—and perhaps (full-bloodedly) normative properties and facts more generally—as response-dependent or as response-independent. Some go for straightforward response-dependent reductions, either on the level of individual responses[38] or of wider, social ones, perhaps in terms of social practices or codes.[39] Some deny any role at all for our moral responses in constituting the fundamental moral or normative truths.[40] Many expressivists—views that the naïve would assume embrace some response-dependence—go to considerable lengths to show that in an important sense, theirs too is a response-independent view, indeed, that *in the only sense* theirs is a response-independent view.[41] Some error theorists can be thought of as reading a commitment to some kind of response-independence into moral or normative discourse, then insisting that no response-independent properties and facts exist—hence the error theory.[42] And the games go on.[43] But regardless of where you stand on these and related issues, at least it's clear that whether moral and normative properties and facts are response-dependent is a live issue, and indeed, that for many, many metaethical views—and not just hyperrealist ones, like my own—accommodating morality's response-*in*dependence, or the appearance thereof, is a major metaethical desideratum.

---

[36] For an error theory about color discourse motivated, roughly, by the thought that it is committed to the kind of response *in*dependence the world does not supply here, see (Boghossian and Velleman 1989).

[37] Indeed, a sufficiently radical idealist view can perhaps be thought of as denying that anything at all is response-independent.

[38] (Firth 1952); (Lewis 1989); (Sobel 2001); (Schroeder 2007). For more references, see, for instance, my "Why Idealize?" (2005).

[39] (Harman 1977); (Copp 1995).

[40] I think what I say in the text here is true of objectivist naturalist Cornell Realists (Sturgeon 1984); (Boyd 1988); (Brink 1989)) as well as of those who reject naturalism (Shafer-Landau (2003), also my TMS), and of so-called quietists, those who think they can have their realism without committing to any non-naturalist metaphysical extravagance (Parfit 2011); (Scanlon 1998); (Kramer 2009); Nagel in some moods (1997)).

[41] See (Gibbard 2003), and especially, (Blackburn 1993). Not all of us are convinced by such efforts. For my related attempt at a critique of quasi-realism, see TMS 35-8.

[42] (Mackie 1977); (Joyce 2001).

[43] Perhaps I should also mention here no-priority response-dependence views, whose precise nature it is especially hard to capture. See (Wiggins 1987) and (McDowell 1985).

I am not aware of any remotely plausible view in jurisprudence that denies the response-dependence of legal validity, say, or that asserts that whether or not a norm is legally valid is constitutively independent of human responses and practices.[44] No one denies, as far as I know, and no one should, that things such as legislation, court decisions, perhaps custom and so on at least partly determine the law. Many do deny, however, that such social practices determine morality (they may, of course, be *morally relevant*. Everything may be *that*, as I've already emphasized above).

And so, we have here some reinforcement to the conclusion of the previous two sections. There I concluded that law is not normative in a way that renders jurisprudence interesting in anything like the way morality's normativity renders metaethics interesting. And now we see one interesting metaethical controversy—the one over response-dependence—where the metaethical and the jurisprudential evidence seems so different that the analogue of the majority view in metaethics is just a nonstarter in jurisprudence. Jurisprudence is just not sufficiently like metaethics.[45]

I don't want to create the false impression that by declaring response-dependence the obvious and uncontested way to go with regard to legality, we've solved all jurisprudential problems. Taking for granted that legal validity often—perhaps always—at least partly constitutively depends on social practices and attitudes, on the attitudes and judgments of officials, and the like, there is still a lot we don't know—we don't know, for instance, *which* social practices and conventions are relevant here. We don't know which responses of which individuals (if any) play this constitutive, perhaps grounding role in the law. We still don't know whether legal validity is *entirely* or only *partly* grounded in such natural facts—and if only partly, what parts, and what else is needed (I take much of the discussion about legal positivism to be precisely about these questions). And so on. Work remains to be done, then, and though some of it can only be done in a jurisdiction-specific way, perhaps some can also be done as a matter of general jurisprudence. Acknowledging response-dependence, then, is not *everything*. But at least in our context, it is *a lot*. Because it shows, first, how jurisprudence is not at all like metaethics, and second, that the remaining questions are not remotely as interesting as the central questions in metaethics.

Once again we can compare the law to other realms. Perhaps fashion is not a good comparison here, because at least arguably fashion-discourse and practice is *entirely* constituted by social facts and personal responses—though the details are in no way trivial to

---

[44] Stepping entirely outside my comfort zone here: I think that according to the natural law tradition, *some* parts of the law are considered valid entirely independently of human practices and responses (though perhaps not of divine ones). Even according to such views, though, *other* parts of the law are at least partly response-dependent.

[45] Kevin Toh suggested that we should perhaps think—both in metaethics and jurisprudence—not in terms of a dependence-independence dichotomy, but in more continuous terms. Even according to metaethicists who reject the global response-dependence of moral facts and properties, presumably some moral facts and properties are response-dependent (such as perhaps those having to do with contractual obligations). I agree that this line of thought—perhaps together with the previous note, according to which it's not uncontroversial that *all* legal facts are response-dependent—may show that it's not obvious how to see the difference here between metaethics and jurisprudence, but a difference surely remains. My suggestion: All moral truths are ultimately morally grounded in response-independent truths. This, I take it, is what the debate in metaethics is about, and there's no analogous debate in jurisprudence.

fill in, and though fashionability is not plausibly considered to be in the eye of the beholder, still it's not clear that there's more to fashionability than the complicated function of social conventions and practices, personal tastes and attitudes, and the like. Perhaps more interesting here is etiquette.

When it comes to etiquette, as with the law, *some* response-dependence is very, very hard to deny. Many etiquette norms constitutively depend on social conventions and practices, and perhaps on people's attitudes as well. A philosophy of etiquette that ignored or denied this obvious fact would be grossly inadequate. But many questions remain. Partly, they are about complexity: the intricate ways in which etiquette-related practices emerge and develop; the way they combine formal normativity with at least some descriptive content (presumably, the etiquette norm that dictates what kind of fork to use with your salad has a world to mind direction of fit when I'm deliberating about what fork to reach for, but a mind-to-world direction of fit when the practice of distinguishing between kinds of forks lapses); the relevant second-order norms (sometimes it's contrary to the norms of etiquette to point out an etiquette violation, sometimes it's contrary to the norms of etiquette not to); and so on: It is going to be very, very hard to get the details of our account of etiquette correctly (and the project will take, by the way, at least as much empirical sociology as it will philosophy).

But perhaps it's not just complexity. For we could ask interesting questions about the relation between the norms of etiquette and real, genuine, counting-in-favor-of norms, norms that merit our allegiance. Clearly, norms of etiquette may be normatively—indeed, morally—relevant. But then again, almost everything can be normatively relevant. More interestingly, perhaps it can be argued that norms of etiquette are *systematically* morally relevant. Or perhaps that given some background conditions (say, that the relevant system of etiquette is not too corrupt or silly), whenever you have an etiquette-reason to do something, you have a reason to do it. Perhaps some etiquette norms are best seen as moral norms themselves. Perhaps while social facts partly determine or ground etiquette facts, they cannot do so on themselves—perhaps, say, a part of the *point* of etiquette is to allow more pleasant interactions among people, and so perhaps a system of social rules resembling etiquette in other ways that fails to do that doesn't even succeed in generating norms of etiquette.

Perhaps these are questions worth thinking about. Myself, I don't find them very exciting—it's hard for me to see what implications their answers may have elsewhere, or—to repeat a point I've been emphasizing throughout—why there is anything *in particular* interesting about etiquette compared to numerous other practices about which we could ask similar questions. The point I want to note here, though, is that the most jurisprudence (of the kind I've been discussing) can hope for is to be as interesting as this study of etiquette. It seems unlikely to me that this hope will be realized—for the ways of etiquette seem to me to be *much* more intricate and complicated and less transparent (perhaps because less institutional) than those of the law. Regardless of this, though, the obvious fact that legal validity is response-dependent places an upper bound on how interesting jurisprudence is—an upper bound that places it far below metaethics, and at most, at the level in which such a study of etiquette can be interesting.[46]

[46] Let me note a way in which jurisprudence may be more interesting than the study of etiquette—because law is more institutional, there may be a practical point to engaging in normative philosophy of law that there isn't

VII. Internal Implications?

One way in which a metadiscourse can be important and interesting is if the object-level-discourse is important and interesting, and if the metadiscourse has implications to the object-level discourse.

In metaethics, there is some discussion of the neutrality of metaethics. Usually, such discussion proceeds by asking whether any interesting first-order, moral implications follow from metaethical claims. Now, I don't think that metaethical claims all by themselves typically entail normative claims. But I don't think that metaethics is morally neutral either. I think that we can show that metaethics makes a difference to normative ethics, by conjoining metaethical claims with normative auxiliary premises, and showing that now we can draw moral conclusions that would not have followed from the auxiliary premises alone. In other words, we can show that metaethics extends normative ethics *non-conservatively*.[47] If this is right, then even if you are interested primarily in normative ethics and not in metaethics, there will be cases in which you should take an interest in metaethics, because what view you end up endorsing in metaethics may make a difference to the availability of views in normative ethics as well.

This criterion for the non-neutrality of a metadiscourse can be generalized so as to apply to other discourses as well.[48] Let's get back to the law, then: Suppose we're either doing positive law, or normative legal theory, asking what the desirable legal arrangement of some matter should be (in a jurisdiction, at a time). Call this—all of this together—the legal project. And so now we can ask—does general jurisprudence have implications to the legal project? Or does it conservatively extend the legal project, so that (roughly) the set of conclusions within the legal project we can draw from a set of premises within the legal project remains the same once we add whatever jurisprudential claims we want to add as premises? If jurisprudence conservatively extends the legal project, this means that we can't secure jurisprudence's interestingness by tying it to the (undeniable) interestingness of the legal project.

If jurisprudence makes a difference to the legal project, it's not going to be easy to see how. The suggestions that come most naturally to the novice seem clearly wrong, and it's a part of our role in teaching jurisprudence to show that this is so: Sure, Hart and Dworkin may differ with regard to the best account of what's going on when a judge exercises (some kind of) discretion, but it's not at all clear that what you should do as a judge in such cases depends on whether Hart or Dworkin are right. Sure, positivists and (some) non-positivists differ on whether sufficiently unjust norms can be legally valid, but the question whether you should obey them will receive its (highly context-dependent) answer regardless of which side is right

to engaging in a similar endeavor regarding etiquette—namely, we can *change* the law. But this difference can motivate not the study of the nature of law, but rather the normative considerations applying to it, as I note in the concluding section.

[47] See "How Objectivity Matters" (2010). And TMS Chapter 2.

[48] It can also be generalized in another way: It can be shown that violations of neutrality of the kind I highlight will occur whenever an object-level-discourse is powerful enough to include second-order statements, that is, in the case of morality, statements in which moral predicates are embedded within the scope of other moral predicates. See Malcai (ms).

about legal validity.[49] Whether there is a rule of recognition, and if so what it is in a specific jurisdiction, whether there is a Kelsenian Grundnorm and what the relations are between it and the constitution of a specific country—we can discuss these questions, of course, but it's not at all clear that the answers will have any implications to questions in normative constitutional theory, such as whether we should have—let alone whether we do have—a court with the power for judicial review. And so on.[50]

This does not, of course, amount to an argument establishing the conclusion that jurisprudence conservatively extends the legal project. I wouldn't know how to argue for this conclusion. But we do have here, I think, a challenge for the friend of jurisprudence, to show how the legal project is or should be affected by what we do when we do general jurisprudence.[51]

Notice that my point here is not an instance of the general impatience with theoretical projects that do not have any practical implications. I'm okay with such projects—they are most of what I do. My point is just that *one* way in which some theoretical projects of this meta-kind are interesting is by having first-order implications, and that this way does not seem a promising one of defending jurisprudence. Combined with the results of the previous sections, this completes my case for the claim that general jurisprudence is not interesting.

VIII. So: What *Is* Interesting?

Different people are interested in different things, and that's all right, of course. And if people continue to take interest in general jurisprudence—in the ways that I've argued above are somewhat unjustified—no disaster will follow. So I don't want to sound alarmist. Nor do I expect to have a wide-ranging influence on the field: In all likelihood, after this chapter

[49] So in particular, in order to answer the question whether or not to obey morally problematic norms that (I'm watching my wording here) seem to have been made into the law of the land by the relevant legal institutions, it just doesn't matter whether you say that they are legally valid, but there may be no moral obligation to obey them (or perhaps there is, but it is outweighed); or (a la Greenberg (2014)) that they are not legally valid norms at all because they haven't had the needed moral impact for that, but of course they are the content of some legal texts; or that there is a legal duty, but not a moral duty, to obey them; or (a la Hershovitz (2015)) that there are no legal duties at all, only moral ones, so there's no duty to obey them of any kind.

[50] Some of the five-and-a-half fallacies Gardner (2001) is out to eradicate regarding legal positivism amount to precisely carelessly drawing implications to the legal project. Also, for similar doubts about making a difference elsewhere (from Dworkin and Greenberg among others) see (Hershovitz 2015, 1200–1201).

Notice, of course, that even if some people—even some judges, or some legal scholars—cite jurisprudential views in supporting interesting results within the legal project, this in no way refutes my points in the text here. Such people may be (and are, I suspect) simply mistaken about the implications of jurisprudential views. They too, in other words, may be falling prey to some of Gardner's five-and-a-half fallacies, or the like.

[51] Greenberg (2014) repeatedly claims that his general jurisprudential theory has implications for a normative theory of interpretation. If this were so, this would have been an example of facing up to the challenge in the text. But this is not so. While Greenberg's theory may have implications to what the right *description* is of what judges do when they interpret, it is *normatively* irrelevant. Greenberg also gives normative arguments supporting his claims about what judges should do when they need to interpret (or, less tendentiously, to do the kind of thing that many of us think of as "interpretation"). These may yet work. But if they do, they do so directly, without relying non-redundantly on Greenberg's theory of the nature of law. *That* part of the story drops out of the picture entirely.

too, people—philosophers of law included—will continue to do what they've always been doing. Still, if I'm right, to an extent they shouldn't.

If we think of general jurisprudence—or of parts within it—as roughly analogous to metaethics, jurisprudence is just nowhere nearly as interesting. The law is not full-bloodedly normative; it is just another, in no relevant way special, instance of formal normativity; some kind of response-dependence view about it is the *obvious* way to go, and we have yet to see any interesting implications from jurisprudence to other areas, including to normative legal theory. I wouldn't mention these results on your next application for research funds.

But this does not mean that *the law* is uninteresting—it doesn't even mean that everything people have been doing under the title "general jurisprudence" is uninteresting. The law is a major character on the political field. Understanding how it works is a major part of understanding how politics works. Understanding the normative constraints and considerations applying to the law and to legal reasoning—or to specific legal domains—is extremely important, and the kind of thing that philosophers can help with.

True, none of this is exactly the metaphysical project of which the wars over positivism are a major part. Such questions are not exactly questions about the nature of law. Jurisprudence *thus* understood is not an analogue of the central parts of metaethics, but is an important part of moral and political philosophy.[52] And much of it will have to be highly context-dependent, and so jurisdiction-dependent, but perhaps some of it will remain for general jurisprudence. Now, that moral and political philosophy is interesting is something we've known all along. Perhaps we can hope that it's also important and worth doing. If in this way jurisprudence takes more of its place as a part of moral and political philosophy, perhaps similar hopes about jurisprudence will not be too out of place.

References

Berman, Mitchell. 2011. ""Let 'Em Play": A Study in the Jurisprudence of Sport," *GEO Law Journal* 99:1325.

Blackburn, Simon. 1993. *Essays in Quasi-realism* (Oxford: Oxford University Press).

Boghossian, Paul A., and J. David Velleman (1989), "Colour as a Secondary Quality," *Mind* 98:81–103.

Boyd, Richard N. 1988. "How to Be a Moral Realist." In *Essays on Moral Realism,* edited by G. Sayre-McCord. (Ithaca and London: Cornell University Press), 181–228.

Brink, David O. 1989. *Moral Realism and the Foundations of Ethics* (Cambridge and New York: Cambridge University Press).

Copp, David. 1995. *Morality, Normativity, and Society* (New York and Oxford: Oxford University Press).

_____. 2007. "Moral Naturalism and Three Grades of Normativity." In his *Morality in a Natural World* (Cambridge and New York: Cambridge University Press), 249–283.

[52] For very different reasons, then, I agree with Hershovitz (2015, 1203) who writes: "The time has come for jurisprudence to drop the metaphysics and take up morals."

Darwall, Stephen. 2006. *The Second-Person Standpoint: Morality, Respect, and Accountability* (Cambridge, MA: Harvard University Press).

Enoch, David. 2005. "Why Idealize?," *Ethics* 115(4):759–787.

_____. 2010. "How Objectivity Matters." In *Oxford Studies in Metaethics*, edited by Russ Shafer-Landau 5:111–152.

_____. 2011a. *Taking Morality Seriously: A Defense of Robust Realism* (Oxford University Press).

_____. 2011b. "Reason-Giving and the Law," *Oxford Studies in the Philosophy of Law* 1:1–38.

Enoch, David and Kevin Toh. 2013. "Legal as a Thick Concept." In *Philosophical Foundations of the Nature of Law*, edited by Will Waluchow and Steffan Sciaraffa (Oxford: Oxford University Press), 257–278.

Firth, Roderick. 1952. "Ethical Absolutism and the Ideal Observer." *Philosophy and Phenomenological Research* 12:317–345.

Gardner, John. 2001. "Legal Positivism: 5 ½ Myths." *The American Journal of Jurisprudence* 46:199–228.

Gibbard, Allan. 2003. *Thinking How to Live* (Cambridge, MA: Harvard University Press).

Greenberg, Mark. 2014. "The Moral Impact Theory of Law." *The Yale Law Journal* 123: 1288–1342.

Harman, Gilbert. 1977. *The Nature of Morality* (Oxford: Oxford University Press).

Hershovitz, Scott. 2015. "The End of Jurisprudence," *The Yale Law Journal* 124:1160–1204.

Joyce, Richard. 2001. *The Myth of Morality* (Cambridge: Cambridge University Press).

Korsgaard, Christine. 1996. *The Sources of Normativity*, edited by Onora O'Neill (Cambridge: Cambridge University Press).

Kramer, Matthew H. 2009. *Moral Realism as a Moral Doctrine* (Chichester and Malden, MA: Wiley-Blackwell).

Lewis, David. 1989. "Dispositional Theories of Value." *Proceedings of the Aristotelian Society* (Supp.) 63: 113–37.

Mackie, John L. 1977. *Ethics: Inventing Right and Wrong* (Harmondsworth: Penguin Books).

Malcai, Ofer. (ms) "Second-Order Normative Propositions and Metaethical Neutrality."

Marmor, Andrei. 2011. "The Nature of Law." *Stanford Encyclopedia of Philosophy*, http://plato.stanford.edu/entries/lawphil-nature/.

McDowell, John. 1985. "Values and Secondary Qualities." In *Morality and Objectivity*, edited by T. Honderich (Boston: Routledge & Kegan Paul), 110–129

McPherson, Tristram. 2011. "Against Quietist Normative Realism." *Philosophical Studies* 154: 223–240.

Mill, John Stuart Mill. 1863. *Utilitarianism*, http://www.earlymoderntexts.com/pdfs/mill1863.pdf/.

Nagel, Thomas. 1997. *The Last Word* (Oxford: Oxford University Press).

Parfit, Derek. 2011. *On What Matters* (Oxford: Oxford University Press).

Plunkett, David, and Shapiro, Scott. (2017). "Law, Morality, and Everything Else: General Jurisprudence as a Branch of Metanormative Theory." *Ethics* 128: 37–68.

Ridge, Michael. 2014. "Moral Non-Naturalism," *The Stanford Encyclopedia of Philosophy*, http://plato.stanford.edu/entries/moral-non-naturalism/#OpeQueArg.

Scanlon, Tim. 1998. *What We Owe to Each Other* (Cambridge, MA: Harvard University Press).

Schroeder, Mark. 2007. *Slaves of the Passions* (Oxford: Oxford University Press).

Shafer-Landau, Russ. 2003. *Moral Realism: A Defence* (Oxford and New York: Oxford University Press).

Sobel, David. 2001. "Subjective Accounts of Reasons for Action," *Ethics* 111:461–492.

Sturgeon, Nicholas L. 1984. "Moral Explanations." In *Morality, Reason and Truth: New Essays on the Foundations of Ethics,* edited by D. Copp and D. Zimmerman (Totowa: Rowman & Allanheld), 49–78.

Toh, Kevin. 2005. "Hart's Expressivism and His Benthamite Project." *Legal Theory* 11: 75–123.

Wiggins, David. 1987. "A Sensible Subjectivism?." In his *Needs, Values, Truth: Essays in the Philosophy of Value* (New York: Oxford University Press), 185–214.

5 Legal Metanormativity

LESSONS FOR AND FROM CONSTITUTIVIST ACCOUNTS IN THE PHILOSOPHY OF LAW

Kathryn Lindeman*

I. The Metanormative Ambitions of Metaethics

Philosophers working in metaethics are gripped by questions about how we think, talk, and come to know facts about ethics and morality and what the nature of its domain could be, given answers to these questions. It is increasingly clear to many that the features of the ethical domain that make these questions so gripping extend beyond it to other domains that might also be properly thought of as normative, dealing with questions not merely of how things are, but of how they ought to be.

This recognition of normativity outside of ethics puts pressure on metaethicists to attend to other normative domains to ensure that their answers to metaethical questions can be extended to provide a natural unified explanation of normative phenomena wherever they occur. Many metaethicists are, then, in the process of turning their sights to see whether their accounts of the metaethical could be extended to metanormative accounts more generally.[1]

* Thanks to Gwen Bradford, Eric Brown, Jill Denton, Billy Dunaway, Chad Flanders, Julia Haas, Sophie Horowitz, Richard Kim, Charlie Kurth, Frank Lovett, Ian MacMullen, Brooke McLane-Higginson, Kranti Saran, Lizzie Schecter, George Sher, Tim Schroeder, Julia Staffel, Brian Talbot, Kevin Toh, Eric Wiland, and audiences at Washington University in Saint Louis, Rice University, and Ashoka University for helpful discussion of and feedback on the arguments in this chapter.

[1] Though what distinguishes normative domains is a matter of controversy, many agree that a domain is normative when it can be understood in terms of reasons. The question "is domain D normative" often is thought to be settled by the answer to the question "are the dictates of domain D reason-giving?" So, Foot's example of sexist club rules would not be normative on this account, because they do not give us reason to accord with them, while the rules of prudence might, though they would not themselves be dictates of ethics. (Foot

Dimensions of Normativity. David Plunkett, Scott J. Shapiro, and Kevin Toh.

It is unsurprising, then, that the domain of legality has increasingly come to the attention of metaethicists. Though metaethicists interested in expanding their account beyond the ethical domain typically focus on the theoretical or epistemic domain, the legal domain has characteristic prescriptive reason-giving normativity that the epistemic domain is often thought to lack.[2] Unlike the epistemic domain, it is inherently practical, and so has features that make it plausibly reason-giving. Because of its reason-giving and evaluative features, the legal domain is a clear candidate for explanation from metanormative extensions of metaethical accounts. It seems important, then, that any metaethical account must be extendable to include an account of the legal domain.[3] However, it complicates matters to include the legal domain among those domains that a metanormative theory is beholden to explain. The greater the number of normative domains and the more diverse their subject matter and normative features, the more sophisticated the metanormative account of them must be. However, one promising metaethical account that seems poised to extend to account for diverse normative domains is constitutivism.

Metaethical constitutivism is a reductive account that takes the constitutive features of some ethical kind to explain or ground the normative ethical facts. So, for example, Korsgaard seeks to explain the reasons agents have (a normative ethical fact) by appeal to the claimed fact that agents are by nature self-constituting, and agents have reasons to do things that would further the success of this constitutive activity.[4] The heavy lifting for constitutive theories is in explaining the constitutive features that all kind-members in a domain share and how that constitutive feature grounds the normative features of the domain. I think of these tasks as the Extension Task and the Norm Explanation Task, respectively.

These two tasks also constrain the metanormative constitutivist's account of normativity generally. The constitutivist's account of normativity must explain the extension of normative domains generally, a correlate of the Extension Task. In addition, the metanormative constitutivist must have the resources to explain the distinctive normative features of each normative domain. So, depending on the set of domains to be explained by the generalized constitutivist account, which I will call the Metanormative Constitutivist account, the constitutivists' task will vary in difficulty. It seems that the more diversity there is in the normative features across domains, the greater the problems for the constitutivist in providing a unified account. So, the metaethical constitutivist with unifying aspirations has an

1972) Considerations of parsimony might lead us to reject this understanding, because many domains that might strike us as having important commonalities with ethics that metanormativity seeks to understand are ruled out on this account. Epistemology, for example, if you are to follow Kolodny, is not normative on this conception because it is not reason-giving in the right way. *Pace* Kolodny, in "Why Be Rational?" *Mind* (2005), I think this result should lead us to reject this reasons-basic understanding of normativity, rather than reject epistemology as normative. For readers who are primarily interested in the reason-givingness of the legal domain, I direct them to Enoch's (2011) "Reason Giving and the Law" that argues that the reasons given by laws are triggering reasons, which bring about conditional reasons.

[2] See, for example, (Wedgwood 2002, 267–297). and (Velleman 2000, 244–81) Kate Nolfi, who calls this view, in epistemology, at least "Normativism" see her: (2015) "How to Be a Normativist About the Nature of Belief.".

[3] Alternately, the metaethicist could provide an Error Theory of the normativity of the legal domain consistent with her general metanormative account.

[4] See (Korsgaard 2009). For other prominent examples of constitutivists, see (Velleman 2000), (Smith 2013), and (Katsafanas 2013).

additional burden: to show that her metaethical story generalizes in some principled way to a metanormative constitutivist account according to which we can understand specific constitutivist accounts in other normative domains.

In this chapter, I look to the legal domain which is both plausibly normative and practical, and in which there are currently accounts that take the general shape of constitutivist explanations I sketched above. I'll look at one such account, Scott Shapiro's, and see how far understanding its strengths and working to avoid its weaknesses can get us toward completing these tasks for the metaethical constitutivist.

II. The Planning Theory of Legal Normativity

In many plausibly normative domains, there are already existing constitutivist-esque accounts that take the nature of individuals in that domain to explain the plausibly normative features of that domain. Perhaps unsurprisingly, there are current positions in the philosophy of law literature that take the general shape of a constitutivist account, grounding the normative features of the legal domain in the nature of laws themselves.[5] This sets the metaethical constitutivist up to incorporate an existing constitutivist account of legal normativity into her metanormative account.[6] Here I'll focus on one account with a constitutivist form recently developed by Scott Shapiro to identify a type of problem faced by constitutivist accounts of the legal domain and what lessons metanormative constitutivists can glean from its struggles.

Shapiro's account is one of the more interesting recent attempts to ground law's normative features in an account of its function.[7] Shapiro's Planning Theory of Law explains normative facts in the law by appealing to the necessary features of the law itself. His account has two general constitutive requirements on being a legal institution. First, developing a position found in the philosophy of action in the work of Michael Bratman, Shapiro understands a

[5] This is, of course, not the only position in current and historical philosophy of law. It is, of course, possible to deny that there *are* normative features of the legal domain. It is also possible to explain the normative features by appeal to those of other normative domains, (e.g., the domain of morality), or from the activities of other normatively authoritative beings (e.g., the commands of deities). Regardless, each of these forms could produce a unified metanormative account, provided the same sort of explanation held of other normative domains. What is at issue, then, seems to be whether the legal domain is *itself* the source of its own normative features, or whether the existence of legal normativity is dependent on the existence of ethical normativity or divine normativity, or perhaps pragmatic normativity, if such a thing exists. There are many interesting questions that turn on this that are beyond the scope of the chapter here.

[6] I'm understanding, "metanormative accounts" to be those that explain, in general, how domains have their normative features, and particular accounts then specify how that metanormative account applies in specific cases. So, e.g., metaethical accounts explain how the ethical domain has the normative features it has, and accounts of how the legal domain explain how legal domains have their normative features. A particular metaethical and legal account can have the same form, e.g., can both be constitutivist accounts, and thus both fall under the same metanormative account.

[7] Shapiro's account is certainly not alone here. See, for example, (Ehrenberg 2015, 247–266). I focus on Shapiro because his book-length treatment lays out the constitutive features of the legal domain and accounts for both how those constitutive features are had and how those features generate norms. It is, to my knowledge, the most explicit and recent development of a full constitutivist legal account.

legal institution as characterized by the Planning Thesis: as social organizations that create, carry out, and enforce social plans. Legal activity, for Shapiro, is thus activity of a sort of social planning. Shapiro writes that "legal institutions plan for the communities over whom they claim authority, both by telling their members what they may or may not do and by authorizing some of these members to plan for others."[8] Certain complex social arrangements lead to what Shapiro calls the "circumstances of legality," situations in which the management of predictability, compensation for ignorance and bad character, and accountability are needed.[9] According to Shapiro, in these circumstances of legality, social planning is needed to set communal standards for behavior via publicly accessible standards. This is the sort of planning that legal institutions are constitutively engaged in as a matter of actual practice. Any institution, in order to be a legal institution, must be engaged in such planning activity.

However, engagement in planning activity is not sufficient to constitute a legal system on Shapiro's account. To fully account for the constitutive requirements of legal systems, Shapiro supplements the Planning Thesis with what he calls the Moral Aim Thesis. The Moral Aim Thesis states that "the fundamental aim of legal activity is to remedy the moral deficiencies of the circumstances of legality."[10] There are institutions that engage in planning activity of the sort the Planning Thesis constitutively attributes to legal institutions and yet are not legal institutions (e.g., the Mafia). On Shapiro's account, these institutions are not legal institutions because they do not have the constitutive moral aim that all legal institutions have. Though many planning institutions coordinate social activity, "only a legal system *is supposed to* address those problems that less sophisticated methods of coordinating social activity and guiding action are unable to resolve."[11]

So, the two constitutive requirements on a legal institution are characterized by the Planning Thesis and the Moral Aim Thesis. Legal institutions must be engaged in a characteristic type of planning activity and they must have a moral aim. The Planning Thesis only requires that legal institutions *actually* engage in planning activity, and so accounting for this requirement only requires that we can determine what an institution does. Determining whether an institution has a moral aim is more difficult. Shapiro reçognizes that many legal institutions fail to achieve their moral aims, and some might even fail to attempt to achieve their moral aims. So he doesn't require that legal institution *actually* achieve moral ends. Instead, he holds that "what makes the law the law is that it *has* a moral aim, not that it *satisfies* that aim."[12] Together, on Shapiro's view, these two constitutive features are shared by all legal institutions and can be used to explain the normative features of the legal domain.

Shapiro develops this view to account for Extension (ruling in all and only pre-theoretical legal institutions) and Norm Explanation (accounting for the normative features of the domain). The Moral Aim Thesis serves both tasks for Shapiro. It helps explain why the Mafia and Yakuza aren't legal institutions, despite being planning institutions, and it helps explain

---

[8] (Shapiro 2011, 195).

[9] (Shapiro 2011, 200).

[10] (Shapiro 2011, 213).

[11] (Shapiro 2011, 214).

[12] (Shapiro 2011, 214). The explanation for how an institution counts as having this constitutive aim is, as yet, unexplained. We'll return to this shortly.

the normative features that govern legal officials. The Planning Thesis, with its behavioral constraint, and the Moral Aim Thesis with its teleological constraint, together generate an account of not only what the law *is*, but also what it *should be*, and importantly for Shapiro, *how it should be used*. He writes "the law is, in the end, an instrument [. . .] and as with all instruments, there are correct and incorrect ways to use the law; if we use it incorrectly, it will not do what it is supposed to do and authorities will not do what they are entitled to do."[13]

III. The Moral Aim Thesis and the Extension Task

Shapiro takes legal officials to be accountable for the accomplishments of the law as well as its uses. The demand to explain these normative features makes Shapiro's Moral Aim Thesis an obviously appealing constitutive requirement for legal institutions. By appealing to the moral aim of law, Shapiro takes himself to be able to explain how those who make and apply laws are also under moral and other practical constraints because of the nature of law.

However, explaining a domain's normative features by appeal to a constitutive feature requires a successful account of how that feature is constitutive of the domain. So, a suitable metaphysical account must be given to explain both *how* the members of a normative domain have this feature and to show that all members of the normative domain in question have that feature. So, how can we tell whether a system has a moral aim, and how can we be sure that all legal systems are going to have such an aim?

On Shapiro's view, we can determine whether an institution is a planning institution by looking to what the institution *does*, but this same strategy can't be used to determine whether an institution has a moral aim. The constitutive requirement is *having* a moral aim, not engaging in any activity that would satisfy or accomplish this aim. Additionally, having the moral aim cannot require satisfaction of the aim, and similarly cannot require minimal satisfaction.[14]

Without a satisfactory account of how legal institutions have their constitutive features, an account cannot succeed in grounding the normative features of the legal domain. One might hope that the Moral Aim Thesis could be accounted for by appeal to the intentions of its designers as is often thought to work for artifacts. Artifacts occupy a plausibly normative domain where the activities of designers seem to determine the domain's normative facts. Because there is a long tradition of understanding legal institutions as particularly complex social artifacts, this route might seem particularly appealing.

However, the turn to artifacts for this work is already concerning to some. Leiter, for example, has worried that legal creators cannot seem to do the metaphysical work that artifactual creators do.

> Often, for artifacts that have identifiable human creators, we appeal to the intentions of the creator, and that works well as long as we have other theoretical reasons for treating the creator's intention as metaphysically decisive. [. . .] Such considerations

[13] (Shapiro 2011, 399).

[14] For an argument for this general position, see (Lindeman 2017).

> will not help, in any case, with law, at least for positivists, since law need not have a creator who intended to create it (think of custom as a source of law, among many other examples). But when we untether artifacts from creators, functions seem hostage to rather variable interests in that artifact. [. . .] I am not aware of a single, widely accepted analysis of the essential properties of any artifact that does not rely on appeal to intentions of the creator in a context where it seems we should defer to those. If there is one, I would like to hear it.[15]

Leiter takes this to be a decisive reason to reject all functional accounts of legal normativity, but here we need to focus on the more fundamental worry: that legal institutions are more varied than an appeal to any shared creator intention could account for. If we searched for one intention that all legal officials shared that could account for the legal nature of their creation, we would come up empty-handed. Shapiro recognizes this, and so instead appeals not to legal officials' *actual* intentions or aims, but to their *avowed* intentions and aims.

Shapiro thinks we can account for legal institutions having constitutive moral aims without falling into the trouble Leiter raises. Instead of appealing to the actual *intentions or aims* of legal officials, he appeals to their *activities* to account for the constitutive moral aim of legal institutions. Specifically, he states that in order for an organization to have a moral aim (and thus to be a legal institution), the high-ranking officials of that organization must *avow* that the organization has a moral aim.[16] This can be done explicitly and implicitly in speeches, preambles to formative documents, such as constitutions, prologues to legal codes, and judicial dicta. It is thus a necessary condition on an institution having a moral aim, on Shapiro's account, that its officials use moral discourse to frame their activities.[17]

Shapiro thus writes "[t]he law possesses the aim that it does because high-ranking officials represent the practice as having a moral aim or aims. Their avowals need not be sincere, but they must be made."[18] So, it is a condition on something's being a legal institution that its high-ranking officials represent it as having a moral aim. This, it seems, is supposed to account for the law having that represented aim, which could then serve to ground the normative facts in the legal domain. Importantly, however, the transition from the claim that high-ranking legal officials avow particular aims to the position that the relevant legal institutions have those aims presupposes some principle such as Aim Transfer.

Aim Transfer: When an individual or set of individuals with creative control over some system or item profess to have aim x, the system or item thereby has aim x in virtue of that profession.

---

[15] (Leiter ms, 5–6).

[16] (Shapiro 2011, 217).

[17] Recently, David Plunkett has challenged Shapiro to account for how the Moral Aim Thesis is fully compatible with the positivist commitment, as Shapiro claims. On this objection the account of the law that Shapiro gives seems to import moral material to account for normative evaluations of law in ways Shapiro seems committed to avoiding. It isn't clear to me that Shapiro has made this mistake, but in any event, my own objection to Shapiro differs from and is prior to Plunkett's. See his "Legal Positivism and the Moral Aim Thesis" (2013, 1–43).

[18] (Plunkett 2013, 216–217).

Aim Transfer avoids the under-accounting problems that resulted from making aims turn on either sincerely held or fully or partially satisfied aims. Unfortunately, because Aim Transfer is highly implausible as a general principle, it will do no better at accounting for how legal systems have constitutive moral aims.

To see how odd Aim Transfer is, consider what commitments we must take on to endorse it in other cases. Suppose propaganda is information disseminated with the function of shaping the views of consumers in ways not sensitive to the truth.[19] A good propagandist is often someone who successfully represents their propaganda as having the aim of disseminating clearly presented truths, and this might involve insincere avowals that the information is being conveyed with the aim of informing consumers about the truth. But, representing propaganda as legitimate unbiased information does not thereby give it that function. Its actual function remains to mislead or otherwise lead the consumers to believe what the propagandist wants, independently of whether it is accurate or best supported by all the evidence.

If by making insincere avowals, I deceive others into thinking I run a legitimate news organization with the aim of disseminating unbiased information, it does not thereby become a legitimate news organization with this aim.[20] However, according to Aim Transfer, my organization would have the aim of disseminating unbiased information. But this is implausible; propaganda cannot become news so easily.

This inability of propaganda to become news via mere avowals should help us see why a possible supplement to Aim Transfer will not help. Even if we were to supplement it with an uptake requirement, according to which the avowed aim only transfers when others believe the avowal. In the case of propaganda, however, we can see that the propaganda does not become news when it succeeds in convincing others that it is news. Even with this strengthening, Aim Transfer cannot account for how things with authors or creators have aims.

We shouldn't be surprised that avowals of legal officials would be unable to account for the aims of legal systems. Even in the case of artifact designers, we don't think their *claims* are of metaphysical significance. Of course, the claims of both artifact designers and legal officials could be defeasible *evidence* that they are engaged in an activity that might be involved in the transfer of an aim. Shapiro relies on the avowals of legal officials to account for the moral aim of legal systems. However, even though it is perhaps plausible that all legal systems will have officials who avow moral aims, accounting for the Moral Aim Thesis via Aim Transfer does not work.[21]

If all legal institutions have a constitutive moral aim, something other than the claims of high-ranking legal officials must be at work to account for it. What seemed to be a promising

[19] I'm not here attempting to develop a sophisticated account of propaganda; the analysis given here is only meant to be a plausible one. Any analysis that similarly takes propaganda to be the sort of thing that a) is not news, and b) can be falsely presented as news, will serve my purposes just as well.

[20] Plunkett presents an alternate to the Moral Aim Thesis he calls the Represented as Moral Thesis: "It is that legal activity involves at least the different forms of surface-level moral presentation identified by that organization meeting the moral-representation criteria (or some slightly revised version of them)." (Plunkett, 2013, 33) This criticism, I think, holds against Plunkett's revision, offered to be more palatable to positivists.

[21] I grant that it is plausible because no matter how plausible, it does not do the needed metaphysical work. Despite this, I am convinced by (Plunkett 2013) that it is not, actually, particularly plausible.

answer to Leiter's worry about what might account for constitutive features of law as an artifact seems to not appropriately account for the functions the Planning Theory attributes to it. So, Shapiro seems not to have provided the metaphysical account needed to support the Moral Aim Thesis.

IV. The Moral Aim Thesis and Norm Explanation

Given the difficulty faced in accounting for the Moral Aim Thesis, it is worth revisiting why Shapiro is interested in this thesis. Shapiro takes it to be important for meeting the two primary tasks facing constitutivist accounts: the Extension and Norm Explanation tasks. First, as we noted above, the Moral Aim Thesis is directly involved in ensuring the Planning Account gives an accurate extension of legal systems. Without the Moral Aim Thesis, according to Shapiro, the Japanese Yakuza or Sicilian Mafia and similarly advanced criminal organizations that perform planning functions laid out in the Planning Thesis would count as legal institutions.[22] Second, in order to satisfy Norm Explanation, the legal constitutivist must account for all the normative features in the legal domain by appeal to its constitutive features. These normative features should include the types of criticism Shapiro takes to be appropriate in the legal domain. He thinks that we believe that legal systems that are unable to solve serious moral problems are criticizable, while we do not make similar judgments about all systems. Moreover, he believes we make moral appraisals of legal officials and make prescriptive judgments about how law-users ought to behave and what lawmakers are entitled to do. If the legal institution has a moral aim, then via some transfer principle, Shapiro thinks that there will be constraints on how we ought to use, bring about, and act in the light of the moral aim of legal institutions.

The two motivations for endorsing the Moral Aim Thesis thus align with the Extension and the Norm Explanation tasks that we saw all constitutivist accounts were tasked with. Shapiro takes these tasks to require something like the Moral Aim Thesis, and yet we saw that Aim Transfer was not a suitable foundation for the Moral Aim Thesis. If Shapiro is right, legal constitutivists need another way to account for the constitutive moral aim of legal institutions. However, given the difficulty Shapiro has accounting for the Moral Aim Thesis, it might be useful to consider whether the Moral Aim Thesis would successfully account for these additional normative features.

It seems that the normative features of the legal domain Shapiro is considering include those concerning what ends the law should be put to, what counts as a correct or incorrect use, and what legal authorities are entitled to do. Moreover, Shapiro seems to think that this is a general account that can be appealed to in artifactual cases more generally, such that when one knows what an instrument is *for*, one is in a position to know how one ought to use it and what one is entitled to do with it.

We've already seen reason to be suspicious that aims, moral or otherwise, can be transferred from avowed aims of creators or authorities. The principle Shapiro needs here is different. In this case, the aim or function of some artifact or system is supposed to transfer to its user

---

[22] (Plunkett 2013, 215).

or designer, to account for their normative constraints. Shapiro's explanation of normative evaluations seems to rely on something like Norm Transfer:

Norm Transfer: When someone is using, creating, or otherwise interacting with some functionally understood individual thing, they are thereby assessible, according practical norms determined by the function of that thing.

There are some attempts in the metaethics literature to argue that the normative features of constitutive kinds constrain the reasons or norms that designers or users of those kinds are bound by. Korsgaard, for instance, argues that the constitutive function of a house constrains the reasons that housebuilders have.[23] On her view, housebuilders have reasons to build houses that are good at sheltering because houses are for sheltering. In explaining this connection, Korsgaard appeals to a further commitment that Shapiro has denied himself in his explanation of the Moral Aim Thesis: that if housebuilders were not *actually* aiming to make something good at sheltering, then they would not be building a house at all. Korsgaard believes that individuals undertaking to create something with a constitutive function must be guided by the kind's norms in order to count as making something with that function. If you build something sufficiently bad at the norms of houses, you are not building a house, and if you are not aiming at building a house, you are not performing the characteristic activity of housebuilding, and so you are not a housebuilder. So, the conclusion is supposed to be that if you are a housebuilder, you are already engaged in an enterprise governed by the aims of housebuilding, because you are already aiming at building a shelter when you undertake to build a house. So, as a housebuilder, you have reason to build houses that are good at serving the function of houses. There is a sort of existential risk in not so aiming: you could cease being a housebuilder.[24]

However, this explanation of the norms governing tool-users or designers seems to require they *actually* have the relevant aim. Because Shapiro does not think legal officials necessarily have a moral aim, this sort of account is not open to him. Shapiro takes high-ranking legal officials to have their status as legal officials in virtue of institutional features, rather than in virtue of their legal activities (as Korsgaard thinks housebuilders have their status as housebuilders). No legal official is a legal official in virtue of their good performance of legal activities, or in virtue of having a moral aim. So there is no existential risk in being a very bad legal official on Shapiro's planning account.

In accepting Norm Transfer, it seems we would need to think (implausibly) that the natures of tools bind their users and creators with norms to further their functions.[25] We can accept that there are correct and incorrect ways to use a tool and facts about what the tool is supposed to do without thinking that has anything to do with what a tool-user is entitled to use it for or what others can rightfully demand of tool designers or users. For example, I have done nothing essentially criticizable when I use a teacup as a potter for a plant, despite it not being the function of the teacup to hold a plant. I have done the right thing when I dismantle

[23] For this argument, see (Korsgaard 2009) Chapter 2.

[24] I think there are good reasons that one should reject this sort of story, independent of the considerations addressed here. For an argument against the identification of the real and the (minimally) good at the heart of this view, see (Lindeman 2017).

[25] We would, that is, need to think that in creating artifacts we normatively enslave ourselves to them.

the bomb, rather than permit it to fulfill its function of exploding when on a crowded public street. If I am designing a pocketknife, I am not criticizable for sacrificing optimal functionality for cost-effectiveness. I need not even be criticizable for sacrificing optimal functionality for my lunch break, though you might disagree if you are my boss. In general, that something has an aim or a function does not imply that it is criticizable to use it for another (even contrary) purpose. That something has an aim or a function does not require that any particular person be co-opted into the furtherance of that function or aim. That something has a function or an aim doesn't even seem to demand of designers that they try to make an excellent instance of that kind of thing.

Even if we could establish the Moral Aim Thesis, it doesn't seem that it could do most of what Shapiro wants it for anyway, because Norm Transfer is false. Absent an explanation like the one provided by Norm Transfer, it's hard to see what could account for the Moral Aim Thesis explaining the practical norms governing legal officials and other individuals under the legal institution. Moral aims, even if we could account for them as a constitutive feature of legal institutions, don't seem to account for the practical constraints on those who are engaged in designing or being governed by them as simply as an artifactual account might have led us to think.

V. Planning Functions Without Moral Aims

Without Norm Transfer, it's thus unlikely that the Moral Aim Thesis will allow us to account for the practical norms governing legal officials as we might want. Even if we could find a way, other than Aim Transfer, to account for the Moral Aim Thesis, it doesn't seem to provide the constitutivists with everything they wanted. We could then, following Leiter, reject appeal to a constitutive function or aim of legal institutions to understand the normativity of the legal domain. First, however, the metanormative constitutivist would do well to take a step further back and consider whether there is another way to understand what artifactual normativity could look like.

So far, we saw Shapiro's Planning Theory involved two constitutive components characterized in the Planning Thesis and the Moral Aim Thesis. The first required actual planning behavior in order to be a legal system. This constitutive feature involved actual performance or properties (e.g., actually performing planning functions). The second required having a moral aim in order to be a legal system. This constitutive feature involved the claims of a creator (e.g., the avowed aims of legal officials). However, these two accounts do not exhaust the ways that functions and aims can be had by individuals or kinds.

This is where the metanormative constitutivist might turn her sights to other domains in which functional accounts are used to explain plausibly normative features. An ecumenical account of normativity might involve not only explicitly practical domains such as morality and legality, or the reason-involving, which would presumably include the epistemic, but also include all domains in which deontic judgments are apt: not just the artifactual, but also the biological, and plausibly the aesthetic.

If we recognize domains in which metanormative constitutivists must account for normative features without recourse to designers at all, we are emboldened to look beyond Aim Transfer and the activities of legal officials to account for the normativity of the legal domain.

The biological domain, for instance, involves no designers who transfer their aims. There are many facts in the biological domain that involve normative assessment, despite their failure to be grounded in the intentions of any designer. Despite lacking a designer, we think livers ought to filter toxins from the blood, that plants are harmed by acid rain, that hearts too weak to adequately circulate blood are bad hearts. These are all claims that are true *because of* the nature of the biological kinds in the subject. There are function claims that underpin each of these assessments, and we need not abandon them for lack of a designer.

We no longer think that explanations of biological organisms must appeal to a creator whose intentional designs gave organs their functions, yet we understand eyes functionally. Eyes have the function of seeing, and my eyes have this function independently of my own use or interest in their having this function. They also have this function independently of how well or badly suited they are to perform this function or whether they are currently being used to see. They have this function because, independently of any intentionally directed intervention, they were created in a process selected to give a form that was suited to serve the function of seeing.[26] Similarly, we can understand the norms of eyes as coming from this function. Eyes ought to be sensitive to light, to present accurate images of visually perceivable phenomena, etc.

In in the philosophy of biology neither actual behavior nor creator intentions or claims are needed to explain etiological proper function.

> For some activity or effect, Z, to be the *etiological proper function* of some x,
> i) x must be created in a process selected to produce individuals with a form F,
> ii) F itself must have been selected over alternatives *because* it was selected to have effect Z.

The etiological proper function of my eyes is to see because they were created in a process selected to produce individuals with the rough physiology of my eyes and that physiology was selected to have the effect of providing sight.[27] Having an etiological proper function, then, is a matter of having been created in a way that relates your form to an end.

This provides the beginnings of a sketch of how we can generate constitutive functions or aims without accounting for them through a transfer from something else that shares the function or aim, as the artifactual story under consideration required. If having a constitutive function is a matter of having a form with the right sort of creation story to account for a proper function, we could do away with the need for appeals to intentions or aims of any particular individual or to any minimal success criteria to account for what it is to have a constitutive function or aim. This account then would hold that being a member of a functional kind requires a history that accounts for the relevant proper function.[28] Nothing has to be

[26] There are many individuals who have eyes that are incapable of serving their function and have no interest in those organs performing their function. Many blind people would not choose to become sighted and yet this does not change the function of their eyes. These people believe they are benefitted in important and meaningful ways because of this difference, and this is almost certainly true. Yet, this also does not change the function of the eyes.

[27] See (Millikan 1993).

[28] Note, not every legal institution must share the same history or same form. It is the sameness of function that groups legal institutions on this account, and different histories or forms can account for this function.

particularly good at performing a function to have it as a proper function. This is particularly useful to the constitutivist who wants proper functions to serve the Extension task, because it would permit, e.g., extremely flawed legal institutions, so long as they had the correct etiological proper function.

To incorporate this approach in the legal domain, we would need to explain the constitutive feature of legal institutions and show that it can satisfy the Extension and Norm Explanation tasks. That is, we would need to find one function or aim that all legal institutions share as a proper function, ensure that all legal institutions are likely to have some historical account that explains their having this as a proper function, and then explain the normative features of legal domains by appeal to this function.

Without a substantial account of the constitutive function of legal institutions, we can't get far in this project, and it is well beyond the scope of the current chapter to fully defend a particular function for this purpose. Instead, in the remaining space, I want to accomplish two tasks. First, using the resources remaining from Shapiro's Planning Theory, we will see how far we can get in understanding what such an account would look like. Second, we will assess whether such an account makes any progress where the Planning Theory seemed to flounder. I aim to show that it does, and that the aspiring metanormative constitutivist should take this success into consideration in her development of a unified metanormative account.

VI. Planning Functions as Proper Functions

The metanormative constitutivist has the hard task of accounting for how specific legal institutions have their forms selected for whatever function legal institutions all share. Of course, she can't just rest here because she doesn't yet have a story for what, specifically, that function is or how, in general, legal institutions could have histories that make them selected to have it.[29] But understanding legal institutions as evolving systems whose large-scale features can be understood as selected for the performance of certain functions could, in principle, adequately account for the extension of legal institutions.

For now, let's assume with Shapiro that it is a constitutive function of legal institutions to be a particular sort of planning institution, of roughly the sort that he claims. The Moral Aim Thesis won't help account for what Shapiro wants, but the constitutivist might fruitfully understand this planning function etiologically to address the Extension and Norm Explanation tasks discussed above.

First, understanding the planning function as an etiological proper function does seem to provide some resources that might help with the Extension task. If the aim or function is had as the result of having a form selected for suitedness to that function or aim, this directs our attention away from the actual behavior of an institution and toward its history to determine what sort of institution it is. Shapiro, of course, thought that actual planning behavior

[29] One account could be to appeal to Hart's transition from pre-legal to legal stages of a community's evolution when the community adopts secondary rules, which establish the legal conditions under which primary rules can be recognized. For this account, see Hart, *The Concept of Law* (1994), especially ch. 5.

was insufficient to count as a legal institution because it ruled in, e.g., the Japanese Yakuza or Sicilian Mafia, which engaged in planning but are not taken to be legal institutions.

But on the etiological account, planning institutions are those institutions that have forms selected to perform planning tasks, not necessarily those institutions that actually do perform those tasks. Legal institutions are, on the Planning Account, social planning organizations with a particular character. Shapiro writes that this social character "creates and administers norms that represent *communal standards of behavior*," via *general policies*, via *publicly accessible standards*.[30] So, on the proper function account, in order for some organization to have this function of social planning it must have been selected to create and regulate communal standards that are general and publicly accessible.

Shapiro describes sophisticated crime syndicates as a form of non-legal planning organization:

> These firms are compulsory planning organizations: their members engage in collective planning designed to further shared criminal ends, they occupy offices (for example, the don, consigliores, capos, lieutenants, bodyguards, hitmen, and so forth), their normativity is institutional in nature (for example, the Yamaguchi-gumi of Japan has tens of thousands of members and as a result has an extremely complex hierarchal structure), and they do not require consent before imposing their demands on their victims.[31]

Is it at all plausible that the Japanese Yakuza or Sicilian Mafia have this organizational form selected for the planning function? It might be possible that these groups have a social planning function selected to serve a larger purpose of facilitating the criminal ends of financial success and dominance of one family or social group over the rest.[32]

But looking at whether they have offices, engage in compulsory planning, etc., involves looking at their current features, rather than *why* they have those current features. Though it isn't obvious that all institutions that we wish to pre-theoretically rule out as potential legal institutions are actually ruled out by this proper function account, it certainly provides additional resources over creator and performance functional accounts. Looking to the historical selection process seems to provide extra resources to the constitutivist to sort the legal from the extralegal, i.e., to serve the Extension task.

---

[30] (Shapiro, 2011, 203).

[31] (Shapiro 2011, 215).

[32] I am not as convinced as Shapiro that this would be an unwelcome outcome. If it turns out that the Yakuza and Mafia share proper functions with legal institutions, we will likely have the resources to account for their serious defects qua legal institutions. Whether having the planning function for some further purpose was a disqualifying trait in a legal institution would then determine whether the Yakuza or Mafia were legal institutions. One could hold that the final proper function of legal institutions must be the social planning function, such that if the social planning function is instituted for some other function, the institution with those functions is not a legal one. I have no real objection to this sort of view, either.

VII. Explanatory Resources of Proper Functions

The extra resources in the etiological proper function account also aid the constitutivist in addressing the Norm Extension task where the Moral Aim Thesis failed. The etiological account of the planning function explains legal institutions as having the function of social planning because their form was selected to engage in the creating, carrying out, and enforcing of social plans for guiding and coordinating the activity of agents.

Legal institutions aren't selected to merely issue prohibitions; they also, as we learn from Hart, characteristically confer powers and establish the apparatus that enables social agents to undertake certain statuses and obligations with respect to each other.[33] Grant, for the moment, that these are part of how legal institutions are selected to fulfill their proper function; it's not something they do accidentally, but something they do because they were selected to do it, and individual legal institutions have the shape and structure they do because that shape and structure was chosen to perform these functions. With this, we have additional resources, though we have not yet explained how we get moral or practical judgments about legal institutions from these facts.

Leslie Green has distinguished what he calls the *internal problem* of how legal institutions perform their given function from the *external problem* of the moral (or social) value of that function.[34] This is an important distinction, because we can certainly see this having been an issue earlier in explaining why artifactual function does not determine the practical norms governing artifact users. In addition to these two problems, we might also see a third problem that we might call the *normative internal problem* of the value of how legal institutions perform their given function. Not only can we ask *how* some institution performs its function, and what the value of *that function* is, we can also ask after the value of *how that institution achieves that function*. Proper functions are uniquely set up to provide space for this last question. The same proper function can be multiply realized by different systems that achieve it in varying ways.

Artifacts provide nice examples of how the same function can be realized by different forms. Of the many ways corkscrews can be designed to perform their proper function, here are two: they can use a lever-system to remove the impaled cork, and they can be set up to allow the force from direct pulling to remove the impaled cork. Both are ways of achieving the same aim of removing corks. The answer to the external question requires us to ask: What's the value of removing corks? Answering this question does not require us to consider the answer to the internal question. However, the answer to the internal question differs between the two cases, and so there could be different answers to the normative internal question. There might be a difference in the value of the *way in which* the two corkscrews remove corks.

Once the function of legal institutions is understood to have social agents as its object, the significance of this normative internal problem is clear. Given that there are numerous ways of engaging in social planning, the normative internal problem can lead us to ask which

---

33 (Hart 1994, 26–78).

34 (Green 1998, 121–122).

is best, and the kind of activity that social planning is—the planning for social agents—can help us understand those constraints. Loading the contents of a moving van is a function that a person might perform, but how it's best to load differs dramatically on whether you're loading feather pillows—toss 'em in—or boxes of priceless porcelain plates—set them down gingerly and carefully secure them ensuring they don't jostle. If the thing you're planning is the social arrangements of people, there are constraints on what makes that arrangement a good one in addition to the external success of whether you end up with a social arrangement.

Unlike corks, the object of the function of corkscrews, agents, and especially social agents, have normative significance. This normative significance is independent of the function of legal institutions to engage in social planning for them. Because the social planning function is planning for these social agents, the normative significance of these social agents is relevant for addressing the normative internal problem for legal institutions. It is not a mere consequence of legal activity that it affects agents that have normative standing; it is part of the function of legal activity that it affects these agents. So, the standards that govern how these agents ought to be treated is internal to the function of legal institutions, because they are essentially engaged in an activity that engages with these agents. Because of this, we should see that it's a mistake to think that moral aims are required to help us satisfactorily answer the normative internal problem for legal institutions. On any plausible constitutive aim or function of legal institution, e.g., bringing individuals into political society or being a social planning organization, any form selected to perform this function will have internal normative standards that involve moral evaluations, because the constitutive activity of that institution is an instance of a more general activity that has normative standards.

Additionally, this move to a proper function account of the planning theory allows us to admit of legal institutions with distinctly immoral aims, more easily accounting for the Extension task. That is, it more easily allows for extensions that not only exclude the Yakuza, but that include distinctly immoral legal systems. For example, a social planning system that structures and coordinates social beings through the oppression of some subset of those beings would be a legal system without a plausible moral aim. Antebellum America had such a legal system. It was structured to commodify and exploit a set of those social beings who were governed by the system. Those of African ancestry, both free and enslaved, were governed by the legal system and had their obligations and rights (such as they were) structured by a system whose aim involved their oppression. It had no moral aim, yet it has a social planning function that could account for it being a legal system.

This also allows a useful resource to answer to the Norm Explanation task by accounting for how legal officials are evaluable because of the proper function of legal institutions. Norm Transfer cannot account for the standards legal officials are held to, but once we reject the Aim Transfer, we can see the activities of legal officials as standing in a special role in legal institutions. Legal officials, qua social agents, have the same general moral obligations to treat other social agents with respect, but criticism of their actions qua social agents is criticism external to the normative features of the legal system. By understanding the function of legal institutions to be accomplished independently of it being accomplished *well*, we have recourse to an internal understanding of the moral criticism of legal officials. The activities of legal officials, qua agents of the legal system, constitute the performance of the institution's planning function, and their actions are thereby evaluable by the internal standards of the legal institution. The actions of legal officials done in their official capacities are not normatively assessable simply because those officials are generally morally assessable according to moral standards external to the legal system, as they are when they go to the store or interact with neighbors. When legal officials are engaged in legal activities, they are engaged in an activity with a function that has moral standards because of the kind of activity it is. Looking at *how* the function is performed opens up the space for internal moral assessment of legal institutions and legal agents, independently of any explicit or implicit moral aim the legal institution might have.

It seems we should then be less concerned about Shapiro's inability to account for a distinctive constitutive moral aim of legal institutions. He adds the Moral Aim Thesis because he thinks it is the only way to account for the extension of legal institutions and to explain the prescriptive and evaluative judgments governing legal officials. But he is unable to satisfactorily account for how legal institutions have moral aims, and it seems to cause rather than solve problems for the Extension and Norm Explanation tasks. We've seen, however, that for constitutivists willing to understand constitutive functions as etiologically understood proper functions, there are more satisfying ways to address these constitutivist tasks for the legal domain. So, given that Shapiro has been unable to account for how the Moral Aim Thesis could be a constitutive aim of legal institutions, and there are alternate ways of accounting for at least some of the normative facts governing how legal systems function and legal officials operate, metanormative constitutivists have reason to turn to developing an account of legal institutions without constitutive moral aims.

VIII. Conclusions for Metanormative Constitutivists

This is relevant not only to the philosopher of law, of course, but also to the interested metaethicist. Metaethical constitutivists interested in expanding their views to other normative domains will be interested in determining whether some feature constitutive of the legal domain can explain its normative features, i.e., explain the evaluative, prescriptive, and deontic facts in the legal domain. Shapiro provided a candidate account, but a central part of his planning theory, the Moral Aim Thesis, seemed both difficult to account for (because of the failure of Aim Transfer) and unable to do what was asked of it (because of the failure of Norm Transfer). In looking more closely at how we should understand constitutive functions, we saw that it is possible for the planning thesis alone to account for the Norm Explanation and Extension tasks that the Moral Aim Thesis was introduced to address.

By turning to etiological proper functions, we have seen that there is hope that this work can be accomplished without a Moral Aim Thesis. Though we were led to think constitutivists needed it because of a particular view of artifactual functions, according to which all normative features are explained by appeal to an explicit aim, this isn't true. We have seen, rather, that things can have functions independently of having any intentionally understood aims, so long as they have a particular history that accounts for a characteristic function. Additionally, we saw that institutions and institutional-members can be morally criticized even if they do not have moral aims themselves, if those institutions have etiologically understood proper functions that constitutively involve moral subjects.

We also have dismissed the concern that because legal institutions were artifacts, their aims must come from the aims of their designers. Shapiro avoided the implausible commitment that all legal institutions had designers who shared aims by retreating to an account based on an aim transfer principle. We've seen that the need for such an account is avoided if we can explain the moral normative facts in the legal domain independently of any specific moral aim. The aspiring metanormative theorist has examples of other normative domains that lack designers all together. These provide models for constitutive features that do not stipulate designers, but rather rely on historical accounts of form. Combined with the need to account for a constitutive moral aim, this should increase the metanormative theorist's confidence that a constitutivist account in the legal domain is possible.

Moreover, this can help the metaethicist who was interested in the two questions that we began with. What is the scope of the set of normative domains, and can metaethical constitutivism generalize to account for every normative domain? One tentative answer to the first question is that there are normative domains wherever there are etiological proper functions, because wherever there are etiological proper functions, there are deontic facts. In this case, the constitutivist is well-poised to give a general account for metanormative constitutivism of the following form: for any domain in which there is an etiological proper function determining the membership in that domain, this constitutive function can be used to explain the normative facts governing that domain.

References

Ehrenberg, Kenneth. 2015. "Law's Artifactual Nature. How Legal Institutions Generate Normativity," In *Reasons and Intentions in Law and Practical Agency*, edited by George Pavlakos and Veronica Rodriguez-Blanco. Cambridge: Cambridge University Press, pp. 247–266.

Enoch, David. 2011. "Reason Giving and the Law," In *Oxford Studies in Philosophy of Law*, Vol. 1, edited by Leslie Green and Brian Leiter. Oxford: Oxford University Press, pp. 1–38.

Foot, Phillipa. 1972. "Morality as a System of Hypothetical Imperatives," *The Philosophical Review*. 81(3):305–316.

Green, L. J. M. 1998. "The Functions of Law," *Cogito*. 117(12):121–122.

Hart, H. L. A. 1994. *The Concept of Law*, 2nd ed. Oxford: Clarendon Press.

Katsafanas, Paul. 2013. *Agency and the Foundations of Ethics: Nietzschean Constitutivism*. Oxford: Oxford University Press.

Kolodny, Nico. 2005. "Why Be Rational?" *Mind*. 114:509–563.

Korsgaard, Christine. 2009. *Self-Constitution: Agency, Identity, and Integrity*. Oxford: Oxford University Press.

Lindeman, Kathryn. 2017. "Constitutivism without Normative Thresholds," *The Journal of Ethics and Social Philosophy*. 12(3):231–258.

Leiter, Brian. ms. "Why Legal Positivism (Again)?" University of Chicago, Public Working Paper No. 442. Available at SSRN: http://dx.doi.org/10.2139/ssrn.2323013.

Millikan, Ruth Garrett. 1993. "In Defense of Proper Functions," In *White Queen Psychology and Other Essays for Alice*. Cambridge, MA: MIT University Press, pp. 13–29.

Nolfi, Kate. 2015. "How to Be a Normativist about the Nature of Belief," *Pacific Philosophical Quarterly*. 96 (2):181–204.

Plunkett, David. 2013. "Legal Positivism and the Moral Aim Thesis," *Oxford Journal of Legal Studies*. 33(3):563–605.

Shapiro, Scott. 2011. *Legality*. Cambridge, MA: Harvard University Press.

Smith, Michael. 2013. "A Constitutivist Theory of Reasons: Its Promise and Parts," *Law, Ethics, and Philosophy*. 1:1–30.

Velleman, David. 2000. "On the Aim of Belief," In *The Possibility of Practical Reason*. Oxford: Oxford University Press, pp. 244–281.

_____. 2000. *The Possibility of Practical Reason*. Oxford: Oxford University Press.

Wedgwood, Ralph. 2002. "The Aim of Belief," *Philosophical Perspectives*. 16(s16):267–297.

6 Robust Normativity, Morality, and Legal Positivism

David Plunkett*

I. Introduction

Lots of possible actions have a determinate legal status, relative to the law of a given jurisdiction. For example, suppose an American citizen is considering whether to pay taxes to the American federal government on the income she has earned this year from teaching physics at a university in California. Is she legally obligated to do so? Or suppose a French citizen is considering killing her neighbors because she doesn't like them. Is she legally permitted to do so? Or suppose a Greek citizen is considering selling her car to a friend in exchange for money. Is she legally empowered to do so? For each of these questions, it is hard to deny that the law of the relevant jurisdiction—e.g., contemporary American law, French law, Greek

* Thanks to Mitchell Berman, Ray Briggs, Samuele Chilovi, Matthew Chrisman, Nico Cornell, Terence Cuneo, Shamik Dasgupta, Tyler Doggett, Luis Duarte D'Almeida, Kenny Easwaran, James Edwards, David Enoch, Max Etchemendy, John Gardner, Jeffrey Helmreich, Scott Hershovitz, Nadeem Hussain, Stephen Leuenberger, Dustin Locke, Euan MacDonald, Tristram McPherson, Michaela McSweeney, Eliot Michaelson, Lucas Miotto, George Pavlakos, Alejandro Pérez Carballo, Mike Ridge, Stefan Sciaraffa, Michael Sevel, Scott Shapiro, Sam Shpall, Sarah Stroud, Kevin Toh, Sabine Tsuruda, Frederick Wilmot-Smith, Kevin Walton, Daniel Wodak, Jack Woods, and Julia Zakkou for helpful feedback and discussion. Earlier versions of this chapter were presented at Stanford University (Legal Philosophy Workshop), University of Vermont (Ethics Working Group), University of Genoa (Tarello Institute for Legal Philosophy), the CLAP reunion workshop, University of Barcelona (Logos Research Group), University College London (Legal Philosophy Forum), the University of Pennsylvania (Legal Theory Workshop), UC Irvine (Legal Theory Colloquium), and University of Edinburgh (Workshop on Metaphysics and the Law and the Ethics Discussion Group). Thanks to everyone who participated in those sessions.

Dimensions of Normativity. David Plunkett, Scott J. Shapiro, and Kevin Toh.

law, etc.—yields a determinate answer. (Yes, no, and yes, respectively).[1] Of course, for many possible actions, the law might be silent on the legal status of that action, or at least not yield a determinate answer on it. The important point is that the law isn't silent or indeterminate about *all* questions about the status of all possible actions. Rather, the law—at least the law of many contemporary legal systems (e.g., American law, French law, Greek law, etc.)—*does* take a stand on the legal status of some possible actions, and moreover one that (in at least some of those cases) yields a determinate answer about the legal status of those actions. Indeed, it often takes such stand on a great many such possible actions.

This has something to do with *the law* itself being a certain determinate way in a given jurisdiction, at a given time. Indeed, it might be that *what it is* for the law to be a determinate way in a given jurisdiction is simply for it to be the case that, relative to the law of that jurisdiction, lots of possible actions have a determinate legal status—e.g., the action is permitted, required, etc.

Everything I have said thus far is relatively uncontroversial in contemporary legal philosophy.[2] Things get *much* more controversial when we ask questions about *in virtue of what* the law is what it is (in a given jurisdiction, at a given time). The basic issue here can be glossed as follows. The law being *this* way, rather than *that* way, in a given jurisdiction (at a given time) isn't a metaphysically fundamental fact, for which there is no further explanation. Rather, any time that the law is one way or another in a given jurisdiction, there is a further explanation of that fact. The relevant notion of "explanation" that I want to target here isn't epistemic. Nor is it causal. It is rather *constitutive* or *metaphysical*. Roughly, it is the kind of explanation that is invoked in the following (purported) explanations: (1) a glass is fragile *in virtue of* being disposed to break in such-and-such conditions, (2) an action is morally right *because* it promotes the greatest expected utility among the possible actions, and (3) a movie is funny *in virtue of* our dispositions to respond to it in certain ways, under certain conditions. For my purposes here, I will use the terminology of *ground* to refer to the basic kind of constitutive explanatory relation here, which (roughly) is a kind of asymmetric metaphysical dependence. On my way of proceeding, to say that "X grounds Y" means "X explains Y" (in the constitutive sense of "explain" I want to target here).[3] The basic question on the table concerns the *grounds* of facts about what the law is in a given jurisdiction at a given time (henceforth, *facts about the content of the law*, or, more simply, the *legal facts*).

Some legal philosophers claim that, necessarily, legal facts are ultimately grounded solely in *social facts* (roughly, descriptive facts of the kind that are the purview of the social sciences), and not *moral facts* (roughly, normative and evaluative facts of the kind that are the

[1] If you want to deny that the law does yield a determinate answer to these *particular* questions (fleshed out in appropriate detail), then I invite you to substitute in your own favorite examples here.

[2] This is not to say that no one would challenge what I have said thus far. For example, some might want to challenge the thesis that the law is *ever* determinate, or at least in any actual legal systems. More radically, some might want to challenge the thesis that the law involves norms (or standards), even in some minimal sense of 'norm'. I will briefly return to this later in the chapter.

[3] For a good overview of the idea of ground, see (Rosen 2010) and (Trogdon 2013). It should be noted that there might in fact be multiple different grounding relations (e.g., "metaphysical" grounding versus "normative" grounding), as argued for by (Fine 2012) and argued against by (Berker 2018). This is one of the many issues about grounding that I am glossing over in this initial setup.

purview of moral and political philosophy). Drawing on one recently influential way of thinking about the positivism/antipositivism dispute in legal philosophy, we can call that thesis *legal positivism*. In turn, we can use the label *legal antipositivism* for the thesis that, necessarily, legal facts are ultimately grounded in both social facts and moral facts.[4] These are competing views not about what law should be, but what about what law *is*. Moreover, they are views about *law*, rather than our *thought and talk* about it.[5]

It is worth emphasizing a few basic points about these formulations of positivism and antipositivism at the start. First, the basic positivist idea is that social facts are relevant *not* because of the obtaining of moral facts. They matter simply because of *what law is*. The parallel point is true for why antipositivists think that moral facts are amongst the grounds of law. (Hence, the use of "necessarily" at the start of the formulation of legal positivism, as with antipositivism). Second, legal positivism does *not* mean that moral facts are never amongst the grounds of legal facts. According to *inclusive* legal positivism, moral facts might be amongst the grounds of legal facts, in some jurisdictions, *because of* the obtaining of contingent social facts. (This is in contrast to *exclusive* legal positivism, which denies that moral facts are ever amongst the grounds of legal facts). The inclusive legal positivist thinks that moral facts *can* be amongst the grounds of the legal facts.[6] But it is still the social facts that "ultimately" matter here, and that have the relevant kind of (relative) explanatory priority.[7] Or at least so the basic thought goes. The use of 'ultimately' in the formulation of legal positivism is meant to make room for this idea of inclusive legal positivism. It does *not* mean that there are no further grounds of the (purportedly) relevant social facts or of the (purportedly) relevant moral facts. At the end of the day, it might well be that using the term 'ultimately' here isn't the best choice. And there are, of course, further issues here to be unpacked about how exactly to understand the nature of inclusive legal positivism. I will return to some of these issues later in the chapter. But, for now, hopefully what I have said is enough to get the basic picture of what positivism and antipositivism are each committed to on the table.

To help get the distinction between positivism and antipositivism in focus, consider the following two different views: (1) necessarily, the legal facts are ultimately grounded solely in descriptive facts about what *shared plans* a group of agents has; and (2) necessarily, the legal facts are ultimately grounded in facts about what best *morally justifies* a set of social practices. The first view (a version of which Scott Shapiro argues for in *Legality*) is an example of a positivist view.[8] The second view (a version of which Ronald Dworkin argues for in *Law's Empire*) is an example of an antipositivist view.[9]

---

[4] This way of defining positivism and antipositivism stems from (Greenberg 2006b), (Rosen 2010), (Shapiro 2011), and (Plunkett 2012). There are many other ways in which the dispute has been formulated. For example, see (Gardner 2001) for another influential way of thinking about the dispute. See (Plunkett 2013a) for discussion of how this way of thinking about legal positivism relates to the way I am discussing it here, as an issue about what grounds what.

[5] I take this debate over positivism to be a "metaphysical" debate. But if you don't like the label 'metaphysical' here, you can replace it with 'object-level'. What I want to highlight is this: the issue is about *law* and not about our thought and talk about it.

[6] See (Waluchow 1994) for a helpful overview and defense of inclusive legal positivism.

[7] See (Shapiro 2011, ch. 9).

[8] (Shapiro 2011).

[9] (Dworkin 1986).

There are well-known motivations and arguments on both sides of this debate. For example, positivists often emphasize the fact that there can be morally bad laws, and, indeed, morally bad legal systems as a whole. At the same time, positivists often emphasize that *all* legal facts seem to be directly under human control, in a way that at least many moral facts are not (e.g., the fundamental moral facts). Positivists often claim to be able to better explain these things than antipositivists. On the opposing side of this, antipositivists often point to the normative significance we give to the law in moral and political thought; a significance that seems different than the kind we give to the rules of social organizations that merely happen to have social power. And they also often point to facts about on-the-ground legal argumentation, in which lawyers and judges seem to freely cite moral facts as justifications for legal opinions about what the law is (and not just what it morally should be). Antipositivists often claim to be able to better explain these things than positivists. (Whether or not the above motivations and arguments are *good* ones is, of course, part of the substantive debate in legal philosophy).

It is not clear that the dispute over legal positivism is best understood as a dispute over what grounds what. For example: the core issue might well be about *real definition* (roughly, about what law *is*) or about *essence* (roughly, about what lies in the nature of law).[10] However, for the purposes of this chapter, I want to focus on the debate over positivism, *understood as* a debate about what grounds what. I want to discuss the following question: Once we agree to focus on this issue of grounding, what are some of the important dividing lines, moving parts, and questions we should pay attention to? And how can this help us better understand, and make progress on, the debate over legal positivism?

I break up my discussion in this chapter into two main parts. In the first part, I argue that, in many contexts when discussing "legal positivism", we should shift our focus from *moral* facts to *robustly normative* facts. This is because, in many contexts, this is really what is driving the debate. I understand *robust normativity* to be the most authoritative kind of normativity that we appeal to in our thinking. It is the kind of normativity we (at least prima facie) seem to appeal to when we make claims about what one *really* should do, think, or feel, all-things-considered. This is in contrast to thinner, more formal notions of normativity, such as the normativity involved in the rules of chess or standards of fashion. (I will say more about this distinction below.)

In the second part, I explore another issue about legal positivism and robust normativity. It concerns the kinds of arguments that legal philosophers give for the (purported) truth of legal positivism. The basic issue is whether (purportedly) robustly normative facts are appealed to as premises in those arguments or not. (A closely connected issue that I will discuss is whether (purportedly) normative facts that bear one or more important *connections* to robustly normative facts are appealed to in premises to those arguments.) In some arguments

---

[10] For example: perhaps legal positivism is best understood (at least partly) as a thesis about the real definition of law. One proposal here would be this: legal positivism is the thesis that one can give a real definition of law in fully nonmoral terms. Real definition and grounding are arguably closely connected topics. For example: facts about the real definition of X might well entail facts about what grounds certain facts (including, importantly, those that we might think are intuitively labeled as the "X facts"). See Gideon Rosen's discussion of the "Grounding-Definition Link" in (Rosen 2015). But that doesn't mean that debates about real definition *just are* debates over what grounds what. See (Rosen 2015) for further discussion on this point.

for positivism (including, I argue, the best way of developing Scott Shapiro's arguments for positivism in *Legality*), such premises do *not* show up in the argument. But I argue that on some key arguments for positivism (including, perhaps, one of Joseph Raz's main arguments for it), such premises *do* show up in the argument. This dividing line raises a host of interesting questions—including, importantly, about whether such arguments really should be thought of as arguments for *positivism* at all. More generally, I argue that thinking about this dividing line helps us better situate the positivist/antipositivist dispute, better understand the space of views in legal philosophy (both actual and possible positions), and better evaluate those views. Moreover, as I emphasize in the conclusion, thinking about it can also help us better diagnose points of agreement and disagreement in legal philosophy, thereby helping us avoid merely verbal disputes.

II. Morality and Robust Normativity

For many of our purposes, the definitions of 'legal positivism' and 'legal antipositivism' that I started with are sufficient. This in the following respect: these definitions are a helpful way to regiment terminology, for the purposes of given agents, in a given context. Such regimentation can be helpful in a context insofar as it helps philosophers in that context make progress within inquiry, given the questions they care about and given their epistemic aims. However, these definitions do *not* always provide us with the tools we need in legal philosophy, *even if* we want to hold fixed that positivism and antipositivism are theories about the ultimate grounds of legal facts.

The main issue I want to focus on here concerns the appeal to "moral facts". Consider the following debate about morality. Some philosophers accept what Stephen Darwall calls *morality/reasons internalism.*[11] (This thesis is also sometimes called a version of "moral rationalism"). Darwall characterizes morality/reasons internalism as follows: "if S morally ought to do *A,* then necessarily there is reason for S to do *A* consisting either in the fact that S morally ought so to act, or in considerations that ground that fact".[12] The core idea is that the demands of morality are necessarily *reason-providing.* The meaning of 'reason' here is meant to pick out the strongest, most normatively loaded sense of "normative reason" we have. In short, the idea is that morality necessarily provides us with *genuine* normative reasons for action, where these are understood as facts that genuinely *count in favor of* certain actions. Genuine normative reasons do not count in favor of simply what you "morally should" do. Rather, they count in favor of what you *really* should do, *full stop* or *all-things-considered. Morality/reasons externalism* is the denial of morality/reasons internalism. It is the claim that it is a *contingent* matter whether morality provides such normative reasons or not. A morality/reasons externalist might hold that morality provides such normative reasons for some people in the actual world, but not all of them. Or she might even hold that morality provides such normative reasons for *everyone* in the actual world, but not certain agents in other possible worlds. The thought, in rough terms, is that a connection to *genuine* normative reasons for action is

[11] (Darwall 1997).

[12] (Darwall 1997, 306). For connected discussion, see (Darwall 2017).

not internal to the nature of morality as such, any more than it is internal to other systems of norms (e.g., the standards of etiquette or the rules of basketball).[13]

This debate over morality/reasons internalism suggests the following. Even if we are confident that morality/reasons externalism is false (as many legal philosophers no doubt are), the fact that many philosophers are drawn to morality/reasons externalism helps bring out an important distinction. On the one hand, there is something along the lines of *genuine* normative reasons for action; roughly, things that contribute to whether an agent *really* should perform an action, all-things-considered. On the other hand, there is the idea of a system that is worth calling a "moral" one. These two things might be necessarily linked, in the way that morality/reasons internalism holds. Moreover, it might even be true that this sort of link is metaphysically necessary, given the nature of morality as such. Or perhaps this link is supported in some way at the *conceptual* level, e.g., given truths about the concept MORALITY.[14] But, even if morality/reasons internalism is true, it might well be that there are additional features of morality that aren't just about the connection that morality/reasons internalism is concerned with, and that help define what morality as such *is*.

What might those features be? There are *many* different theories on offer in the philosophical literature. Here are a few them worth flagging, to appreciate the range of views on offer. First, maybe morality is distinctive in part because of the *content* of the norms (or values) at issue. For example: perhaps the content of the norms (or values) at issue concern certain kinds of conduct.[15] Second, perhaps morality is distinctive in part because it involves a distinctively impersonal "moral point of view".[16] Third, maybe morality has to do with the purported *grounds* of the norms (or values) at issue; e.g., that these are norms that we could justify to others under certain conditions, or which people, in certain conditions, could not reasonably reject.[17] Fourth, maybe morality purports to provide categorical, mind-independent reasons in a particular way, which helps to (at least partially) set it apart from other normative systems.[18] Fifth, maybe morality involves issues about the warrant of distinctive emotions (such as blame and guilt).[19] Sixth, maybe morality involves distinctive kinds of inter-personal demands, such that it involves *second-personal* reasons of a certain sort.[20]

Morality/reasons externalists can (and often do) also grant that some of these things are necessary features of *morality* as such. Indeed, they might grant that they are truths not just about morality, but also truths about what we (or at least some of us) *mean* when we use the term 'morality' or think thoughts using the concept MORALITY. After all, externalists need

---

[13] For some examples of views that accept morality/reasons internalism, see (Korsgaard 1996), (Smith 1994), (Darwall 2006), and (Markovits 2014). For some examples of views that accept morality/reasons externalism, see (Railton 1986), (Boyd 1997), (Foot 1972), and (Brink 1989).

[14] In this chapter, I use small caps to designate concepts. Single quotation marks are used strictly to mention linguistic items. Double quotation marks are used for a variety of tasks including quoting others' words, scare quotes, and mixes of use and mention.

[15] See (Smith 1994), (Jackson 1998), and (Foot 1978) for this kind of proposal.

[16] See (Railton 2003).

[17] See (Scanlon 1998).

[18] See (Williams 1985) and (Finlay 2014).

[19] See (Gibbard 1990).

[20] See (Darwall 2006).

not deny that morality exists, or that it is a distinctive "normative system" (or "normative schema") in some sense.[21] Rather, they just deny something about its intrinsic importance for settling what agents really should do, all-things-considered.[22] The same might be true of someone who thinks that there are normative facts about what agents really should do, but who denies that morality even *contingently* provides us with weighty normative reasons in the actual world. This kind of "moral skeptic" might grant that some of these above things are necessary features of morality as such—as, indeed, many moral skeptics of this sort have (e.g., Nietzsche).[23] The point is just that not everyone interested in "morality" will agree on the idea that it has necessary or even significant normative import for agents like us, in terms of settling what we *really* should do.

In light of this, we then need to ask the following: When we as legal philosophers use the term 'morality' in the context of arguments about *legal positivism*, what really matters most to us? Are we concerned about something along the lines of *real* or *genuine* normative reasons for action (which many, though not all, think morality necessarily provides)? Or are we concerned about some of the other features I glossed above, which many—though, again, not all—think are features of morality? Or are we concerned about both things at once? Here is a conjecture: different legal philosophers involved in the contemporary debate over legal positivism care more about some of these things than others. One reason to take this idea seriously is that people in *general*, including those in *ethics* and *moral philosophy*, seem to have pretty different things in mind when they use the term 'morality', or at least strikingly different theories about morality. These philosophers are not inventing their proposals out of thin air. Each of them draws on important strands of usage of the term 'morality' in our social/historical context, and highlights properties that many closely associate with morality (regardless of whether they take those properties to be *necessary* or *essential* features of it).[24]

To bring this out, consider the following thesis: necessarily, legal facts are ultimately partly grounded in moral facts (in addition to social facts). Without knowing anything more about what moral facts are like, would *all* contemporary legal antipositivists think establishing this thesis would really vindicate their core idea, and see the establishment of it as a victory for their side of the debate over positivism? I suspect that at least many of them would *not*. Similarly, I suspect that many contemporary legal positivists would not see the establishment of this thesis as a defeat for their side of the debate. Rather, I think, many would think the following crucial questions remains: First, are the legal facts ultimately partly grounded in facts about *genuine* normative reasons for action or facts about what agents *really* should do, all-things-considered? Second, even if they are not, are the legal facts ultimately partly grounded in facts that *bear some important connection* to facts about *genuine* normative reasons for action or facts about what agents *really* should do, all-things-considered? The idea

[21] The idea of "schema" is meant to indicate that the collection of norms might not be fully *systematic* in some ways, and might be tied together in loose ways. For connected discussion of "normative schemas" versus "normative systems", see (Railton 2019).

[22] If morality provided *genuine* normative reasons for action in the sense we have in mind here, then it would follow that it had such import. This is because such reasons necessarily contribute to whether or not an agent *really* should perform an action, all-things-considered.

[23] See (Nietzsche 1887/1994). For connected discussion on this point, see (Williams 1985).

[24] For connected discussion, see (McPherson and Plunkett Forthcoming).

of "some important connection" will need to then be specified in some further way. One possibility here is this: the normative facts under discussion play a major role in grounding the facts about what agents *really* should do, all-things-considered. (And perhaps necessarily so). Putting sociological questions about the current dispositions of current legal philosophers aside, the more important point is this: I think these are crucial questions to ask about the grounds of legal facts.

Should these questions *replace* our original question about the ultimate grounds of legal facts, which was formulated in terms of "moral facts"? Not necessarily. For example, we might care about the relationship between the legal facts and the moral facts *not* because of anything having to do with the (purported) normative significance of moral facts, but rather because of other (purported) similarities between law and morality. For example, consider the following thought: both law and morality seem to regulate a wide swath of human action, both seem to claim some kind of authority not claimed by all systems of norms (or values), and both seem to involve a certain family of concepts— e.g., having to do with rights, duties, and obligations—that (at least prima facie) don't seem to show up across all normative systems (or schemas) in the same way, or to the same extent. These kinds of (purported) similarities suggest that, in many contexts, we might really be *more* interested in the (purported) features of morality that the morality/reasons internalist, the morality/reasons externalist, and the moral skeptic can *agree to*. We might be wondering about whether the law is grounded in moral facts, when morality is understood in *that* sort of way (one that is neutral on core issues about the normative significance of morality as such).

To further this line of thought, consider the following. In some cases, people use the term 'morality' to refer to facts about the conventions and practices of a given community for regulating key parts of conduct, including through cultural attitudes. We might call the target here the *mores* of a given community, or its *conventional morality*. Of course, in other cases (as evidenced in much of the discussion over morality/reasons internalism), it seems quite clear that when people use the term 'morality' they want to refer to something that is distinct from the "conventional morality" of a given society. Rather, they aim to refer to something distinct that can (and *should*) be used to critically assess different "conventional moralities", and to do so because it is normatively privileged in a key way. Most recent legal philosophers use the term 'morality' to refer to this latter thing (which we might call "critical morality"), rather than conventional morality.[25] But this isn't always the case. [26] Moreover, philosophers who work on morality (in the "critical" sense) *disagree* about its relation to mores. Certain kinds of cultural relativists, for example, might draw them *very* closely together.[27] We might well want to know about the relation between law and *mores*, just as much as we want to know about the relation between law and *critical morality* (which, as I have emphasized, might be something that provides genuine normative reasons for action or not).[28] Historically, both of

---

[25] For critical discussion here, which brings "conventional" and "critical" morality much closer together than I am presenting things here, see (Woods 2018). For connected discussion, see also (Walden 2017).

[26] See (Hart 1961/2012) for connected discussion about the relevance of this distinction between "conventional" and "critical" morality to general jurisprudence.

[27] See, for example, (Harman 1996). For discussion of possible close connections here, see (Walden 2017).

[28] We might, for example, want to know about how the social facts that ground conventional morality relate to those social facts that ground legal facts.

these are questions that legal philosophers have asked about. And, importantly, both of them are ones that might well be (and I think are) *worth* asking about.

Based on this, I want to make the following methodological suggestion. In many contexts in legal philosophy, we would often do best *not* just to use the term 'morality' but to be *more specific* about which purported feature(s) of morality we care about. In short: Which of the various features that different philosophers associate with "morality" are the ones we want to be focusing on in the context at hand? We would often be best off to focus on those things, and then talk about them *directly*. In many contexts, we might well want to ask whether the legal facts are grounded in the *moral facts*, where, other than specifying that we are talking about facts of "critical morality" and not "conventional morality", we just leave it completely open what exactly the moral facts are like. (Roughly, we just let the chips fall where they may in moral philosophy on this topic.) But we might well have something more specific (purported) feature of morality in mind, based on a particular view about what morality is like: e.g., that morality *necessarily* provides genuine normative reasons for action, or that it provides *categorical* as opposed to *hypothetical* reasons for action, or that its content is *not* grounded in any facts about "conventional morality". If so, we should just talk about *that feature* (or *these features*) directly, and make that the focus of our debate.

With that in mind, let's return to the idea of what an agent *really* should do, all-things-considered. This use of 'really' here is meant to bring in the idea of a distinctive kind of normative authority. What exactly does that idea amount to? It would be great to have an answer to that question. But it is also well beyond the scope of this chapter to attempt anything like a worked-out answer to it. For my purposes here, what I want to do is simply flag a contrast between two kinds of normativity: a contrast that, I claim, is at the core of much of the debate over legal positivism. The contrast is between (A) the most authoritative notion of normativity we have (roughly, the kind we seem to often invoke when we talk about "genuine normative reasons for action" in ethics, or "genuine normative reasons for belief" in epistemology) and (B) the generic idea of a standard that someone (or something) can fail to conform to, and which (in many cases) can thus be used as a guide for behavior and action. Let's put this in terms of a contrast between *robust* normativity (or, equivalently *authoritative* normativity) and *formal* normativity (or, equivalently, *generic* normativity).[29]

At least prima facie, it seems that formal normativity is plentiful in the world. The rules of board games have formal normativity. So do rules of etiquette, and standards of fashion. But most of us think that there is an important difference between failing to conform to standards of fashion and failing to conform to the all-things-considered ethical norms. Those latter norms are meant to be (somehow) more authoritative, *as a normative matter*. We can mark that by saying that they are meant to be *robustly normative*. Robust normativity might, of course, be a chimera in the end: perhaps there is just no such thing, or perhaps we can't even unpack the metaphors here to make sense of it as a coherent concept.[30] These are

[29] My terminology here draws from (McPherson 2011) and (McPherson 2018). McPherson's distinction here draws from (Copp 2005). For further discussion of this distinction within the philosophy of law (including how it shows up in theories of legal thought and talk, and not just in legal metaphysics), see (Plunkett and Shapiro 2017). See also (McPherson and Plunkett 2017).

[30] For skeptical discussion here, see (Tiffany 2007), (Copp 1997), and (Baker 2018). For some recent defenses, see (McPherson 2018) and (Wodak 2018).

important challenges. For our purposes here, what matters is the broad idea of a contrast between formal and robust normativity, which seems to show up in much of our *thinking* about normativity (even if the contrast can't be vindicated in the end). I take it that this gives us an important contrast to begin to work with, and clear enough in broad outlines for my limited purposes at hand.

With the distinction between robust and formal normativity on the table, let's return to the debate over the grounds of legal facts. It is generally common ground that the law, whatever else it is, involves standards that have *at least* formal normativity (insofar as anything does). Indeed, I find it difficult to make sense of exactly how one could really deny this thesis, without changing the subject from talking about *the law*. After all, whatever else it is, the law seems something that we can act in accordance with (e.g., by *conforming to* or *following* the law) or not (e.g., by *breaking* the law). That entails that the law involves *at least* formal normativity.[31]

A more controversial, and more crucial, dividing line in theories of law isn't about formal normativity. It is about whether the law involves robust normativity in some important way. There are various ways that one might propose that it does. For example, one might think that a parallel of morality/reasons internalism is true (call it "legality-reasons internalism" or "legal rationalism"). That thesis faces obvious important challenges, including, for example, the existence of *many* bad laws in *many* legal systems that agents don't have genuine normative reasons to follow (even if they are in the group of agents the law is meant to apply to).[32] But, for now, we can put discussion about this thesis to the side. For our purposes here, the more important kind of connection to robust normativity concerns the *grounds* of legal facts. Consider here the work of Ronald Dworkin and Mark Greenberg. They think that the facts that ultimately ground legal facts are not just ones worth calling "moral", but facts about *what really is valuable*. This suggests that they think that legal facts are ultimately grounded in robustly normative facts—or at least facts that bear an important, fundamental connection to such facts.[33]

For our purposes here, we can think of the concept of *real normative reasons* (for an action, for a belief, for emotions, etc.) as picking out something that contributes to what you *authoritatively* ought to do. (And, moreover, is picked out *under that description*.) It is thus one of a number of connected notions—including, for example, the idea of *real* value, that

---

[31] This is not to say that there aren't possible dissenters on this point. For example, Scott Hershovitz argues that it is a mistake to think that "our legal practices make something—the content of the law" (Hershovitz 2015, 1199). He also argues that it is a mistake to think that "there is a body of "existing law", which encompasses the entire set of legal rights, obligations, privileges, and powers in force in a legal system at a given time". (Hershovitz 2015, 1200). Perhaps then, Hershovitz should count as a dissenter. But, if he is, then I think there is good reason to think he thereby accepts a form of *nihilism* or *error theory* about law. Moreover, it is not clear to me exactly how to unpack Hershovitz's ideas. For instance, some of what Hershovitz writes seems ultimately *not* to be about an *object-level* (or "metaphysical") issue about *law* at all, but rather about a *representational-level* issue about our thought and talk. For example, he writes: "To be clear, I do not object to talking about what the law requires. What I object to is the supposition that there is a single entity called the law to which all such talk refers". (Hershovitz 2015, 1202). If that is right, Herhsovitz's core point might well be a thesis about language and reference, and not about law as such.

[32] For connected discussion about the problems with legality-reasons internalism, see (Enoch 2011).

[33] See (Dworkin 2011) and (Greenberg 2014).

can be seen as part of a connected cluster of ideas involving robust normativity. So, with that in mind, we can put a thought I proposed earlier in a new way, now in terms of the idea of *robust normativity* and not just in terms of the idea of real normative reasons for action. The thought is this. One issue that the positivism/antipositivism debate brings up is whether legal facts are ultimately grounded partly in *robustly normative* facts. Second, on a related front, we can ask whether legal facts are grounded in facts that (even if not robustly normative themselves) bear an important, fundamental connection to such facts; a connection of a sort lacked by many *merely formal* normative facts. (For example, perhaps a connection that is parallel to that suggested by morality/reasons internalism.)[34]

I am inclined to think that, for many of our purposes, in many contexts, we would be best off regimenting our use of the labels 'positivism' and 'antipositivism' to refer to competing views about one of these issues about the grounds of law and robust normativity, thus not using the term 'morality' at all in defining them.[35] But I don't here want to argue at length for that proposal about our use of the labels going forward. Moreover, given the diversity of epistemic aims we have in different contexts, I doubt there is a *single* best way to regiment use here across *all* contexts in legal philosophy where we currently use these labels of 'positivism' and 'antipositivism'.[36] Rather, what matters most to me here is simply that we have clearly identified a range of different issues that matter for discussion about the metaphysics of law.

We can also here note that much of my argument about "morality" above might well also apply to "robust normativity". In other work, McPherson and I have suggested that, in the end, there might not be a single thing that all philosophers are after in discussing "robust" or "authoritative" normativity.[37] Rather, there might be a cluster of different features that we tend to group together, but that are really distinct. Some of these might have to do with the normative import or authority of facts themselves, as I have gestured to above. But on that topic, there might in fact be a range of relevant features here we discuss under the idea of "robust normativity". Other features might have to do with thought and talk (e.g., the kinds of speaker-endorsement that expressivists are likely to take as markers of engaging in robustly normative thought and talk). It is not clear that metaethicists (or metanormative theorists) all target the same thing—or even if they are all talking about something at the object-level rather than the level of thought and talk—when they talk about "normativity", in the robust sense. So, just as with talk about "morality", those of us involved in debates about the metaphysics of law would often do well to be more specific about what exactly we have in mind with "robust normativity", insofar as we in fact have something more specific in mind (which we will often not).

There are further issues we can and should ask about the definitions of 'legal positivism' and 'legal antipositivism' that I started with. Let me here briefly mention a few of them, which interact with my discussion of robust normativity in interesting ways. One important question

[34] This resonates with Greenberg's own way of thinking about what is really crucial in the positivism/antipositivism debate. This is suggested by his use of "value facts" and "moral facts" as interchangeable terms for his purposes. See (Greenberg 2006b) and (Greenberg 2006a).

[35] For further discussion of this suggestion, see (Plunkett and Shapiro 2017).

[36] In this regard, I think the case about our use of the term "legal positivism" is on all fours with many terms we use in philosophy.

[37] See (McPherson and Plunkett 2017). For connected discussion, see (Finlay 2019) and (Silk 2019).

is what exactly counts under the heading of "social facts". For example, does it include all descriptive facts, or just some subset of them? And do facts about the meaning of texts, or about mental content count as "descriptive" ones here or not, given that many philosophers accept some version of the claim that "meaning is normative"? Legal philosophers tend to go for a capacious view here, where pretty much anything other than moral facts (or whatever the relevant alternative category here really is—e.g., robustly normative facts) gets put into the bucket of "social facts". That might be the right thing to do in many contexts. But maybe doing so obscures important dividing lines here, which will matter to us in some of our inquiries in legal philosophy.[38] And, in any case, it is not at all clear that this capacious way of using 'social facts' is a helpful way to talk about the facts that we are really concerned with here, whatever those turn out to be. There are various relevant things we could mean by 'social facts' once we aim to get more fine-grained about it. For example, perhaps we are after facts about practices that are specifically *social* in nature, where that is understood as (in some sense) set apart from other descriptive facts (e.g., biological facts, or facts about the meaning of texts).[39] Thus, the question of what counts as a "social fact" might well involve many similar complications to the question of what counts as a "moral fact" that I have discussed above. Thus, in many contexts, we will be best off by being more precise about which purported features of "social facts" we have in mind—e.g., that they are *not* robustly normative facts, or that they somehow are grounded in descriptive facts about the shared behaviors or attitudes of agents, etc.

Another crucial question is what we mean by the phrase 'ultimate grounds'. At the start of this chapter, I briefly discussed what legal philosophers have roughly had in mind here. But there are still different ways of unpacking the core idea. One thing we might want to focus on is this: take the social facts and moral facts, *whatever* turns out to ground each of those things, and then state this is the level at which we start doing this localized part of metaphysics.[40] Or we might have something different in mind, where we are concerned with what facts do or don't show up in a more fundamental explanatory story of the legal facts (where facts about what grounds moral facts and social facts, respectively, will matter a lot).[41] The best way to proceed is not entirely clear.

How we proceed here in terms of our discussion of "ultimate grounds" will intersect with the following thesis: moral facts are fully grounded in social facts. This turns out to be true on certain views in moral philosophy, such as, for example, views that combine the following two theses: (1) Humeanism about normative reasons for action, according to which an agent A's normative reasons for action are fully explained by facts about A's contingent psychological states (e.g., her desires); and (2) the thesis that morality can be explained in terms of

---

[38] For example: What if someone thinks that "meaning is normative" not only in the formal sense of "normative", but also in some more robust sense? (See, for example, (Gibbard 2012)). I think such a view is implausible. But, if it were right, it would lead to a view on which certain facts about the content of mental states, or the linguistic content of texts or utterances, might well count as "robustly normative", in a way that would depart from how those facts are normally thought of in the debates over positivism.

[39] For a discussion of the nature of the "social" as such, which suggests something along these lines, see (Haslanger 2016). For connected discussion, see (Epstein 2015).

[40] See (Shapiro 2011).

[41] See (Greenberg 2006b) and (Greenberg 2006a).

reasons for action (e.g., as concerning a subset of those reasons).[42] Suppose the moral facts are fully grounded in social facts, and legal facts are ultimately partly grounded in moral facts. Would that be a victory for positivism, or for antipositivism? One way to go here would be to claim that what the positivist and antipositivist both care about are the social facts *other* than the *specific set* of them that grounds the moral facts (insofar as any do). As I have argued elsewhere, I think that is a good way to go for many of our purposes.[43] But notice how this loops back into my earlier discussion of what we care about when talking about "morality". If the features we are interested in are *not* morality's (purported) ties to robust normativity, perhaps this isn't what we should say here about this possibility of the moral facts being fully grounded in the social facts. Or, more precisely: different philosophers will likely care about different things on this front, depending on what was driving them to engage in the debate over positivism in the first place. Our goal should be to zero in on the issues that are philosophically interesting and significant, and then talk about those issues directly.

If my above thoughts in this section are on the right track, one of the core lessons is this: there are *multiple different* philosophically interesting dividing lines in theories about what grounds the legal facts. For many of our purposes in doing legal philosophy, it might be okay—relative to our epistemic aims at hand—to not worry about all of these dividing lines, and just focus on the very broad dividing line with which I started, when I introduced the initial definitions of 'legal positivism' and 'legal antipositivism'. But for our purposes in many contexts, we will often need to pull these different issues apart, and then focus on the *particular* ones that we think matter most.

III. A Role for Robust Normativity in Arguments for Legal Positivism?

For now, let's suppose that we regiment the term 'legal positivism' to mean the following thesis: necessarily, social facts alone (and not robustly normative facts) ultimately ground the legal facts. I now want to focus on a new issue about legal positivism and robust normativity. The issue is about arguments for legal positivism that appeal to (purported) robustly normative facts, or at least normative facts that bear an important connection to such facts (of a sort lacked by many normative systems). (For example, the kind of connection that morality/reasons internalists claim morality has.)

For many working in legal philosophy, this idea of appealing to robustly normative facts in arguments for legal positivism might seem to suggest a form of *prescriptive* or *normative* legal positivism. The rough idea of prescriptive legal positivism is that that we *should* create a legal system (or legal systems) in which the law is "positivist". This means roughly, that the law (in *the relevant jurisdictions*) is ultimately determined by social facts alone, and not robustly normative facts.[44] Prescriptive legal positivism is a claim *not* about what law is, but rather about what it should be (either in all cases, or in certain specified circumstances). Thus, it is not really about legal positivism at all, in the sense of "legal positivism" I have been using in this chapter. This is because positivism, as I have been discussing it in this chapter, is a descriptive

[42] For an example of such a view, see (Schroeder 2007).

[43] See (Plunkett 2012).

[44] See, for example, (Campbell 2004).

claim (rather than a normative one) about what, necessarily, in fact grounds the legal facts. It is a descriptive claim about the grounds of law in all possible legal systems. Prescriptive legal positivism is a thesis about a different topic.

The topic that prescriptive legal positivism *is* about interacts in important ways with the debate over legal positivism (as I am understanding that debate here). For example, consider that for prescriptive legal positivism (understood in the way I am understanding it here) to make sense, it must be *possible* for the law (in a given jurisdiction) to be fully determined by social facts alone. If positivism (as I am understanding it in this chapter) is true, then "prescriptive legal positivism" would be an uninteresting claim, since it would be impossible to have law that wasn't ultimately fully determined by social facts alone (and not robustly normative facts). In order to be interesting, prescriptive legal positivism, as I am understanding it here, must therefore rest on a theory of law of (roughly) the following sort: the nature of law is such that it is possible for the law in a given jurisdiction to be ultimately grounded either in a) a combination of social facts and robustly normative facts *or* b) social facts alone (and not robustly normative facts). Thus, the view is also committed to the following claim: facts about the nature of law (or the essence of law) do not determine whether a) or b) is true. This is incompatible with *both* positivism and antipositivism, as I am understanding those theses here, since they are theses about what kind of facts *necessarily* ground legal facts. Moreover, it is in tension with the way I introduced the discussion of legal positivism at the start of the chapter. As I said earlier in the chapter, the basic positivist idea is that social facts are relevant *not* because of the obtaining of robustly normative facts: they matter simply because of *what law is*. This is not to say that we must throw out the idea of "prescriptive legal positivism" as such, only that it will take care to state it in a way that makes it both coherent and interesting, and that it is likely going to assume a controversial view about the nature of law.[45]

But however prescriptive legal positivism is ultimately best formulated (and whatever the view exactly amounts to), it is uncontroversial that it will need centrally to be about a normative topic about what *should* be the case (perhaps authoritatively should, or perhaps from a "moral point of view", or perhaps some other kind of "should" claim). In contrast, legal positivism, as I am considering it here, isn't making a "should" claim of any sort. What I am interested in is the possibility of an argument that appeals to robustly normative facts in defending *positivism* as such (when understood in the way I am understanding it here), rather than the distinct position of prescriptive positivism. Can positivists coherently make such an argument? And, if they can, *should* they?

On this front, I want to turn to Joseph Raz's main argument in favor of exclusive legal positivism. For our purposes here, we can understand that as the thesis that robustly normative facts are never amongst the grounds of legal facts. The argument that I want to discuss, which

[45] Another important question about prescriptive legal positivism is this. Suppose the prescriptive legal positivist says (as I think she must) that facts about the nature of law (or, similarly, the essence of law) don't settle whether robustly normative facts are part of the "ultimate grounds" or not, or whether it is social facts alone (and not robustly normative facts). We can then ask: Which facts *do* settle this? If the answer is social facts that are contingently tied (in an appropriate way) to the legal jurisdiction in question, then the view appears to rest on a form of *inclusive* legal positivism. If the answer is robustly normative facts, then the view might turn into a form of antipositivism. The answer might, of course, be neither social facts nor robustly normative facts. But then the question remains: Which *other* facts exactly then do the work? For connected discussion, see (Waldron 2001).

Raz gives in *The Authority of Law*, is directed both against inclusive legal positivists *and* leading forms of antipositivism.[46] Thus, in addition to being an argument for exclusive legal positivism, it also functions as an argument for positivism as such (of one form or another). The point that I want to bring out is that Raz makes *substantive* normative claims about the nature of practical authority in order to defend exclusive legal positivism (in a sense of "substantive claim" I will explain later). Or at least this is one straightforward way of unpacking what Raz is up to. Because of this, I will argue, he can be fruitfully read as developing an argument for positivism that appeals to (purportedly) robustly normative facts in the premises of that argument, or at least to facts that bear an important relationship to such facts (of the kind that morality/reasons internalists hold that moral facts have, for example). If that is right, it is an interesting (and I think underappreciated) feature of Raz's views on positivism. Moreover, it is a feature that might well mean that we should reject the resulting form of positivism—indeed, potentially reject it as not even a form of positivism at all. It might also mean that we should rethink our understanding of where the action really is in debates over positivism, as well the divide between inclusive and exclusive legal positivists. Or at least so I will argue.

Drawing on the conceptual distinctions I have introduced in the first section, we can reconstruct Raz's main argument for exclusive legal positivism in broad outline as follows.[47] According to Raz, having *practical authority* involves having the ability to create genuine obligations in virtue of one's directives. Having this kind of authority is meant to be conceptually distinct from being an *epistemic* authority (as in when one person knows more about a subject matter than another). For X to have practical authority over Y, Raz claims, it will normally be the case that Y would do better at conforming to her genuine reasons for action (that she already has prior to X's commands) by following X's commands, rather than trying to deliberate herself about the issues at hand. This is what Raz calls "the normal justification thesis".[48] This thesis is tied to Raz's "service conception" of authority, according to which the role of practical authorities is to *serve* their subjects. On Raz's view, they should do so by helping subjects better conform to their genuine normative reasons for action, and thus what they *really* should do (where this use of 'really' is meant to invoke the idea of what I am calling "robust" or "authoritative" normativity).[49]

From the normal justification thesis, it follows that, if an agent X in fact *has* practical authority over Y, then Y should not deliberate herself about what she should do, but rather follow the commands directly. This would be the case, for example, if *the law* in fact had practical authority over its subjects. On Raz's view, however, the law often does *not* have such authority—and, in any case, whether it does or not is a separate normative question, not to be settled by this part of Raz's theory. But—and this is the part where Raz begins to

[46] (Raz 1979/2002).

[47] The argument I sketch below is a reconstruction of the core argument from (Raz 1994). Note that there are other arguments for exclusive legal positivism that Raz gives that I won't be discussing here.

[48] See (Raz 1985). See (Hershovitz 2011) for a helpful overview of Raz's normal justification thesis, and for Raz's views on authority in general.

[49] Note that, as this discussion of Raz underscores, it is important to conceptually keep separate different ways the terms 'authority' and 'authoritative' are used in this paper. In particular, it is important to keep conceptually distinct (1) the idea of "practical authority", in the Razian sense; and (2) the idea of "authoritative normativity", used in McPherson's sense (where this is equivalent to talking about "robust normativity").

links these claims about practical authority to his views on the nature of law—Raz holds it is part of the nature of law that it *claims* such authority. From this, he thinks it follows that the law must be set up in a way as to make having practical authority *possible*. This possibility would be vitiated, he thinks, if the law instructed agents to deliberate directly about the normative issues at hand (in order to figure out what the law is). Rather, he argues, agents must be able to identify the content of the law *without* engaging in all-things-considered practical reasoning about what to do, or about what they *really* should do (where the "really" here is, again, meant to invoke the idea of robust normativity). This is an epistemological constraint, which Raz thinks supports a particular view of the metaphysics of law: namely, he thinks it supports exclusive legal positivism. This is because, Raz argues, the alternative views (inclusive legal positivism and Dworkinian antipositivism), suggest that the law is (at least sometimes) partly grounded in robustly normative facts. And if that is so, Raz reasons, the epistemology of legal reasoning (i.e., figuring out what the law is) would involve agents engaging in normative reasoning about what they really should do. So, Raz concludes, we have an important reason to think that exclusive legal positivism is correct.

We can flesh this argument out with a bit more detail to highlight the aspect of Raz's argument that I want to discuss. The core of Raz's main argument for exclusive legal positivism can be put as follows:

- P1) The law claims practical authority.
- P2) Insofar as something claims practical authority, it must be capable of having it.
- P3) Law must be capable of having practical authority. (From P1 and P2).
- P4) A is capable of having practical authority over B only if:
  - a) One can identify the content of A's directives without reference to the considerations on which they are based (e.g., without reference to the genuine normative reasons for and against the directive). (This is sometimes called *the identification condition.*)
  - b) The directives must represent an agent's view (e.g., agent A's view) about what B should do. (This is sometimes called the *agency condition.*)
- P5) Inclusive legal positivism and Dworkinian antipositivism fail to meet the identification condition and the agency condition. (The same arguably holds true of all other leading forms of antipositivism).
- C) Therefore, there is an important reason to favor exclusive legal positivism over inclusive legal positivism and antipositivism.

There is also obviously a lot to ask about at each step of the way in the argument I have sketched. (For example: why accept P2?). My goal here, however, is not to evaluate Raz's overall argument. Rather, the key point is about *the broad kind* of argument he gives for P4. Raz's argument for P4 is explicitly based on the service conception of practical authority, and the normal justification thesis in particular. Importantly, the normal justification thesis and the service conception are, I submit, best read as *substantive* ethical/political views about how we *really* should live, and what sort of social/political institutions we *really* should have. The views, in other words, are substantive views about robustly normative topics. If we think there are robustly normative "facts", then it seems fair to say that they are views about such facts.

To see what I mean by this, distinguish between two different projects. On the one hand, consider the following explanatory project. Take the entirety of actual ethical thought and talk, and what (if anything) it is distinctively about (e.g., perhaps such things as ethical obligations, ethical facts, or ethical properties). We can then ask how to explain how actual ethical thought and talk—and what (if anything) it is distinctively about—fit into reality. (By 'reality' I mean, roughly, something along the lines of the following: the totality of what there is and what is the case.) This explanatory project is what we can call the project of "metaethics" or "metaethical inquiry".[50] The aim of this overarching metaethical project isn't to answer ethical questions (although engaging in it might help do so). Rather, it is a descriptive, hermeneutic project aimed at explaining our actual ethical thought and talk, and what (if anything) it is distinctively about.

Contrast the metaethical project with a project that *explicitly* aims at answering ethical questions, either extensional ones (e.g., "am I ethically required to be a vegetarian?") or explanatory ones (e.g., "what explains why ethically right actions are right?"). Or consider a project that aims to illuminate the nature or essence of important ethical phenomena, facts, properties, etc. Consider, for example, projects that aim to explain what *justice* really is, or what *exploitation* really is, or what *promising* really is. Explaining that sort of thing could be done in the service of trying to complete the broader metaethical project—as, indeed, it often is. But, in many cases, philosophers propose such theses *without* thinking they will be a part of the best overall metaethical theory (or follow directly from it), even if the theses place important constraints on which metaethical theory is correct. Moreover, many theses of these kind, when advanced on their own, are ones that could be embedded in radically different more general metaethical views, or accepted by people who explicitly endorse a rival overall metaethical view. For example: the claim that "the essence of justice is that it concerns issues about fairness in cooperation" could be accepted by someone who is an expressivist about thought and talk of this kind (e.g., ethical thought and talk, or ethical/political thought and talk), or someone who is a non-naturalist realist about it, or someone who is a fictionalist about it.

With these distinctions in mind, let's return now to Raz's service conception of authority. This is a contentious view of authority, which explicitly is developed as an alternative to other well-known theories on the topic in (e.g., consent-based views). It is perhaps unsurprising then that Raz aims to establish this view of practical authority *not* by giving a straightforward descriptive or hermeneutic analysis of our actual ethical (or political) thought and talk. Instead, he argues for it based partly on normative arguments about which ethical/political thoughts are *true* or *correct*.

This feature of Raz's argument is somewhat obscured insofar as Raz presents his relevant views on authority as "conceptual" ones. That might suggest a close tie to the explanatory project of metaethics. But in the final part of "Authority and Justification", Raz claims that his "conceptual" work is deeply intertwined with substantive normative work in moral/political philosophy, and is not merely a form of descriptive conceptual analysis.[51] Regardless of Raz's explicit views here, we can also just focus on the following point: the service conception

[50] I here draw on (McPherson and Plunkett 2017) and (Plunkett and Shapiro 2017).

[51] (Raz 1985).

is best understood (whatever Raz may or may not say) as a substantive normative view that doesn't follow simply from the correct metaethical theory (whatever that turns out to be), or the correct purely descriptive account of our ethical/political concepts. The same holds for the normal justification thesis. If that is right, it seems like that is a good reason to think these are "substantive views" about normative facts here, in a way that is similar to (for example) how Rawls's views about the nature of justice in *A Theory of Justice* are substantive views about normative facts.[52] And, moreover, the relevant normative facts here (in at least Raz's case) are ones that are most straightforwardly read as *robustly* normative. They are not about what we should do from such-and-such point of view, or about what we have reason to do, relative to some system of norms. Rather, they concern what we *really* or *authoritatively* should do, full stop.

If this is right, it suggests that Raz's argument here for exclusive legal positivism appeals to (purportedly) robustly normative facts. It thus, it seems, appeals to *exactly* the kind of facts that the positivist claims are *not* ultimately part of the grounds of the legal facts. At the same time, the conclusion of Raz's argument is about a *descriptive* topic, in the following sense. The conclusion of this argument is something about what we have normative reason to believe. In that sense, the conclusion of the argument is about something normative. But the idea is that we have normative reason to believe a descriptive theory (about the nature of law), rather than a normative theory (e.g., that law *should* be made in such-and-such way).

Whether I have ultimately put forward the right reading of Raz depends on a number of issues here. These issues include how to best read Raz's understanding of the "conceptual" nature of his claims, how much of the service conception Raz really needs to make his argument work, and how to best understand what relation between a given thesis (e.g., the normal justification thesis) and different projects (e.g., the overarching explanatory project of metaethics versus the substantive project of figuring out what one really should do) is relevant in the current context.[53] So I don't want to claim that I have given anything like a knockdown argument here about how to best read Raz. I certainly have not. However, what is important for me in the end is the *kind* of position this reading of Raz suggests, even if it is ultimately not Raz's own position. With this in mind, putting issues about Raz interpretation aside, we can ask the following: What should we make of that kind of argument (wherein one appeals to (purported) robustly normative facts to support the (purported) truth of legal positivism)? In particular: Even if such arguments fail, do they make sense as *possible* arguments for legal positivism that we should take seriously? And what (if anything) can we gain in our understanding about the debate over legal positivism by thinking about such arguments?

A. A Dividing Line within Arguments for Positivism or Antipositivism

The first thing to note is how this kind of argument *differs* from many arguments for positivism or antipositivism. Paying attention to this difference suggests an important dividing

[52] (Rawls 1971/1999).

[53] For further discussion of this last issue, see (McPherson and Plunkett 2017). We there argue that different such relations are relevant in different contexts.

line within theories that (purport) to support either positivism or antipositivism.[54] It is worth pausing to note that this is not merely a dividing line in *hypothetical* arguments for positivism (or antipositivism), but arguably brings out an important distinction among existing influential arguments in the debate over positivism.

First, consider arguments that *do* appeal to (purported) robustly normative facts in order to argue for the (purported) truth of legal positivism. On the positivist side, we should note that there are different routes by which someone might end up with this sort of argument, other than the Raz-inspired one I have sketched here. Consider here the debate about whether law should be understood as having a specific kind of *function*, or whether it lacks a necessary function and should instead be understood, rather, in terms of the *means* it uses to carry out its ends. Leslie Green has argued (I think correctly) that this is a crucial debate within legal philosophy.[55] Importantly, both kinds of view might yield the claim that robustly normative facts are appealed to as premises in an argument for legal positivism. For example: one might deny that law necessarily has a certain function, but claim (with Raz) that it necessarily *claims* practical authority. This is a view about the *means* that law has for accomplishing its ends. One can then follow the Razian argument for exclusive legal positivism that I sketched above. Alternatively, one might follow John Finnis and think that law should be understood in terms of the "focal case" of law, and that this "focal case" involves the law promoting the common good of a community. Promoting the common good, Finnis claims, is the proper *function* of law, and having the content of law be based in social facts alone (and not robustly normative facts) helps it achieve this function.[56] Insofar as facts about the common good are (or bear an important link to) robustly normative facts, this yields a potentially different way of getting to the idea that robustly normative facts are premises in a good argument for legal positivism.[57]

Let's now turn to arguments for antipositivism that appeal to (purported) robustly normative facts. Consider Ronald Dworkin's view in *Law's Empire*.[58] Dworkin there argues for (roughly) the following antipositivist view: legal facts are, necessarily, ultimately grounded in facts about what would best justify the relevant set of social practices (e.g., people engaging in arguments in courtrooms, legislators writing things down in official documents,

---

[54] I say "purport" here because, as I will discuss below, it might be that this kind of argument is ultimately inconsistent with legal positivism as such.

[55] (Green 2010).

[56] See (Finnis 2011) for the main statement of Finnis's view that I am reconstructing here. See also (Finnis 2013).

[57] Two notes here. First, I am not claiming that *any* argument about the proper function of law of this kind is going to yield an argument of this sort—i.e., one that aims to support legal positivism by appeal to robustly normative facts. Rather, I just aim to illustrate the possibility of such an argument going in that direction. Second, it should be noted that Finnis doesn't discuss positivism in exactly the same way I am understanding it there, as a thesis about the ultimate grounds of legal facts. But he uses a definition that is quite close, and then endorses legal positivism. For example, he writes that "in relation to the settled positive law, natural law theory . . . shares the principal thesis of contemporary legal positivists, that laws depend for their existence and validity on social facts". (Finnis 2016). As Finnis notes, this is a point about his version of natural law theory that is recognized by many contemporary legal positivists, including (Raz 1980, 213) and (Gardner 2001, 227). It is worth emphasizing, however, that *Finnis's version* of "natural law theory" is just one version of it—and not all versions of "natural law theory" will end up with the same relation to legal positivism.

[58] (Dworkin 1986).

the history of judicial decisions, etc.).[59] This view—the core of his "interpretivism" about law—is *itself* supported, according to Dworkin, by thinking about what would best justify our practices of engaging in a set of relevant social practices of talking about "the law". Dworkin's interpretivism, in other words, operates at two levels, and both levels involve appeal to normative facts about justification—facts that, at least when understood in one way, invoke (or are closely bound up with) the idea of robust normativity. Dworkin's argument for antipositivism thus bears an important similarity to the Raz-inspired argument for positivism that I sketched above: both involve appeal to (purported) robustly normative facts in a similar (and important) place in the argument.

In contrast, consider arguments for positivism or antipositivism that don't appeal to robustly normative facts. Consider here one way of reading Scott Shapiro's argument for legal positivism in *Legality*.[60] Shapiro argues that legal institutions are a particular kind of organization involved in the activity of shared planning. According to Shapiro, this is a fact about a particular kind of institution, which we learn from doing a combination of conceptual analysis of LAW (and related concepts), metaphysical inquiry, and social scientific study of the world we live in, without doing any kind of inquiry into robustly normative facts. Shapiro then argues that laws are the particular plans those institutions have.[61] The relevant plans here aren't plans the legal institution has just for itself, but rather also for ordinary people who aren't involved in the creation, adoption, or enforcement of the plans. (Think here of how an agent A might make plans for what agents B and C will do next week, without B and C having a say about this planning activity). Laws *are* plans on this picture. In general, the facts about what plans an agent has, and what kinds of things conform to them or not, depend on social facts alone, and *not* robustly normative facts. (Or at least so Shapiro argues.) Since laws *are* plans, the same is true of laws. When we talk about "the content of the law", Shapiro claims, this is just one way of talking about what these particular plans are, and relational facts what does or does not conform to them (e.g., whether a possible action is permitted by the relevant plans). Thus, legal positivism is true.[62]

On the antipositivist side, consider Mark Greenberg's arguments for what he calls "the Moral Impact Theory of Law". According to this theory, legal facts are a subset of moral facts: roughly, those that are brought about (in the right way) by the activity of legal institutions.[63] The idea, roughly, is that some moral facts (e.g., that we have a moral obligation

---

[59] I here follow the basic reading of Dworkin's view in *Law's Empire* given in (Greenberg 2006b) and (Greenberg 2014). See (Hershovitz 2015) for a way of reading Dworkin that pushes in a different direction, on which the real thrust of Dworkin's view is that we should deny that there are legal facts whose ultimate grounds we should ask about.

[60] (Shapiro 2011).

[61] Shapiro also argues in (Shapiro 2011) that "planlike norms" (including norms of custom) can be laws too, if there are relevant plans to follow them. But this detail doesn't matter for my purposes here.

[62] This is one of way of reconstructing Shapiro's main argument for legal positivism. My reconstruction here parallels my basic reconstruction of Shapiro's views in (Plunkett 2013b) and (Plunkett 2013c). Hershovitz has recently argued in (Hershovitz 2014) that Raz's and Shapiro's arguments for positivism share a deep similarity, which pushes Shapiro's work in a different way, closer to the Razian view I discussed in the last subsection—and possibly also to a form of prescriptive legal positivism. (For connected discussion on this later possibility, see also (Toh 2018)). I leave discussion of the important strands of Shapiro's work that Hershovitz and Toh discuss aside for my purposes here.

[63] See (Greenberg 2014).

not to drive on a given side of the road in X place) are brought about by recognizably "legal" activities, and that those resulting moral facts simply *are* the law. When Greenberg speaks of "moral facts" here, he has in mind robustly normative facts—or at least that is one straightforward way of understanding his view. Unlike Dworkin, Greenberg never appeals to robustly normative facts in arguing for his theory of law. Rather, he argues that his theory is the best way to explain certain social facts, including actual practices of legal argumentation and legal reasoning. Dworkin makes these kinds of arguments too (for example, in considering how to account for the nature and extent of actual legal disagreements).[64] The difference is that Dworkin *also* cites robustly normative facts in arguing for why antipositivism is true. Greenberg does not. Taken at face value, this suggests that Greenberg (unlike Dworkin) does not think that robustly normative facts are part of the best argument for legal antipositivism.

All of this suggests the following: even before we get to *evaluating* the idea of appealing to (purported) robustly normative facts in arguments in favor of positivism or antipositivism, we can appreciate how this idea helps to bring out an important division within arguments in legal philosophy. Moreover, as my examples above underscore, it is a division that (at least appears) to crosscut the divide over positivism and antipositivism.

B. *Evaluating The Raz-inspired Kind of Argument*

With that in mind, let's now turn to evaluating the kind of argument I used Raz to introduce: that is, an argument that brings in premises about robustly normative facts to support the (purported) truth of legal positivism.

First, one thing that is striking about this argument is the particular way it mixes "ought" and "is" claims. Many doubt that you can derive an "ought" *solely* from an "is". It is perhaps even harder to see how the reverse could work: that is, how one could derive an "is" *solely* from an "ought". One way to go is to insist that the Razian is not trying to do so. Instead, one might want to insist that all that is going on is a sort of "wide reflective equilibrium", wherein we try to have all of our different views, on a range of different topics, mesh together into a rationally defensible and justified overall package of views. As part of this, we might insist that claims of all different kinds bear on each other in different ways, such that some of the normative claims we want to hold put pressure on us to accept certain descriptive claims. But it is not at all clear that this picture is correct for the relevant arguments at hand. Thus, if one remains skeptical of a supposedly valid argumentative move from an "ought" to an "is", then there is some pressure to think that claims about what X "is" might be best understood as involving covert "ought" claims of some sort. Consider claims about "exploitation", "democracy", "promising", or "lying". We can think of these as picking out purely sociological kinds—that is, the kinds of things we study for the purposes of sociological inquiry (or related inquiry in the social sciences). But we can (and often do) think of them as picking out important *normative* or *evaluative* kinds—kinds that matter for the purposes of determining or explaining the robustly normative facts. These kinds might well be bound up with "ought" claims in some way (where the "ought" is the "ought" of robust normativity). It is confusing why one might support a claim about what "exploitation is" with normative arguments if

[64] See (Dworkin 1986).

one thinks of it as a sociological kind. However, it is less confusing (and perhaps not at all) if one thinks of it as a normative/evaluate kind in some way. Perhaps the Raz-inspired view that I sketched above is best understood as involving using the term 'law' to pick out a normative kind in some way. (If not, we should ask: Is Raz trying to derive an "is" from an "ought" in an objectionable way?) If this is the right way to understand Raz, it raises questions about whether the proponent of the Raz-inspired view is in some sense *changing the subject* from what many involved in general jurisprudence thought they were investigating (including, crucially, many positivists).[65] I will return to this thought more below, in the conclusion.

Second, consider that some are drawn to positivism because they believe it will help them secure a fully naturalistic account of legal metaphysics, and also because it fits smoothly into a fully naturalistic account of metaphysics in general.[66] But this result is not obviously secured when positivism is combined with the kind of Raz-inspired argument I just sketched, on which this argument relies on (purported) robustly normative facts. If there isn't some further naturalistic account of *those normative facts*—or else some deflationary (e.g., quasi-realist expressivist) meta-treatment of our talk of "facts" here—then this kind of argument turns out to not be that naturalist-friendly after all. [67] This helps bring out the following: not all motivations for legal positivism sit well with this *kind* of argument for legal positivism, which appeals to robustly normative facts.

Third, we should ask the following. Let's assume that legal positivism is correct. Call the fact *that* legal positivism is true "fact F". If robustly normative facts are relevant to *figuring out* that fact F obtains, *why* would that be? Or, as is in the case of the Raz-inspired argument I have sketched above, *why* would it be that robustly normative facts (about ethics and politics) are used as premises in an argument that has fact F as its conclusion (or, which, relatedly, where the conclusion is that we have normative reason to believe fact F)? One possibility that I want to consider here involves the *grounds* of fact F. In raising this issue, I do *not* mean to suggest that, in all sound arguments, the premises *ground* the fact that the conclusion is correct. But I do think that this is *sometimes* true of the relationship between the facts cited in premises and those facts cited in conclusions in sound arguments. (At least insofar as it makes sense to go in for grounding in metaphysics in the first place). And, importantly, raising it as a possibility here helps bring out what I think is an interesting and underappreciated question in general jurisprudence.

Take the question: What grounds fact F? To be clear: in asking this, I want to use the *same* notion of "ground" that we did in the debate over positivism itself. Thus, we are *not* asking

---

[65] For connected concerns, see (Hershovitz 2014).

[66] See, for example, (Hart 1961/2012).

[67] On this front, it is worth noting that Raz endorses a form of *non*-naturalist realism in metaethics. Roughly, he thinks that ethical thought and talk are about real properties and facts in the world—in a straightforward, descriptivist sort of way—but that such properties and facts cannot be explained in fully naturalistic terms. (See (Raz 1999)). There is obviously a further question about what exactly it would take for there to be a suitably "naturalistic" account of these facts. For example, some philosophers see the issue as one about *ground*, whereas others see it as one primarily about *real definition* or *essence*. See (McPherson 2015), (Leary 2017), and (Rosen 2017) for some of the recent discussion on this topic. We can leave these complications aside here. For the core point is just this: *whatever* it takes to be a non-naturalist about robustly normative facts, we can see that it might be possible to hold that position about robustly normative facts while also being a legal positivist.

about an epistemic or causal explanation here. Rather, we are asking about a constitutive explanation of fact F, of the kind that is at the heart of much recent work in metaphysics.

Not everyone will grant that this kind of question is a meaningful one. But, for now, let's suppose that it is. Here, we face a choice: Are robustly normative facts part of the grounds of fact F or not? It might be that positivists should say "no". Indeed, I think many should, given their other commitments, and given the motivations that they cite for positivism in the first place. (On this front: consider what I said above, for example, about wanting to secure naturalism about legal metaphysics, in combination with the fact that non-naturalism is at least a serious going option in metaethics). An interesting question, though, is whether they *need* to say "no", given their commitment to positivism as such. In earlier work, I briefly discussed this idea, and expressed some skepticism about whether such a view is ultimately compatible with legal positivism.[68] But I think I there moved too quickly.

One crucial issue here concerns ground in general. Suppose we want to defend the idea that it is at least possible that robustly normative facts ground the fact that legal positivism is correct. To do so, we might start by saying the following: legal positivism is strictly a view about what grounds the legal facts. Legal positivism need not involve a view about what grounds the fact that it is itself correct, since that latter issue is simply a different issue that doesn't bear directly on the possibility of legal positivism being true or not. To defend this view, one would need to take on some general questions about the grounds of grounding facts. Suppose that the A facts ground the B facts. What, if anything, does that mean in terms of what we should say about this fact itself (that is, the fact that the A facts ground the B facts)? Some philosophers, including Karen Bennett and Louis deRossett, have argued for the following view about this fact (that is, the fact that the A facts ground the B facts): it too is grounded in the A facts.[69] Positivism is a view of the following form: the A facts, and *not* the C facts, ground the B facts. Thus, if the Bennett/deRossett view is right, then positivists *need* to say "no" when asked whether fact F is partly grounded partly in robustly normative facts. For if they say "yes", then this would be in conflict with positivism. Bennett and deRossett's views about grounding here are, not surprisingly, hardly the only views on offer on this topic. For example: Shamik Dasgupta argues that, in many crucial cases, facts about *essence* (e.g., facts about the essence of X) ground the relevant fact here (namely, the fact that the X facts ground the Y facts).[70] But the point here isn't that Bennett and deRossett are correct. It is only that one would need to reject their view, if one wanted to defend the possibility that robustly normative facts ground the fact that legal positivism is correct.

A second issue connects to the question of how to best formulate inclusive legal positivism, and what it means for thinking about the discussion of "ultimate" grounds in formulating the debate over legal positivism. Recall the basic idea of inclusive legal positivism, formulated now in terms of a focus on robustly normative facts (rather than formulated in terms of moral facts, as is more standard). The thesis is this: contingent social facts can *make it the case* that

[68] See (Plunkett 2012, 177–178). See also section VI, subsection C of (Coleman 2011) for connected discussion that also develops my basic line of worry, and which also extends it in numerous distinct ways.

[69] See (Bennett 2011) and (deRosset 2013).

[70] See (Dasgupta 2014). For a related view, see (Rosen 2015).

robustly normative facts are amongst the grounds of legal facts. In other words: *if* robustly normative facts are amongst the grounds of the legal facts in a given jurisdiction (at a given time), then it is *in virtue of* or *because of* the obtaining of certain contingent social facts. How exactly should this idea be unpacked? It might be that inclusive legal positivism involves the following claim: in legal systems where certain robustly normative facts are amongst the grounds of legal facts, social facts ground the fact that this is so.

If that is the case, then inclusive legal positivism would be structurally parallel to a view that stated the following: in legal systems where certain social facts are amongst the grounds of legal facts, robustly normative facts ground the fact that this is so. Suppose one adopted this latter view and then insisted that robustly normative facts weren't themselves amongst the grounds of the legal facts. Rather, they *only* grounded the fact that such-and-such social facts (as opposed to other social facts) are amongst the grounds of law. It is very tempting to think that such a view should count as a form of antipositivism. And, indeed, if we take inclusive legal positivism to really be a form of positivism, then it seems we should say this. But then we have a worry. Maybe positivism and antipositivism are, after all, not really just about what grounds the legal facts, but *also* at least partly about the facts that ground the fact that the legal facts are grounded in such-and-such facts.[71] Based on this, one might be tempted to the following line: positivism involves the view that, necessarily, robustly normative facts are *neither* amongst the grounds of legal facts *nor* amongst the facts that ground the facts about *which* social facts the legal facts are grounded in.

If that conclusion is right, it raises the stakes for wondering about *why* the Razian argument appeals to robustly normative facts to begin with. Suppose the proponent of the Razian argument makes such an appeal because she thinks that robustly normative facts are amongst the grounds of fact F. Then, if the conclusion above about the nature of legal positivism is correct, it means that it vitiates her ability to have a form of positivism *at all*. This raises the stakes also for the interpretation of Raz. Raz is, after all, standardly taken to be one of the leading positivists of our time. As he puts it: "the positivist social thesis is that what is law and what is not is a matter of social fact".[72] This is a thesis he accepts, and which he takes to be the backbone of his (purportedly) thoroughgoing positivism. If we go down this road for interpreting inclusive legal positivism, this then gives us some good reason to think my interpretation of Raz's argument for legal positivism is wrong. Or perhaps, if the reading of Raz that I sketched earlier is on track, it gives us reason to be worried about whether Raz's view is really one worth thinking of as "positivist" after all—as opposed to, say, a version of prescriptive legal positivism of some sort, or perhaps even an antipositivist position.[73] Since *that* result would be quite surprising indeed (and one which we arguably should want to avoid), this then gives us further reason to think more about what we mean by 'legal positivism', and what we *should* mean by it going forward.

[71] Thanks to Samuele Chivoli and Stephan Leuenberger for helpful discussion on this point.

[72] (Raz 1979/2002, 37).

[73] This point here connects back to the worries driving my discussion in (Plunkett 2012, 177–178), where I wondered whether Raz's view of law was really a "positivist" one in the end or not. See also connected worries in (Hershovitz 2014).

One thing that might be said here at this juncture is this.[74] I have been discussing two different issues about ground here. First there is the "level 1" issue of what grounds legal facts. Second there is the "level 2" issue of what grounds the fact that legal facts are grounded in such-and-such facts. This second level concerns *why* certain facts are amongst the grounds of legal facts. But perhaps two levels simply isn't enough to help us appreciate the array of existing positions on the table here, and where the important divisions between those positions are. Perhaps the key to understanding the Razian view I have been discussing (and understanding it *as* a form of positivism)—as well as the key to getting some of what we want from the talk of "ultimate" grounds in our formulation of the debate over positivism—is to move to the "third level" issue: namely, the issue of what grounds the facts at the second level above. That is: What grounds the facts that, in turn, ground the fact that the legal facts are grounded in such-and-such facts? We might then be able to distinguish positivism from antipositivism, and distinguish inclusive from exclusive legal positivism, as follows.

At the first level ("what grounds legal facts?"), we can distinguish three positions. The exclusive positivist position is that, necessarily, it is social facts alone, and not robustly normative facts. The inclusive positivist position is that, necessarily, it is social facts and possibly also robustly normative facts. Or perhaps the inclusive legal positivist could even go for a less committal view, where they claim that is entirely contingent what kinds of facts are amongst the grounds here. And, finally, the antipositivist position is that, necessarily, it is social facts and robustly normative facts (or perhaps *just* robustly normative facts).

At the second level ("what grounds the fact that the legal facts are grounded in such-and-such facts?"), we can distinguish two positions. The positivist position is that, necessarily, it is social facts alone, and not robustly normative facts. In contrast, the antipositivist position is that, necessarily, it is social facts and robustly normative facts (or perhaps *just* robustly normative facts).

Finally, at the third level, this is where one might want to say that some of the key different positivist views we have been considering again part ways. Some legal philosophers (perhaps Raz and Dworkin) say that robustly normative facts are amongst the grounds here. Others (perhaps Shapiro and Greenberg) say they are not.

If *that* three-level picture is correct, it would capture the inclusive legal positivist idea that it is *because of* the obtaining of social facts that robustly normative facts are (or are not) amongst the grounds of legal facts. In so doing, it would also help get us (at least some of what) we wanted from talk of "ultimate grounds" in the discussion of legal positivism. Finally, *if* Raz is really best read as denying that robustly normative facts play a role in the second level, but granting that they do in the third level, it would explain the sense in which the Razian view I have discussed in this section is a positivist one, despite convergence with Dworkin (and some other antipositivists) at the third level.

I leave it for future discussion to assess whether this proposed three-level picture is really what we want here—as well as how to interpret Raz. What I hope to have shown is the need to move to *some* kind of multi-tiered picture—involving *at least* two levels—to bring out important connections and differences between different views in the debate over legal positivism. Many of these connections and differences are ones that we will miss if we stay

[74] Thanks to James Edwards for helpful discussion on what follows in the rest of this section.

focused on simply the issue of positivism versus antipositivism. And many of them are ones that involve issues about robust normativity, rather than (or perhaps in addition to) issues about morality. Or at least so I have argued. [75]

IV. Conclusion

Suppose two legal philosophers agree on legal positivism. But they disagree about whether robustly normative facts figure into the best argument for legal positivism. There appears to be a serious difference between the views of these two philosophers. In fact, it is the kind of difference that should make us wonder whether these people are even offering theories of the *same thing*, or rather talking about different things entirely. One diagnosis of this is as follows. One the one hand, we might think of the term 'law' as picking out something within a normative theory about what we really should do (where the "should" is that of robust normativity). On the other, we might think of it as picking out something within a descriptive *sociological* theory. For example, we sometimes talk about the "rule of law" as an ideal within moral and political philosophy, where this is a kind of moral and political achievement, and where it is assumed that this bears heavily on what we (authoritatively) should do. In contrast, we distinguish "law" from other ways of organizing human behavior, within sociology and anthropology, without this involving any normative endorsement of this way of organizing human behavior. It might well be that for many facts in the first category, robustly normative facts play a role in the "second level" here as follows: they ground the fact that the X facts are grounded in Y facts. (Or, similarly, perhaps robustly normative facts play a role in the "third level" of the sort I discussed in the last section.) However, in contrast, it might be that robustly normative facts play no such role for *sociological* facts. In both cases, for both sociological facts and those in the first category, it might still be that (at least some instances of) facts in that category are fully grounded in social facts.[76]

Suppose one philosopher is making a claim about a fundamentally *normative kind* (where, again, the relevant notion of "normative" is *robustly* normative), and another making a claim about a purely *sociological kind*. If that is right, then both of these philosophers might well be correct in terms of the theses they each advance about the respective thing they are talking about. Such theses might well be the core of the literal content of what each of them says (that is, in terms of the semantics of what they say). This might be true either in terms of what they say about whether or not positivism is true, as well as what they say about what (if anything) grounds the fact that it is true (or false). We might recognize this, and then the appearance of disagreement between these two speakers might start to fade. It might be, for example, that the only reason we thought they were disagreeing (or the speakers themselves thought they were disagreeing) was based on a false presumption of shared literal meaning

---

[75] Note that, if we go down this road of exploring "multitiered" views here, there are other options that we might consider than the one I have sketched here. For example, (Epstein 2015) thinks that there are "anchoring" facts that are distinct from facts that ground grounding facts, but that are closely related in terms of the basic explanatory role they play.

[76] This is assuming, for now, that this is consistent with what grounds grounding relations. (Recall my earlier discussion of the views from Bennett and deRosset here that would push against this).

in the case at hand. We might then say that such speakers were engaged in a "merely verbal dispute" of a familiar kind.[77]

However, this need not always be the result. The fact that two speakers both speak truly in terms of what they literally say doesn't mean that there are not further issues between them over which they genuinely disagree. Moreover, as I have argued in other work (including, most importantly, in joint work with Tim Sundell), those disagreements might well be ones those speakers express in the linguistic exchange in question.[78] This is because, in addition to expressing disagreements via the semantics of what we say, we also do so via pragmatic mechanisms—e.g., via implicature or presupposition.[79]

Consider the following. It might be that we are best off using the term 'law' in certain ways when doing sociology, history, and anthropology, and other ways when engaged in normative theorizing about how we (authoritatively) ought to live, or how we (authoritatively) ought to organize our social/political institutions.[80] Suppose that both legal philosophers in our above scenario agree to that. That still doesn't settle *which ways* those are. Thus, as I argue in other recent work, legal philosophers in this sort of situation might disagree about the *normative* issue of which way we *should* use the term 'law' moving forward in the context at hand.[81] Issues about the normative and evaluative assessment of concepts—including, centrally normative issues about which concepts we should use, and which words we should use to express those concepts—are issues in what Alexis Burgess and I call *conceptual ethics*.[82] In the case at hand, one legal philosopher might think, for example, something along the following lines: "the relevant concept we should be using in this context for our inquiry is obviously concept X". Or the legal philosophers in our scenario might disagree about the *descriptive* issue about which context they are actually in. These are further substantive issues, and ones that can often be well worth debating about. Moreover, given the rich pragmatic mechanisms we have for communicating such disagreements (including what Sundell and I, borrowing from Chris Barker, call "metalinguistic" usages of terms) these legal philosophers might in fact actually be expressing such disagreements in their actual linguistic exchanges—but just not through the literal semantic content of what they say.[83] In turn, insofar as legal philosophers disagree about these issues, they will likely be tied to further ones they disagree about as well. In particular, it is rare to find a disagreement in conceptual ethics that is also not tied to some further disagreement about something other than conceptual ethics. For example, there might be a further disagreement about a descriptive issue about the way things are, or a normative one about what agents should do, think, or feel.[84]

---

[77] For helpful discussion of the idea of "merely verbal disputes", see (Chalmers 2011) and (Jenkins 2014).

[78] See (Plunkett and Sundell 2013a) and (Plunkett and Sundell 2013b). See also (Plunkett 2015).

[79] In addition to (Plunkett and Sundell 2013a), see also (Finlay 2014), (Khoo and Knobe 2016), and (Thomasson 2016) for other recent work that emphasizes the importance of this fact.

[80] For more on this idea, see (Plunkett 2016). For related discussion, although in an importantly different theoretical framework, see (Dworkin 2006).

[81] See (Plunkett 2016).

[82] See (Burgess and Plunkett 2013a) and (Burgess and Plunkett 2013b).

[83] See (Plunkett and Sundell 2013a) and (Plunkett and Sundell 2013b), drawing on (Barker 2002).

[84] I discuss this at greater length in (Plunkett 2015), (Plunkett and Sundell 2013a), and (Plunkett and Sundell 2013b).

But, crucially, these are issues that might well be ones that the speakers themselves are only implicitly aware of in their actual dispute. Focusing on them, and bringing them into explicit discussion, might well help us make philosophical progress.[85]

Doing so might bring in another, different place where robustly normative facts (including ones about how we should live, and how we should set up our social/political institutions) enter the picture in a serious way. One might argue the following: *which* aspects of reality we should choose to focus our attention on when doing legal philosophy should be determined by how we (authoritatively) ought to live, or how we (authoritatively) ought to set up our social/political institutions. (In other words: considerations of the kind that many in moral and political philosophy are concerned with.) In turn, this might be used as the basis for a claim about how we should be using the term 'law': namely, we should be using it to pick out a feature of social reality that is ethically/politically important (perhaps in addition to it being important for purposes of anthropological/sociological explanation).[86] That view in conceptual ethics doesn't entail anything about what arguments there are for why positivism is true of X (whatever it is), where X is what we should be talking about. The fact that *we should be thinking and talking about the X facts* is different than *the X facts themselves*. The argument for the former might involve robustly normative facts, but without that entailing anything about whether robustly normative facts are amongst the ultimate grounds of the X facts. To see this, consider the following kind of view: we (authoritatively) ought to talk about facts that, necessarily, are ultimately solely grounded in social facts alone. The argument for *why* those facts are solely grounded in social facts need not involve appeal to any robustly normative facts.

Perhaps some arguments about legal positivism really are ultimately best understood as metalinguistic negotiations, where the underlying issue is one in conceptual ethics. And perhaps then the various issues driving the differences in view in conceptual ethics (including, perhaps, issues in ethics and politics *not* about words and concepts) will bring us to shared subject matter where (at least many) positivists and antipositivists disagree. At the same time, it is worth keeping in mind the possibility I mentioned earlier. This is that it might turn out that, for many exchanges between legal philosophers that seem to be explicitly talking about different things (a sociological kind we call "law" versus a normative kind we call "law"), they simply do not have any further disagreement here, once it becomes clear to them that one is talking about a sociological kind, and the other a normative kind. Thinking about different views on what grounds the fact that positivism is true (or antipositivism is true, if it is) can help us here. In particular, it can help us better appreciate whether these are the sorts of issues at play here; and, thus, it can help us better identify which issues need to be addressed in order to help us make progress within legal philosophy.

---

[85] I discuss this kind of issue at greater length in (Plunkett 2015) and (Plunkett 2016). For closely connected discussion, see (Chalmers 2011).

[86] For further discussion of this kind of view, see (Plunkett 2016). For connected discussion, see also (Murphy 2008) and (Stoljar 2013). It is worth noting here, that as I discuss in (Plunkett 2016), Hart endorses a version of this kind of view at the end of (Hart 1961/2012).

References

Baker, Derek. 2018. "Skepticism about Ought Simpliciter". In *Oxford Studies in Metaethics, Vol. 13*, edited by R. Shafer-Landau. Oxford: Oxford University Press.

Barker, Chris. 2002. "The Dynamics of Vagueness". *Linguistics and Philosophy* 25:1–36.

Bennett, Karen. 2011. "By Our Bootstraps". *Philosophical Perspectives* 25(1):27–41.

Berker, Selim. 2018. "The Unity of Grounding". *Mind* 127(507):729–777.

Boyd, Richard. 1997. "How to Be a Moral Realist". In *Moral Discourse and Practice*, edited by S. Darwall, A. Gibbard, and P. Railton. New York: Oxford University Press.

Brink, David. 1989. *Moral Realism and the Foundations of Ethics*. Cambridge: Cambridge University Press.

Burgess, Alexis, and David Plunkett. 2013a. "Conceptual Ethics I". *Philosophy Compass* 8(12):1091–1101.

_____. 2013b. "Conceptual Ethics II". *Philosophy Compass* 8(12):1102–1110.

Campbell, Tom. 2004. *Prescriptive Legal Positivism: Law, Rights and Democracy*. London: Cavendish.

Chalmers, David J. 2011. "Verbal Disputes". *Philosophical Review* 120(4):515–566.

Coleman, Jules L. 2011. "The Architecture of Jurirsprudence". *The Yale Law Journal* 121(2):2–80.

Copp, David. 1997. "The Ring of Gyges: Overridingness and the Unity of Reason". *Social Philosophy and Policy* 14(1):86–106.

_____. 2005. "Moral Naturalism and Three Grades of Normativity". In *Normativity and Naturalism*, edited by P. Schaber. Frankfurt: Ontos-Verlag.

Darwall, Stephen. 2017. "Ethics and Morality". In *The Routledge Handbook of Metaethics*, edited by T. McPherson and D. Plunkett. New York: Routledge.

Darwall, Stephen L. 1997. "Reasons, Motives, and the Demands of Morality: An Introduction". In *Moral Discourse and Practice: Some Philosophical Approaches*, edited by S. L. Darwall, A. Gibbard, and P. A. Railton. New York: Oxford University Press.

_____. 2006. *The Second-Person Standpoint: Morality, Respect, and Accountability*. Cambridge, MA: Harvard University Press.

Dasgupta, Shamik. 2014. "The Possibility of Physicalism". *The Journal of Philosophy* 111(9):557–592.

deRosset, Louis. 2013. "Grounding Explanations". *Philosophers' Imprint* 13(7):1–26.

Dworkin, Ronald. 1986. *Law's Empire*. Cambridge, MA: Belknap Press.

_____. 2006. *Justice in Robes*. Cambridge, MA: Harvard University Press.

_____. 2011. *Justice for Hedgehogs*. Cambridge, MA: Harvard University Press.

Enoch, David. 2011. "Reason-Giving and the Law". In *Oxford Studies in Philosophy of Law*, edited by L. Green and B. Leiter. Oxford: Oxford University Press.

Epstein, Brian. 2015. *The Ant Trap: Rebuilding the Foundations of the Social Sciences*. Oxford: Oxford University Press.

Fine, Kit. 2012. "Guide to Ground". In *Metaphysical Grounding: Understanding the Structure of Reality*, edited by F. Correia and B. Schnieder. Cambridge: Cambridge University Press.

Finlay, Stephen. 2014. *Confusion of Tongues: A Theory of Normative Language*. Oxford: Oxford University Press.

_____. 2019. "Defining Normativity". In *Dimensions of Normativity: New Essays on Metaethics and Jurisprudence*, edited by D. Plunkett, S. Shapiro, and K. Toh.

Finnis, John. 2011. *Natural Law and Natural Rights*. Oxford: Oxford University Press.

_____. 2013. *Philosophy of Law: Collected Essays Volume IV*. Oxford: Oxford University Press.

_____. 2016. "Natural Law Theories". In *The Stanford Encyclopedia of Philosophy (Winter 2016 Edition)*, edited by E. N. Zalta. https://plato.stanford.edu/archives/win2016/entries/natural-law-theories/.

Foot, Philippa. 1972. "Morality as a System of Hypothetical Imperatives". *Philosophical Review* 81(3):305–316.

_____. 1978. *Virtues and Vices*. Berkeley: University of California Press.

Gardner, John. 2001. "Legal Positivism: 5 1/2 Myths". *American Journal of Jurisprudence* 46(199):199–228.

Gibbard, Allan. 1990. *Wise Choices, Apt Feelings: A Theory of Normative Judgment*. Cambridge, MA: Harvard University Press.

_____. 2012. *Meaning and Normativity*. Oxford: Oxford University Press.

Green, Leslie. 2010. "Law as a Means". In *The Hart-Fuller Debate in the Twenty- First Century*, edited by P. Cane. Oxford: Hart.

Greenberg, Mark. 2006a. "Hartian Positivism and Normative Facts: How Facts Make Law II". In *Exploring Law's Empire: The Jurisprudence of Ronald Dworkin*, edited by S. Hershovitz. New York: Oxford University Press.

_____. 2006b. "How Facts Make Law". In *Exploring Law's Empire: The Jurisprudence of Ronald Dworkin*, edited by S. Hershovitz. New York: Oxford University Press.

_____. 2014. "The Moral Impact Theory of Law". *The Yale Law Journal* 123(5):1288–1342.

Harman, Gilbert. 1996. "Moral Relativism". In *Moral Relativism and Moral Objectivity*. Malden, MA: Blackwell.

Hart, H. L. A. 1961/2012. *The Concept of Law* 3rd ed. Oxford: Oxford University Press.

Haslanger, Sally. 2016. "What Is a (Social) Structural Explanation?" *Philosophical Studies* 173(1):113–130.

Hershovitz, Scott. 2011. "The Role of Authority". *Philosophers' Imprint* 11(7): 1–19.

_____. 2014. "The Model of Plans and the Prospects for Positivism". *Ethics* 125(1):152–181.

_____. 2015. "The End of Jurisprudence". *The Yale Law Journal* 124(4):1160–1204.

Jackson, Frank. 1998. *From Metaphysics to Ethics: A Defence of Conceptual Analysis*. Oxford: Clarendon.

Jenkins, C. S. I. 2014. "Merely Verbal Disputes". *Erkenntnis* 79(1):11–30.

Khoo, Justin, and Joshua Knobe. 2016. "Moral Disagreement and Moral Semantics". *Noûs* 50(2):109–143.

Korsgaard, Christine M. 1996. *The Sources of Normativity*. New York: Cambridge University Press.

Leary, Stephanie. 2017. "Non-naturalism and Normative Necessities". In *Oxford Studies in Metaethics Vol. 12*, edited by R. Shafer-Landau. Oxford: Oxford University Press.

Markovits, Julia. 2014. *Moral Reason*. Oxford: Oxford University Press.

McPherson, Tristram. 2011. "Against Quietist Normative Realism". *Philosophical Studies* 154 (2):223–240.

_____. 2015. "What Is at Stake in Debates among Normative Realists?" *Noûs* 49(1):123–146.

_____. 2018. "Authoritatively Normative Concepts". In *Oxford Studies in Metaethics Vol. 13*, edited by R. Shafer-Landau. Oxford: Oxford University Press.

McPherson, Tristram, and David Plunkett. 2017. "The Nature and Explanatory Ambitions of Metaethics". In *The Routledge Handbook of Metaethics*, edited by T. McPherson and D. Plunkett. New York: Routledge.

_____. Forthcoming. "Conceptual Ethics and the Methodology of Normative Inquiry". In *Conceptual Engineering and Conceptual Ethics*, edited by A. Burgess, H. Cappelen, and D. Plunkett. Oxford: Oxford University Press.

Murphy, Liam. 2008. Better to See Law This Way. *New York University Law Review* 83(4):1088–1108.

Nietzsche, Friedrich Wilhelm. 1887/1994. *On the Genealogy of Morality*. New York: Cambridge University Press.

Plunkett, David. 2012. "A Positivist Route for Explaining How Facts Make Law". *Legal Theory*, 18(2):139–207.

_____. 2013a. "Legal Positivism and the Moral Aim Thesis". *Oxford Journal of Legal Studies* 33(3):563–605.

_____. 2013b. "The Planning Theory of Law I: The Nature of Legal Institutions". *Philosophy Compass* 8(2):149–158.

_____. 2013c. "The Planning Theory of Law II: The Nature of Legal Norms". *Philosophy Compass* 8(2):159–169.

_____. 2015. "Which Concepts Should We Use?: Metalinguistic Negotiations and the Methodology of Philosophy". *Inquiry* 58(7–8):828–874.

_____. 2016. "Negotiating the Meaning of 'Law': The Metalinguistic Dimension of the Dispute over Legal Positivism". *Legal Theory* 22(3–4):205–275.

Plunkett, David, and Scott Shapiro. 2017. "Law, Morality, and Everything Else: General Jurisprudence as a Branch of Metanormative Inquiry". *Ethics* 128(1):37–68.

Plunkett, David, and Timothy Sundell. 2013a. "Disagreement and the Semantics of Normative and Evaluative Terms". *Philosophers' Imprint* 13(23):1–37.

_____. 2013b. "Dworkin's Interpretivism and the Pragmatics of Legal Disputes". *Legal Theory* 19 (3):242–281.

Railton, Peter. 1986. "Moral Realism". *The Philosophical Review* 95:163–207.

_____. 2003. *Facts, Values, and Norms: Essays toward a Morality of Consequence*. New York: Cambridge University Press.

_____. 2019. " 'We'll see you in court!': The Rule of Law as an Explanatory and Normative Kind". In *Dimensions of Normativity: New Essays on Metaethics and Jurisprudence*, edited by D. Plunkett, S. Shapiro, and K. Toh. New York City: Oxford University Press.

Rawls, John. 1971/1999. *A Theory of Justice (revised edition)*. Cambridge, MA: Harvard University Press.

Raz, Joseph. 1979/2002. *The Authority of Law: Essays on Law and Morality*. Oxford: Oxford University Press.

_____. 1980. *The Concept of a Legal System: An Introduction to the Theory of Legal System*. 2d ed. Oxford: Oxford University Press.

_____. 1985. "Authority and Justification". *Philosophy and Public Affairs* 14(1):3–29.

_____. 1994. "Authority, Law, and Morality". In *Ethics in the Public Domain: Essays in the Morality of Law and Politics*. Oxford: Oxford University Press.

_____. 1999. *Engaging Reason: On the Theory of Value and Action*. New York: Oxford University Press.

Rosen, Gideon. 2010. "Metaphysical Dependence: Grounding and Reduction". In *Modality: Metaphysics, Logic, and Epistemology*, edited by B. Hale and A. Hoffmann. Oxford: Oxford University Press.

_____. 2015. "Real Definition". *Analytic Philosophy* 56(3):189–209.

_____. 2017. "Metaphysical Relations in Metaethics". In *The Routledge Handbook of Metaethics*, edited by T. McPherson and D. Plunkett. New York: *Routledge*.

Scanlon, T. M. 1998. *What We Owe to Each Other*. Cambridge, MA: Harvard University Press.

Schroeder, Mark. 2007. *Slaves of the Passions*. Oxford: Oxford University Press.

Shapiro, Scott. 2011. *Legality*. Cambridge, MA: Harvard University Press.

Silk, Alex. 2019. "Normativity in Language and Law". In *Dimensions of Normativity: New Essays on Metaethics and Jurisprudence*, edited by D. Plunkett, S. Shapiro, and K. Toh. Oxford: Oxford University Press.

Smith, Michael. 1994. *The Moral Problem*. Cambridge: Blackwell.

Stoljar, Natalie. 2013. "What Do We Want Law to Be? Philosophical Analysis and the Concept of Law". In *Philosophical Foundations of the Nature of Law*, edited by W. J. Waluchow and S. Sciaraffa. Oxford: Oxford University Press.

Thomasson, Amie L. 2016. "Metaphysical Disputes and Metalinguistic Negotiation". *Analytic Philosophy* 57(4):1–28.

Tiffany, Evan. 2007. "Deflationary Normative Pluralism". *Canadian Journal of Philosophy* 37(5):231–262.

Toh, Kevin. 2018. "Plan-Attitudes, Plan-Contents, and Bootstrapping: Some Thoughts on the Planning Theory of Law". In *Oxford Studies in Philosophy of Law Vol. 3*, edited by J. Gardner, L. Green, and B. Leiter. Oxford: Oxford University of Press.

Trogdon, Kelly. 2013. "An Introduction to Grounding". In *Varieties of Dependence*, edited by M. Hoeltje, B. Schnieder, and A. Steinberg. Munich: Philosophia Verlag.

Walden, Kenneth. 2017. "Mores and Morals: Metaethics and the Social World". In *The Routledge Handbook of Metaethics*, edited by T. McPherson and D. Plunkett. Oxford: Oxford University of Press.

Waldron, Jeremy. 2001. "Normative (or Ethical) Positivism". In *Hart's Postscript: Essays on the Postscript to* The Concept of Law, edited by J. L. Coleman. Oxford: Oxford University Press.

Waluchow, Wilfrid. 1994. *Inclusive Legal Positivism*. Oxford: Oxford University Press.

Williams, Bernard. 1985. *Ethics and the Limits of Philosophy*. Cambridge, MA: Harvard University Press.

Wodak, Daniel. 2018. "Fictional Normativity and Normative Authority". *Canadian Journal of Philosophy*. DOI: 10.1080/00455091.2018.1433795.

Woods, Jack. 2018. "The Authority of Formality". In *Oxford Studies in Metaethics Vol. 13*, edited by R. Shafer-Landau. Oxford: Oxford University Press.

7 Of Law and Other Artificial Normative Systems

Mitchell N. Berman*

IT IS WIDELY believed that a central task of jurisprudence—arguably *the* central task—is to explain what makes it the case that legal norms have the contents that they do, or, in rough equivalence, to explain what renders legal propositions true when they are true. I will call a theory that aims to accomplish this task a "constitutive theory" of law. A constitutive theory would explicate what Ronald Dworkin famously called the "grounds of law,"[1] and provide an account as well of the grounding relationship or function. It would explain, in Mark Greenberg's felicitous phrase, "how facts make law."[2] Jurisprudential schools can thus be distinguished by the constitutive theories they provide. By scholarly tradition, the first cut at classifying theories separates positivism from natural law. Broadly speaking, philosophers from the natural law or non-positivist traditions insist that moral norms have

* Leon Meltzer Professor of Law, and Professor of Philosophy, the University of Pennsylvania. Email: mitchberman@law.upenn.edu. I am indebted to the editors of this volume for inviting me to contribute, and to David Enoch, Mark Greenberg, Scott Hershovitz, Lewis Kornhauser, David Plunkett, Stefan Sciaraffa, and Kevin Toh for extremely helpful comments on previous drafts. I am also grateful to participants at a workshop at the Wharton School, and to Rob Hughes, Stephen Perry, Daniel Singer, Fred Wilmot-Smith, and Daniel Wodak, for very useful feedback and conversations. I apologize to anyone whose contributions I have overlooked.

[1] (Dworkin 1986, 4).

[2] (Greenberg 2004, 157–198). I acknowledge that language of constitution and grounding suggests at least a minimal realism about legal norms. I think that's the dominant view among legal theorists and philosophers of law. Still, I don't mean to prejudge realism about legal norms. Expressivists about legal norms who accept some standards of correctness need the sort of theory I'm referencing, even if they'd not characterize such a theory as "constitutive."

Dimensions of Normativity. David Plunkett, Scott J. Shapiro, and Kevin Toh.

an ineliminable role to play in the constitution of legal norms, whereas positivists maintain either that moral norms play no such role or that, insofar as they do, that is a consequence of contingent nonmoral facts.

Although this is the conventional way to carve up the field, it's not obviously the most illuminating one, surely not for all theoretical purposes. A given inclusive positivist account and a given natural law one might agree on all the features possessed by legal systems with which we are familiar. It's not clear that it will prove most useful to place the two theories on the opposite side of the field's fundamental cleavage solely because some basic feature that the latter treats as conceptually necessary the former views as contingent though practically inevitable. Nor is it clear that all theories that assign *some* necessary role to *some* aspect of morality should be classed together no matter how radically disparate are the roles and the aspects that they pick out.

In this essay, I offer an alternative path of entry into the terrain, one that tries to foreground differences in the basic pictures that theories of law advance, assume, or presuppose about our normative landscape and law's place within it. Here's what I mean. At least on the surface of things, we inhabit a multiplicity of normative systems—law and morality, of course, but also sports and games, prescriptive grammar and fashion, etiquette, religious ritual, families, militaries, corporations, and so on. The multiplicity of normative systems seems a plain fact of our lives.[3] But it is a fact that can be interpreted, or made sense of, in countless ways. Instead of starting by asking whether morality necessarily contributes to legal content, I invite us to adopt a wider-angled perspective on our normative landscape.

I will not offer a taxonomy of ways to make sense of the apparent fact of multiple normative systems. Instead, I will try to make more visible and concrete a commonsensical picture of our normative situation that, I believe, reflects basic positivistic beliefs and presuppositions yet has no obvious champion among leading contemporary legal philosophers and finds itself increasingly under attack. I will call it the "Standard Positivist Picture" (SPP). It is, as I have said, a picture of our normative landscape and law's place within it. For ease of discussion, I'll introduce these two aspects of the view separately, even at the risk of some artificiality.

The picture of "the normative landscape" tries to vindicate surface appearances: The social world is densely populated by countless normative systems of human construction. The core functions of such systems are to generate and maintain norms—oughts, obligations, powers, rights, prohibitions, and the like. The norms that these constructed or "artificial" normative systems output are (or may be) substantively independent from each other, and may conflict. Because artificial norms possess only "thin" or "formal" normative force, whether you "really" ought to comply with any system's norms is always an askable question that the system at issue cannot on its own terms resolve. I will call this picture of a multiplicity of independent artificial normative systems the "Independent Systems Picture" (ISP). I hope and expect that it will resonate with some readers.

To the ISP, the SPP adds that legal systems comprise a subclass of artificial normative systems and, as such, are characterized by the features that the ISP maintains are generally true of artificial systems. That is, legal systems are (or may be) substantively independent

---

[3] Think of Philippa Foot's picture in "Morality as a System of Hypothetical Imperatives" (1972, 305–316), putting aside her controversial views about morality.

from other normative systems, generate thin or formal norms, and so on. I'll call this understanding of law, inelegantly, "legal non-exceptionalism." The SPP conjoins the general picture of the normative landscape that I'm calling the ISP and a particular claim that law and legal systems are, in a relevant sense, non-exceptional.

My ambition in this chapter is to shine light on this SPP and to identify and criticize a slate of arguments for rejecting it. The SPP looks right to me. It forms the backdrop to the constitutive theory that I advance elsewhere.[4] Yet even if the SPP reflects one common (but far from universal) implicit understanding of our multiple-systems landscape, it remains oddly marginalized, nearly invisible, in the current legal-philosophical debates. That is unfortunate. We should have the ordinary commonsensical positivistic picture more clearly in mind before we abandon it.

* * *

Section I introduces and elaborates upon the SPP. The two sections that follow identify and briefly assess challenges to it. Section II addresses legal-exceptionalist theories that are possibly compatible with the ISP, but insist that law is in important respects different from (other) artificial normative systems. My goal will not be to disprove the varied theories according to which law—unlike games, fashion, and other artificial systems—is dependent upon morality (conceptually or necessarily), but to highlight how such accounts rest upon ambitious and contested claims about the purpose or nature of law. If the SPP coheres well with the commonsensical understanding of the landscape of artificial normative systems captured by the ISP, we have some reason to resist more sectarian accounts of law's function.

The arguments canvassed in Section II attack the SPP at the branch, not the root, for they accept (at least arguendo) that the features that I am collectively dubbing the ISP characterize artificial normative systems other than law. But scholars in increasing number are casting doubt on the ISP even as applied to, say, chess, advancing in its place a view that, following Dworkin, I will call the "One-System Picture" (OSP). Section III addresses this more fundamental challenge to the SPP, concentrating on recent work by Scott Hershovitz that represents the most forceful rejection of the ISP to date.

Collectively, the first three sections aim to make salient features of the normative landscape that I believe fit with widespread background assumptions, even if inchoate, and to cast doubt on several prominent arguments given for rejecting that picture or for endorsing competing accounts. As readers should expect, the SPP bears a distinctly Hartian hue. That said, the SPP is *not* "the Hartian Account." All in all, I think that it coheres well with *The Concept of Law*. But even if so, it is manifestly inconsistent with some of Hart's later writings, in particular his final settled position on legal obligations. Section IV explains Hart's change of view and defends early Hart against later Hart.

---

[4] On the account I call "principled positivism," derivative and reasonably determinate legal norms ("legal rules") are constituted by the interaction of normatively fundamental legal norms ("legal principles"), that are themselves directly grounded in complex social behaviors. I maintain that the central features of this account—that rules are determined by principles, and that principles are normatively fundamental, inevitably plural, and inescapably dynamic—are true not only of legal systems but of all artificial systems of practical normativity. Legal rules are determined by legal principles, fashion rules are determined by fashion principles, baseball rules are determined by baseball principles, and so on. See (Berman 2018) (Berman and Toh 2013, 1739–1784).

Section V draws forth some metanormative lessons. The fundamental implication of the SPP is that law is not meaningfully different, in some or most of the ways that should interest metanormative theorists, from other "artificial" normative systems, and therefore that jurisprudes should work the idea that law is one among a large group of normative systems closer to the center of their thinking, and not attend to this fact only in an ad hoc manner.[5] In particular, I propose that we can make progress on the central jurisprudential task of explaining how legal norms gain their contents (or are what they are) by exploring how the norms of sports and games gain theirs (or are what *they* are).

I. The Standard Positivist Picture

Normativity concerns what people ought to do, believe, feel, and so on. Its central notions include *ought, obligation, permission, power, right, rule, reason,* and *good.* Beyond this vague common ground, however, almost everything is unclear or disputed. Or so it seems to me. I'd like to avoid committing myself on any contested matters at the outset. Better that they emerge as we proceed.

In lieu of theoretical ground-clearing, let's start with the uncontroversial observation that the norms we encounter, or many of them, appear to belong to systems or collections. Everyone recognizes that our linguistic practices, at least, suggest a multiplicity of normative systems, a system being a set of interconnected component parts that collectively form a complex whole. We routinely deploy normative concepts qualified by descriptive adjectives that signal systems, domains, institutions, or practices. "You are morally obligated to keep your promises"; "it is a principle of law that voluntary agreements will be respected"; "in basketball, a defensive player has a right to maintain his position"; "etiquette prohibits children from addressing their elders unless spoken to"; "the rules of Monopoly permit players to trade properties." We do not always speak this way. But even when we employ normative terms unmodified, a particular normative system or domain is usually implied.

One first step toward making sense of this apparent multiplicity of normative systems is to distinguish artificial normative systems from natural or non-artificial ones. Precision might be hard, and I won't strive for it. That a distinction of some sort can be drawn along these lines seems highly intuitive.[6] To a first pass, systems are "artificial" if they are, as Kevin Toh puts it, "products of our own making."[7] Sports and games, prescriptive grammar, manners, fashion, ceremony and ritual, are all artificial systems. Presumably, prudence and rationality, if they comprise systems at all, are non-artificial. The chief function of artificial systems of practical normativity is to create and sustain norms that are sufficiently salient

[5] For brief defense of my contention that serious engagement with sports can pay dividends for legal theory see (Berman 2011, 1330–1331).

[6] Accord (Toh 2011).

[7] (Toh 2011). To say that a system of normativity is artificial is not to say that its existence is accidental or a matter of chance. Many artificial systems may be inevitable for beings constituted as we are. But even if all people everywhere have, say, games and etiquette, the existence of such systems and the contents of their norms depends upon the actual choices and behaviors of persons.

and determinate to effectively guide people's conduct. Legal positivists, at least, view legal systems as artificial systems of practical normativity.

In this section, I sketch an account or picture of the features or characteristics of artificial normative systems. I do not propose a test or definition. Instead, I offer the following five "hallmarks" or "features" of the picture:

- *Systemic fundamentality:* artificial normative systems are analytically and explanatorily prior to the norms they comprise, and do not depend on other systems for their norm-making power;
- *Ostensible normativity:* the normative force that artificial normative systems confer upon their norms is only "thin," "formal," or "ostensible"; artificial norms do not confer "real" normative force, and thus are not *really* binding—whatever, exactly, it *is* for a norm to be *really* binding;
- *Content independence:* the contents of the norms of one system are not necessarily dependent on the norms of other systems;
- *Normative isomorphism:* the basic normative concepts (e.g., right, obligation, ought) share structure and function across normative systems even if they differ in normative force; and
- *Inter-systemic conflict:* norms of artificial systems may conflict with one another and with non-artificial norms.

This section elaborates. I do not claim that each feature is strictly necessary to the picture, that all are comparably important, that no equally or more important features have been overlooked, or that these features could not be derived from a more concise list. It strongly bears emphasis, throughout this essay, that I am trying to convey a fairly general understanding of the normative landscape, not to articulate, let alone to defend, a precise thesis. I'm painting a painting, not building a building.

Before jumping in, let me clarify what I will mean by "morality," given the term's notorious ambiguity. I will mean the set of interconnected norms that principally govern our obligations to others—not "positive" or "conventional" morality (mores), but norms that comprise a system distinguished by their content or subject matter. This usage contrasts with an alternative according to which "moral" norms are those with real normative force, regardless of their content. On the second usage, prudence is a subset of morality such that it is accurate, if nonstandard, to say that morality directs that you should brush your teeth if that's what the balance of (genuine) reason directs. My usage does not prejudge whether morality is an artificial or non-artificial system, or whether norms that it supplies have real normative force (see Section I.B).

A. Systemic Fundamentality

It is widely accepted that an artificial system is prior to its norms, and is in some sense fundamental. Two distinct aspects of this common idea can be teased apart.

First, the norms of a normative system gain their contents and their normative character—the fact that they *are* norms and bear on what agents ought to do—from the normative system, not vice versa. The normativity of the system has *priority* over the normativity of the system's discrete norms. This was something upon which both Hart and Kelsen insisted. In her masterful biography of Hart, Nicola Lacey explains that he felt that "the idea of rules valid by reason of their source" was in some sense the "key" to his account of law.[8] In a notebook entry, Hart described as "revelatory" "the notion of a rule binding valid [sic] by virtue of its '*source*' not content."[9] Indeed, I am tempted by the thought that artificial and natural normative systems differ precisely in that artificial systems are systems of norm-generation, whereas natural systems are systems of norm-collection. An artificial normative system is a system whose principal functions include the production and maintenance of norms and that is partly composed by the norms that it produces and maintains.

If artificial normative systems are conceptually prior to the norms they sustain, a related but distinct idea is that each normative system stands on its own normative bottom. It gains capacity to invest the norms that it generates and maintains directly from social facts. Artificial normative systems typically do not depend upon any other normative systems of a different type, artificial or natural, for their power to create norms.[10]

How do artificial normative systems gain their norm-making power? Although very much about the story remains to be worked out, I do not myself find the rudiments mysterious. An ordinary person is naturally endowed with the normative power to create oughts, or non-instrumental reasons, for herself. By the same token, she has the normative power to confer such power—the power to make norms *for her*—upon others, be they individuals or institutions. I believe that this is a function of oaths of obedience, for example.

A normative system is a type of institution. It arises and is sustained by persons conferring upon it the power to promulgate norms for its subscribers. One invests a system with normativity, or subscribes to a system already invested with normative power, by taking Hart's "internal point of view" toward the system and its outputs. This is not to say that a norm ϕ is normative for P if and only if P takes an internal point of view toward ϕ. A norm ϕ of system S can be normative for P just so long as P takes an internal point of view toward the normative outputs of S, i.e., by "subscribing" to S. Ordinary (committed) normative statements are thus analyzable as containing both a cognitivist and noncognitivist prong. For example, in making an internal, non-detached statement to the effect that the law prohibits ϕ, the speaker expresses both (a) acceptance of the normativity for herself of the legal system, and (b) a belief that prohibition of ϕ is a norm of that system.[11] In short, people confer normative power upon a system which in turn invests its outputs with normative force. In this way, a normative system possesses normative priority over the norms that constitute the system.

---

[8] (Lacey 2004, 227).

[9] (Lacey 2004, 227).

[10] In a hierarchical arrangement of normative systems belonging to the same class, a subordinate system may gain its normativity from a superordinate system. For example, in a federal political system, the national legal systems might confer normative authority upon the state legal systems. The qualifier "of a different type" is intended to accommodate cases of this sort.

[11] Contrast the two-prong analysis attributed to Hart in (Toh 2005, 75–123, at 88), and compare the quasi-expressivist construal proposed in (Finlay and Plunkett 2018).

B. *Ostensible Normativity*

In what sense are artificial normative systems, or their norms, "normative"? What is claimed by "you ought not to end a sentence with a preposition," or "mixed martial arts fighters are permitted to land elbow blows to opponents' heads"? Presumably, such claims aren't that ending a sentence with a preposition is *really* proscribed, or that it is *truly*, or all-things-considered, permitted to elbow others in the face. Such claims could be true, but that's not what speakers generally mean to assert. To make sense of artificial normative systems, then, requires that we distinguish between norms that are genuinely or truly binding upon us regardless of our desires, and norms that are not.

As David Enoch rightly emphasizes in his contribution to this volume, the distinction, while familiar, eludes precise articulation.[12] Instead, authors tend to make heavy use of adjectives and italics. They distinguish "real," "genuine," "robust," "full-blooded," or "not-merely-claimed-or-supposed" normativity from "formal," "thin," "weak," "apparent," or "generic" normativity.[13] Although many of these terms would work equally well, I favor a nomenclature that makes clear that the difference is one of kind, not degree. Accordingly, I will call these two flavors or grades of normativity "real" and "ostensible," respectively.[14] It is widely thought both that prudence, rationality, and (perhaps) interpersonal morality are all really normative if anything is, and that all artificial normative systems generate only ostensible normativity. I share those judgments.

It is essential to the ISP that whether there are artificial normative systems and, if so, whether we really ought to comply with the norms they generate are distinct questions. It seems to me that skepticism about the ISP is often rooted in the supposition that a putative norm that lacks real normative force is not a norm. On this view, real normative force figures somehow into the existence conditions for norms. The ISP operates upon a different understanding of what it is to be normative. On the notion of normativity that the ISP accepts, it is a truism, and not a reasonably contestable substantive claim, that volleyball, fashion, grammar, and law are normative.

We could stipulate that putative normative systems that do not generate real normativity do not count as normative systems at all and that their outputs are not norms. Such linguistic or conceptual legislation would be revisionary. More important, it would make no *substantive* difference. It would only create a need for a new name for what I am calling artificial normative systems (systems that I concede generate only ostensible normativity). Call them, if you'd prefer, "shnormative systems."[15] All that I want to ask and claim about "artificial normative systems" could be asked and claimed about "shnormative systems." Most notably, the

[12] The Kantian distinction between "categorical" and "hypothetical" imperatives does not quite mark the distinction we are seeking. See (Foot 1972, 308–309).

[13] See, e.g., (McPherson 2011, 223–240); (Copp 2004); (Gardner 2012a, 134).

[14] I eschew McPherson's use of "formal" for what I'm calling "ostensible" because I will use "formal," to designate a subclass of artificial normative systems (a subclass that includes most legal systems and most sports and games, but not, e.g., fashion or etiquette) that warrants particular attention from jurisprudes. See Section V. That is, on my terminology, it is not the case that all systems that generate only ostensible normativity are formal, although the converse is true: all formal systems generate only ostensible normativity.

[15] Compare (Enoch, 2006, 169–198).

central jurisprudential task would not be substantively different: it would be to explain how legal shnorms gain the contents they have.

C. Content Independence

Whether any norm of a normative system S partially determines the content of any norm of a normative system Q is a contingent fact about system Q. This does not mean that systems are closed to each other. Systems can and frequently do incorporate norms of other systems. Precisely because the norms of artificial systems are, in an important sense, "the products of our own making" (which is not to say that they are necessarily within anyone's conscious or purposive control), it would be extraordinary if our normative systems, albeit distinct, did not overlap and interpenetrate in thick and complex ways. Surely, as Hart emphasized, legal systems are bound to address certain topics, and to have some morally infused content, given basic truths about the constitution of human beings.[16] That does not undermine the straightforward point that the contents of a system's norms are generally not dictated or constrained by other systems of norms. The principles of a legal system, for example, are simply that—legal principles. Whether and to what extent they overlap with, or incorporate, moral principles is entirely contingent, even though significant overlap is a near-certainty in systems that enjoy significant popular input.[17]

The suggestion that normative systems are distinct from one another and generate norms that do not necessarily share content, should evoke the "separation thesis" that Hart famously claimed to be definitional of legal positivism.[18] Yet the ISP differs from the separation thesis as canonically formulated—there is "no necessary or conceptual connection" between law and morality in breadth and modesty.

First, whereas the separation thesis concerns the relationship (or lack thereof) between law and morality, content independence is a feature of all artificial normative systems. This is a noteworthy difference, not a quibble, because it is a central claim and premise of this essay that, for many or most of their purposes, jurisprudential and metanormative theorists should expand their focus from law and morality alone to the wider domain of practical normativity. Second, to describe normative systems as independent and distinct is to make less extravagant and more precise claims about the systems to which these characterizations apply than the separation thesis (as formulated) claims about law and morality. As leading positivists have urged, the contention that there is "no necessary connection" between law and morality (or between *any* normative system and morality) is implausibly strong partly because *connection* is such a capacious notion.[19] To take a single proffered disproof: in contrast to some things (e.g., Thursday, the color orange), legal norms are necessarily morally evaluable. In saying that normative systems are distinct, I do not contend that normative systems are necessarily "unconnected" (and neither did Hart).[20]

---

[16] See generally (Hart 1961, ch. 9).

[17] See (Berman 2018).

[18] (Hart 1982, 18); (Hart 1958, 57 n.25).

[19] See, e.g., (Green 2008, 1035–1058).

[20] See (Gardner 2012c, 48–49).

D. Normative Isomorphism

Does "obligation" "mean the same thing" in law and morals? Hart struggled with this question throughout his academic life.[21] But of course the answer might depend on what is meant by "meaning the same thing," and Hart did not stick to a clear or consistent interpretation of this phrase, nor did he consistently employ the same vocabulary. The ISP maintains that obligation *does* "mean the same thing" in law and morality in a sense that I will try to clarify.[22] Moreover, generalizing from *obligation* to all normative concepts, and from law and morality to all normative systems, the ISP maintains that any given norm type (obligation, reason, ought, right, power, etc.) "means the same thing" in any given normative system (interpersonal morality, law, etiquette, cricket, etc.). Call this feature of the ISP *normative isomorphism*.

Normative isomorphism holds that the normative elements that a normative system comprises or generates (rule, power, right, reason) are definable in terms that are invariant across normative systems. If the Razian analysis of obligation as a protected reason is correct, then it applies to legal obligations and moral obligations. If it is part of the relevant concepts that rights correlate with duties, that is true of moral rights and rights in backgammon. If weight is a necessary characteristic of principles, then principles have weight across normative systems. The concepts of rule, right, permission, etc. are graspable in the abstract, detached from the countless normative systems in which tokens of these concepts appear. *Isomorphism* does not maintain that the entire panoply of normative elements occur in every normative system. For example, some systems may contain *oughts*, but no *obligations* at all. Possibly, as Hart suggests, etiquette and grammar are like this.[23] The idea is only that if system S contains any tokens of norm-type T, then those tokens *have the same normative composition and function* in S as they do in any other normative system in which such tokens appear. This is what Hart had in mind, I think, when maintaining that there exist a "general idea of obligation" (and of permission, right, etc.) that is "a necessary preliminary to understanding it in its legal form."[24]

E. Inter-systemic Normative Conflict

From *systemic fundamentality* and *content independence*, it follows that a norm of one normative system, S, may conflict with a norm of another system, Q. To be sure, the mere existence of multiple systems does not ensure that normative conflict will be rife. Conflicts can be avoided in at least two ways. First, systems may claim non-overlapping jurisdiction. A ball that touches the boundary line is out of play in gridiron football but in play in association football. Nonetheless, the rules of these two sports do not conflict because they do

---

[21] (Lacey 2004) brings this out especially effectively. See esp. (225–229, 249–253, 325, 335–337, 354).

[22] Obviously, the sense will not be that legal and moral obligations have the same normative force. See Section I.B. Normative force is not an aspect of a norm-type's "meaning." See Section IV.

[23] (Hart 1961, 86).

[24] (Hart 1961, 85). This is not to say, e.g., that "legal obligation" means the same thing as "moral obligation," but that "obligation" contributes the same meaning to the compound phrases "legal obligation" and "moral obligation."

not simultaneously govern any token event. Second, where normative systems do claim overlapping jurisdiction, conflict is avoided cooperatively if one system claims dominance in cases of (apparent) conflict and the other concedes subordinacy, as is true of national and state or provincial legal systems in a federal system of government. That said, inter-systemic conflict remains possible. It may be, say, that a game requires attire that flouts norms of fashion, or that interpersonal morality prohibits conduct that the law mandates.

That is straightforward.[25] How if at all are inter-systemic normative conflicts resolved? Here are the three most eligible possibilities:

First, *if* any norms possess real normative force, presumably they take precedence over conflicting norms possessed only of ostensible normative force. If interpersonal morality is really normative, and if all artificial norms are only ostensibly normative, then when a moral norm conflicts with a norm of an artificial system, we (really) ought to follow the moral norm.

Second, it could be that normativity is always and only ostensible—for morality as well as for artificial normative systems—and that normative resolution of inter-system conflict is not forthcoming. It could be that, on a given occasion, your legal obligations conflict with your moral obligations, or that what you ought to do from a baseball perspective conflicts with what you ought to do from a fashion perspective, and that, prudence aside, there is nothing more of a normative nature to say. You may face a practical necessity to choose one course of action or the other, but which course you choose is necessarily ungoverned by norm or reason: there's no "ought" of the matter.

Third, even if all normative systems generate only ostensible normativity, the normative systems that populate the ISP could collectively constitute a supersystem that generates rules or principles that adjudicate conflicts between the member systems. This is one way to understand the domain of what is variously termed "all-things-considered ought," or "ought, period," or "ought-sans-phrase," even without attributing real normativity to that domain. Put another way, inter-systemic normative conflict might be resolvable from an all-things-considered perspective even if normativity is ostensible all the way down.

In my view, the SPP is compatible with each of these three possibilities, and perhaps others too. The ISP is agnostic about whether real normativity resides anywhere in our normative landscape, and the SPP is not committed to any particular view regarding whether, and how, inter-systemic normative conflict involving law is (normatively) resolved.

---

[25] And to keep it simple, the examples I invoked instantiate what I call "strong conflict": system S prohibits ϕ, and system Q prohibits $\neg\phi$. A second form of conflict—"weak inter-systemic conflict"—exploits a distinction between what some legal theorists and deontic logicians call "weak" and "strong" permission, and what I will instead call "allowance" and "permission," respectively. An allowance is the mere absence of an obligation, duty, or requirement. A permission is something more, though it is hard to say precisely what more is required. Compare, e.g., (von Wright, 1963, 86) and (Bulygin 2015). Putting details aside, if we accept the likely cogency of *some* allowance/permission distinction, it follows that conflict might arise when one system prohibits what another system permits.

II. Legal Exceptionalism

Section I sketched what I am calling the "Standard Positivist Picture," an account of the normative landscape designed to reflect basic positivist sensibilities. We may parse it into two pieces: a picture of the landscape of artificial normative systems that I am calling the "Independent Systems Picture," and a claim that legal systems are artificial systems in the manner that the ISP describes. Accordingly, two paths toward rejecting the SPP can be distinguished. The first broadly accepts the ISP but maintains that legal systems are not artificial, or that they differ from other artificial systems in some or all of the respects I have highlighted. A second path rejects the account of artificial normative systems that the ISP reflects, even as a description of paradigmatic artificial systems such as games and fashion. I consider "legal exceptionalist" rejections of the SPP in this section, and more radical rejections of the ISP in Section III.

A. Arguments from Law's Purpose or Function

Many jurisprudential theories deny that one or more hallmarks of the ISP apply to legal systems. It is not always clear, however, that other artificial normative systems fare the same. For example, Dworkin's view, circa *Law's Empire,* denies that legal systems respect content independence, on the ground that moral norms or facts are necessarily part of law. But it does not simultaneously maintain that such facts are necessarily part of games or fashion or grammar. Similarly, Mark Greenberg denies that legal norms can ever conflict with moral norms, while accepting that norms of other artificial systems frequently do. These are possible examples of views that reject the SPP without frontally attacking the ISP.

What explains these forms of legal exceptionalism? They stem from an effort to explain what distinguishes the subclass of legal systems from other artificial normative systems. Dworkin argues that law's purpose or function is to morally justify the use of coercion.[26] And Greenberg contends "that it is part of the nature of law that a legal system is supposed to change our moral obligations in order to improve our moral situation."[27] Thus, legal exceptionalists can reject the SPP without incurring the cost in "plausibility points"[28] of taking on the ISP by drawing out implications from particular purposes that are supposedly baked into law's nature.

Defenders of the SPP are likely to endorse sparer conceptions of law's purpose. In the Postscript, Hart rejected Dworkin's claim that "the purpose of law is to justify the use of coercion," observing that positivist theories generally "make[] no claim to identify the point or purpose of law and legal practices as such." Indeed, he deemed it "quite vain to seek any more specific purpose which law as such serves beyond providing guides to human conduct and standards of criticism of such conduct."[29]

---

[26] See, e.g., (Dworkin 1986, at 93).

[27] (Greenberg 2014, 1288–1342, 1294).

[28] See (Enoch 2011).

[29] (Hart 1961, 248–249).

Kenneth Ehrenberg has commented on this apparent "tension between Hart's claim that positivists make no claim to identify law's function and his claim that it is to guide behavior," concluding that "the best way to square these passages is to say that Hart believed the 'primary function' he attributed to law was so thin that nothing much of theoretical value could be derived from it."[30] While Ehrenberg is right as far as he goes, I'd go further. The function that Hart seems to attribute to law is simply the function common to all artificial normative systems. His claim is that no functions feature in the differentia that distinguish legal systems from other members of that larger class.

What then does distinguish legal systems from other artificial normative systems? Although the SPP may be able to accommodate a range of answers, I anticipate that many proponents would distinguish legal systems from their cousins principally in terms of their relationship to a state or other political community. Too briefly: legal systems are artificial normative systems established and maintained by political communities and designed to serve a potentially limitless range of functions, characteristically including those of resolving disputes between community members, and preserving public order and punishing breaches.[31] Legal systems are political communities' normative Swiss Army knives.

I cannot argue for this sparer account of law's nature or purposes in an already overlong essay that aims not fully to defend the SPP, but only to revive it as a genuine jurisprudential option. I'll merely announce my belief that, insofar as we are seeking *our* concept of law, the SPP will fare well when measured by its fit with pre-theoretical data. Accounts that attribute to law significantly thicker or different essential functions have the feel of theory-driven overlays that can be resisted. This is true not only of antipositivist theories of law such as Dworkin's and Greenberg's, but also of Joseph Raz's exclusive-positivist theory rooted in his contention that law necessarily claims to be a legitimate practical authority, in the sense of mediating between its subjects and the (real) reasons that antecedently apply to them. That is admittedly a contention, not an argument.

B. Dworkin's One-System Picture and the Argument from Circularity

The upshot of Section II.A is that, if the ISP correctly describes features of most artificial normative systems, rejection of the SPP depends upon claims about the nature or functions of law that are ambitious and controversial. Whilst Dworkin's account (or Greenberg's, or whoever's) could be correct, they should not move us too quickly from a more bare-bones account of law's function or nature that the standard positivist picture embodies. It is perhaps revealing, then, that in his last major jurisprudential work, *Justice for Hedgehogs,* Dworkin purported to defeat the SPP on logical grounds, not on contested substantive claims about law's function or nature.[32]

---

30 (Ehrenberg 2013, 447–456, 454 n.8).

31 In the Postscript, Hart offers a different suggestion: "the distinctive features of law are the provision it makes by secondary rules for the identification, change, and enforcement of its standards and the general claim it makes to priority over other standards." (Hart 1961, 249). This is not promising, for the first supposedly distinguishing feature is common to all "formal" artificial normative systems. See Section V, below. Sports leagues, for example, generate primary rules of conduct and also maintain secondary rules governing change and enforcement.

32 See (Dworkin, 2011, ch. 19).

In *Hedgehogs*, Dworkin identified, and rejected, an "orthodox picture" of the normative landscape in which "'[l]aw' and 'morality' describe different collections of norms."[33] Calling this vision "the two-systems picture," Dworkin argued that it should be rejected in favor of a "one-system picture" in which law is just "a part of political morality," not a distinct normative domain with distinct normative upshots.[34] The contention itself was not novel. But Dworkin's argument for it was:

> There is a flaw in the two-systems picture. Once we take law and morality to compose separate systems of norms, there is no neutral standpoint from which the connections between these supposedly separate systems can be adjudicated. Where shall we turn for an answer to the question whether positivism or interpretivism is a more accurate or otherwise better account of how the two systems relate? Is this a moral question or a legal question? Either choice yields a circular argument with much too short a radius.
>
> Suppose we treat the question as legal. We look to legal material . . . and we ask: What does the correct reading of all that material declare the relationship between law and morality to be? We cannot answer that question without a theory in hand about how to read legal material, and we can't have such a theory until we have already decided what role morality plays in fixing the content of the law. . . .
>
> If we turn to morality for our answer, on the other hand, we beg the question in the opposite direction. We can say: Would it be good for justice if morality played the part in legal analysis that interpretivism claims it does? Or is it actually better for the moral tone of a community if law and morals are kept separate as the positivists insist? These questions certainly make sense . . . . [But] [i]f law and morals are two separate systems, it begs the question to suppose that the best theory of what law is depends on such moral issues. That assumes we have already decided against positivism.[35]

This long passage represents nearly the entirety of Dworkin's argument against a picture that he acknowledges to be orthodox.[36] Although Dworkin claims that his one-page argument presents "*decisive* objections to the two-systems picture,"[37] I am skeptical that it scores any points.

---

[33] (Dworkin, 2011, 400).

[34] (Dworkin, 2011, 405).

[35] (Dworkin, 2011, 402–403).

[36] I say "nearly" because Dworkin does speculate that the "logical difficulty" he identifies—namely, that the two-systems picture "poses a question that cannot be answered other than by assuming an answer from the start"—explains the "turn in Anglo-American jurisprudence . . . to the surprising idea that the puzzle about law and morals is neither a legal nor a moral problem but instead a *conceptual* one." (Dworkin, 2011, 403). I will not examine his (highly condensed) arguments for the conclusion that this "supposed escape from the circularity problem is no escape at all" (404), because, as I argue in the text, the supposed circularity problem is no problem at all.

[37] (Dworkin 2011, 410).

Dworkin's argument from circularity is undermined by his initial assumption that, on the two-systems picture, the relationship between law and morality presents a *single* question to which either law or morality must supply the *single* answer. However, as he had explained one page earlier, there are at least two questions here, not one: (1) Are citizens or subjects of a legal system morally obligated to obey the law's requirements? (2) Are legal norms partly constituted by moral norms?[38] If there are two questions, not one, the possibility arises that law supplies the answer to one and morality answers the other.

The SPP suggests just that. Question (1) is the traditional problem of "political obligation." It is for morality to answer. The dominant contemporary philosophical opinion is that there is no moral (or "real") obligation to obey the law, as such, but the SPP can accommodate either answer.

Question (2) presents either a first-order legal question, or a metalegal question, depending upon how it's understood. It is a metalegal, or jurisprudential, question, if it asks whether it is necessary, possible, or impossible for the norms of a legal system to be partly constituted by the norms of morality. Or, if we believe that it is possible, but not necessary, for the norms of a legal system to be partly constituted by the norms of morality, we might be asking whether the norms of *this* legal system are partially so constituted. That is a legal question.

So a proponent of the SPP can supply distinct answers to the two questions that Dworkin raises but mistakenly reduces to one. To repeat: the question of political obligation is answered by morality; the jurisdiction-general question of how moral norms can possibly contribute to the content of legal norms is a metalegal question, and the regime-specific question of how the legal norms of a given legal system are constituted is a legal question. These are answers to the *jurisdictional* questions regarding which domain answers a substantive question, and not to the *merits* questions (1) whether and under what circumstances legal obligations are morally obligatory, or (2) whether moral considerations bear constitutively on the contents of legal norms. They confront no flaws of circularity.

To be sure, moral considerations could bear constitutively on the contents of legal norms in that all legal obligations, properly so called, are moral obligations, and that, as a consequence, people are morally obligated to obey the law. That is Dworkin's view, as well as Greenberg's. I am unpersuaded, though I cannot take them on in this chapter. The important point at present is that the case for Dworkin's "interpretivist" theory of law, or for Greenberg's "moral impact theory of law," or for other views in the vicinity, depends upon controversial claims about law's nature or function. If the SPP is mistaken, on this reasoning, that would not be due to any argumentative circularity, as Dworkin claims. Rather, the SPP's infirmity would arise as the product, not an argumentative ground, of the conclusion that interpretivism, or the moral impact theory, or what-have-you, is correct. And whatever might be said of the arguments that would deliver interpretivism, and related accounts of law, that they traverse a short arc is not among them. Dworkin might have sound substantive arguments against the SPP, but he has not shown that a picture in which law and morality are independent is logically defective.

[38] See (Dworkin 2011, 401).

III. One-System Pictures

Prescind now from Dworkin's circularity-based argument for the OSP to the picture itself. If we start by thinking of the normative landscape as a whole, rather than of law and morality alone, Dworkin's rejection of a "two-systems picture" and concomitant embrace of a "one-system picture" becomes ambiguous. On one interpretation, the putatively distinct systems of law and morality constitute one system, but this single system fits within a landscape populated by *other* normative systems (sports, fashion, etc.) that are independent from that one system and from each other. The second interpretation recognizes just a single system of practical normativity: all systems of practical normativity, not only law, constitute branches of a single normative system.

Of legal philosophers writing within a Dworkinian tradition, Mark Greenberg steers in the first direction. Like Dworkin, Greenberg maintains that "legal obligations are a certain subset of moral obligations."[39] But his arguments rest on claims about law's particular function and therefore have no obvious implications for other artificial normative systems. Scott Hershovitz takes the second route. For Hershovitz, as for Dworkin and Greenberg, "legal obligations just are moral obligations generated by legal practice."[40] But the same holds for obligations generated by any other normative system. A's golf obligations—what golf rules require of A—are what A morally ought to do given all relevant facts, including facts about what participants expect of each other and about what makes the joint activity "go better," as by contributing more to human flourishing.

A *true* one-system picture (a picture that is more Hershovitz than Greenberg) flatly rejects core elements of the ISP. Most conspicuously, because the obligation created by *any* system is a moral obligation, inter-systemic normative conflict is impossible.[41] On the OSP, not even baseball or fashion issues norms that lack genuine normative force and are substantively independent from the dictates of morality.

A. The Argument from Practicality

The core argument against the ISP starts from the premise that, ultimately, what we care about is what we ought to do—not what we ought to do from a legal, or a tennis, or a fashion perspective, but what we *really* ought to do. Therefore, we have no practical need ever to ask what the law provides. Rather, we need only ask how the various non-normative facts that constitute legal-normative facts (whatever those facts, and the constitution relationship, may be) bear on what we (really) ought to do. Call this the argument from practicality. It recommends that we adopt a one-step decision protocol (asking ourselves what we really

---

[39] (Greenberg 2014, 1290).

[40] (Hershovitz 2015, 1160–1204, 1192).

[41] Hershovitz can be read to contend otherwise, for he allows that legal and moral obligations "can conflict, sometimes in terrible ways." (Hershovitz 2015, 1187). Understandably, Enoch finds this passage puzzling, for it seems inconsistent with the thrust of the OSP. (Enoch 2019, 73 n.25). But the type of conflict Hershovitz has in mind is simply the conflict that can arise between *any* pro tanto moral obligations. See (Hershovitz 2015, 1189). Hershovitz denies that an agent can have a genuine legal obligation that isn't even a pro tanto moral obligation.

ought to do) in lieu of a two-step protocol that first asks what this or that artificial normative system requires and only then asks what we really should do. Recent proponents of a one-step protocol, or of some variant of the practicality-based objection to the ISP, include Jeremy Waldron and Lewis Kornhauser, in addition to Hershovitz.[42]

The argument from practicality does not threaten the SPP. First, it assumes that there is a domain of real normativity, or of ought-sans-phrase, that governs or guides our actions. This is highly controversial, and I have said that the SPP is agnostic. Second, even assuming real normativity, nothing in this line of argument supports an error-theoretical conclusion about the outputs of artificial normative systems. That is, the (supposed) fact that we don't *need* artificial normative facts does not establish that we don't *have* them. Our social world contains countless things that we don't need and may lack value for us.

Beyond that, artificial norms can make real normative differences. Suppose that A promises her father to "always obey the rules of basketball." The standard view is that, by making this promise, A puts herself under a moral obligation to obey all basketball rules. Exactly why a voluntary promise has that moral upshot is controversial. But for present purposes we can help ourselves to the assumption that A has such a moral obligation without bothering with the details. It would seem to follow that whether A comports with her moral obligation will be a function of ordinary facts about her behavior combined with normative facts about what the rules of basketball prohibit. This assumes that there are such normative facts.

An opponent of the ISP might propose that we construe A's promise <to obey the rules of basketball> as a promise <to do what the rulebook says>. Yet this would be entirely revisionist, for it might not be that the norms of a practice are entirely determined by the communicative contents of provisions in an authoritative text. Consider intentional fouls in professional basketball committed by the losing team near the game's end in order to stop the clock. Not only the semantic content, but also the full communicative content, of the relevant provision in the official NBA rulebook provides that such conduct is prohibited.[43] But most basketball insiders believe that it is permitted—not just morally, but in terms of basketball's own norms, rightly understood. Indeed, the nominal prohibition is not merely a normative permission, it's a *power*. The fouling team has a valid complaint if the referee refuses to whistle the play dead. This would not be so if some communicative content of the text of the basketball rulebook determined (or mirrored) the content of the basketball rule.

Or, to switch sports, consider Major League Baseball Rule 3.09, which, in relevant part, reads: "Players of opposing teams shall not fraternize at any time while in uniform." Yet opposing players fraternize while in uniform routinely (as during pregame batting practice) without anybody believing that this violates an applicable norm. Of course, this conventional understanding among baseball players could be mistaken but it seems probable that they are right, possibly because the normative system that is associated with Major League Baseball includes a principle of desuetude, even though such a principle does not correspond to the communicative content of any provision within the rulebook.

The case of promising to obey rules of a game thus suggests that there are rules of a game and that such rules do not necessarily set forth moral obligations. Now, people rarely

[42] See (Waldron 2013, 14–16); (Hershovitz 2015, 1193–1195); (Kornhauser 2015, 15).

[43] "A player shall not hold, push, charge into, impede the progress of an opponent . . ." NBA Rule 12B, Section I(a).

promise to obey the rules of a game. But the lesson I aim to draw is not *limited* to cases of promising. We might think that participants often make *commitments* to obey the rules, where commitments have more lenient existence conditions than promises and different moral upshots. Your commitment to play by the rules is intelligible only on the assumption that there are rules to commit to, and your commitment can make a moral difference to your situation only if the rules are not already moral obligations for you.

Furthermore, the argument from practicality is infirm even putting promises and commitments aside. For insofar as it seeks to cause trouble for the ISP, the argument rests upon a heroic conception of the human condition and of human capacities that defenders of the ISP may fairly reject as implausible. Suppose, again, that all we really should care about is what we really ought to do. Making this determination is frequently hard, and the felt need to undertake the effort, and to accomplish it successfully, can be stressful, even paralyzing. We may find that we navigate the world more successfully and happily by voluntarily subscribing, as it were, to diverse systems of norms that output directives for particular contexts. Doing so does not require that we abdicate responsibility to reason morally. It's not that we must subject ourselves slavishly to the normative outputs of diverse (artificial) normative systems, but only that we have prudential reason to follow these artificial norms ordinarily, proceeding to the second step of the two-step protocol—consulting other (real) reasons that might weigh against the norms of the system we are first consulting—*only when there are unusual grounds to do so*. This was Hart's view about judging: judges not only follow their legal obligations in each case,

> but are committed in advance in the sense that they have a settled disposition to do this without considering the merits of so doing in each case . . . . So although the judge is in this sense committed to following the rules his view of the moral merits of doing so . . . is irrelevant. His view of the merits may be favourable or unfavourable, or simple absent, or, without dereliction of his duty as a judge, he may have formed no view of the moral merits.[44]

Compare Daniel Kahneman's account of the two systems involved in ordinary mental processing: the fast, intuitive, and emotional System 1, and the slow, deliberative, and more logical System 2.[45] As Kahneman explains, human beings do not and could not consistently kick decisions up to System 2. I'm making a similar claim about the considerations we consult when we are already operating from within the second of these psychological systems. When operating within a domain that we take to be governed by one or another artificial normative system, we ordinarily engage with the norms that that system delivers, and then consult the norms of morality (or real reasons) only when a particular reason to do so impinges upon our deliberative field. Whatever those impinging reasons consist of, my key point is simply that agents who subscribe to multiple systems (almost everybody) do not engage in a "two-step process" in the routine case—and that's okay. It's fun to play baseball. It's easier to gain the potential benefits that the practice offers by acting on a general disposition to follow its rules, which is to take the baseball rules as normative for you. A two-step decision procedure in which we reach the second step only occasionally has real-life benefits for organisms constituted as we are.

[44] (Hart 1982, 158–159).

[45] (Kahneman 2011).

B. *Hershovitz's Argument from Games*

That is my response to the argument from practicality. Before closing this section, however, let us tarry a little longer over Hershovitz's argument, because of all recent jurisprudential writings, his is the most sustained and forceful attack on the ISP. As I have emphasized, more explicitly than Dworkin, and in contrast to Greenberg, Hershovitz challenges a picture of our landscape that recognizes *any* truly independent and distinct normative systems. Yet more significantly, Hershovitz's argumentative strategy is to bolster the OSP precisely by broadening our focus from legal systems in particular to the fuller normative landscape. He argues that expanding our attention from law alone to other purportedly normative domains (chiefly games) *bolsters* the OSP's plausibility and thereby allows us to *inter* the central jurisprudential question of how legal norms gain the contents that they have—hence his article's provocative title: "The End of Jurisprudence."[46] I argue, in contrast, that consideration of sports and games substantially *diminishes* the OSP's plausibility. And I further propose that careful attention to sports and games will facilitate progress in *accomplishing* (not avoiding) this basic task for legal philosophy. Because Hershovitz and I start from nearly identical premises to reach nearly opposite conclusions, it may be revealing to identify just where we part ways.

Hershovitz's article is long and subtle. I cannot address it all. I will focus on the portion that deals most squarely with games. In his chief hypothetical, Hershovitz imagines that, while playing a game of chess, you pick up a pawn in your left hand and place it back on the board with your right. Your opponent objects. Citing a provision in the FIDE rulebook that says that "[e]ach move must be made with one hand only,"[47] she charges you with an illegal move—that is, a move that the rules prohibit. However, says Hershovitz, "we need to know more about the context of the game" in order to determine whether your opponent's objection is sound. "If you're playing in a FIDE-sanctioned tournament, for example, then you are presumably obligated to follow the rules."[48] But "[t]he picture looks rather different if you are playing a casual game with a friend." In that case, he concludes, "FIDE's adoption of a rule requiring players to make moves with one hand only has no normative consequences for [you]."[49]

So far, we are in agreement. An inhabitant of the ISP might explain things as follows. "Chess" is not a single undifferentiated normative system, but a tightly knit family of systems that are unified by a large number of constitutive and regulative rules but that also

[46] See also (Hershovitz 2015, 1194) (explaining, as "a welcome consequence" of his version of legal eliminativism, that "[i]f we deny that legal practices give rise to a distinctively legal domain of normativity . . . we relieve ourselves of the burden of explaining just what that domain is and how its content is constituted").

[47] (World Chess Federation 1988, § 4.1).

[48] (Hershovitz 2015, 1183). By "obligated" here, Hershovitz means *morally* obligated. He is therefore assuming that your voluntary participation in the tournament puts you under a moral obligation to obey the FIDE rules. I think that more needs to be said to establish that you are in fact morally obligated to follow the FIDE rules, but I also suspect that Hershovitz would agree. Although there will no doubt be controversial cases at the margins, I accept that a set of conditions could be articulated the satisfaction of which would, according to most observers, put a participant in a FIDE-sanctioned tournament under at least a pro tanto moral obligation to comply with the FIDE rules.

[49] (Hershovitz 2015, 1183).

exhibit some degree of diversity. This is familiar. Although we usually speak of basketball, for instance, as though it were a single game governed by a single set of rules, the rules that govern play in the NBA are not identical to those that govern in the WNBA, the NCAA, in international basketball competitions, or in pickup ball. Similarly, we commonly reference "American tort law," or "Anglophone tort law," while knowing that the rules vary across jurisdictions. In the same way, "the rules of chess" is a slight misnomer, and the rules that govern a particular token game will depend upon which member system of the chess game family the game in question is a token. A proponent of the ISP has no difficulty concluding, with Hershovitz, that "[a] casual game of chess seems more apt to be governed by the widely known rules of chess than it does by FIDE's more complete set of rules, absent an antecedent agreement about what rules are in play."

Of course, what the rules of casual, friendly chess are may be significantly less determinate, and less easily ascertained, than what the rules of FIDE-sanctioned chess matches are. That's why it is useful for authorities in a normative system to "write the rules down," even if doing so may not perfectly fix the contents of the rules. It's also why, when folks play a game that they intend not to be governed by the entire panoply of rules formally promulgated by an official organization, they often specify the rules to govern particular situations. When acquaintances play a casual game of pool, for example, they often expressly agree at the outset on the rules to govern scratches and other fouls.

In short, I take Hershovitz's example to illustrate that our normative universe is even more complicated and densely populated than one might otherwise suppose, for there is not a single normative system denominated chess, or baseball, or basketball, but potentially a multiplicity of systems under each label. But he draws a different lesson—that "we can navigate these situations [involving disputes that arise in the course of game play] just fine without supposing that the FIDE rules give rise to a non-moral FIDE obligation to make each move with one hand only . . . [or] that the FIDE rules give rise to their own distinct domain of normativity."[50] Now we have parted ways. On the ISP, there *is* a nonmoral FIDE obligation to make each move with one hand only." And the FIDE rules *do* make out a distinct normative domain.[51] It's just that casual, friendly chess (call it "CFC") is also a normative domain, and it happens to be false that there is a nonmoral *CFC* obligation to make each move with one hand only.

Importantly, Hershovitz does not fully deny this. He doesn't say that there are no such things as FIDE rules or CFC rules, where rules are norms that possess only ostensible normative force ("shnorms" if you must). He just says that we can manage fine without attending to them, that talk of such entities is "superfluous."[52] But talk of artificial norms is not superfluous; we cannot navigate nearly as well when we do without. Suppose that players in a casual game of eight ball have failed to take the common precaution of clarifying rules in advance. Player A has table scratched and Player B makes to remove the cue ball, noting that the penalty allows her to place it anywhere on the table. A disagrees. Acknowledging that

---

[50] (Hershovitz 2015, 1184).

[51] I would not, however, describe this domain, as Hershovitz does, as involving "a new sort of normativity." (Hershovitz 2015, 1184). The sort of normativity at issue is ordinary "ostensible" normativity.

[52] (Hershovitz 2015, 1184).

that's the prescribed penalty in games governed by rules promulgated by official bodies such as the World Pool-Billiard Association (WPA), A maintains that casual rules, or "American pub rules," provide that the only penalty for table scratches is loss of turn, the cue to be played where it is, and that they should be playing under those rules. We can envision the conversation between A and B going in many directions. They may disagree (or not) about what WPA rules provide. They may disagree (or not) about what American pub rules are, or about what local rules or house rules require. They may disagree (or not) about whether they should follow this or that set of rules, either for the remainder of the game, or in this initial disputed instance. But of one thing we can be reasonably sure: A and B will not find it convenient to abandon all talk of what this or that set of rules "are" or "provide."

So the charge of superfluity does not stick. And I find it revealing that Hershovitz doesn't rest his case on it: "we shouldn't avoid this sort of talk just because it is superfluous. We should avoid it because it risks a great deal of confusion." To see why, Hershovitz asks us now to suppose that the chess game we have been imagining does occur during a FIDE-sanctioned competition. "[E]ven in those circumstances," he observes,

> it is possible that play is not governed by the standards expressed in the FIDE rules. Instead, play may be governed by the standards that FIDE intended to adopt, which may or may not have been fully or accurately captured in the text that its officials had in front of them when they voted. Or it may be that play is governed by the standards that would best serve the purposes that FIDE had when it adopted the text, even if those standards are slightly different than the standards reflected in the text. Or it may be that some combination of these things is true, depending on the phase of play or the context of the match. This should all feel familiar, as these possibilities are also at play in debates over statutory interpretation. And here, just as there, the question which standards govern is a question about the normative significance of a set of social facts.[53]

All that Hershovitz says here is right and important. But it does not undermine the ISP. To the contrary, it suggests that the common notion that rules of a normative system are necessarily fully constituted by the communicative content (or by *a* communicative content) of utterances in a rulebook is much too naïve.[54] (This is why I said a few paragraphs ago that transcribing "rules" "may not perfectly fix" their contents.) It further suggests, as a consequence, that it remains to discover what determinants *do* give the norms of artificial normative systems the contents that they have. And that, I have been emphasizing, is widely viewed as a principal task of general jurisprudence. Hershovitz counsels legal philosophers to abandon this task out of concern that *their* taking artificial norms seriously risks nourishing *others'* mistaken belief that those artificial norms must be whatever an authoritative text expresses.[55] *That* is the confusion that acceptance of the ISP risks. I think that risk is slight, and, in any event, that the strong medicine Hershovitz recommends is a cure worse

---

[53] (Hershovitz 2015, 1184–1185).

[54] See generally, e.g., (Greenberg 2011a, 39–106); (Berman 2017, 783–808). For elaboration on the parenthetical, see (Greenberg 2011b, 217).

[55] (Hershovitz 2015, 1186).

than the disease. The fact to which Hershovitz rightly points—that norms of a game might differ, even in formal, official, competitive contexts, from what authoritative texts say—only reinforces the need for jurisprudes to explain how the norms of artificial normative systems (e.g., municipal legal systems, games) are constituted. It does not entail that there are no such norms, or that legal philosophers should assume them away.

IV. A Change of Hart

Thus far I have tried to foreground, and modestly sharpen, a sense of our normative situation that I claim to constitute the "standard positivist picture." I have also claimed that the picture too often lies dimly in the background of our thinking and wants for explicit defense. Why, if the picture is as intuitive and commonsensical as I claim, is it no more vivid and robustly defended in the jurisprudential literature? Part of the answer, I suspect, is that, although the SPP coheres well with *The Concept of Law*, Hart disavowed key elements of the picture in later work. Moreover, he did so in response to pressures exerted by his student and fellow positivist, Joseph Raz. This section identifies and explains Hart's change in view, and argues that it was a wrong turn.

In "Legal Duty and Obligation," a chapter in his 1982 volume *Essays on Bentham*, Hart advanced an arrestingly new account of legal obligation.[56] Rejecting "a cognitive interpretation of legal duties in terms of objective reasons," Hart proposed a noncognitivist interpretation in which "to say that an individual has a legal obligation to act in a certain way is to say that such action may be properly demanded or extracted from him according to legal rules or principles regulating such demands for action."[57] Hart reaffirmed this position in a 1987 interview with the Spanish-language journal *Doxa*, stating: "I now think that this idea of a legitimate response to deviation in the form of demands and pressure for conformity is the central component of obligation." Acknowledging that this is a "new account," he nonetheless insisted that "it is still compatible with the views which I have always held and which most of my critics reject that the concept of legal obligation is morally neutral and that legal and moral obligations are conceptually distinct."[58]

It is true that Hart's "final, modified position on the nature of legal obligation and its relationship to moral obligation"[59] preserves the core positivist idea that "legal obligation is morally neutral." But it is hard to square with the view of legal obligation that he had set forth in *The Concept of Law*. There he had made clear that the primary function of legal obligations, as with other types of primary legal norms, is to guide the conduct *of those to whom the obligation applies*. Yet Hart's revised view turns the citizen's legal obligation to ϕ into a liability condition to be subjected to criticism or sanction for failing to ϕ, provoking Raz to object that "this sudden Kelsenian twist to Hart's view of legal duties implies that duty-imposing laws are instructions (or perhaps merely permissions) to courts to apply sanctions or remedies against people who are guilty of breach of duty."[60] If Hart's final view maintains the core idea

[56] For a helpful discussion, though reaching conclusions I reject, see (Kramer 1999, 375–407).

[57] (Hart 1982, 159–160). This was a revision of an essay first published in 1966, in Italian.

[58] Excerpts from the interview, in English, are presented in Lacey (2004, 354).

[59] This is Lacey's characterization, (Lacey 2004, 354), not Hart's own.

[60] (Raz, 1984, 123–131, 131).

that "legal obligation" and "moral obligation" are conceptually distinct, it renders obscure what makes the former a type of *obligation*. The obligatoriness—even the oughtness—of legal obligation is lost.

What explains this striking change? Hart's own answer was that he had realized that it was impossible to jointly maintain three discrete theses: (1) "that 'obligation' and 'duty' have the same meaning in legal and moral contexts";[61] (2) "that legal and moral duties [are] conceptually independent"; and (3) that judgments about moral duties express beliefs that the duty holder has "objective" reasons for action "in the sense that they exist independently of his subjective motivation."[62] In combination, these premises "would involve the extravagant hypothesis that there were two independent 'worlds' or sets of objective reasons, one legal and the other moral."[63] Hart thought that the solution was to abandon the first premise and replace it with his novel "Kelsenian" interpretation of statements of legal obligation.

Putting aside whether Hart's proposal solved the problem he identified, it's unclear why he saw a problem in need of solving. I have claimed (Section I) that what Hart describes as "conceptual independence" (the essence of which I have captured by *systemic fundamentality* and *content independence*) fits entirely comfortably with his same-meaning thesis (captured by *normative isomorphism*). And positivists may accept that the norms inhabiting these independent domains are "objective" in Hart's sense of being independent of a purported duty-holder's subjective motivation. As Philippa Foot observed, rules of artificial normative systems do "not *fail to apply* to someone who has his own good reasons for ignoring [them], or who simply does not care about what, from the point of view of [that system], he should do."[64] I think, therefore, that Hart's own analysis of the problem misses something of importance. What troubled Hart was the possibility of distinct sets of *reasons,* and the reason that this troubled him was Razian.[65]

Earlier and only in passing, I noted worries about Raz's contention that law necessarily claims to be a practical authority (Section II.A) Here I'll focus on Raz's general views about normativity. Raz maintains that all normativity starts with reasons: "The normativity of all that is normative consists in the way it is, or provides, or is otherwise related to reasons."[66] Reasons are the basic normative concept: they are not reducible to any more basic normative element, and they constitute the building blocks for more complex normative elements (obligations, rights, etc.). Reasons also possess "real" normative force (Section I.B); there are no merely "ostensible" reasons. Influenced by this account of normativity, Hart worried that cognitivist analyses of claims about legal obligations must be claims either about moral obligations (as Dworkin maintained) or about law's *claims* about moral obligations (as Raz contended). Disliking both options, Hart defended his noncognitivist analysis as the best among three alternatives, all of which he clearly found suboptimal.[67]

---

[61] "Legal Duty and Obligation" (Hart 1982, 147).

[62] "Commands and Authoritative Legal Reasons" (Hart 1982, 266–267).

[63] (Hart 1982, 267).

[64] (Foot 1972, 308).

[65] For a distinct but broadly compatible account, see (Toh 2007, 403–427, esp. 414–420).

[66] (Raz 1999, 354–379, 354).

[67] See "Commands and Authoritative Legal Reasons" (Hart 1982, 267–268) for his manifest lack of enthusiasm for his own proposal.

Hart was right to have qualms. On the Razian view, normativity concerns reasons, and reasons are real; therefore, for a system to be "normative" (as law plainly is), it must be, in some fashion, concerned with our (real) reasons. John Gardner, operating from within this Razian paradigm, is led to conclude that the game of Monopoly claims that its "obligations, permissions, rights, powers, and liabilities" have real normative force, that they capture what its players really ought to do.[68] That's a striking conclusion, but not plainly wrong on Razian premises, for Monopoly too is (in some sense) normative. The ISP resists Gardner's conclusion about Monopoly by maintaining that artificial normative systems, as such, need not concern themselves at all with what we "really" ought to do. Hart's mistake, then, was to conflate the question of whether a reason—or, if you prefer, a "shmeason"[69]—is objective or subjective with the separate question of whether it has genuine normative force. We can have the trio of theses Hart rightly wanted—cognitivism, systemic non-dependence, and normative isomorphism—if we detach normative force from the "meaning" that norm-types share across normative systems.

V. Implications

Suppose that the SPP is broadly correct: we live enmeshed in an overlapping multiplicity of distinct normative systems, many of which are artificial and that we choose to inhabit. We have powers and disabilities, liabilities and immunities, privileges, rights, and duties furnished by morality, law, family, games, etiquette, and so on. It is not an existence condition of an artificial norm that it possesses real normative force. In this final section, I offer four suggestions regarding possible lessons for metanormative investigations of law.

First, on many topics that have traditionally occupied the field, jurisprudes should broaden their focus. If legal systems constitute a subclass of artificial normative systems, jurisprudes will sometimes learn more by looking carefully at artificial normative systems generally.

Second, as I have emphasized from the start, a principal task for jurisprudence remains to explain how legal norms have the contents that they do. Our need for such an explanation cannot be elided by observing that artificial systems generate norms with only ostensible normative force and that what we want to know at the end of the day is what we really should do.

Third, this makes jurisprudence important *if* different accounts of what gives legal norms their contents have at least some different first-order legal implications. Do they? That's a common view.[70] David Enoch casts doubts, however, in his contribution to this volume. Consider a putative or apparent legal norm that is morally unjust. Different jurisprudential accounts might generate different answers to the question of what the law does require. But what we really care about, Enoch says (echoing proponents of the one-step protocol, Section III.A), is what a judge should do. Because that is ultimately a moral question (or a question about ought-sans-phrase), the same answer should obtain regardless of how we answer the legal question: either (depending upon the details), the law requires other than

[68] (Gardner 2012b, 136).

[69] See (McPherson 2011, 233).

[70] See, e.g., (Shapiro, 2011, 25).

it superficially appears to require, and comports with justice, in which case the judge should enforce it; or what the law requires is unjust, in which case the judge should not enforce it.[71]

I find Enoch's doubts about whether positions in jurisprudence have first-order implications misplaced, for two reasons. First, even if judges (really) should care only about what they (really) should do, whether that is all they *do* care about is an empirical question. If a nontrivial number of judges try to follow the law, then what they will do will be shaped by what they take the law to be, which will be partly a function of the account of the determination of legal norms that they accept, consciously or not. Second and independently, Enoch overlooks cases in which different constitutive theories yield different legal norms both of which (or all of which) are morally allowable.[72] A judge will often find herself within a sea of moral allowability: ruling for plaintiff or for defendant would each be morally permissible (in fact, or as far as the judge can discern), and the critical question confronting the judge is: What does the law provide? What it provides is partly a function of general truths about how norms of that particular legal system are constituted. And truths about how the legal norms of that jurisdiction are constituted will be partly a function of, or at least must be consistent with, yet more general truths about how norms of legal systems as a group are or can be constituted. Thus, different jurisprudential theories—that is, different accounts of how the norms of legal norms are constituted—will generate different views about what the system's norms provide, which will in turn generate different conclusions about what the judge should do.

Fourth, notwithstanding my first observation, it need not be that *all* normative systems are comparably illuminating for the metanormative study of law. At this point a typology of systems of practical normativity would be useful. Without any pretense of exhaustiveness,[73] here are six dimensions on which normative systems vary: (1) systems can be "artificial" (depending upon actual human practices) or "non-artificial" (practice-independent); (2) systems can generate "real" normativity or only "ostensible" normativity; (3) systems can be "formal" (involving norm-creating texts) or "informal" (lacking them); (4) systems can be "institutional" in authorizing particular persons or assemblages to perform particular tasks, such as to change or enforce norms and to adjudicate alleged violations, or "non-institutional"; (5) systems can be "limited" in the behaviors or areas of life that they purport to govern, or "comprehensive"; and (6) systems can be "consensual"—i.e., issue norms that purport only to govern persons who voluntarily subject themselves to the system's jurisdiction—or "extra-consensual"—purporting to govern persons regardless of their consent.

Law and interpersonal morality are like each other, and unlike many or most other systems of practical normativity, with respect to the latter two dimensions: they are comprehensive and extra-consensual. I suspect that these two features lead many jurisprudes to believe that, among all normative systems, morality is the most useful or illuminating comparison for the metanormative study of law. On the other hand, law is unlike morality, and like many

[71] (Enoch 2019, 65–86).

[72] See *supra* note 25.

[73] For a different take, see (Raz 1999, 107–123).

sports and games[74] on the four other dimensions noted: law and games are artificial, ostensible, formal, and institutional. Morality (on most accounts) is none of these things. There are reasons to believe that formality and institutionalization are two especially important dimensions for purposes of understanding the grounds and grounding of law. If so, formal and institutionalized sports and games will be especially fertile sources for jurisprudential investigations.

The importance of formality should be obvious. Formal normative systems contain authoritative formally promulgated texts. Law, rugby, and Clue are formal systems; morality, fashion, and etiquette are informal. The communicative contents of authoritative texts have some constitutive role to play in the determination of a formal system's norms. But the suggestion that the communicative contents of a legal system's authoritative texts necessarily *fully* determine the law of that system is heterodox and wildly implausible.[75] It likely follows that legal norms are constituted by some combination or interplay of semantic facts and other facts, possibly including facts about historical practices and moral principles. Informal normative systems cannot shed light on this complex determination relationship; other formal normative systems potentially can. Think of the famous "pine tar incident" from a 1983 baseball game between the New York Yankees and the Kansas City Royals.[76]

Although most formal normative systems are institutional and most institutional normative systems are formal, institutionalization is a distinct characteristic of distinct significance. Some skeptics of the ISP claim support for their views from the apparent fact that the various participants in a legal system are frequently not governed by the same set of norms. The driver of a motor vehicle might be subject to a legal prohibition against traveling faster than 65 mph, while a traffic cop might be subject to a legal directive to allow driving as fast as 75 mph. Or Congress might have legal power to regulate intrastate activity only if the activity substantially affects interstate commerce, while courts are legally enjoined to uphold legislation so long as they determine that Congress *could rationally conclude* that the activity being regulated substantially affects interstate commerce. Kornhauser concludes, on the basis of examples such as these, that

> It is not clear that there is a single norm that we might call the law that governs the decision of each of the agents [that make up the legal system]. The separation of governance tasks and the complex institutional relations make it unlikely that we can usefully distill a single norm from the web of decisions that individual public officials make.[77]

That is a conceivable lesson: possibly, legal systems direct members of the public to comply with (or conform to) a set of norms that differ somewhat from the norms that govern one class of government agents (say, executive officers), which differ as well from the norms

---

[74] Exactly what games and sports are, and what the relationship between the two is, are controversial matters. See (Berman forthcoming 2019a). A rough pre-theoretical sense of sports and games is good enough for now.

[75] See supra note 54.

[76] The incident is described and discussed in (Hershovitz 2015, 1185 n.49); (Berman 2018, 1370–76).

[77] (Kornhauser 2015, 17); see also, e.g., (Hershovitz 2015, 1202–1203).

that govern another class of government agents (say, judicial officers), and so on: there is no commonality to these divergent sets of norms. An alternative explanation is that differently situated agents are subject to different norms *regarding how they are to engage with a single norm*. On this latter view, a legal system can consist of a welter of *norms about norms:* primary norms that regulate the behavior or the system's subjects as well as secondary norms that regulate how enforcers (e.g., police officers) are to enforce those primary norms, and how adjudicators (e.g., judges) are to adjudicate claimed violations of those primary norms. Just to identify these distinct possibilities suggests that, in order to understand how norms of legal systems are constituted, jurisprudes might need, as well, to excavate the normative structure or architecture of legal systems. There is a substantial, and growing, legal-theoretic literature on just this subject.[78] And on this topic, once again, other normative systems that have a complex *institutional* structure may prove a source of useful insights, analogies, and contrasting cases that informal normative systems cannot similarly provide due to their comparatively flat institutional configuration.

Jurisprudes have many tools in their toolbox. Among the small handful of analytic strategies that he identifies, Scott Shapiro recommends the effort "to stimulate thought through the heavy use of comparisons on the premise that examining institutions and practices that are similar, but not identical, to law, such as games, organized crime, religion, corporations, clubs, etiquette, popular morality, and so forth, will better equip us to appreciate the distinctive aspects of law itself."[79] I am suggesting that philosophers of law zoom out from law to other normative systems to better understand, not what is distinctive about law, but what isn't.

References

Berman, Mitchell N. 2004. "Constitutional Decision Rules." *Virginia Law Review* 90:1–160.

_____. 2011. "'Let 'em Play': A Study in the Jurisprudence of Sport." *Georgetown Law Journal* 99:1330–1331.

_____. 2017. "The Tragedy of Justice Scalia." *Michigan Law Review* 115:783–808

_____. 2018. "Our Principled Constitution." *University of Pennsylvania Law Review* 166:1325–1413.

_____. 2019a. "Sport as a Thick Cluster Concept." In *Games, Sports, and Play: Philosophical Essays*, edited by Thomas Hurka. New York: Oxford University Press.

_____. 2019b. "For Legal Principles." In *Moral Puzzles and Legal Perplexities: Essays on the Influence of Larry Alexander*, edited by Heidi Hurd. Cambridge: Cambridge University Press.

Berman, Mitchell N., and Kevin Toh. 2013. "Pluralistic Non-originalism and the Combinability Problem." *Texas Law Review* 91:1739–84.

Bulygin, Eugenio. 2015. "Permissory Norms and Normative Systems." In *Essays in Legal Philosophy*. Oxford: Oxford University Press,

[78] See, for an entry into it, (Berman 2004).

[79] (Shapiro 2011, 19). Shapiro calls this the "Comparative Strategy." I'd use that term for the strategy I am proposing and rename the approach Shapiro identifies the "Contrastive Strategy." Jurisprudes should help themselves to both.

Copp, David. 2004. "Moral Naturalism and Three Grades of Normativity." In *Normativity and Naturalism*, edited by Peter Schaber. Frankfurt: Ontos-Verlag.

Dworkin, Ronald. 1986. *Law's Empire*. Cambridge, MA: Harvard University Press.

_____. 2011. *Justice for Hedgehogs*. Cambridge, MA: Harvard University Press.

Ehrenberg, Kenneth. 2013. "Functions in Jurisprudential Methodology." *Philosophy Compass* 8:447–456.

Enoch, David. 2006. "Agency, Shmagency." *Philosophical Review* 115:169–198.

_____. 2011. *Taking Morality Seriously: A Defense of Robust Realism*. New York: Oxford University Press.

_____. 2019. "Is General Jurisprudence Interesting?". In *Dimensions of Normativity: New Essays on Metaethics and Jurisprudence*, edited by David Plunkett, Scott Shapiro, and Kevin Toh. Oxford: Oxford University Press.

Finlay, Stephen, and David Plunkett. 2018. "Quasi-expressivism and Statements of Law: A Hartian Theory." *Oxford Studies in Philosophy of Law* 3, edited by Leslie Green and Brian Leiter.

Foot, Philippa. 1972. "Morality as a System of Hypothetical Imperatives." *The Philosophical Review* 81(3):305–316.

Gardner, John. 2012a. *Law as a Leap of Faith*. Oxford: Oxford University Press.

_____. 2012b. "How Law Claims, What Law Claims." In his *Law as a Leap of Faith*. Oxford: Oxford University Press, pp. 125–48.

_____. 2012c. "Legal Positivism: 5½ Myths." In his *Law as a Leap of Faith*. Oxford: Oxford University Press, pp. 48–49.

Green, Leslie. 2008. "Positivism and the Inseparability of Law and Morals." *New York University Law Review* 83: 1035–1058.

Greenberg, Mark. 2004. "How Facts Make Law." *Legal Theory* 10:157–198.

_____. 2011a. "The Standard Picture and Its Discontents." *Oxford Studies in Philosophy of Law* 1:39–106.

_____. 2011b. "Legislation as Communication? Legal Interpretation and the Study of Linguistic Communication," In *Philosophical Foundations of Language in the Law*, edited by Andrei Marmor and Scott Soames. New York: Oxford University Press.

_____. 2014. "The Moral Impact Theory of Law." *Yale Law Journal* 123:1288–1342.

Hart, Herbert Lionel Adolphus. 1958/1983. "Positivism and the Separation of Law and Morals." In *Essays in Jurisprudence and Philosophy*. Oxford: Oxford University Press.

_____. 1961. *Concept of Law*. Oxford: Clarendon Press.

_____. 1982. *Essays on Bentham: Jurisprudence and Political Theory*. Oxford: Oxford University Press.

Hershovitz, Scott. 2015. "The End of Jurisprudence." *Yale Law Journal* 124(2015): 1160–1204.

Kahneman, Daniel. 2011. *Thinking, Fast and Slow*. New York: Farrar, Straus and Giroux.

Kornhauser, Lewis A. 2015. "Doing without the Concept of Law." NYU School of Law Public Law and Legal Theory Working Paper.

Kramer, Matthew H. 1999. "Requirements, Reasons, and Raz: Legal Positivism and Legal Duties." *Ethics* 109:375–407.

Lacey, Nicola. 2004. *A Life of H. L. A. Hart: The Nightmare and the Noble Dream*. New York: Oxford University Press.

McPherson, Tristram. 2011. "Against Quietist Normative Realism." *Philosophical Studies* 154: 223–240.

National Basketball Association. 2013–14. Official Rule Book.

Raz, Joseph. 1984. "Hart on Moral Rights and Legal Duties." *Oxford Journal of Legal Studies* 4: 123–31.

_____. 1999. "Explaining Normativity: On Rationality and the Justification of Reason." *Ratio* 12: 354–379.

_____. 1999. *Practical Reason and Norms*. Oxford: Oxford University Press.

Shapiro, Scott J. 2011. *Legality*. Cambridge, MA: Harvard University Press.

Toh, Kevin. 2007. "Raz on Detachment, Acceptance and Describability." *Oxford Journal of Legal Studies* 27:403–427.

_____. 2005. "Hart's Expressivism and his Benthamite Project." *Legal Theory* 11:75–123.

_____. 2011. "Artificial Norms and Interstitial Reasoning." Unpublished manuscript.

von Wright, G.H. 1963. *Norm and Action: A Logical Inquiry*. London: Routledge.

Waldron, Jeremy. 2013. "Jurisprudence for Hedgehogs." NYU School of Law Public Law and Legal Theory Working Paper.

World Chess Federation. 1988. *Laws of Chess*. Lucerne: FIDE.

8 How to Argue for Law's Full-Blooded Normativity

George Letsas*

I. Introduction

Very many questions can be pursued under the heading of "the normativity of law," not all of which are worthy of philosophical attention. The *Rule of Law Index* is a project that collects data on how the Rule of Law is experienced and perceived by the general public across the globe.[1] Denmark, who topped the index for 2016, can be said to have the most normative legal system in the world. But that is hardly the sense in which philosophers are interested when they ask whether law is normative. We can ask questions about the normativity of law even in conditions of widespread disobedience: Does law contain norms? Does law claim to obligate? Does law purport to give reasons?

Some of these questions can be pursued as part of more general inquiries about the nature of authority or the nature of rules, assuming of course that law—properly understood—claims authority or is made up of rules. We can then learn about the normativity of law in a derivative way, through studying the normativity of these other phenomena. There is, for instance, a distinct sense in which making a plan is normative for the person whose plan it is: I would have had less reason to become an academic, had I not planned my entire educational

* Professor of the Philosophy of Law, UCL. I would like thank Mitch Berman, Ruth Chang, David Enoch, Scott Shapiro, and Kevin Toh for extremely helpful comments and suggestions on an earlier draft. Earlier versions of this essay were presented at the Surrey Centre for Law and Philosophy (2017) and the Oxford Jurisprudence Discussion Group (2018). I am really grateful to the organizers and the audiences for extremely valuable comments, suggestions and criticisms.

[1] https://worldjusticeproject.org/our-work/wjp-rule-law-index.

Dimensions of Normativity. David Plunkett, Scott J. Shapiro, and Kevin Toh.

path with that goal in mind. So Scott Shapiro's claim that law consists in plan-like norms[2] would, if true, teach us a great deal about the normativity of law.

This way of proceeding drives a wedge between the normativity of law and the normativity of what we might call objective moral standards. It may be a mafia rule that new members must commit murder as part of their initiation. They may have made it their plan to murder, or they may have been ordered to do so by the relevant authorities. None of this changes the fact that one has an objective moral duty not to murder. In fact, insofar as rules, plans, or orders give people reasons, those reasons seem to belong to a different category altogether. They neither compete with, nor reinforce objective moral standards, whatever we might go on to say about the normativity of morality at a metaethical level.

It is in this vein that recent literature distinguishes between two kinds of normativity: *formal* and *full-blooded*.[3] Formal normativity is said to pertain to man-made norms that govern conventional practices (such as games, fashion, and etiquette) or activities such as planning or exercising authority. Full-blooded normativity, by contrast, is said to be an essential attribute of moral norms. The main difference between formal and full-blooded normativity is said to relate to their reason-givingness: man-made rules do not necessarily give objective reasons for action, whereas norms of critical morality necessarily do. You really do have to abide by morality's requirement to refrain from murdering others, but you do not really have to follow fashion's requirement to wear denim this year.

In his contribution to this volume, David Enoch argues that law lacks full-blooded normativity, because the claim that law necessarily gives genuine reasons for action is manifestly false: all it takes to falsify the claim is a real or conceivable case of exceptionally stupid or morally evil legal rules. These are cases where there is a legal rule requiring A to φ, yet A does not thereby acquire a reason to φ. The morally abhorrent laws of Nazi Germany or apartheid South Africa are the textbook example here. Enoch couples this argument with the observation that the normativity of law leaves open a question that the normativity of morality does not. He says that we find it odd when someone accepts that he has a moral reason to φ, yet questions whether he should be bothered with it. By contrast, he thinks that it is perfectly open for us to question whether we should be bothered with whatever law requires of us.

The view that law possesses formal normativity has become somewhat of an orthodoxy in legal philosophy. Yet the contrary view, that law exhibits the same full-blooded normativity as morality, gets a short shrift in the relevant literature. It is usually construed as the proposition that one has moral reason to follow each and every legal rule simply in virtue of the fact that they are valid. Yet this is just one way to entertain the proposition that law possesses full-blooded normativity, and it is far from the most plausible one. In principle, nothing keeps law from providing us with objective, non-contingent, moral reasons. Law has a factual dimension and, as David Enoch argues, it is non-normative facts that trigger moral reasons. The fact that I promised to write this essay triggers my moral duty to do so. In a functioning legal system, law populates our non-normative landscape with a myriad of facts (legislative enactments, court decisions, executive measures) and it would be extremely

---

2 (Shapiro 2011).

3 David Enoch (2018) and (Plunkett and Shapiro 2017). Other terms used in the literature for full-blooded normativity include "robust," "high-octane," or "strong."

surprising if these facts, like the movement of distant planets, triggered no moral reasons. Where law's claim to full-blooded normativity appears to falter is not at its general capacity to trigger moral reasons (*any* fact has that potential), but at the suggestion that legal facts *necessarily* serve, in virtue of being legal, as moral triggers. What we count as legal facts and what kind of reasons for action they trigger is therefore crucial.

In this contribution, I aim to motivate the view that law possesses full-blooded normativity in a top-down way. I want to begin from morality and unpack the view that a practice may be necessarily normative, in a full-blooded sense. Here is the dialectic of my inquiry: What would have to be true of morality, for the claim that some specific practice is full-bloodedly normative to be plausible? I will assume that the practice of morality as a whole has full-blooded normativity in the sense that its requirements give one genuine reasons to act irrespective of one's subjective wants, desires, and beliefs. My focus will be on what it means to say of a *specific* practice that it partakes of morality's normativity. The reason is simple: it should be an open question whether this or that practice has full-blooded normativity. For if it is not possible for *any* particular practice to have full-blooded normativity, then the question of whether *law* has full-blooded normativity would make no sense from the get-go. We need, in other words, an independent account of what it means for a practice to partake of morality's full-blooded normativity.

The account I shall put forward builds on the idea of obligations of role. A practice, I shall argue, has full-blooded normativity when it instantiates a distinct set of obligations, one that pertains to people in a particular capacity, such as friends, parents, doctors, or teachers. The proposition that there are distinct moral practices, which are not reducible to a single moral concern, is of course disputed territory in moral philosophy. But if we accept this proposition, we can ask, by analogy, whether legal practice exhibits the necessary elements for full-blooded normativity. This way of proceeding perceives the relationship between law and metaethics differently: it shows that law's claim to full-blooded normativity ultimately depends on contestable assumptions about the nature of morality as a whole.

II. Not the Positivism Debate Again

The proposition that law necessarily gives reasons needs some unpacking. Enoch understands it as the claim that for each and every legal rule that one must φ, one thereby has a moral reason to φ. This raises the immediate objection that the claim loads the dice in favor of legal positivism. For it assumes that law is made up of individual rules that owe their existence to their mode of origin rather their moral merits; it assumes in other words that legal standards are very much unlike moral standards, lacking a necessary connection to genuine reason-giving. But this is a contested issue in general jurisprudence. For over 40 years, Ronald Dworkin has challenged the idea that law consists in rules, understood as a finite set of standards identifiable by virtue of social facts alone. If laws are rules thus understood, then it is both conceivable and possible that I am legally required to do stupid or morally atrocious things, and yet I acquire no reason to do them. The chances of law having full-blooded normativity are then zero from the get-go.

I am not sure how much this objection should detain us. It would be unfortunate if we are unable to make headway on the issue of the normativity of law before we take up (yet again!)

the positivism versus non-positivism debate. Besides, it is not clear how taking the other side of that debate would help here. Suppose we accept, with Dworkin, that law is partly determined by the moral principles that best fit and justify a community's past political practice. It would then make little sense to ask whether law necessarily gives real reasons. If these principles are moral principles, then it would follow that they have full-blooded normativity built into them; they ground pro tanto moral obligations. The question is begged in the other direction.

But there is an important lesson here. If we take rules, descriptively identified, to be the candidate element for normativity then it is not an open question whether law's normativity is full-blooded. No set of rules, descriptively identified, can make it the case that the relevant practice in which they figure necessarily gives genuine moral reasons for action. If normativity pertains to rules then it is *not* an open question whether we should necessarily be bothered with what law requires of us. For we shouldn't necessarily be bothered with what *any* rule-based practice requires of us. Likewise, if we take true moral principles to be the locus of normativity then law cannot *but* possess full-blooded normativity. This is because moral principles have a necessary connection to the moral reasons for action that they ground. But then any practice in which moral principles are picked out in virtue of the fact that they are applicable would possess full-blooded normativity. And since morality governs every practice and everything we do, then law's (and any practice's) claim to full-blooded normativity would not be an open question either.

Yet we need to start somewhere. And the idea that non-normative facts about the world trigger normative reasons seems to me like a good place to start. Moral reasons to do, or not to do things are triggered by non-normative facts in the world. If this is true, then it makes perfect sense to ask whether certain non-normative facts confer full-blooded normativity on certain practices, the type of normativity that other practices lack. Fashion is for instance no doubt a practice, but it is hard to see how its requirements bear a necessary connection to the type of reasons morality gives. Though there might occasionally be genuine moral reasons to dress fashionably, they bear a contingent connection to the practice of fashion. By contrast, parenthood is a practice heavily loaded with assumptions about one's moral rights and duties. So we can ask whether the non-normative fact of having a child necessarily confers full-blooded normativity on the practice of parenthood. In so asking, we inquire into whether parenthood is best understood as a normative role that has explanatory priority over the moral rights and duties that the practice of parenthood generates. Then we can proceed to ask, by way of analogy, whether some non-normative fact about law has the same effect on legal practice. We might end up asking whether each and every legal rule to the effect that one must φ, triggers a moral reason to φ. But we might not. In either case, we are not committed to a particular view about the metaphysics of legal standards.

The above seems to me to be a fresh and promising way of looking at the nature of law, as part of doing general jurisprudence. It bypasses some of the questions with which legal philosophers have been preoccupied for some time now, such as what determines the content of the law[4] or what makes propositions of law true.[5] And I am hoping that it will allow

[4] See (Greenberg 2011, ch. 2).

[5] (Dworkin 1998); (Stavropoulos 2014).

me to lay out the case for law's full-blooded normativity without begging any questions against legal positivism.

III. Reasons and Facts: Triggering versus Constituting

Some preliminary remarks about the relationship between facts and reasons are in order. I think Enoch is right to focus on the reason-givingness of non-normative facts, but I am somewhat skeptical of his formulation that facts trigger preexisting reasons. Let us take the case of parental reasons. As a general proposition, that parenthood necessarily creates reasons for action rings true: parents have a number of genuine moral reasons, such as to care for their children, show them love and affection, look after their health and well-being, educate them, and the like. These reasons are conditional on becoming a parent. This much is relatively uncontroversial. But there are problems. On Enoch's triggering model, conditional reasons are to be explained using a wide scope, rather than a narrow one. The former means that the reason exists prior to, and independently of any facts, and that facts condition when the reason obtains. The latter, by contrast, means that reasons obtain only if, and in virtue of, a fact obtaining. On the triggering model, people have preexisting (Enoch calls them "dormant"[6]) parental reasons, reasons that are triggered by the non-normative fact of becoming a parent.

This strikes me as an odd proposition. To begin with, parental reasons are directed; they are owed to one's adopted or biological child. Prior to adoption, the identity of the child need not be known, whereas prior to conception, the person to whom the reason is owed does not even exist. So when the parental reason is dormant (i.e., prior to the triggering fact of adoption or birth), the reason is undirected. And when it wakes up, so to speak, the reason is directed. But then it is a mystery how the dormant reason has explanatory priority over the triggered reason. Nothing about the dormant reason can explain the directedness of the triggered reason.

True, we might try to give a definite description of the people toward whom these preexisting parental duties are owed (e.g., whoever is born out of one's genetic material) and certainly the idea of duties owed to future generations is generally unproblematic. But, at least in the case of parenthood, it seems that the identity of the person is an essential part of the duties owed. Parents owe their children duties because of a special relationship that holds between them. By contrast, we owe future people a duty to act on climate change, not because of any special relation, but because they are those who will be affected by what we now do to the environment.

There is another concern as well. Talking of preexisting or dormant reasons seems misleading. It might suggest that I have a reason to make it the case that these reasons get triggered or that it is a good thing when they are triggered. But this is a contested issue. On some overtly teleological views about the good life, everyone has reason—perhaps even a duty—to have children. Less moralistic views about the good life would however reject this: some people have reason to become parents because it is right for them, or a good time for them, or

[6] (Enoch 2011, 4).

what have you. But many others have no reason to acquire parental reasons, so to speak, and it seems odd to say that these people have dormant parental reasons. Prior to the triggering fact occurring, what actions are their dormant reasons, reasons *for*? If the answer is nothing, then the idea of a dormant reason sounds oxymoronic. This is also evident in cases of people who cannot have or adopt children. If ought implies can, then how is it possible for them to have parental reasons—reasons that cannot but be forever dormant?

The triggering model may here resort to a strategy of abstraction: suppose we say that people have a general, preexisting, reason to develop valuable personal relationships with other human beings. Having a child is just one way in which this reason can be pursued but there are other ways too, such as having friends or partners. So it might make sense to say—with the teleologists—that we all have the same general reason: to seek out and develop personal relationships. This reason is far from dormant and it explains why say, the fact that one acquired a friend triggers normative reasons. This strategy would salvage the idea of preexisting reasons, but at some significant cost. It would imply that one's parental reasons are no different in kind from friendship reasons, or reasons of romantic love. This would distort the important ways in which caring for one's friends or partner differs from caring for one's child. Not only are the reasons for action different in each case, but also the moral considerations to which we will appeal to explain them differ.

A way to avoid the above worries is to adopt what we might call a *constitutive* model of reasons, according to which the relevant non-normative facts simply *are* reasons.[7] The fact that one had a child constitutes one's reason to care for her. He had no such reason before, not even dormant. I do not mean this to be a form of reductivism: that all moral considerations are reducible to non-normative facts. Nor is this a form of a category mistake, or deriving an ought from an is, flouting Hume's law. On the contrary: moral considerations are to explain *why* some non-normative fact is a reason. It is just that reasons are the *explanandum* not the *explanans*. When we ask for an example why having a child makes a moral difference to one's reasons we expect the answer to contain reference to moral notions such as justice, fairness, well-being, and the like. Sometimes such references are implicit. For example, when we assert that one ought not to impose the cost of one's choice on others, we imply that doing so would be unfair or unjust.

Moreover, in seeking to provide an explanation of why parenthood makes a difference we are likely to rely on a plurality of moral considerations, such as the following: the needs of vulnerable or helpless people have priority; people have a strong ethical interest in developing child-parent relationships; it is generally unfair if the cost of having a child is shifted entirely on others; parents are on average better placed to care for their kids than strangers are; following existing cultural representations of child/parent relations are ethically vital for children's well-being; justice requires to assist parents with their child-rearing responsibilities. These considerations, taken together, explain the reason-giving property the fact of becoming a parent has. And so there needn't be a one-to-one correlation between the normative significance of a fact and the moral considerations that explain why it has that significance.

---

[7] I believe this is the model followed by Gardner and Macklem (2002).

It may be objected that the constitutive model is no different to the triggering one: all these considerations can be redescribed as preexisting, dormant, reasons. I doubt however that the idea of dormant reasons can capture each and every of the considerations to which we appeal when we seek to justify reasons for action. Take the proposition that it is unfair if the cost of being a parent is shifted entirely onto others. The proposition states a principle of fairness and applies it to childcare costs. What dormant, preexisting, reason do persons with no children have with respect to this proposition? We can perhaps say that they have a general reason to be fair or to reject an unfair allocation of anything—including childcare costs—but that sounds like we just repeated the principle without adding any salient information. Presenting the principle as a preexisting moral reason—even if it is possible to do so—is an additional task we might undertake and one that lacks any explanatory salience.

So I will proceed using the constitutive model as the basis for asking whether law necessarily gives reasons. I will assume that non-normative facts are reasons, that they are so in virtue of moral explanations, and that such explanations are in principle complex and pluralistic, comprising a rich set of moral considerations (such as fairness, justice, and equality). And since reasons are constituted (or if you still prefer, triggered) by facts, then we are asking whether there are any non-normative facts in the world, of which it is necessarily true that they confer obligations of role upon a particular practice. We can then move on to ask whether some non-normative legal facts (in a sense to be determined) are amongst those.

IV. Subdomains of Morality and Obligations of Role

When we assert that parenthood necessarily gives moral reasons for action we do so at a general level. We rely on our pre-theoretical concepts of what it means to have a child or become a parent. There are standard cases where people choose to have a biological child or to adopt a child. But there are other cases where the element of choice is diminished or absent, or where there is a prior agreement not to assume the role of a parent (e.g., donation of genetic material). We operate at the same level of conceptual generality when we refer to the reasons for action one acquires in virtue of parenthood. We say for instance that having children gives parents a general moral reason to care for them, and we will not cite their concrete reason to read them the same bedtime story for the tenth time, until they finally decide to go to sleep.

But there are problems. There are borderline cases where parenthood, be it biological or adoptive, appears insufficient to ground a duty to care, or at least the typical duties of care associated with parenthood. Think of the case where someone's genetic material was stolen and used for reproduction unbeknownst to him, or against his will. Or think of a case where an adopted child chooses to go and live with her newly discovered biological parent. There are also cases where parental duties amount to very little in practical terms. The parental duties of soldiers conscripted to fight decade-long wars in distant countries, though persisting, consist in a very limited number of required actions. Parental duties may vary enormously depending on context. The parental duties of people living in impoverished countries, with no schools or welfare support, are very different compared to parental duties in developed countries. The parental duties of biological parents typically kick in since the child's birth, whereas those of adoptive parents need not. So it might be objected that the proposition that parenthood necessarily gives reasons is either false or too general to be philosophically interesting. It is false if there is one (real or conceivable) case in which one is a parent yet acquires no reasons whatsoever vis-à-vis her child, that is reasons grounded on the fact of parenthood; this would entail that having a child may, but need not, be normatively relevant. And the proposition is philosophically uninteresting if the normative relevance of parenthood is too diffuse: it is relevant for different moral considerations depending on one's situation, and it grounds very many different reasons for action.

The objection has the same shape as some of Enoch's arguments against law's having full-blooded normativity. Enoch remarks that it would not do to show that law may *sometimes* be normatively relevant. For one thing, this would not satisfy the modal condition that law *necessarily* gives reasons. Call this the *necessity objection*. But that law is sometimes relevant would also be philosophically uninteresting because this much is true, he remarks, about pretty much everything.[8] Any fact can become normatively relevant and some pretty mundane facts, such as the weather, might be normatively relevant for all, or most, of us and systematically so. For example, every single day, weather conditions affect what people have reason to wear. Weather is necessarily reason-giving in that sense. Enoch thinks that there is nothing philosophically interesting here. Call this the *triviality objection*.

These objections however can be deflected. Take the *triviality objection* first. It is true that any fact can be normatively relevant. But we can, and should, attend to the different ways in which certain facts are normatively relevant. Parenthood is not normatively relevant in the same way the weather or the stock market are relevant. To begin with, parenthood reasons are necessarily other-regarding, unlike the weather. They are necessarily owed to others; they belong to the moral, not the prudential realm. When we ask whether law is reason-giving, we are likewise interested in its capacity to generate moral reasons because that is how law presents itself to us. It claims to obligate morally.[9]

Second, parenthood is not just a normatively relevant event that occurs. It is something that you *become*, rather than something that happens to you or in the world, such as an illness or a thunder storm. It is what philosophers refer to as a normative *role* one occupies.[10] This role comes with a package of duties, rights, and responsibilities, all of which have internal connections. This is why moral philosophers talk about the ethics of parenthood[11] or the human right to family life. We do the same when we talk about the ethics of friendship, or the ethics of being a doctor or a teacher. Morality comes in domains, or spheres, and these are some of them. We do not, by contrast, talk about the ethics of weather, even if the weather systematically changes people's reasons for action. There is no package of weather duties, rights, and responsibilities—no role that one occupies in virtue of the weather being hot or cold. This is so despite the fact that there are things we can call weather practices,

8 (Enoch 2018).

9 No doubt law also gives one prudential reasons to do things in order to avoid going to prison or losing one's money, and some philosophers have sought to explain law's normativity in that way. But since the work of H. L. A. Hart there has been wide consensus amongst legal philosophers that prudential reasons cannot account for law's normativity.

10 (Hardimon 1994, 333–363).

11 See (Archard and Benatar 2010).

which include things people routinely do in relation to the weather, including institutional practices such as weather forecasting.

We must also note here a distinction in kind between moral reasons and moral duties. What one has most moral reason to do can never outweigh one's deontic moral duty.[12] Suppose my students' interest in education and learning is a reason for me to schedule an additional revision class and that, on the balance of moral reasons, I should offer it to them. That is different from saying that I have a moral duty to offer the students a revision class, say because I promised or because it is part of my employment duties. In case of conflict, deontic duties take precedence over what one has most reason to do. The distinction is relevant to discussion of normativity: it is one thing to ask whether a practice triggers moral reasons and a different thing to ask whether it triggers moral duties. Practices in which one occupies a normative role are special in that they trigger deontic duties as opposed to (mere) moral reasons. And hence their normativity is of an even stronger type.

Obligations of role moreover are considered agent-relative. They are owed only by those who occupy the role and in virtue of some special relationship they have with others, such as friendship or love. Few philosophers doubt that such relationships ground genuine reasons, but there has been a long-standing debate about whether one of the main moral theories, consequentialism, can account for why these reasons are agent-relative or special.[13] Within a thoroughly consequentialism framework, the normative significance of such relationships is contingent on whether engaging in them will have the consequence of advancing or maximizing some good state of affairs; no normative significance is attached merely on the fact that someone is my friend or my child, and none would be if it turns out that I am a terrible friend or parent. I shall return to this issue later, but it is important to flag up now that some general debates in moral theory bear on the nature of reason-giving, and that law's (or parenthood's) full-blooded normativity may depend on where one stands on these debates.

To recap: there are facts that may be normatively relevant in a trivial or contingent sense: the fact that it is sunny today gives me (and perhaps everyone in the vicinity) reason to go for a walk; or the fact that I pay for a gym subscription gives me more reason to exercise. But there are also facts that are normatively relevant in the special sense of conferring a normative role, a role that comes with a package of moral rights, duties, and responsibilities. And this distinction helps to deflect *the triviality objection*: some normatively relevant facts trigger reasons in a nontrivial way; they confer normative roles upon people. This is a promising model for testing law's normativity because it allows us to ask whether having a legal system confers upon us, or some of us, a normative role consisting in a package or rights, duties, and responsibilities. This is the route I shall pursue here.

Consider now the *necessity objection*. Is parenthood necessarily reason-giving? Take the case of someone whose genetic material was stolen and used against his will to create another human being. We will naturally pause to question whether that person has acquired any parental reasons as a result of this blatant wrongdoing. The absence of choice or control seems troubling here, and it might suggest that parental obligations are entirely voluntarist: they obtain if, and only if, one has chosen to assume them. A long tradition in political

[12] See (Darwall 2006).

[13] (Nagel 1970); (Parfit 1984).

philosophy has thought something similar about law: legal or political obligation obtains if, and only if, one has voluntarily given one's consent to government. The Lockean strand in this tradition stretches the notion of consent to the breaking point, in order to support the view that most of us have political obligations. But other strands are happy to accept that political obligations are owed by very few, perhaps just the officials who have what Hart called the "internal point of view." Yet there is much controversy here, and the voluntarist model of parental obligations is subject to some powerful criticisms.[14]

First, even on the voluntarist model, people do not need to have accepted the obligations of parenthood, one by one, in order to have them; it suffices that they have exercised some voluntary control over the choice of becoming a parent, even if they do not or would not accept all the reasons that parenthood entails. In other words, there is no control over the *content* of parental reasons; the normative role of a parent is what it is, so to speak. Second, the voluntarist model does not explain why people who have taken great care to avoid having biological children feel the pull of parental responsibility nonetheless. Nor does it explain why caring for a child for long periods, and developing a relationship with her, triggers parental responsibilities even in the absence of a voluntary choice to become her parent. Finally, we must not forget that few—if any—doubt that children have reasons to care for their parents despite the fact that they have exercised no voluntary control over coming into existence—let alone over being a particular person's child. We are very comfortable with the idea that the normative role of children can be triggered without voluntary control, and it would be odd if the triggering conditions of parental and child responsibilities were substantially asymmetrical.

A lot more needs to be said of course about the kind of relationship that triggers parental reasons and the conditions under which one may—involuntarily—assume parental responsibility. I have no such theory to offer here. There are no doubt hard cases in which one has involuntarily acquired biological children, or has deliberately sought not to acquire parental obligations (as in the case of anonymous donation of genetic material). But they are insufficient to falsify the proposition that parenthood—just like other normative roles such as friendship or family—*necessarily* gives reasons. For it will still be an open question whether, in these cases, one has become a parent. There is a difference in kind between being a sperm donor and deciding to have children but it is not to do with different types of parenthood (one with acquired duties and the other without). Parenthood tracks a subset of moral reasons, not the other way around.

To sum up: certain factual circumstances in which people develop relationships with others are reason-giving in the special sense that they confer normative roles. Such roles demarcate distinct domains of morality; they come with a package of rights, duties, and responsibilities and they are, in that sense, necessarily reason-giving. I do not mean to suggest the stronger thesis that *all* genuine moral reasons track obligations of role. For instance, the duty not to torture or the duty to perform an easy rescue are not duties we have in virtue of acting in a particular capacity. My focus is on full-blooded normativity that tracks a subset of moral rights and duties, those held in virtue of occupying a normative role.

---

[14] See (Prusak 2001, 61–75).

V. The Myth of Formal Normativity

Normative roles contain various rights, duties, and responsibilities, and these are typically described at an abstract level. We say for instance that the role of parents is to show love and care for their children. Such propositions convey meaningful information about one's moral profile, without the need to list concrete actions that a parent has reason to do, such as to read small children bedtime stories or take them regularly to the park. The general reason to show care and love for one's children has explanatory priority over the concrete actions that parents have reason to take. If a parent has reason to read her child a bedtime story every day, this is because that is the proper way for her to fulfill her role, given the circumstances in which she is found: she knows how to read, she has access to books, reading is beneficial to her child, there are no alternative ways to teach the child language skills and excite their imagination, etc.

We could perhaps say that there are necessarily parental reasons to take certain concrete actions, but only if we take for granted a number of things about contemporary life, such as that there are books and that people do not live in the woods. Contemporary Western culture is full of attempts to provide rulebooks that new parents can use as guidance in fulfilling their role ("never wake up a sleeping baby," "give small children multiple meals throughout the day," etc.). Such rules are widely accepted and used, and they bear the hallmarks of formal normativity: within the practice of childrearing, they set standards of correctness. But even if such rules provide good guidance, it would be a mistake to think that there is necessarily reason to follow each and every one of these rules. Such rules will necessarily make a number of implicit assumptions about the standard or typical circumstances of parents and children. As a result, they will not apply to each and every case, nor are they supposed to. No rulebook can capture what concrete actions that the general duty to care for one's children demands in specific circumstances. A parent who lives in the countryside, and has had no formal education, has no reason to read to her child or take him to the park. She can fulfill her normative role by other means, and be no less of a good parent.

So here is what the example of normative roles teaches us about the relationship between formal and full-blooded normativity: in testing whether a practice (e.g., parenthood) has full-blooded normativity, we are not meant to take some list of rules (to the effect that one ought to φ, χ, and ψ) and then ask whether it is true of *these* rules that give full-blooded moral reasons to φ, χ, and ψ. The existence of these rules are not the relevant fact that constitutes (or if you like, triggers) one's parental reasons for action; It is *parenthood* that triggers those reasons. Nor is abiding by the rulebook what makes someone a good parent. Good parents are those who perform well their normative role, and strict adherence to the rulebook may, or may not, help them do so (most likely it will not). In other words, we are not here asking whether some practice of formal normativity (e.g., the parental rules accepted by contemporary parents or the community at large) is full-blooded normative. If we want to know whether parenthood has full-blooded normativity, the rules of formal normativity inhabiting the practice of parenthood are neither here nor there. At best, they provide epistemic reasons to think that some important normative role is in play.

Enoch remarks that formal normativity is not a prerequisite for full-blooded normativity, because things that lack formal normativity, such as the weather, can give genuine reasons for action. He is half right: we should say that even for practices with formal normativity, their full-blooded normativity—if there is one—is not necessarily *attached* to their formal normativity.[15] At least in the case of parenthood, full-blooded normativity is not formal normativity *plus* some missing ingredient. It is not like the beef that you need to add to a list of other ingredients in order to make a burger, and without which it could not possibly qualify as one. Rather, formal normativity is to full-blooded normativity what fool's gold is to gold.[16] It is no part of the real thing.

But we should be careful. Other cases are different. As we saw, it *can* be the case that rules of formal normativity are part of one's moral reasons. The fact that skinny ties are in fashion coupled with the fact that I promised my employer to dress fashionably gives me a reason to follow this fashion rule. The morality of promising explains here why this rule of fashion acquires normative significance. But other practices of so-called formal normativity have an even closer connection to full-blooded normativity. Consider etiquette. The fact that rules of etiquette require people to shake hands when making someone's acquaintance, coupled with the fact that people expect this greeting ritual as a form of expressing respect, gives me a moral reason to do it. If I do not, I risk causing offense to others, acting impermissibly. Moral considerations to do with respect and protecting reasonable expectations explain why rules of etiquette acquire this normative significance systematically, and for most people. Even rules seemingly indifferent from a moral point of view, such as the rules of grammar, have such moral significance: the need to ensure accurate and truthful communication explains why people have reason to follow the rules of grammar. These rules allow us to express nuances in meaning that would otherwise be lost, risking miscommunication. The reason to follow grammar rules does not of course have a huge amount of moral weight, and can be outweighed easily, but it is a full-blooded reason nevertheless.

The same applies to games: people have strong ethical interests in pursuing the values of play and sociability. Games enable us to do so but only if everybody follows the same rules and knows that others will do the same. The fact that the rules of various games that people invented (out of an infinite number of possible ones) have become salient, forms part of my reasons for following them when I choose to play for fun. But if the context is different, as in the case of teaching chess to a beginner, then some of the rules can be ignored: the teacher still plays chess when he, unlike the student, plays the game without the queen.

So some of the paradigm examples of formal normativity, such as etiquette, language, or games, turn out to be not so formal at all: a plethora of moral considerations explains why their rules systematically form part of our moral reasons for action. This, I think, is the hallmark of the practices we call conventional; they exist because they enable us to comply with our full-blooded reasons.[17] Nor is the moral significance of these conventional practices *contingent*: we could do with different grammar rules or different games but we could not do without language or games altogether. I have always found it puzzling that the normativity of conventional practices such as etiquette, language, or games is being contrasted to morality's

---

[15] This point is different from Dworkin's argument that the rules of a practice do not exhaust the obligations one has in virtue of the practice.

[16] I borrow these apt metaphors from Stephen Finlay who used them at the Yale workshop in May 2015.

[17] I here draw on material from Letsas (2014).

full-blooded one. There is a contrast here no doubt, but it is one *within* full-blooded normativity: sometimes our moral reasons for action do not include what others do and accept by way of convention; sometimes however they do, and they might also include the rules that are held valid within the practice.

That is not to say of course that there is reason to follow *each and every rule* found in conventional practices: in my view, there is no reason to follow evil conventional rules,[18] just like there is no reason to keep evil promises.[19] Whichever moral considerations explain why some conventional rules are reason-giving will confer no normativity upon rules that are morally atrocious. Enoch thinks that the existence of a real (or conceivable) evil rule suffices to deprive a conventional practice from having full-blooded normativity. I disagree. Most rules of etiquette or language bear a systematic connection to full-blooded normativity: they are amongst the facts that necessarily constitute (or trigger) one's reasons for action, according to available moral explanations. Why should irregular facts about evil rules be counted amongst those that make up a practice, only to discount them as lacking full-blooded normativity? Indeed, on the triggering model, wouldn't such facts have to be *made* relevant for us?

But perhaps all this is terminological. It matters little if we say that etiquette, properly understood, is necessarily reason-giving, or whether we say that most etiquette rules, together with some other facts, are necessarily reason-giving. The important point seems to me to be this: full-blooded normativity is central even in practices of so-called formal normativity, such as etiquette, language, or games. It is not that these practices *aim* or *claim* to give us reasons; they *in fact* do and, properly understood, they do so necessarily and systematically.

So formal normativity, insofar as it is meant to be contrasted with full-blooded normativity, ends up being a myth. For it is about rules, and rules are just that: a bunch of facts about what is accepted and practised, and these facts may or may not be reason-giving. Rule-based practices are either irrelevant to full-blooded normativity (as in the case of parenthood), or they *just are* full-bloodedly normative (as in the case of conventions). In neither case do we begin from some rulebook, descriptively identified, and then ask whether each and every rule found therein possesses full-blooded normativity. We shouldn't do this about law either, insofar as we are genuinely interested in the question of whether it is necessarily reason-giving.

VI. How Law Is Necessarily Reason-Giving: Three Steps

Earlier sections have sought to establish that certain facts are necessarily reason-giving, in the special sense of conferring a normative role that comprises a package of rights, duties, and responsibilities. The normative attributes of the role are not within the control of the person occupying it, nor is occupying the role necessarily the product of the exercise of one's will. We are now ready to ask, by way of analogy, whether some non-normative fact is such that it

[18] For the opposite view see Andrei Marmor.

[19] (Altham 2009). For the contrary view see (Searle 2001, 193–200). Also more recently see (Owens 2012, 245–249).

triggers obligations of role bearing this type of full-blooded normativity. This, unlike asking about the normativity of rules or principles, is an open question.

But which fact? Legal philosophers have had difficulty resisting the thought that the relevant fact is the enactment of certain rules according to a legal system's criteria of validity. They ask whether morality could make it the case that there is necessarily reason to follow each and every one of those rules. I mentioned earlier that this naturally makes the chances of law possessing full-blooded normativity slim from the get-go. It is effectively a matter of whether legal rules can be filtered or massaged to become bearers of full-blooded normativity. And it seems to me that even those who want to make law's claim to full-blooded normativity go through, also begin from the bottom up: they take legal rules as their starting point if only to show that some revised conception of them (e.g., the principles underlying them) is the true candidate for full-blooded normativity.[20] This is akin to modeling law's normativity on that of conventional practices such as language, etiquette, or games. Conventionalist accounts of law are well known in the literature and they cut across the divide between positivism[21] and non-positivism.[22] But my focus in this chapter is on the top-down strategy I have sketched in previous sections: I want to explore whether some special normative role is necessarily triggered by a set of facts that can be said to be distinctively legal. On this model, the rulebook (what people refer to as formal normativity) is a red herring.

I do not however think that the prospects of the top-down strategy are at the outset more promising. There are a number of difficulties. The normative roles with which we are familiar belong to personal, not political, morality. They pertain to agent-relative obligations that arise in the context of special relationships, such as being someone's friend or parent. They carve out a sphere of partiality, within a moral universe of impartial concern for all human beings. Law, by contrast, is usually perceived as the antithesis of special relations. Impartiality and equality before the law are hailed as legal values. It is not obvious to which special relationship legal obligation pertains and in virtue of which normative role one has legal obligations.

One way to proceed here is by looking for legal facts that might have some special normative significance. We could for instance ask whether having a state with legal institutions (legislature, judiciary etc.), as an alternative to having anarchy, is necessarily reason-giving. But this is inevitably too coarse-grained. What actions does the fact of statehood give us reason to take? Hobbesian accounts of the normative significance of the state usually overreach, culminating in an unqualified duty to obey the sovereign. It seems to me better to begin by asking whether any distinctive normative roles are found in law's neighborhood, roles that pertain to special relationships, and then ask which facts trigger those roles. Insofar as these facts can be conceptualized as legal facts, law will come out possessing full-blooded normativity. No doubt, the case for law's full-blooded normativity, thus understood, requires complex argumentation. But it is important to explore what the various steps in the argument are, and where exactly people who are skeptical of law's full-blooded normativity might get off the ladder.

---

[20] See (Dworkin 1978, chs. 2 and 3).

[21] (Hart 2012); (Coleman 2001); Marmor (2009).

[22] For non-positivist accounts of legal conventionalism see (Kyritsis 2008); (Letsas 2014).

So are there any such normative roles and special relationships in law's neighborhood? The best candidate here is citizenship, understood as membership to a political community, rather than the technical notion of holding a country's passport or having a certain nationality. Migrants who permanently reside and live in another country become members of that country's political community, whatever their legal status might be. Citizenship is typically understood in this moralized, non-formal sense. We speak for instance of civic duties and the ethics of citizenship and debate what it means to be a good citizen, not only within a country but also within particular organizations such as universities. Citizenship is not yet a distinctively legal role, but it is close enough to law to serve as a starting point. It would be odd if an account of citizens' rights, duties, and responsibilities said nothing about law. And it would be surprising if the best account of the normative role of citizenship required unconditional contempt for law. Anarchists who deny that there is a duty to obey the law typically also dispute the category of citizenship duties altogether. So insofar as some inherent link exists between citizenship and law, we can make headway in understanding law's normativity by starting with the normative role of a citizen.

This argumentative path echoes Ronald Dworkin's well-known claim that legal obligation is, like parental or familial obligation, associative. But it differs from Dworkin's account in that it does not begin from legal practice, asking what makes propositions of law true within that practice; nor does it assume that the point of law is to justify state coercion.[23] It begins in political philosophy and it asks whether certain political circumstances are necessarily reason-giving in the full-blooded sense of triggering obligations of role. It is premised on the priority of political theory to legal theory.

Citizenship obligations share three important features with parental or familial obligations: first, they are agent-relative in that they only hold between people having a particular relationship. Second, they need not be triggered voluntarily. People do not choose which country to be born in, and ability to emigrate is the exception, not the norm. Third, they have relative priority vis-à-vis obligations owed to people outside that relationship. Most people think that we owe fellow citizens more than we owe foreigners, just like we owe our family members more than we owe strangers.

The idea of obligations of citizenship is of course contested territory in moral philosophy. As mentioned already, consequentialists who deny that special relationships are inherently reason-giving will not in principle accept them. It is not an accident that some well-known consequentialists are cosmopolitans, arguing that the moral demands of your fellow citizens are on an par with those of the distant needy.[24] And some non-consequentialists, who accept in principle that special obligations exist, are also cosmopolitans because they think that citizenship—unlike family—does not ground agent-relative obligations.[25] This is not the place to defend the view that obligations of justice are bounded by citizenship.[26] But we should note that, just like with familial obligations, the widely shared intuition is that citizenship carves out a sphere of partiality within a universe of impartial concern toward the

[23] (Dworkin, 1998, 93).

[24] (Singer 2009).

[25] (Pogge 1992, 48–75); (Pogge 1994, 195–224); (Pogge 2001, 6–24).

[26] See, e.g., (Nagel 2005, 113–147).

whole of humanity. Cosmopolitanism is seeking to debunk that intuition, to make us see that it is a prejudice, or an accident of history.

So the first step in the argument is to establish that citizenship constitutes a distinct normative role: it comes with a package of rights, duties, and responsibilities and it holds in virtue of some special relationship that holds between people of a particular state or political community. Which facts confer this role requires further argumentation. Some philosophers think the fact of being under the coercive control of a particular state is a necessary condition, but others dispute that.[27] It most certainly involves attitudes that people have toward one another, though it is hard to pinpoint what exactly these are.[28] Ronald Dworkin for example speaks of an attitude of equal respect and concern that members of a true community have toward one another.

As with parental obligation, I have no theory to offer here. What we should note is that the attitudes or emotions that we take to trigger citizenship reasons are not supposed to be the same as the ones that trigger reasons of friendship or family. The latter typically involve emotions of love and affection toward specific people. Citizenship by contrast does not—at least these days—require having such strong patriotic feelings toward one's fellow citizens or one's country. Perhaps patriotic love is a good thing for justice, or even essential for the stability of just institutions.[29] But that is different from saying that it is a necessary condition for duties of citizenship to kick in. Raz's objection to the idea of associative political obligations,[30] that not all of us identify with our country in this strong way, seems to me off the mark since the argument for political obligation being associative need not be grounded on this type of identification.

So let us assume, for the sake of the argument, that the category of citizenship obligations is genuine. It is a normative role that is necessarily reason-giving, in the sense of triggering special reasons to respect fellow citizens and treat them fairly in the distribution of collective resources, goods, and opportunities. Now it seems to me that it is a short distance from this proposition to the proposition that law necessarily has normative significance for our normative role as citizens. This is the second step in the argument for law's full-blooded normativity and it goes along the following line.

Law forms part of what John Rawls has called the basic structure of society:[31] its institutions are a means through which political decisions are made about how to distribute freedoms,

---

[27] See (Sangiovanni 2012, 79–110).

[28] Here is Mill's effort to capture them: "A portion of mankind may be said to constitute a Nationality, if they are united among themselves by common sympathies, which do not exist between them and any others—which make them cooperate with each other more willingly than with other people, desire to be under the same government, and desire that it should be government by themselves, or a portion of themselves, exclusively. This feeling of nationality may have been generated by various causes. Sometimes it is the effect of identity or race and descent. Community of language, community of religion, greatly contribute to it. Geographical limits are one of its causes. But the strongest of all is identity of political antecedents; the possession of national history, and consequent community of recollections; collective pride and humiliation, pleasure and regret, connected with the same incidents in the past. None of these circumstances, however, are necessarily sufficient by themselves," in (Mill 1977, 546) as quoted by (Rawls 1999, 23).

[29] See (Nussbaum, 2015).

[30] See (Raz 2006).

[31] See (Rawls 1999). There is disagreement however over whether the whole of law, and in particular private law, is part of the basic structure. For a recent discussion see (Scheffler 2015). See also (Dworkin 2008b).

goods, and opportunities across different persons. This is a weaker view than asserting the familiar Kantian thesis that law is a *necessary* tool for carrying out our responsibilities of justice, and securing individual rights. Once law is in place and it is practiced, people rely on how it distributes burdens and benefits, and form reasonable expectations around them. And since citizenship—we have now assumed—requires a fair distribution of burdens and benefits amongst the members of each political community, law becomes necessarily relevant. Which actions are required of us qua citizens depends on what the background distribution is, and the background distribution is in part determined by law. Think of taxation law: not only do we have reasons of justice to have it but also we have reasons of justice stemming from what *content* taxation law has, once it is enforced: in a country without progressive taxation rich people have citizenship reasons to share more of their wealth with their fellow citizens, and all citizens have reason to campaign and vote in favor of tax reform. Put differently, the fact that there is a legal rule requiring people to φ (e.g., pay a flat-rate tax of 10 percent) gives them a full-blooded reason to ψ (e.g., donate to charity and vote for progressive taxation).

Enoch concedes the possibility that legal rules to φ may necessarily give reasons to ψ,[32] and he also allows for the possibility that law systematically has normative relevance. He writes:

> Perhaps it can even be said that the law is more systematically normatively relevant: Perhaps it affects not just what it makes sense for you or me to do, but what it makes sense for all of us (for some "us") to do. And perhaps it affects what we have reason to do not in some anecdotal way but a more holistic way (within a specified domain).[33]

I find this difficult to square with his claim that law lacks full-blooded normativity. At the very least his claim must be weakened as follows: the fact that there is a legal rule requiring one to φ does not necessarily give one a moral reason to φ. But as we saw in the example of parenthood, that is not the way to test whether a practice has full-blooded normativity. It is a mistake to assume that a practice has full-blooded normativity if, and only if, there is moral reason to follow each and every one of its rules. Enoch does not find it philosophically interesting that law may have systematic relevance for what we have reason to do. But if I am right that this relevance—and the reason that it is systematic—is due to the normative role of citizenship, this is a mistake. We are asking whether law is necessarily reason-giving, and there is at least one important sense in which we can say that it is: it has necessary relevance for what citizens owe one another. Shouldn't philosophers be interested in the different domains of political morality and the duties of citizenship? And isn't the very idea of special normative roles at the heart of debates about consequentialism and deontology? If that is not of philosophical interest, I do not know what is.

But I sense a different worry here: legal philosophers want something more from the claim that law has full-blooded normativity than that it is relevant to what citizens owe one another as matter of justice. Even if this moral relevance is systematic or even necessary, it appears to be extrinsic to law. After all, even evil legal rules necessarily give citizens some type of reason: they give them reasons to oppose them and fight to repeal them. And

---

[32] (Enoch 2011, fn. 36).

[33] (Enoch 2018).

many non-legal facts affect what citizens have reason to do, such as natural catastrophes or fluctuating oil prices. Isn't the domain of law meant to determine *exclusively* a set of duties, rights, and responsibilities that are properly called legal? Put differently, aren't legal facts meant to trigger a normative role of their own?

I think the worry is valid and relates to the autonomy of law as a domain of political morality. Law, assuming it is by and large followed and enforced, manipulates (some of) the non-normative circumstances that pertain to what citizens owe one another, as a matter of justice. But why should we follow and enforce law in the first place, particularly if it changes the non-normative circumstances of justice in less than ideal ways?

This, I think, is the third and most difficult step toward establishing that law has full-blooded normativity. It is also, to my mind, the most important part of Ronald Dworkin's theory of law. Dworkin has argued that in striving for justice, political communities have a duty to act with integrity: they are required to act under principled consistency with their past decisions, to follow a coherent scheme of principles of justice, fairness, and due process across time. Put differently, citizens use law to pursue justice and, in pursuing justice, they are constrained by what they have done in the past. Integrity speaks to what citizens' duties are within the ordinary conditions of politics, where law has existed and practiced, rather than in ideal conditions. It computes the normative effect that political history (legislation, executive action, judicial judgments) has on obligations of justice. In Gerald Postema's apt phrase, integrity is justice in workclothes.[34] It makes facts about legal practice necessarily relevant to what we now have a duty to do qua citizens. And for Dworkin, courts have a responsibility to enforce only those citizens' obligations that are based on integrity.

The specifics of Dworkin's account however are not so important here, as the dialectic of his argument is clear. Citizenship is a normative role. As part of that role we must ask whether facts about our past political practice are relevant for how we are to pursue justice collectively, through our institutions. And part of that question involves which obligations of justice courts may enforce. Unless we deny outright that past political practice is relevant to what reasons of justice we now have, we owe an account of how that practice (which includes legal facts to do with statutes, judgments, executive acts) shapes the content of the duties of citizenship. And unless we deny outright that courts' primary responsibility is to enforce genuine obligations of justice, we owe an account of *which* obligations of justice courts may enforce. So let us assume that we do not deny any of that. And let us call *legal** all the reasons for action that citizens and courts have in virtue of their normative role, and that are in part constituted (or triggered) by facts to do with past political decisions. *Legal** facts would then be necessarily reason-giving in the most full-blooded sense possible.

Now are *legal** facts different from legal facts? The short answer might be: Who cares? If we have discovered that there is an animal, *law**, whose normativity is full-blooded, then who cares about that other animal, law, whose normativity is merely formal? Let us urge legal philosophers to dig their teeth into *law**, which is philosophically the interesting concept, and bury the concept of law in the philosophical graveyard. I have great sympathy for the short answer, but I also see the motivation of those convinced that there is no difference

[34] (Postema 2004).

between *law** and law: they want to establish not only that *law** best explains salient features of legal practice (such as the presence of non-factual disagreement in adjudication), but also the more general thesis that conceptual inquiries track moral inquiries.[35] They want to show for instance that even the concept of a *rule* is moralized: disagreement over the moral reasons that a practice gives, bottoms out to disagreement over what the rules of the practice are.[36] This is a worthy battle, but I do not think it is one we have to fight if reason-givingness is our main concern.

VII. Conclusion

We are familiar with the idea that certain facts trigger special normative roles, roles that contain moral rights and duties in a full-blooded moral sense. Citizenship is arguably one such role, and it grounds duties of justice and fairness to members of a political community. It can be argued further that facts about political practice (such as legislatures enacting statutes and courts handing down judgments) necessarily shape the obligations of justice that citizens have toward one another. Finally, it can be argued that the normative role of the judge is to enforce only those obligations of justice that have been shaped by past political practice. If successful, these arguments establish that some dimension of legal practice is necessarily reason-giving, for both citizens and judges.

Those who want to deny that law is necessarily reason-giving have the ball on their court. They can deny that special normative roles exist on consequentialist or other grounds, or they can accept that normative roles exist and are necessarily reason-giving, but deny that political morality contains any such special normative roles, or deny that *citizenship* is one of them. Finally, they can accept the category of special reasons of citizenship, but deny that facts about legal practice are necessarily relevant to the reasons for action citizens and judges have, as part of their normative roles.

I have argued in this chapter that it is with these arguments that we need to engage when we ask whether law has full-blooded normativity. By contrast, debating whether the normativity of legal rules is formal or full-blooded is like debating whether fool's gold is gold: the answer is obvious and the question is uninteresting. If I am right, this is good news for general jurisprudence. Its philosophical battles turn on such foundational questions as the merits of consequentialism, the nature of special normative roles, and the structure of political morality. Being foundational, these questions inevitably engage metaethical assumptions about the structure of morality as a whole. Far from being close to a divorce, general jurisprudence and moral philosophy are enjoying an exciting and long-lasting relationship.

References

Altham, Jimmy E.J. 2009. *Wicked Promises*. In *Exercises in Analysis: Essays by Students of Casimir Lewy*, edited by Ian Hacking. Cambridge: Cambridge University Press.

---

[35] See (Dworkin 2004); (Dworkin 2008a) and (Coleman and Simchen 2003).

[36] Dworkin, 1978, ch. 3.

Archard, David, and Benatar, David (eds.). 2010. *Procreation and Parenthood: The Ethics of Bearing and Rearing Children.* Oxford: Oxford University Press.

Coleman, Jules. 2001. *The Practice of Principle.* Oxford: Oxford University Press.

Coleman, Jules, and Simchen, Ori. 2003. "Law." *Legal Theory* 9(1): 1–41.

Darwall, Stephen. 2006. *The Second Person Standpoint: Morality, Respect and Accountability.* Cambridge, MA: Harvard University Press.

Dworkin, Ronald, 1978. *Taking Rights Seriously.* London: Duckworth.

_____. 1998. *Law's Empire.* Oxford: Hart.

_____. 2004. "Hart's Postscript and The Character of Political Philosophy." *Oxford Journal of Legal Studies* 24 (1): 1–37.

_____. 2008a. "The Concepts of Law". In *Justice in Robes*, edited by Ronald Dworkin and Frank Henry Sommer. Cambridge, MA: Harvard University Press, pp. 223–240

_____. 2008b. "Rawls and the Law". In *Justice in Robes*. Cambridge, MA: Harvard University Press, pp. 241–261.

Enoch, David. 2011. "Reason-Giving the Law." In *Oxford Studies in the Philosophy of Law,* Vol. I, edited by Leslie Green and Brian Leiter. Oxford: Oxford University Press.

_____. 2018. "Is General Jurisprudence Interesting?" in this volume.

Gardner, John, and Macklem, Timothy. 2002. "Reasons." In *The Oxford Handbook of Jurisprudence and Philosophy of Law,* edited by Jules Coleman and Scott Shapiro. Oxford: Oxford University Press.

Greenberg, Mark. 2011. "The Standard Picture and its Discontents." In *Oxford Studies in the Philosophy of Law,* Vol. I, edited by Leslie Green and Brian Leiter. Oxford: Oxford University Press.

Hardimon, Michael, 1994. "Role Obligations." *The Journal of Philosophy* 91: 333–363.

Hart, H. L. A. 2012. "Postscript." In *The Concept of Law,* 3rd ed. Oxford: Oxford University Press.

Kyritsis, Dimitrios. 2008. "What Is Good about Legal Conventionalism?" *Legal Theory* 14(2): 135–166.

Letsas, George. 2014. "The DNA of Conventions." *Law and Philosophy* 33 (5): 535–571.

Marmor, Andrei. 2009. *Social Conventions: From Language to Law*. Princeton: Princeton University Press.

Mill, J. S. 1977. "Considerations on Representative Government." In *John Stuart Mill: Collected Works*, Vol. 19, edited by J. M. Robson. Toronto: University of Toronto Press.

Nagel, Thomas. 1970. *The Possibility of Altruism.* Oxford: Clarendon Press.

_____. 2005. "The Problem of Global Justice." *Philosophy and Public Affairs* 33(2): 113–147.

Nussbaum, Martha. 2015. *Political Emotions.* Cambridge, MA: Harvard University Press.

Owens, David. 2012. *Shaping the Normative Landscape*. Oxford: Oxford University Press.

Parfit, Derek. 1984. *Reasons and Persons*. Oxford: Oxford University Press.

Plunkett, David, and Shapiro, Scott. 2017. "Law, Morality and Everything Else: General Jurisprudence as a Branch of Metanormative Inquiry." *Ethics* 128(1): 37–68.

Pogge, Thomas, 1992. "Cosmopolitanism and Sovereignty." *Ethics* 103(1):48–75.

_____. 1994. "An Egalitarian Law of Peoples." *Philosophy and Public Affairs* 23(3): 195–224.

_____. 2001. "Priorities of Global Justice." *Metaphilosophy* 32(1/2): 6–24.

Postema, Gerald. 2004. "Justice in Workclothes." In *Dworkin and His Critics,* edited by Justine Burley. London: Blackwell.

Prusak, Bernard G. 2001. "The Costs of Procreation." *Journal of Social Philosophy* 42:61–75.

Raz, Joseph. 2006. "Revisiting the Service Conception of Authority." *Minnesota Law Review* 90:1003–1044.

Rawls, John. 1999. *A Theory of Justice*, rev. ed. Cambridge, MA: Harvard University Press.

Sangiovanni, Andrea. 2012. "The Irrelevance of Coercion, Imposition and Framing to Distributive Justice." *Philosophy and Public Affairs* 40(2):79–110.

Scheffler, Samuel, 2015. "Distributive Justice, the Basic Structure, and the Place of Private Law." *Oxford Journal of Legal Studies* 35(2):213–235.

Searle, John R. 2001. *Rationality in Action.* Cambridge, MA: MIT Press.

Shapiro, Scott. 2011. *Legality*. Cambridge, MA: Harvard University Press.

Singer, Peter. 2009. *The Life You Can Save*. New York: Random House.

Stavropoulos, Nicos. 2014. "Legal Interpretivism." *The Stanford Encyclopedia of Philosophy* (Summer 2014 Edition), edited by Edward N. Zalta. https://plato.stanford.edu/archives/sum2014/entries/law-interpretivist/.

9 Defining Normativity

Stephen Finlay

IN RECENT JARGON, *metanormative theory* explores fundamental questions crosscutting ethics, political and legal philosophy, aesthetics, epistemology, and more. It is described as the study of *normativity*, suggesting there is something, called 'normativity', that is the common object of the competing theories of the philosophers working in this field. The literature on "normativity" has in a short time become overwhelmingly huge.[1,2] A curious layperson might reasonably ask, "So, what is this *normativity*, then?" This innocent little question might already be interrogation enough to make philosophers squirm and sweat, because it is hard to find any definition that every metanormative theorist can agree on, as we'll see. At least one leading practitioner, Derek Parfit, has recently gone so far as to claim that many philosophers who appear to disagree with him about the nature of normativity must be using their terms with different meanings, and talking about something else entirely.[3] One may reasonably be skeptical, as I previously was. Dismissing opponents' claims as not even about the same subject seems to foreclose on the possibility of substantive theoretical disagreement prematurely. This chapter finds, in partial agreement with Parfit, that philosophical discussion about "normativity" is plagued by systematic ambiguities contributing to significant confusion, as there are many things that "normativity" can reasonably be taken

[1] A *Philosopher's Index* search on 'normativity' (January 12, 2017) returns 2,171 records, 1,076 published in the 2010s (to 2016) alone, from 23 records in the 1980s and 216 records in the 1990s.

[2] I use single-quote marks to refer to words and expressions, and double-quote marks for both scare quotes and ordinary quotation.

[3] E.g., (2011, 439f).

Dimensions of Normativity. David Plunkett, Scott J. Shapiro, and Kevin Toh.

to be.[4] However, it ultimately finds cause for optimism, against Parfit, that very different theoretical positions are nonetheless engaged in substantive disagreements over common questions.

Some readers may be exasperated. Can't language get out of our way and let us think and talk directly about the thing itself? Every philosopher understands the importance of scrutinizing our (meta) language for equivocations and other ways our thinking can be led astray by its linguistic garb. But surely not every philosophical issue conceals significant semantic perils, and the study of normativity might be thought safe for the semantics-averse, since 'normativity' is a term of art recently introduced specifically to get a terminological grip on something elusive in ordinary language. Nonetheless, I've come to believe that debates about "normativity" are mired in equivocation and terminologically-induced confusion, and can only be moved forward by reflecting on the meaning(s) of the word.

This chapter aims to advance understanding of the nature of normativity—or rather, of various things that may go by the name. Because my concerns are ultimately metaphysical rather than semantic, I largely avoid making claims about what 'normativity' *should* be used to mean. Neither will I try to give a complete taxonomy of senses. Instead, I'll put pressure on three major fissures, in order to cast light on some central controversies. I start with the distinction between the "normativity" ascribed to (i) language and thought, and (ii) facts and properties, in order to explore the possibility of univocity between cognitivists' and noncognitivists' claims about "normativity". Then I examine the possibility of univocity between different kinds of cognitivists, such as non-naturalists, subjectivist naturalists, and objectivist naturalists, by examining two further distinctions: between (a) abstract versus substantive senses of 'normativity', and (b) formal versus robust senses. This leads to a special kind of hybrid view of normative judgment I'll call *perspectivism*, which has the resources to explain how different cognitivists could be united by interest in a common phenomenon, while at the same time potentially using 'normativity' with significantly different meanings. Whether or not this perspectivism is correct, observing the option casts helpfully disambiguating light on the debates over at least the nature, existence, extension, and analyzability of "normativity".

I. Preliminaries

First I need to explain and defend my basic assumptions. This chapter addresses two words: the noun 'normativity' and the adjective 'normative'. Since 'normativity' is just the nowadays-preferred nominalization of the adjective 'normative',[5] one might expect these to be interdefinable as follows: to describe something as 'normative' (in a particular sense) is to ascribe it a property that is denoted by 'normativity' (in a corresponding sense). We'll

---

[4] This aligns with a central theme of my 2014 book, that metaethical debates largely stem from a "confusion of tongues". However, there I was insufficiently sensitive to the ambiguities in the word 'normativity' itself, leading to some seemingly inconsistent claims, and inviting skepticism about my claims to have reductively analyzed normativity (e.g., Dowell 2016; Laskowski 2014). This chapter is partly a mea culpa and an attempt to clarify those claims.

[5] Overtaking 'normativeness' in the early 1970s, per Google's ngram viewer.

encounter some important exceptions to this rule, but I will shift between noun and adjective as suits the context.

I will argue that these words are multiply ambiguous, as used by metanormative theorists (subsequently, "theorists"). Readers might be skeptical that any systematic ambiguities would go unnoticed by so many trained philosophers. When we think about lexical ambiguity, we typically consider forms of simple *homonymy*: identically spelled and pronounced words with unrelated meanings, such as 'hide' (animal skin versus to conceal), or the standard example of 'bank' (financial institution versus sloping landform). However, the ambiguities at issue here are cases rather of *polysemy*: identically spelled and pronounced words with distinct but closely related meanings, as classically illustrated by Aristotle's example of 'healthy' (as of food versus as of organisms). Polysemies are often subtle and easily overlooked even by sophisticated thinkers, as well as being ubiquitous in natural language,[6] and therefore pose a much greater equivocation risk in philosophy. So denying that metanormative theory is unified by interest in a common object of inquiry does not imply, implausibly, that it is a Frankenstein's monster stitched together out of unrelated parts, akin to "Hideology", the (imaginary) study of concealment and animal skins. I suspect many theorists are aware 'normative' is polysemous, but that few realize how much this has confused metanormative debate.

In identifying different possible senses for 'normativity', I will be offering *descriptive definitions*. In particular, I will be seeking what I'll call theorists' *effective* definitions, which articulate the concepts that theorists are employing. Such a definition is reference-fixing for a theorist (or use-fixing, for words with nondescriptive functions) and therefore "nonnegotiable": to talk about something that doesn't satisfy the description is necessarily to change the subject.[7] Effective definitions must be sharply distinguished from theorists' *official* definitions, or what they explicitly offer as definitions, whether analytic or synthetic. This distinction is important because theorists' official definitions often constitute substantive theories of the nature of their objects, even when ostensibly offered as analytic or nonsubstantial. Official definitions are therefore "negotiable", and a theorist can in principle come to recognize hers as incorrect and needing revision. Ascribing effective definitions is a difficult and often presumptuous task: I will offer tentative hypotheses about what various theorists' concepts may be on the basis of their statements, but these must be weighed against the alternative possibility that those statements are merely mistaken.

The proposal to offer "definitions" may elicit concerns that some crucial questions are being begged from the outset. These concerns can be allayed, because I'll take a broad, ecumenical approach to the practice of definition.[8] One concern is on behalf of non-naturalists such as Parfit, who often claim that normativity is "indefinable", because primitive and sui generis. However, I allow that an adequate definition of 'normativity' need only individuate the

[6] As (Fogal 2016) points out in rebuke of my 2014 book.

[7] Following (Joyce 2001, 3–4). A definition's being nonnegotiable in this sense doesn't preclude the theorist from accepting a change of subject, even under the same terminology. Note that concepts in my sense are different from David Copp's (2017) "ways of thinking", which are not reference-fixing and can misrepresent their objects.

[8] A possible exception is the idea of reference-magnetism. I assume that it is something about the practice, mind, or situation of the speaker that determines what she is talking about, rather than the nature of the object itself.

property in question (perhaps only privately), and needn't constitute an analysis of it.[9] For example, I take seriously *ostensive* definitions of the following kind: *that* property (mentally ostending something being cognized, perceived, remembered, or imagined). Definitions of this kind are both compatible with and familiar from the writings of non-naturalists.

A second concern comes from semantic externalists, who may complain that for a term, such as 'normativity', to successfully refer to something, there needn't be any description that every competent user of the term has in mind or associates with the word; i.e., that no description or concept has the status of being the word's conventional meaning. 'Normativity' might rather be the *name* of something. However, I don't assume that an adequate definition of 'normativity' must identify its conventional meaning, and I allow that different people might employ different, perhaps private, definitions or concepts for the same word. This might appear to make claims of ambiguity too cheap, but I'll also assume it is sufficient for univocity between two speakers that their different concepts contingently pick out the same reference; i.e., that sameness of meaning requires only that they are talking about the same thing. Finally, semantic externalists might also object that speakers could use a term such as 'normativity' to refer without having any concept or description of the reference in mind at all; e.g., by virtue of their use standing in a causal chain with other uses. While skeptical, I allow for this too: an adequate definition for a particular use of 'normativity' might simply be a description of the facts that fix the reference for that use, such as facts about the causal chain.

II. Univocity between Cognitivists and Noncognitivists

The lack of any agreed-upon characterization of "normativity" might be thought simply an unsurprising consequence of metanormative theory's being an area of live debate, in which there are competing views about its nature. But researchers in disputed fields don't generally have any difficulty agreeing on some characterization of their common object of inquiry. Scientists disputing the chemical composition of water in the eighteenth century, for example, could agree at least that water is the stuff that flows in Earth's rivers, fills its oceans, and falls from the sky in the form of rain. If we are to find a common object for metanormative theorizing, it will presumably be through examining the common ground: What can all parties to the metanormative debate agree on?

The possible answers to this question are seriously constrained by the fact that the field includes significant numbers both of theorists who claim that "normativity" is a property of facts, properties, and relations (such as ought-facts, goodness and rightness, and being-a-reason-for), and also of theorists who deny there are any "normative" facts, properties, and relations, but nonetheless don't generally deny that some kinds of things are "normative" or that there is "normativity". Prima facie it might seem that common ground can be found in applications to language and thought—as I have previously assumed. This includes linguistic and mental *entities* such as words, sentences, concepts, and beliefs, and *acts* such as

[9] In particular, it need only identify it by an individuating property *of* normativity. Even if Parfit is talking about a non-natural property, I can think and talk about the same property in virtue of the definition or concept, *the property Parfit is talking about*.

utterances, assertions, claims, and judgments, but I'll write in conveniently fudgy terms of "expressions and judgments".

A. The Normativity of Language and Thought

Surely all theorists agree that some language and/or thought is normative? At least, I know of none who refuse to classify any expressions or judgments as 'normative'. But are they all predicating the same property with the term? This question might be thought to stir up needless trouble. Metanormative theorists are members of one contiguous linguistic community, thinking and writing in close engagement with each other, and largely assuming that they are all talking about the same thing. While there is considerable disagreement about the proper extension of the term (exactly *which* expressions and judgments are normative?), this arguably resembles either garden-variety vagueness or substantive disagreement over borderline cases, since there is also convergence on many central cases, such as the words 'ought', 'wrong', and judgments about reasons to act. While I agree that these considerations lend a default presumption of univocity, this is undermined by closer scrutiny.

What does it mean to classify an expression or judgment as "normative"? Many theorists, who I'll call *cognitivists*, seem to favor an answer along the following, representationalist lines: an expression or judgment is "normative" just in case (or at least, only if) it is *about* something in the world of a special kind. What kind? The obvious answer is: of a "normative" kind. This answer is significant here for two reasons. First, it introduces us to an initial ambiguity (polysemy), just within cognitivists' use. Second, it casts doubt on the univocity of different theorists' talk about "normative" expressions or judgments.

This approach requires an ambiguity in 'normative', because whatever it is for something to be a "normative" fact or property, it can't be *to be about something normative*—or about anything at all, since facts (or states of affairs) and properties aren't in the business of being "about" things. Rather, it requires us to distinguish between *ontological* and *representational* senses of 'normative', as follows:[10]

> NORMATIVE$_{ont}$: (As of facts and properties); Having a property P of some special kind.
> NORMATIVE$_{rep}$: (As of expressions and judgments); Being about something normative$_{ont}$.

(To help readers, my definitions are collected together at the chapter's end.) These entries may need to be divided further into different ontological and representational senses, but for now let's suppose this is sufficiently fine-grained.[11] The relationship between NORMATIVE$_{rep}$ and NORMATIVE$_{ont}$ manifests a common pattern, or *regular polysemy*, which can also be

---

[10] Cf. (Eklund 2017, 64). Some theorists ("quietists") purport to recognize the existence of normative facts and properties without incurring any "ontological" commitments (e.g., (Parfit 2011); (Scanlon 2014)), while disavowing "quasi-realism" (as defined in (Blackburn 1993)). For discussion see (Dreier 2016); (Streumer 2017). Since I understand ontology simply as the study of what exists, I ignore this complication here.

[11] Recognizing these senses is metaphysically noncommittal. Perhaps there is no property P, or nothing instantiates it; then nothing is normative$_{ont}$. Or perhaps there are no normative$_{rep}$ expressions or judgments.

observed, for example, in the adjectives 'mythological' and 'aesthetic'. Mythological$_1$ language (= language about mythology) needn't itself be mythological$_2$ (= existing only in cultural imagination); aesthetic$_1$ language (= language about aesthetic qualities) needn't itself be aesthetic$_2$ (= possess aesthetic qualities).

We can't stop with just these two senses of 'normative', because they apparently fail to accommodate the claims of *noncognitivists*, who acknowledge the existence of "normative" expressions and judgments, but deny that they are about "normative" facts and properties. This includes both *nondescriptivists* who deny that "normative" expressions and judgments are about or represent anything at all, and virtually all so-called *hybrid theorists*, who allow that "normative" expressions and judgments are representational, but attribute their status as "normative" not to their representing something normative$_{ont}$, but to some other (noncognitive) function or property they have. As this makes clear, my distinction here between "cognitivism" and "noncognitivism" differs importantly from the usual distinction drawn in these terms. The issue here is not whether normative judgments have cognitive (representational, descriptive) content per se, but whether their status *as normative* is due to their cognitive content.[12]

Noncognitivists are obviously committed to holding that there are no normative$_{rep}$ expressions or judgments, at least in our ordinary "normative" language and thought. So when noncognitivists classify an expression or judgment as "normative", they must mean something other than NORMATIVE$_{rep}$. Indeed, while being normative$_{rep}$ would evidently entail being descriptive, many theorists use the words 'normative' and 'descriptive' as terms of direct contrast. Noncognitivists' talk about "normative" expressions and judgments seems to require a definition conforming to the following schema:

> NORMATIVE$_{funct}$: (As of expressions or judgments); Having the nonrepresentational function F.

There is a wide variety of noncognitivist theories about function F, although I presume they all construe it as a broadly psychological function. For example, it could be the function of *expressing the speaker's motivational attitudes*, or the function of *motivating attitudes or behavior*: "putting pressure on choice and action" (Blackburn 1993). So this entry itself might need to be divided into distinct functional senses of 'normative', implying a failure of univocity even between different noncognitivists' talk about "normativity", although I'll ignore this complication here. Whatever F might be, however, its nonrepresentational character entails that whether an expression or judgment is normative$_{funct}$ is a completely different issue from whether it is normative$_{rep}$.[13]

If I have correctly albeit roughly identified the effective definitions underlying cognitivists' and noncognitivists' talk about "normative" expressions and judgments, then it seems there is indeed no real common ground over whether there is normative language and thought, only a "verbal agreement" consisting in superficial overlap in application of an ambiguous vocabulary. If this was the best hope for finding common ground and thereby a

---

[12] Cf. (Ridge 2014, 79–80); (Streumer 2017, 91–92).

[13] Cf. (Copp 2007, 266); (Streumer 2017, 128).

common object for theories of "normativity", as we were supposing, then perhaps there is no common object at all. Since noncognitivists deny that "normative" language and thought derive their claim to "normativity" from representing special kinds of facts, they can be expected to deny that anything is normative$_{ont}$. And since cognitivists deny that "normative" language and thought derive their "normativity" from a special nonrepresentational function they possess, they can be expected at least to deny that normativity$_{funct}$ is what their investigations are concerned with. So with respect to cognitivists' and noncognitivists' claims about "normativity", Parfit's radical pessimism might seem vindicated: they are just talking about completely different things.

It is too early to draw this conclusion, however, because we can dig deeper to try to locate an underlying univocity between cognitivists and noncognitivists. Even philosophers who explicitly endorse definitions along the lines of NORMATIVE$_{rep}$ or NORMATIVE$_{funct}$ might not be identifying their effective definitions, and their official definitions may turn out to represent competing, substantive, falsifiable theories of a common subject-matter.

B. *Making Do*

I'll now explore a solution that might initially seem promising but I think ultimately fails, before introducing a better solution in the next section. We might hope to find univocity by identifying the cognitivist's normativity$_{ont}$ with the noncognitivist's normativity$_{funct}$. In principle, the extremely thin definitions above aren't incompatible: having some nonrepresentational function *is* a property of a special kind. So might cognitivists and noncognitivists be unified by common interest in a single functional property, normativity$_{ont/funct}$? Their differences would then consist in a substantive disagreement about this property: cognitivists maintain that it is a property of facts and properties, while noncognitivists maintain that it is exclusively a property of expressions and judgments.

For illustration, consider the familiar but vague identification of "normativity" with *prescriptivity*, glossed as the function of *guiding* agents or "telling them what to do."[14] A noncognitivist might claim that only expressions and/or judgments prescribe or tell agents what to do. A cognitivist might think that prescriptivity is "objective", and a function of some part of the "world itself", if of anything at all.[15] From noncognitivists' point of view, cognitivism is substantively mistaken because it attributes a property of expressions and judgments to facts and properties in the world—perhaps due to committing the "projective fallacy" of mistaking our subjective reactions to the world for objective qualities that prompt those reactions.[16] From cognitivists' point of view, noncognitivism is substantively mistaken because it attributes a property of facts and properties to certain of our expressions and judgments, which are instead about things with that property—perhaps due to committing the "psychologistic fallacy" of analyzing something objective in terms of our subjective reactions to it.

---

[14] Cf. (Copp 2012). I suspect the intuitive appeal of this proposal is due to this language of "prescriptivity" and "guidance" being ambiguous in exactly the same way.

[15] E.g., (Mackie 1977, 23).

[16] E.g., (Hume 1739/1896); (Nietzsche 1882/1974); (Mackie 1977); (Blackburn 1998).

Could metanormative theory consist in substantive disagreements over a common object such as normativity$_{ont/funct}$? One problem comes, ironically, from what we began by supposing the best hope for common ground: that certain expressions and judgments are "normative". For cognitivists cannot mean to say that these expressions and judgments are normative$_{ont/funct}$. They certainly *may* hold that language or thought is normative$_{ont}$, which is plausibly what is at issue in the debates over the "normativity of meaning" in the philosophy of language (e.g., whether a word's having a particular meaning has entailments about how it *ought* to be used), and over the normativity of intentional attitudes in the philosophy of mind (e.g., whether a particular kind of mental state constitutively involves being *rationally required* to behave in some way[17]). But this could not be what cognitivists mean in classifying certain expressions (such as 'ought') and judgments as "normative". First, cognitivism as such is neutral on the debates over the normativity of meaning and attitudes, and so clearly isn't committed to holding that expressions or judgments in general are normative$_{ont}$. Yet no cognitivist denies there are any "normative" expressions or judgments. Second, cognitivists' classification of certain expressions or judgments as "normative" or "nonnormative" makes no sense on the supposition that they mean NORMATIVE$_{ont/funct}$, because there is no good reason to think that only (e.g.) words that by the cognitivists' lights are *about* normativity$_{ont}$, such as 'ought', 'wrong', etc., and not others such as 'tall' or 'blue', are themselves normative$_{ont}$. This is not a plausible alternative to NORMATIVE$_{rep}$ as an interpretation of cognitivists' claims.

This approach fails to find univocity in cognitivists' and noncognitivists' talk of "normative" expressions and judgments, but you might think this needn't be a serious problem. From cognitivists' point of view, the most important sense of "normativity" is normativity$_{ont}$. From noncognitivists' point of view, the important sense is normativity$_{funct}$. If in fact these are the same thing, normativity$_{ont/funct}$, then we have found a common, central object for cognitivists' and noncognitivists' claims. If cognitivists' talk about "normative" expressions or judgments has to be understood in an idiosyncratic, derivative sense, this may be interesting but not very important.

However, we began by thinking that the apparent agreement that certain expressions and judgments are "normative" was the most promising place to find common ground. If this rather turns out to be equivocal, we have to seriously ask whether we have any good reasons to think that cognitivists and noncognitivists are talking about the same thing. The evidence all seems to point the other way. First, as already noted, they locate "normativity" in entirely different places. Cognitivists find it in facts and properties, disagreeing among themselves whether it is also ever to be found in language or thought (generally), while noncognitivists deny it can ever be found in facts and properties, locating it only in language or thought (of a specific class). Second, there is some reason to doubt they are even talking about the same classes of expressions and judgments, since there is disagreement even over the exemplars of "normative" language. Noncognitivists often take *imperatives* such as 'Keep off the grass!' to be central and particularly naked examples of normativity$_{funct}$, but cognitivists characteristically deny that they are "normative" at all.[18]

[17] E.g., (Wedgwood 2007).

[18] Cf. (Parfit 2011, 291), on W. D. Falk.

Finally, cognitivists' theories about the nature of normativity$_{\text{ont}}$ are generally radically different from noncognitivists' theories about the nature of normativity$_{\text{funct}}$. (i) Many cognitivists are *non-naturalists*, holding that "normativity" can't be reduced to or identified with anything natural, whereas noncognitivists hold that the "normativity" of expressions and judgments is naturalistically analyzable. (ii) Cognitivists typically don't deny that "normative" language and thought characteristically has the natural properties that noncognitivists identify with normativity$_{\text{funct}}$, such as expressing attitudes and putting motivational pressure on agents. They just deny that this is the property of normativity$_{\text{ont}}$ they're thinking about. (iii) Whereas cognitivists all think that some fact or property's being "normative" has essential entailments about what (e.g.) someone *ought* or *has reason* to do, noncognitivist identifications of some expression or judgment as "normative" involve no such commitments on the part of the theorist. Suppose a sadist judges that *the suffering of innocents is good*; noncognitivists may identify this as a normative$_{\text{funct}}$ judgment, but typically would deny that it follows from this that there is anything that the sadist herself, or anybody else, ought or has a reason to do. Noncognitivists do not necessarily or generally claim, for example, that if an agent makes the "normative" judgment that *she herself ought to* φ, then she ought to ϕ, or be motivated to ϕ, etc.—although something of the kind would be implied by the judgment's being normative$_{\text{ont}}$ rather than merely normative$_{\text{funct}}$.

Given all these differences over the bearers, the exemplars, the nature, and the implications of "normativity", if cognitivists and noncognitivists were talking about the same property, normativity$_{\text{ont/funct}}$, then one party or the other would have to be extremely confused. We should prefer a more charitable interpretation, if one can be found.

C. *Ostending Normativity*

Many other kinds of effective definitions could be considered in the hope of leveraging the superficial convergence in classifying expressions and judgments as "normative" into a common subject-matter for cognitivists' and noncognitivists' claims about "normativity". Rather than surveying a variety of approaches that ultimately fail, I'll now sketch the approach I consider most promising. This takes the form of ostensive, natural (or non-natural) kind definitions, which look to one or more samples of expressions or judgments to pick out some underlying common characteristic, the identity and nature of which is open to dispute. Schematically:

> NORMATIVE$_{\text{lang/judg-ost}}$: (As of expressions/judgments); Having the common property of samples $n_1, n_2, \ldots$

Theorists who appeal to different samples would be operating with different versions of this kind of definition, but this is no barrier to univocity in talk of "normative" expressions or judgments so long as their definitions pick out the same underlying property or kind.

This approach has a number of things in its favor as an interpretation of metanormative theory. First, it can be motivated by the plausible observation that metanormative inquiry typically begins from reflection on an ordinary, ubiquitous practice of making a certain kind of claim or judgment. Second, many theorists endorse it either explicitly[19] or implicitly by

---

[19] E.g., (Wittgenstein 1930/1997), which predates adoption of the term 'normative', but clearly addresses the same topic.

the way they introduce their quarry. Parfit, for example, appeals to a particular judgment (*I ought to jump*) in a particular scenario (*Burning Hotel*—in which one's hotel is on fire and the only way out is through the second-story window) to fix on the kind of judgment that interests him.[20] Third, it plausibly locates a common object for cognitivists and noncognitivists, who can agree (mostly)[21] on what is and isn't a paradigm of "normative" language or thought, and that this class of expressions or judgments shares some philosophically important property that is (part of) what interests them. We could then interpret the parties as disagreeing substantively over whether normativity$_{\text{lang/judg-ost}}$ is to be identified as normativity$_{\text{rep}}$ or rather as normativity$_{\text{funct}}$; i.e., whether the common property that unifies the class of normative$_{\text{lang/judg-ost}}$ language and thought is the property of being about something that is normative$_{\text{ont}}$, or the property of having some nondescriptive function F.

Obstacles to this approach remain, however. These seem best overcome by opting for a thought- or judgment-based definition (NORMATIVE$_{\text{judg-ost}}$) rather than a language-based one (NORMATIVE$_{\text{lang-ost}}$).[22] This is partly because the words commonly identified as "normative" are at least often ambiguous between normative and nonnormative uses or senses, making it difficult to ostend "normativity" by linguistic samples alone.[23] We can plausibly identify a derivative, theory-neutral sense of 'normative' as applying to language, as follows:

> NORMATIVE$_{\text{lang-exp-judg}}$: (As of language); Having the property of being conventionally used to express normative$_{\text{judg-ost}}$ judgments.

So, we might hope, cognitivists and noncognitivists can agree that they are interested in normative$_{\text{judg-ost}}$ judgments, and derivatively, normative$_{\text{lang-exp-judg}}$ language.

Some cognitivists may seem to resist this attempt at assimilation. Parfit, for example, insists that he's fundamentally interested in a certain property of *facts and properties* that he is directly acquainted with (perhaps picked out by an ostensive ontological definition, NORMATIVITY$_{\text{ont-ost(Parfit)}}$), and derivatively in judgments about that property (i.e., normative$_{\text{rep(Parfit)}}$ judgments), as in his *Burning Hotel* example. He expresses uncertainty about whether his opponents ever make these kinds of judgments, or whether ordinary natural language even contains normative$_{\text{rep(Parfit)}}$ words.[24] Taking Parfit at his word, if his suspicions are correct then he and his opponents would indeed be talking about different things. However, if his suspicions are incorrect then, even taking him at his word, this approach can secure common objects for theorists' talk of "normative" expressions

---

[20] (Parfit 2011, 326–327) (elsewhere, however, he focuses on second-personal/advice versions of the scenario); (Wedgwood 2007, 1); (Thomson 2008, 1).

[21] This approach is robust enough to survive some disagreement over exemplars. For example, the parties might be able to agree that whether imperatives such as 'Keep off the grass!' are properly classified as "normative" depends on whether they share the underlying property of declaratives such as 'You ought to keep off the grass'.

[22] This focus is championed in (Laskowski 2017). My previous work focuses on language instead.

[23] Here I have in mind not so much the distinction between "robust" and "formal" senses of normative terms (addressed in Section III.B, but that between normative and epistemic uses of modals such as 'must' and 'ought', and between normative and (merely) explanatory uses of 'reason', etc.

[24] (Parfit 2011, 293, 304, 369); see also (Moore 1903).

and judgments—for example, if parties on both sides are employing effective definitions of the form NORMATIVE$_{\text{judg-ost}}$ using samples that are as a matter of fact of the same kind. Optimism seems justified, given that we are (1) all human agents with the same cognitive faculties, (2) who (at least in English-speaking metanormative theory) are members of the same linguistic community, (3) largely apply "normative" vocabulary in the same ways, to the same objects and actions in the same scenarios,[25] and (4) employ these words similarly in regulating our conduct and communicating with others.

The main problem facing this approach is that ostension of samples alone might not be enough to fix on a particular underlying kind or property. The same set of samples can, and presumably will, be exemplars of multiple different kinds. A flat-footed example is that most theorists provide samples of words that have in common that they are members of the kind, *words of English*. Of course, we can easily narrow in on a more plausible range of kinds by including examples of what is excluded; e.g., *the common property shared by words such as 'ought' and 'good', but not by words such as 'tall' and 'blue'.* But even here we might reasonably worry that the samples ostended underdetermine a particular reference for normativity$_{\text{judg-ost}}$. Perhaps, for example, the samples feature both normativity$_{\text{funct}}$ *and* normativity$_{\text{rep}}$ (cognitivists do not generally deny that these words have the functions that noncognitivists describe, after all); do our definitions then pick out one, the other, both, or neither?

Is there any way of narrowing in on the relevant kind of judgment that doesn't exclude either cognitivists or noncognitivists? Common ground can arguably be found over the role of normative judgment in practical deliberation.[26] Approximately, normative judgments are the kinds of judgments that we aim at reaching to close our deliberations, and on which we directly base our decisions or actions. This is certainly something that at least some cognitivists and noncognitivists agree about. For example, David Enoch (2011a) is a non-naturalist cognitivist who claims that normative judgments are "deliberatively indispensible"; i.e., one simply isn't deliberating if not employing normative concepts and reasoning toward normative judgments. The naturalist noncognitivist Allan Gibbard (2003) agrees: normative judgments just *are* deliberative judgments about what to do. Enoch and Gibbard substantively disagree about the nature of the judgments that play this role: Enoch thinks they are judgments about certain kinds of facts and properties, while Gibbard thinks they are noncognitive attitudes of a certain kind (roughly, plans or intentions).

---

[25] This may seem to overlook Parfit's disagreement with Humeans such as Bernard Williams over whether there are any "external" reasons unconnected to an agent's motivations. However, this may reflect less first-order disagreement than one might expect. Williams' (1981) famous example of alleged external reasons (of family tradition) would presumably be rejected by Parfit too, and internalists often accept the reasons that theorists such as Parfit allege to be external (e.g., moral and prudential reasons), rather claiming they are internal.

[26] E.g., (Schroeter and Schroeter ms): "What's distinctive of the normative is a characteristic psychological role played by certain concepts in deliberation and action"; (Wedgwood 2007); (Eklund 2017, 38); (McPherson 2018). See (Silverstein 2017) for a dissenting view on which normative concepts are rather *about* (sound) deliberation; cf. (Williams 1981). Note also that this strategy looks problematic in application to (e.g.) epistemic or aesthetic normativity. Here we might either try to find some epistemic/aesthetic analog to deliberation, or deny that these are "normativity" in the same sense (perhaps, for example, they are merely "formally normative"; see Section III.B).

It may seem a problem that not all cognitivists agree that "normative" judgments are deliberatively indispensable. We're already noted Parfit's skepticism about whether all agents even make (what he means by) "normative" judgments.[27] Since he never denies that all agents deliberate and make decisions, he would presumably allow that some of us may close our deliberations or base our decisions on something other than "normative" judgments. I expect he and others would insist that normative judgments are merely the kind of judgments that *rational* agents aim to base decisions on, or that agents *ought* to aim to base decisions on, and would charge my attempted characterization with the psychologistic fallacy. This is a reason not to try to turn our proposed platitude into an *analytic* definition, true in virtue of meaning. However, an ostensive-style definition can accommodate it. Parfit would surely agree that normative judgments are a kind of judgment that *some* agents aim to close their deliberation with and base their decisions on. We could identify these agents under some normative classification (e.g., *rational*) or simply ostensively (e.g., *me*). Indeed, in Parfit's paradigm of a normative judgment in *Burning Hotel*, the judgment is playing exactly this deliberative role (2011: 326–327). So long as theorists are using ostensive definitions, picking out *that kind of judgment* (whichever it is) that actually satisfies the characterization they have in mind, they can be talking about the same kind of judgment even if they have different characterizations in mind (i.e., they disagree about the class of agents for whom it plays that role).

I therefore suggest that in NORMATIVE$_{\text{judg-ost}}$ we have identified a kind of concept that could, at least in principle, provide a common object for cognitivists' and noncognitivists' claims about "normative judgments", despite the enormous differences between them. Similarly, in NORMATIVE$_{\text{lang-exp-judg}}$ we have a potentially unifying concept for their claims about "normative language". There is thus reason for optimism about the univocity of at least these parts of metanormative discourse. I hesitate to draw the stronger conclusion that this is the kind of concept all theorists actually employ, and thereby that claims about "normative judgments" are actually univocal—although if a principle of charity operates at the level of a whole field we might invoke it here.

What about the "normativity" of facts and properties, which cognitivists identify as the ultimate object of their investigations? The ostensive definitions I've proposed don't provide a common object here; cognitivists clearly don't mean to classify these facts and properties as normative$_{\text{judg-ost}}$, and so we still need another sense of 'normative' to accommodate these claims along the lines of NORMATIVE$_{\text{ont}}$—perhaps of the following, derivative kind:

> NORMATIVE$_{\text{ont-judg-rep}}$: Having the property P that is common to all and only the kinds of facts and properties that normative$_{\text{judg-ost}}$ judgments (and normative$_{\text{lang-exp-judg}}$ expressions) are about.

Here our previous conclusions seem to stand. Noncognitivists are committed to denying that anything is normative$_{\text{ont-judg-rep}}$, since they reject the presupposition that normative$_{\text{judg-ost}}$

[27] Consider also philosophers such as (Broome 2013); (Arpaly and Schroeder 2013); (Silverstein 2017) who deny that deliberation typically has normativized *content*: e.g. we look to close deliberation by identifying our reasons, not by identifying them *as* reasons/reaching the judgment that something is a reason.

judgments as such are about any special kind of property. From their point of view, cognitivists are engaged in a wild goose chase, led astray by their signature misinterpretation of the underlying nature of these judgments. Their positive claims about the nature of "normativity", therefore, are not claims about normativity$_{\text{ont-judg-rep}}$, the primary object of cognitivist's metanormative claims. Regarding this, Parfit's claim that noncognitivism is "close to nihilism" (2011, 267) therefore seems right or even overly cautious.

Which side is right? This is a difficult question, as the past century of metaethics attests. The cognitivists' claim can seem compelling. In Parfit's *Burning Hotel* scenario it seems phenomenologically correct to say that one looks for and recognizes a *fact*, of a distinctively normative$_{\text{ont}}$ kind, about what one ought or has most reason to do, and that this is what our normative$_{\text{judg-ost}}$ judgment is *about*. But the noncognitivists' positive claim can seem compelling too: that normative$_{\text{judg-ost}}$ judgments are distinguished as a kind by having a special nonrepresentational property or function. Another option, however, is a widely overlooked kind of *hybrid* position: that normative$_{\text{judg-ost}}$ judgments are distinguished as a kind by the combination of *both* (i) being about a special normative$_{\text{ont}}$ kind of property, *and* (ii) having a special nonrepresentational property or function. This is importantly different from the familiar kind of "hybrid theory", very much in fashion today, which attributes normative$_{\text{judg-ost}}$ judgments both cognitive content and noncognitive properties. These familiar, *first-order* hybrid theories are generally not hybrid regarding the second-order question that is at issue here, concerning a judgment's status as *normative*.[28] Instead, they adopt a straightforwardly noncognitivist answer to this question, assigning normative$_{\text{judg-ost}}$ judgments ordinary, "nonnormative" contents, rejecting the cognitivist (in our sense) view that they are distinguished by being normative$_{\text{rep}}$ or about properties of a normative$_{\text{ont}}$ kind. We'll see below that the option of a *second-order* hybrid theory, about what distinguishes a judgment as being normative$_{\text{judg-ost}}$, significantly complicates the possible interpretations of cognitivists' claims about normativity$_{\text{ont}}$.

III. Univocity among Cognitivists

I turn now to examine the prospects for univocity in talk about "normativity" among cognitivists. These are commonly divided into two broad camps: *naturalists* who claim that "normativity" is identical or reducible to ordinary "natural" properties, and *non-naturalists* such as Parfit who deny it. Here we can ignore the difficult issue of how to understand the relevant concept of naturalness, as the most salient difference for our purposes is that non-naturalists generally deny that "normativity" can be analyzed or reduced in "nonnormative" terms at all.[29] The camp of naturalists can be further divided into *subjectivists*, who analyze "normativity" in broadly or partly psychological terms (e.g., involving counterfactual

[28] Possible exceptions articulating potentially second-order hybridist views include the "de dicto cognitivism" of (Tresan 2006) (about "moral" judgments) and the "relational expressivism" of (Toppinen 2013); (Schroeder 2013); also (Laskowski 2017); (Copp 2017); and cf. (Finlay 2004, 2010, 2014). As I understand Mike Ridge's distinction between "ecumenical" cognitivism and noncognitivism (2014, 6–7), this form of (perfect) hybridism falls in the gap between them.

[29] *Primitivism* is therefore a better, though less familiar, label for this family of views.

motivation or relations to desires or agency), and *objectivists* who analyze "normativity" in terms of some nonpsychological natural property.[30] Cognitivists have generally assumed that there is something that they all call "normativity", the nature of which is at issue between them. But after many years of arguing against (particularly subjectivist) forms of naturalism, Parfit has come to the conclusion that theorists who appear to disagree with him about the nature of normativity, or of "reasons", must instead be using a different concept and talking about something else entirely. He identifies as many as *five* different senses (2011, 267–268), and claims that naturalism, like noncognitivism, is "close to nihilism," the view that there are no normative$_{ont}$ facts and properties (2011, 368).

The previous section provides some reason to suspect this to be unduly pessimistic. We might reasonably suppose that whatever their differences, cognitivists should all agree that the object of their theories is normativity$_{ont\text{-}judg\text{-}rep}$: the special property, whatever it might be, possessed by all and only the facts and properties of the kind that our normative$_{judg\text{-}ost}$ judgments are about. But among non-naturalists it is commonly thought that the normativity$_{ont}$ that interests them is *just too different* (as David Enoch puts it)[31] from natural facts and properties to be naturalistically analyzable, and some go so far as to claim that this is so self-evident that nobody could seriously suppose otherwise. On this basis, Parfit concludes that charity requires interpreting naturalists' claims as addressed to a different object altogether. How else could the dramatic differences between the theories be explained?

Below I examine the prospects for univocity between different cognitivists' claims about the "normativity" of facts and properties. I start by exploring two straightforward polysemies in ontological senses of "normativity": (i) an abstract/substantive distinction, and (ii) a formal/robust distinction. Reflection on these will lead us to a second-order hybrid option with significant but ambiguous implications for univocity in metanormative theory. On one hand, against Parfit's pessimism it suggests an alternative, univocity-compatible explanation of why different philosophers are drawn to such radically different theories. But on the other hand, it also suggests a range of subtly but importantly different things that these theorists could be talking about under the label of "normativity", *despite* their shared interest in a single, cognitive kind of normative$_{judg\text{-}ost}$ judgment.

A. Abstract versus Substantive

Before we can get to grips with the nature of "normativity" we need to observe an often overlooked distinction between *normative properties* and (the property of) *normativity*. To bring it into view, consider the question of what things are normative. "Normativity" can seem totally ubiquitous. Anything that is a (normative) reason can appropriately be called "normative", for example, and any kind of ordinary fact whatsoever can be a normative

[30] Objectivist views commonly take broadly Aristotelian forms (e.g., Foot 2001; Thomson 2008); I have often understood my own views (e.g., Finlay 2010, 71; 2014, 79) as non-Aristotelian objectivist naturalism; see also (Copp 2007). Note that subjectivism as understood here needn't imply that what is normative *varies* from agent to agent, and includes universalist views appealing to idealized or normalized psychology, such as (Hume 1739/1896); (Smith 1994).

[31] (Enoch 2011a, 105–109) (see also his references in n.27, and Huemer 2005, 94–95); for discussion see (Laskowski 2017, ch. 3).

reason (e.g., a reason to believe something). Similarly, diverse properties can apparently be normative$_{ont}$, such as the property of being painful, or of being what you were asked to do. However, we can distinguish between facts and properties that are *inherently* normative$_{ont}$ (or whose very nature it is to be normative$_{ont}$), and those that are only *derivatively* normative$_{ont}$.[32] Derivatively normative$_{ont}$ facts and properties are "normative" in virtue of either contingently or necessarily having properties that are inherently normative$_{ont}$. A reason to act, such as the fact that it's raining, is derivatively normative$_{ont}$ because it has the inherently normative$_{ont}$ property of being a reason for some action, like opening your umbrella. Physical sensations of pain are derivatively normative$_{ont}$ because they have the inherently normative$_{ont}$ property of being *bad*.

This means we need to distinguish *three* levels of facts or properties. At the first level are the ordinary facts and properties that can be (e.g.) reasons, or valuable, or obligating: the derivatively normative$_{ont}$ facts and properties. Cognitivists' claims that there are "normative" facts and properties are not usually about this level; what distinguishes cognitivists from noncognitivists is not their claims that some facts are reasons, or that some properties are valuable, but their recognition of properties such as being-a-reason and goodness. At the second level are these special facts and properties—of what somebody ought to do, or of being-a-reason, goodness, etc.—which are inherently normative$_{ont}$. At the third level is the abstract property of normativity$_{ont}$ (being normative$_{ont}$) itself, the common feature of all the facts and properties of the second level (inherently) and the first level (derivatively).

So cognitivists' claims about "normativity" are about this third-level property, right? Not so fast. Theorists commonly proceed straight from an analysis of (e.g.) what it is to be a reason, or an analysis of ought-facts, to the claim to have analyzed "normativity", or from the claim that the reason-relation or ought-facts are unanalyzable, to the claim that "normativity" is unanalyzable.[33] Many claims about "normativity" are clearly about the *second-level* facts and properties, i.e., about the things that are (inherently) normative$_{ont}$ such as ought-facts, the reason relation, and the property of goodness, rather than about what it is to *be* normative$_{ont}$. (Occasionally, one comes across a particularly flatflooted identification of "normativity" with the first-level or derivatively normative$_{ont}$ facts and properties, as in the claim that "normativity" is natural because things such as pain and the fact it is raining are natural.)

This could be interpreted as a simple fallacy of conflation; failing to observe the difference between a property (normativity$_{ont}$), and that which has that property (the things that are normative$_{ont}$).[34] Perhaps more charitably, we might recognize it as a further form of regular polysemy in uses of 'normativity'. Nouns formed by nominalizing adjectives

[32] This distinction is drawn in various terms; e.g., (Schroeder 2007, 80); (Parfit 2011, 278); (Audi 2012, 171). It should not be confused with the familiar distinction between extrinsic and intrinsic value, which arises at the second level described below, rather than the third.

[33] For a culprit I needn't look further than my own claims (e.g., Finlay 2010, 2014) to have analyzed "normativity" as *end-relational* on the basis of end-relational analyses of what it is to be *good*, a *reason*, etc. This invites the criticism in (Eklund 2017, 71).

[34] Cf. (Parfit 2011, 329). This is, in fact, one of the ways G. E. Moore (1903) characterizes the "naturalistic fallacy": confusing substantive and adjective, perhaps on the basis of failing to distinguish the 'is' of identity and the 'is' of predication. Ironically, many contemporary non-naturalists (among others) may be committing the mistake Moore cautioned against!

('normative'→'normativity') are often ambiguous, used to refer either to the higher-order or *abstract* property P predicated by the adjective, or to any of a set of lower-order or *substantive*, P-making, properties (or tropes/property-instances). For example, we might identify the "nutritiousness" of a carrot substantively with its vitamin-A content and the "nutritiousness" of a potato substantively with its carbohydrate content, whereas the abstract property of nutritiousness, which the carrot and the potato share in virtue of their respective vitamin and carbohydrate content, is approximately the property of being disposed to promote a person's health when consumed.[35]

Use of 'normativity' (= "normativeness") presents the same polysemous pattern. First-level normative$_{ont}$ facts and properties (e.g., the fact that it's raining, the property of being painful) have the abstract (third-level) property of normativity$_{ont}$ because they have second-level normative$_{ont}$ properties (e.g., being a reason to open your umbrella, being bad). Accordingly, 'normativity' is apt to be used in a substantive sense to refer to the second-level normative$_{ont}$ properties in virtue of which the first-level facts and properties are normative$_{ont}$. In the substantive sense, "normativity" would not strictly be a property, but rather something such as a *kind* or *set* of properties, relations, etc., or a *domain* of reality: "the normative".[36] We can therefore distinguish a further dimension of ambiguity in the noun, between abstract and substantive senses:

NORMATIVITY$_{ont-ab}$: The property of being normative$_{ont}$;
NORMATIVITY$_{ont-sub}$: The properties (etc.) that are inherently normative$_{ont}$ ("the normative").

Recognizing such a polysemy only gets charity so far, however. It still seems we have to recognize widespread equivocation or confusion in metanormative theory. Notice that it doesn't necessarily follow from a fact or property at the second level (such as goodness, or being-a-reason-for) having a certain property (such as being analyzable, unanalyzable, natural, or non-natural) that the property at the third level (normativity$_{ont-ab}$) also has that property, or vice versa. For example, non-natural second-level properties, if there are any, can have the arguably natural third-level property of *being thought about by us*.

Conceivably, therefore, normative$_{ont-sub}$ properties such as *being-a-reason* could be non-natural while the property of normativity$_{ont-ab}$ is entirely natural, or vice versa. It is open to non-naturalists about the reason-relation or value to identify normativity$_{ont-ab}$ as the property of *being the kind of property that agents look to in order to close their deliberations*, for example. This looks like an entirely natural third-level property, although it could conceivably be possessed only by non-natural second-level properties. A rival suggestion is that to be "normative" is to *reduce to facts about reasons*,[37] which is clearly addressing normativity$_{ont}$ in

[35] Cf. (Finlay 2001, 48f). Substantive uses or definitions of nouns are common in metanormative theory. For example, Judy Thomson (1996) identifies moral "goodness" with the various *ways* of being morally good, such as being generous, being just, etc. This could be interpreted as conflating a second-level property (goodness) with first-level (goodness-making) properties. See also (Railton 1990) ('seaworthiness' analogy), (Mackie 1977, 56).

[36] Moltmann (2013) argues that nominalized adjectives (of the form 'F-ness') don't refer to abstract properties (of F) at all, but this seems to overlook their abstract uses.

[37] E.g., (Hampton 1998, 115); (Raz 1999, 67); (Schroeder 2007, 79f).

the abstract sense. This would make normativity$_{\text{ont-ab}}$ a reductively analyzable property, but would presumably refer questions about its naturalness back down to the second-level issue concerning the naturalness of the reason-relation.

This possibility of "ticket-splitting" has not been widely recognized,[38] and even theorists who draw the distinction explicitly seem to assume without argument that the questions of naturalness or analyzability must have the same answer at both levels. Parfit himself may be a case in point. He objects to theories that analyze normative properties such as *being-a-reason* as a natural property N that they face a fatal "lost property" problem, of explaining what it is that we would learn about N if we were to learn that N is the normative property of being-a-reason. A naturalist about reasons could reply that we learn that N has the property of normativity$_{\text{ont-ab}}$, or of being normative$_{\text{ont}}$; perhaps, for example, that N is a property that certain agents (or even Parfit himself) looks to in order to settle deliberation.[39]

Observing this distinction presents us with a fork in the road. Should the problem of univocity in cognitivists' talk about "normativity" be understood in the abstract sense, or the substantive sense—or both? The various familiar positions, like non-naturalism, subjectivist and objectivist naturalism, seem primarily to be theories of the nature of inherently normative$_{\text{ont}}$ facts and properties, i.e., of normativity$_{\text{ont-sub}}$. Privileging instead the abstract property of normativity$_{\text{ont-ab}}$ would make for strange bedfellows and an unfamiliar, topsy-turvy metanormative landscape where the self-described "non-naturalist" David Enoch might be able to agree with self-described "naturalists" such as David Copp (2012) and Laura and Francois Schroeter (ms) that "normativity" is reductively analyzable as the property of *being the kind of thing that agents look toward to close deliberation*, in opposition to the self-described "naturalist" Mark Schroeder and the self-described "non-naturalists" Tim Scanlon (1998) and Parfit who might agree that it is the property of *reducing to facts about reasons*.[40] So the familiar battlelines drawn between cognitivists over the nature of "normativity" seem best interpreted, by and large, in terms of normativity$_{\text{ont-sub}}$, or the nature of inherently normative$_{\text{ont}}$ facts and properties. By comparison, the question of what normativity$_{\text{ont-ab}}$ is has drawn relatively little attention.

Despite revealing what looks like rampant equivocation over "normativity", observing this ambiguity may actually be a promising development for the prospects of unity in metanormative theorizing. This is because even if the different theories of "normativity" in the substantive sense turn out to be about radically different facts and properties, they could still be unified by the common aim of describing those facts and properties, whichever they are, that have the further, third-level property of normativity$_{\text{ont-ab}}$ that theorists are largely assuming rather than analyzing. The radical differences between the camps could then be explained by divergence in opinion about which facts and properties those are. Of course,

[38] One exception is (Eklund 2017, 65), who also takes Parfit to task on this point.

[39] See also (Copp 2007, 2012), who appears to infer immediately from normative$_{\text{ont}}$ properties being natural to normativity$_{\text{ont-ab}}$ being natural. On one page (2012, 26), he writes both that "the fundamental issue is whether the *normativity* of moral facts and properties can be understood naturalistically," and that "The arguments I consider . . . attack the thesis that *normative properties* are natural properties" (emphasis added). The distinction is much sharper in (Copp 2017, 32–33).

[40] I'm not claiming that these theorists all accept these analyses of normativity$_{\text{ont-ab}}$, merely that they are broadly consistent with what they say in some places (see Copp 2017, 32–33 for a clearly different account).

this hope hinges on different theorists assuming the *same* third-level property, which is possible even if they do or would endorse different official definitions of it, but we have yet to identify decisive evidence for or against this. I take up this issue below.

B. *Formal versus Robust Normativity*

The way forward may seem clear. In Section II.C, I suggested that what unifies cognitivists and noncognitivists is a common interest in a particular kind of judgment we all make. What unifies all cognitivists against noncognitivists, I provisionally suggested, is the view that these are representational judgments, about normative$_{\text{ont}}$ properties and facts. So we might suppose that univocity can be secured by defining normativity$_{\text{ont-ab}}$ as normativity$_{\text{ont-judg-rep}}$: the property, whatever it might be, shared by all and only the facts and properties of the kind that normative$_{\text{judg-ost}}$ judgments are about,[41] and by defining normativity$_{\text{ont-sub}}$ as the facts and properties that have this property inherently. However, I will now argue that matters aren't so straightforward. The difficulty will emerge from reflection on a further, much-discussed ambiguity in talk about "normativity", between *robust* and *formal* senses.

Cognitivists encounter difficulties in identifying the object of their investigations, normativity$_{\text{ont}}$ (whether abstract or substantive), to others in uncontroversial terms, due to the lack of agreement over its nature. These difficulties are particularly acute for non-naturalists, since they deny that "normativity" can be analyzed, defined, or explained in "non-normative" terms. Attempts to pick it out therefore generally rely on either the mention (in language-based ostensions) or use (in judgment-based ostensions) of normative$_{\text{lang-exp-judg}}$ language: "normativity" is the special property or domain of what "ought to", "should", "must", or "may" be, or of "obligation", "right" and "wrong", "correct" and "incorrect", "value", "good" and "bad", or—the present favorite—of "reasons".[42] Allan Gibbard identifies the target by reference to "a circle of ought-like terms," for example, and Mark Schroeder defines it as what is reducible to "reasons".[43]

Inconveniently however, at least much of this normative$_{\text{lang-exp-judg}}$ vocabulary turns out to be apparently ambiguous. As John Broome puts it,

> I could not explain the term 'normative' except in terms of 'ought'. 'Normative' means 'to do with ought', but this ought has to be a normative one, of course. So this definition gets us nowhere if we cannot already identify the normative ought. I simply have to assume you know a normative ought when you meet one. (2013, 10)

There are ordinary uses of 'ought', 'must', 'may', 'should', 'obligation', 'right', 'wrong', 'correct', 'incorrect', 'value', 'good', and 'bad' that apparently describe facts and properties that most non-naturalists readily allow are naturalistic and reductively analyzable (e.g., Parfit 2011,

---

[41] This picks out normativity$_{\text{ont-ab}}$ by a *fourth*-level property it possesses, leaving open the intrinsic nature of the third-level property, and allowing theorists to pick it out by their own, idiosyncratic concepts.

[42] This is not to say it is unsolvable; I proposed a solution above in terms of normativity$_{\text{ont-judg-rep}}$.

[43] 'Ought' is also favored in (Broome 2013), while 'reason' is also favored in (Raz 1999); (Parfit 2011); (Scanlon 1998).

308), and subjectivists readily allow are nonpsychological. For example, "oughts" of etiquette, "right" answers to exam questions, "good" moves in chess, and (more controversially) legal "obligations". Philosophers therefore commonly deny that these statements are about the normative$_{\text{ont}}$ facts and properties that are the objects of their metanormative investigations.

One might think the quarry can be identified, extensionally if not helpfully, as what the *normative* uses of 'ought', 'right', 'good', 'value', etc. are about. The need for a general term to capture this "fugitive thought" eluding our grasp in ordinary normative$_{\text{lang-exp-judg}}$ language may be a primary motivation for theorists largely abandoning talk of "value", "obligation", etc. since the 1970s in favor of 'normativity' as a term of art. But if so the move has been an ironic failure, because today exactly the same distinction is observed for the term 'normative' itself. As Broome continues,

> The terminology in this area is confusing because so many words have both normative and nonnormative senses. Even the word 'normative' has a nonnormative (in my sense) sense. (2013, 11)

This distinction is marked with various terminology; here I'll adopt the relatively theory-neutral labels of *formal* versus *robust* normativity$_{\text{ont}}$.[44] "Mere" formal normativity$_{\text{ont}}$ is said to be ubiquitous (found in law, etiquette, games, shopping lists, and more), naturalistic, and nonsubjective, but also of little philosophical interest. Robust normativity$_{\text{ont}}$ is said to be the important kind of normativity$_{\text{ont}}$ of special interest to ethics, epistemology, and other branches of "normative" philosophy.

Some theorists think this ambiguity problem can be solved by identifying a special subset of normative$_{\text{lang-exp-judg}}$ vocabulary that is unambiguously robust, lacking any formal sense. 'Reason' has been the most popular candidate. Parfit, for example, distinguishes robust normativity as "reason-implying" from formal normativity as "rule-implying". I think this attempt to disambiguate 'normativity' fails to cut the phenomena at the joints. We can legitimately talk about merely institutional *reasons*, such as legal reasons, or reasons of chess,[45] and some domains of allegedly robust normativity, such as morality, seem to imply robustly normative *rules* such as the Categorical Imperative or the Principle of Utility. This claim might be rejected, or a theorist might appeal to some other normative$_{\text{lang-exp-judg}}$ word instead.[46] While the jury is still out on this strategy, I'll sketch an alternative way of looking at the relationship between formal and robust normativity, one that treats the parallel vocabularies as an important datum to be explained rather than a problem to be circumnavigated or explained away.[47]

---

[44] (McPherson 2011). Formal normativity has also been labeled 'rule-implying' (Parfit 2011), 'pseudo', 'institutional' (Joyce 2001), and 'generic' (Copp 2007), while robust normativity has been labeled 'reason-implying' (Parfit 2011), 'genuine' (Joyce 2001), 'true' (Broome 2013), and 'authoritative' (Copp 2007), inter alia.

[45] E.g., (Joyce 2001); (Finlay 2006); (Enoch 2011b); (Copp 2017); (McPherson 2018). A certain chess move might be a *good* move because it is likely to provoke one's opponent into a rash response, which is a *reason* to make it, but doesn't obviously imply any *rule*. Similarly, some philosophers acknowledge the existence of *moral reasons* while denying they are necessarily robustly normative; e.g., (Finlay 2006); (Copp 2007).

[46] For example, 'rational', 'matters', or 'important'. For discussion, see (Finlay 2006, 2014, 252f); cf. (Korsgaard 1996, 42–44).

[47] A speculative diagnosis: (1) The original sense of 'normative'/'normativity' was the formal one, as suggested by etymology (from 'norm'). (2) Moral philosophers, interested in a particular (robust) subset of formally

My goal is not to establish that this view is correct (although I believe it is), but to show how it greatly complicates the task of defining normativity$_{\text{ont}}$.

Are formal and robust normativity$_{\text{ont}}$ both forms of "normativity" in the same sense? Or do the qualifiers here function to disambiguate different senses of a word, as in 'river banks and financial banks'? The parallel vocabularies are a strong reason to think the former.[48] But this prompts a second question: What kind of adjectives are the labels 'formal' and 'robust' here? In particular, do they function *subsectively*? (An adjective A is subsective just in case being an A N entails being an N.) For example, 'formal' might function *anti*-subsectively like 'fake' (or *non*-subsectively like 'alleged'), in which case even if there is one common meaning of 'normativity' at issue, formal normativity isn't really (or necessarily) normativity at all. We could then presume that 'robust' is *exhaustively* subsective, and equivalent to 'true' or 'genuine' (e.g., Broome 2013); all normativity would then be robust normativity. Or 'formal' might function subsectively, so that formal and robust normativity are each subclasses of normativity$_{\text{ont}}$ in a general and common sense.

Many theorists are attracted to the anti-subsective or non-subsective views. Among legal philosophers, for example, it is a popular idea that legal "normativity" (abstract) consists in law as such necessarily *purporting* to be genuinely (or robustly) normative.[49] However, this view faces difficulties. It is controversial even in the philosophy of law, and seems much less plausible for other instances of "formal normativity", such as games of chess and football, grocery lists, or exam rubrics. (Is calling an exam answer "wrong" really to pretend or allege that it is "robustly" prohibited?) Additionally, there are popular and plausible analyses of what it *is* to be formally normative that make it out to be something real rather than fake or putative. It's commonly and plausibly said that what it is for something to be "formally normative" is just for it to provide a standard, rule, or norm—in the etymologically original senses of *yardstick, ruler*, or *builder's square*—against which other things can be compared.[50] So for example, a code of laws describes a set of (ideal) behaviors, against which actual behavior can be compared, and a shopping list describes a set of possible purchases, against which actual purchases can be compared. Formal normativity$_{\text{ont-ab}}$ would then be roughly *norm-relativity*.

Along such lines, in my own work I have claimed to provide a reductively naturalistic, objectivist analysis of "normativity" (in a substantive sense) as consisting in *end-relational* properties of increasing/decreasing the probability of some outcome or "end", and *rule-relational* properties of conforming/nonconforming with some proposition or "rule".[51]

normative judgments, began using the adjective 'normative' to distinguish these from ordinary, "descriptive" judgments, then (3) in the late 1970s started using the noun 'normativity' derivatively in a new, robust (abstract) sense, intending to refer to a property shared by the objects of those robust judgments that previously lacked a clear label.

[48] Note also that drawing the distinction doesn't seem awkward without repeating the noun. Compare 'formal and robust normativity' (natural) with 'river and financial banks' (odd).

[49] E.g., (Raz 1979); for extension to formal normativity generally, see (Wodak forthcoming). Within the philosophy of law it is disputed whether legal normativity as such is formal or robust; for some recent discussion see (Enoch 2011b); (Plunkett and Shapiro 2017).

[50] See especially (Railton 2003, 322–323); cf. (Copp 2007, 267).

[51] For my account of end-relational normativity$_{\text{ont-sub}}$, see (e.g.) (Finlay 2006, 2009, 2010, 2014). For rule-relational normativity$_{\text{ont-sub}}$, see (Finlay and Plunkett 2018).

I subsume these with what Kant called "hypothetical imperatives of skill", or claims about what has to happen in order that some outcome obtains. This invites the objection that my account is about the wrong kind or sense of normativity$_{ont}$.[52] Other self-described cognitivists, like non-naturalists and subjectivists, are interested in *robust* normativity$_{ont\text{-}sub}$, or what our normative$_{judg\text{-}ost}$ judgments are (apparently) about. So Parfit's pessimistic conclusion might seem partially vindicated: at least one of his supposed cognitivist opponents isn't talking about "normativity" in the same sense at all.

However, this conclusion may be too hasty. I have advanced my claims about "normativity" in full awareness of the formal/robust distinction, and that my fellow metanormative theorists are typically interested only in the latter. My reductivist, objectivist claims about "normativity" are based on the belief that "robustly normative" judgments and expressions are about exactly the *same kind* of facts and properties as "formally normative" judgments and expressions. So my claims are concerned with (substantive) normativity$_{ont\text{-}judg\text{-}rep}$, the facts and properties that normative$_{judg\text{-}ost}$ judgments are about, which we were supposing to be the common object of cognitivist theories.[53]

This view might seem absurd: surely there is a clear difference between formal and robust normativity$_{ont}$! I agree, at least, that there is a clear difference between mere judgments about formal normativity$_{ont\text{-}sub}$, such as many ordinary judgments about the requirements of law, games, and etiquette, and (robustly) normative$_{judg\text{-}ost}$ judgments, such as (perhaps) those about the requirements of morality or rationality.[54] But it doesn't follow that those judgments are about different kinds of facts and properties. Here we may recall the noncognitivists' views about what distinguishes a judgment as normative$_{judg\text{-}ost}$, and the availability of a (second-order) hybrid theory of this. Perhaps what distinguishes a judgment as robustly normative is not *merely* what it is about, but also some other, nonrepresentational property it has.

For concreteness, I'll just assume my own preferred view here: that robustly normative$_{judg\text{-}ost}$ judgments are distinguished from nonrobust judgments about normative$_{ont}$ facts and properties by *being made from a relevantly motivated perspective*.[55] A judgment with end-relational content (concerning the probability of some outcome) is "robust" in case the judge contemporaneously desires the end in question, and a judgment with rule-relational content (concerning what conforms with some general proposition), such as a legal judgment, is "robust" in case she contemporaneously accepts the rule in question as a guide to conduct. In Parfit's *Burning Hotel* scenario, for example, there is apparently no deliberation or question over whether to live or die; the goal of living is simply assumed. Within this deliberative context, the judgment "[In order to live], I ought to jump!" qualifies as robustly normative$_{judg\text{-}ost}$. On this view, an amoralist's "moral judgments" would be "merely formal" judgments—despite possibly having the same *content* as the moral judgments of ordinary

[52] Cf. (Dowell 2016). This might be attributed to my focusing on (ambiguous) normative$_{lang\text{-}exp\text{-}judg}$ *language*, as opposed to normative$_{judg\text{-}ost}$ judgments; cf. (Gregory 2015, 2).

[53] See (Woods 2018) for a detailed account of formal normativity along similar lines.

[54] Similarly, this doesn't identify robust normativity$_{ont\text{-}ab}$ (being robustly normative) with formal normativity$_{ont\text{-}ab}$ (being formally normative).

[55] For similar views, see references in note 28. This corresponds to H. L. A. Hart's distinction in the philosophy of law between "internal" and "external" legal judgments or statements (as interpreted in Finlay and Plunkett 2018); cf. (Raz 1993); (Smith 1994, 81).

people[56]—while the committed mafioso's judgments of familial obligation are robustly normative$_{\text{judg-ost}}$ judgments. I'll call this kind of hybrid view of normative$_{\text{judg-ost}}$ judgments a *perspectivist* account, tipping my hat to Nietzsche who (to my knowledge, and by my reading) was the first to propose it.

I reiterate that my purpose in introducing perspectivism here is not to establish it as correct (although I believe it is), but rather to explore what recognizing this overlooked part of theoretical space implies about the univocity of metanormative theory. It is worth noting, however, that the option has far more explanatory power on the hypothesis that it is correct. I also believe it escapes at least most of the objections that have been directed against other views.

C. *A Perspectivist Diagnosis of Metanormative Disagreement*

From the perspectivist's point of view, metanormative theorists are unified by interest in a kind of judgments that exist, and can be properly understood, only within the two-dimensional space generated by the twin axes of subjective psychology or motivation, and objective world. This gives perspectivism the resources to explain why different theorists could have come to such starkly opposed views of a common subject matter: each of the positions correctly perceives part of the phenomenon but fails to see the whole, and so goes wrong in trying to analyze something essentially two-dimensional in just a single dimension, as depicted in Figure 9.1 below. Furthermore, each camp is sensitive to the errors committed by their opponents, which, given ignorance of the perspectivist alternative, serves to further strengthen their conviction that their own views must be correct.[57]

From this vantage point, *noncognitivism* is explained as the result of recognizing the noncognitive dimension of robust normative$_{\text{judg-ost}}$ judgment (e.g., that they are made from a motivated perspective), but—perhaps blinded by this insight—missing the cognitive dimension, of what those judgments are about. As Parfit complains against Gibbard,

<table>
<tr><td colspan="3" rowspan="2"></td><td colspan="3">Recognizes Cognitive Dimension?</td></tr>
<tr><td colspan="2">Yes</td><td>No</td></tr>
<tr><td rowspan="5">Recognizes Noncognitive Dimension?</td><td colspan="2">Yes</td><td colspan="2">Perspectivism</td><td>Noncognitivism</td></tr>
<tr><td rowspan="2">No</td><td rowspan="2"></td><td colspan="2">Recognizes Content is Nonpsychological?</td><td rowspan="4"></td></tr>
<tr><td>Yes</td><td>No</td></tr>
<tr><td rowspan="2">Sensitive to Noncognitive Dimension/ Robustness?</td><td>Yes</td><td>Non-naturalism
Error Theory</td><td>Subjectivism</td></tr>
<tr><td>No</td><td>Obj. Naturalism</td><td></td></tr>
</table>

FIGURE 9.1 What makes a judgment robustly normative?

[56] Cf. (Tresan 2006); (Finlay 2004).

[57] For example, Parfit never addressed a theory of this kind, to my knowledge.

normative judgment isn't a matter of arbitrary choice or preference, but (in part) of discovering antecedently existing facts (2011, 386f, 408).

Objectivist naturalism, whether of neo-Aristotelian (e.g., Foot 2001, Thomson 2008) or non-Aristotelian (e.g., Copp 2007, Finlay 2014) forms, is explained as a result of recognizing both the cognitive dimension and (broadly) the essentially nonpsychological nature of its content (what robustly $\text{normative}_{\text{judg-ost}}$ judgments are about), but perhaps failing to sufficiently heed the (noncognitive) difference between robustly $\text{normative}_{\text{judg-ost}}$ judgments and mere judgments of formally $\text{normative}_{\text{ont}}$ facts and properties.[58] Hence the charge commonly leveled against such views, that they have left out the "normativity" altogether. As Parfit approvingly quotes Darwall, "For the philosophical naturalist, concerned to place normativity within the natural order, there is nothing plausible for normative force to be other than motivational force" (2011, 363).

Subjectivist naturalism, whether Humean or Kantian, can be explained as a result of sensitivity to the (noncognitive) dimension that differentiates robustly $\text{normative}_{\text{judg-ost}}$ judgments from mere judgments of formal $\text{normativity}_{\text{ont}}$, as well as recognition of the cognitive dimension, but failing to recognize that these are two separate dimensions, and therefore misinterpreting the noncognitive dimension in terms of cognitive content, incorrectly analyzed in psychological terms (psychologistic fallacy). As Parfit complains against his subjectivist opponents such as Williams, Darwall, Korsgaard, and Schroeder, $\text{normative}_{\text{judg-ost}}$ judgments simply aren't about anybody's psychological attitudes or dispositions, actual or counterfactual, or what satisfies them.[59]

Non-naturalism, finally, can be explained as also being sensitive to both dimensions though failing to distinguish them, but also recognizing that the content is nonpsychological, and as a result misinterpreting the specially robust character of these judgments in terms of their being *about* something of a special robust character (projective fallacy).[60] Also recognizing that no other kind of ordinary, natural property is such that being about it would be sufficient to give $\text{normative}_{\text{judg-ost}}$ judgments their special robust character, non-naturalists mistakenly but understandably conclude that these judgments must be about special, *non-natural* properties, the implausible mysteriousness of which encourages *error theorists* to maintain that all positive $\text{normative}_{\text{judg-ost}}$ judgments are untrue.

Perspectivism therefore provides an alternative explanation of how metanormative theorists could come to such starkly different views, one that has promise to rescue us from Parfit's pessimism about the unity of metanormative debate. However, once we return to address explicitly what cognitivists might mean by 'normativity', the case for ambiguity is bolstered. For this two-dimensional, perspectivist view on $\text{normative}_{\text{judg-ost}}$ judgment brings to light a large number of alternative things that these different theorists might reasonably mean by 'normativity'. Rather than dismissing the various camps as mistaken about the

[58] Although my own work (like Copp's) has been informed by the difference, I have often ignored it when making claims about "normativity", assuming the concept of $\text{NORMATIVITY}_{\text{ont-judg-rep}}$.

[59] (2011, 324f, 431f). See also (Dancy 2005); (Enoch 2011a).

[60] Cf. (Copp 2017, 48). Perspectivism also offers a potential explanation of many non-naturalists' barely comprehensible *quietist* claims that "normativity" exists/is a property, but not in any "ontological" sense (e.g. (Parfit 2011); (Scanlon 2014)), as a confused attempt to reconcile the facts that (i) robustly $\text{normative}_{\text{judg-ost}}$ judgments are about a particular kind of facts and properties, but (ii) there *is no property* of robust $\text{normativity}_{\text{ont}}$.

nature of "normativity", we might rather identify different concepts they could be using on the basis of their sensitivity to different parts of the complex phenomenon of normative$_{\text{judg-ost}}$ judgment as understood by the perspectivist.[61]

D. *The Many Possible Faces of Normativity*

Start with the concept we introduced above (separated into substantive and abstract senses);

NORMATIVITY$_{\text{ont-judg-rep-sub}}$: The facts and properties of the kind that normative$_{\text{judg-ost}}$ judgments are about.

NORMATIVITY$_{\text{ont-judg-rep-ab}}$: The property shared by all and only the facts and properties of the kind that normative$_{\text{judg-ost}}$ judgments are about.

According to perspectivism, objectivist naturalism (of the kind advocated in my own work) provides the correct account of normativity$_{\text{ont-judg-rep-sub}}$, which turns out to be exactly the same kind of facts and properties that merely "formally normative" judgments are about. So if non-naturalists (such as Parfit) and subjectivists are employing the same effective definition in their talk about "normativity", as hypothesized above, then their metanormative claims are false. They err about the nature of normativity$_{\text{ont-judg-rep}}$ because they wrongly attribute the special character of their (robust) normative$_{\text{judg-ost}}$ judgments to it. Of course, they would deny that they are talking about "mere formal normativity." But this would be mistaken, just like somebody who wonders "what is this stuff?" upon encountering ice for the first time denying they were talking about "mere" water or H2O.[62] According to non-naturalists and subjectivists, on the other hand, perspectivism errs about normativity$_{\text{ont-judg-rep}}$ because it wrongly attributes this difference to an alleged noncognitive or nonrepresentational property of normative$_{\text{judg-ost}}$ judgments.[63]

However, there is some evidence that the "robustness" of the property itself may be non-negotiable for at least some cognitivists' concepts of "normativity". For example, some non-naturalists declare that either "normativity" is irreducible, or else it doesn't exist at all (e.g., Parfit 2011, 267). These claims might simply reflect what (from the perspectivist's point of view) is the non-naturalists' mistake, but they could instead point toward other, more discriminating effective definitions. For example, sometimes non-naturalists—together with *error theorists* about "normativity"[64]—seem to employ concepts along the following lines:

NORMATIVITY$_{\text{ont-judg-rep-robust-sub}}$: The facts and properties of the kind that normative$_{\text{judg-ost}}$ judgments are about, in virtue of which they are (robustly) normative$_{\text{judg-ost}}$.

---

[61] For similar speculation, see (McPherson & Plunkett forthcoming).

[62] For discussion of such opacity in normative thought and language, see (Copp 2012); (Laskowski 2017).

[63] The most pressing worry might be that perspectivism, like noncognitivism, cannot adequately account for practices of wondering or deliberating about final ends or intrinsic value (e.g., Olson 2011). See (Finlay 2014, 204) for brief discussion. It also must deal with the contextualist's/relativist's well-known problem with normative disagreement; see (Finlay 2014, ch. 8) for one response.

[64] A once-rare but increasingly popular position; e.g., (Biehl 2008); (Streumer 2017); (Bakka 2015).

NORMATIVITY$_{\text{ont-judg-rep-robust-ab}}$: The property shared by all and only the facts and properties of the kind that normative$_{\text{judg-ost}}$ judgments are about, in virtue of which they are (robustly) normative$_{\text{judg-ost}}$.

Or alternatively, a directly ostensive ontological definition:

NORMATIVITY$_{\text{ont-ost-robust}}$: *That* property (ostending a "robust" property being cognized, perceived, or imagined).

In either case, the perspectivist will conclude that the projective fallacy infects the very concepts that non-naturalists are employing, and that "normativity" in the non-naturalists' substantive sense neither exists, nor (contra some error theorists) is what our ordinary normative$_{\text{judg-ost}}$ judgments are about.[65]

Now consider the subjectivists. They could conceivably be employing any of the effective definitions already surveyed in this section. In this case, perspectivism agrees with non-naturalists such as Parfit that subjectivist theories are in error, on the grounds that whatever normative$_{\text{judg-ost}}$ judgments are about (and whether or not it also explains their robustness), it isn't generally something psychological. Parfit doubts that anybody with his concept of (robust) normativity$_{\text{ont}}$ could reasonably believe it to be psychological, and so charity leads him to pessimism about a common object of inquiry between himself and subjectivists such as Williams, Darwall, Korsgaard, and Schroeder.[66]

Perspectivism casts helpful light here too. For it implies that whenever somebody makes a first-personal normative$_{\text{judg-ost}}$ judgment (e.g., about what she herself has a reason to do, or ought to do),[67] the propositional content of that judgment is true if and only if the object of judgment has a corresponding *subjective* property: roughly, a property of being instrumentally related to the satisfaction of a desire of the agent. Furthermore, according to perspectivism this subjective property may be the *only* property that is tracked by all first-personal normative$_{\text{judg-ost}}$ judgments as a kind, since different judgments are about different properties (as relevant to different motivated perspectives). It would therefore be understandable that a theorist might identify substantive normativity$_{\text{ont-judg-rep}}$ (what normative$_{\text{judg-ost}}$ judgments are about) or substantive normativity$_{\text{ont-judg-rep-robust}}$ (the facts and properties they are about in virtue of which they are robust) with this subjective property—even though this would be an error because, as non-naturalists insist, normative$_{\text{judg-ost}}$ judgments are nonetheless not *about* such subjective properties.

While this provides a possible explanation of how theories as different as non-naturalism (e.g., Parfit) and subjectivism (e.g., Williams) could be aimed at exactly the same object—and even by means of the same concepts—it *also* reveals how subjectivists' claims about "normativity" could be about a subtly but importantly different property or domain. Perhaps subjectivists are not using any of the above concepts at all, but rather a concept such as

[65] Perhaps there is a corresponding abstract property, but if so it would be uninstantiated.

[66] E.g., (Parfit 2011, 294).

[67] The significance of this restriction to first-personal judgments will be taken up below.

NORMATIVITY$_{\text{ont-judg-relation}}$: The relation that obtains between an agent and an action iff a first-personal, robustly normative$_{\text{judg-ost}}$ judgment about that agent and that action would be true.[68]

According to perspectivism there is indeed such a relation, and a subjectivist or instrumentalist theory of it is correct (for first-person judgments, at least)—although subjectivists are mistaken if they claim that this is what normative$_{\text{judg-ost}}$ judgments are *about*. Non-naturalists could also be employing this concept too, but if so then (the perspectivist will think) the non-naturalists' claims about normativity$_{\text{ont-judg-relation}}$ are false.[69]

Once we recognize a concept of normativity$_{\text{ont-judg-relation}}$, we will also need to recognize additional, related concepts, and potential further polysemies in talk about "normativity". Consider what a subjectivist might then mean by talk about "normative" facts and properties. Presumably, a fact or property would be "normative" in a relevant sense if and only if it stands in this relation to some agent. So "normativity", understood as the abstract property of being "normative" in this sense, will not be the relation itself, but the *relational property* of standing in this relation to some agent or subject. Or more precisely, 'normativity' will be an essentially relativistic or context-sensitive term, such as 'tall' or 'big', referring to any of a whole family of relational properties: something could be *normative/normativity-relative-to-*s_1, or *normative/normativity-relative-to-*s_2, etc., but nothing would ever be *normative-simpliciter*.[70] So we have:

NORMATIVITY-RELATIVE-TO-S: The property of standing in the relation of normativity$_{\text{ont-judg-relation}}$ to s.

If there is such a relation as normativity$_{\text{ont-judg-relation}}$, which is tracked by our (first-personal, robust) normative$_{\text{judg-ost}}$ judgments, then why *not* think that this is normativity$_{\text{ont-judg-rep}}$, or what our normative$_{\text{judg-ost}}$ judgments are about? An answer arises from considering what the extension of the relevant class of judgments is. While the central paradigms of normative$_{\text{judg-ost}}$ judgments are first-personal judgments, concerning what "I" have a reason or ought to do, etc., I don't know anybody who denies that there are second- and third-personal "robustly normative" judgments, e.g., about what "you", "he", or "they" ought to do. But this introduces

---

[68] This interpretation is consistent, for example, with the way Mark Schroeder (2007, 1) introduces his subjectivist theory of reasons, in terms of the psychological difference between Ronnie who has a reason to go to a party, and Bradley who doesn't.

[69] Something like this is presumably what Parfit has in mind when he says that he understands what Williams means (by a "reason"), but that it isn't what he means (2011, 271).

[70] This shouldn't be confused with the relation of *being-a-reason-for*. Looking beyond first-personal judgments, it allows for reasons *for* s_1 that are normative-relative-to-s_2 but not normative-relative-to-s_1. For example, reasons for Hitler not to commit genocide might be normative-relative-to-us, but not normative-relative-to-him (cf. Finlay 2006). This account also shouldn't be confused with a "constructivism" that analyzes F's being "normative-relative-to-*s*" in purely psychological terms of *s*'s *taking* F to be normative (e.g., Street 2008), any more than x's being "to the left-relative-to-s" can be analyzed in terms of *s*'s *believing* x to be to the left. Rather, "s_1 believes that p is a normative reason for s_2 to ϕ relative-to-s_3" is parallel to "s_1 believes that x is to the left of s_2 relative-to-s_3".

a significant complication, because these judgments can be motivationally "internal" or "external" in two fundamentally different ways, corresponding to the two dimensions distinguished by perspectivism.[71] A judgment could be about normative$_{\text{ont}}$ facts and properties that stand in an internal relation either to the specified *agent's* desires or agency ("agent-internalism"), or to the *judge's* desires or agency ("judge/speaker-internalism").

First-personal "robust" normative$_{\text{judg-ost}}$ judgments are internal both to the judge and to the agent, being one and the same individual, whereas paradigmatic judgments of "merely formal normativity" are external both to the judge and to the agent. Taking first-personal normative$_{\text{judg-ost}}$ judgments as one's paradigm of robust normativity therefore conceals the fundamental dilemma that faces us here in trying to define (robust) "normativity". This dilemma comes into view when we consider second- and third-personal judgments, in which agent-relativity and judge-relativity can come apart. Which kind of internality determines a judgment as being of the relevantly "robust" or normative$_{\text{judg-ost}}$ type?

By attributing the robustness of normative$_{\text{judg-ost}}$ judgments to their tracking or being about a partly psychological relationship between the agent and the action, subjectivists commit themselves to denying that any judge-internal judgment about normative$_{\text{ont}}$ facts and properties is a normative$_{\text{judg-ost}}$ judgment if it isn't also agent-internal. This gets subjectivists into trouble, with their opponents (non-naturalists, noncognitivists, and others) objecting that second- and third-personal *moral* judgments are "robustly normative" yet also *categorical*, their truth-value being independent of any instrumental relationship to the agent's desires or agency. Perspectivism understands these objections as a result of privileging instead the judge-internal relation, and classifying a judgment as "robustly normative" only if it is internally related to the judge's own desires or agency (even if non-naturalists misinterpret it due to the projective fallacy). Here perspectivism agrees with the noncognitivists: this relation lies wholly on the dimension of motivated perspective, rather than that of cognitive content.[72]

Perhaps, then, subjectivists really are employing a different concept of "robust normativity"? If so, then the perspectivist will think that they should stand their ground and insist that morality indeed isn't necessarily "normative" (e.g., that Hitler may not have had any genuinely "normative" reason not to engage in genocide),[73] explaining away the indignant reactions such claims provoke as results of misunderstanding their (nonendorsing) sense of "normative". We can grant that there were *exceptionally good* reasons for Hitler not to engage in genocide, even if these weren't normative-relative-to-Hitler. However, subjectivists sometimes respond to this kind of objection by instead trying to accommodate the "normativity" of moral judgments by denying that they really are agent-external—a move that typically strikes their opponents as desperate and implausible. This perceived need to accommodate

[71] This point is widely observed; e.g., (Dreier 1990); (Harman 1996).

[72] This contrasts with unpopular *judge*-subjectivism (not to be confused with the *agent*-subjectivism under discussion here) that analyzes normative$_{\text{judg-ost}}$ judgments as *introspectively* psychological; e.g., (Westermarck 1932); (Jackson 2008).

[73] (Harman 1975); see also (Foot 1972); (Joyce 2001).

the "normativity" of morality may be evidence that they are partly concerned to capture a kind of robustness that is actually agent-external.[74]

Since there are no facts and properties that all and only these judge-internal judgments are about (different judges being related in this way to different sets of formally normative$_{ont}$ facts and properties), and no special "normative" property shared by all the facts and properties in this (empty) set, this implies that no property of "robust normativity" along these lines, such as normativity$_{ont\text{-}judg\text{-}rep\text{-}robust\text{-}ab}$, is ever instantiated. So we might conclude that the only robust kind of "normativity" to be found in the world is the noncognitivist's notion of normativity$_{funct}$: the nonrepresentational, purely psychological property (or properties) of normative$_{judg\text{-}ost}$ judgments and normative$_{lang\text{-}exp\text{-}judg}$ language. However, there is at least one further possibility. We might still make sense of talk about "robustly normative facts and properties" by construing 'normative' as itself a (robustly) normative$_{lang\text{-}exp\text{-}judg}$ term.[75] This would be to adopt a *quasi-realist* concept of normativity$_{ont}$, which could be defined, in the expressivist's "sideways-on" style, roughly as follows:

> NORMATIVITY$_{quasi\text{-}ont}$: To apply this concept to some facts or properties involves having or expressing a favorable attitude toward them.

So for example, judging a fact F to be a normative$_{quasi\text{-}ont}$ reason to do A might be to approve of weighing F in favor of doing A.

This quasi-realist concept of "normativity" is presumably different from the concept that the subjectivist employs in claiming that "normativity" is always relative to or dependent on the relevant agent's desires. That is, unless the subjectivist happens (unusually and perversely) to approve of agents always acting in ways that instrumentally serve the agent's own desires, even if, for example, the desires in question are genocidal.[76] However, as Gibbard points out (2003, 184f), the concept of normativity$_{quasi\text{-}ont}$ does a reasonable job of modeling the claims of non-naturalists, who unlike subjectivists generally describe a fact, property, or consideration as "normative" only if they approve of an agent's being guided by it. So it could be argued that the metanormative claims of non-naturalists such as Parfit actually employ the concept of normativity$_{quasi\text{-}ont}$, attributing their disavowals of noncognitivism either to a lack of self-understanding,[77] or to their metanormative claims being aimed at primarily practical rather than theoretical effect (i.e., "bullshitting"). In addition to being highly uncharitable, however, this interpretation is at odds with non-naturalists' claims that "normativity" isn't a natural property, rather predicting identifications of "normativity" with whatever natural properties the theorist favors as a basis for decision. More plausibly, therefore, non-naturalists employ genuinely cognitivist concepts of the "normativity" of facts and properties, of one or another of the kinds surveyed above.

---

[74] E.g., (Schroeder 2007) (cf. Parfit 2011, 361). Another response is to "democratize" subjectivism (Manne 2016), allowing that *any* agent's desires are "normative" for any agent.

[75] E.g., (Gibbard 2003).

[76] Although the implication that they do arguably lies behind the perceived outrageousness of subjectivist claims about (e.g.) what normative reasons monsters such as Hitler might have.

[77] Parfit concedes that he "cannot exclude the possibility" (2011, 272).

Having exposed these potential ambiguities in talk about "normativity", we are now able also to identify potentially insidious cases of equivocation within familiar and influential lines of philosophical reasoning. It is commonplace today for theorists to recognize the distinction between mere "formal normativity" (which is neither judge- nor agent-internal; symbolically: ○), and "robust normativity". But what has usually not been noticed is that (if the proposals of this chapter are correct) there are three distinct kinds of robustness: that involving judge-internality only (symbolically: ⦶), that involving agent-internality only (⊖), and that involving both judge- and agent-internality (⊕). Failure to recognize this may lead us into the following kinds of inferences:

> *Anti-Instrumentalist Inference*: Moral oughts are robustly normative (⦶). Moral oughts do not depend on agents' attitudes. Therefore, it is not the case that robust normativity (⊖) depends on agents' attitudes.
>
> *Moral Instrumentalist Inference*: Robust normativity (⊖) depends on agents' attitudes. Moral oughts are robustly normative (⦶). Therefore, moral oughts depend on agents' attitudes.
>
> *Moral Nihilist Inference*: Robust normativity (⊖) depends on agents' attitudes. Moral oughts do not depend on agents' attitudes. Therefore, moral oughts are not robustly normative (⦶).
>
> *Noncognitivist Antirealist Inference*: Judgments are robustly normative (⦶) in virtue of the judge's attitudes, not in virtue of being about a particular class of facts or properties. Therefore, there are no robustly normative (⊖) facts or properties.
>
> *Moral Rationalist Inference*: Moral oughts are robustly normative (⦶). If an agent believes they ought to do A, and that 'ought' is robustly normative (⊖/⊕), then they are irrational if they are not motivated to do A. Therefore, if an agent believes they morally ought to do A, then they are irrational if they are not motivated to do A.
>
> *Anti-Egoist Inference*: Harm and pain are bad in a robustly normative way (⊖). All else being equal we robustly ought (⊕/⦶) to prevent whatever is bad in a robustly normative way (⊕/⦶). Therefore, all else being equal we robustly ought (⊕/⦶) to prevent harm and pain.

Isn't it a violation of the principle of charity to think that philosophers ever equivocate in these ways? Our reason to suspect equivocation is that while each of these premises is quite plausible (perhaps even compelling) under the suggested, equivocal disambiguations, each argument contains a premise or conclusion that is far less plausible (and perhaps even very implausible) under the disambiguation required for validity.

IV. Conclusion

What do philosophers mean by 'normative' and 'normativity', and can the univocity of metanormative theory be saved? I first argued that univocity between cognitivists' and noncognitivists' talk about "normative" thought and language could plausibly be secured by an ostensive, judgment-focused concept. Plausibly, all metanormative theorists are united by interest in a common kind of judgment we all make. I then asked whether univocity in claims about the "normativity" of facts and properties between different kinds of cognitivists could be secured by a derivative concept, concerning what those normative judgments were about. My findings here were more ambiguous. First, I showed how a perspectivist, hybrid theory of normative judgments offers an explanation of how philosophers could come to such radically different views on this common subject-matter, potentially saving us from Parfit's pessimism about metanormative theory. But second, I showed how from this point of view we could alternatively distinguish a range of interrelated though different things that these theorists could plausibly mean by 'normativity'—which would save the truth of many of their superficially conflicting claims, but at the expense of implying that many metanormative debates do indeed involve us talking past each other. One way of looking at this is that metanormative theory is centrally concerned with a complex network of interrelated properties and relations, and the words 'normative' and 'normativity' are commonly used, polysemously, to pick out different parts of this network by different theorists and at different times—as I have concluded that I myself have done. My hope is that this investigation helps advance metanormative debate by aiding the disambiguation of different claims about "normativity" and thereby the avoidance of equivocations and mere verbal disputes.[78]

Glossary of Definitions

NORMATIVE$_{ont}$: (As of facts and properties); Having a property P of some special kind.

NORMATIVE$_{rep}$: (As of expressions and judgments); Being about something normative$_{ont}$.

NORMATIVE$_{funct}$: (As of expressions or judgments); Having the nonrepresentational function(s) F.

NORMATIVE$_{lang/judg\text{-}ost}$: (As of expressions/judgments); Having the common property of samples $n_1, n_2, \ldots$

NORMATIVE$_{lang\text{-}exp\text{-}judg}$: (As of language); Having the property of being conventionally used to express normative$_{judg\text{-}ost}$ judgments.

NORMATIVE$_{ont\text{-}judg\text{-}rep}$: Having the property P that is common to all and only the facts and properties of the kind that normative$_{judg\text{-}ost}$ judgments (and normative$_{lang\text{-}exp\text{-}judg}$ expressions) are about.

NORMATIVITY$_{ont\text{-}ab}$: The property of being normative$_{ont}$.

NORMATIVITY$_{ont\text{-}sub}$: The properties (etc.) that are inherently normative$_{ont}$ ("the normative").

NORMATIVITY$_{ont\text{-}judg\text{-}rep\text{-}sub}$: The facts and properties of the kind that normative$_{judg\text{-}ost}$ judgments are about.

[78] For helpful comments and discussion I am grateful to David Copp, Jerry Hull, Nick Laskowski, Neil Mehta, David Plunkett, Mark Schroeder, Bart Streumer, Kevin Toh, Jack Woods, and participants of the Yale Law and Metaethics Workshop in 2015; a meeting of the Princeton Workshop on Normative Philosophy in 2017; talks at the University of Oslo, University of Stockholm, and University of Uppsala in 2018; and my 2018 graduate seminar on normativity at USC. After writing the original version of this chapter I found some similar points made in (Eklund 2017) and (Copp 2017) (although they don't take the threat of polysemy seriously). I owe special thanks to Derek Parfit for awakening me from this particular dogmatic slumber, and deeply regret the loss of the opportunity to hear his reactions.

NORMATIVITY$_{\text{ont-judg-rep-ab}}$: The property shared by all and only the facts and properties of the kind that normative$_{\text{judg-ost}}$ judgments are about.

NORMATIVITY$_{\text{ont-judg-rep-robust-sub}}$: The facts and properties of the kind that normative$_{\text{judg-ost}}$ judgments are about, in virtue of which they are (robustly) normative$_{\text{judg-ost}}$.

NORMATIVITY$_{\text{ont-judg-rep-robust-ab}}$: The property shared by all and only the facts and properties of the kind that normative$_{\text{judg-ost}}$ judgments are about, in virtue of which they are (robustly) normative$_{\text{judg-ost}}$.

NORMATIVITY$_{\text{ont-ost-robust}}$: *That* property (ostending a "robust" property being cognized, perceived, or imagined).

NORMATIVITY$_{\text{ont-judg-relation}}$: The relation that obtains between an agent and an action iff a first-personal, robustly normative$_{\text{judg-ost}}$ judgment about that agent and that action would be true.

NORMATIVITY-RELATIVE-TO-S: The property of standing in the relation of normativity$_{\text{ont-judg-reason}}$ to s.

NORMATIVITY$_{\text{quasi-ont}}$: To apply this concept to some facts or properties is to have or express a favorable attitude toward them.

References

Arpaly, Nomy, and Timothy Schroeder. 2013. *In Praise of Desire*. (Oxford: Oxford University Press).

Audi, Robert. 2012. "Can Normativity Be Naturalized?" In *Ethical Naturalism,* edited by S. Nuccetelli and G. Seay. (Cambridge: Cambridge University Press), 169–193.

Bakka, Conrad. 2015. *A World without Reasons*. MA Thesis, University of Oslo.

Biehl, Joseph. 2008. "The Insignificance of Choice". In *Moral Psychology Today*, edited by D. Chan. (Dordrecht: Springer), 110–175.

Blackburn, Simon. 1993. *Essays in Quasi-realism*. (Oxford: Oxford University Press).

_____. 1998. *Ruling Passions*. (Oxford: Oxford University Press).

Broome, John. 2013. *Rationality through Reasoning*. (Malden, MA: Blackwell).

Copp, David. 2007. *Morality in a Natural World*. (Cambridge: Cambridge University Press).

_____. 2012, "Normativity and Reasons". In *Ethical Naturalism,* edited by S. Nuccetelli and G. Seay. (Cambridge: Cambridge University Press), 24–57.

_____. 2017. "Normative Naturalism and Normative Nihilism". In *Reading Parfit,* edited by S. Kirchin. (New York: Routledge), 28–53.

Dancy, Jonathan (2005), "Nonnaturalism". In *Oxford Handbook of Ethical Theory*, edited by D. Copp. (Oxford: Oxford University Press).

Dowell, Janice. 2016. Review of *Confusion of Tongues, Mind* 125(498):585–593.

Dreier, James. 1990. "Internalism and Speaker Relativism", *Ethics* 101(1):6–26.

_____. 2016. "Another World". In *Passions and Projections,* edited by R. Johnson and M. Smith. (Oxford: Oxford University Press), 155–171.

Eklund, Matti. 2017. *Choosing Normative Concepts*. (Oxford: Oxford University Press).

Enoch, David. 2011a. *Taking Morality Seriously: A Defense of Robust Realism*. (Oxford: Oxford University Press).

_____. 2011b. "Reason-Giving and the Law". In *Oxford Studies in Philosophy of Law,* edited by L. Green and B. Leiter. (Oxford: Oxford University Press), 1–38.

Finlay, Stephen. 2001. *What Does Value Matter?* PhD Dissertation, University of Illinois.

_____. 2004. "The Conversational Practicality of Value Judgement", *Journal of Ethics* 8(3):205–223.

_____. 2006. "The Reasons That Matter". *Australasian Journal of Philosophy* 84(1): 1–20.

_____. 2009. "Oughts and Ends". *Philosophical Studies* 143(3): 315–340.

_____. 2010. "Normativity, Necessity, and Tense: A Recipe for Homebaked Normativity". In *Oxford Studies in Metaethics* 5, edited by R. Shafer-Landau. (Oxford: Oxford University Press), 57–85.

_____. 2014. *Confusion of Tongues*. (Oxford: Oxford University Press).

Finlay, Stephen, and David Plunkett. 2018. "Quasi-expressivism about Statements of Law". *Oxford Studies in the Philosophy of Law*, Vol. 3, edited by J. Gardner, L. Green, and B. Leiter. (Oxford: Oxford University Press).

Fogal, Daniel. 2016. Review of *Confusion of Tongues*, *Ethics* 127(1):281–288.

Foot, Philippa. 1972. "Morality as a System of Hypothetical Imperatives", *Philosophical Review* 81(3):305–316.

_____. 2001. *Natural Goodness*. (Oxford: Oxford University Press).

Gibbard, Allan. 2003. *Thinking How to Live*. (Cambridge, MA: Harvard University Press).

Gregory, Alex. 2015. Review of *Confusion of Tongues*, *Analysis* 75(4):687–689.

Hampton, Jean. 1998. *The Authority of Reason*. (Cambridge: Cambridge University Press).

Harman, Gilbert. 1975. "Moral Relativism Defended", *Philosophical Review* 84 (1): 3–22.

_____. 1996. "Moral Relativism". In G. Harman and J.J. Thomson, *Moral Relativism and Moral Objectivity*. (Oxford: Blackwell).

Huemer, Michael. 2005. *Ethical Intuitionism*. (Houndmills: Palgrave MacMillan).

Hume, David. 1739/1896. *A Treatise of Human Nature*, edited by L. Selby-Bigge. (Oxford: Clarendon Press).

Jackson, Frank. 2008. "The Argument from the Persistence of Moral Disagreement", *Oxford Studies in Metaethics, Vol. 3*. (Oxford: Oxford University Press), 75–86.

Joyce, Richard. 2001. *The Myth of Morality*. (Cambridge: Cambridge University Press).

Korsgaard, Christine. 1996. *The Sources of Normativity*. (Cambridge: Cambridge University Press).

Laskowski, Nicholas. 2014. "How to Pull a Metaphysical Rabbit out of an End-Relational Hat". *Res Philosophica* 91(4):589–607.

_____. 2017. *Rethinking Reductive Realism in Ethics*. PhD Dissertation, University of Southern California.

Mackie, J. L. 1977. *Ethics: Inventing Right and Wrong*. (London: Penguin).

Manne, Kate (2016), "Democratizing Humeanism". In *Weighing Reasons*, edited by E. Lord and B. Maguire. (Oxford: Oxford University Press), 123–140.

McPherson, Tristram. 2011. "Against Quietist Normative Realism", *Philosophical Studies* 154(2):223–240.

_____. 2018. "Authoritatively Normative Concepts". In *Oxford Studies in Metaethics, Vol. 13*, edited by R. Shafer-Landau. (Oxford: Oxford University Press), 253–277.

McPherson, Tristram, and David Plunkett. forthcoming. "Conceptual Ethics and the Methodology of Normative Inquiry". In *Conceptual Engineering and Conceptual Ethics*, edited by A. Burgess, H. Cappelen, and D. Plunkett. (Oxford: Oxford University Press).

Moltmann, Frederike. 2013. *Abstract Objects and the Semantics of Natural Language*. (Oxford: Oxford University Press).

Moore, G. E. 1903. *Principia Ethica*. (Cambridge: Cambridge University Press).

Nietzsche, F. W. 1882/1974. *The Gay Science*. W. Kaufman trans. (New York: Random House).

Olson, Jonas. 2011. "In Defense of Moral Error Theory". In *New Waves in Metaethics*. edited by M. Brady (Houndmills: Palgrave MacMillan), 62–84.

Parfit, Derek. 2011. *On What Matters, Vol. 2*. (Oxford: Oxford University Press).

Plunkett, David, and Scott Shapiro. 2017. "Law, Morality, and Everything Else: General Jurisprudence as a Branch of Metanormative Inquiry", *Ethics* 128(1): 37–68.

Railton, Peter. 1990. "Naturalism and Prescriptivity". *Social Philosophy and Policy* 7(1):151–174.

_____. 2003. "Normative Force and Normative Freedom". In *Facts, Values, and Norms*. (Oxford: Oxford University Press).

Raz, Joseph. 1979. *The Authority of Law*. (Oxford: Oxford University Press).

_____. 1993. "H. L. A. Hart (1907–1992)". *Utilitas* 5(2):145–156.

_____. 1999. *Engaging Reason: On the Theory of Value and Action*. (Oxford: Oxford University Press).

Ridge, Michael. 2014. *Impassioned Belief*. (Oxford: Oxford University Press).

Scanlon, T. M. 1998. *What We Owe to Each Other*. (Cambridge, MA: Belknap Press).

_____. 2014. *Being Realistic about Reasons*. (Oxford: Oxford University Press).

Schroeder, Mark. 2007. *Slaves of the Passions*. (Oxford: Oxford University Press).

_____. 2013. "Tempered Expressivism". In *Oxford Studies in Metaethics* 8, edited by R. Shafer-Landau. (Oxford: Oxford University Press).

Schroeter, Laura, and Francois Schroeter. ms., "Deflationary Normative Naturalism".

Silverstein, Matthew. 2017. "Ethics and Practical Reasoning", *Ethics* 127(2):353–382.

Smith, Michael. 1994. *The Moral Problem*. (Malden, MA: Blackwell).

Street, Sharon. 2008. "Constructivism about Reasons". In *Oxford Studies in Metaethics* 3, edited by R. Shafer-Landau. (Oxford: Oxford University Press).

Streumer, Bart. 2017. *Unbelievable Errors*. (Oxford: Oxford University Press).

Thomson, Judith Jarvis. 1996. "Moral Objectivity". In G. Harman and J.J. Thomson. *Moral Relativism and Moral Objectivity*. (Oxford: Blackwell).

_____. 2008. *Normativity*. (Chicago: Open Court).

Toppinen, Teemu. 2013. "Believing in Expressivism". In *Oxford Studies in Metaethics* 8, edited by R. Shafer-Landau. (Oxford: Oxford University Press).

Tresan, Jon. 2006. "De Dicto Internalist Cognitivism", *Noûs* 40(1):143–165.

Wedgwood, Ralph. 2007. *The Nature of Normativity*. (Oxford: Oxford University Press).

Westermarck, E. 1932. *Ethical Relativity*. (London: Kegan Paul).

Williams, Bernard. 1981. "Internal and External Reasons", reprinted in *Moral Luck: Philosophical Papers 1973–1980*. (Cambridge: Cambridge University Press), 101–113.

Wittgenstein, Ludwig. 1997. "Lecture on Ethics". In *Moral Discourse and Practice*, edited by S. Darwall, A. Gibbard, and P. Railton. (Oxford: Oxford University Press).

Wodak, Daniel. forthcoming. "Mere Formalities". In *Canadian Journal of Philosophy*.

Woods, Jack. 2018. "The Authority of Formality". In *Oxford Studies in Metaethics* Vol. 13, edited by R. Shafer-Landau. (Oxford: Oxford University Press), 207–229.

10 Legal Philosophy à la carte*

Kevin Toh

I. Introduction

Many contemporary legal philosophers characterize their own and others' positions in legal philosophy by employing certain metaphysical idioms. If "social facts" were taken to mean behavioral and psychological facts, some of which may amount to certain social practices among groups of people, then many contemporary legal philosophers characterize legal positivism in one or more of the following ways, or some close variations thereof:

(P1) Legal facts are *dependent* only *on* social facts.
(P2) Legal facts are *grounded* only *in* social facts.
(P3) The fact that the law is such-and-such obtains only *in virtue of* social facts.
(P4) The fact that the law is such-and-such is *constituted* only *by* social facts.
(P5) Social facts wholly *determine* what the law is.
(P6) Social facts are the sole *truth-makers* of legal claims.

* This chapter was substantially written in Winter 2009–2010 after an email correspondence with Brian Leiter and a particularly useful conversation with Mitch Berman. I am grateful for the comments and questions from audiences at Binghamton University, two sessions of the Law and Philosophy Workshop at the University of Chicago, San Francisco State University, the Nature of Law Conference at McMaster University, and the Annual Meeting of the Australian Society of Legal Philosophy held in 2014 at Murdoch University where a version was presented as a keynote address. I also benefited from helpful written comments on prior drafts from Mitch Berman, John Deigh, Bill Edmundson, David Enoch, Jeff Goldsworthy, Ben Laurence, Brian Leiter, Eliot Michelson, Gerhard Nuffer, David Plunkett, Scott Shapiro, and Dale Smith. An earlier and shorter version of the chapter was published in Spanish as Toh (2012). Thanks to Alejandro Calzetta for the translation.

Dimensions of Normativity. David Plunkett, Scott J. Shapiro, and Kevin Toh.

I will hereinafter call these theses, and their variations, the "P-theses". Legal antipositivism[1] is in turn often conceived as denials of one or more of the P-theses—e.g., that legal facts are often dependent on moral or normative considerations, that the fact that the law is such-and-such obtains often in virtue of moral or normative considerations, etc.

It may turn out that according to the best meta-moral or metanormative theory that we can muster, moral and other normative considerations are, or are wholly constituted by, natural facts of certain sorts, and even behavioral and psychological facts that are social facts. Throughout this chapter, however, I will be assuming that this is *not* the case. In other words, I will be assuming throughout that moral and other normative considerations are not, or are not wholly constituted by, natural facts. Strictly speaking, I do not need this assumption for much of this chapter; I need it only in Section VI. Elsewhere in the chapter, I could have done with a much weaker and less controversial assumption that, even if moral and other normative considerations were or consisted of natural and even social facts, there would have been a cleavage between, on the one hand, the social facts that legal positivists have deemed the only determinants of the law; and on the other, any facts, even social ones, that amount to the moral and other normative considerations of the sort that antipositivists insist are partial determinants of the law. But proceeding with this weaker assumption (and suspending it in favor of the stronger assumption in Section VI infra) would have made my exposition much more cumbersome and confusing than I want it to be. I will therefore rely throughout on the stronger assumption characterized above. Given that my primary goal in this chapter is to delineate and explore what I consider a hitherto neglected option in legal philosophy, I hope making the stronger assumption—which moreover, though controversial, is far from outlandish—would not be deemed too high a price for entry.

Now, some philosophers would balk at facile reliance on the metaphysical notions with which the P-theses are formulated above, and call for translations of these theses into those that rely on the more familiar and tractable modal notions of necessity and possibility. But recently a number of philosophers (e.g., Fine 2001 and 2012; Rosen 2010; Schaffer 2010) have made quite compelling cases for admissibility and even indispensability of the notions exemplified above, and I shall follow their lead. I do want to clarify the nature of the competing theses in legal philosophy. But I do not propose to do so by replacing the above-instanced metaphysical idioms with some others that contemporary philosophers in general have come to feel more comfortable handling. Even assuming the intelligibility and good philosophical hygiene of the theses as formulated above, I shall argue, contemporary debate about the nature of law has proceeded while overlooking an important theoretical option. And that overlooked option becomes quite obvious once we examine carefully what motivations there really are for adopting legal positivist theses like the P-theses.

For convenience, let me simply call the relations of the sort that, according to the P-theses, obtain between social facts on the one hand and legal facts on the other "determination"

[1] I use "antipositivism" instead of the more familiar "natural law theory" given that the most prominent alternative to legal positivism in recent years has been Ronald Dworkin's conception of the nature of law, which is not unproblematically classified as a natural law theory. See (Dworkin 1982).

relations. Determination is not the same as supervenience, which is one of the modal notions with which philosophers have recently developed some degree of comfort. For one thing, supervenience, as philosophers usually conceive it, is neither symmetric nor asymmetric. In other words, a supervenience relation may hold between two sets of facts or properties in only one direction, or in both directions; whereas determination seems invariably asymmetric. Second, determination seems to imply ontological priority of one set of facts or properties, which is not invariably the case with supervenience. Third, very important for our purposes, the difference between legal positivism and legal antipositivism, *as that distinction has usually been conceived in recent years*, may go missing if we relied solely on supervenience, or any other such modal notions.[2] Two paragraphs ago, I talked of meta-moral or metanormative views that conceive moral or normative considerations as, or as constituted by, the behavioral and psychological facts that are social facts. But even those who favor a different kind of meta-moral or metanormative position—i.e., those who favor a naturalism of a different sort, a non-naturalism, or even non-factualism for the metaphysics of moral or normative considerations—could be committed to necessary covariance of moral or normative facts on the one hand, and behavioral and psychological facts on the other.[3] When any of such meta-moral or metanormative positions are in play, we would lack the ability to mark the distinction between legal positivism and legal antipositivism in terms of supervenience of legal facts on social facts. The idiom and metaphysics of determination can get us out of the bind. Even when legal positivists and legal antipositivists share a commitment to the supervenience of legal facts on social facts, their difference, as usually conceived in recent years, can be formulated as follows. Legal positivists believe that social facts are the sole determinants of legal facts; whereas legal antipositivists believe that some moral or normative considerations, along with social facts, are determinants of legal facts. These are compelling considerations for thinking that the P-theses and their denials could not be reduced to theses couched in supervenience or some other such modal notions. In any case, I will be relying on the idiom and metaphysics of determination both to characterize the standard conception of the distinction between legal positivism and legal antipositivism that I have just discussed, and also to formulate my pitch for its revision subsequently in this chapter.

II. Hart on the Existence of Laws

Yet a fourth difference between supervenience and determination is that supervenience relations are not plausibly thought as brute, and instead must be explained (see, e.g., Blackburn 1983, 118–119; Kim 1993, 167–168); whereas some determination relations could be thought

---

[2] As Gideon Rosen has helpfully pointed out. See (Rosen 2010, 113–114), and some related discussion in (Rosen 2015, 203, 205–207).

[3] I do not go for a somewhat stronger claim (i.e., use "would" instead of "could") here not only because some do not buy supervenience, but also because some may be committed to a supervenience of moral or normative facts on natural facts that include in the supervenience base natural facts other than social facts. In the latter case, a meta-moral or metanormative theorist would not necessarily be committed to a necessary covariance of moral or normative facts on the one hand and social facts on the other. Even when all the social facts were the same, the moral or normative facts could be different because some other subvening natural facts are different.

brute. Still, in most cases, determination relations call for an explanation. And any determination relation of the sort articulated by the P-theses, it appears, should be susceptible to an explanation of why it holds (see Rosen 2010, 130–133). For such an explanation, contemporary legal positivists would appeal to the nature of law. And their conception of the nature of law would rely to a great extent on the arguments that H. L. A. Hart marshaled in *The Concept of Law* (1961/1994). In the relatively narrow confines of legal philosophy, Hart's legal theory has hardly been rivaled in its explanatory powers before or since. Hart sought to explain, and is widely thought to have succeeded in explaining, the following, among other things:

(F1) Some laws are power-conferring rules (as opposed to duty-imposing rules).
(F2) Some customary rules are laws even before being recognized as such by legal officials.
(F3) Some communities governed by laws are without legislators whose legal powers are unlimited.
(F4) Some laws retain their binding force even after the deaths of the lawmakers who enacted those particular laws.[4]

It is the failure of command theories of law—proposed by Jeremy Bentham, John Austin, and others—to explain satisfactorily facts of these sorts that motivated Hart to seek out an alternative theory of law.

Hart argued that facts like the above could be explained by conceiving laws in the following way. Laws (or *legal* rules) come in hierarchically structured packages, with some specific kinds of second-order rules, or rules governing the operation of the rules within the package. These second-order rules—which Hart calls *secondary rules* to distinguish them from *primary rules* that directly govern conduct—include: the *rules of change,* which regulate any modification in the rules of the system; the *rules of adjudication,* which regulate settling of disputes about the content and application of the rules of the system; and the *rule of recognition,* which regulates the identification of the rules of the system. A legal system exists or prevails in a community if some powerful subset of the members of the community—call them the "officials" of that community—*accept* the secondary rules (in the sense to be specified presently) and follow them as the result, and the rest of the community at least follow the rules that are valid according to the rule of recognition prevailing in that community. A person accepts a rule, or takes an "internal point of view" to use the terminology Hart made famous, when he believes there to be reasons to follow it. Such acceptance is constituted by the person's dispositions to regulate his own conduct in accordance with the rule, to justify his own and others' conduct by appeals to that rule, and to criticize his own and others' deviance by appeals to that rule. Presumably, to treat a rule of recognition as reason-giving is to treat generally the rules that are valid according to that rule of recognition as reason-giving. Hart does not go into how thoroughly a person must be disposed to treat each valid law as reason-giving to count as accepting a rule of recognition, but we can assume that some general tendency must be there.

[4] Just to be clear, this is not meant to be an exhaustive list of Hart's explananda.

In effect, according to Hart, the existence of laws (or a legal system) in a community of people consists ultimately, and entirely, of certain behavioral and psychological facts, or social facts, prevailing in that community. It is for this reason that legal positivists avow one or more of the P-theses. Joseph Raz once characterized Hart as "regard[ing] the existence and content of the law as a matter of social fact whose connection to moral or any other values is contingent and precarious" (1985, 194). In this respect, Hart's conception of law is not different from the older positivist ones implicated by Bentham's and Austin's command theories.[5] But given its clear explanatory superiority over the older theories, it does a much better job of underwriting the determination relation between social facts and legal facts summed up by the P-theses. It can be said therefore that contemporary legal positivists' acceptance of the P-theses is ultimately based on the impressive explanatory powers of Hart's conception of the nature of law.

III. More Recent Developments

This is not to say that contemporary legal positivists rest content with what Hart offered. Many legal philosophers believe that there are facts in addition to (F1)–(F4) and their ilk that a legal theory should explain, and some of them have thought that Hart's theory falls short in explaining some of these important additional facts. Among these are the following:

(F5) A thriving legal system may exist in a community even in the absence of a law-identifying rule that is commonly or jointly accepted by the community's officials.
(F6) Even in hard cases—i.e., those cases in which decisions are not clearly determined by jointly accepted legal rules and their clear consequents—judges often consider their decisions as completely constrained by preexisting laws.
(F7) Laws create genuine reasons (and even duties or obligations) to behave as the laws say.
(F8) It is possible for unconfused people to have genuine legal disagreements (as opposed to disagreements about what the law should be) that persist despite their agreements on all social factual issues.

A very large portion of contemporary legal philosophy can be characterized as various combinations of attempts to tinker with the Hartian framework to account for these additional facts, or attempts to deny the need to account for some of these facts.

(F7) and (F8) have been particularly important in motivating and shaping contemporary legal philosophical debates since the 1970s, and (F8) in particular will feature importantly in the rest of this chapter as well. (F5) is also an important consideration, but Hart arguably had resources to account for it, and in fact did so at least in a preliminary way in the largely unread last chapter of *The Concept of Law*.[6] (F6) is the alleged feature of our legal practice

---

[5] According to Raz, "[i]t is common ground to all legal positivists . . . that the content and existence of the law can be determined by reference to social facts and without relying on moral considerations" (1979, 53). Raz is here making an epistemological point, but it seems safe to think that this epistemological point is parasitic on the metaphysical point summed up in various ways by P-theses. See (Greenberg 2004, 158).

[6] For slightly greater elaboration of this point, see (Toh 2010a, esp. 339–340).

that Dworkin (1967) emphasized early on in his criticisms of Hart's legal theory, but his later criticisms emphasized (F7) and (F8) instead. At a couple of places in *Law's Empire* (1986, viii, 234), Dworkin suggests that (F6) and (F8) really amount to the same thing. I am not sure that that is entirely the case, but I will in the rest of this chapter pay attention only to the aspects of (F6) that complement (F8).

(F7) is the putative feature of law that usually goes by the term "the normativity of law". Dworkin (1972 and 1986) set the scene on this issue by first articulating the complaint that even if the kind of social facts that according to Hart amount to the existence of a legal system in a community were to obtain, that would not necessarily mean that the members of that community have reasons and obligations to behave as their laws say. Since then, others have reiterated this criticism or proffered their own variations on it (see, e.g., Raz 1975/1990, 56–58; Green 1999). And in response, legal philosophers of the positivist bent have proposed, in order to account for the normativity of law, a number of ingenious variations on and/or specifications of the configuration of behavioral cum psychological facts that according to Hart amount to the existence of a legal system.[7] Setting aside the issue of whether any of these proposals succeed in their intended task, it is far from clear that (F7) really should be considered a non-contingent feature of laws or legal systems, and David Enoch (2011) has recently made a very strong case for doubting that that is the case.[8]

Moving on to (F8), once again, it was Dworkin who initiated the program of devising a conception of law that accounts for this fact. His term for the kind of legal disagreements that allegedly could persist despite lawyers and judges' total agreement on social factual issues is "theoretical disagreements". Since Dworkin broached the issue in the first chapter of *Law's Empire*, a number of legal positivists have made attempts to account for theoretical disagreements within the confines of the positivist framework (see, e.g., Raz 1998; Marmor 1998/2001; Coleman 2001, lecs. 7–8, 11; Shapiro 2007). Difficulties that such attempts encounter appear quite large, and that fact seems to be one motivation behind Brian Leiter's (2009) forceful recent arguments to cast doubt on the idea that (F8) should be thought a real explanandum that legal theories should seek to account for.

These recent and not-so-recent activities in legal philosophy indicate that while many contemporary legal positivists are not *completely* happy with the details of Hart's legal theory, they on the whole have great degrees of trust in the framework for conceiving the existence of laws and legal systems that Hart's theory furnished. They appear to think that Hart's theory has sufficient explanatory powers to warrant further tinkering with his theory, or its basic outlines, in attempts to extend its explanatory reach to cover some of the "data" that his theory fails to explain. They further appear to think that the tinkering could be done, and the framework's explanatory powers sufficiently extended, without thereby abandoning the view that the existence of laws or a legal system in a community consists entirely of the existence

[7] See, e.g., (Postema 1982); (Marmor 1998/2001 and 2009); (Shapiro 2002 and 2011). Marmor and Shapiro put interesting spins on their conceptions of the normativity problem, and they may resist the characterization of it that I give in the text. I discuss their versions of the normativity problem, their proposed solutions, and my reservations in (Toh 2010c and 2018).

[8] I myself have cast doubt on the alleged problem of the normativity of law, as that problem is usually put or understood by the likes of the legal philosophers I listed in the preceding footnote. See (Toh 2005, 77; 2010a, 331 and n.1).

in that community of certain social facts. That is their ground for subscribing to one or more of the P-theses.

IV. The Fallacy of Double Duty

I want, however, to question whether the explanatory powers of Hart's legal theory, or some variation thereof, really warrant a commitment to the P-theses, at least as those theses are usually understood.

Let us use the generic name "Hartian theories" to refer to legal theories patterned along the lines that Hart has proposed. A successful Hartian theory would, while positing only the social facts of the sort that Hart referred to, explain the features of laws that need to be explained—namely, those that really are important invariable or non-contingent features of communities with laws. The set of such features would certainly include (F1)–(F5). For the moment, let us remain agnostic about the other facts discussed in the preceding section. Given the forceful arguments that Enoch and Leiter have made recently, we do not want to jump too quickly to the presumption that a successful legal theory would need to explain (F7) and (F8) as well.

Hart's particular Hartian theory can be summed up roughly as follows:

(H) A community is governed by laws when its members regulate their behavior and practical thought by a set of rules, which set includes some higher-order rules governing the following types of operations of the rules of the set: (i) revision of the rules of the set; (ii) resolution of disputes about the rules of the set; and (iii) identification of the rules that belong to the set.

Other Hartian theories that have been proposed and discussed more recently can be considered variations or specifications of this template. If we were to find one such theory credible on explanatory grounds, then that in turn would clearly warrant a commitment to the following:

(L1) Whether a community has, or is governed by, (a system of) laws is a matter only of certain social facts existing in that community.

The idiom "a matter of", as used here, belongs to the family of metaphysical idioms that were used to formulate the P-theses at the beginning of the chapter. (L1) could be formulated using some of the other idioms instead—i.e., in terms of "dependent on", "grounded in", "in virtue of", etc. But then is not (L1) just a P-thesis? And does not the fact that (H), or some better version of it, implies (L1) indicate that a successful Hartian theory would warrant a commitment to the P-theses?

Not quite. For contemporary legal positivists are unlikely to rest content with (L1) alone. Instead, those who endorse one or more of the P-theses are likely to construe those theses as implying the following as well:

(L3)[9] Whether some (first-order) legal claim is true or correct is a matter only of certain social facts existing in the relevant community.

[9] The reason for this numbering should become obvious presently.

Here are some instances in which contemporary legal positivists appear to infer (L3) from (H), or from (L1):

> [I]f Hart is correct, and social practices explain how legal systems are possible, then legal reasoning must always be traceable to a social rule of recognition. Arguments about who has authority to do what, what rights individuals have, which legal texts are authoritative, and the proper way to interpret them must ultimately be resolved by reference to the sociological facts of official practice. (Shapiro 2011, 102)

> [T]he Rule of Recognition, on Hart's view, is a social rule, meaning its content—that is, the criteria of legal validity—is fixed by a complex empirical fact, namely, the *actual practice* of officials (and the attitude they evince towards the practice). So it looks like the only dispute about the criteria of legal validity that is possible, on Hart's view, is an empirical or "heads count" dispute: namely, a dispute about what judges are doing, and how many of them are doing it, since it is *the actual practice of officials and their attitudes towards that practice* that fixes the criteria of legal validity according to the positivist. (Leiter 2009, 1222)

> Especially, but not only where a legal system has no canonical text, it is common to say that ultimate constitutional questions are questions of practice (or *realpolitik*), not questions of law. Hart exposed this as a false contrast. That a question is one of practice does not mean that it is not one of law. For some law is made by what people do . . . . (Gardner 2008, 69–70)

It may be thought that we are warranted in inferring (L3) as well as (L1) from a successful Hartian theory. After all, from such a theory, we should be able to infer the following:

> (L2) Whether a particular rule is a law (or a legal rule) in a community is a matter only of certain social facts existing in that community.

According to (H), for example, the existence of a legal system in a community requires the members of that community (or their officials more specifically) to employ a particular rule of recognition—i.e., a rule that sets out the criteria that rules need to meet for them to belong to that legal system. And whether a community has a law with a particular content is a matter only of a rule with that content meeting the criteria that the prevailing rule of recognition delineates.[10] It would follow that the social facts that amount to the existence of a legal system in a community include whatever social facts that amount to the existence of any particular law in that community. And (L3) seems to follow straightaway from (L2). In fact, it may be thought, (L3) is just another formulation of (L2).

---

[10] Things would get more complicated if we were dealing with a Hartian theory that has the capacity to account for (F5). But since I am here articulating a line of thinking that I am about to question, let me just bracket such complications.

I think that this or something very close to it is the line of reasoning that practically all contemporary legal positivists have followed or presupposed. But this line of reasoning is fallacious. I think the fallacy can be put into sharp relief by looking at certain moral analogues of both (H) and the three L-theses. We could get a sense of what kinds of social facts could be taken as amounting to the existence of a *morality* (or a set of mores) in a community by invoking certain meta-moral views. According to Allan Gibbard's (1990) influential conception of morality, for example, the rules of morality can be distinguished from other rules by the fact that the rules of morality have to do with the warrant of guilt and impartial anger.[11] We can sum up the resulting conditions for the existence of a morality as follows:

(G) A community is governed by mores when its members regulate their emotions of guilt and impartial anger by a set of rules, and those emotions of guilt and impartial anger in turn regulate the members' behavior and practical thought.

We do not have to try to assess (G), as we are using it merely as an example. It seems safe to assume that something like (G)—i.e., some thesis that says that the existence of some kinds of social facts amount to or constitute the existence or prevalence of a set of mores in a community—will have to be true. And from that fact, we could infer the following:

(M1) Whether a community has, or is governed by, (a set of) mores is a matter only of certain social facts existing in that community.

Furthermore, it would follow from (G) that whether a particular rule of morality exists or prevails in a community would depend only on whether the members of that community think that guilt on the part of a person and impartial anger on the part of others would be warranted in the event of that person's noncompliance with the relevant rule. In other words, the following could be inferred from (G) as well:

(M2) Whether a particular rule is a mos[12] (or a rule of morality) in a community is a matter only of certain social facts existing in that community.

In sum, both a community's having a morality, and its having a particular rule of morality, are ultimately and fully determined by the existence in that community of certain behavioral and psychological facts.

The following, however, is a different story altogether:

(M3) Whether some (first-order) moral claim is true or correct is a matter only of certain social facts existing in the relevant community.

---

[11] For similar conceptions of morality, see (Brandt 1979, ch. 9); (Williams 1986, ch. 10); (Skorupski 1993). See also (Hart 1961/1994, ch. 8) for a more rudimentary conception along a similar line. Although Gibbard is an expressivist when it comes to the semantics of moral discourse, his expressivism is detachable from his conception of morality, about to be approximated in the text as (G).

[12] "Mos" is the singular of "mores", as Gerhard Nuffer pointed out to me.

If (G) were to imply (M3) as well as (M1) and (M2), then it would in effect be a particular *first-order* or *substantive* moral thesis[13] according to which the rightness or wrongness of an action depends only on whether the rules that prevails in the (agent's or assessor's) community say that guilt and impartial anger are warranted when a person carries out such an action. That is certainly a very implausible view, and does a very poor job of competing against, for example, the standard utilitarian and Kantian views. But what is more important—i.e., more important than the fact that social-factualist first-order moral views of the sort just sketched are implausible—is that (M3) is not implicated by (M1) and (M2). A person can without inconsistency or any kind of theoretical tension believe (M1) and (M2) and reject (M3). Gibbard for instance while espousing (M1) and (M2) believes that whether some first-order moral claim is true or correct is not merely a factual matter; he believes that it is partly a normative matter.[14] But if this is the case with the three M-theses, should we not, by way of *the principle of parity*, think the same of the trio of L-theses? Should we not think that a person can without inconsistency or theoretical tension believe (L1) and (L2), and reject (L3)? And that would mean that (L1) and (L2) do not imply (L3).[15]

One might balk at this last suggestion by questioning the applicability here of the principle of parity. One might argue that whereas first-order *moral* social factualism like (M3) is quite implausible, first-order *legal* social factualism like (L3) is quite plausible.[16] I am not

[13] By speaking of a "first-order" or "substantive" moral thesis here, what I want to distinguish it from are meta-moral theses (or what are more commonly called "metaethical" theses). What I am talking about is a thesis that makes claims *in* morality, not claims *about* morality.

[14] Gibbard happens to be a utilitarian. He believes that the moral status of actions—their moral rightness or wrongness—depends not only on whether those actions are likely to lead to most human well-being, but also on the principle of utility, which is a rule or a norm. It follows that according to him the truth or correctness of first-order moral claims is not simply a matter of facts, but also of norms (or at least *a* norm).

[15] I should emphasize that I am not by any means assuming that any plausible conceptions of the nature of morality—i.e., any plausible competitor to (G)—have to be limited or devoid of first-order or substantive implications as (G) is. Some influential conceptions of morality have named the properties that constitute or ground the properties of moral goodness or rightness. See, e.g., Sturgeon (1985); Railton (1986); Boyd (1988); Smith (1994). And some have even suggested that the sentences enumerating certain nonmoral or non–normative facts have analytic implications for sentences of moral goodness or rightness. See, e.g., (Foot 1958–1959); (Jackson 1998 and 2003); see also (Lewis 1970 and 1989). All I am arguing in the text is that legal philosophers have all too readily and without argument have assumed that Hart's (H) is analogous to these latter metanormative theories in its first-order or substantive implications, when in fact it is quite open and plausible to think that it is more analogous to Gibbard's (G) in *not* having such implications.

[16] In his very helpful comments on a prior draft, David Plunkett pressed this point. He suggested that laws are like rules of games, and for this reason first-order legal social factualism is quite a bit more plausible than first-order moral social factualism. Plunkett further suggested that the implication is that what I deem a fallacious move on the part of many contemporary legal positivists is better conceived as a case of suppressed unargued-for premise. I believe what follows in the text is responsive to Plunkett's worry.

I should add that first-order social factualism about game rules, apparently very widely shared among philosophers, is not obvious to me. Dworkin (1975, 101–105) offers, to my mind, very plausible and instructive discussion of a chess dispute that indicates that what chess rules call for is not best conceived as purely a social factual matter. Also very much relevant here are games of make-believe that children play, and that Kendall

sure if this last point is right, but either way, this point does not undermine my contention. My contention is that commitments to (L1) and (L2) do not require in their wake a commitment to (L3) as well; the trio of L-theses are not a package deal. For all I have said, (L3) may be plausible in its own right. But a Hartian theory that implies (L1) and (L2) need not imply (L3) as well. That happens to be the case with (H), Hart's own theory, for example. The explanatory considerations that Hart marshaled to argue for his (H) support a theory that implies (L1) and (L2), but not (L3). If (L3) is to be taken on board, if a Hartian theory of the sort that implies (L3) as well as (L1)–(L2) is to be favored or sought after, that is something that needs to be motivated on separate or additional explanatory grounds.

It may also be thought that whereas the transition from (M2) to (M3) is obviously illicit, the transition from (L2) to (L3) is quite a bit more plausible.[17] If some particular rule is a law, then, it appears, a legal claim stating the content of that rule is true or correct. And the set of facts in virtue of which some particular rule qualifies as a law would be the same set of facts in virtue of which the corresponding legal claim is true or correct. I believe, however, that the intuitive appeal of this last line of reasoning, and the temptation to deny the parity between (L2) and (L3) on the one hand and (M2) and (M3) on the other stems mainly from a terminological quirk. We are not tempted to infer (M3) from (M2) because the mere fact that some rule is a mos in a community does not warrant the conclusion that that rule is morally right. The term "mos" clearly designates what *is treated as* morally right, not what *is* morally right. The term "law", on the other hand, is much more ambiguous, and it could mean either what *is treated as* legally valid or what *is* legally valid. Perhaps there is then a need to disambiguate (L2) as follows:

(L2a) Whether a particular rule *is treated as* legally valid in a community is a matter only of certain social facts existing in that community.

(L2b) Whether a particular rule *is* legally valid in a community is a matter only of certain social facts existing in that community.

The convenient availability of the term "mos" (and "mores") makes this kind of disambiguation unnecessary when we are discussing morality. An unfortunate fact is that we do not have an analogous term for our discussion about law. But this terminological quirk need not

Walton invokes to explain our interactions with works of representational art. According to Walton (1990, 12), works of representational art function as props in games of make-believe the way that dolls and teddy bears function as props in children's games of make-believe. As a child is prompted by a doll to imagine that she has a baby, we are prompted by a novel by Arthur Conan Doyle to imagine that a man of Sherlock Holmes's description lives on Baker Street in London and is involved in various exploits. How such games of make-believe are to be played—i.e., what the rules of any such games of make-believe are—is a difficult and fraught question. But first-order social factualism about such rules is unlikely to be the most plausible of possible positions to take. See (Stevenson 1950); (Walton 1979, 212). The relevant discussion in Walton (1990, 38, ch. 4) gives the impression that Walton is committed to a first-order social factualism about fictional truths in that work. But in a conversation, he indicated that he still subscribes to the older view indicated in Walton (1979). Given the considerations of the sort just outlined, I find myself disinclined to accept a clean distinction between "robust" (or "full-blooded") normativity and merely "formal" (or "internal") normativity, which a number of other contributors to this volume embrace.

[17] Thanks to Mitch Berman and David Enoch for flagging the worry addressed in this paragraph.

trip us up or lead us astray. Notice that what we need to infer (L3) is (L2b); (L2a) is not good enough for that purpose. On the other hand, what we can infer from (L1), and more fundamentally from the explanatory considerations that warrant our acceptance of (L1), is (L2a), not (L2b). (L2a) is the legal analogue of (M2), and neither of these two warrants the first-order conclusion of (L3) or (M3). I initially formulated (L2) the way I did because I wanted the reader to feel the temptation to make the slide that I believe that many contemporary legal philosophers have made. But once we disambiguate (L2) as I have recommended, the temptation to make the slide should subside. (In subsequent paragraphs, I shall continue to speak in terms of "(L2)"; but I should be taken to mean "(L2a)" rather than "(L2b)".)

In sum, I believe that a majority of contemporary legal philosophers, antipositivists as well as positivists, are guilty of a fallacy. They have conceived legal positivism in terms of Hartian theories. And they have thought that a successful Hartian theory supports (L3) as well as (L1) and (L2). But that is not necessarily the case. A successful Hartian theory could support (L1) and (L2), but not (L3). Almost no one I know of makes the mistake of thinking that (G) entails or supports (M3). But the mistake of thinking that (H) entails or supports (L3) has been endemic among legal philosophers. The relevant fallacy could be called "the fallacy of double duty". In effect, legal philosophers have been assuming that theories like (H) do double duty both as a theory that specifies the facts that amount to or constitute a community's having a legal system or a law, and as a theory that specifies the truth- or correctness-conditions of first-order legal claims. We can conclude that (H) and its close variations do support the P-theses, only if the P-theses were interpreted to mean no more than (L1) and (L2); but they do not support the P-theses if these theses were interpreted to imply (L3) as well.[18]

V. From a Fallacy to an Oversight

The fallacy of double duty is responsible for contemporary legal philosophers' oversight of a quite significant theoretical option in legal philosophy. That is the possibility of having a conception of legal positivism that numbers among the grounds or determinants of legal

[18] The mistake that I am accusing many recent legal philosophers of making is related to the mistake of thinking that desires always feature in agents' "foreground" rather than being in the "background" when they act, to use Philip Pettit and Michael Smith's terminology. See (Pettit and Smith 1990); cf. (Schroeder 2007: ch. 2). As Pettit and Smith observe, even if actions are always causally explained by beliefs and desires of agents, as the intentional conception of human actions says, that does not mean that the relevant desires (or the prospects of satisfying those desires) always figure as justifying reasons in agents' deliberations. Desires can figure strictly in the background as causes of actions, without figuring in the foreground of deliberations. The view I am putting forward in the text could be put as follows: The psychological and behavioral facts that amount to the existence of legal systems and laws in a community of people may figure strictly in the background of those people's adherence to their laws, without the same set of facts figuring in the foreground of their legal deliberations. Warren Quinn (1993), for one, attacked certain philosophers for taking desires as chief justifying reasons. It turns out that Quinn was mistaken in construing these philosophers as thinking of desires as always figuring in the foreground of practical deliberations. In my opinion, Dworkin and others following him have been similarly mistaken in construing the psychological and behavioral facts that, according to Hart, amount to the existence of legal systems and laws in a community as always figuring in the foreground of legal deliberations.

truth or correctness normative considerations as well as social facts. That may strike many readers as paradoxical, but let me explain.

Let us go back to the language of determination. According to one of the P-theses,

(P5) Social facts wholly *determine* what the law is.

I have been using the term "determinants" to talk about the facts that do the determining. Now, let "resultants" be the facts that are determined. In committing the fallacy of double duty, contemporary legal positivists are conflating two different sets of resultants. Each of the first set of resultants is the fact that some rule *is treated* by a community of people as legally valid. Each of the second set is the fact that some rule *is* legally valid. In the preceding section, I have argued that Hartian theories tell us that social facts fully determine the fact that certain rules *are treated as* the law in a community; but they do not necessarily tell us that social facts fully determine what rules *are* the law in a community. In morality, we readily distinguish between what is treated by a community of people as morally called for and what is morally called for. Contemporary legal positivists do not seem to recognize an analogous distinction between what is treated as the law and what is the law. If what is treated as the law really is equivalent to what is the law, then that is something that needs to be shown or argued for. My point is that Hart's legal theory, and the explanatory considerations that he marshaled to argue for that theory, do not get us to that conclusion. Of course, a Hartian theory different from (H) may get us to that conclusion; but that alternative theory would have to have some extra features that are motivated by explanatory considerations that are different from or additional to the ones that motivated (H).[19]

Once we distinguish the two kinds of resultants, we see that the two kinds may be determined by, or obtain in virtue of, disparate sets of determinants. One salient possibility is that whereas the determinants of the fact that some rules are treated as the law in a community are all social facts, the determinants of the fact that some rules are the law may include some normative considerations. According to many moral philosophers, that is how things are with moral rightness and wrongness. For example, the resultant that some action is morally right could be deemed to have two determinants: (i) the fact that such an action is likely to produce the greatest balance of happiness over unhappiness, and (ii) the principle of utility. Or the same resultant could be thought to have the following two determinants: (i) the fact that the maxim (or the intention) with which the relevant agent would carry out that action could be willed as a universal law of nature, and (ii) the categorical imperative. Either way, there would be a normative determinant—(ii) in each example—that partly determines the resultant that the relevant action is morally right. Furthermore, moral philosophers of either

[19] The fact that Hart himself did not conflate the two kinds of resultants—i.e., the fact that he himself was not guilty of the fallacy of double duty—is clearly indicated by his constant insistence that we distinguish internal legal statements from external legal statements. See, e.g., (Hart 1961/1994, vi, 89–91, 102–105); cf. (Bulygin 1982). Internal legal statements are statements of what the law is, whereas external legal statements are statements of what rules are treated as the law by the members of a community. Hart emphasized the importance of this distinction in the preface to *The Concept of Law*, and throughout the book and also in his other writings. Contemporary legal philosophers' neglect of this distinction, in my opinion, has come with a great cost.

utilitarian or Kantian stripe could happily grant at the same time that the determinants of the resultant that some action is *treated as* or *considered* morally right are without exception social facts. An analogous combination of views about the two legal resultants is certainly a possibility. It makes sense to think that the determinants of the fact that the law is thought or considered such-and-such are all social facts. But we can at the same time think that the determinants of the fact that the law *is* such-and-such are not all social facts, but include some normative considerations.

It may be complained here that the conception of law that is implicated by this last combination of views is not a legal positivist one. It may be thought that whenever the ultimate determinants of what the law is are thought to include normative considerations, the resulting view is an antipositivist one. But such a diagnosis would be too hasty and arguably question-begging. I grant that such a diagnosis is what is motivated by the recently standard conceptions of legal positivism and legal antipositivism. But I believe that these recent conceptions are dispensable, for we can capture the crucial underlying motivations for the distinction without them. First, notice that with the particular combination of views that I am putting forward, we would still be of the opinion that the prevalence of a legal system or of a particular law in a community is wholly a matter of social facts, contrary to what some prominent antipositivists think.[20]

Second, in suggesting that the determinants of what the law is include normative considerations, I am not suggesting that the included normative considerations are necessarily moral ones. There are normative considerations other than moral ones, including prudential, epistemological, aesthetic, and perhaps even etiquette and fashion ones.[21] Why not think that the normative determinants that are some of the ultimate determinants of what the law is are a separate category of normative considerations—namely, *legal* considerations? For example, the fact that a particular legal position is correct could be characterized as having the following two kinds of determinants: (i) the fact that courts have repeatedly and consistently adhered to such a position, and (ii) the doctrine of precedent. Here, the doctrine of precedent is a legal rule that is an ultimate determinant of the truth or correctness of the relevant legal conclusion. It is not a moral rule—i.e., it is not a rule that is meant to govern the rationality of guilt and impartial anger, to borrow from (G) once more. Instead, it is a rule that is meant to be a part of a hierarchically organized set of rules with some specific sorts of the higher-order rules that (H) specifies. It is a nonmoral normative consideration that is one of

---

[20] In addition to Dworkin's important writings, see, e.g., (Finnis 1980, ch. 1). At the risk of muddying the waters a bit, it should be pointed out that even some avowed legal positivists have made concessions to the antipositivist take on this issue. See e.g. (Raz 1983, § IV; 1985, § VI); cf. (Postema 1986, § 9.4).

[21] The following passage from Dashiell Hammett's *The Glass Key* is instructive on this point:

> Ned Beaumont . . . was looking at the blond man's outstretched crossed ankles. He said: "You oughtn't to wear silk socks with tweeds."
>
> Madvig raised a leg straight out to look at the ankle. "No? I like the feel of silk."
>
> "Then lay off tweeds. . . ."

(Hammett 1933, 642). Beaumont is not saying here that Madvig ought to feel guilty and that others are entitled to resent him for wearing silk socks with tweeds. He is not making a moral judgment about Madvig's supposed mistake.

the ultimate determinants of the relevant legal conclusion.[22] It follows that a person who is trying to figure out whether a particular rule is the law in his community would test the legal validity of that rule by applying a nonmoral normative test. He would not think that some moral test always applies. We have here a position that captures the core commitments of legal positivism.[23]

VI. Some Features of the Overlooked Option

Let me now point out some additional aspects of this hitherto neglected (legal positivist) position that I am putting forward. First, notice that according to this position, social facts—e.g., the fact that courts have repeatedly and consistently adhered to certain positions—could be some of the ultimate determinants of what the law is. But such social facts can be ultimate determinants only in tandem with some legal rule—e.g., the doctrine of precedent. So it is not exactly wrong to say that social facts are some of the ultimate determinants of what the law is. That is sometimes the case. But it is quite misleading to suggest that social facts can by themselves determine what the law is.

Second, not only social facts, but also moral considerations could be some of the ultimate determinants of what the law is. For example, the fact that a particular regime of criminal punishment is unconstitutional in the United States seems to have the following two ultimate determinants: (i) the fact that this regime of punishment is cruel and unusual, and (ii) the Eighth Amendment of the U.S. Constitution. Here, (i) is (partly) a moral fact that is one of the ultimate determinants of the unconstitutionality of the relevant regime of punishment. But like social facts, moral considerations can be ultimate determinants of the law only in tandem with some legal rule—e.g., the Eighth Amendment prohibition of inflictions of cruel and unusual punishments. In either case, social facts or moral considerations (or any other kinds of considerations)[24] can partly determine what the law is only if some fundamental legal rule makes such non-legal considerations legally relevant.

Third, according to the view that I am putting forward, certain legal rules are the most fundamental determinants of what the law is.[25] These legal rules, together with any other kinds of facts or considerations that they render legally relevant, fully determine all other legal facts in a jurisdiction. And while they are the ultimate determinants of all other legal conclusions, they themselves are not determined by other more fundamental legal or non-legal determinants. (The ultimate legal rules *supervene* on natural and even social facts. But as noted in the last paragraph of the introductory section, that is quite a different story.)

---

[22] In case the reader thinks that the doctrine of precedent is not one of the most fundamental rules of our legal system, such a reader would likely be able to think of some other rule that he thinks is one of the most fundamental rules of our legal system.

[23] Despite what I have said in the last two paragraphs, I really do not care in the end whether the position that I am sketching is a legal positivist one. I am more concerned to show that it is a viable option in legal philosophy that has been neglected and should be considered.

[24] For example, rules of etiquette among hunters or customs among whalers could be some of the determinants of the law. See Pierson v. Post, 3 Cai. R. 175 (N.Y. 1805); Ghen v. Rich, 8 F. 159 (D. Mass. 1881).

[25] For a conception of fundamental epistemic norms (e.g. that of modus ponens) that is similar to the conception of fundamental legal norms that I am about to sketch in the text, see (Horwich 2005 and 2008).

A conjunction or schedule of all such ultimate legal rules could be deemed what Hart called "the rule of recognition" of the relevant jurisdiction. Now, once again, whether some rule *is treated as* the rule of recognition in a community is wholly a matter of social facts. But whether some rule *is* the rule of recognition is not. In fact, while the truth or correctness of any other legal conclusions is ultimately a matter of what the rule of recognition says (along with other facts or considerations that it makes legally relevant), what the rule of recognition itself says is not a matter of anything else.

Fourth, that the rule of recognition, or the component rules that make up the rule of recognition, of a community do not themselves have any determinants would not mean that there is no way to argue for the identification of some rule as the rule of recognition of a community, or a component rule thereof.[26] We can here analogize our legal reasoning to moral reasoning. According to utilitarians, for example, the principle of utility is the most fundamental moral principle; and it, together with other facts and considerations that it makes morally relevant, determine all other moral facts. Now, while some utilitarians believe that the principle of utility itself has some more fundamental determinants, some others believe that that principle is the normative bedrock and does not itself have further determinants.[27] We do not here have to adjudicate this last issue. The important point is that even if a utilitarian were to take the latter position, he is not foreclosed from various ways of arguing for identifying the principle of utility as the most fundamental principle of morality. A utilitarian could argue for the principle of utility as the most fundamental principle of morality not by appealing to its determinants, but instead by appealing to its resultants. He could argue that this principle has implications that are more plausible than the implications of alternative fundamental moral principles. Better yet, he could argue that the principle of utility does a better job of meshing with our considered moral judgments than alternative candidates for the most fundamental moral principles.[28] This is the method of epistemic justification called "reflective equilibrium" that philosophers like John Rawls (1951 and 1971) and Nelson Goodman (1953/1983) have formulated and advocated. And analogous

---

[26] I could put this point by saying that we should not confuse metaphysics with epistemology. But that would be misleading for the reasons that I will be specifying in my sixth point below.

[27] Chapter 4 of Mill (1861) is often read as arguing for the view that certain psychological facts are the determinants of the principle of utility. But there are indications elsewhere that Mill may have been closer to the view that that principle lacks determinants. See (Mill 1843, bk. 6, ch. 12, esp. §§ 6–7). Hare (1986, part II) argues that certain semantic facts—more specifically, the facts about the meaning of moral terms, or "the logic of moral concepts", as Hare calls them—determine the principle of utility. For some compelling criticisms of this view, as well as Hare's replies, see the papers collected in (Seanor and Fotion 1986), especially the papers by Allan Gibbard, Thomas Nagel, and Bernard Williams. For an influential and more general argument that could be read as showing that the ultimate principles of morality should not be thought to have determinants, see (Prichard 1912).

[28] Similar moves are available for Kantians. Kant himself and many of his followers have taken the position that the most fundamental principle of morality—i.e., Kant's categorical imperative or something like it—has as its determinants certain facts of rational agency or practical reasoning. But even a Kantian who takes a more Prichardian line about the determinants of the ultimate principle of morality (or the lack thereof) may rely on reflective equilibrium to argue for the identification of the categorical imperative (or something like it) as the most fundamental principle of morality, by showing that that principle meshes better with our considered moral judgments than any other available candidate fundamental principle.

ways of arguing by way of reflective equilibrium are available for identifying certain rules as components of a community's rule of recognition. The mere fact that a community's rule of recognition does not have determinants would not foreclose the possibility of arguing for particular rules as making up that rule of recognition by showing that these rules do a better job of meshing with considered legal judgments than any alternative candidates for components of the rule of recognition.[29]

Fifth, it is quite possible for there to be no rule that is treated by the members of a community as the rule of recognition of their legal system. This is why (F5) should be considered an explanandum of a plausible legal theory. But given the aforementioned distinction between what is treated by the members of a community as their rule of recognition, and what is the rule of recognition in that community, the fact that there is no rule that is commonly accepted as the rule of recognition would not mean, by itself, that there is no rule of recognition in that community. Some rule may be the rule of recognition of a community despite the lack of a common recognition or acceptance of it, by the community's members or officials, as the community's rule of recognition. And an astute lawyer, judge, or legal scholar may be able to show that that rule is the rule of recognition of the relevant community, despite the members' or officials' failure up to that point to recognize and accept it as such, by showing that it meshes better with the considered legal judgments than any alternative candidate rule. The possibility of carrying out such an argument for the whole rule of recognition of a community seems rather remote given the probable massive size and complexity of the rule of recognition of any real community. But the possibility of carrying out such an argument for a particular *component* of the rule of recognition—say, in favor of a particular version among several competing versions of the Eighth Amendment—seems well within the capacities of a well-functioning legal community.

Sixth, and finally, notice that according to the view I am putting forward, both the legal rules that are the determinants of the truth or correctness of legal conclusions and the resultant facts represented by legal conclusions are normative facts. But some philosophers may be reluctant to posit any normative facts in the world.[30] Such philosophers would be inclined to refrain from talking about normative facts by going non-factualist about both the determinant legal rules and their resultants. Such philosophers would also be inclined to take up an expressivist semantics to go along with such non factualist metaphysics. And according to such an expressivist semantics, an utterance of a legal conclusion or of a legal rule would not be a description of some normative fact: instead, it would be an expression of a noncognitive or motivation-laden psychological state—e.g., an acceptance of the relevant legal rule.[31] Here, we can take notice of the fact that the metaphysical idioms employed in

---

[29] I am eager to prevent a particular misunderstanding of the method of reflective equilibrium. The considered judgments that serve as evidence for identification of some principle as a fundamental principle have evidentiary weight not because they are commonly accepted, but instead because of the high degree of confidence we have in them. It is not their prevalence, but instead their high degree of credibility that does the crucial epistemological work. Rawls himself sometimes gives the impression of understanding considered judgments in the former, mistaken, way. For a helpful corrective, see (Scanlon 2003).

[30] Unless, that is, they were conceiving normative facts as "facts" in some deflationary or minimalist sense.

[31] In some of my prior works, I have attributed such an expressivist analysis of (internal) legal statements to Hart, and also developed the outlines of my own expressivist analysis meant to get around some problems that beset Hart's analysis. See (Toh 2005 and 2011).

formulating the P-theses could be blinding, or apt to mislead, in at least two ways. First, as I have argued at length above, they may blind us to the distinction between two different sets of resultants—i.e., between certain rules being the law, and certain rules being treated as the law. Second, they could blind us to the possibility that both the resultants and some of the determinants are not facts. Instead, they may be non-factual normative statuses, and our attributions of such statuses may be non-fact-positing psychological attitudes and uses of language. Ubiquitous employments of the terms like "determination", "constitution", etc. may blind us to the possibility that the relevant determination relation between legal determinants and legal resultants is not really (or at least not in the first instance) metaphysical, but instead normative.

To reiterate, the following combination of views should be considered a live option in legal philosophy. The fact that certain rules are treated as legally valid in a community is determined solely by social facts. But the "fact" that certain rules *are* legally valid in a community is not ultimately determined solely by social facts, and is determined partly by normative considerations. We could take up a factualist or a non-factualist metaphysics for this latter "fact". If we were to take up the latter option, then we could adopt an expressivist semantics to characterize statements of such "facts".

VII. Theoretical Disagreements

So far in this chapter, I have been trying to carve out a logical space for a conception of legal positivism that is different from the standard conception. From here on, for the balance of the chapter, I will argue that the new conception has certain explanatory powers that the standard conception lacks.

In specifying what a successful Hartian theories would need to explain in Section III above, one of the explananda that we bracketed for the intervening discussion is the following:

(F8) It is possible for unconfused people to have genuine legal disagreements (as opposed to disagreements about what law should be) that persist despite their agreements on all social factual issues.

The kind of disagreements that I am describing here is what Dworkin (1986, ch. 1) has called "theoretical disagreements" in law. Dworkin invoked such disagreements and argued that legal positivism lacks resources to account for such disagreements. Over the years, a number of legal positivists have taken up Dworkin's challenge, and have proposed several ways to account for such disagreements, but without much success in my opinion.[32] More recently, Brian Leiter (2009) has argued that theoretical disagreements may not be things that need to be explained by a satisfactory theory of law; instead, according to him, their *appearances* could be explained *away*. I believe that we can take advantage of the preceding arguments to devise a more satisfying way of answering Dworkin's challenge than what his legal positivist respondents, including Leiter, have so far provided.

[32] My worries about Raz's (1998) particular proposal are indicated in Toh (2010b, § 7).

Dworkin describes theoretical disagreements as disagreements among discussants (judges, commentators, etc.) about "the grounds of law" (1986, 4). Some other writers have characterized such disagreements as ones about "the criteria of legal validity". An example would be a disagreement between judges who agree that a particular statute is determinative of the outcome of a case, but disagree as to how the statutory text should be read or interpreted. One group may think that the statutory text should be read literally, and the other may think that it must be read in light of counterfactual intentions of legislators. Disagreements of this sort would differ markedly from what Dworkin calls "empirical disagreements", or disagreements in which judges and other agree about the grounds of law, but disagree about certain facts that the grounds refer to—e.g., what the literal meaning of the statutory text is, or what legislators would have intended.

In reaction, Leiter concedes that theoretical disagreements *appear* to occur in actual legal settings. He also agrees with Dworkin that if any of the legal positivist theories were right, such disagreements could not occur. What Leiter has in mind by "legal positivist theories" are Hart's legal theory and those patterned on that theory, and he explains the supposed impossibility of theoretical disagreements according to such legal theories as follows (in the passage that I have already quoted in Section IV above):

> [T]he Rule of Recognition, on Hart's view, is a social rule, meaning its content—that is, the criteria of legal validity—is fixed by a complex empirical fact, namely, the *actual practice* of officials (and the attitude they evince towards the practice). So it looks like the only dispute about the criteria of legal validity that is possible, on Hart's view, is an empirical or "heads count" dispute: namely, a dispute about what judges are doing, and how many of them are doing it, since it is *the actual practice of officials and their attitudes towards that practice* that fixes the criteria of legal validity according to the positivist. (2009, 1222; emphases in the original)

The language of "fixing" here closely resembles the metaphysical idioms that were used to formulate the P-theses.[33] And notice that Leiter conflates two types of resultants in exactly the way that I described earlier. It is true that, according to Hart, any existing fact that the members of a community *treat* some rule as the rule of recognition (or the "criterion of legal validity") is wholly "fixed" or determined by the complex empirical facts of the sort that Leiter refers to. But as I have argued, that does not mean that what the law is, or what the rule of recognition says (i.e., its content), is wholly "fixed" or determined by the same kind of empirical facts.

Leiter is here guilty of the fallacy of double duty that I have been accusing many legal positivists of, and this fallacy is responsible for his overlooking what in retrospect is a quite salient way of accounting for theoretical disagreements. Using the terminology that I have been employing in this chapter, theoretical disagreements could be characterized as the ones in which discussants disagree about the ultimate normative, and more specifically legal, determinants of what the law is. The fact that there is no joint acceptance among judges or legal officials for a particular ultimate legal determinant of the law—e.g., that statutes must

[33] Leiter also speaks in terms of "constitution". See, e.g., (Leiter 2009, 1215, 1221).

be read in light of counterfactual legislative intentions—would not mean that there could not be genuine legal disagreements about what the law is, or that any disagreements would turn into disagreements about what the law should be. As I have argued above, such a joint acceptance among judges or officials fully determines (and is necessary for the existence of) the fact that some particular legal determinant is treated by the members of the relevant community as (a component of) their rule of recognition. But such a joint acceptance does not fully determine (and is not necessary for the existence of) the fact that some particular legal determinant is (a component of) a community's rule of recognition. To invoke the analogy to morality once again, genuine moral disagreements would not become impossible or problematic even if there were no set of rules governing guilt and impartial anger that the members of community generally accept. Even if I were to come across a completely amoral group of people (e.g., some thoroughgoing Nietzscheans), I could start to discuss with them whether it makes sense to feel guilty for acting in certain ways. Similarly, genuine legal disagreements would not become impossible or problematic even if there were no rule that is commonly accepted by the members of a community as the rule of recognition of their community.

In many instances, lawyers or judges can argue for some legal conclusions not by appealing to these conclusions' determinants, but by appealing to their resultants. They can, for example, try to justify a particular rule of statutory interpretation by appealing to the legal conclusions, in which we have very high degrees of confidence, that would follow from the relevant rule of statutory interpretation, but not from alternative interpretive rules. In other words, as I pointed out in the preceding section, lawyers or judges could rely on the epistemic method of reflective equilibrium, and appeal to considered legal judgments to argue for the fundamental rules or principles that best account for or that mesh best with such judgments. They could appeal to such considered judgments while allowing for possibilities of making adjustments either in those judgments or in the relevant fundamental principles, or in both, with the epistemic aim of arriving at a conflict-free and mutually supporting set of fundamental principles and considered judgments. In other words, each discussant in a theoretical disagreement could be characterized as arguing for a particular rule as one of the ultimate determinants of the law of his community by arguing that that rule meshes best with the relevant set of considered legal judgments. It follows that theoretical disagreements about even the ultimate legal determinants are quite possible despite the absence of any more fundamental determinants to which discussants could appeal.[34]

VIII. The Rewards of Going à la Carte

Leiter is unfazed by the fact that the legal positivist position that he favors is incompatible with non-debunking explanations of theoretical disagreements. Instead of trying to explain "the face value" of such disagreements, he seeks to cast doubt on Dworkin's assertion that theoretical disagreements are genuine phenomena, and proposes that the appearances

[34] There is the possibility of discussants arriving at different equilibrium points. Nothing in the method of reflective equilibrium forecloses such a possibility. For a conception of legal judgments that allows for genuine theoretical disagreements even in such eventualities, see (Toh 2011).

of their occurrences could be explained *away* as: (i) instances of discussants behaving disingenuously—i.e., acting as if they are disagreeing about what the law is, when in fact they are actually arguing about what the law should be; or (ii) instances in which discussants are motivated by their ignorance of the jurisprudential fact that certain social facts fully determine what the law is.

I am not here in a position to react fully or adequately to the various considerations that Leiter enumerates for doubting the reality of theoretical disagreements. The considerations that Leiter invokes are aimed mainly at throwing into doubt Dworkin's specific descriptions of several actual legal cases as supporting his view that theoretical disagreements actually occur and are quite common. The admittedly ad hominem nature of Leiter's arguments limits their implications for the general question of whether theoretical disagreements are genuine and common legal phenomena. I myself surmise that such disagreements are quite common and unremarkable phenomena. The debate among judges and constitutional theorists about originalism (see, e.g., Scalia 1998), and the debate about the appropriate level of generality at which the substantive rights protected by the Fourteenth Amendment ought to be defined (see, e.g., Tribe and Dorf 1991), to name just two, seem to me to fit Dworkin's conception of theoretical disagreements pretty well.[35] But in order to substantiate more adequately my own surmise, I would have to write a separate and far different paper enumerating various empirical considerations. I will here opt for a different tack, and pick on a different step in Leiter's argument.

Leiter argues that however many points that Dworkin's antipositivist theory of law scores by explaining "the face value" of theoretical disagreements, Hart's legal theory (combined with the two aforementioned debunking explanations of theoretical disagreements) explains a whole lot more. It would be an epistemological folly, he suggests, to give up all the explanatory rewards of Hart's legal theory merely because it fails to explain the face value of theoretical disagreements, and to adopt Dworkin's theory merely because it succeeds in doing so. It should come as no surprise to the reader at this point that I believe that Leiter is presenting a false choice here. In effect, Leiter is laying out two package deals. Let me remind the reader of the following trio of theses:

(L1) Whether a community has, or is governed by, (a system of) laws is a matter only of certain social facts existing in that community.

(L2) Whether a particular rule is a law (or a legal rule) in a community is a matter only of certain social facts existing in that community.[36]

---

[35] I also believe that given the history of twentieth century philosophy, we should be extremely wary of any denials—especially those driven by philosophical theories—of the possibility of genuine fundamental disputes within any domain of inquiry. Some of the most significant developments in twentieth century philosophy were those works that highlighted such possibilities, contrary to the preceding consensus opinions denying such possibilities. See, e.g., (Quine 1951); (Kuhn 1962/1996); (Burge 1979). For some interesting and suggestive recent reflections on this and related themes, see (Friedman 2001); (van Fraassen 2002). Given his Quinean sympathies, Leiter is a particularly surprising source of the suggestion that genuine disagreements about the most fundamental laws could not take place.

[36] Once again, (L2) should be read as:

(L2a) Whether a particular rule *is treated as* legally valid in a community is a matter only of certain social facts existing in that community.

(L3) Whether some (first-order) legal claim is true or correct is a matter only of certain social facts existing in the relevant community.

Leiter is in effect recommending that we choose all three of these L-theses (along with his two debunking explanations of theoretical disagreements) over Dworkin's denials of all three and his explanation of theoretical disagreements. But these are not our only options. Instead of going with one of these package deals, we can go à la carte, and opt for (L1) and (L2) along with not-(L3). By rejecting (L3), and thereby conceiving what the law is as having some normative ultimate determinants, we can reap all the explanatory benefits that come with (L1) and (L2)—e.g., the benefits that Hart's legal theory furnishes us—while also maintaining an ability to explain (the face value of) theoretical disagreements. None of the explanatory benefits that Leiter associates with Hart's legal theory seems to require our adopting (L3) as well as (L1) and (L2).

The upshot is that the alternative conception of legal positivism that I have been delineating accounts for (F8) better than the more standard conception that involves commitments to all three L-theses. But once again, I have not in this chapter established, though I surmise that it is quite true, that theoretical disagreements are real phenomena that must be explained by any satisfactory theories of the nature of law.

IX. "The Normativity of Law"

In the new conception of legal positivism that I have been delineating, we have a conception of the nature of law that explains (F1)–(F5) and (F8). As I indicated in Section III, I am in this chapter treating (F6)—the fact having to do with the phenomenology of adjudicating hard cases—as not different from (F8). That probably is not entirely the case, but in any event I believe that the new conception of legal positivism can account for (F6) as well.

Now, what about (F7), the purported normativity of law? On this point, I quite agree with David Enoch (2011) that although legal philosophers have often talked about the so-called normativity of law, it is far from clear what they have had in mind, and that the problem of explaining the normativity of law is quite obscure. In seeking such an explanation, legal philosophers have often sought some extralegal grounds for acting as the laws say. Legal antipositivists, for example, have sought to offer a conception of law according to which there invariably are moral reasons and even obligations to act as the laws say. And in many instances, legal positivists who purport to specify only social-factual determinants of the law could be accused of being covert antipositivists. In pursuing their advertised goal of identifying the social-factual determinants of the law, they have often singled out in their proposals configurations of psychological and behavioral facts—e.g., coordination conventions, shared cooperative activities—that plausibly generate some moral or at least prudential reasons to act as the laws say. But setting aside the issue of whether these proposals succeed in their endeavors,[37] it is far from clear why there should be any presumption that

[37] I quite agree with Leslie Green who has steadfastly argued over the years that conventionalist conceptions of what the law is that many legal positivists have proposed are inadequate to capture the normativity of law. See e.g. (Green 1983 and 1999); cf. (Dickson 2007). I am not entirely sure where my disagreements with Green

there are moral or any other kinds of extralegal reasons to act as the laws say. I doubt that such a presumption is reasonable, and for this reason I believe that the problem of accounting for the normativity of law, as it is often articulated or understood by legal philosophers, is largely a pseudo-problem.[38]

I do think, however, that there is a phenomenon that many legal philosophers were misconstruing in construing it as the extralegal normativity of law. It is not the case that there always are extralegal reasons or obligations to do as the laws say. But according to the new conception of legal positivism that I have been sketching, there always are some normative, and more specifically legal, determinants of what the law is. And this means that there always are *legal* (as opposed to moral or any other kinds of extralegal) reasons to do as the laws say. The strengths of these reasons, and whether there are all-things-considered reasons to act as the laws say in any given situation depend very much on how compelling the relevant legal reasons are, and on what other kinds of reasons are applicable in the given situation. We can put my main point here in a somewhat different way. In order for there to be the facts that amount to the existence of a legal system in a community, the members of the community must treat the laws as giving them reasons to act as the laws say. That is because they must treat the laws as having among their ultimate determinants some normative determinants. Only if they do could they have the kind of theoretical disagreements that Dworkin highlighted. In sum, the members of a community with a legal system must treat their laws as generating reasons for action. This fact is not really so much an explanandum, but is instead a part of an explanans to explain the explanandum of (F8). So, there is something real that many legal philosophers were getting at when they sought to explain (F7); but it is not exactly (F7).

X. Conclusion

By drawing a distinction between two kinds of legal resultants, we can delineate a new conception of legal positivism that does a nice job of explaining many of the invariable features of communities with legal systems that seem worth explaining. That seems to speak in favor of making the distinction, and for the new conception of legal positivism. It would be a significant progress in legal philosophy, I believe, to add this new conception of legal positivism to the list of contenders.

begin. My guess is that my disagreements are with the following of his commitments: (i) despite the failure of conventionalist solutions, the problem of the normativity of law is a genuine problem; (ii) some social factualist, albeit non-conventionalist, conception of what the law is probably right; and (iii) legal positivism is committed to such a social factualism about what the law is. See (Green 2003). It seems to me that with my distinction between the two types of resultants, we can move past the intramural social factualist debate that Green has had with conventionalist legal positivists. My understanding, based on my conversations with him, is that Leiter's position on the issue of the purported normativity of law is not different from Green's. In that case, (i)–(iii) would also be Leiter's commitments with which I disagree.

[38] I delve into this set of issues at a greater length in (Toh 2018).

References

Blackburn, Simon. 1983. "Moral Realism", reprinted in Blackburn, *Essays in Quasi-Realism*. Oxford: Oxford University Press, 1993.

Boyd, Richard. 1988. "How to be a Moral Realist". In *Essays on Moral Realism*, edited by Geoffrey Sayre-McCord. Ithaca, N.Y.: Cornell University Press.

Brandt, R.B. 1979. *A Theory of the Good and the Right*. Oxford: Clarendon Press.

Bulygin, Eugenio. 1982. "Norms, Normative Propositions, and Legal Statements". In *Contemporary Philosophy: A New Survey*, Vol. 3, edited by Guttorm Fløistad. The Hague & Boston: M. Nijhoff, 1982.

Burge, Tyler. 1979. "Individualism and the Mental", reprinted in Burge, *Foundations of Mind*. Oxford: Clarendon Press, 2007.

Coleman, Jules L. 2001. *The Practice of Principle*. Oxford: Oxford University Press.

Dickson, Julie. 2007. "Is the Rule of Recognition Really a Conventional Rule?". *Oxford Journal of Legal Studies* 27: 373–402

Dworkin, Ronald. 1967. "The Model of Rules I", reprinted in Dworkin (1977).

_____. 1972. "The Model of Rules II", reprinted in Dworkin (1977).

_____. 1975. "Hard Cases", reprinted in Dworkin (1977).

_____. 1977. *Taking Rights Seriously*. Cambridge, MA: Harvard University Press.

_____. 1982. "'Natural' Law Revisited". *University of Florida Law Review* 34: 165–188.

_____. 1986. *Law's Empire*. Cambridge, MA: Harvard University Press.

Enoch, David. 2011. "Reason-Giving and the Law". In Green & Leiter (2011).

Fine, Kit. 2001. "The Question of Realism". *Philosophers' Imprint* 1: 1–30.

_____. 2012. "Guide to Ground". In *Metaphysical Grounding: Understanding the Structure of Reality*, edited by Fabrice Correia and Benjamin Schnieder. Cambridge: Cambridge University Press.

Finnis, John. 1980. *Natural Law and Natural Rights*. Oxford: Clarendon Press.

Foot, Philippa. 1958–1959. "Moral Beliefs", reprinted in Foot, *Virtues and Vices*. Berkeley and Los Angeles, CA: University of California Press, 1978.

Friedman, Michael. 2001. *Dynamics of Reason*. Stanford, CA: CSLI.

Gardner, J. 2008. "Some Types of Law", reprinted in Gardner, *Law as a Leap of Faith*. Oxford: Oxford University Press, 2012.

Gibbard, Allan. 1990. *Wise Choices, Apt Feelings*. Cambridge, MA: Harvard University Press.

Goodman, Nelson. 1953/1983. "The New Riddle of Induction", revised and reprinted in Goodman, *Fact, Fiction, and Forecast*, 4th ed. Cambridge, MA: Harvard University Press, 1983.

Green, Leslie. 1983. "Law, Co-ordination and the Common Good". *Oxford Journal of Legal Studies* 3: 299–324.

_____. 1999. "Positivism and Conventionalism". *Canadian Journal of Law and Jurisprudence* 12: 35–52.

_____. 2003. "Legal Positivism". In *Stanford Encyclopedia of Philosophy*, edited by Edward Zalta. (http://plato.stanford.edu/entries/legal-positivism/).

Green, Leslie, and Brian Leiter (2011). *Oxford Studies in the Philosophy of Law*, Vol. 1. Oxford: Oxford University Press.

Greenberg, Mark. 2004. "How Facts Make Law". *Legal Theory* 10: 157–198.

Hammett, Dashiell. 1933. *The Glass Key*, reprinted in Hammett, *Complete Novels*. New York: The Library of America, 1999.

Hare, R. M. 1986. *Moral Thinking*. Oxford: Clarendon Press.

Hart, H. L. A. 1961/1994. *The Concept of Law*, 2nd ed. Oxford: Clarendon Press.

Horwich, Paul. 2005. "Meaning Constitution and Epistemic Rationality". In Horwich, *Reflections on Meaning*. Oxford: Oxford University Press.

_____. 2008. "Ungrounded Reason", reprinted in Horwich, *Truth-Meaning-Reality*. Oxford: Oxford University Press, 2010.

Jackson, Frank. 1998. *From Metaphysics to Ethics: A Defense of Conceptual Analysis*. Oxford: Clarendon Press.

_____. 2003. "Cognitivism, A Priori Deduction, and Moore". *Ethics* 113: 557–575.

Kim, Jaegwon. 1993. "Postscripts on Supervenience". In Kim, *Supervenience and Mind*. Cambridge: Cambridge University Press.

Kuhn, Thomas. 1962/1996). *The Structure of Scientific Revolutions*, 3rd ed. Chicago: University of Chicago Press, 1996.

Leiter, Brian. 2009. "Explaining Theoretical Disagreements". *University of Chicago Law Review* 76: 1215–1250.

Lewis, David. 1970. "How to Define Theoretical Terms", reprinted in Lewis, *Philosophical Papers*, Vol. 1. Oxford: Oxford University Press, 1983.

_____. 1989. "Dispositional Theories of Value", reprinted in Lewis, *Papers in Ethics and Social Philosophy*. Cambridge: Cambridge University Press, 1999.

Marmor, Andrei. 1998/2001. "Constitutive Conventions", revised and reprinted in Marmor, *Positive Law and Objective Values*. Oxford: Oxford University Press, 2001.

_____. 2009. *Social Conventions: From Language to Law*. Princeton, NJ: Princeton University Press.

Mill, John Stuart. 1843. *A System of Logic, Ratiocinative and Inductive*. Toronto: University of Toronto Press, 1974.

_____. 1861. *Utilitarianism*. Indianapolis: Hackett Publishing Co., Inc., 2001.

Pettit, Philip, and Michael Smith. 1990. "Backgrounding Desire", reprinted in Frank Jackson, Philip Pettit, and Michael Smith, *Mind, Morality, and Explanation*. Oxford: Clarendon Press, 2004.

Postema, Gerald J. 1982. "Coordination and Convention at the Foundations of Law". *Journal of Legal Studies* 11: 165–203.

_____. 1986. *Bentham and the Common Law Tradition*. Oxford: Clarendon Press.

Prichard, H. A. 1912. "Does Moral Philosophy Rest on a Mistake?", reprinted in Prichard, *Moral Writings*. Oxford: Clarendon Press, 2002.

Quine, W. V. O. 1951. "Two Dogmas of Empiricism", reprinted in Quine, *From a Logical Point of View*, 2nd ed. Cambridge, MA: Harvard University Press, 1980.

Quinn, Warren. 1993. "Putting Rationality in Its Place", reprinted in Quinn, *Morality and Action*. Cambridge: Cambridge University Press, 1993.

Railton, Peter. 1986. "Moral Realism". *The Philosophical Review*, 14: 5–29.

Rawls, John. 1951. "Outline of a Decision Procedure for Ethics", reprinted in Rawls, *Collected Papers*. Cambridge, MA: Harvard University Press, 1999.

_____. 1971. *A Theory of Justice*. Cambridge, MA: Harvard University Press.

Raz, Joseph, 1975/1990. *Practical Reason and Norms*, 2nd ed. Princeton, NJ: Princeton University Press.

_____. 1979. "Legal Reasons, Sources, and Gaps", reprinted in Raz, *The Authority of Law*. Oxford: Clarendon Press, 1979.
_____. 1983. "The Problem About the Nature of Law", reprinted in Raz (1994).
_____. 1985. "Authority, Law, and Morality", reprinted in Raz (1994).
_____. 1994. *Ethics in the Public Domain*. Oxford: Clarendon Press.
_____. 1998. "Two Views of the Nature of the Theory of Law: A Partial Comparison", reprinted in Raz, *Between Authority and Interpretation*. Oxford: Oxford University Press, 2009.
Rosen, Gideon. 2010. "Metaphysical Dependence: Grounding and Reduction". In *Modality*, edited by Bob Hale and Aviv Hoffmann. Oxford: Oxford University Press.
_____. 2015. "Real Definition". *Analytical Philosophy*, 56: 189–209.
Scalia, Antonin. 1998. *A Matter of Interpretation: Federal Courts and the Law*. Princeton, NJ: Princeton University Press.
Scanlon, T. M. 2003. "Rawls on Justification". In *The Cambridge Companion to Rawls*, edited by Samuel Freeman. Cambridge: Cambridge University Press.
Schaffer, Jonathan. 2010. "On What Grounds What". In *Metametaphysics: New Essays on the Foundations of Ontology*, edited by David Chalmers, David Manley, & Ryan Wasserman. Oxford: Clarendon Press, 2010.
Schroeder, Mark. 2007. *Slaves of the Passions*. Oxford: Oxford University Press.
Seanor, Douglas and N. Fotion eds. 1986. *Hare and Critics*. Oxford: Clarendon Press.
Shapiro, Scott. 2002. "Law, Plans, and Practical Reason". *Legal Theory*, vol. 8: 387–441.
_____. 2007. "The 'Hart-Dworkin' Debate: The Short Guide for the Perplexed". In *Ronald Dworkin*, edited by Arthur Ripstein. Cambridge: Cambridge University Press.
_____. 2011. *Legality*. Cambridge, MA: Harvard University Press.
Skorupski, John. 1993. "The Definition of Morality", reprinted in Skorupski, *Moral Explorations*. Oxford: Oxford University Press, 1999.
Smith, Michael. 1994. *The Moral Problem*. Oxford: Blackwell Publishing.
Stevenson, C. L. 1950. "Interpretation and Evaluation in Aesthetics". In *Philosophical Analysis*, edited by Max Black. Ithaca, NY: Cornell University Press.
Sturgeon, Nicholas 1985. "Moral Explanations". In *Morality, Reason, and Truth*, edited by David Copp and David Zimmerman. Totowa, N.J.: Rowman and Allanheld.
Toh, Kevin. 2005. "Hart's Expressivism and His Benthamite Project". *Legal Theory* 11: 75–123.
_____. 2010a. "The Predication Thesis and a New Problem about Persistent Fundamental Normative Controversies". *Utilitas* 22: 331–350.
_____. 2010b. "Some Moving Parts of Jurisprudence". *Texas Law Review* 88: 1283–1321.
_____. 2010c. Review of Marmor (2009). *Ethics* 120: 617–622.
_____. 2011. "Legal Judgments as Plural Acceptances of Norms". In Green & Leiter (2011).
_____. 2012. "La Falacia del Doble Deber y los 'Desacuerdos Teóricos' en el Derecho" ("The Fallacy of Double Duty and 'Theoretical Disagreements' in Law", translated into Spanish by Alejandro Calzetta). In *Acordes y Desacuerdos*, edited by Pau Luque Sánchez and Giovanni Ratti. Madrid: Marcial Pons.
_____. (2018). "Plan-Attitudes, Plan-Contents, and Bootstrapping: Some Thoughts on the Planning Theory of Law". In *Oxford Studies in Philosophy of Law*, Vol. 3, edited by John Gardner, Leslie Green, and Brian Leiter. Oxford: Oxford University Press.
Tribe, Laurence and Michael Dorf. 1991. *On Reading the Constitution*. Cambridge, MA: Harvard University Press.

van Fraassen, Bas C. 2002. *The Empirical Stance*. New Haven, CT: Yale University Press.

Walton, Kendall. 1979. "Categories of Art", reprinted in Walton, *Marvelous Images: On Values and the Arts.* Oxford: Oxford University Press, 2008.

______. 1990. *Mimesis as Make-Believe.* Cambridge, MA: Harvard University Press.

Williams, Bernard. 1986. *Ethics and the Limits of Philosophy.* Cambridge, MA: Harvard University Press.

11 Theoretical Disagreements in Law: Another Look

Brian Leiter

JUST WHEN DWORKIN'S decades-long campaign against legal positivism seemed moribund (cf. Leiter 2005 for a summary of where things stood), a new Dworkin-inspired challenge, with new champions, arrived on the scene. Shapiro (2007) argued that positivists had not responded adequately to the argument from theoretical disagreement (TD) in Dworkin (1986). I agreed with Shapiro that the argument from TD demanded a systematic positivist reply, and offered one (Leiter 2009). Since then, a number of other writers have expressed doubts about this reply, some from a position sympathetic to positivism, some less so (Toh 2013; Levenbook 2015; Duarte D'Almeida 2016). I begin by reviewing Dworkin's criticism of the positivist account of TD and my original response to it, and then turn to the doubts raised by the critics. I hope, once again, to lay the problem of TD to rest.

I. The Problem Stated

Judges sometimes agree on the applicable criteria of legal validity (e.g., they agree the intention of the legislature controls), but disagree on its application (e.g., what did the legislature *really* intend?). Dworkin (1986) noted judges sometimes appear to disagree about what the applicable criteria of legal validity are (the "grounds of law" in Dworkin-speak) (Dworkin 1986, 5). Dworkin claimed that positivists could not explain such disagreements—though his *real* objection was that they could not explain such disagreements *without explaining them away*, i.e., without offering an interpretation of those disagreements that did not see them as involving a mistake. In many contexts, the best explanation of a phenomenon does involve attributing a mistake to the parties (cf. Leiter 2009, 1238–1241), so the fact that

Dimensions of Normativity. David Plunkett, Scott J. Shapiro, and Kevin Toh.

positivists *explain away* TDs settles nothing. The question is always what is the *best* explanation of the phenomenon.

Take *Riggs v. Palmer* (a late nineteenth-century case from the highest court in the state of New York, and Dworkin's favorite example for decades), which considers the question whether the grandson (Elmer) who murdered his grandfather in order to inherit under the latter's will should be permitted to do so. According to Dworkin, the majority and dissent are having a dispute about the *criteria of legal validity* ("the grounds of law"). The majority and dissent, according to Dworkin, agree that the statutes governing wills control this case, but the majority opinion by Judge Earl (denying the inheritance) argues as though the *meaning* of the statute is given by the *counterfactual intention* of the legislature (i.e., what the legislators would have intended had they thought of this sordid case, in which case Elmer loses), while the dissenting opinion by Judge Gray (allowing the inheritance) argues as though the *meaning* of the statute is given by the *plain meaning* of its provisions, in which case Elmer inherits.

On the positivist view, where a legal system exists, there exists a rule of recognition (hereafter RR) that specifies the criteria of legal validity for that system. The RR is, itself, merely a "social rule": its content is fixed by (i) a convergent pattern of behavior, and (ii) acceptance of a rule describing that behavior from an "internal point of view" (i.e., treating the behavior described by the rule as obligatory). In the case of the RR, this means its content will consist in (i) the criteria of legal validity on which judges actually converge, and (ii) which they also treat as obligatory. So the existence of an RR is just a complex psychosocial fact about officials of the system.

Let us now suppose that officials in the New York legal system at the time of *Riggs* did not converge upon either the *counterfactual intention* theory of statutory meaning or the *plain meaning* theory. It follows, then, on the positivist view, that there is no fact of the matter about which criterion of legal validity is correct. Insofar as Judge Earl, writing for the majority, and Judge Gray, writing for the dissent, think there is a fact of the matter, they are both mistaken: perhaps an innocent error, perhaps not so innocent (i.e., perhaps they know there is no fact of the matter, and are really trying to change the content of the RR or are simply trying to get their preferred outcome in the case).

According to Dworkin (1986), what the law is follows from the best "constructive interpretation" of the institutional history of the legal system (the latter being, roughly, the authoritative sources a positivist theory might identify: legislative enactments, prior court decisions, a constitution, executive orders. etc.). A constructive interpretation identifies moral principles that explain a sufficient amount of that institutional history and then decides the present case in a way consistent with the explanatory moral principle that provides the best moral justification for that history (i.e., shows that history in its best "moral" light). A TD for Dworkin, then, is just a case of conflicting constructive interpretations. Is that really the best explanation of the phenomenon Dworkin identifies?

II. The Problem Resolved from a Positivist Point of View

In Leiter (2009), I argued that the positivist had a better explanation of TD in cases such as *Riggs*. The fact that the positivist explanation of *Riggs* treats the judges as mistaken in thinking there was a fact of the matter about the meaning of the statute is no objection to it as an explanation: the better explanation of a phenomenon, as we have already noted, often treats the surface phenomena as misleading or illusory. (Even Dworkin's reading of the dispute in *Riggs* does violence to the actual dispute between the majority and the dissent: neither side, for example, even acknowledges the opposing reading, so neither side writes *as if* this is a dispute about the best constructive interpretation of the statutory materials, *contra* Dworkin's reading.) A good explanation should not only make sense of what the judges said and did in *Riggs,* but what they said and did in other cases: this is the explanatory virtue of *consilience.* But as soon as we look beyond *Riggs,* we find that Judge Gray is often an intentionalist about interpretation, and Judge Earl is usually a severe textualist, with little enthusiasm for speculations about counterfactual intentions (Leiter 2009, 1244). Their rhetorical posturing in *Riggs* turns out to be wholly opportunistic, driven by underlying legal and political differences that far transcend the particulars of *Riggs* (Judge Earl was really trying to salvage some remnants of the "civil death" doctrine recently repudiated by the New York Court of Appeals, while Judge Gray was simply vindicating his absolutist view of property rights against government meddling [it is not for the courts to correct the murdered grandfather's foolish decision to leave his wealth to his felonious grandson]). The positivist, with some legal realist instincts, offers a much more plausible account of what is really going on precisely by *not taking seriously* the TD on which the Dworkinian focuses.[1]

How a particular jurisprudential theory explains a particular TD is not, despite Dworkin's framing, sufficient for deciding its theoretical merits. Even though the positivist has a more consilient explanation than Dworkin of the judicial behavior in *Riggs,* that does not show that positivism is a more plausible theory of law, precisely because theoretical disagreements are only one kind of phenomenon a theory of law should explain, and a relatively marginal one at that (being confined largely to the upper reaches of appellate litigation). *Massive agreement* about what the law is remains the most striking feature of functioning legal systems, and positivism has always had the most straightforward explanation of that phenomenon. Legal professionals agree about what the law requires so often because, in a functioning legal system, *what the law is* is fixed by a discernible practice of officials who decide questions of legal validity by reference to criteria of legal validity on which they recognizably converge and that they treat as obligatory. If what the law is were really what follows from the best constructive interpretation of the institutional history of the legal system, then one would expect controversy about what the law is to break out all the time and everywhere, given how contestable constructive interpretations are. But beyond the fact of massive agreement,

[1] Tim Macklem presses on me a different kind of positivist response: namely, that a RR identifies the sources of law, but does not adjudicate among all the ways of interpreting them. Here I agree, I take it, with Dworkin (as well as Shapiro): namely, that this austere conception of the RR would be inadequate to discharge the functions of an RR as Hart originally conceived them, namely, eliminating some (if not all) uncertainty about the valid legal norms are in a particular system. I thus agree (infrequent as that may be) with Dworkin that saying the duly enacted statute is a source of law is not enough for a RR that resolves uncertainty: it is necessary that the RR provide guidance as to what norms the statute enacts as legally valid. This, of course, can be done by content-neutral criteria: e.g., the intent of the legislature, the plain meaning of the text, and so on. And, indeed, these content-neutral criteria can come in hierarchical orderings, such that some sources trump others. But an RR that did not resolve some number of TDs would not, in fact, be adequate to support a functioning legal system.

positivism also fares better at explaining other familiar features of modern legal systems, such as the distinctions everyone recognizes between what is *legally* binding and what is *morally* required, between legal expertise and general "good judgment," and so on. Moreover, legal positivism offers explanations that do not depend, unlike Dworkin's, on tendentious (perhaps incredible?) metaphysical commitments, such as the existence of objective moral truths (e.g., Leiter 2001, 2015).

A number of writers (e.g., Toh 2013; Levenbook 2015; Duarte D'Almeida 2016) think this kind of reply to the argument from TD is the wrong response. Crucial to my account (and also to the restatement of Dworkin's challenge in Shapiro 2011) was the supposition that Dworkin is correct that on a positivist view, a dispute about the criteria of legal validity is a dispute about the *content of the rule of recognition*, and that since the content of the RR is fixed by the criteria of legal validity on which officials converge and that they accept from an internal point of view, a *genuine* dispute about the criteria would be nothing more than a "head count" dispute (Leiter 2009, 1222), that is, a dispute about what the actual "internal point of view" practice of the officials was. Kevin Toh has posed the most direct challenge to that latter assumption, so I begin by considering his view (especially since D'Almeida depends crucially on it).

III. Toh's Basic Objection

I should note at the start that debating with Toh on this issue is complicated by his hermeneutic posture. He denies offering a "correct understanding" of Hart, only "an alternative to the standard understanding," one supposedly vindicated by "the new possibilities in legal philosophy that it opens up, rather than on its fidelity to what Hart actually said or thought" (2015, 335).[2] Toh is happy to ascribe "commitments" to Hart on the basis of remarks in essays prior to *The Concept of Law*, even when Toh admits that "Hart himself was not always consistent in" honoring the alleged commitments subsequently and, indeed, that some of the alleged commitments "are only implicit in Hart's writings" (2015, 334). And when Hart's explicit statements in *The Concept of Law* are in tension with Toh's "alternative" understanding, Hart is sometimes deemed to be guilty of an "unforced error" (2015, 344) or we are simply advised to "dispense with Hart's view" on a particular question (2015, 344). Indeed, when what Hart actually says is flatly incompatible with one of the alleged commitments Toh deems central to Hart, Toh warns us against being "easily blind[ed]" to the commitment by what Hart actually writes (2015, 360).[3] My interpretive posture is different: I think we should take seriously what Hart actually says, especially in *The Concept of Law* (unless recanted later)

---

[2] What those possibilities actually are is, in the end, not entirely clear. Of particular concern here is what the alternative account of TD would look like. Toh (2013, 2015) does not address this directly, though one can infer the general structure of the account. TDs would be disagreements in "attitudes," namely, attitudes about RR-acceptance. But from a Dworkinian perspective that would be as bad as the error-theoretical interpretation, since the disagreement is not factual, but attitudinal and, more seriously, it obscures the fact that the TD disputants in Dworkin's examples are arguing *about the content of the RR purportedly accepted*, not the subsidiary rules validated by that RR.

[3] I return to this last case, below.

and especially as it bears on the question of TDs. We should be loath to attribute error to him based on alleged "commitments" that Hart himself does not honor or sometimes even explicitly embrace. Until the clear theoretical advantages of an alternative approach are demonstrated, discounting Hart's actual views seems to me unwarranted.

Toh (2013) thinks the assumption that a dispute about the content of the RR must be resolved by appeal to the actual practice of officials wrongly ignores Hart's distinction between "internal" and "external" statements about law. That a RR exists is an "external" fact about the behavior and attitudes of officials in some society; but it is not true, says Toh, that these external facts about behavior and attitudes set the correctness conditions for "internal" judgments of legal validity made by officials in the system. (An "*internal statement*" manifests "the internal point of view"—the view of someone who accepts the rules as standards of conduct—and "is naturally used by one who, accepting the RR and without stating the fact that it is accepted, applies the rule" in deciding a question of legal validity (Hart 2012, 103–112).[4]

Thus Toh (2013) claims that Hart accepts the following proposition: "(L1) A community's being governed by (a system of) laws consists only of certain social facts existing in that community." But Hart purportedly rejects (or at least does not endorse) "(L3) Any first-order legal judgment is correct ultimately in virtue only of certain social facts existing in the relevant community" (461).[5] Toh claims that "there is no explanatory payoff from accepting (L3) that Hart ever discusses—that is, there is no explanandum that would require (L3) as a part of the explanans" (2013, 461). This, I will argue, is mistaken as a matter of Hart exegesis, a point to which we return shortly.

Toh (2013) proposes an analogy to metaethical noncognitivism like that defended in Gibbard (1990). While it might be true, says Toh, that a community has a "morality" only in virtue of certain complex psychosocial facts obtaining—e.g., "when its members regulate their emotions of guilt and impartial anger by a set of norms, and those emotions of guilt and impartial anger in turn regulate the members' behavior and practical thought" (Toh 2013, 462)—it would be a non sequitur on the preceding to say (as a matter of first-order and internal moral judgment) that "any first-order moral judgment is correct ultimately in virtue only of certain social facts existing in the relevant community" (Toh 2013, 462). Toh's worry, then, is that Dworkin's challenge to Hart, as well as my response on behalf of Hartian positivism, involves precisely that non sequitur.

IV. Toh's Basic Objection: Moral versus Legal Conventionalism

Toh's analogy to metaethical noncognitivism of the Gibbard variety is misconceived. Let us call "Moral Conventionalism" the view that what is morally right and wrong depends

---

[4] Cf. (Hart 2012,101): "In the day-to-day life of a legal system its RR is very seldom expressly formulated as a rule . . . but its existence is *shown* in the way in which particular rules are identified." As Hart will say elsewhere, it is "presupposed." I will have more to say about presupposition in the text, below.

[5] I take it "correct" in (L3) means that the judgment is a true statement of the law in the jurisdiction, and nothing more. So (L3) can be both an "external" judgment in Toh's sense and a first-order judgment about which propositions of law are true. Presuppositions can perform this semantic function, as discussed later.

ultimately on the behavior and attitudes of most members of a community. So, for example, action X is morally right if most members of the community act as if X is right and, when pressed, will affirm that X is indeed something that ought to be done. The metaethical view in Gibbard (1990) is *not* committed to this kind of Moral Conventionalism, and perhaps Moral Conventionalism is false. The key question is whether the legal analogue to Moral Conventionalism is also false, that is, that law is not conventional in precisely the sense that morality would be on the Moral Conventionalist view. I take it to be central to the positivist theory as defended by Hart and others that law is conventional in precisely the way the Moral Conventionalist thinks morality is conventional. In other words, the positivist view is that which norms are legally valid in any society, and thus which judgments of legal validity are correct, depends ultimately on the conventional practice of officials, that is, on the criteria of legal validity on which they converge and accept from an internal point of view (i.e., it depends on their behaviors and attitudes): roughly, Toh's (L3).

Crucial to Toh's position is the claim that (L3) ("Any first-order legal judgment is correct ultimately in virtue only of certain social facts existing in the relevant community") has "no explanatory payoff" in Hart's theory. But his argument for this again exposes his odd hermeneutic posture vis-à-vis Hart's texts. According to Toh (2013, 2015), (L3) does not help explain the kinds of phenomena that Hart thought Bentham's and Austin's theories could not adequately explain, and that Hart focused on in Chapters 2 through 4 of *The Concept of Law*: for example, the transfer of sovereign power, the continuity of laws across sovereigns, the existence of power-conferring rules, and so on. Hart's theory, of course, aims to explain these phenomena, and does so more successfully, by almost universal consensus, than his positivist predecessors. But from this it simply does not follow that (L3) has no explanatory power in Hart's theory: the idea that what needs explaining are only the phenomena that Bentham and Austin failed to explain is unmotivated. For it is precisely Hart's more complicated theoretical apparatus of a union of primary and secondary rules—and secondary rules understood as social rules—that leads Hart to be committed to Toh's (L3) or what I have been calling legal conventionalism. Let me explain.

Although Hart is offering an analysis of the concept of law, one supposedly adequate to what an ordinary person familiar with a modern municipal legal system understands, we also know the analysis has a revisionary dimension, aiming to purge the folk concept of incompatible elements in favor of a more satisfactory and coherent theoretical account (for discussion of this aspect of Hart's methodology, see Langlinais and Leiter 2016, 678–679). For example, the folk—not to mention theorists from Austin to Kelsen—think there is some kind of necessary connection between law and coercion, but that aspect of the folk concept cannot be reconciled with the idea of *obligations* to act as the law requires, as Hart famously argues. But legal conventionalism, in particular, is necessary to explain an even more prosaic set of observations. Where legal systems exist, we can distinguish between those norms that are legally valid and those that are not. A theory of law should explain this. Hart's theory does so by noting that for a legal system to exist there must be a special kind of secondary rule, a rule of recognition specifying the criteria of legal validity, which is itself simply an instance of the phenomenon that Hart calls a "social rule": a convergent practice of behavior (e.g., judges applying particular criteria of legal validity) and acceptance of the rule describing that practice from an internal point of view (e.g., judges treat applying such criteria as obligatory). But the introduction of the idea of a rule of recognition naturally raises Dworkin's worry: sometimes judges in modern legal systems engage in TDs, i.e., disputes about the content of the rule of recognition or the criteria of legal validity. How are we to explain what's going on in such disputes? Hart answers this question as well: he is explicit that internal judgments of legal validity *presuppose* the RR that validates them, and we already know that an RR exists only if the relevant internal-point-of-view practice exists.[6] If there is a dispute about the presuppositions of a legal judgment—a TD in Dworkin's sense—then there is only one way to resolve it on Hart's view. Consider the following three claims made by Hart:

(1) Hart says that an internal judgment of legal validity that "makes use of a RR which [the legal official] accepts as appropriate for identifying the law" (108) also presupposes that this RR is "actually accepted and employed in the general operation of the system. *If the truth of this presupposition were doubted, it could be established by reference to actual practice: to the way in which courts identify what is to count as law, and to the general acceptance of or acquiescence in these identifications*" (108, emphasis added). In other words, internal judgments of legal validity presuppose that the RR has a particular content, and if that were "doubted" (as it would be in a TD), the content would be established by empirical facts about "actual practice." This, I take it, is a direct endorsement of what Toh calls (L3), and what Dworkin (1986), Leiter (2009), and Shapiro (2011) are all assuming is a feature of Hart's view.

(2) In addressing uncertainty about the content of the RR—about the "ultimate criteria of legal validity" in a legal system (149), using the English rule about the sovereignty of Parliament as his example—Hart says that its content "is an empirical question concerning the form of rule which is accepted as the ultimate criterion in identifying the law. Though it is a question about a rule lying at the base of a legal system, it is still a question of fact to which at any given moment of time, on some points at least, there may be a quite determinate answer." He concludes, based on the practice of the English courts, "that the presently accepted rule is one of continuing sovereignty, so that Parliament cannot protect its statutes from repeal" (150). In this case, then, the *content* of the RR is explicitly established by Hart by appeal to statements of fact about official practice—once again, demonstrating an explanatory role for Toh's (L3), since the first order judgment that Parliament cannot protect its statutes from repeal is established by answering this "empirical question."

(3) Hart goes on to say that "the fact that the rule of parliamentary sovereignty is determinate at this point [in time] does not mean that it is so at all points. Questions can be raised about it [i.e., about the content of the RR with respect to parliamentary sovereignty] to which at present there is no answer which is clearly right or wrong. These can be settled only by a choice, made by someone

[6] I agree with Toh (2013, 2015) that the existence of an RR is a matter of external fact, and that there is no sense to the question whether an RR is legally valid, but as far as I can see, that is wholly irrelevant to the TD problem, which is not about the "legal validity" of the RR, but about its content. I should add that I also agree with Toh (2015, 349–353) that the supposed problem of the "normativity of law" is a pseudo-problem (though not quite for all Toh's reasons).

> to whose choices in this matter authority is eventually accorded" (150). (Hart's example concerns legislation that imposes special voting rules for its own repeal.) So here "we are in the area of open texture of the system's most fundamental rule . . . a question may arise to which there is no answer—only answers" (151), and some court may subsequently make "determinate . . . the ultimate rule by which valid law is identified" (152). In these cases—cases of TD in Dworkin's sense—"when courts settle previously unenvisaged questions concerning the most fundamental . . . rules, they *get* their authority to decide them accepted after the questions have arisen and the decision has been given. Here all that succeeds is success" (153). In other words, a new official practice (converging on particular criteria of legal validity) settles the questions about the content of the RR, and thus settles disputes about presuppositions such as the kind we saw in (2), above—which is exactly the supposition of my positivist account of TD (Leiter 2009).

As the last two preceding passages (2 and 3) indicate, for Hart, judgments about the content of the RR can be first-order judgments about the content of the law.[7] That is because they are not judgments that *"presuppose"* the RR, they are judgments about the RR itself, and those are, as Hart says, factual or empirical, but the truth of these factual judgments, according to Hart, are "presupposed" by the internal judgment that the law is X. And, as the first quote makes clear, a dispute about that presupposition is resolved by "reference to actual practice," or what I glossed as a "head count."

V. Presuppositions

Since Toh's claim that legal conventionalism (i.e., his L3) plays no explanatory role in Hart's theory is flatly contradicted by what Hart says, perhaps we should consider a different tact: namely, What is the best way to understand Hart's talk of "presupposition"? Perhaps there is a reading of Hart's talk about presupposing the RR that can be explained in a way that supports Toh's position.

Toh (2015) addresses this question, but makes two mistakes in his treatment of it. First, after noting correctly that Hart criticized "Kelsenian talk of presuppositions [as] misleading" and that Hart argued instead that the "'existence' of rules of recognition [is] a complex empirical fact" (2015, 359), Toh goes on to claim that "Whatever the real or full nature of Kelsen's notion of presupposition, it seems to bear sufficient resemblance to the one that Hart himself deploys for [Hart's] simple dismissal of Kelsen's talk of presupposition of the basic norm to be quite misleading" (2015, 359–360). Here Toh betrays his excessive enthusiasm for dismissing what Hart actually says.

---

[7] "Ultimate" rules such as the RR are neither valid nor invalid, but "We can ask whether it is the practice of courts, legislatures, officials, or private citizens . . .actually to use this rule as an ultimate RR" (2012, 107). But when we ask such questions we are "no longer attempting to answer the same kind of question about it as those which we answered about other rules with its aid" (107), precisely because "we have moved from an internal statement of law asserting the validity of a rule of the system to an external statement of fact" (108). But that external statement answers the first-order question.

Kelsen's and Hart's talk of presuppositions are, to start, completely different. Kelsen is a NeoKantian: his talk of "presupposition" is talk of a transcendental condition on the possibility of the intelligibility of some judgment (in the legal case, the possibility of ultimate judgments about legal validity). That is not surprising when one remembers that Kelsen's was supposed to be a "pure" theory of law, one untainted by empirical claims: whatever exactly transcendental conditions on the possibility of judgment are, they are not empirical facts. Hart, by contrast, is no NeoKantian, and he has no use for talk of transcendental conditions on the possibility of judgment. Hart's is plainly not a "pure" theory of law: unlike Kelsen, it grounds a legal system in complex psychosocial facts about the behavior and attitudes of officials, not in talk of transcendental conditions. More precisely, Hart was influenced by ordinary language philosophy—appeal to how people actually speak—so his references to "presuppositions" has an empirical dimension, one grounded in the pragmatics of ordinary language. That is utterly absent from Kelsen. We will return to that crucial aspect of Hart's ideas about "presupposition" shortly.

Toh's second mistake in his treatment of presupposition follows not from the misunderstanding of Kelsen, but in his willingness to disregard what Hart says. According to Toh's rendering of Hart's "oblique" analysis of "internal" legal judgments, a judgment by an official of the system that "This rule is the law" can be analyzed as follows:

> [He] expresses his acceptance of some rule that he deems validated by the rule of recognition of his community's legal system, and furthermore *presupposes* (i) the content of that rule of recognition, and also (ii) the efficacy of that rule of recognition . . . [He thus] presupposes not only the content of the rule of recognition of his community, but also that the relevant rule of recognition is accepted and followed by the officials of his community. *The content of this second, factual presupposition—as opposed to the first, normative presupposition—is the same as the content of the external legal statement about the existence of the relevant rule of recognition.* (Toh 2015, 360; emphasis added)

In other words, it seems that, even on Toh's view, an official of the system who judges that "This rule is the law" presupposes that "any first-order legal judgment is correct ultimately in virtue only of certain social facts existing" (Toh 2013, 461, stating his [L3]), and thus presupposes what Toh calls the "external legal statement about the existence of the relevant rule of recognition." This might suggest, of course, that someone engaged in a TD is disputing precisely the factual statement about the practice constituting the RR, and the truth of that statement is an empirical question as Hart put it in the passage from page 108 of *The Concept of* Law that I quoted earlier. Toh, no doubt realizing that this analysis defeats his claims, cautions us not to be "easily blind[ed]" (2015, 360) to Hart's real view. The other possibility, of course, is that Hart has expressed his real view accurately, and Toh simply wants to distort our perception of what Hart said.

Toh's attempt to have us disregard what Hart actually says depends on two claims. First, Toh (2015, 362) quotes a lengthy passage from Hart's 1959 essay on "Scandinavian Realism" in which, on Toh's gloss, "Hart . . . warns explicitly against conflating internal and external statements," which is correct, but the conflation Hart is reacting to is Ross's (supposed) claim that statements of law are just predictions of official behavior,[8] not the problem of TDs, which are cases in which the presuppositions are explicitly in dispute. Second, Toh goes on to note that "presuppositions are defeasible and could be cancelled" in ordinary language (2015, 362–363). But in TDs, they are not canceled, they are directly disputed, so the phenomenon of cancelation is not relevant.

If Toh's argument that what Hart actually says "blinds" us to his real meaning is not compelling, then let us see whether we can take seriously what Hart actually says. We should begin with the fact that Hart, unlike Kelsen, is plainly thinking of "presupposition" in the empirical manner of ordinary language philosophers, who were always sensitive to the pragmatics of language use, a theme that has come to the fore in subsequent philosophy of language and linguistics. One familiar view about presuppositions in this tradition, the "semantic" view, requires that presuppositions hold even when the statement that presupposes them is negated: so "a proposition that *P* presupposes that *Q* if and only if *Q* must be true in order that *P* have a truth value at all" (Stalnaker 1999, 48). The proposition ("P") that "It is unconstitutional to execute juveniles in the United States" clearly presupposes that the United States has a constitution, and that presupposition does survive negation of (P): it cannot be true that it is really constitutional to executive juveniles in the United States unless the United States also has a constitution! But in Hart's view, (P) also presupposes something else, namely, ("Q") "A Supreme Court decision about the constitutionality of such executions under the Eighth Amendments is decisive," which is one small part of the general RR of the American legal system. That presupposition cannot be a semantic presupposition of (P) since some negations of P do not require it: for example, some speakers might simply deny (Q) and endorse "Z": "Such executions are constitutional unless they are really cruel." So it looks like a judgment about the unconstitutionality of executing juveniles in the United States, in which Q is presupposed, cannot be a presupposition *in the semantic sense*.

There is a different view of presuppositions that is, I will suggest, more adequate to Hart's usage, but before setting that out explicitly, it will be useful to imagine how a dispute about the preceding propositions *P*, *Q*, and *Z* might actually go between two lawyers, call them Leslie and Jeremy. Leslie asserts, "It is unconstitutional to execute juveniles in the United States." Jeremy retorts, "No it isn't." They continue:

LESLIE: "Of course it is, the Supreme Court settled the issue with its decision in *Roper v. Simmons* in 2005."

JEREMY: "I know the Court made that decision, of course, but that doesn't mean it is really unconstitutional, it depends on whether it is *really* cruel."

LESLIE: "No, its constitutionality in the United States right now has been settled by the Supreme Court. Your opinion, or anyone else's, about its cruelty isn't relevant, unless you can persuade the High Court to reverse itself."

JEREMY: "Why do you talk as if the Supreme Court's decision in *Roper* settles anything about the constitutionality of executing juveniles?"

LESLIE: "Are you being serious? That issue has been settled at least since *Cooper v. Aaron* in 1958!"

---

[8] Ross, as we now know, did not proffer this as a claim about the ordinary concept of law, but as a kind of reforming definition meant to reconcile the intelligibility of law in a world naturalistically conceived. Cf. (Leiter (2013, 951–953) and the references therein.

JEREMY: "Just another court decision, who cares?"

LESLIE: "Did you pass a bar exam? Supreme Court decisions about constitutionality are binding on the lower courts and the other branches of government."

JEREMY: "Says you!"

LESLIE: "No, says all the courts and other lawyers in this jurisdiction."

JEREMY: "But they could all be wrong!"

LESLIE: "I'm not even sure what that would mean."

JEREMY: "It means they're all wrong about what the law really is."

LESLIE: "I understand you would like the law to be different, and so maybe you want the High Court to overrule itself, but the law right now is settled."

JEREMY: "No it's not, it only *appears* to be settled because of the consensus among the lower courts following the High Court."

LESLIE: "But that's just what the law is today!"

To be sure, someone might really press Jeremy's line against Leslie's, and if it were false that the content of the RR is settled by actual practice, then Jeremy's pressing this line of criticism would not be ridiculous. But the latter is not our immediate question here; our question is whether it could be Hart's view that the *actual practice of officials* settles questions about the content of the RR—i.e., Leslie's position in this debate (which I do take to be both the positivist's posture and the ordinary lawyer's posture). And in assuming that the actual practice does settle that, as Leslie does, it seems wholly in line with what Hart actually says in the passages quoted earlier. Hart holds the view that actual practice settles the question of the content of the RR in contested cases, and such a view is compatible with how a putative disagreement between a positivist and Dworkinian lawyer would go, as the case of Leslie and Jeremy illustrates. Moreover, if I am right that Leslie's position is the ordinary lawyer's position in this debate, and that Jeremy's position is as puzzling as Leslie finds it, then that would also count in favor of Hart's view as against Dworkin's.[9]

Now there is a view of presupposition in ordinary language, the pragmatic view, that comports much better with how Hart is thinking about "presupposition" when he treats the empirical fact that the RR has such-and-such a content as the presupposition of first-order legal judgments. According to the pragmatic view, "Presuppositions . . . are something like the background beliefs of the speaker—propositions whose truth he takes for granted, or seems to take for granted, in making his statement" (Stalnaker 1999, 48). Leslie starts the debate with Jeremy assuming that it is "common ground" between them that a Supreme Court decision about constitutionality settles the legality of executing juveniles. Their dispute breaks down, and descends into Leslie's incredulity, precisely because Jeremy seems to reject the idea that any competent American lawyer accepts, namely, that since maybe *Marbury* and certainly *Cooper v. Aaron*, the Supreme Court has the final word on constitutional validity. Leslie, like Hart in *The Concept of Law*, takes it for granted that *official practice* is decisive, which in the American context, with regard to constitutionality of legislation, means decisions of the U.S. Supreme Court. From this point of view, as already noted, Jeremy's dissent from what Leslie (speaking for Hart) took to be the "common ground" appears mysterious.

[9] Of course, Jeremy might reasonably be understood to be arguing that the Supreme Court *got the law wrong*, a point to which I return below, in the text.

Although on the pragmatic view, "[p]resupposing is . . . not a mental attitude like believing, but is rather a linguistic disposition—a disposition to behave in one's use of language as if one had certain beliefs, or were making certain assumptions" (Stalnaker 1999, 52), this "does not rule out a semantic *explanation* for the fact that a certain presupposition is required when a certain statement is made" (1999, 53), though the pragmatic view does not require it. On the pragmatic view, presuppositions can vary by context of utterance and, more importantly, presupposition and logical entailment can go together or come apart. On the semantic view, *A* presupposes *B* iff *both A* and its denial require *B*. But the pragmatic account allows for the fact that "sometimes when a presupposition is required by the making of a statement, what is presupposed is also entailed, and sometimes it is not" (1999, 54), and this is helpful when it comes to the dispute between Leslie and Jeremy. For Jeremy denies that executing juveniles is unconstitutional, but does *not* presuppose, as Leslie does, that a Supreme Court decision settles the matter. Their disagreement results precisely from presupposition and entailment coming apart. Leslie believes that (A) it is unconstitutional to execute juveniles, presupposes (B) constitutionality is settled by decisions of the U.S. Supreme Court, such that someone who denies (A) must still presuppose (B). But Jeremy denies (A) while also rejecting (B), meaning that he denies Leslie's presupposition and thus is having a TD. Yet, as we have seen, on Hart's view, that kind of dispute is settled by reference to the empirical facts about official practice. So we can say that on Hart's view, any first-order judgment presupposes pragmatically an official practice constituting the relevant rule of recognition, while Dworkin denies that.

Perhaps that is too quick, though. Cannot a lawyer *intelligibly* argue that a question of American constitutional law settled by the U.S. Supreme Court was wrongly resolved and should be overruled in a subsequent decision? The simple answer is, of course, yes, any lawyer can so argue, and that person may well be right: perhaps the law would be morally improved by being overruled; or perhaps the High Court misunderstood the law. Only the latter claim is at issue (anyone can argue that the law would be morally better if construed differently, of course). But the latter claim involves a TD, which according to Hart is resolved by reference to actual practice, which is what the Dworkinian denies, of course. But this just shows that arguments for overruling based on "what the law *really* requires" are not neutral datapoints for adjudicating between competing accounts of the content of the RR. Legal arguments for overruling earlier decisions in a common-law system are even less frequent datapoints requiring explanation than TDs themselves, which occur against the background of massive agreement about the law, as noted earlier

VI. Some Other Objections and Concluding Remarks

Once we see that Hart assumes that the RR, as fixed by official practice, functions as a pragmatic presupposition of first-order legal judgments, we can dispense with Duarte D'Almeida's objections (2016) fairly easily. Duarte D'Almeida follows Toh in thinking the internal/external judgment distinction is crucial, and notes that when officials make what he calls "general internal statements" (176)—statements of the form, "This decision is legally required because of this criterion of legal validity" (e.g., in the example I have been using, "A state cannot execute a juvenile because the U.S. Supreme Court has deemed such executions unconstitutional")—they do not *justify* them by appeal to the fact that officials accept such a criterion (193). But in ordinary discourse, one does not *justify* one's statements by reference to their pragmatic presuppositions: one takes the *common ground* to actually be the common ground of the discourse! Of course judges do not claim the correctness of their "statements of law depends on everyone else or even a majority agreeing with them" (Duare D'Almeida 2016, 193); the correctness of their statements of law depends on their correctly applying the criteria of legal validity, which in cases of constitutionality, presupposes that the criteria are fixed by Supreme Court decisions (where the Supreme Court has ruled on the matter). Even Duarte D'Almeida concedes that judges do "presuppose the truth of the external statement that that rule [that criterion of legal validity] is actually generally accepted as appropriate for that purpose" (2016, 194), which is to concede the point: the external fact that the RR is what it is based on official practice is pragmatically presupposed as the common ground of the debate. That issue, of course, does not arise when speakers agree about the law; it only arises when they *disagree* about the common ground, which is why, *contra* Duarte D'Almeida, one would not expect the character of theoretical agreement and disagreement to be symmetrical.

By contrast, Levenbook (2015, 5) echoes Shapiro's attempt to motivate Dworkin's critique (2011, 290–291) in claiming that since "criticism for engaging" in TDs "is notably absent," it is not plausible that those engaged in them are being disingenuous. The idea would be that if dispute about the common ground was mere pretense—an attempt to change the law, rather than dispute its fundamental grounds—then we would expect criticism of judges for engaging in what look like Dworkinian TDs, but she thinks there is none. In fact, some scholars do criticize judges on this ground (e.g., Fallon 2008), but put that to one side since there is a more basic point. To argue against the error-theoretical interpretation of TD it is never enough to appeal to the ordinary practice of those committing the error, including those acceding to it. Many objections have been made against Mackie's error theory of ethical discourse, but no one, to my knowledge, has argued that Mackie *must* be wrong because those engaged in ethical discourse think their claims are true. Error-theoretic treatments of religious and theological discourse are an even better case: such discourse generally does not admit of noncognitive analysis (as ethical discourse does), and yet no one would seriously argue that because many participants in the discourse think, e.g., that there is a real question about how one being, God, could be realized in three distinct "divine" beings, the Father, the Son, and the Holy Spirit, that the error-theoretic interpretation of the discourse is misguided. Legal positivism stands to theoretical disagreements about law, as error-theoretic naturalism stands to theological debates about the Trinity. One can forgive, and even explain, how participants in these discourses come to make the mistakes they do, and in the legal case, it is quite a bit easier, given that neither the judiciary nor practitioners have a reason to have well-developed views on the foundational questions about their practice (why would judges need to recognize the truth of legal conventionalism?), so their error in these unusual cases may well be innocent. Moreover, judges and lawyers have obvious practical motivations for misconceiving their disputes, something that is also true of other discourses that warrant error-theoretic treatment. In the end, as I argued originally (Leiter 2009), the *only* relevant question is whether the *best explanation* of law and legal systems is one that involves an error-theoretic interpretation of TDs, when they actually occur. That is also the question we are left with by what Hart actually says.[10]

References

Duarte d'Almeida, Luis. 2016. "The Grounds of Law." In *The Legacy of Ronald Dworkin*, edited by W. Waluchow and S. Sciaraffa. (Oxford: Oxford University Press).

Dworkin, Ronald. 1986. *Law's Empire.* Cambridge, MA: Harvard University Press.

Fallon, Richard. 2008. "Constitutional Precedent Viewed through the Lens of Hartian Positivist Jurisprudence," *North Carolina Law Review* 86:1107–1164.

Gibbard, Allan. 1990. *Wise Choices, Apt Feelings: A Theory of Normative Judgment.* Cambridge, MA: Harvard University Press.

Hart, H. L. A. 1961, 2012. *The Concept of Law*, 3rd ed. Oxford: Clarendon Press.

Langlinais, Alex and Brian Leiter. 2016. "The Methodology of Legal Philosophy." In *The Oxford Handbook of Philosophical Methodology*, edited by H. Cappelen, T. Gendler, and J. Hawthorne. Oxford: Oxford University Press, 671–689.

Leiter, Brian. 2001. "Objectivity, Morality, and Adjudication," reprinted in Leiter, *Naturalizing Jurisprudence.* Oxford: Oxford University Press, 2007.

_____. 2005. "The End of Empire: Dworkin and Jurisprudence in the 21st-Century," *Rutgers Law Journal* 35:165–181.

_____. 2009. "Explaining Theoretical Disagreement," *University of Chicago Law Review* 76:1215–1250.

_____. 2013. "Legal Realisms, Old and New," *Valparaiso University Law Review* 47:949–964.

_____. 2015. "Normativity for Naturalists," *Philosophical Issues: A Supplement to Nous* 25:64–79.

Levenbook, Barbara Baum. 2015. "Dworkin's Theoretical Disagreement Argument," *Philosophy Compass* 10(1): 1–9.

Shapiro, Scott. 2007. "The Hart/Dworkin Debate: A Short Guide for the Perplexed." In *Ronald Dworkin*, edited by A. Ripstein. Cambridge: Cambridge University Press.

_____. 2011. *Legality.* Cambridge, MA: Harvard University Press.

Stalnaker, Robert. 1999. *Context and Content: Essays on Intentionality in Speech and Thought.* Oxford: Oxford University Press.

Toh, Kevin. (2013). "Jurisprudential Theories and First-Order Legal Judgments," *Philosophy Compass* 8(5):457–471.

_____. 2015. "Four Neglected Prescriptions of Hartian Legal Philosophy," *Law and Philosophy* 34:333–368.

[10] A very early version of this chapter benefitted from discussion at the conference on "Deep Disagreements" at the Humboldt University in Berlin in June 2015. I can recall particularly useful questions and comments on that occasion from Don Loeb, Ralf Poscher, and Ernie Sosa. A later version benefitted from detailed comments by Kevin Toh. The current version was improved by discussion at a legal and political philosophy workshop with faculty from Chicago, King's College, London, and the National University of Singapore at the University of Chicago in May 2016—especially Ryan Doerfler, Ben Laurence, Tim Macklem, and John Tasioulas—and by written comments from Max Etchemendy. Finally, I am grateful to Tim Grinsell for guidance on linguistic presuppositions; to Taylor Coles, University of Chicago Law School Class of 2018, for research assistance; and to the Alumni Faculty Fund of the Law School for research support.

12 Hybrid Dispositionalism and the Law

Teresa Marques*

I. Introduction

Among the many things that humans disagree about, disputes over so-called matters of fact are often described as an idealized paradigm—there is an objective fact of the matter. Either we get the facts right or we don't. And when we disagree, we can't both be right. At least one of us is wrong when I believe that *p* and you believe that not-*p*. In turn, this requires the existence of a common content of belief over which we can disagree.

This idealization is simplistic and unrealistic. First, it is not clear if it applies to all "matters of fact."[1] Second, other concerns arise once we focus on presumably more anthropocentric issues. For example, in spite of the saying *de gustibus non est disputandum*, disagreements

* Thanks are due to Andrea Altobrando, Caroline Arruda, Hrafn Asgeirsson, Carla Bagnoli, Sara Bernstein, Gunnar Björnsson, Massimiliano Carrara, Bianca Cepollaro, Sam Chilovi, Janice Dowell, John Eriksson, Ragnar Francén Olinder, Manuel García-Carpintero, Kathrin Glüer-Pagin, Sanna Hirvonen, Torfinn Huvenes, Dan López de Sa, Genoveva Martí, Robin McKenna, Lucas Miotto, Josep Joan Moreso, Peter Pagin, George Pavlakos, Federico Penelas, Diana Perez, David Plunkett, Mike Ridge, Jonathan Schaffer, Laura Schroeter, François Schroeter, Andreas Stokke, Isidora Stojanovic, Caj Strandberg, Tim Sundell, Marco Tiozzo, Kevin Toh, Veronica Tozzi, Chiara Valentini, Pekka Vayrynen, Jack Woods, and Dan Zeman. Work funded by the European Commission, for projects CAND and DIAPHORA [Grant agreements numbers PIEF-GA-2012-622114; H2020-MSCA-ITN-2015-675415]; Ministerio de Economía y Innovación for projects ABOUT OURSELVES and CONCEDIS [Grant agreements: FFI2013-47948-P; FFI2015-73767-JIN], and AGAUR de la Generalitat de Catalunya for Grup Consolidat LOGOS.

[1] One possible source of scepticism comes, for instance, from reflection on the pervasive vagueness of language, which raises doubts about the existence of such a thing as the right answer to each and all factual question.

Dimensions of Normativity. David Plunkett, Scott J. Shapiro, and Kevin Toh.

over matters of taste are pervasive in our social life. If we have different standards of taste, it is pretentious to insist that one of us is wrong, or that there is a single right answer about what is of good taste. Similar pervasive and persistent disagreements occur in other domains, from aesthetics to knowledge attributions. The simple model described above does not appear to be well-suited to all such disputes. It is questionable if in each of those domains there is one single correct answer to the question of what is the case. It is not clear that in all cases either one gets the facts right or one doesn't.

These concerns intersect various kinds of questions. First, there's the metaphysical question of what, if anything, distinguishes matters of fact from matters of value, and of matters of personal taste. Second, there is the epistemic question of whether it is the case that we can disagree without either of us being at fault.[2] Also, there is the semantic question of what the content of our mental states and speech acts must be for us to disagree or have a conflict.

One possible answer to the metaphysical question makes these facts dependent on our perspectives. For instance, one could say after Hume 1775/1966 that beauty is "no quality in things themselves," or that moral values are projections we make onto the world (Hume 1777/2004). To capture the perspectival nature of taste, beauty, or moral value, various authors argue for dispositional or response-dependent theories of value.[3]

Different answers to the metaphysical question recommend different answers to the semantic question. It is possible that in some domains there is near universal convergence on responses that have an appearance of objectivity. But it is hard to make the case that, across the board, from personal taste to morality, there's one right answer for each evaluative or normative question. Insofar as answers to the metaphysical question recommend the dependence of normative and value facts on our perspectives, affective responses, or dispositions, the answer to the semantic question about the content of normative discourse and thought may likewise require semantic dependence on perspectives or standards.

However, semantic solutions that incorporate ontological perspective-dependence face substantial objections. One central objection concerns the explanation of speakers' intuitions about disagreement: if two people do not refer to the same standards, how can they intelligibly disagree? A theory that makes norms and values dependent on the perspectives from which they are valid puts forward contents that can be accepted by anyone. If we can all accept the same contents, we apparently don't disagree. Another objection concerns the motivational force of evaluative and normative discourse and thought. It seems that it is possible to accept that something is a value, or a norm, given certain standards or sets of norms, and not be motivated to act by that value or norm. Yet, evaluative and normative thought is motivational in a way that merely descriptive thought is not.

In Section II, I offer a brief summary of the problem of legal disagreements for social or collective accounts of the Law. In Section III, I present hybrid dispositionalism, and show how it offers an account of three core features of evaluative discourse, and solutions for resilient conflicts and disagreements. My view combines a contextualist semantic account

---

[2] In the last decade, there has been an intense debate about whether disagreement without fault is possible. E.g., (Kölbel 2004b); (Moreso 2009); (Egan 2010); (MacFarlane 2014); (Marques and García-Carpintero 2014), among many others.

[3] See, e.g., (Lewis 1989/2000); (Smith 1989, 2002); and more recently (Egan 2012) and (Marques 2016a).

with a dispositional account of the value properties denoted. I suggest that the properties denoted are response-dependent *de nobis* properties (properties *about ourselves*). The view is complemented with expressive conversational implicatures, which I argue are inferable and pass two relevant tests. The last section suggests that an adaptation of this model to legal discourse results complements Toh's 2011 proposal of legal statements as expressions of shared acceptance of norms.

II. Social Practice and Collective Agency: The Problem of Legal Disagreements

Legal positivism is, briefly, the thesis that facts about the existence and content of the law at a jurisdiction are ultimately determined by social facts, in particular by facts about the actions and dispositions of members of the legal community in a jurisdiction. On Hart's 1961/2012 view, a legal system exists just in case:

On the one hand, those rules of behaviour which are valid according to the system's ultimate criteria of validity *must be generally obeyed*, and, on the other hand, its rules of recognition specifying the criteria of legal validity and its rules of change and adjudication *must be effectively accepted as common public standards of official behaviour by its officials*. (Hart 1961/2012, 116) (emphasis added)

A *rule of recognition* is a higher-order rule that specifies the features that other rules must have to be part of the legal system (Hart 1961/2012, 94).

Hart also distinguished between internal and external legal statements. *Internal legal statements* are statements of law—*normative statements made from the point of view of the participants within a legal system*. Any given legal sentence—e.g., "It is illegal for civil servants to leave the country without government authorization"—might be true in a given legal system, but not in another. This sentence is not *about* social facts. *External legal statements*, on the other hand, are about individual laws or other aspects of legal systems—*descriptive statements about social facts that are made from the point of view of an external observer*.

Now, Dworkin distinguished between two kinds of legal dispute about what the law is in a jurisdiction. Disputes of the first kind—theoretical disagreements—are about the content of the rule of recognition. Disputes of the second kind—empirical disagreements—are about whether the conditions set out in the rule of recognition have obtained in a particular case. In empirical disagreements, parties agree on the conditions for something's being a law, but disagree about whether those conditions are met in the case at hand. However, in theoretical disagreements, legal actors have different views about what the law is, even though they may fully agree about the empirical facts.

In so-called hard cases (Dworkin 1977, Ch. 3), officials within a system disagree even though they don't share *a common understanding* of their public standards of behavior. Whenever legal officials *do not share ends*, or *interpret their commitments in different ways*, they don't constitute a cohesive group linked by "the same normative relations." Therefore, there is no shared rule of recognition that is "generally obeyed." Legal officials nonetheless take themselves to disagree, and these disagreements are pervasive in the practice of the law. Hence, the law can't reduce to what a community of officials at a jurisdiction accepts as the law.

In *Law's Empire*, Dworkin illustrates the argument with the famous example of *Riggs v. Palmer*. In this New York state civil court case, Mrs Riggs and Mrs Preston tried to invalidate their father's will. The defendant of the case, Elmer E. Palmer, had killed his grandfather to inherit the estate. At the time, the New York statute of wills said nothing explicitly about whether someone named in a will could inherit if he had murdered the testator. Palmer's aunts, Riggs and Preston, sued the administrator of the will, demanding that they, and not Palmer, should inherit the property. Judge Gray, who wrote the dissenting opinion in the trial, argued for a *literal* interpretation of the law, which made no exception for murderers, and argued that Palmer was already being punished for the murder. Judge Earl, who wrote for the majority, argued that the legislators couldn't have *intended* murderers to benefit from their crimes. The *statute*, on this interpretation, would not be merely the written text, but rather that text interpreted according to the intentions of the legislators, which would exclude the interpretation on which a murderer could benefit from the crime. Judges Gray and Earl hence had different interpretations of what the law fundamentally is:

> If two lawyers are actually following *different* rules in using the word "law," using different factual criteria to decide when a proposition of law is true or false, then each must mean something different from the other when he says what the law is. Earl and Gray must mean different things when they claim or deny that the law permits murderers to inherit: Earl means that his grounds for law are or are not satisfied, Gray has in mind his own grounds, not Earl's. So the two judges are not really disagreeing about anything when one denies and the other asserts this proposition. They are only talking past one another. Their arguments are pointless in the most trivial and irritating way, like an argument about banks when one person has in mind savings banks and the other riverbanks. (Dworkin, 1986, 43–44)

Theoretical disputes raise a challenge to legal positivism—legal officials often and fundamentally disagree about what norms they have a duty to apply. Since there is no *single set of obligations* that is accepted by all legal officials, there should be no law. But there is. Hence, the law cannot be merely what is accepted as such by legal officials. Dworkin's argument fundamentally rests on the premise that the best way to explain how an exchange between two speakers expresses a disagreement is to suppose that *speakers mean the same thing*—that is, express the same concepts—with the words they use in that exchange.

In contrast, Dworkin argues for *interpretivism*. Dworkin claimed that the concept LAW, like other concepts (DEMOCRACY, EQUALITY, FREEDOM), is an *interpretative concept*, and that in theoretical disputes participants disagree about the concept's correct application. Interpretivism is the thesis that the law includes not only the rules *accepted by a community*, but also *"the principles that provide the best moral justification for those enacted rules"* (Dworkin 2011, 402). Interpretivism contradicts legal positivism because the *content* and *existence* of the law is to be determined by things other than social facts about what legal officials are disposed to accept.

III. Hybrid Dispositionalism

In recent work (Marques 2016a), I argue for a hybrid form of *contextualism* about aesthetic predicates. My account is committed to a dispositional metaphysical account of aesthetic properties, which is close to Lewis's conditionally relative dispositional theory. Lewis's theory allows for value pluralism, but does not require it. It also allows us to be mistaken about what is a value. Both are desirable features in a theory of value. I suggest that a contextualist semantic implementation of Lewisian dispositionalism about values has the resources for a comprehensive explanation of value discourse: it can help explain its cognitive role, its expressive role, and its connection-building role. Moreover, a contextualist implementation of dispositionalism allows people that prima facie disagree and are in conflict to denote different value properties. People may simply not share perspectives. This gives a reply to objections to contextualism similar to Dworkin's objection to legal positivism: that in situations like this, people "are only talking past one another."

In that article, I argued that the action-guiding nature of the dispositional value properties denoted in discourse, when supplemented by expressive conversational implicatures, explains unifying features of evaluative and normative discourse. Moreover, the additional expressive dimension can be the focus of resilient normative or evaluative disagreements.

A. Dispositionalism and Contextualism

Many philosophers have thought that facts about values are tied to facts about us, i.e., to the responses elicited from us under certain conditions. David Lewis's (1989/2000) dispositional account of value offers one way to cash out this idea. For Lewis, "something of the appropriate category is a value if and only if we would be disposed to value it under ideal conditions" (Lewis, 1989/2000, 103), and a value property is something of the following kind:

> *x* is a value iff *x is disposed to elicit response R in group of agents G in circumstances C.*

Or, to the same effect,

> *x* is a value iff *we are disposed to give response R to x in circumstances C.*

For Lewis, the elicited response *R* is a certain kind of motivational action guiding state, *desiring to desire. We* are the relevant group of agents *G*, and *C* are conditions of full imaginative acquaintance. Although Lewis's account has been disputed, it has virtues. The theory is cognitivist, naturalist, internalist about motivation, and it is subjectivist, in that it is tied to facts about *us* (Lewis, 2000, 68–69). The view is also conditionally relative:

> I say *X* is a value; I mean that all mankind are disposed to value *X*; or anyway all nowadays are; or anyway all nowadays are except maybe some peculiar people on distant islands . . . or anyway you and I, talking here and now are; or anyway I am . . . What I mean to commit myself to is conditionally relative: relative if need be, but absolute otherwise. (Lewis, 2000, 129)

Which semantic implementation fits conditionally relative dispositionalism? Semantic invariantism could be adopted under the empirical precondition that there is universal (or near universal) convergence in the relevant responses under ideal conditions (of imaginative acquaintance).[4] But there is plenty of evidence against uniformity in evaluations. Taste and humor are clear cases; and there is cross-cultural variation in specific moral codes.[5] If this is right, it puts pressure on any account that postulates a uniform *right* answer to all matters of value. Semantic contextualism can accommodate this possible variability in value standards.[6]

Contextualism about evaluative predicates holds, first, that they have denotation relative to an evaluative standard. A value standard may be absolute or not. If it is absolute, it does not vary with context. If it is not absolute, some feature of the context of the use of the word must contribute to determine the relevant standard of the context. In spite of contextual variation, a dispositional contextualist theory should accommodate the core features of value terms that justify the membership of a word in the category *evaluative term*. The core features are, in summary, that value terms communicate cognitive descriptive contents, they play an expressive and motivational role, and finally that uses of evaluative discourse contribute to build connections among discourse participants.

Arguments for contextualism about evaluative discourse are often supported by semantic considerations. Recently, McNally and Stojanovic (2014) and Liao et al. (2016), have investigated common features of value adjectives that support a context-dependent treatment, specifically of aesthetic and personal taste adjectives. Drawing on work on gradable adjectives, McNally and Stojanovic (2014) offer a taxonomy of aesthetic adjectives. They argue that some of the features that are typical of relative gradable adjectives are also present in aesthetic adjectives.[7] Relative gradable adjectives, such as "big" or "long," are multidimensional. The same object can be big in some respect, dimension, or with respect to some comparison class, but not on other dimensions or comparison classes. Relative gradable adjectives are also *measurable*: they have degrees and thresholds of application that vary with contexts. The context of use of a relative gradable adjective requires that relevant parameters be supplied by the local conversational context. We can say that something is *big for an X*, we can use modifiers such as *very big*, comparatives such as *X is bigger than Y*, etc. Relative gradable adjectives also allow certain inferential patters. For instance, "Mary is richer than Betty" entails neither "Mary is rich" nor "Betty is not rich" Kennedy and McNally (2005).

Now, value terms such as "good" or "beautiful" also admit modifications with "very," "more . . . than . . . ," ". . . in some respect," and "for an X." "Good" is to "rich" like "better" is to "richer." The same patterns of inference of relative gradable adjectives are also manifest with aesthetic and taste predicates. For instance, "Bob is prettier than Meg" similarly entails neither "Bob is pretty" nor "Meg is not pretty."

---

[4] For a defense of such a view for aesthetic and taste predicates, see Schafer (2011).

[5] See for instance recent results in Sarkissian et al. 2011, and (Khoo and Knobe 2016).

[6] (Marques 2016a); (Marques and García-Carpintero 2014); (Brogaard 2008); and (Schaffer 2009) argue for contextualism about value predicates. Contextualism about the semantics of evaluative and normative language is sometimes classified as relativism (cf. Harman 1975; and Dreier 1990).

[7] In recent presentations, Stojanovic has proposed to generalize the taxonomy to different evaluatives. Liao et al. (2016) make the case that aesthetic adjectives don't pair neatly with relative or absolute gradable adjectives. Aesthetic adjectives are like relative gradable adjectives in the sense that their standards of application derive from aesthetic comparison classes. But they are unlike relative gradable adjectives because the relevant comparison classes are not contingent on the immediate situational context of their use.

One of the main objections to semantic contextualism about evaluative and normative discourse appeals to intuitions about disagreement that competent speakers allegedly share.[8] The examples typically report an interchange that prima facie presents a real disagreement. The contextualist analysis would arguably deprive interlocutors of a common subject matter over which to disagree.

Also, Andy Egan (2012) challenges the contextualist semantic implementation of a dispositional theory of value. His objection rests on the possibility of non-converging dispositions. Egan rightly argues that it is not clear that *everybody* would desire to desire alike under the same conditions of full imaginative acquaintance. If "we" refers to everybody, then there is a risk that *there will not be any values*, since it may be that there is *nothing* that elicits the relevant response in the right circumstances from absolutely everybody (Egan 2012, 558). On the other hand, if what "we" refers to is conditionally relative, then there will be a relativity of values: values$_{\text{humans}}$, values$_{\text{martians}}$, values$_{\text{them}}$, values$_{\text{us}}$, etc. The same value predicate will express different values in different contexts. There will be no common-subject matter for evaluative discourse and thought when evaluative standards diverge. But, Egan says, when I say *x* is a value and you say it is not, our assertions and thoughts should be in conflict, "our difference should count as a disagreement" (Egan 2012, 568).

B. *The Role of Evaluative Discourse: Cognitive, Expressive, and Connective*

Evaluative and normative discourse performs three very important roles: (i) it expresses people's evaluative and normative beliefs. Let us call this its *cognitive role*. (ii) It also (normally) expresses speakers' action-guiding conative attitudes, which have motivational effects; we can call this its *expressive role*. And finally, (iii), value talk normally establishes commonalities that, quoting Egan, are a "substantial part of the process of building and maintaining interpersonal relationships" (Egan 2010, 260). We can call this *the connective role* of evaluative discourse.

A dispositional contextualist theory has the resources to give a straightforward explanation of evaluative discourse. It claims that evaluative terms denote value properties, that those properties are response-dependent, and that we can believe correctly or incorrectly that those properties apply to their objects. The dispositional theory hence captures the *cognitive role of evaluative talk*. The theory does not face the Frege Geach problem, which purely expressivist theories arguably face.[9] Additionally, the theory must explain how the denoted properties relate to the expressive and connective roles of evaluative talk. Finally, it must also explain the impression of persistent evaluative and normative disagreements.

If we accept that something has the property *what* we *desire to desire (in way w, under conditions C . . .)*, we accept that we share desire-like attitudes. We hence implicitly accept that we have common responses under similar conditions. Attributing value to something, by the nature of value properties themselves, is essentially a way of establishing commonalities. Yet, although we may be similarly disposed, we are fallible in our value judgments, and our

---

[8] See, e.g., (Egan et al 2005, Egan 2010, 2012); (Kölbel 2004b, 2004a); (Kolodny and MacFarlane 2010); (MacFarlane 2014).

[9] See (Schroeder 2008).

fallibility is in itself a possible source of disagreement. It is possible that many persistent disputes are the result of the difficulty of assessing what we should value.

> I say that to be valued by us means to be that which we desire to desire. Then to be a value—to be good, near enough—is that which we are disposed, under ideal conditions, to desire to desire. . . . It allows, as it should, that under less-than-ideal conditions we may wrongly value what is not really good. (Lewis 1989/2000, 71)

However, we may not be disposed alike, and in such cases we will not have the same perspectives. In the previous section, I mentioned the problem of non-converging dispositions raised by Egan. One of the possible consequences of non-convergent dispositions is that there may be no values at all, or that we lose a common subject matter. Egan suggests that a solution for the Lewisian dispositional account of value is to modify the nature of the dispositional value properties. He argues that if dispositional properties are *de se* properties that we self-ascribe, then we guarantee common content. The *de se* dispositional theory's central claim is that the content of a belief that x is a value is the property of the form *being disposed to have response* R *to* x *in* C. As Egan claims, this version retains the good features of dispositionalism (Egan 2012, 571), and it avoids the problems of non-convergence, because it avoids both an error theory and guarantees a common *de se* subject matter.

Egan defends an independently motivated Stalnakerian account of assertion (Stalnaker 1978). On Stalnaker's account, assertions add the content they communicate to the conversational common ground. In felicitous contexts, interlocutors accept the asserted content as part of the common ground. And thus,

> On a *de se* dispositionalist theory of value, the role of evaluative discourse is going to be to get the participants in the conversation on the same page with respect to how they think they would respond to the objects of evaluation under the appropriate conditions. (For example, on the *de se* version of Lewis's view, the role of evaluative assertion will be to get the parties to the conversation aligned with respect to what they think they would desire to desire under conditions of full imaginative acquaintance.) (Egan 2012, 574)

De se evaluative thought allegedly does not face the challenges of lost disagreement that the contextualist dispositional theory faces.[10] *De se* thoughts are incompatible when it is subjectively irrational to self-ascribe the two centered properties that are the content of those thoughts. The subjective incompatibility of the thoughts grounds intersubjective incompatibility: if a *de se* property *p* is asserted in a given context, it cannot be coherently

[10] The difference between believing classical propositions and believing centered, or *de se* propositions (on the Lewisian understanding of *de se* propositions that Egan relies on) comes down to this. To believe a classical proposition p is to believe that p is true at the actual world; e.g., that Bea eats the last piece of cake. In contrast, to believe a centered proposition is to believe that a property, q, is true of oneself at the actual world; e.g., eating the last piece of cake. The difference exists also in desires, where to desire a classical proposition p is to desire that p be true at the actual world; e.g., that Bea will eat the last piece of cake. In contrast, to desire a centered proposition is to desire that a property, q, be true of oneself at the actual world; e.g., eating the last piece of cake.

accommodated in the conversational common ground by speakers who already self-ascribe (accept) a *de se* property not-*p*. Egan also suggests that disagreement need not always be cognitive—it may involve disagreements (or conflicts) in attitude, and that is what is to be expected in the evaluative case anyway, since value properties are constituted by desire-like states.

Disagreement about values depends thus on three factors: (i) there is disagreement in discourse, on the assumption that Stalnaker's account of assertion as providing uptake conditions on the common ground is correct, coupled with an account of *de se* content. (ii) The *de se* contents expressed allow for (a sort of) *disagreement in thought* when the desires of the different interlocutors do not converge (it is a sort of disagreement in thought in the sense that it is not rational for an individual to self-ascribe *p* and not-*p*). (iii) In cases where people in dispute have non-converging desires, there is also disagreement *in attitude*, i.e., there are also conflicts of desires. The explanatory priority goes from (iii) to (i): it's because there's a conflict of dispositional attitudes that there is (a sort of) disagreement in thought, and it's because there's a disagreement in thought that there is a disagreement in discourse (because of incompatible uptake conditions).

I don't have the space in the present chapter for a full discussion of why I think that the *de se* implementation of dispositionalism does not work.[11] I will just give a summary of why I think the view is problematic. My objection to Egan focuses on the fact that (iii) above is ungrounded. As I argue in Marques (2016b), a purely first-personal subjective rationality constraint does not guarantee that pairs of desire-like states are in conflict. Suppose that I hate liquorice, and have no wish to eat it. You, however, tolerate eating liquorice; in fact you enjoy it. As long as I'm not forced to eat it, our different dispositions do not conflict. Now, the desires that Egan claims are relevant for value properties are purely *de se*. But this example about liquorice shows that there need not be any intersubjective conflict of *de se* attitudes when two people's dispositions do not "converge." In short, having different *de se* preferences is neither necessary nor sufficient for having conflicting attitudes. If so, we cannot explain the presumed intersubjective disagreement in thought that Egan says occurs, and hence we don't motivate the expression of disagreement in discourse.

When I first introduced Lewis's account, I said that a main worry for the theory concerned who *we* are. Egan's objection targeted this concern. If we allow, as I think we should, for possibly variable perspectives, we have to explain the apparent persistent disagreements between people who don't share standards. But the objection from possibly non-convergent attitudes leading to "no common subject matter" ignores alternative sources of communicated content and of possible disagreement. I stand by the contextualist implementation of dispositionalism, in spite of Egan's criticism.

In my view, we have action-guiding attitudes that are essentially *de nobis*, not *de se*.[12] We may not be entirely aware of the content or the character of these attitudes, but they play an important explanatory role in our lives. The relevant dispositional *de nobis* attitudes for

[11] I give a full discussion in Marques (2017c).

[12] Frith and Frith (2012) review work in cognitive science and psychology on various "mechanisms of social cognition." Ongoing research on these mechanisms of social cognition reveals the role they play in learning, cooperation, and language acquisition.

value properties are (higher-order) attitudes *about ourselves*.[13] A value property involves the relevant group to which the speaker belongs, but it does not depend on the speaker's self-identification. Speakers may be in error about what they value. So, the question is, who are *we* in a value property, and in the content of the implicatures?

There are three alternatives. First, *we* may be the current interlocutors in a conversation. We can engage in dialogue with people who don't share our standards. In a dispositional property, *we* does not depend on who our conversational partners happen to be. Second, then, *we* must be *those of us who share a perspective* or *a standard*. Finally, *we* may be all of us who are *peers* in a more fundamental sense, for instance moral peers deserving of equal respect.[14]

We, qua conversational partners, are also peers qua people equally deserving of respect, although we (in either of these previous senses) may not all be disposed alike. The hypothesis hybrid dispositionalism offers is that, through discourse, the speaker conversationally implicates (through a generalized conversational implicature[15] both that she accepts certain standards, and a desire that we—interlocutors—come to share the same standards.

I think that a semantic contextualist implementation of the Lewisian account is compatible with the expression of additional content. We can call the supplemented account *hybrid dispositionalism*, HD:

HD If a speaker *S* asserts the sentence '*x* is good', then *S* denotes a dispositional property *what we desire to desire in way w in ideal conditions C* by 'good' and:
(i) In asserting 'x is good', *S* implicates that she desires *x* (in way *w*); and
(ii) *S* implicates that she desires that we desire (to desire) *x* (in way *w*).

There is some linguistic evidence that these implicatures are associated with evaluative assertions. Imagine that Ana and Bea have the disagreement below:

(3)
a. Ana: It is good to respect the sanctity of life.
b. Bea: No, it's not good to respect sanctity of life. It's absurd to insist that terminally ill patients in extreme pain have to cling to life to matter what.[16]

---

[13] In Marques (2015), I advanced a conjecture about the evolutionary origin of *de nobis* attitudes. I suggest that coordination problems are at the root of our having, as humans, evolved to have the *de nobis* dispositions we have. However, I don't understand *de nobis* attitudes as "self-ascribable properties." There are different theories of *de se* contents, and not all regard *de se* contents as centered propositions. For discussion, see for instance (Recanati 2009).

[14] In recent work, Carla Bagnoli (2016) revises Nozick (2001)'s proposal of an ethics of respect, which he claimed is rooted in our evolutionary history. Bagnoli favors both the idea that we have irreducibly different moral standards, and that we share a basic commonality—that we are moral peers, not epistemic peers, in that our parity status is rooted fundamentally on the respect owed to each of us (Bagnoli 2016, 17–18).

[15] (Strandberg 2012); (Fletcher 2014).

[16] In personal conversation, Mike Ridge raised the following objection: Often we only say that we desire something when we don't currently have it. "I want a yacht" implies I will (all else equal) seek a yacht, but it doesn't entail that I have one. In fact, it tends to imply the opposite—I seek it because I don't have it yet. So we get an implicature that the speaker will try to acquire a first-order desire that *x*, not that she has one already—unless desires are special in being easy to control. But this isn't obvious. When I am on a diet, I wish I desired to

If Ana and Bea share value perspectives, they contradict each other and have a straightforward disagreement. One of them may "wrongly value what is not really good." But they may not share perspectives, and still appear to disagree. How can the contextualism-dispositionalism combo explain this? How do we justify the claim that the implicatures (i) and (ii) are associated with value statements? Is there any evidence of their existence, and can we explain how they are rationally calculated from the meaning of the used sentences and the conversational contexts where they occur? And do these implicatures play a role in the explanation of persistent disagreement and conflict?

The implicatures (i) and (ii) appear to pass several tests of so-called not-at-issue content.[17] For instance, they appear to be *cancelable*, and they pass the *Hey, wait a minute!* test.

First, they are cancelable. There is no contradiction in Ana complementing (3a) by uttering the sentence in (4).

(4) Ana: It's good to respect the sanctity of life, but there are some people who should *just die.*

It is equally not contradictory for Ana to utter (5), somewhat pedantically:

(5) Ana: It's good to respect the sanctity of life, but I don't expect you to respect it.

The implicatures also pass the *Hey, wait a minute!* test, which is usually regarded as a *necessary* but *not sufficient* condition for presuppositionality:

> [I]f π is presupposed by *S*, then it makes sense for an audience previously unaware of π to respond to an utterance of S by saying 'Hey, wait a minute, I didn't know that π'. (Yablo, 2006, 165)

Thus, implicature (i) passes the test:

(6)

a. Ana: It is good to respect the sanctity of life.
b. Bea: *Hey, wait a minute!* I didn't know you felt so strongly about this!

---

not eat chocolate and that I desired to exercise more. But my first-order desires quite often do not cooperate. Upshot: The proposed mechanism may not deliver the needed implicature. I think that the objection does not apply to my view. We can have desires that are expressible with infinitives—which arguably denote ongoing processes, and those desires can be continuous. My desire to have a family does not cease to exist when I have a family. At no point do I not desire having a family. Also, our failing to desire as we should is predicted by the Lewisian dispositional story; hence there is no objection from one desiring as one shouldn't.

[17] See (Potts 2007, 2005), and (Tonhauser et al. 2013) for discussion of projective not-at-issue content. Potts has a project that tracks uses of "hey, wait a minute," or similar phrases, in transcripts from CNN. http://www.christopherpotts.net/ling/data/waitaminute/.

And (ii) also passes the test:

(7)
a. Ana: It's a good thing to respect the sanctity of life.
b. Bea: *Hey, wait a minute!* You can't expect me to respect all lives equally in any circumstances!

Yablo (2006) and von Fintel (2004) discuss further presuppositionality tests, namely the ... *and what's more* ... test. If a sentence triggers a presupposition, it is *infelicitous* to follow an utterance of that sentence with that presupposition. For instance,

(8) It was John who ate all the cookies. [Presupposition: someone ate all the cookies]
(9) # It was John who ate all the cookies, and what's more, someone ate all the cookies.

Now, whereas (i) and (ii) are cancelable and pass the *Hey, wait a minute!* test, they don't seem to pass the ... *and what's more* ... test. On the contrary, it is *felicitous* to add reinforcing information to the sentence, as in (10) and (11).

(10) Ana: It is good to respect the sanctity of life; actually, I hope to always respect it, even when I'm terminally ill.
(11) Ana: it is good to respect the sanctity of life, and I hope we all respect it, as we should.

The fact that the speaker's commitment to (i) and (ii) can be reinforced suggests that the contents implicated are not semantically encoded (as a presupposition or a conventional implicature would be). A feature of conversational implicatures is, precisely, that they are reinforceable, as (10) and (11) illustrate (Potts 2007, 669–670).

This supports the idea that value statements pragmatically communicate content that expresses the speaker's conative states (approval or endorsement of a certain standard), and that the speaker desires others to share the same standards.

If (i) and (ii) are conversational implicatures, they should be inferable from the literal content of the sentence used, in agreement with the theory's supposition that what is denoted is a dispositional property. My explanation is similar to Caj Strandberg's in his (2012) paper.

First, we can calculate that by saying that it is good to respect the sanctity of life, Ana communicates that she herself desires to respect the sanctity of life. How? Let us assume that Ana is cooperative and rational, and follows the maxim of Relevance: *make your contribution so as to be relevant in order to fulfill the purposes of the conversation*. Ana utters a sentence to the effect that respecting the sanctity of life is good, thereby saying that *we* (the set of people that share her perspective) are disposed to value respecting the sanctity of life. Since she is one of the people referred to, she implicates that she herself *desires to desire* respecting life. Normally we seek to satisfy our desires, and hence, normally she would seek desiring to respect the sanctity of life. Hybrid expressivism can thus explain how the expressive role of evaluative discourse falls off the content of the evaluative statements: by making an assertion the speaker expresses a desire.

Second, Ana may find herself in conversations where she knows *that her interlocutor does not share her perspectives*. Now, Ana cannot be implicating *that her interlocutor shares her perspective*, since she already knows (or may know) *that* to be false. Nevertheless, she persists and asserts that it is good to respect that sanctity of life, thereby saying that respecting the sanctity of life is something *we* desire to desire. Since we have no reason to believe that she does not conform to the maxim of Relevance, we can infer that she *desires her audience to share the same standards.* Thus, even if Ana and Bea don't have the same standards, Ana's assertion plays a *connection-building role.* Hybrid dispositionalism can account for the cognitive, the expressive, and the connection-building roles of evaluative discourse, even when speakers are not disposed alike.

The theory can also explain the impression of resilient disagreements and conflicts of attitudes, even when interlocutors are not disposed alike. Let us assume that Bea has no desire to share the same perspective with Ana. But Ana desires *that we come to share the same perspective.* In that case, Ana and Bea have desires that *cannot be jointly satisfied*, and thus have *conflicting conative attitudes.* Hybrid dispositionalism has hence the resources to account for conflicts of attitudes that follow from the very nature of evaluative disputes. A further positive aspect of the account is that the expression of conflicts is the direct consequence of the failure of the connective role of value talk.

We may wonder if a variation of the Frege-Geach problem also arises for the conversational implicature account.[18] We disagree not only when I say "X is good" and you say "X is not good." We also disagree when I say "If X is good then Y is good" and you assert "X is good but Y is not," etc. *But* the story about attitude implicature, which is meant to explain the disagreement facts, seems to work only for simple atomic assertions of value. Asserting the conditional appears to be compatible with nihilism.

The problem is merely apparent, however. Conversational implicatures survive under embeddings, unless they're canceled. Sentences such as "*It is better to* get married and get pregnant *than to* get pregnant and get married," or "*Bill thinks that* there were four children at the party" show how conversational implicatures survive under embeddings. Each of the conjunctions in the first sentence conversationally implicate that one event temporally precedes the other. Those implicatures are preserved under the embedding in "it is better to . . . than to . . . " Likewise, the sentence embedded under "Bill thinks that . . ." conversationally implicates that there were exactly four children.

Moreover, what is evaluative on hybrid dispositionalism is *the asserted content* itself. Hence, the conditional "If X is good then Y is good" is evaluative in virtue of the meaning of the words uttered. The conversational implicatures are only expressive of the attitudes a speaker is presumed to have in virtue of making an evaluative assertion.

IV. Hybrid Dispositionalism and "Shared Acceptance of Norms"

Recent social accounts of the law use resources from social ontology to account for the existence and content of the law as the result of a joint activity of a community of legal officials. Among the current versions that rely on input from theories of collective action,[19] Toh (2005) offered an expressivist interpretation of Hart's view of internal legal statements. In his 2011 paper, Toh's account offers a defense of an expressivist version of legal positivism

[18] I'm grateful to Mike Ridge for raising this question.

[19] For instance, (Shapiro 2002); (Kutz 2001); (Sanchez-Brígido 2009 and 2010).

that relies on the idea of *shared norm acceptance*, and that has core aspects in common with hybrid dispositionalism. In this section, I suggest how hybrid dispositionalism can complement Toh's proposal.

Toh suggests that committed internal legal statements are *explanatorily primary*, and that *external* and *detached internal* legal statements are to be explained derivatively (110). External legal statements would be "attributions" of norm acceptances and of their expressions, and detached internal legal statements would be "expressions of psychological attitudes that simulate norm acceptances" (fn. 5). Although this is not explicitly stated, it seems to entail that legal statements are semantically ambiguous. However, I take it that Grice's modified Occam's razor should be followed whenever possible: *don't multiply meanings beyond necessity*.

On the noncognitivist interpretation of Hart's account of internal legal statements, where *R* is the norm that she considers the rule of recognition of the legal system of her community, a speaker that makes a legal statement:

(i) *Expresses* her acceptance of a particular norm that is valid according to some fundamental legal norm *R* of her community and
(ii) *Presupposes* that *R* is generally accepted and complied with as the 'fundamental legal norm' by the members of her community.

Yet, Toh voices concerns about how to interpret Hart:

> What Hart says is that in making a legal statement, a speaker (i) expresses his acceptance of a particular norm that is valid according to the most fundamental legal norm of his community, or, as Hart calls it, the rule of recognition of his community; and (ii) presupposes that that particular norm is accepted and employed as the rule of recognition by the officials of his community. We can entertain two different interpretations of what Hart means here depending on how we conceive the effect of any possible failure in the factual presupposition of (ii). First, we can think of such a presuppositional failure as rendering the whole legal statement defective. In such a case, a speaker who discovers that the particular rule of recognition that he appeals to is not accepted by the officials of his legal system would be disposed to withdraw his legal statement. Alternatively, we can think of the factual presupposition of (ii) as the usual but not an invariable accompaniment of the more primary normative component of (i). In this latter case, a speaker would not be disposed to withdraw his legal statement upon recognizing a presuppositional failure. (Toh 2011, 116–117)

I agree that the presuppositional failure of (ii) is problematic. But I confess I have some trouble seeing how the option of focusing on the "primary normative component of (i)" is helpful, once we assume the failure of (ii). So, given the presuppositional[20] failure, a speaker

[20] There are accounts that postulate a presupposition of commonality with the content that a rule or perspective is commonly accepted and complied with by the members of a community, or the interlocutors in context. See for instance, López de Sa's 2008 account.

who makes a legal statement accepts a particular norm that is valid according to *a* fundamental legal norm *R'*, since we agree that there is no unique fundamental legal norm of the community. The fact that the speaker accepts a norm that is valid-according-to-a-rule-of-recognition-*R'* is insufficient to fully account for the problem of legal disputes. Those who disagree with the speaker can certainly accept *that a particular norm N is valid-according-to-a-rule-of-recognition-R'*, and accept *that the speaker expresses her acceptance of norm N that is valid-according-to-a-rule-of-recognition-R'*.

Toh suggests that a further worry concerns how expressivism explains normative and legal disagreement. Dworkin's objection to Hart's legal positivism emphasizes the problem of theoretical disagreements. These legal disputes occur frequently, whenever people do not agree on the fundamental rules of recognition. So the question here is whether (i) can carry the needed explanatory weight, or whether a modification of (ii) is required.

Toh says that expressivists have the resources, in principle, to explain why people may have conflicts that survive factual agreement. One speaker can accept *R* and another accept another rule of recognition *R'*.[21] Toh has in mind pragmatic accounts such as Gibbard's, where it is rational to make conversational demands in contexts where there are no shared norms only if engaging in such interactions can produce benefits that come with the resulting convergence in normative opinions (Gibbard 1990, ch. 12). The problem, however, is that such interactions do not present themselves clearly as *normative disagreements* (or legal disagreements, in the case that concerns us presently). Gibbard's proposal does not distinguish between negotiations among peers who try to coordinate on which fundamental rule to follow, and the goading of one's interlocutors into accepting the rules we want followed. The concern is that the latter is not a genuine normative or legal dispute.[22]

Instead of (i) and (ii), Toh suggests that speakers express a first-personal plural norm acceptance, through which a speaker *invites* the audience to share the same fundamental norms. He assumes that *speaker and audience aim at a joint acceptance of the same set of fundamental norms*, adding that joint acceptances are maintained only when there is sufficient uptake:[23]

> [I]nstead of thinking of the joint acceptance of the fundamental norms as something that is always presupposed, it can be thought of as something that the speaker is sometimes trying to instigate (Toh, 2011, 118–119).

The "content of the norm acceptance" is as follows:

> *Let us φ, on the assumption that: you, of your own accord, think or will come to think likewise, partly as the result of your recognition of this attitude*! (Toh 2011, p. 122)

---

[21] I have doubts that accepting different fundamental rules in and by itself suffices for the existence of "disagreements in attitude" (see Marques 2017c). Schroeder (2008) voices a similar worry. (Schroeder 2008, 587).

[22] This problem does not arise for hybrid dispositionalism, since there are cognitive contents that are evaluative, and the conversational implicatures are inferable from the nature of the evaluative debate itself.

[23] Plural acceptance of norms differs from a mere joint acceptance of norms, and the attitudes at stake are acceptance states, not intention states. This modification guarantees a substantial difference between Toh's 2011 proposal and Shapiro's 2002 proposal of legal practice as a joint intentional activity.

I'm sympathetic to what Toh is trying to formulate, and I think that what he spells out as the content of norm acceptance is an instance of an expressive conversational implicature "*S* implicates that she desires that we desire (to desire) *x* in way *w*," which as I suggested in the previous section accompanies evaluative statements in general, unless they are canceled. In effect, what Toh is proposing is that the speaker expresses a desire that *we come to accept the same fundamental norms*. However, Toh builds in the content of the norm acceptance the additional features that will guarantee that his account does not suffer from the problem he raises to Gibbard's.

How does the expression of an invitation to share norm acceptances relate to the making of legal statements? Either the joint norm acceptance is semantically encoded in the content of legal statements, or it is expressed pragmatically. Is there any linguistic evidence of which option is the correct one?

Normative claims are often expressed with deontic modals such as "ought," "might," "should," etc. On Kratzer's canonical semantics of deontic modals (1977, 1991), modal expressions such as "might," "may," "must," or "ought" function as quantifiers over possibilities, in which the domains of quantification are contextually restricted. Modal sentences contain parameters that require context to determine a circumstantial accessibility relation on a world of evaluation *w*. This determines a modal base, i.e., a set of worlds accessible from *w* that are circumstantially like *w* in relevant ways. Furthermore, context must supply a standard or ordering source as a function of *w*—i.e., a standard that orders the worlds in the modal base as better or worse. Thus, context contributes to determining a proposition by determining both a modal base and an ordering standard.

The standard Kratzerian semantics can apply to normative or prescriptive statements in general, and to the semantics of deontic legal statements in particular. The standard, or ordering source, for particular legal statements would be provided by the rule(s) of recognition of the local jurisdiction. This can be made explicit by preceding the legal sentence with an explicit relativization to the local jurisdiction. For simplicity, roughly, a statement made by a legal official of "According to the law, it must/may be that φ" assumes that there is a local jurisdiction (a set of existing norms and rule(s) of recognition) and asserts that φ follows from/is compatible with) the law at the jurisdiction.

Silk (in a chapter in this volume) offers a uniform account of internal and external deontic legal statements based on standard semantics for deontic modal claims, which I'm sympathetic to.[24] As desired here, the semantics is descriptivist—it assigns truth-conditions to deontic claims—the apparent normativity of claims of law follows from a contextualist interpretation of the standard semantics for modals, along with general principles of interpretation and conversation, elucidating the social and interpersonal function of legal discourse.

Normative sentences can be used to make *committed* statements or *uncommitted* statements. For instance, (12) seems to be a committed statement. But if we omit the parenthetical contextual information at the end, (12) no longer seems to be committed. A similar

---

[24] Also, in recent work, Chilovi and Moreso (2016) offer an account of sentences of the form "according to the law, ϕ" where "according to the law" works as an intensional operator that quantifies over a prejacent, ϕ, and denotes a function that maps any proposition to the truth-value 1 if that proposition is compatible with the content of the law at that jurisdiction.

ambiguous prescription of etiquette can be made with (13), although it does not contain a deontic modal.

(12) In Spain, one *shouldn't* eat with one's mouth open. [uttered in Spain by a Spaniard.]
(13) In Spain, it's *rude* to eat with one's mouth open [uttered in Spain, and/or by a Spaniard]

Toh illustrates the putative ambiguity with examples of legal sentences. We can imagine situations where each of (14) and (15) can have a committed reading or an external descriptive reading.

(14) A leasehold interest is not freely alienable.
(15) The Fourteenth Amendment allows states to regulate bakery employees' work hours.

The parallelism between the legal case and other normative statements with deontic modals, or words such as "rude,"[25] suggests that committed readings can be inferred with conversational maxims. In general, any utterance of these sentences has a descriptive semantic content. The meaning of the words used requires sets of norms or value standards to be provided in context. Additionally, we can infer the committed reading (and we generally do) given sufficient information from context about the identity, location, and background of the speaker and the audience, while assuming that the speaker is being cooperative and rational, and is saying something that is relevant for the discussion.

In the legal case, if the speaker is a legal official addressing her peers, the fact of *peerage* is part of the common ground. Legal officials within a jurisdiction form a well-demarcated group. Their status is not just what *results* from each person's interpretation of her commitments in a jurisdiction. Rather, the status *being a legal official* is partly constituted by an existing and ongoing *practice*, and the social roles or positions created by that practice. What is required for someone to be a legal official is for there to exist a (partly) external causal-historical chain of events through which some legal and social conventions have been enacted, and which enable a person to occupy a position as an official within the jurisdiction, qua social structure or matrix.[26] It is of course correct to say that,

> [I]t is difficult to maintain that people are committed to the most fundamental laws of their legal system as a matter of convention when there is no convention (or any other type of convergent practice) of following those laws because there exists instead persistent controversies about such laws. (Toh, 2011, 126–127)

[25] Words such as "rude" ("dainty," "cruel," "lewd," etc.) are normally described as thick value words—words that combine a descriptive content and an additional evaluative component, by contrast with thin value words such as "good" that arguably are not descriptive.

[26] On the notion of social matrix, see (Haslanger 2012). A legal official can be described as someone who is constitutively of a social kind, where X is socially constructed constitutively as an F iff such that in order for X to be F, X must exist within a social matrix that constitutes Fs) (Haslanger 2003, 317–318).

However, meeting the condition *being a legal official* does not require that legal officials make the same interpretation of their commitments to the fundamental rule of recognition. It is not required that each official interpret all her duties as an official in the jurisdiction in the same way. Once someone is actually invested as an official, she becomes one.[27] So, the conversational peers in a jurisdiction are the interlocutors who satisfy the *legal peerage* condition, but not necessarily those people who satisfy the condition *people committed to the same fundamental laws*. The situations where the implicature is entailed are those that present legal statements as *committed*.

My suggestion is that it is part of common ground that a speaker addresses her legal peers, but not that she addresses only those who make the same interpretation of their commitments. This understanding of the condition is essential to the very expression of the plural norm acceptances, since "us" must denote the interlocutors who are legal officials at the jurisdiction—*we* cannot be just those of us who accept the same interpretation of fundamental rules (if that were the case, the content of plural norm acceptance would be infelicitous). So, we need legal peers to engage in debate and to be under the requirement, as Toh suggests quoting Rawls, to be "ready to explain the basis of their actions to one another in terms each could reasonably expect that others might endorse as consistent with their freedom and equality" (Rawls 1993, 218; Toh 2011, 130).

In Dworkin's example, Judge Earl and Judge Gray have a theoretical disagreement concerning how to interpret the statute of wills. Judge Earl persists in asserting, "Elmer should not inherit the estate." If Earl's statement is valid according to the (intentionalist) rule of recognition that he accepts, what he states is correct, and there is no reason for Gray not to accept that statement as true. That statement implicitly relies on the rule of recognition that Earl accepts. Moreover, Earl does not presuppose that Gray accepts and employs the same rule of recognition. Both Earl and Gray know that *this*—that they accept and employ the same rule of recognition—is false.

The description of the conversation in the previous paragraph assumes that what Gray (or Earl) expresses is merely *his personal* acceptance of a fundamental legal norm. This is insufficient to explain their disagreement. I suggest that the plural norm acceptance that Toh proposes is expressed is conversationally implicated, and imposes a conversational requirement on their context. So how is a plural norm acceptance instigated through a conversational implicature? Let's assume that Gray states that *according to the law, Elmer may receive the inheritance*. Given the semantics of deontic sentences, we require a contextually provided set of fundamental norms of their jurisdiction to have a complete proposition. Through his assertion, Gray is conveying that this set of fundamental norms is compatible with Elmer inheriting. It is common knowledge that Earl and Gray are peers in the dissent, and that the court in their jurisdiction will enact a single decision. Since they are not merely talking past each other, they must be doing something else. On the assumption

[27] As the US government in 2017 and 2018 abundantly illustrates, the behavior of government officials, or candidates to those positions, may ignore unwritten norms that were previously assumed to regulate their office. Their status as government officials is guaranteed by the institutional historical practices that placed them in their positions as officials, not on their individual understanding of their roles or responsibilities. Katerina Wright keeps up a weekly updated list of democratic norms being eroded in the blog Just Security: https://www.justsecurity.org/author/wrightkaterina/.

that Judge Gray is rational and cooperative, and follows the maxim of Relevance: *make your contribution so as to be relevant in order to fulfill the purposes of the conversation*, we can infer that he *desires his peers to accept the same rule of recognition*. So, we can explain the expression of a desire of a plural norm acceptance. With Toh, by saying that Elmer may inherit the estate, Gray expresses that the rule of recognition *R*, that justifies his divergent opinion, is the rule that is to be jointly accepted as their shared standard.[28,29]

If plural norm acceptances are conversationally implicated, they should pass tests for conversational implicatures, namely the cancelability test and the *Hey, wait a minute!* test. This would provide additional support for the proposal. The implicature that there is a joint norm acceptance passes the *Hey, wait a minute!* test. For instance, we may conceive Judge Earl replying to Judge Gray saying,

(14) Judge Earl: *Hey, wait a minute*! I didn't know you were a literalist!
(15) Judge Earl: *Hey, wait a minute*! You can't expect me to endorse a literalist interpretation of the law!

The implicature can also be canceled:

(16) Judge Earl: The lawmakers couldn't possibly intend that murderers benefit from their crimes . . . but I no longer expect you to accept an intentionalist interpretation of the law.

There is also support to the claim that the plural norm acceptance is conversationally implicated, and not semantically encoded, in the fact that the implicature can be reinforced:

---

[28] Silk (forthcoming) offers a very similar reconstruction of the underlying reasoning in the dispute between Earl and Gray, based on the semantic properties of deontic modals and on the assumption that the participants are rational and follow the maxim of Relevance (Silk, pp. 12–13 of the final draft). I also agree with Silk when he says that these disputes are not properly described as *metalinguistic* or about how to use words (Plunkett and Sundell 2013a, 2013b); they are disputes about "what basic legal norms to accept" (Silk, 15). Elsewhere, I have expressed my scepticism about the extent and usefulness of metalinguistic negotiations in normative, evaluative, and legal domains (Marques 2017a, 2017b).

[29] Finlay and Plunkett (2018) argue for *quasi-expressivism*, an alternative descriptivist theory of normative and legal sentences, based on Finlay's (2014) end-relational theory or normative discourse. "Good" or "ought" statements would assert propositions about the statistical relations in which actions stand to ends/potential states of affairs. On this view, if an agent has a desire toward end *e*, she will be motivationally disposed toward what she believes stands in an instrumental relation to *e*. An "ought" statement would express a pragmatic presupposition: that the speaker has a favorable attitude toward end *e*. I'm skeptical of this proposal because I don't see how if what "*S* ought to do *A* (in order to *e*)" means is "*e* is more likely if *S* does *A* (than anything else)," it should follow that we can infer in context that the speaker has a favorable attitude/desire toward end *e*. Moreover, I don't think that the pragmatic content can be this presupposition, since it can be accepted into the common ground by an interlocutor who still disagrees with the speaker. This interlocutor can accept what *S* says and that pragmatic presupposition—accept that doing *A* is the most effective way for us to bring about *e*, and accept that speaker *S* desires that we bring about *e*, while disagreeing that we ought to *A*.

(17) Judge Earl: The lawmakers couldn't possibly intend murderers to benefit from their crimes; in fact, it would be desirable for us to interpret what the law requires, in this and other cases, by taking into account the intentions the lawmakers might reasonably have had.

The reinforcement, as the previous section indicated, would be infelicitous if plural norm acceptances were part of the semantic content of legal statements, or semantically entailed by them.

The cancelation of committed readings can explain further properties of legal statements. Raz distinguished between *committed* and *detached* internal legal statements, where the latter would not display the speaker's commitment or endorsement of a legal system (Raz, e.g., 1975/1990, 172–173). The speaker explicitly stating that she doesn't endorse the rule in question can cancel the conversational implicature. Toh gives the example of a libertarian lawyer's tax advice to a client (Toh, 2011, 109). In (18) the libertarian lawyer would be canceling the conversational implicature that he accepts that the government has the right to collect taxes:

(18) You must pay your income taxes before the end of this month . . . although, just between us, I actually think the state has no right to collect income taxes.[30]

Following my suggestion, detached internal legal statements can be explained as statements that cancel a conversational implicature. This allows us to respect Grice's modified Occam's razor: *do not multiply meanings beyond necessity*. We do not need legal statements to be semantically ambiguous to explain internal committed, internal detached, and external legal statements.

Besides passing tests for conversational implicated content, plural norm acceptances must contribute to explain resilient theoretical legal disagreements. So, if we say that, in making a legal statement, the speaker conversationally implicates that she desires the joint acceptance of the same fundamental legal norms by her peers—i.e., that she desires *us all, "of our own accord, to think or come to think likewise,"* we can describe theoretical legal disputes over fundamental legal criteria as involving conflicts of attitudes, or, as Stevenson (1963) would say, "disagreements in attitude"—disagreements where disputants' desire-like states cannot be jointly satisfied. (1962, 1–2). This offers a reply to Dworkin that does not force the legal positivist to interpret legal officials as making the same interpretation of their commitments, or to accept that moral considerations are part of the background that determines the content of the law.

V. Concluding Remarks

In this chapter, I claimed that hybrid dispositionalism shares some important features with Toh's (2011) account of legal statements as expressions of shared acceptances of norms.

[30] Notice that it would be misleading to regard the lawyer's statement in this case as *non-normative* or *merely descriptive*. The obligation to pay taxes still exists and is expressed in (18), in spite of the lawyer not accepting all of the background norms.

I suggested that Toh's idea of a *shared acceptance of a norm* is an instance of a *de nobis* attitude type. Yet, there are some structural differences between my proposal and the expressivist account that Toh offers. Toh claimed that committed internal legal statements are *explanatorily primary*, and external and detached internal legal statements are to be explained derivatively (Toh 2011, 110). My proposal takes seriously the Gricean recommendation of avoiding semantic ambiguity, if possible. I tried to make the case that hybrid dispositionalism about evaluative discourse offers some theoretical resources that can be applied to legal discourse. In particular, we can make assumptions about legal peers and about the function of legal practice to explain how we infer conversational implicatures with contents that are essentially *plural norm acceptances*, i.e., *de nobis* attitudes.

This proposal differs from other accounts that rely on presuppositions of commonality, where these presuppositions have the content that a rule or standard is commonly accepted and complied with by the members of a community. Unlike proposals of this kind, my suggestion distinguishes between the conditions for being a *peer*, and the conversational implicature that we desire our peers to come to share the same standards or accept the same fundamental rules. I argued that there's good evidence in support of the hypothesis that we communicate *de nobis* contents with conversational implicatures when we make evaluative statements, and legal statements.

In spite of the structural differences, my positive suggestion for the legal case can supplement Toh's expressivist proposal. In normal contexts, background information from context, the identity of the interlocutors, or other surrounding sentences, will make it clear whether the speaker is just making a description, making a committed normative statement, or making a normative statement in spite of canceling her own endorsement of the background normative standard. My suggestion also helps in defusing the objections from theoretical legal disputes against legal positivism, without compromising positivism

References

Bagnoli, C. 2016. "The Principle of Coercive Respect". Manuscript.

Brogaard, B. 2008. "Moral Contextualism and Moral Relativism." *Philosophical Quarterly* 58(232): 385–409.

Chilovi, S., and J. J. Moreso. 2016. "The Semantics and Pragmatics of 'According to the Law.'" In *Pragmatics and Law: Philosophical Perspectives on Pragmatics, Philosophy and Psychology*, edited by A. Capone and F. Paggi. Basel: Springer.

Dreier, J. 1990. "Internalism and Speaker Relativism." *Ethics* 101(1):6–26.

Dworkin, R. 1977. *Taking Rights Seriously*. London: Duckworth.

_____. 1986. *Law's Empire*. Cambridge, MA: Harvard University Press.

_____. 2011. *Justice for Hedgehogs*. Cambridge, MA: Belknap Press Harvard University Press.

Egan, A., J. Hawthorne, and B. Weatherson. 2005. "Epistemic Modals in Context." In *Contextualism in Philosophy: Knowledge, Meaning, and Truth*, edited by G. Preyer & G. Peter. Oxford: Oxford University of Press, pp. 131–168.

Egan, A. 2010. "Disputing about Taste." In *Disagreement*, edited by T. Warfield and R. Feldman. Oxford: Oxford University Press, pp. 247–286.

_____. 2012. "Relativist Dispositional Theories of Value." *Southern Journal of Philosophy* 50(4):557–582.

Finlay, S. 2014. *Confusion of Tongues: A Theory of Normative Language*. Oxford: Oxford University Press.

Finlay, S., and D. Plunkett. 2018. "Quasi-expressivism about Statements of Law: A Hartian Theory." *Oxford Studies in Philosophy of Law, Vol. 3*.

Frith, C., and U. Frith. 2012. "Mechanisms of Social Cognition", *Annual Review of Psychology* 63: 287–313.

Gibbard, Allan (1990). *Wise Choices, Apt Feelings*. Cambridge, Massachusetts: Harvard University Press.

Harman, G. 1975. "Moral relativism defended". *Philosophical Review* 84 (1):3–22.

Hart, H. L. A. 1961/2012. *The Concept of Law*, 3rd ed. Oxford: Oxford University Press.

Haslanger, S. 2003. "Social Construction: The 'Debunking' Project." In *Socializing Metaphysics*, edited by F. Schmitt. Oxford: Rowman and Littlefield, pp. 301–325.

_____. 2012. *Resisting Reality: Social Construction and Social Critique*. Oxford: Oxford University Press.

Hume, D. 1757/1966. "Of the Standard of Taste." In *Of the Standard of Taste and Other Essays*, edited by J. W. Lenz. Indianapolis: Bobbs-Merrill.

_____. 1777/2004. *An Enquiry concerning the Principles of Morals*. Amherst, New York: Prometheus Books.

Kennedy, C., and L. McNally. 2005. "Scale Structure and the Semantic Typology of Gradable Predicates", *Language* 81(2):1–37.

Khoo, J., and J. Knobe. 2016. "Moral Disagreement and Moral Semantics", *Noûs* 00:0 , 1–35.

Kolodny, N., and J. MacFarlane. 2010. "Ifs and oughts." *The Journal of Philosophy* 107(3): 115–143.

Kölbel, M. 2004a. "Faultless Disagreement." *Proceedings of the Aristotelian Society* 104(1):53–73.

Kölbel, Max. (2004b). "Indexical Relativism vs Genuine Relativism", *International Journal of Philosophical Studies* 12:297–313.

Kratzer, A. 1977. "What 'Must' and 'Can' Must and Can Mean." *Linguistics and Philosophy* 1(3):337–355.

Kratzer, A. 1991. "Modality." In *Semantics: An International Handbook of Contemporary Research*, edited by A. von Stechow and D. Wunderlich. Berlin: De Gruyter, pp. 639–650.

Kutz, C. 2001. "The Judicial Community." *Noûs* 35(1):442–469.

Lewis, D. 1989/2000. "Dispositional Theories of Value." *Proceedings of the Aristotelian Society* 63:113–137. (Reprinted in *Papers in Ethics and Social Philosophy*, Cambridge: Cambridge University Press, 2000 (q.v.)).

Liao, S., L. McNally, and A. Meskin. 2016. "Aesthetic adjectives lack uniform behavior." *Inquiry* 59 (6): 616–631.

López de Sa, D. 2008. "Presuppositions of Commonality." In *Relative Truth*, edited by M. Kölbel and M. García-Carpintero. Oxford: Oxford University Press, pp. 297–310.

MacFarlane, J. 2014. *Assessment Sensitivity: Relative Truth and Its Applications*. Oxford: Clarendon Press.

Marques, T. 2015. "Disagreeing in Context", *Frontiers in Psychology* 6 (257): 1–12.

_____. 2016a. "Aesthetic Predicates: A Hybrid Dispositionalist Account." *Inquiry* 59(6):723–751.

_____. 2016b. "We Can't Have No Satisfaction." *Philosophy South—Unisinos Philosophy Journal* 17(3): 308–314.

_____. 2017a. "What Metalinguistic Negotiations Can't Do." *Phenomenology and Mind* 12:40–48.

_____. 2017b. "Can Metalinguistic Negotiations and 'Conceptual Ethics' Rescue Legal Positivism?" In *Pragmatics and Law: Practical and Theoretical Perspectives*, edited by Alessandro Capone and Francesca Poggi. Barcelona: Springer, pp. 223–241.

_____, 2017c. "*De se* dispositions and conflicting attitudes". Manuscript

Marques, T., and M. García-Carpintero. 2014. "Disagreement about Taste: Commonality Presuppositions and Coordination." *Australasian Journal of Philosophy* 92(4):701–723.

McNally, L. and Isidora Stojanovic. 2014. "Aesthetic Adjectives." In *The Semantics of Aesthetic Judgment*, edited by James Young. Oxford: Oxford University Press.

Moreso, J. J. 2009. "Legal Positivism and Legal Disagreements." *Ratio Juris* 22(1): 62–73.

Nozick, R. 2001. *Invariances, the Structure of the Objective World*. Cambridge, MA: The Belknap Press of Harvard University Press.

Plunkett, D., and T. Sundell. 2013a. "Disagreement and the semantics of normative and evaluative terms". *Philosophers' Imprint*, 13(23): 1–37.

_____. 2013b. "Dworkin's interpretivism and the pragmatics of legal disputes". *Legal Theory*, 19(3): 242–281.

Potts, C. 2005. *The Logic of Conventional Implicatures*. Oxford: Oxford University Press.

Potts, C. 2007. "Into the Conventional Implicature Dimension." *Philosophy Compass* 2/4: 665–679.

Rawls, J. 1993. *Political Liberalism*. New York: Columbia University Press.

Raz, J. 1975. *Practical Reason and Norms*. London: Hutchinson.

Recanati, F. 2009. "*De re* and *de se*." *Dialectica* 63(3):249–269.

Sánchez-Brígido, R. 2009. "Collective Intentional Activities and the Law." *Oxford Journal of Legal Studies* 29(2): 305–324.

_____. 2010. *Groups, Rules and Legal Practice*. Basel: Springer.

Sarkissian, H., J. Park, D. Tien, J. Cole, and J. Knobe, 2011. "Folk Moral Relativism," *Mind and Language* 26: 482–505.

Schafer, K. 2010. "Faultless Disagreement and Aesthetic Realism," *Philosophy and Phenomenological Research* 82: 265–286.

Schaffer, J. 2009. "Perspective in Taste Predicates and Epistemic Modals." In *Epistemic Modality*, edited by A. Egan and B. Weatherson. Oxford: Oxford University Press, pp. 179–226.

Shapiro, S. 2002. "Law, Plans, and Practical Reason." *Legal Theory* 8(4): 387–441.

Schroeder, M. 2008. "How Expressivists Can and Should Solve their Problem with Negation". *Noûs* 42:4 (2008) 573–599.

Silk, A. "Normativity in Language and Law," forthcoming, this volume.

Smith, M. 1989. "Dispositional Theories of Value." *Proceedings of the Aristotelian Society* 63:89–174.

_____. 2002. "Exploring the Implications of the Dispositional Theory of Value." *Philosophical Issues* 12 (1):329–347.

Stalnaker, R. 1978. "Assertion," In *Syntax and Semantics* 9, edited by P. Cole. New York: Academic Press, pp. 315–332. Also in R Stalnaker, *Context and Content*, Oxford:University Press, 1999, pp. 78–95, which I refer.

Stevenson, C. L. 1963. *Facts and Values: Studies in Ethical Analysis*. New Haven and London: Yale University Press.

Strandberg, C. 2012. A Dual Aspect Account of Moral Language. *Philosophy and Phenomenological Research 84* (1): 87–122.

Toh, K. 2005. "Hart's Expressivism and His Benthamite Project." *Legal Theory* 11(2): 75–123.

_____. 2011. "Legal Judgments as Plural Acceptance of Norms." In *Oxford Studies in Philosophy of Law, edited by* L. Green and B. Leiter. Oxford: Oxford University Press.

Tonhauser, J., D. Beaver, C. Roberts, and M. Simons, 2013. "Toward a Taxonomy of Projective Content." *Language* 89 (1):66–109.

von Fintel, K. 2004. "Would You Believe It, The King of France Is Back." In *Descriptions and Beyond*, edited by M. Reimer and A. Bezuidenhout. Oxford: Oxford University Press.

Yablo, S. 2006. "Non-catastrophic Presupposition Failure." In *Content and Modality*, edited by J. J. Thomson and A. Byrne. Oxford: Oxford University Press, pp. 164–180.

"We have fulfilled our obligation under the law."
"It's wrong."
"No. We follow the law, Alicia. Sometimes it's wrong,
sometimes it's right. But we always follow the law."
(*THE GOOD WIFE*, "Fixed")

13 Normativity in Language and Law

Alex Silk*

I. Introduction

Here are two not implausible claims about the law:

A. *Normativity of Law:* The law of a community is intended to guide the behavior of the members of that community.
B. *Sociality of Law:* Facts about the existence and content of the law are grounded in social facts—facts about judicial rulings, legislative enactments, the attitudes and actions of lawmakers and community members, and so on.

Rough-and-ready support for (A): Legal claims are a paradigm type of normative claim. Statements about people's legal rights and duties and about what they must do in view of the law, such as (1)–(3), are prototypically directive.

(1) Alice has a legal right to privacy.
(2) It is Bert's legal duty to pay the fine.
(3) In view of the law, Chip must repay his debt.

Such statements are intended to guide, influence, regulate what we do.

* Thanks to participants in the 2015 Yale Workshop on Metaethics and Philosophy of Law for helpful discussion, and to Stephen Finlay and David Plunkett for detailed comments on a previous draft. Some of the material in this paper is drawn from portions of Silk (2015a, 2016).

Dimensions of Normativity. David Plunkett, Scott J. Shapiro, and Kevin Toh.

Rough-and-ready support for (B): It should be possible to describe a law without endorsing it. It would be surprising if one couldn't investigate the law of a community without making normative or ethical evaluations of it. Interpreting language in context doesn't ordinarily involve engaging in substantive normative or ethical theorizing (think: Natural Language Processing). Why should interpreting language in legal contexts be any different? Or, at least, why should legal interpretation call for normative or ethical theorizing over and above any such theorizing involved in interpretation more generally? Legal scholars needn't be moral saints.

Though the ideas in (A) and (B) are perhaps individually plausible, there is a prima facie tension between them. Suppose (A) is true. But if legal claims are paradigmatically normative, then how could claims about the (social) facts which make them true not be normative too? How could there be true claims about, say, the interpretation of a legal text that weren't directive in the way that the legal claims which it issues are directive? On the flip side, suppose (B) is true. Then it would seem that claims about the law are ultimately about the obtaining of certain social facts. But claims about such facts aren't paradigmatically normative. So whence the normativity of legal claims? Why should the normativity of legal claims go beyond any normativity in claims about content or interpretation more generally?

I have been intentionally sloppy in formulating our puzzle (hackles, be thou unraised). There are various things one might say in reply. For instance, one might distinguish issues concerning the meaning and use of legal language from issues concerning the nature and metaphysics of law. Following H.L.A. Hart, and Joseph Raz after him, we might distinguish "external" from "internal" legal claims (Hart 1961/1994: vi, 89, 102–103). *Internal* legal claims, according to Hart, are claims of law made from the "point of view" of an adherent of a given legal system; *external* legal claims are claims about a body of law made from the point of view of an observer. The former are normative, whereas the latter are merely descriptive. One can make external claims about the content of a body of law without thereby endorsing the prescriptions that would be issued in internal uses of those claims. Correspondingly, even if substantive normative or ethical facts aren't among the fundamental grounds of legal facts, as positivism insists, one may still use legal language to express one's normative or ethical views when taking an internal point of view. Hence, one might conclude, the normativity of legal language in its internal use is compatible with the sociality of law in its metaphysical grounds.

The above characterization of the tension between the "normativity" and "sociality" of law may have been sloppy, but it targets what some have regarded as *the* central problem in philosophy of law (Kelsen 1967)—what Raz called the "problem of the normativity of law" (Raz 1975/1990: 170). Our not-altogether-hypothetical reply brings out important distinctions for theorizing about the nature of law and legal discourse and interpretation. Yet there is still more to explain. Can the distinction between internal and external legal claims be implemented in a rigorous semantic theory? How are we to cash out the metaphorical appeals to "points of view"? What exactly do we mean in calling legal language "normative"? How is the putative normativity of internal legal claims derived from their conventional meaning? What is the relation between the meanings of internal and external legal claims, such that the explanation of the normativity of the former doesn't carry over to predict normativity of the latter? What is the relation between the meanings of legal claims and the grounds of law that make these claims true or false?

Progress can be made on these questions, I think, by viewing them as instances of more general questions about the nature of normative uses of language and the relation between the metaphysics and semantics of normative thought and talk. A promising strategy is to look to advances in metaethics, philosophy of language, and formal semantics and pragmatics, and see what lessons we can extract for philosophy of law. My aim in this chapter is to develop an improved account of the meaning and use of various types of legal claims, and to use this account to inform debates about the normativity and metaphysics of law. The account is contextualist (in a sense to be explained), and draws on a more general framework for implementing a contextualist theory, called *Discourse Contextualism*, which I have developed elsewhere (Silk 2015a, 2016, 2017). I will argue that we can derive the apparent normative features of internal legal claims from a particular contextualist interpretation of an independently motivated formal semantics, along with general principles of interpretation and conversation (Sections III–IV). Though the semantics is descriptivist, I will argue that it avoids Ronald Dworkin's influential criticism of so-called "semantic theories of law," and elucidates the nature of "theoretical disagreements" about the basic criteria of legal validity. The account sheds light on the social, interpersonal function of normative uses of language in the law, as highlighted in Kevin Toh's expressivist interpretations of Hart. It also gives precise expression to Hart's and Raz's intuitive distinctions among types of legal claims (internal/external, committed/detached), while giving them a uniform type of analysis. The proposed semantic/pragmatic account provides a fruitful framework for further theorizing in ethics, metaethics, and philosophy of law—for instance, concerning the normativity and metaphysics of law, the relation between law and morality, and the nature of legal judgment (Section V). Delineating these issues in Raz's "problem of the normativity of law" can help refine our understanding of the space of overall theories. This can illuminate new ways the dialectics may proceed. A Discourse Contextualist account of the meaning and use of legal language is thus of interest to a range of theorists, regardless of their specific normative and metaphysical commitments. The project isn't to show that no other theory can succeed. It is to investigate one avenue for developing an improved linguistic basis for a broader theory of normativity and law.

Normative uses of language aren't limited to expressions of a single category. To fix ideas I will focus specifically on deontic readings of modal verbs—so-called *deontic modals*—such as in (3).[1] Though I think the proposed framework can be applied to expressions of other categories ('obligatory', 'duty', 'right', etc.), I won't argue for this here (see Silk 2016).

II. Theoretical Disagreement about the Law

An important function of language is to create and develop interpersonal relationships in communication. Language affords a variety of normative and evaluative resources for doing so. For instance, in using sentences such as (1)–(4), speakers can express their normative

[1] I use 'deontic' as a catchall term for any kind of practical normative reading. In calling a use 'deontic' I am not assuming that it need be performative or issue a directive/permissive speech act; more on this in Sections IV.E–V. I will assume that legal language is a register of ordinary natural language.

views and coordinate on what norms to accept—sometimes in agreement, sometimes in disagreement, as in (5).

(4) Morally speaking, we must help reform our prison system.
(5) *A:* Morally speaking, we must help reform our prison system.
B: Yeah you're right. What should we do?
B': No, it's fine the way it is.

In communication we shape our identities as thinkers and feelers in a social world; we coordinate on how to act, what to feel, and whom to be.

Some theorists claim that the dependence of our evaluation of (e.g.) (4) on what moral norms we accept derives from a dependence of the interpretation of (4) on a contextually relevant body of norms. *Metaethical contextualism*, as I will understand it, treats this context-dependence as a dependence of semantic (conventional) content on features of the context of use. Sentences such as (1)–(4) are treated as context-sensitive in the same kind of way as sentences with paradigm context-sensitive expressions (pronouns, demonstratives, etc.). What information is conventionally conveyed by, say, 'She won a medal' depends on which female is most salient in the discourse context. Likewise, the conventional content of (4) is treated (to a first approximation) as the proposition that such-and-such moral norms in the discourse context require us to help reform our prison system.[2]

Contextualism about normative language, in this sense, often goes under the heading of 'Metaethical Relativism' (e.g., Stevenson 1963, Dreier 1990). The view has a checkered past. Serious objections have been raised, both on linguistic and on substantive (meta)normative grounds. One prominent objection to contextualism is that it cannot account for certain normative disagreements. A version of this objection can be discerned in Ronald Dworkin's influential criticism of Hart's account of internal legal claims and other so-called "semantic theories of law" (1986, ch. 1; cf. 2011, ch. 8). In this section I briefly describe the objection and note several constraints on an adequate response. The depth of the problem raised by disagreement phenomena is often inadequately appreciated by contextualists. In Sections III–IV I will develop (what I regard as) a more successful contextualist account. In Section V I will show how the resulting semantics and pragmatics is compatible with a positivist theory, such as Hart's, of the conventionality of the criteria of legal validity.

(NB: My aim here isn't to do Dworkin (or Hart) exegesis.[3] What matters for present purposes is the content of the objection to be described. Though I construe the objection

[2] We will make this more precise shortly. I use terms such as 'conversation', 'discourse', and 'utterance' broadly to include uses of language in texts and deliberation, not simply in spoken dialogue. For now I gloss over the distinction between sentences-in-context and utterances (see Section V); my talk about the semantic properties of utterances can be understood as short for talk about the semantic properties of the sentences uttered in the contexts of those utterances. Following Yalcin (2014), there may be reasons to avoid using '(semantic) content' as a label for a compositional semantic value in context; my use of 'content' for this type of object makes no assumptions about its broader theoretical role.

[3] See, e.g., Raz (1998), Coleman (2001), Coleman and Simchen (2003), Leiter (2007), Shapiro (2007), Kramer (2008), Plunkett and Sundell (2013b).

as an objection to certain semantic theories, this isn't to deny that there are nonlinguistic construals of the objection or ways in which fundamental legal disagreement might undermine a Hartian positivist metaphysics.)

Dworkin asks us to consider the U.S. judicial case *Riggs v. Palmer*. The question was whether Elmer was entitled to the inheritance provided by his grandfather's will, given that Elmer had murdered his grandfather in order to claim the inheritance. Judge Earl held that Elmer wasn't entitled to the inheritance; Judge Gray dissented. The judges agreed on the relevant empirical facts of the case, the plain meaning of the statute of wills, and the intentions of the legislators who enacted the statute. The disagreement was a *fundamental legal disagreement*, what Dworkin calls a *theoretical* disagreement. The disagreement was centered not on the particular implications of agreed-upon general legal norms, but on the content of the fundamental legal norms themselves, which determine the existence and content of the law. Earl held that Elmer wasn't legally entitled to inherit in light of the "No one may profit from his own wrong" principle, and on the grounds that the original legislature wouldn't have intended a murderer to benefit from his crime in this way. Gray rejected the fundamental status of this principle and the legal relevance of such counterfactual intentions: the grandfather's will was valid, hence Elmer was legally entitled to inherit. We can imagine the following simplistic dialogue between Earl and Gray:

(6) *Earl:* In view of the law, Elmer may not receive the inheritance.
Gray: No, legally, Elmer may receive the inheritance.

The worry for contextualism is that there doesn't seem to be any way of specifying the contextually relevant body of legal norms that captures how Earl and Gray can felicitously express their fundamental legal disagreement in this way.

Dworkin sums up the worry well:

> If two lawyers are actually following *different* rules . . . , then each must mean something different from the other when he says what the law is. Earl and Gray must mean different things when they claim or deny that the law permits murderers to inherit: Earl means that his grounds for law are or are not satisfied, and Gray has in mind his own grounds, not Earl's. So the two judges are not really disagreeing about anything when one denies and the other asserts this proposition. They are only talking past one another. Their arguments are pointless in the most trivial and irritating way. (Dworkin 1986, 43–44)

In other words: If Earl's utterance of (7) is just a claim about the basic legal norms he accepts—that they forbid Elmer from inheriting—then it is unclear how Gray can reasonably disagree with him. It is unclear how in uttering (8) Gray is disagreeing with Earl if they are both making claims about their own respective norms.

(7) In view of the law, Elmer may not receive the inheritance.
(8) No, legally, Elmer may receive the inheritance.

Earl and Gray can agree about whether Elmer's inheriting is compatible with their respective legal norms, R_E, R_G, while disagreeing with what one another says. Gray's denial in (6) is felicitous, whereas *B*'s denial in (9) is not.

(9) *A:* In view of R_E, Elmer may not receive the inheritance.
B: #No, in view of R_G, Elmer may receive the inheritance.

This puts pressure on the claim that the sentences used in (9) explicitly specify the semantic contents of the respective sentences used in (6).

Several clarificatory remarks: First, Earl and Gray's disagreement is "fundamental" in the sense that it concerns the basic criteria of legal validity, which determine the very content of the law. As Dworkin puts it, the disagreement is not about "what [the law] should be" but rather about "what the law is" (1986, 7). In *Law's Empire* Dworkin often seems to treat theoretical disagreements as disagreements about the proper methods of interpreting authoritative sources of law. What is important here is simply that the disagreements are about the fundamental grounds of law.[4] Such disagreements may be rooted in issues about proper methods of interpretation, but I won't require this in what follows. (Terminology in this area is fraught. I will use expressions such as 'fundamental grounds of law', 'criteria of legal validity', 'basic legal norms', 'rule of recognition', etc. largely interchangeably. Differences among these notions won't matter for present purposes.)

Second, it isn't uncontentious what the basis of Earl and Gray's actual disagreement was. (Indeed the above exposition ran together two readings of the case, emphasized in Dworkin's "The Model of Rules I" and *Law's Empire*, respectively.) For dialectical purposes I assume that fundamental legal disagreements are possible—and common enough to warrant theorizing about them (cf. Leiter 2009)—and that the disagreement between Earl and Gray is an example of such a disagreement.

Third, I will focus specifically on discourse disagreements, though of course not all disagreements are expressed in linguistic exchanges.[5] The task here isn't to provide a general philosophical account of the nature of disagreement, or of fundamental legal disagreement at that. For our purposes what is to be explained is a certain discourse phenomenon: the systematic licensing of expressions of linguistic denial ('no', etc.) in discourses such as (6). These expressions signal the speaker's rejection of some aspect of the previous utterance. Not all cases in which speakers intuitively disagree can be marked in this way. *B*'s "disagreement in attitude" with *A* in (10) couldn't typically be signaled with a linguistic denial.

(10) *A:* I like Mexican food.
B: #No, I don't. I like Thai.

[4] Cf.: "a theoretical disagreement is a disagreement about the criteria of legal validity, that is, about the content of what Hart calls the Rule of Recognition" (Leiter 2007, 3); it "involves conflicting claims about what the grounds of law are" (Shapiro 2007, 36). See also n. 3.

[5] For discussion of inter-conversational disagreement, see MacFarlane (2007), Silk (2016, §3.4.2), and references therein. See also Section IV.B.

Our task is to generate a representation of discourses such as (6) that correctly predicts the felicity of expressions of linguistic denial and the discourse moves they mark.

The epicycles from here are involved; I simply wish to flag one not uncommon reaction.[6] I am sympathetic with the informal impression that in discourses such as (6) the speakers are disagreeing about what sort of context to be in. Intuitively, Earl and Gray are disagreeing, not about whether Elmer's receiving the inheritance is permitted by such-and-such basic legal norms, but about what basic legal norms *to accept*. Yet simply noting this is insufficient. The question isn't whether such "discourse-oriented" negotiations are possible. The challenge is to explain why they are so systematic with normative uses of language, given that a contextualist semantics is correct.

According to contextualism, sentences such as (7)–(8) have ordinary representational contents; they have a mind-to-world direction of fit. Even if we find examples of ordinary descriptive claims sometimes having normative implications—consider 'It's cold in here' ⇝ 'You should shut the window'—it's not as if they systematically trigger those particular normative implications across uses. Why, then, should uttering a sentence that conventionally describes given legal norms systematically communicate something about what legal norms to accept? 'I'm hungry' doesn't (systematically) imply that the addressee ought to be hungry. 'That [demonstrating *b*] is a cute baby' doesn't (systematically) imply that the addressee ought to be demonstrating *b*. Denials such as *B*'s in (11)–(12) are typically infelicitous.

(11) *A:* I'm hungry.
B: #No, I'm not hungry.

(12) *A:* That is a cute baby. [said demonstrating *b*]
B: #No, that isn't a cute baby. [said demonstrating *b′*]

When speakers use paradigm context-sensitive expressions with different intended asserted contents, the norm isn't disagreement but talking past.

In sum, the worry is that the distinctive role of internal legal claims is unexpected given the contextualist's semantics. Although many contextualists have offered pragmatic diagnoses of disagreement in terms of non-conventional aspects of use, little attention has been paid to what specific mechanisms are involved and how they are linguistically constrained. The challenge is to explain how the (dis)agreement phenomena can be derived from the sentences' specific contents and general conversational principles and features of contexts of use, and why the phenomena can be systematically derived with deontic modals but not with paradigm context-sensitive language. The force of this challenge has been underappreciated by contextualists.[7]

---

[6] For prescient early discussion, see Moore (1912, ch. 3), Stevenson (1937). For discussion in the broader literature, see Gibbard (1990, 2003), Kölbel (2004), Lasersohn (2005), von Fintel and Gillies (2008), Richard (2008), Dreier (2009), MacFarlane (2014), Silk (2014, 2015a, 2016); see also nn. 7, 19.

[7] In the broader literature, see Cappelen (2008), Björnsson and Finlay (2010), von Fintel and Gillies (2011), Sundell (2011), Plunkett and Sundell (2013a, 2013b), Finlay (2014). Plunkett and Sundell nicely highlight

III. Deontic Modals in Legal Contexts

The general consensus is that the objection from discourse disagreement is devastating for standard versions of contextualism (cf. Egan et al. 2005, 149; MacFarlane 2010, 1, 11; 2014, 248–249). I am more optimistic. The following sections briefly motivate a contextualist framework, developed in greater detail elsewhere (Silk 2015a, 2016, 2017), and apply it to uses of deontic modals in legal contexts. I call the framework *Discourse Contextualism*. The strategy is to start with a particular contextualist interpretation of a standard semantics for modals, and show how this formal semantics generates constraints on the interpretation of deontic modals and predicts distinctive features of their use. With a more nuanced understanding of the role of context in interpretation, we can provide an improved contextualist account of the function of deontic modals in managing an evolving body of norms. This section develops the basics of a Discourse Contextualist treatment of internal legal claims and theoretical disagreements. Section IV elaborates on various features of this account. Section V examines how the proposed semantic/pragmatic framework can be integrated with broader theorizing about the normativity and metaphysics of law (Section I). We will see that, *pace* Dworkin, it's not the case that "our jurisprudence [i.e., legal positivism] has no plausible theory of theoretical disagreement in law" and hence "distorts legal practice" (1986, 6, 15).

A. From Formal Semantics to Interpretive Constraints

It is standard in linguistic semantics to treat modal verbs as semantically associated with a parameter or variable that ranges over sets of premises (propositions) (see esp. Kratzer 1977, 1981, 1991). Broadly deontic readings call for a premise set that encodes the content of a body of norms (n. 1). For instance, a moral premise set might include propositions such as that no one steals, that everyone keeps one's promises, etc. In the case of legal readings, we can leave open the precise relation between basic legal norms, such as a Hartian rule of recognition, and any subsidiary norms that are "validated" by them (e.g., Hart 1961/1994, 107–110). What is important here is simply that the premise sets in the semantics of legal readings represent the full content of a body of law. Roughly put, for a given premise set P, 'Must φ' says that φ follows from P, and 'May φ' says that φ is compatible with P.[8]

---

examples of discourse disagreement over non-truth-conditional content. On this basis they claim *that* speakers negotiate about the values of contextual parameters, and "pragmatically advocate" for their proposed values in using normative language (2013a, 13–19, 28; 2013b, 262–263, 267). However, it isn't part of their aim to explain precisely how this happens, given the contextualist's semantics, or why normative language contrasts with paradigm context-sensitive language in its tendency for this kind of use. (Thanks to David Plunkett (p.c.) for clarifying this.) For further discussion of these issues, see Silk (2014, 2016, 2017).

[8] Kratzer's semantics uses two premise sets, calculated as a function of the world of evaluation: a "modal base" $F(w)$ that represents a set of background facts in w, and an "ordering source" $G(w)$ that represents the content of some ideal in w. These complications won't be relevant here; I treat modals as evaluated with respect to a single finite, consistent premise set. I generally suppress world-indexing on premise sets; talk about a proposition p "following from (/being compatible with) P" can be understood as short for saying that p follows from (/is compatible with) $P(w)$, for any relevant world w. I use 'φ,' 'ψ,' etc. both as schematic letters to be replaced with

It is also common to include in a model of context a parameter representing norms accepted for the purposes of conversation (esp. Portner 2007; cf. e.g. Lewis 1979, Lochbaum 1998, Starr 2010).[9] In conversation we not only share information in coordinating our beliefs about the world; we express our normative views and coordinate our plans. Inquiry is, in part, inquiry about what to do. Yet normative inquiry isn't limited to norms of a single category. We investigate the nature of morality, nonmoral value, the law, and so on. It isn't uncontroversial how these domains are related. Bracketing this issue for the moment, we can treat the contextual norms parameter as consisting of a sequence of premise sets, representing different types of norms that may be relevant in the conversation (cf. Portner 2007). It is natural to treat the uses we have been considering as calling for deontic premise set variables (moral, legal, etc.) which represent the same sorts of norms represented in this discourse-level parameter. For instance, the use of 'must' in (3) 'In view of the law, Chip must repay his debt' calls for a variable $\mathbf{P}_l$ that represents the legal norms endorsed in the conversation. This reflects the paradigmatic roles of deontic modals in communal planning and deliberation, and in coordinating on an overall normative view. (Complications to these natural moves will follow shortly.)

Treating deontic modals as semantically associated with a deontic premise set variable places constraints on their felicitous use and interpretation. When the variable is free, a value must be contextually supplied in order for the sentence to have a specific interpretation in context. For communication to succeed, the hearer must be able to infer how the speaker takes the discourse context to be such that it determines such-and-such content for her utterance. Uttering 'The baby is laughing' assumes that—at least after one's utterance (Stalnaker 1978, 2002, 2014)—context supplies a salience ordering on which such-and-such individual *b* is the most salient baby, and asserts that *b* is laughing. Likewise uttering (3) 'In view of the law, must (/may) φ' assumes a value for $\mathbf{P}_l$, say P_l,[10] and asserts that φ follows from (/is compatible with) P_l.

To be clear, I am *not* suggesting that the standard semantic framework for modals calls for contextualism about deontic modals.[11] All parties can accept that certain modal verbs, qua lexical items, are context-sensitive in the sense that the context of utterance determines what type of reading the modal receives (see Silk 2016, §3.1). What is at-issue in debates about contextualism (as I am understanding it) is whether, given a certain type of normative

---

declarative sentences, and for the possible-worlds propositions they denote. I use bold for variables, and italics for their values in context; any subscripts are included simply for expository purposes to indicate the intended assignment and interpretation of the variable. (See Silk 2016, 2017, 2018 for refinements and further details on the formal semantics.)

[9] We needn't commit to a particular account of the nature and representation of context. For instance, I am not assuming that contexts are determined wholly by speaker attitudes. What is important here is simply that contexts determine premise sets for the interpretation of modals. See Wróblewski (1983) for discussion of various notions of context in legal interpretation.

[10] Or, in some cases, at least a relevant range of values (for discussion, see Silk 2016, §§3.3.6, 3.5–3.6, 4.4, 5.2.5, 6.3; see also nn. 2, 8, 14).

[11] On this I disagree with sentiments in von Fintel and Gillies (2008), Finlay (2009, 2014), Björnsson and Finlay (2010), Dowell (2011, 2012).

reading (e.g., moral), some specific body of norms supplied by context is used in calculating the sentence's semantic content, or compositional semantic value.

B. Managing the Context

Before returning to the discourse disagreement with Earl and Gray, I would like to briefly look at agreement and disagreement phenomena more generally. Perhaps better understanding the role of context in collaborative action will shed light on the role of deontic modals in managing the context and what norms to accept.

Suppose it's common knowledge between Clara and Dan that several days ago she said something to him that could have been construed as rude. Clara isn't sure whether Dan took what she said that way, and, if he did, whether he is offended. She doesn't want to bring up their previous interaction explicitly since she wouldn't want to make something out of nothing. So the next time she sees Dan she acts as though everything is normal between them. She is warm and open as usual. Since Dan wasn't offended by Clara's earlier remark, he responds in kind to Clara. Since Clara knows that Dan wouldn't respond this way if he was annoyed, and Dan knows that she knows this, etc., it becomes common ground that they are on good terms and that he didn't take her remark as rude.

Now consider a variant on the case. Suppose that Dan was in fact offended by Clara's remark, and, though he didn't say so at the time, Clara knows this. Nevertheless she still doesn't want to bring up their previous interaction. She wants to avoid the potential conflict if she can. So she acts as if everything is copacetic, even though she knows it isn't. However, Dan doesn't want to go along with Clara's behavior. He *might* object by making their clash in attitudes explicit. He could say something like, "Why are you acting as if everything is okay between us? Don't you remember what you said?" Or perhaps, "I know you're just trying to get everything back to normal, but, listen, it isn't." But Dan needn't object in this way. Instead he simply acts aloof. In return Clara might continue to act amiably, hoping that he will eventually respond in kind. Clara and Dan can thus manage their assumptions about the status of their relationship without explicitly raising the issue.

My point in considering these examples is to highlight how commonplace a certain sort of reasoning about context is. The appropriateness of our actions often requires that circumstances are a certain way. *In acting*, we can thus exploit our mutual world knowledge and general pragmatic reasoning skills to communicate information and manage our assumptions about these circumstances. This streamlines collaborative action. The lesson: *by acting in such a way that is appropriate only if the context is a certain way, one can implicitly propose that the context be that way.* If the other party accommodates by proceeding in like manner, it can become taken for granted that the context is that way. If she doesn't, negotiation over the state of the context may ensue. Crucially, this can all happen without explicitly raising the issue of what the context is like.

I suggest that the linguistic case—the case of linguistic action, discourse, and interpretation—is a special instance of these phenomena. Deontic modal utterances presume an implicit, conventionally unspecified body of norms. By reasoning from deontic modals' semantically generated constraints, interlocutors can integrate relevant features of the (past, present, and projected future) conversational situation to interpret deontic modals, share information, and coordinate on an evolving normative view.

With these points in mind, let's reconsider Earl and Gray's discourse disagreement in (6). Earl utters (7) 'In view of the law, Elmer may not receive the inheritance'. Upon hearing Earl's semantically underspecified utterance, Gray might (tacitly) reason roughly as follows (where i is the proposition that Elmer receives the inheritance):

(13) "Earl is intending to say something about the possibility i. In order to do so, given the grammatical properties of modals, a set of premises must be contextually supplied. Since Earl wouldn't intend to say something false, he must be assuming a premise set P that is incompatible with i. The current question under discussion concerns whether Elmer is legally entitled to inherit. Since Earl is cooperative, his utterance of (7) must be relevant and realize an intention to provide at least a partial answer to this question. Assuming P_l as a value for $\mathbf{P}_l$ would do so by ensuring that the legal norms endorsed in the discourse forbid Elmer from inheriting. So, Earl must be assuming a value for $\mathbf{P}_l$, P_l, and have meant that P_l is incompatible with i."

Rather than formalize this reasoning here, let's simply observe its principal features.[12] Given the grammatical properties of modals, Earl's utterance assumes a body of legal norms relevant for the particular task at hand: resolving the question of whether Elmer is legally entitled to inherit. The appropriateness of Earl's linguistic act of uttering (7) requires that the legal norms operative in the context be incompatible with Elmer's receiving the inheritance. Since it's mutually presupposed that Earl is obeying the conversational maxims (Grice 1989), in uttering (7) Earl implicitly proposes that it become taken for granted that such norms be accepted in the discourse. In accepting an utterance one normally accepts what the speaker committed to in uttering it. So, since it's common knowledge that Earl can expect Gray to undergo an abductive reasoning process like (13), it's also common knowledge that he will object if he has relevantly different views on the criteria of legal validity, given their common goal of settling on what the law provides. So if Gray doesn't object, this will confirm that the context is as the appropriateness of Earl's act requires, and the discourse-level legal norms parameter can be updated to a value that is incompatible with i.

However, since Gray accepts an incompatible legal view, he objects.[13] He says (8) 'No, legally, Elmer may receive the inheritance'. For reasons parallel to those above, his doing so

[12] For rigorous formalizations in artificial intelligence and logic of this sort of process and the tacit reasoning behind it, see, e.g., Hobbs et al. (1993), Asher and Lascarides (2003), Thomason et al. (2006). As these literatures have documented, we are quite skilled at inferring one another's intended context and coordinating accordingly (see Railton 2009 for rich related discussion of our fluency in tacit reasoning and integrating it in action). Research in psycholinguistics also establishes the ease with which speakers coordinate on linguistic meaning and use, both at the level of individual conversations in establishing local sublanguages (entrainment) and at the level of communities in establishing more stable linguistic conventions (e.g., Clark and Wilkes-Gibbs 1986, Garrod and Doherty 1994). See Stalnaker (2014) for discussion of relevant philosophical motivations.

[13] The fact that Earl and Gray disagree doesn't imply that they aren't engaged in a "cooperative" conversation, in the sense relevant for interpreting their utterances; denials are compatible with Gricean cooperativity (Asher and Lascarides 2013; *pace* Finlay 2014, 124, 180). *Pace* Marmor (2008), strategic conversations needn't call for novel interpretive or pragmatic mechanisms.

is appropriate only if the legal norms operative in the context are compatible with Elmer's inheriting. As expected, Earl goes through an analogous abductive reasoning process and infers that he must wish to take for granted that these discourse-level legal norms are that way. If Earl accepts Gray's justification for his denial, it can become taken for granted that the context is as their present actions mutually require. If he doesn't, further negotiation may ensue. By producing utterances that assume incompatible values for the contextual variable $\mathbf{P}_I$—i.e., by acting in ways that would be appropriate only if $\mathbf{P}_I$ was assigned such-and-such contrary values—Earl and Gray can manage their assumptions about the conversational situation. In using deontic modals Earl and Gray exploit their mutual grammatical knowledge, and general pragmatic reasoning skills, to negotiate over what basic legal norms to accept.

IV. Basic Features

This basic Discourse Contextualist account sheds light on various aspects of the use of modal language in the law.

A. Justified Use

First, Discourse Contextualism captures how speakers such as Earl and Gray are in a position to make their deontic modal claims. Since Earl can reasonably expect Gray to undergo the sort of pragmatic reasoning in (13) and retrieve his intended interpretation, he needn't be overstepping his bounds in using 'may' and assuming a value for the discourse-level legal norms parameter. Similarly, since Gray knows that Earl has similar semantic and pragmatic competencies, he can express his disagreement with Earl's assumption with a direct denial—that is, by performing an act, the linguistic act of uttering (8), which assumes an incompatible value for $\mathbf{P}_I$. In assuming a value for the contextual variable $\mathbf{P}_I$ one needn't believe that the assumed norms are in fact (already) commonly accepted. (As far as individual attitudes go, a speaker needn't even believe that there are correct basic criteria of legal validity, determined by whatever means.) The relevant attitude toward the proposition that the context is thus-and-so isn't belief but acceptance for purposes of conversation (Stalnaker 1974; Thomason 2002)—in our examples, acceptance for purposes of legal discourse and practice. Given how skilled we are at inferring one another's intended context (n. 12), we can use deontic modals as a way of testing one another's normative views, inviting them to object if they accept different norms.

B. Locus of Disagreement

The account makes sense of how speakers can express disagreements about the law in discourses such as (6). For all I have said, the intended contents of Earl's and Gray's utterances may be compatible. It may be the case both that Earl's assumed value for $\mathbf{P}_I$, P_E, is incompatible with the proposition *i* that Elmer inherits, and that Gray's assumed value for $\mathbf{P}_I$, P_G, is compatible with *i*. Even so, contextualism needn't treat Earl and Gray as talking at cross-purposes (*pace* Toh 2005). Uses of context-sensitive expressions reflect speakers' assumptions about relevant content-determining features of context. Although the compositional semantics takes as given a particular abstract representation which supplies values for (e.g.) pronouns/variables, what contextual resolution is determined can become at-issue, or have main-point status, in concrete utterances (Thomason et al. 2006, Simons 2007, Silk 2014, 2016; more on this in Section V). Our model of the discourse dynamics represents Earl and Gray as disagreeing over the grammatically backgrounded content of what value for the contextual deontic premise set variable $\mathbf{P}_1$ is determined by the conversational situation; their utterances carry incompatible assumptions about what body of legal norms is operative in the context and represents the norms endorsed for purposes of legal discourse and practice.[14] *Pace* Dworkin, the contextualist can locate a "fulcrum of disagreement" (1994, 14) when there is controversy about the basic grounds of law.

It is important to be clear about the level, if any, at which Earl and Gray's disagreement is "about the context." The present challenge for contextualism is to explain the licensing of expressions of linguistic denial in discourses such as (6), and to represent how the hearer rejects the speaker's discourse move and issues a countermove (Section II). For purposes of responding to this challenge what is important is that our formal pragmatics locates a specific incompatibility in the updates from Earl's and Gray's utterances: their utterances make incompatible assumptions about the conversational situation (n. 14). This needn't imply that the disagreement is fundamentally "about the context," how to use words, etc. More fundamentally, Earl and Gray's disagreement is about what basic legal norms to accept and why; Earl and Gray disagree about what to presuppose about the concrete features determining what legal norms are operative in their situation. It is this substantive normative disagreement which grounds the incompatible representations of context presupposed by their utterances. For these reasons I avoid classifying Discourse Contextualism as a "metacontextual" or "metalinguistic" account of discourse disagreement.[15]

C. *Force and Function in Context*

Discourse Contextualism elucidates the informal ideas from Section II concerning the role of internal legal claims in managing what legal norms to accept. Following C.L. Stevenson, Allan Gibbard observes that when making a normative assertion, the speaker "is making a

---

[14] Slightly more formally: One effect of accepting Earl's utterance is that the Context Set—the set of worlds compatible with what is taken for granted in the conversation (Stalnaker 1978)—is updated to include only worlds in which (among other things) the concrete conversational situation determines a value for $\mathbf{P}_1$ that is incompatible with i, i.e. worlds in which the interlocutors presuppose legal norms which imply $\neg i$; whereas one effect of accepting Gray's utterance is that the Context Set is updated to include only worlds in which (among other things) the concrete conversational situation determines a value for $\mathbf{P}_1$ that is compatible with i. In discourse there may be various ways of accommodating a value for $\mathbf{P}_1$ that bears the stated relation to the embedded proposition given the speakers' existing commitments; our purposes often don't require us to commit for the future course of the discourse to a particular body of norms (n. 10). This observation helps capture how interlocutors needn't accept precisely the same norms in cases of *agreement* over particular legal issues. In an agreement with (say) Earl, although different norms may be determined by the concrete conversational situation in different worlds in the Context Set, the norms will be alike in implying i. The basis for the speakers' agreement is their attitudes regarding the legal status of Elmer's inheriting.

[15] Cf. Plunkett and Sundell (2013a, 2013b), Plunkett (2015).

conversational demand. He is demanding that the audience accept what he says, that it share the state of mind he expresses" (1990, 172)—albeit in a "more subtle, less fully conscious way" than by using an imperative (Stevenson 1937, 26). In making normative assertions we *make claims on* our interlocutors. "Their typical use is to provide guidance by criticizing, commending, demanding, advising, approving, etc." (Raz 1981, 300). Discourse Contextualism locates this feature of normative discourse in the presuppositions of normative utterances.

Though the truth conditions of deontic modal sentences are ordinary representational contents, speakers can use deontic modals to communicate normative claims about what norms to accept. Since deontic modal sentences require a value for a contextual variable in order to express a proposition, the assignment of such a value is a precondition for making a deontic modal assertion. Doing so thus creates a new discourse context in which that precondition is taken for granted.[16] This puts pressure on the hearer to conform her legal views to the assumed deontic premise set. In cooperative conversations, exerting such conversational pressure will be able to be supported by some justification for why it would be reasonable to rely on the relevant presupposed norms, or why it would be reasonable to treat one as relevantly authoritative on the issue in question. This can promote consensus about the law. Consensus isn't always in the offing, but that is no different from the ordinary non-normative case.[17]

The interpersonal aspect of legal practice is emphasized in Hart's understanding of the rule of recognition and in Kevin Toh's expressivist interpretation of Hart (Toh 2005, 2011; cf. Raz 1981, 1993). A characteristic feature of internal legal claims, on Hart's view, is that they presuppose that the speaker's assumed rule of recognition is also generally accepted and complied with in the community (e.g., Hart 1959, 167–168; 1961/1994, 108). Such a view raises the question of how legal claims are interpreted in contexts of disagreement where this presupposition isn't satisfied.[18] On the account developed in this chapter, what is assumed by one's utterance is a value for a contextual parameter representing legal norms accepted for the purposes of legal discourse and practice; what is assumed is the body of norms. As we have seen, speakers needn't believe that these norms are already mutually accepted. Interlocutors can manage their views on what legal norms to accept in *using* expressions such as deontic modals. Discourse Contextualism captures Toh's expressivist idea that "joint acceptance of the fundamental [legal] norms . . . [is] something that the speaker is . . . trying to instigate," rather than "something that is always presupposed" (2011, 119).

The nature of deontic modal sentences' truth conditions may help explain their propensity for discourse-oriented uses (see Silk 2016 for extended discussion). The truth-conditional contents of deontic modal sentences are propositions about logical relations (e.g., implication, compatibility) between propositions and premise sets. Such logical matters can be at-issue when working out the specific content of a body of general legal norms given the

[16] Cf. Stalnaker (1978, 2002, 2014) on the "commonplace effect" of speech acts: "the context on which an assertion has its essential effect is not defined by what is presupposed before the speaker begins to speak, but will include any information which the speaker assumes his audience can infer from the performance of the speech act" (1978, 86); cf. Thomason et al. 2006, Silk 2016, §§3.5, 5.2.5, 6.2.2, 6.3.

[17] For further discussion, see Gibbard (1990, Part III). See Forrester (1989) for developments of a "pragmatics of deontic speech," along with applications to legal discourse.

[18] Cf. Silk (2016, §3.5.3) in reply to theories invoking a "presupposition of commonality."

non-normative facts. Such is the case in what Dworkin calls "empirical disagreements"—disagreements about whether certain agreed-upon criteria of legal validity are satisfied in a particular case (1986, 4–5). But, as Dworkin emphasizes, such empirical matters aren't always what is at-issue in legal inquiry. What is often interesting in a speaker's deontic modal utterance is the assumption that the discourse-level legal norms, hence value for $\mathbf{P}_l$, are such as to make the utterance true. Given the ease with which we can retrieve one another's intended interpretation (as described above), using a deontic modal affords an efficient means of managing our assumptions about these norms. General pragmatic principles concerning efficiency and effectiveness in communication enjoin us to do so (cf. Levinson 1987, Grice 1989, Heim 1991). So, it wouldn't be surprising if a primary function of deontic modals in legal discourse came to be to facilitate coordination on a body of legal norms. Capturing this is often taken to be a distinctive advantage of expressivist theories.[19] Discourse Contextualism captures it in terms of a contextualist semantics and general pragmatic effects of using sentences with this semantics.

D. *Expressing States of Mind*

Expressivist accounts highlight another important feature of legal claims: their role in expressing speakers' states of mind. "The use of unstated rules of recognition . . . in identifying particular rules of the [legal] system," Hart writes, "is characteristic of the internal point of view. Those who use them in this way thereby manifest their own acceptance of them as guiding rules" (1961/1994, 102). An internal legal claim "expresses its speaker's endorsement," or "acceptance . . . of standards of behaviour towards conformity with which the statement is used to guide its addressee" (Raz 1981, 300; 1993, 148). A common complaint against contextualism is that it incorrectly treats normative utterances as reporting, rather than expressing, speakers' states of mind.[20] Discourse Contextualism avoids this worry.

Common characterizations of contextualism notwithstanding,[21] deontic modal sentences, on the present account, aren't fundamentally about an individual or group. They make claims about the logical properties of a given deontic premise set. Earl's utterance of (7) assumes a value for a contextual variable, $\mathbf{P}_l$, that represents the legal norms operative in the conversation. Given their assumed common goal of settling on what norms to accept, Gray can reasonably infer from Earl's act that Earl accepts basic legal norms which, given the facts of the case, imply that Elmer is not to receive the inheritance. Earl expresses his state of mind in the sense of performing an act that is appropriate only if he is in that state of mind (cf. Bach and Harnish 1979). His utterance expresses his acceptance of certain legal norms via what it asserts *and* presupposes. Discourse Contextualism can capture the core expressivist claim that normative uses of language express the speaker's state of mind.

[19] See Stevenson (1937), Hart (1961/1994), Gibbard (1990), Toh (2005, 2011); in the broader literature, see, e.g., Richard (2008), Yalcin (2012), Swanson (2016).

[20] See, e.g., Ayer (1936), Stevenson (1937), Gibbard (1990); cf. Hart (1961/1994, 102–103).

[21] E.g., Silk 2013, 212–213, MacFarlane 2014, 146–147, a.m.o.

E. *The Varieties of Legal Claims: Internal, External, Detached*

So far we have focused on what Hart called *internal* legal claims—claims of law made by adherents of a legal system. But, as Hart observed, some legal claims are descriptive; they simply describe the laws of a given community. To capture this distinction, Hart, and Raz after him, posited a distinctive "internal point of view" on the law. It is only when taking up the internal point of view that one's claims are genuinely normative. The present account provides a framework for capturing Hart's and Raz's insights about internal and external legal claims, and cashing out the metaphorical talk of "points of view." (We will return to Hart's and Raz's accounts of the internal point of view and the normativity of internal legal claims in Section V.)

Not all uses of deontic modal expressions are prescriptive or express the speaker's endorsement of certain norms or values. Following Lyons (1977, 1995), it is common to distinguish (what I will call) *endorsing* uses of modals, such as in (6), where the speaker is presented as endorsing the considerations with respect to which the modal is interpreted, from *non-endorsing* uses, such as in (14)–(15), where the speaker isn't presented in this way.[22] The non-endorsing use in (15) reports what Ernie's parents' rules require; these rules needn't be accepted by the speaker. The claims in (14)–(15) can be paraphrased with an explicit 'according to'-type phrase, as in (16).

(14) Bert has to pay a fine. Isn't that crazy? I wouldn't do it if I were him.
(15) Ernie has to be home by 10. Aren't his parents stupid? I'd stay out if I were him.
(16) According to Ernie's parents' rules, Ernie has to be home by 10.

The endorsing uses of deontic modals in (5)–(6), by contrast, present the speaker as endorsing the norms that justify the modal claim. *A*'s utterance in (5) expresses her acceptance of norms implying that Sally contribute to prison reform. Hart's distinction between "internal" and "external" legal claims can be viewed as an instance of the general, independently attested distinction between endorsing and non-endorsing uses of modals.

We can capture the distinction between internal and external legal claims while giving them a uniform type of analysis. In both kinds of uses the modals are interpreted with respect to a contextually supplied set of premises. The difference lies in what the relevant premise set variable represents. The external use of 'have to' in (14) calls for a variable $\mathbf{P}_{NH}$ that refers to (say) New Haven traffic law. Uttering (15) assumes that context determines a value for a deontic premise set variable $\mathbf{P}_{hr}$, P_h, that encodes Ernie's parents' house rules, and asserts that P_h implies that Ernie be home by 10 (n. 8). These rules may be accepted in the context, but they need not be. What distinguishes internal uses is that they call for a discourse-level variable that represents norms accepted for purposes of the conversation. Internal legal claims don't simply say what is permitted, required, etc. according to a given body of legal norms; they assume that the norms are to be endorsed in the context. The distinctive features of internal uses can be derived from the contextualist semantics as explained in the previous sections.[23]

---

[22] This distinction has been noted in many areas under various labels; see also, e.g., Hare (1952), von Wright (1963), Narrog (2005), Verstraete (2007), Silk (2016).

[23] Toh (2005, 2007, 2011) and Raz (1975/1990, 1977) treat the meanings of internal claims as primary, and explain the meaning of external claims in terms of the meaning of internal claims (cf. Forrester 1989).

This treatment sheds light on a further distinction which Raz draws between internal normative claims that are *committed* and those that are *detached* (1975/1990, 171–177). *Committed* internal claims are internal claims in Hart's sense. Yet Raz notes that not all claims of law made within a legal community are endorsed by the members of that community. This observation leads Raz to posit a class of *detached* internal claims: claims that are normative although they don't express the speaker's acceptance of the relevant norms. In a detached internal claim the speaker merely pretends or simulates such acceptance. For instance, an anarchist lawyer may advise her client that he "must pay the fine," though she doesn't endorse the laws that imply that he do so. By analogy, Raz considers a meat-eater uttering (17) to a vegetarian.

(17) You shouldn't eat this dish. It contains meat.

The meat-eater's statement is made "from the point of view of a vegetarian," but without endorsing that point of view. In this sense, the meat eater's utterance of (17) is "detached," whereas a vegetarian's utterance of (17) would be "committed."

I agree with Raz that there is a distinction here, but I would not be the first to be puzzled by his way of drawing it. I find it hard to see a helpful sense in which detached claims are genuinely "normative" even though (like external claims) they are neither directive nor expressive of the speaker's own views. Such properties are often regarded as definitional of normative uses of language.[24] More helpful, I suggest, is to treat Raz's detached internal claims instead as a species of external claims—specifically, external claims made in contexts in which (i) what is at-issue is the specific implications of a general body of norms given the relevant circumstances, where (ii) these norms may be endorsed by certain relevant individuals in the context, though not necessarily by the speaker. For instance, the meat eater's utterance of (17) makes a claim about vegetarian moral norms that are endorsed by the addressee. The variable $\mathbf{P}_v$ with respect to which the modal is interpreted, which represents the content of these norms, needn't be identified with the discourse-level variable representing the moral norms endorsed in the conversation—hence the "external" nature of the claim, and how it needn't express the speaker's endorsement of vegetarianism. Yet insofar as the addressee is a committed vegetarian, she may take the content of the speaker's assertion—that P_v implies that she not eat the dish—to have direct practical implications, and she may guide her behavior accordingly. The speaker may even endorse that she do so, perhaps in light of a higher-order norm enjoining individuals to act in accordance with the moral norms they take to apply to themselves regarding meat-eating. Analogous points hold for Raz's examples of detached internal claims in legal contexts.

The account developed here gives both types of claims a common underlying contextualist semantics, and explains the distinctive features of internal claims as effects of using sentences interpreted with respect to a discourse-level norms variable.

[24] See Forrester (1989, ch. 3); Korsgaard (1996, 8, 226); Thomson (1996, 130–131, 147–150); Gibbard (1990, 33; 2003, ix–x, 9–10, 137–139); Field (2009, 286); Parfit (2011, 284, 288, 291; Railton (2012, 25). For critical discussion, see Silk (2015b, §6).

F. Recap

I have argued that a more nuanced understanding of the role of context in interpretation provides the basis for an improved contextualist theory of uses of deontic modals in legal contexts. The aim of Discourse Contextualism is to start with a particular contextualist interpretation of a standard semantics for modals, and derive distinctive discourse properties of deontic modals from this formal semantics and general conversational principles. Semantically, normative uses of deontic modals—"internal" uses, in Hart's terminology—are associated with a contextual parameter representing norms endorsed for purposes of conversation. Pragmatically, the "discourse-oriented" effects of such uses arise via general pragmatic reasoning from (inter alia) the requirement that a value for this parameter be assumed as input to semantic interpretation. In using deontic modals, speakers can exploit their mutual grammatical and world knowledge, along with general pragmatic reasoning, to manage an evolving normative view.

V. Legal Language and a Theory of Law: The "Problem of the Normativity of Law," Revisited

Sections II–IV focused on the meaning and use of modal language in legal discourse. This section examines how the Discourse Contextualist semantics/pragmatics from Sections III–IV can integrate fruitfully with broader theorizing about the normativity of law, the relation between law and morality, and the nature of law and legal judgment.

Our discussion of Raz and internal normative claims brings us back to our puzzle from Section I. What motivated Raz to posit a distinct category of detached internal legal claims was that it provided a response to what he called "the problem of the normativity of law"—the problem of explaining "the use of normative terms to describe the law and legal situations" in a manner consistent with legal positivism (1975/1990, 169). The challenge was to reconcile the *normativity* of law with the *sociality* of law (Section I). The worry for positivism, Raz argues, is this: Claims of law use "normative terms like 'a right', 'a duty', 'ought' " (1977, 158). If these terms "are used in the same sense in legal, moral, and other normative statements" (1977, 158), then legal statements must be "normative statements in the same sense and in the same way that moral statements are normative" (1981, 303). But this seems to imply that legal statements are just "ordinary moral statements" (1981, 306), contrary to the positivist thesis that "legal rights and duties . . . may and sometimes do contradict moral rights and duties" (1979, 38).

Hart's reply was to deny that 'must', 'right', 'duty', etc. have the same meaning in moral and legal contexts (e.g., 1982, 153–161). Positing a class of internal but non-endorsing legal claims allows Raz to maintain that such expressions have the same meaning in legal and moral contexts, and that claims of law are genuinely normative, while denying that legal claims need have directive moral force: "Detached" legal claims are merely made from the "point of view" of someone who treats the relevant legal norms as morally justified; they needn't express endorsement of that point of view. Hence, though "made by the use of ordinary normative terms, [they do] not carry the same normative force of an ordinary legal statement" (Raz 1977, 156).

Our Discourse Contextualist framework brings into relief an alternative, and I think more attractive, line of reply to Raz's "problem of the normativity of law." We can reconcile a positivist theory of the nature of law with the idea that 'must', 'ought', etc. have the same meaning in legal and moral contexts, and without positing a spurious class of non-endorsing/non-directive normative claim.

First, let's reconsider how Raz sets up the problem. It is misleading to talk about "normative *terms*" (expressions, vocabulary) as such (Raz 1977, 158; emphasis added). There is nothing essentially "normative" in lexical items such as 'must', 'ought', 'duty', etc. Many modal expressions can receive various types of readings, as in (18). As we saw in Section IV.E, even broadly deontic readings needn't be used endorsingly or with directive force, as in (19).

(18) a. (Given when she left,) Sally must have arrived by now. [epistemic]
b. (To get to the concert on time,) you can take a cab. [teleological]
c. (Given the state of my nose,) I have to sneeze. [circumstantial]

(19) [Context: We're teenage siblings. It's 10:30 p.m., and we plan on staying out and going to a party. We know our parents are already asleep.]
You: When is curfew, again? We need to make sure that we tell Mom we got back before then if she asks.
Me: We have to be home by 11. Aren't her rules stupid? C'mon, let's go.

Although modals can be put to different uses such as these, I am sympathetic with the standard view among formal semanticists that "there is something in the meaning [of the modal] which stays invariable" (Kratzer 1977, 340). The linguistic meaning of (e.g.) 'must' in moral and legal contexts is the same: roughly put, given such-and-such set of premises P, 'Must φ' is true iff φ follows from P (Section III.A). What is normative, rather, are *uses* of expressions such as 'must' in certain contexts (cf. Silk 2015b, §6). Raz's move to frame the "problem of the normativity of law" as a problem about "normative language" (1975/1990, 170) is unfortunate. Plausibly, what was of primary interest to legal theorists such as Hart and Raz wasn't a linguistic issue, an issue about the conventional meanings of certain natural language expressions. It was a substantive issue about the normativity of law—whether facts about law provide (possibly moral) reasons for action, how the law can justifiably claim to guide behavior, etc. The remainder of this section shows how Discourse Contextualism can provide a framework for integrating issues about the meaning and use of language in legal contexts with issues about the normativity and nature of law.

The project of compositional semantics is to give an account of the following: given an assignment of values to context-sensitive expressions, what are the conventional contents of expressions, and how are the conventional contents of complex expressions calculated as a function of the conventional contents of their parts (n. 2). Crucially, compositional semantics—the representation of conventional meaning and speakers' semantic competence—*takes as given* an abstract representation that assigns values to free variables and other context-sensitive expressions. The compositional semantics leaves open the broadly metasemantic question of what makes it the case about a concrete conversational situation that such-and-such abstract context (or perhaps range of abstract contexts; n. 10) represents it. The conventional meaning of deontic modals leaves open what makes it the case that such-and-such deontic premise sets represent the operative norms (legal, moral, etc.)—and thus that such-and-such values for $\mathbf{P}_l$, $\mathbf{P}_m$, etc. are determined—in a concrete discourse context.

Distinguishing questions about the metasemantics of deontic modals suggests precise ways of posing substantive questions about the nature of law and legal judgment. For instance:

Metaphysics of law
What property, if any, do all and only lawful actions have? Fundamentally, what determines which body of legal norms (hence value for $\mathbf{P}_l$) is operative in a given concrete context? Are moral properties among the fundamental grounds of law? Or are norms part of the law only in virtue of their social source? Can we provide purely source-based criteria of legal validity?

Normativity of law
What is the relation between the operative legal norms (hence value for $\mathbf{P}_l$) determined in a concrete context and agents' normative reasons for action? Does the fact that, in view of the law, one must α necessarily provide one with a normative reason to α? For instance, is it the case that, for any concrete context C, if the value for $\mathbf{P}_l$ determined in C implies that x pays a fine, then x has a normative reason to pay a fine?

Law and morality
What is the relation between the operative legal and moral norms (hence values for $\mathbf{P}_l$ and $\mathbf{P}_m$) determined in a concrete context? Does the fact that, in view of the law, one must α imply that, in view of morality, one must α, or that one has a moral reason to α? For instance, is it the case that, for any concrete context C, if the value for $\mathbf{P}_l$ determined in C implies that x pays a fine, then the value for $\mathbf{P}_m$ determined in C implies that x pays a fine?

Legal judgment
What is involved in accepting a body of legal norms, or making discourse moves that presuppose such acceptance? Does accepting a body of legal norms essentially involve having certain motivational dispositions or emotional capacities? What must a concrete context be like for an utterance to call for being interpreted with respect to a variable representing a discourse-level legal norms parameter? Must the use play a regulative, directive role in the planning and practical reasoning of the community? Does accepting 'In view of the law, I must α'—accepting that the operative legal norms (hence value for $\mathbf{P}_l$) determined in one's concrete context implies that one does α—necessarily involve taking oneself to have a normative (and perhaps moral) reason to α?

Metaethicists and philosophers of law can all accept Discourse Contextualism in giving a formal semantics and pragmatics for broadly normative uses of language. Where they will differ is on these sorts of further philosophical questions. I won't defend particular answers to such questions here. However, for purposes of illustration it may be helpful to outline what one sort of Discourse-Contextualist-based overall theory might look like.

Delineating the above issues brings into relief an overall theory which adopts a positivist metaphysics and yet treats judgments about the law as essentially practical, perhaps even as a kind of moral judgment. We might see Hart and Raz as offering theories of precisely this kind. Consider the following combination of views:

(i) The law of a community needn't always provide the members of the community with genuine normative or moral reasons for action. It is possible for there to be a concrete context C which determines operative bodies of legal norms P_l, moral norms P_m, and all-things-considered norms P_n such that P_l implies that one does α, but neither P_m nor P_n implies that one does α (even in the absence of any defeating circumstances).

(ii) Moral facts (properties, truths) aren't among the fundamental grounds of law.

(iii) Accepting a body of legal norms essentially involves having certain motivational dispositions to act in accordance with those norms. In order for a belief ascription about the law ('x believes that, in view of the law, φ') to be correctly interpreted with respect to $\mathbf{P}_l$, and for the subject's state of mind to characterize a given value P_l, the subject must intend and be disposed to act in accordance with P_l, criticize others for failing to act in accordance with P_l, not criticize others for criticizing, and express one's criticism with evaluative and directive uses of language (cf. Shapiro 2006, 1163).

(iv) In order for a body of legal norms P_l to be determined by a concrete community C, it must be the case that the legal officials in C take up the sort of practical attitude toward P_l described in (iii).

Claims (iii)–(iv) plausibly reflect the central roles of the internal point of view in Hart's theory: they specify a kind of motivation that individuals take toward the law,[25] they provide a necessary condition for the existence of law in a community, and they capture apparent assumptions about the normativity of law in legal discourse and practice (Shapiro 2006). These claims about the nature of legal judgment are compatible with the positivist theses about the nature and normativity of law in (i)–(ii).

To be clear, I am not suggesting that Discourse Contextualism commits one to a positivist metaphysics or to treating legal judgment as essentially practical. It doesn't. Discourse Contextualism offers a way of representing the conventional meanings of deontic modals, and of modeling how uses of deontic modals conventionally change the context. It doesn't commit one to substantive views about the nature of law or legal judgment. These are extra-semantic issues in (meta)normative theory, philosophy of law, and psychology. Maintaining this sort of neutrality is often taken to be a distinctive feature of expressivist theories (and their kin);[26] Dworkin (1986, 2011) arguably claims it for his version of interpretivism. Yet we can now see that contextualism—even a version of contextualism supplemented with a positivist theory of law—can capture the idea as well.

Bringing our discussion full circle, let's return to Raz's "problem of the normativity of law." Various Discourse-Contextualist-based accounts of legal discourse and practice are possible depending on one's broader philosophical commitments. Some readers may find this conclusion unsatisfying. ("I was looking for a paper on law, not 'law'!" says a frustrated reader.) Such a reaction would be premature. In this section we have seen how, perhaps contrary to initial appearances, the positivist can coherently maintain that expressions such as 'must', 'ought', etc. have a constant meaning in moral and legal contexts, without necessarily treating

25 See Toh (2005, 2011) for further discussion of the psychology and practical character of legal judgment in Hart's theory. For general discussion of the psychology of norm acceptance, and of legal norm acceptance in particular, see Gibbard (1990) and Railton (this volume), respectively.

26 See, e.g., Gibbard (1990, ch. 1; 2003, ch. 2), Chrisman (2007, 243), Silk (2013).

legal discourse as committing one to moral approval of the law or treating legal judgment as a species of moral judgment. Examining Raz's argument highlights a more general lesson and feature of the account. Discourse Contextualism provides a framework for perspicuously articulating questions about the nature of law and legal judgment. Delineating these issues, and distinguishing them from the semantics proper, can free up our inquiry to better track philosophical issues of primary concern. This can motivate clearer answers and a more refined understanding of the space of overall theories.[27] Discourse Contextualism provides a solid linguistic foundation for a broader (meta)normative theory and theory of law.

VI. Conclusion

The central aims of this chapter have been twofold: first, to begin to develop an improved account of the meaning and use of various types of legal claims, focusing on deontic modals; second, to illustrate how this account can help advance dialectics in debates about the normativity and metaphysics of law. The proposed account draws on a more general framework for developing a contextualist theory, which I call *Discourse Contextualism* (Silk 2016). I have argued that we can derive various discourse properties of deontic modals in legal contexts from a particular contextualist interpretation of a standard semantics for modals, and general principles of interpretation and conversation. Discourses expressing fundamental legal agreement and disagreement can be understood in terms of speakers' assumptions about what body of legal norms is determined by their conversational situation. Claims of law, or Hartian "internal" legal claims, presuppose a lexically unspecified value for a discourse-level parameter representing the legal norms operative in the context. In using deontic modals speakers can exploit their mutual grammatical and world knowledge, and general pragmatic reasoning skills, to manage the value of this parameter and coordinate on evolving normative view.

The proposed treatment of deontic modals' meaning and discourse function can be integrated with broader theorizing in philosophy of law and (meta)normative theory. Discourse Contextualism provides a framework for posing further questions about the nature and normativity of law, the relation between law and morality, and the practical character of legal language and judgment. Delineating these issues can refine our understanding of the space of overall theories and motivate more fruitful ways the dialectics may proceed. Notably, our discussion brings into relief a kind of overall theory which combines features many have argued to be incompatible: a positivist metaphysics, a treatment of legal judgment as essentially practical and action-guiding, and a semantics/pragmatics of fundamental legal disagreement. A Discourse Contextualist account of deontic modals' meaning and use provides a linguistic foundation for a broader account of legal discourse and practice.

[27] For points in a similar spirit, see Forrester (1989, chs. 2, 13), Plunkett and Sundell (2013b, 275–277), Silk (2013, 2015a, 2015b, 2016), Plunkett and Shapiro (2017). See Silk (2016, §§3.6, 5.4, 7.5) for further discussion on the relations among the formal semantics, metasemantics, and (meta)normative theory, and the role of truth-value judgments in semantic theorizing.

The development and defense of Discourse Contextualism in this chapter is by no means complete. For instance, I have focused only on deontic modal verbs. Yet there are important differences among normative readings with different categories of expressions. It is nontrivial how precisely to implement a Discourse Contextualist account in each case. Objections concerning disagreement are certainly not the only challenges facing contextualist semantics. More thorough comparisons of the discourse properties and embedding behavior of various types of paradigm context-sensitive expressions and normative uses of language is required. (For starts on these issues, see Silk 2016, 2017, 2018.) Developing a Discourse-Contextualist-based overall theory will require careful examination of how the semantic, metasemantic, and extralinguistic issues interact and constrain theory choice. Detailed comparison with alternative frameworks will be necessary. I leave developments of a more general Discourse Contextualist account, and evaluation of its prospects, for future research.

References

Asher, Nicholas, and Alex Lascarides. 2003. *Logics of Conversation*. Cambridge: Cambridge University Press.

_____. 2013. "Strategic Conversation." *Semantics and Pragmatics* 6:1–62.

Ayer, A.J. 1936. *Language, Truth, and Logic*. New York: Dover.

Bach, Kent, and Robert Harnish. 1979. *Linguistic Communication and Speech Acts*. Cambridge, MA: MIT Press.

Björnsson, Gunnar, and Stephen Finlay. 2010. Metaethical Contextualism Defended. *Ethics* 121:7–36.

Cappelen, Herman. 2008. "Content Relativism and Semantic Blindness." In *Relative Truth*, edited by Manuel García-Carpintero and Max Kölbel. Oxford: Oxford University Press, pp. 265–286.

Chrisman, Matthew. 2007. "From Epistemic Contextualism to Epistemic Expressivism." *Philosophical Studies* 135:225–254.

Clark, Herbert H., and Deanna Wilkes-Gibbs. 1986. "Referring as a Collaborative Process." *Cognition* 22:1–39.

Coleman, Jules L. 2001. *The Practice of Principle*. Oxford: Oxford University Press.

Coleman, Jules L., and Ori Simchen. 2003. "Law." *Legal Theory* 9:1–41.

Dowell, J. L. 2011. "A Flexible Contextualist Account of Epistemic Modals." *Philosophers' Imprint* 11:1–25.

_____. 2012. "Contextualist Solutions to Three Puzzles about Practical Conditionals." In *Oxford Studies in Metaethics, Vol. 7*, edited by Russ Shafer-Landau. Oxford: Oxford University Press, pp. 271–303.

Dreier, James. 1990. "Internalism and Speaker Relativism." *Ethics* 101:6–26.

_____. 2009. "Relativism (and Expressivism) and the Problem of Disagreement." *Philosophical Perspectives* 23:79–110.

Dworkin, Ronald. 1986. *Law's Empire*. Cambridge, MA: Harvard University Press.

_____. 1994. Hart's Posthumous Reply. (ms), New York University.

_____. 2011. *Justice for Hedgehogs*. Cambridge, MA: Harvard University Press.

Egan, Andy, John Hawthorne, and Brian Weatherson. 2005. "Epistemic Modals in Context." In *Contextualism in Philosophy: Knowledge, Meaning, and Truth*, edited by Gerhard Preyer and Georg Peter. Oxford: Oxford University Press, pp. 131–168.

Field, Hartry. 2009. "Epistemology without Metaphysics." *Philosophical Studies* 143:249–290.

Finlay, Stephen. 2009. "Oughts and Ends." *Philosophical Studies* 143:315–340.

_____. 2014. *Confusion of Tongues: A Theory of Normative Language*. New York: Oxford University Press.

von Fintel, Kai, and Anthony S. Gillies. 2008. "CIA Leaks." *The Philosophical Review* 117:77–98.

_____. 2011. "'Might' Made Right." In *Epistemic Modality*, edited by Andy Egan and Brian Weatherson. Oxford: Oxford University Press, pp. 108–130.

Forrester, James William. 1989. *Why You Should: The Pragmatics of Deontic Speech*. Hanover, NH: Brown University Press.

Garrod, Simon, and Gwyneth Doherty. 1994. "Conversation, Co-ordination and Convention: An Empirical Investigation of How Groups Establish Linguistic Conventions." *Cognition* 53:181–215.

Gibbard, Allan. 1990. *Wise Choices, Apt Feelings: A Theory of Normative Judgment*. Cambridge, MA: Harvard University Press.

_____. 2003. *Thinking How to Live*. Cambridge, MA: Harvard University Press.

Grice, Paul. 1989. *Studies in the Ways of Words*. Cambridge, MA: Harvard University Press.

Hare, R.M. 1952. *The Language of Morals*. Oxford: Oxford University Press.

Hart, H.L.A. 1959. "Scandinavian Realism." In Hart 1983, *Essays in Jurisprudence and Philosophy*. Oxford: Oxford University Press, pp. 161–169.

_____. 1961/1994. *The Concept of Law*, 2nd ed. Oxford: Oxford University Press.

_____. 1982. *Essays on Bentham: Jurisprudence and Political Theory*. Oxford: Clarendon Press.

Heim, Irene. 1991. "Articles and Definiteness." In *Semantics: An International Handbook of Contemporary Research*, edited by Arnim von Stechow and Dieter Wunderlich. Berlin: de Gruyter, pp. 487–535.

Hobbs, Jerry R., Mark Stickel, and Paul Martin. 1993. "Interpretation as Abduction." *Artificial Intelligence* 63:69–142.

Kelsen, Hans. 1967. *The Pure Theory of Law*. Berkeley: University of California Press.

Kölbel, Max. 2004. "Indexical Relativism versus Genuine Relativism." *International Journal of Philosophical Studies* 12:297–313.

Korsgaard, Christine M. 1996. *The Sources of Normativity*. Cambridge: Cambridge University Press.

Kramer, Matthew H. 2008. Review of Arthur Ripstein (ed.), *Ronald Dworkin. Notre Dame Philosophical Reviews*, https://ndpr.nd.edu/news/ 23307-ronald-dworkin/.

Kratzer, Angelika. 1977. "What 'Must' and 'Can' Must and Can Mean." *Linguistics and Philosophy* 1: 337–355.

_____. 1981. "The Notional Category Of Modality." In *Words, Worlds, and Contexts: New Approaches in Word Semantics*, edited by Hans-Jürgen Eikmeyer and Hannes Rieser. Berlin: de Gruyter, pp. 38–74.

_____. 1991. "Modality/Conditionals." In *Semantics: An International Handbook of Contemporary Research*, edited by Arnim von Stechow and Dieter Wunderlich. New York: de Gruyter, pp. 639–656.

Lasersohn, Peter. 2005. "Context Dependence, Disagreement, and Predicates of Personal Taste." *Linguistics and Philosophy* 28: 643–686.

Leiter, Brian. 2007. "Beyond the Hart/Dworkin Debate: The Methodology Problem in Jurisprudence." In *Naturalizing Jurisprudence: Essays on American Legal Realism and Naturalism in Legal Philosophy*, edited by Brian Leiter. Oxford: Oxford University Press, pp. 153–184.

_____. 2009. "Explaining Theoretical Disagreement." *University of Chicago Law Review* 76:1215–1250.

Levinson, Stephen C. 1987. "Minimization and Conversational Inference." In *The Pragmatic Perspective,* edited by Jef Verschueren and Marcella Bertuccelli Papi. Amsterdam: John Benjamins, pp. 61–130.

Lewis, David. 1979. "Scorekeeping in a Language Game." *Journal of Philosophical Logic* 8:339–359.

Lochbaum, Karen E. 1998. "A Collaborative Planning Model of Intentional Structure." *Computational Linguistics* 24:525–572.

Lyons, John. 1977. *Semantics, Vol. 2*. Cambridge: Cambridge University Press.

_____. 1995. *Linguistic Semantics: An Introduction*. Cambridge: Cambridge University Press.

MacFarlane, John. 2007. "Relativism and Disagreement." *Philosophical Studies* 132:17–31.

_____. 2010. Epistemic Modals: Relativism vs. Cloudy Contextualism (ms). Chambers Philosophy Conference on Epistemic Modals, University of Nebraska.

_____. 2014. *Assessment Sensitivity: Relative Truth and Its Applications*. Oxford: Clarendon Press.

Marmor, Andrei. 2008. "The Pragmatics of Legal Language." *Ratio Juris* 21:423–452.

Moore, G.E. 1912. *Ethics*. Oxford: Oxford University Press.

Narrog, Heiko. 2005. "Modality, Mood, and Change of Modal Meanings: A New Perspective." *Cognitive Linguistics* 16:677–731.

Parfit, Derek. 2011. *On What Matters, Vol. 2*. Oxford: Oxford University Press.

Plunkett, David. 2015. "Which Concepts Should We Use? Metalinguistic Negotiations and the Methodology of Philosophy." *Inquiry* 58:828–874.

Plunkett, David, and Scott Shapiro. 2017. "Law, Morality, and Everything Else: General Jurisprudence as a Branch of Metanormative Inquiry." *Ethics* 128:37–68.

Plunkett, David, and Tim Sundell. 2013a. "Disagreement and the Semantics of Normative and Evaluative Terms." *Philosophers' Imprint* 13:1–37.

_____. 2013b. "Dworkin's Interpretivism and the Pragmatics of Legal Disputes." *Legal Theory* 19:242–281.

Portner, Paul. 2007. "Imperatives and Modals." *Natural Language Semantics* 15:351–383.

Railton, Peter. 2009. "Practical Competence and Fluent Agency." In *Reasons for Action*, edited by David Sobel and Steven Wall. Cambridge: Cambridge University Press, pp. 81–115.

_____. 2012. "Nietzsche's Normative Theory? The Art and Skill of Living Well." In *Nietzsche, Naturalism, and Normativity*, edited by Christopher Janaway and Simon Robertson. New York: Oxford University Press, pp. 20–51.

_____. this volume. "'We'll see you in court!': The Rule of Law as an Explanatory and Normative Kind."

Raz, Joseph. 1975/1990. *Practical Reason and Norms*, 2nd ed. Oxford: Oxford University Press.

_____. 1977. "Legal Validity." In Raz 1979/2009, *The Authority of Law*, 2nd ed. Oxford: Clarendon Press, pp. 146–159.

_____. 1979. "Legal Positivism and the Sources of Law. In Raz 1979/2009, *The Authority of Law*, 2nd ed. Oxford: Clarendon Press, pp. 37–52.

_____. 1981. "The Purity of the Pure Theory. In Raz 1979/2009. *The Authority of Law*, 2nd ed. Oxford: Clarendon Press, pp. 293–312.

_____. 1993. "H.L.A. Hart (1907–1992)." *Utilitas* 5:145–156.

_____. 1998. "Two Views of the Nature of the Theory of Law: A Partial Comparison." *Legal Theory* 4:249–282.

Richard, Mark. 2008. *When Truth Gives Out*. Oxford: Oxford University Press.

Shapiro, Scott J. 2006. "What Is the Internal Point of View?" *Fordham Law Review* 75:1157–1170.

_____. 2007. "The 'Hart-Dworkin' Debate: A Short Guide for the Perplexed." In *Ronald Dworkin*, edited by Arthur Ripstein. Cambridge: Cambridge University Press, pp. 22–55.

Silk, Alex. 2013. "Truth-Conditions and the Meanings of Ethical Terms." In *Oxford Studies in Metaethics, Vol. 8*, edited by Russ Shafer-Landau. New York: Oxford University Press, pp. 195–222.

_____. 2014. "Accommodation and Negotiation with Context-Sensitive Expressions." *Thought* 3:115–123.

_____. 2015a. "Normative Language in Context." In *Oxford Studies in Metaethics, Vol. 12*, edited by Russ Shafer-Landau. Oxford: Oxford University Press, pp. 206–243.

_____. 2015b. "What Normative Terms Mean and Why It Matters for Ethical Theory." In *Oxford Studies in Normative Ethics, Vol. 5*, edited by Mark Timmons. Oxford: Oxford University Press, pp. 296–325.

_____. 2016. *Discourse Contextualism: A Framework for Contextualist Semantics and Pragmatics*. Oxford: Oxford University Press.

_____. 2017. "How to Embed an Epistemic Modal: Attitude Problems and Other Defects of Character." *Philosophical Studies* 174:1773–1799.

_____. 2018. Semantics with Assignment Variables (ms). University of Birmingham, https://goo.gl/kFVhw3.

Simons, Mandy. 2007. Presupposition and Cooperation (ms). Carnegie Mellon University.

Stalnaker, Robert. 1974. "Pragmatic Presuppositions." In Stalnaker 1999, *Context and Content: Essays on Intentionality in Speech and Thought*. Oxford: Oxford University Press, pp. 47–62.

_____. 1978. "Assertion." In Stalnaker 1999, *Context and Content: Essays on Intentionality in Speech and Thought*. Oxford: Oxford University Press, pp. 78–95.

_____. 2002. "Common Ground." *Linguistics and Philosophy* 25:701–721.

_____. 2014. *Context*. New York: Oxford University Press.

Starr, William. 2010. *Conditionals, Meaning, and Mood*. PhD thesis, Rutgers University.

Stevenson, Charles L. 1937. "The Emotive Meaning of Ethical Terms." *Mind* 46:14–31.

Stevenson, Charles L. 1963. "Relativism and Nonrelativism in the Theory of Value." In Stevenson, *Facts and Values: Studies in Ethical Analysis*. New Haven, CT: Yale University Press, pp. 71–93 .

Sundell, Timothy. 2011. "Disagreements about Taste." *Philosophical Studies* 155:267–288.

Swanson, Eric. 2016. "The Application of Constraint Semantics to the Language of Subjective Uncertainty." *Journal of Philosophical Logic* 45:121–146.

Thomason, Richmond H. 2002. "Combinations of Tense and Modality." In *Handbook of Philosophical Logic, Vol. 7*, 2nd ed., edited by Dov M. Gabbay and Franz Guenthner. Dordrecht: Kluwer, pp. 205–234.

Thomason, Richmond H., Matthew Stone, and David DeVault. 2006. "Enlightened Update: A Computational Architecture for Presupposition and Other Pragmatic Phenomena." In *Presupposition Accommodation*, edited by Donna Byron, Craige Roberts, and Scott Schwenter. Columbus, OH: OSU Pragmatics Initiative.

Thomson, Judith Jarvis. 1996. "Evaluatives and Directives." In *Moral Relativism and Moral Objectivity*, edited by Gilbert Harman and Judith Jarvis Thomson. Cambridge: Blackwell, pp. 125–154.

Toh, Kevin. 2005. "Hart's Expressivism and His Benthamite Project." *Legal Theory* 11:75–123.

_____. 2007. "Raz on Detachment, Acceptance, and Describability." *Oxford Journal of Legal Studies* 27:414–421.

_____. 2011. "Legal Judgments as Plural Acceptances of Norms." In *Oxford Studies in Philosophy of Law*, edited by Leslie Green and Brian Leiter. Oxford: Oxford University Press, pp. 107–137.

Verstraete, Jean-Christophe. 2007. *Rethinking the Coordinate-Subordinate Dichotomy: Interpersonal Grammar and the Analysis of Adverbial Clauses in English*. Berlin: Mouton de Gruyter.

von Wright, Georg Henrik. 1963. *Norm and Action: A Logical Inquiry*. London: Routledge and Kegan Paul.

Wróblewski, Jerzy. 1983. *Meaning and Truth in Judicial Decision*, 2nd ed. Helsinki: A-Tieto Oy.

Yalcin, Seth. 2012. "Bayesian Expressivism." *Proceedings of the Aristotelian Society* 112:123–160.

_____. 2014. "Semantics and Metasemantics in the Context of Generative Grammar." In *Metasemantics: New Essays on the Foundations of Meaning*, edited by Alexis Burgess and Brett Sherman. Oxford: Oxford University Press, pp. 17–54.

14 Authority and Interest in the Theory of Right

Katharina Nieswandt*

I. Introduction: A Tale of Two Incompatible Theories and a Counterproposal

There currently are two dominant theories of right, the *Will Theory* and the *Interest Theory*. Both theories have long-known problems, and both are commonly regarded as incompatible with the other.[1] According to Will Theory, to possess a right is to be able to enforce or waive some duty on the part of another person.[2] Thus, Will Theory's main claim says:

(W) *X* possesses a right *R* iff *X* is able to enforce (or waive) a duty of another person, where this duty is correlative to *R*.

Section IV discusses what it would mean to "be able to enforce (or waive) a duty of another person," but at the current stage our formulation of *W* must be vague enough so as to include a number of different interpretations of Will Theory.

* I am deeply grateful to the many colleagues who commented on earlier drafts: Thomas Breed, Michael Goodhart, Steven Engstrom, Michael Kessler, Oded Na'aman, Josiah Ober, Japa Pallikkathayil, Michael Thompson, Kevin Toh, Grégoire Webber, and particularly to Ulf Hlobil. Your advice and questions were invaluable. I furthermore thank the Andrew W. Mellon Foundation for funding my research during this time.

[1] See, e.g., Cruft (2013a, 196–198). Strictly speaking, the names "Will Theory" and "Interest Theory" denote families of theories. Given that I am only interested in the central idea uniting each family, I shall use the singular.

[2] See, e.g., Steiner (2013, 231); Steiner (1998, 238); (Simmonds (1998, 214–215); or: Preda (2012, 230). The locus classicus is (Hart 1982, 182–183).

Dimensions of Normativity. David Plunkett, Scott J. Shapiro, and Kevin Toh.

Will Theory's main historical root is Kant's "Doctrine of Right." Kant regards freedom from the interference of others as a prerequisite of human agency. He infers from this a *right* to this freedom, which we cannot deny to anyone without contradicting ourselves. All other rights, Kant argues, are justified restrictions of this freedom right, and their justification lies in the protection of the freedom rights of other people.[3] Some contemporary Will Theorists take this idea one step further. They argue that human agency requires a whole set of basic rights.[4] One attraction of the Kantian framework is that it promises to give a non-normative and hence less contested justification for something that is normative and is highly contested: Mere metaphysical considerations about agency are supposed to justify a substantial catalogue of basic rights. One problem with Will Theory's main claim, *W*, however, is its implication that people who are unable to enforce any duties (such as comatose patients or babies) are unable to possess any rights.

According to the competing Interest Theory, to possess a right is to possess an interest that puts another person under some duty.[5] Thus, Interest Theory's main claim says:

(I) *X* possesses a right *R* iff *X* has an interest that grounds a duty of another person.

Sections VI–VIII discuss what it would mean for someone's interest to "ground a duty of another person," but at the current stage *I*, too, must remain sufficiently vague.

Interest Theory starts from the plausible idea that rights serve a function and that rights usually benefit the right-holder. Bentham is often cited as the first proponent of this idea,[6] but there are virtue ethicist versions, too.[7] One attraction of Interest Theory is that it grants rights to everyone who has interests, which certainly includes comatose patients and babies and which could easily be extended to animals, too. One problem with Interest Theory's main claim, *I*, however, is its implication that we are unable to possess rights that exclusively or mainly protect the interests of others. (An example is the right to governmental child support, which is a right of parents, but intended to protect the interest of their children).[8] Most Will and most Interest Theorists see their theory as incompatible with the other; "the debates between them are often intense [. . .][and] seemingly interminable."[9]

Against this standoff, I offer the following proposal: (1) Will and Interest Theory are falsely seen as complete (and hence incompatible) theories of right. We need Will Theory's

---

[3] (Kant 1909/1797, 230–232). H. L. A Hart (1955) gives a defense of these claims without presupposing the larger Kantian framework in "Are There Any Natural Rights?."

[4] See especially the work Alan Gewirth (1962), such as *Human Rights: Essays on Justification and Applications*, James Griffin's (2008, 29–51) *On Human Rights* also grounds human rights in action-theoretic considerations, but Griffin does not regard all denials of these rights as contradictory (Griffin, 4).

[5] See, e.g., Kramer (2013, 246); Kramer (2010, 32); (May 2012, 116, 25); Raz (2007, 235–236); and Raz's (1986, 166) influential *The Morality of Freedom*. The original proposal is by David Lyons (1969, 173) "Rights, Claimants and Beneficiaries."

[6] See Lyons (1969, 173).

[7] Most influential among these has been John Finnis (1980), *Natural Law and Natural Right*, see especially (198–225).

[8] This counterexample is by Raz himself, who tries to solve it through the idea of doubly harmonious interests; see Raz (1994, 50) "Rights and Individual Well-Being."

[9] (Wenar 2011/2005, see section 2.2.2, §13.)

key concept of *authority*, in order to *specify what it is* to possess a right, while we must appeal to *interests*, in order to *justify* rights. (2) Will Theory's misconception of the role of authority and Interest Theory's misconception of the role of interest both result from a failure to distinguish three questions: What prohibitions, commands and permissions does a given right authorize? What interests does this right protect?, and: Who possesses this right? In other words, both Will and Interest Theory fail to distinguish between the *definition* of rights, their *justification* and their *possession*. (3) Once we make these distinctions, we can redefine the roles of authority and interest in a way that avoids Will and Interest Theory's standard problems. I shall call the resulting theory the *Modal Theory of Right*, since the proper understanding of authority and interest will turn out to be through understanding a specific use of modal auxiliary verbs.

I proceed as follows: Section II argues that the most recent and refined attempt to show the incompatibility of Will and Interest Theory fails. Section III distinguishes three questions that any complete theory of right would have to answer: the above-mentioned questions of the definition, the justification, and the possession of rights. Section IV then discusses Will Theory. I show that Will Theory's standard problem is larger than commonly discussed and that it stems from a missing explanation of how rights authorize. I suggest such an explanation, which I summarize as the first claim of Modal Theory, *M1* (Section V). The suggested understanding of the relation between authority and rights avoids Will Theory's standard problem, and it answers the definition question. Section VI then turns to Interest Theory. I suggest an alternative understanding of the relation between interests and rights, which I summarize as the second claim of Modal Theory, *M2*. *M2* answers the justification question. I then show that *M2* avoids Interest Theory's standard problem, and that it captures the actual role of interest in debates about rights, while Interest Theory misconstrues this role (Section VIII). As a last step, Section IX addresses the question of possession, the answer to which is *M3*, the third and last claim of Modal Theory. Section X summarizes my results.

I start from the premise that authority and interest are key elements of any correct theory of right. My argument hence is conditional: if authority and interest are to play a central role in the theory of right, it will be the one described below.

II. *Excursus:* Will and Interest Theory Have Not Been Shown to Be Incompatible

Neophytes to the debate might be surprised to learn that Will and Interest Theory are commonly regarded as incompatible: Don't they stress different aspects of rights, rather than contradict each other? Couldn't we hold, for example, that to possess a property right in one's savings is (among other things) to be able to enforce a bank clerk's duty to pay out the respective amount *and* at the same time hold that the bank clerk's duty is grounded in one's interest? In other words, is it not plausible to assume that rights are characterized by both, the authority they confer over other people's behavior *and* the fact that this authority protects an interest? This understanding does indeed come close to the view I shall offer below. The current section is intended to alleviate principled worries regarding the very idea of such a hybrid theory. Readers who are unfamiliar with the history of the debate might want to skip this meta-dialectical excursus and proceed to Section III.

Previous hybrid proposals (such as Gopal Sreenivasan's)[10] have been criticized by both Will and Interest Theorists.[11] This criticism, however, has not established that Will and Interest Theory's key ideas are indeed incompatible. The most developed and probably best-known principled objection to hybrid theories of right is by the Interest Theorist Matthew Kramer. Kramer argues that the incompatibility of Will and Interest Theory is readily apparent from the following formulations of the two theories: A Will Theorist considers it "necessary and sufficient" that a right-holder, *X*, be "competent and authorized to demand/waive the enforcement of the duty that is correlative to the right." By contrast, an Interest Theorist considers this "neither necessary nor sufficient," while fulfillment of a second criterion is "necessary," viz. that the duty correlative to the right "normatively protects some aspect of *X*'s situation that on balance is typically beneficial for a being like *X*."[12] In short, Kramer argues that Will Theory's claim that a certain condition is "necessary and sufficient" is incompatible with the claim that there is a further necessary condition—specified by Interest Theory.[13] But this inference is invalid: If a first criterion, C_W, is sufficient for *X* to have a right, this does not logically exclude that a second criterion, C_I, is necessary for *X* to have a right, since C_W and C_I might not be independent of each other. For the two criteria in question such a dependency is indeed not just possible, but highly plausible: One of the main claims of the theory I suggest below is that the relevant type of authority (demanded by C_W) only exists where the relevant type of interest does (demanded by C_I). (See Section VI for this.)

In addition, nothing about the two criteria themselves suggests that either of them is sufficient. In the case of our property example, we could consider it necessary for the customer to be "competent and authorized" to demand payment *and* consider it necessary for this payment to be in her interest, in order for the customer to have a right to the payment. Prima facie, there is no problem with the assumption that the two criteria are compatible, while none of them alone suffices.

The most developed principled argument for "the untenability of a sophisticated hybrid theory of rights"[14] hence depends on two implausible assumptions: first, that the relevant kind of authority, demanded by the Will-Theoretic criterion, does not derive from facts about the right-holder's interests; second, that this criterion must be understood as a sufficient condition. There hence seem to be no principled objections against the project of a hybrid theory.

---

[10] See (Sreenivasan 2005).

[11] See, e.g., Kramer and Steiner (2007, 308–310).

[12] (Kramer 2013, 246–247).

[13] Kramer repeats this argument in various places, for example in his contribution to Whittington, Kelemen, and Caldeira (2008, 417–418). There (see propositions *I-1* and *W-1*), as well as in the above-quoted article (see propositions *I-2* and *W*), he actually states Interest Theory in such a way that the negation of Will Theory is an independent und unconnected part of Interest Theory. Given that *any* theory, regardless of its content, could be made incompatible with Interest Theory through adding the negation of Interest Theory to it, this part of the discussion shall be ignored here.

[14] (Kramer 2013, 245).

III. Three Questions for a Theory of Right

In the introduction, I distinguished three questions, which we can ask with respect to any given right *R*:

(Definition) What prohibitions, commands and permissions does *R* authorize?
(Justification) What interests does *R* protect?
(Possession) Who possesses *R*?

The debate so far, I believe, suffers from a failure to distinguish these three questions. A recast version of Will Theory, I suggest, would answer the definition question. A recast version of Interest Theory would answer the justification question. And once these two questions are answered, the possession question becomes a simple empirical question.

Recently, Will and Interest Theory are often understood as attempts to answer the possession question. Following Wenar,[15] this interpretative shift is a reaction to their decade-long standoff: We might be able to explain what rights are, by explaining their Hohfeldian logical correlative, duties.[16] Right-based duties, some believe, differ from other duties—for example, duties of benevolence—in that they are *directed* at (i.e., owed to) the possessor of the right.[17] (The bank clerk's duty to pay the money, e.g., is directed at *me*.) The hope is that an explication of "directed duty" could then serve to explicate the concept "right." On this understanding, Hohfeld has given us an analysis of rights through duties, but has failed to separate right-based duties from other duties, such as duties of benevolence.

I doubt whether the distinction of right-based versus other duties does indeed line up with the distinction of directed versus non-directed duties.[18] All right-based duties might be directed, but it seems that at least some other duties are directed, too: Isn't, e.g., my duty to offer my seat on the bus to the pregnant passenger now entering owed to *that* passenger? But unless I happen to sit on a seat reserved for people with special needs, she certainly has no right to my seat.

The interpretation of Will and Interest Theory as different theories of the possession of rights, however, is also problematic for a further reason: If what I shall say below about rights is correct, then it would render both theories superfluous. We simply do not need a theory of the possession of rights anymore if we have a theory of their definition and their justification.

IV. Will Theory's Main Problem: What Means "Can Enforce?"

The standard accusation against Will Theory says that it denies rights across the board to certain groups of people. Those who are generally unable to enforce any rights—such as patients

[15] (Wenar 2011/2005, section 2.2.2, §§16–17.)

[16] (Hohfeld 1913, 9).

[17] See, e.g., Cruft (2013b), and Căbulea May (2012).

[18] For a summary of counterarguments against the explication of rights through directed duties see Hedahl (2013, 2).

in a coma or babies—cannot have any rights within Will Theory. This accusation, I shall argue, points to a consequence of Will Theory's basic problem rather than its root. Will Theory's basic problem runs much deeper: Any possible interpretation that we can give of the concept "ability to enforce" in a moral context is either false (in that it denies rights to people who seem to have them) or is empty.

Modern Will Theory started as a descriptive account of the role of rights within Anglo-Saxon law.[19] In other words, its original aim was to analyze the form and function of *legal* rights (within one particular legal system). Inspired by Kant, Hart famously characterized legal rights as restrictions on the freedom of others, which the right-holder may *enforce*. It is the holder of such a legal right "who is a small scale sovereign" for Hart.[20] In this legal context, *to enforce* simply means *to sue*, should the other party not willfully heed to your demand.[21]

Contemporary Will Theory has extended its domain of application: Will Theory now is a theory of rights in general: moral rights, legal rights and more—some current discussions of rights even include the "rights" of players in games.[22]Where moral rights are concerned, Will Theory has furthermore become a normative theory: The right-holder is morally entitled to restrict the choices of others, and these others *wrong* the right-holder if they don't comply. At the same time, Will Theory has kept Hart's characterization of the right-holder as sovereign and of rights as demands against others which the right-holder is able to enforce. Outside of a legal framework, however, it becomes unclear what it means *to be able to enforce* such a demand (or to be *authorized and competent* to do so, as Kramer puts it). In the legal case, an official system of rules is in place, as are institutions that watch over these rules, change them, promulgate them, punish transgressions, settle disagreements about the rules etc. Within such a rule-governed practice with permanent social institutions, "enforcement" has a clear meaning: The holder of a legal right is able to enforce that legal right in the sense that she has standing to sue. Should she be unable to do so (e.g., because of a cognitive deficiency) some proxy will have standing on her behalf. In some situations, she (or the proxy) might decide to waive the right, or it might turn out that the legal institutions are malfunctioning, so that she cannot obtain due process. What it means for her to have the respective right, however, is very clear, even in such cases: There is a legal procedure that can be initiated—an institutional machinery that can be turned on, so to speak—with the aim of extorting what the right-holder has been denied.

---

[19] See Edmundson (2004, 122–125) (Edmundson claims that the problem even occurs within the purely legal context; see 124.)

[20] (Hart 1982, 182.)

[21] "The idea is that of one individual being given by the law exclusive control, more or less extensive, over another person's duty so that in the area of conduct covered by that duty the individual who has the right is a *small scale sovereign* to whom the duty is owed. The fullest measure of control comprises three // distinguishable elements: (i) the right holder may waive or extinguish the duty or leave it in existence; (ii) after breach or threatened breach of a duty *he may leave it 'unenforced' or may 'enforce' it by suing* for compensation or, in certain cases, for injunction or mandatory order to restrain the continued or further breach of duty; and (iii) he may waive or extinguish the obligation to pay compensation to which the breach gives rise." (Hart 1982, 182–183, emphasis added.)

[22] E.g., Wenar (2013, 202.)

One important respect in which moral rights differ from legal rights is that such an official system of rules and social institutions is lacking in the moral case. Without such a system, however, it becomes unclear what it means to say that *X is able to enforce* against *Y* the demands that her right *R* entails. There is no similar set of rules and, more importantly, no machinery in place that *X* could use against *Y*. As far as I can see, enforcement could mean either of three things in the moral case: (1) *X* is *justified* (by the rules of the respective moral practice?) in demanding that *Y* respect the demands that *R* entails *and* she is *able to force Y* to respect the demands that *R* entails. (2) *X* is *justified* in demanding that *Y* respect the demands that *R* entails *and* she is *able to demand* that *Y* respect the demands that *R* entails. (3) *X* is *justified* in demanding that *Y* respect the demands that *R* entails.

None of these three interpretations, though, yields a result that is both plausible *and* interesting: The third interpretation is empty, while the other two also expropriate healthy adults of most of their (apparent) rights. To demonstrate this, let me spell out the result of each interpretation for two exemplary cases: Case 1 are the much discussed comatose and babies. For the second case, imagine the following scenario: *X* leaves the room in the public library and another person, *Y*, takes her unattended laptop computer. Assume furthermore that *X* indeed has a moral and not just a legal right to this computer. Case 2 thus is a scenario where *X* possesses a right, but is unable to defend this right because she is not present to do so. Table 14.1 lists the results for the two scenarios under each of our three interpretations: Let's look at each of the three columns in turn.

Column 1 says that any demand of yours can only count as a right if you are in a position to force others to respect it. This assigns no rights to those in *row 1*, since they are unable to force anyone to do anything. But equally unable is the healthy adult from *row 2*, who, given her absence, cannot force *Y* to respect her (supposed) right in the computer. She, too, has no right on this interpretation. But few would assume that our property rights cease as soon as we leave the room; so this first interpretation seems implausible.

Notice two things about the first interpretation before we proceed: (1) The problem that absent healthy adults lose their property rights cannot be solved by interposing a proxy—say,

TABLE 14.1

Outcome *(right/no right)* for two scenarios on three interpretations of Will Theory

		Interpretation 1	*Interpretation 2*	*Interpretation 3*
		X is "able to enforce" her right *R* against *Y* if . . .		
		. . . *X* is *justified* in demanding that *Y* respect the demands that *R* entails and *X* is *able to force Y* to respect the demands that *R* entails.	. . . *X* is *justified* in de-manding this and *X* is *able to demand* this.	. . . *X* is *justified* in demanding this.
Case 1	*X* is comatose or a baby.	—	—	√
Case 2	*X* is a healthy, absent adult.	—	—	√

the police or "the state." For this proxy incurs the same problem as *X* herself; that is, it will not always be able to force *Y* to respect the demands that *X*'s right entails. (The police, for instance, might never catch *Y*.) (2) Notice also that *X* would not have a right either if she were present but less powerful than the thief. The first interpretation, in fact, turns all rights into "rights of the strongest."

Column 2, like the previous column, awards no rights to the comatose and babies, as both are unable to demand anything. What about the absent adult from *row 2*? Given her absence, she, too, is unable to demand that the other respect those demands that her property right in the computer entails (such as: not to take this item without her permission). Hence, she, too, has no right on the second interpretation, and hence this second interpretation is as implausible as the first. (Notice that a proxy-solution would fail for the same reason as before: the proxy will not always be able to demand of *Y* that *Y* respect the demands that *X*'s right entails.)

At his point, Will Theorists might object by saying that I misunderstand what "being able to" means in our context. A Will Theorist might say: "Healthy adult *X* is *currently* not in a position to demand that *Y* leave her computer alone, because of certain accidental circumstances—*X* happens to have left the room. But if *X* returned the next moment, she would be able to demand this. The inabilities of those in *row 2* are accidental, while the inabilities of those in *row 1* are inabilities in principle; hence it seems unfair to assign the same negative outcome to both. For while Will Theory admittedly has a problem with the comatose and babies, the suggested problem with the absent adult could easily be solved if we added 'in principle' to the interpretation listed in *column 2*." Following this reply, *column 2* would be modified so as to read: "*X* is justified in demanding this and *X* is, in principle, able to demand this." Presupposing that our Will Theorist can spell out a suitable notion of "in principle," this modification would indeed allow absent adults to keep their property rights. Nevertheless, this modification is not an option as it would make the well-known problem from *row 1* unsolvable: Prior to our modification, the claim that babies and comatose adults cannot have any rights was just an unwelcome consequence of Will Theory, which its proponents could still hope to circumvent in the future. But once we define right-holders as those who are *in principle* able to demand what their right entails, we rule out rights for babies and comatose adults by definition. Thus, the suggested modification only worsens Will Theory's situation.[23] Our Will Theorist might react to this by altering her proposal as follows: "Let's keep the supplement 'in principle', but give it a different reading. Instead of saying that the comatose and the baby's inability constitute inabilities in principle and that this is what distinguishes their inability from that of the healthy adult, let's treat both groups alike, as originally suggested, and say that they all are 'in principle able, though currently unable' to demand what *R* entails: the healthy adult could demand this if she were to step into the room, the comatose if she were to awake from her coma, the baby, had she already grown up." This second modification would indeed give us the desired result;

[23] Will Theorists sometimes react to this criticism by saying that they are prepared to bite the bullet of denying rights to the comatose and babies. This move, however, simply means to declare Will Theory the winner in this long-standing debate through claiming that the main objection leveled against Will Theory is insignificant or pales beside its advantages.

that is, those in both rows could now possess rights.[24] Effectively, however, this modification collapses *column 2* into *column 3*. For what could the resulting claim that *X* has a right if "*X* is justified in demanding this and *X* is in principle able to demand this" mean, on our new understanding of "in principle," except that the respective person would be justified in demanding what *R* entails, were she ever factually able to demand this? In other words, what would it say more than that she would be *justified in demanding this*? The latter, however, is precisely the interpretation given in *column 3*—and as the following considerations will show, it is not a tenable interpretation of Will Theory either.

Column 3, in giving a less fastidious criterion, avoids all previous difficulties. Here, someone has a right if she would be justified in making a particular sort of demand. Whether she is able to make this demand (as *column 2* required) or whether she is able to force others to obey her demand (as *column 1* required), any such empirical fact is irrelevant for the question of whether she would be justified in making it. In other words, on the third interpretation, someone's abilities are irrelevant for whether she has a right. What result does this claim yield for our two rows? Since inability does not matter, the fact that those in *row 1* are in principle unable to make demands does not matter; that is, the third interpretation finally allows us to assign rights to comatose and babies. And since inability does not matter, the fact that the absent adult of *row 2* is currently unable to make a demand does not matter; that is, the third interpretation finally allows us to assign her a property right in the computer. Thus, the third interpretation gives the desired result for both test cases and hence seems highly plausible.

The third interpretation, however, deprives Will Theory of all characteristic content. For if we think that "to be *justified* in demanding" has nothing to do with an *ability* to demand (not with a cognitive ability, or with a suitable occasion, or with actual power), then to say: "*X* has a right *R* against *Y* if *X is justified in demanding* that *Y* respect the demands that *R* entails" simply is to say: "*X* has a right *R* against *Y* if *Y is under a duty to respect the demands* to which *R* entitles *X*." *X* has a right against *Y* if *X* is justified in demanding of *Y*, and for *X* to be justified in demanding of *Y* is for *Y* to be under a duty to do as demanded by *X*. On the third interpretation, *X* thus has a right *R* against *Y* if *Y* is under a correlative duty toward *X*. This means, however, that the third interpretation collapses Will Theory into the thin conceptual analysis of the primary meaning of *right* given by Wesley Newcombe Hohfeld.[25] Hohfeld's analysis is almost universally accepted. Most important, it is accepted by Will and Interest Theorists alike. Therefore, if Will Theory does not go beyond Hohfeld's analysis on any point, it ceases to be an independent theory of right at all. Everything that was characteristic of Will Theory—that the right-holder is comparable to a "sovereign," who rules over others (albeit in a very limited domain)—has been removed. The third interpretation

[24] Even this modification would still exclude a type of right that I completely bracketed in this paper: animal rights.

[25] "Recognizing, as we must, the very broad and indiscriminate use of the term, 'right,' what clue do we find, in ordinary legal discourse, toward limiting the word in question to a definite and appropriate meaning? That clue lies in the correlative 'duty,' for it is certain that even those who use the word and the conception 'right' in the broadest possible way are accustomed to thinking of 'duty' as the invariable correlative. [...] In other words, *if X has a right against Y* that he shall stay off the former's land, *the correlative (and equivalent) is that Y is under a duty* toward *X* to stay off the place." (Hohfeld 1913, 9) (emphasis added.)

reduces Will Theory to a definition that its main competitor as well as other, lesser-known alternatives willingly accept—that they, in fact, already contain.

Our result regarding Will Theory's criterion therefore is that, on any nontrivial reading (*columns 1* and *2* of Table 14.1), Will Theory denies most people many of the rights that we take them to have. The commonly discussed cases are just a tiny selection of all the counterexamples that Will Theory actually incurs, and new counterexamples can be generated systematically by imagining situations in which people are currently unable to defend their rights.

V. An Alternative Role for Authority: Claim 1 of the "Modal Theory of Right"

Despite Will Theory's problems, there is something to be said for the claim that what characterizes rights is that rights create a special kind of authority. Rights indeed authorize certain prohibitions, commands, and permissions. Thus, one true description of what it is for *X* to possess a right is that *X* enjoys certain permissions, while others are under certain demands—demands that can be expressed as prohibitions and commands such as the following: "You can't take that—it's *X*'s" (*X* has a property right); "He must do so—he assured *X* that he would" (*X* has a right as promisee); "You can't use that—you'll hurt somebody" (people in general, including *X*, have a right not to be harmed); "You will do such-and-such—and that's an order!," said by *X* herself (*X*, as superior officer, has a right to be obeyed); and so forth . . .

Elizabeth Anscombe regarded the semantics of such prohibitions and commands as the key to an analysis of what rights are. She called them "stopping modals" and "forcing modals," after the modal auxiliary verbs that such expressions contain.[26] Anscombe did not coin a name for the third type of relevant modal claim here, viz. those phrases by which we express the permissions for the holder of the right. Following Roger Teichmann, I shall call these "permitting modals."[27] The first part of my solution builds on Anscombe's idea that an analysis of rights must proceed through an analysis of the use of such deontic modals. The example of property rights might serve to illustrate that idea: For *X* to have a property right in a certain computer means: (1) No one *may* take it without her permission (*prohibition* or "*stopping modal*"); (2) if someone destroys it, this person *must* compensate *X* (*command/forcing modal*), while (3) *X* herself *can* destroy the computer if she feels like it (*permission/permitting modal*); (4) she *may* sell it to others (*permission/permitting modal*); and so forth. If *X* has a *right*, then certain prohibitions and commands apply for others, while certain permissions apply for her. Imagine we were to explain the very idea of property rights to a traveler, in whose culture private property did not exist. We could do so by giving her a list of prohibitions, commands, and permissions—or: *stopping*, *forcing* and *permitting modals*—just like the ones mentioned: "See, if this is my 'property,' it means that (1) no one *can* take it

[26] See particularly Anscombe (1981a); but also Anscombe (1981b, 138–146); Anscombe (1981c, 118–121).

[27] (Teichmann 2008. 79). Anscombe uses the adjective "permissive" to describe those modals in "The Question of Linguistic Idealism" (118). As Teichmann points out, "A permitting modal, such as 'may' can be defined as the negation of a stopping modal." This might explain the absence of a name for the third group

unless they've asked me; that (2) others *must* compensate me, if they break it; that (3) I *may* make changes to it as I like, while they . . . " A complete such list would be a complete specification of what my right consists in; in other words, it would be an explication (of this particular type) of property right.[28] It would thereby answer our first question for any theory of right, the question of definition. The first claim of the new theory of right that I want to suggest here can hence be put as follows: [29]

(M1) Any right *R* can be defined through a set of stopping and forcing modals.

By first sight, one might think that *M1*, just like the third reading of Will Theory on p. 323 above, does not go beyond Hohfeld's analysis of rights through duties either. This objection is unwarranted, for the following three reasons: (1) Hohfeld's analysis explicates the concept "right" through its "invariable correlative," "duty,"[30] whereas *M1* explicates "right" through the special usage of an independent class of expressions, modal auxiliary verbs. Hence, in *M1, explicans* and *explicandum* are independent of each other, whereas Hohfeld elucidates the relation *X has a right against Y* through the converse relation *Y has a duty against X.* (2) The explicans in *M1* elucidates through something that is much more basic than the explicandum. After all, modal auxiliary verbs are among the vocabulary that we learn when we first acquire language: We are told as toddlers that we "must" do certain things, "can't" do others, "may" or "may not" do this-and-that; that is, we learn such concepts long before we can be introduced to such demanding concepts as "a right" or "a duty." To define rights through modal auxiliary verbs hence is to define rights through something very simple and fundamental in comparison. (3) The explicans elucidates through something that is not specific to the explicandum, something with which we are familiar from many other contexts (and on which we hence have a much firmer grip). For the normative use of modal auxiliary verbs is in no way limited to rights-contexts: people *cannot* take what belongs to another (property right), and they *need* to feed their offspring (right to life). But philosophers *cannot* infer that such-and-such if doing so would be to affirm the consequent (requirement of theoretical rationality), and chess players *need* to move the king when he's in check (rule of a game); an applicant *cannot* be late for her interview if she intends to make a good impression

[28] It would not be an explication of "property right" in general, because this category comprises a wide variety of rights. There are different types of property rights, and the way to differentiate them is precisely by differentiating the sets of deontic modals as which they can be explicated. Thus, the property right I have in my computer entails that I *may* set it on fire, which my property right in my house or my horse does not. For a discussion of types of property see Waldron (1988, 26–61).

[29] There recently is much debate about "bipolar judgments" and whether those are reducible to "monadic judgments"—see, e.g., Thompson (2004, 335). Given that my above modal claims (such as "You can't take that!") address only one person, some readers might wonder whether Modal Theory entails such a reduction. The answer is that it does not. If you regard moral bipolar judgments as irreducible to monadic ones, you will think that all monadic formulations, such as *X has a right to* . . . , have a logical counterpart (in this case *Y has a duty to* . . .), and that although the individual judgment is monadic, its truth presupposes the truth of this counterpart-judgment, and you will hold that this does "the work of importing bipolarity into the equation" (349).

[30] (Hohfeld 2013, 9).

(requirement of practical rationality), and in some countries one *needs* to reject two times before accepting an invitation (rule of etiquette).

Contrary to Hohfeld's definition (and to the third interpretation of Will Theory), *M1* thus explicates through concepts that are independent of the concept "right," more basic than it and familiar from other and diverse contexts. Against *M1*, the triviality accusation hence seems unwarranted.[31]

VI. An Alternative Role for Interest: Claim 2 of Modal Theory

According to *M1*, to give a complete description of a right is to give a complete list of the stopping and forcing modals that correlate to this right. What place can this new theory allocate to the idea that rights protect interests? After all, Interest Theory does seem to capture an important aspect of rights: if, for instance, women in Saudi Arabia demand the right to drive or if homosexuals demand the right to marry, then they certainly take the thing demanded to protect a justified interest.

Interest Theory refers to interests in order to describe what rights *consist in*, but on our new account this conception must be false. Within Modal Theory, we do not need to refer to *X*'s interests if asked to specify what rights *X* has or what it is for *X* to have a right. We neither need interest to define the general term "right" nor to define any right *R*, say, "right to drive." *R* will simply be defined through a set of stopping and forcing modals $m_1, \ldots, m_n$, and a right is what can be thus defined.

Now that we defined rights as sets of modals, however, a second question poses itself, viz.: What *justifies* the usage of such a set of modals? If, to return to our old example, I have a property right in a certain computer, then others must ask my permission to use it, can't use it without this permission, and so forth—but *why* are they under these constraints? After all, somebody else might need my computer more urgently then I do, or I might even do harmful things with it. If there is a place for interest in a theory of right, I shall argue, then interest will be what justifies the usage of the set of modals in which a given right consists. More precisely, I argue that interests justify at the level of the general right, not of its instantiation for a given individual.

This claim constitutes the second part of Modal Theory, and the idea for it is again inspired by Anscombe.[32] A full-blown defense of this account would require a self-standing treatment. But my aim here simply is to outline a new framework that avoids the standard difficulty of current theories of right.

We must distinguish two kinds of justifications of rights, which, within our new framework, can be put as follows: First, there is the question of why a certain set of modals applies with respect to a certain individual. Second, there is the question of why this set of modals ever applies with respect to anyone. Take again the example of *X*'s private property right in

---

[31] There is a fourth reason that *M1* does not collapse into Hohfeld's analysis, viz. that it entails a strong metaphysical commitment about rights. It can be shown that if *M1* is true, then rights only exist where usage of the relevant class of modal expressions does, in other words, where there is a corresponding social practice. But such a demonstration requires a self-standing treatment. (Please see Nieswandt 2016.).

[32] Particularly by Anscombe (1981d).

a certain computer: There is the question of why we should use—with respect to *X* and for the case of this computer—the set of modals whose application would mean to grant *X* a property right in this item. And then there is the question of why we should ever use this set of modals with respect to anyone for any item, that is, why we should ever grant people property rights. The first question asks whether the general right *R* is instantiated in a given case. The second question asks what justifies *R*. One way to conceive of this difference is as the difference between justification *within* and *of* the "private property game," i.e., justification within and of a certain social practice and its rules.[33] I claim that we must appeal to interest in order to answer the second question. More precisely, I believe that rights are granted within practices, and the justification of such a practice as a whole, as well as of the rights granted within it, must ultimately appeal to interests. If there is a justification for why we should have the practice of private property, for example, and why this practice should assign the rights that our version of it does assign, then this justification will be that (our version of) this practice protects an interest that merits protection. Interest Theory seems to err in that it is not the instantiated but the general right, for which we need to draw on interest, and in that the protected interests must not necessarily be those of the right-holder. We can state this second part of Modal Theory as follows:

(M2) The usage of the set of modals that define right *R* must be justified by appeal to an interest protected through this usage.

Notice three things about *M2*: (1) *M2* does not imply that a right automatically arises as soon as there is an interest to be protected. All it says is that it is interest by which rights are justified. (2) M2 is compatible with a wide variety of ethical views because it is compatible with a wide variety of theories about the interests to be protected. (3) According to *M2*, it is not the individual right R_i that is justified by appeal to interest, but the general right *R*. In the library scenario, for instance, it would not be my individual right in *this* particular computer, but the general right in personal belongings that forms part of our current practice of private property, which must be justified by interest.

VII. Avoiding the "Wrong Kind of Reason" Objection

The view that I suggest belongs to a category sometimes called "practice views" or "conventionalist views."[34] Practice views have been accused of giving the "wrong kinds of reasons" for actions and beliefs, so let me briefly explain why my particular view avoids this objection.

There actually are two such objections. First, Thomas Scanlon has argued that John Rawls mistakenly depicts any practice-internal duty as "a general obligation to the members of the group who have contributed to and benefit from the practice."[35] Rawls indeed justifies the duties that correspond to an individual right R_i through a general duty of fairness that the

---

[33] For this distinction, see Rawls (1955).

[34] See, e.g., Habib (2014/2008) http://plato.stanford.edu/entries/promises/. (See section 5.3.)

[35] (Scanlon 1990, 221).

holder of this duty has toward all other participants in the respective practice.[36] An analogous move is made by rule-consequentialists: They, too, justify the duties that correspond to an individual right R_i through a general duty to comply with the respective practice, only that this general duty is not justified by fairness but by the good which that practice furthers.

No such indirect justification of individual rights and duties is implied by the view I suggest here. Section IX below lays this out in more detail.[37] In a nutshell, I say: R_i must be justified through some empirical fact for which the rules of the practice assign R to people (and hence assign the corresponding duties to others). For instance, the justification for why *I* have a right in *this* computer could be that *I bought this computer*—an empirical fact for which the rules of our practice of private property assign me such a right and put all others under corresponding duties. The justification of the practice of private property itself has no role in justifying my individual right, not even an indirect role.

Second, inspired by Gregory Kavka's toxin puzzle,[38] it has become a common place that considerations showing that it would be good to believe or intend something are not always the right kind of consideration to serve as reasons for believing or intending said thing. Suppose, you promised me a fortune if I believed that the moon is made of cheese: This would give me a (pragmatic) reason for intending to believe that the moon is made of cheese (or for attempting to get myself to believe it, e.g. by visiting a hypnotist), but it does not give me any (epistemic) reason to actually believe this. Similarly, even if *Y* believed that there are good reasons to comply with the practice of private property and hence good pragmatic reasons to intend *to believe that this computer is X's*, this would not provide good epistemic reasons for *Y* to believe that *the computer indeed is X's*.

Kavka's puzzle poses a problem for Rawls and for rule-consequentialists, but not for the view I suggest. On my account, *Y*'s reason for believing that the computer is *X*'s will be some empirical fact, such as that *X* bought the computer, or that *X* received the computer as a present, or that *X* won the computer in a lottery, etc. It has nothing to do with legitimate interests that the practice of private property protects, not even indirectly.

All social practices, I believe, have this structure: There are two levels of justification—justification of the practice and justifications within the practice. What provides a good justification for beliefs or actions regarding the practice does not (at least not usually) provide a good justification for beliefs or actions *within* that practice and vice versa. Take the example of a social practice for which this is more obvious than it might be for private property: money. Most anthropologists think that human beings adopt money where there is need to trade with people whose credit history is unknown and with whom one has no social bonds.[39] From the outside, money resembles a great social illusion: The currency itself often is of little material value; nevertheless all those engaged in the practice highly value the currency. So a human community can have *good reason* to believe that they should introduce money. And once the practice is in place, every single member has *good reason* to believe that the respective paper pieces are valuable. This second good reason differs from the original

[36] See Rawls (1999/1971, sections 18 and 52).

[37] See also Nieswandt (2018).

[38] (Kavka 1983, 36).

[39] For an overview, see Graeber (2011, ch. 2).

good reason for adopting money: it consists in the fact that others, too, treat the paper pieces as valuable, e.g. by accepting them in exchange for desirable objects. Not only, however, do the two good reasons differ, but the good reason for beliefs about the paper pieces does not draw on the good reason for beliefs regarding the practice—not even indirectly. In fact, individual agents might hold no beliefs at all regarding the question of what money in general is for, and they would still have good reason to believe in the value of the pieces of paper. Similarly, *Y* can have good reason to believe that, e.g., this is *X*'s computer, or that he, *Y*, must not take the computer without *X*'s permission, without holding any beliefs about the question of what private property in general is for.

VIII. Interest Theory's Main Problem: The Possessor of a Right Might Not Be Its Beneficiary

As mentioned in the introduction, the standard problem for Interest Theory is that it cannot allow that we possess rights that exclusively or mainly serve the interest of others. Much-discussed examples are the rights of legal guardians or the rights of officeholders. (Thus, a policeman's right to arrest someone does not serve this policeman's personal interest, but the interest of the political entity that employs him.) As for Will Theory, however, the set of counterexamples to Interest Theory is much larger than commonly discussed: Any justification of a right for subgroups through appeal to the general interest contradicts Interest Theory. Such appeals, however, are frequent in political discourse, and they seem to be correct as a form of argument (even if their respective content will sometimes be questionable).

Take the following example: In recent years, young people worldwide protested for the right to study without fees (in Chile, Germany, and Hungary, for instance)[40] or at an affordable fee (for example in the UK, United States, Canada, Liberia, Nigeria, and Taiwan).[41] The right that they demand is free or affordable access to higher education. Their main justification for this demanded right can be rendered as follows: It is in the interest of all members of society that access to higher education be determined by talent, not money (and hence family background). For, first, to regulate access in this way furthers good research and national productivity, and those are aims in which all members of society have an instrumental interest. Second, to regulate access in this way is an important aspect of promoting social justice—given that today access to education determines access to all kinds of other resources—and it is in the interest of all members of society to live in a just society. Whether you agree with these claims or not, the example illustrates two things:

1. Interest is usually brought in at the justificatory stage. It is not part of the specification of the right itself. "We (students) demand the *right* to φ (study without or at affordable fees). The reason we give for this is that granting us this right would further this-or-that *interest* (national productivity, social justice)." In this, as in most other cases, the right itself can be specified without reference to interest, here

[40] See, e.g., Long (2011); ([unnamed] 2013); or Than (2012).

[41] See, e.g., Coughlan (2011); Tylor (2012); Hallward (2012); Tongai (2013); Nasiru (2013); Loa (2013).

as: "the right to study without/at affordable fees." Interests are mentioned in the attempt to justify the specified right: it is *because of* all those benefits that granting the right would be rational.

2. Often, it is not the right-holder's interest that serves to justify a right. True, in the above example it is *also* in the interest of all those to whom the right would be granted that they should have this right. (That is, all students and aspiring students profit from no or low fees.) But the given justification does not even mention these potential right-holders. It says that *all* members of society, most of whom have no intention of attending university and will hence never possess the right, will benefit. It is this general interest that justifies the right (if it does). This pattern of justification seems to be typical for many of the discussions about rights that we actually have: Very often, (claims for) rights for subgroups of a population are defended by appeal to the interest of the whole population. And Interest Theory has given us no reason to believe that this form of argument is generally invalid.

Notice that the first point, about specification, also holds where rights are denied. (The second point, about justification, does, too, of course—that is, it is not necessarily the right-holder's interest that serves to justify denial of the right to her—but that seems obvious.) Consider the example of the recent large-scale protest in France against the right of homosexuals to adopt children.[42] Protesters claimed that granting the discussed right to group *A* (adult homosexuals) would negatively affect the mental health of another group *B* (the children they adopt). Again, whether you agree with this claim or not (and many found it outrageous), the right under discussion can be specified without reference to anybody's interests—as "the right to adopt children"—and the point to bring in interest is where one is pressed for a justification: this right must *not* be granted, because it would violate an important and legitimate interest.

M2 separates the question of the justification of rights from the question of their possession. It allows us to distinguish the bearer of a right from those whose interests this right generally protects, thereby allowing us to avoid Interest Theory's standard problem. As the above examples illustrate, however, it also has a further advantage: it captures the role that interest plays in actual public discussions about rights.

IX. The Possession of Rights

I defined rights through sets of deontic modal claims, and I argued that the general right, but not its individual instantiation, must be justified through interests. This leaves us with our third and last question, the question of the possession of rights.

As with the question of justification, the answer to the question of possession must start from a distinction between the general right and its individual instantiation (see p. 327). A property right in *this* item exists if (1) no one except ___ can use it, (2) ___ may destroy it, (3) all other must compensate ___ if they destroy it, etc. The person who *has* this property right is the person whose name qualifies to fill in the blanks of these deontic modals. Who,

[42] See, e.g., Laurent (2013).

in turn, qualifies for that will be a matter of empirical facts on the one hand and the rules of the practice to which the general right belongs on the other. According to the rules of our current property practice, for instance, you can come to qualify as the possessor of a property right through buying the item in question, through receiving it as a gift, through winning it as a prize etc. Whether you did this, is an empirical question. (Did you, *in fact*, draw the lottery ticket with the winning number, e.g.?) The possessor of a right hence is the person whose name can fill out the possessor blank (or: who can instantiate the possessor variable) that the deontic modals contain as which the right can be defined.

(M3) *X* possesses right R_i just in case "*X*" can correctly be used to instantiate the modals that define *R*, where correct means: in accordance with the rules of the practice to which *R* belongs, applied to the empirical facts.

Anscombe summarizes her own conception as follows: "I have located the generation of the concept of a right in a certain kind of use of a stopping modal [. . .]. We have here a very special use of the name of a person, or a very special way of relating something to a person, which explains (not is explained by) the general term 'right.' Something is *N*'s to do, *N*'s to receive (as: a message), *N*'s to kill—as an ancient Roman would say about *N*'s children: the *patria potestas*. The general term 'right' is constructed because, as it were, our language feels the need for it. As, for example, a general term 'relation' was invented."[43]

X. Conclusions

I have outlined a new role for authority and interest in the theory of right—the key concepts of the two currently dominant theories, Will and Interest Theory. The resulting Modal Theory of Right comprises three central claims:

(M1) Any right R can be defined through a set of stopping and forcing modals.

(M2) The usage of the set of modals that define right R must be justified by appeal to an interest protected through this usage.

(M3) *X* possesses right Ri just in case "*X*" can correctly be used to instantiate the modals that define *R*, where correct means: in accordance with the rules of the practice to which *R* belongs, applied to the empirical facts.

(1) I have argued that if we conceive of rights in this way, we can avoid the problems of Will and Interest Theory. (2) I hope to have shown that Will Theory's problems derive from a misconception of the connection between authority and rights, those of Interest Theory from a misconception of the connection between interests and rights. And instead of ad hoc patches for those problems, I have tried to provide a systematic solution. (3) Although I have not demonstrated that authority and interest need to be part of a correct theory of right, I have tried to endow the new alternative with some independent credibility: Modal Theory, I argued, analyzes rights through very basic and familiar concepts (p. 325); it accurately

[43] (Anscombe 1981b, 142).

reflects actual public discourse about rights (Section XIII), and it is compatible with a wide variety of ethical views (p. 327). Given that it puts very few constraints on the relevant kind of interest, it can be combined with any ethical theory that can accommodate rights and that allows for rights to be grounded in interests. This would include virtue ethics, for instance, certain forms of consequentialism, and also many of the contemporary Kantian accounts, which stress the role of *Glückseligkeit.*

Modal Theory becomes available once we distinguish three questions: First, in what does a right consist? Second, what justifies rights? And, third, who possesses a certain right? On our alternative understanding, we need the concept "authority" to answer the first question, while we need "interest" to answer the second.

References

[unnamed]. 2013. "Das Ende der Studiengebühren," *Frankfurter Rundschau*, February 1.

Anscombe, G. E. M. 1981a. "Rules, Rights and Promises." In *Ethics, Religion and Politics (The Collected Philosophical Papers of G. E. M. Anscombe, Volume 3)*. Oxford: Blackwell.

_____. 1981b. "On the Source of the Authority of the State." In *Ethics, Religion and Politics (The Collected Philosophical Papers of G. E. M. Anscombe, Vol. 3)*. Oxford: Blackwell.

_____. 1981c. "The Question of Linguistic Idealism." In *From Parmenides to Wittgenstein (The Collected Philosophical Papers of G. E. M. Anscombe, Vol. 1)*, Oxford: Blackwell.

_____. 1981d. "On Promising and Its Justice and Whether It Need Be Respected *in Foro Interno.*" In *Ethics, Religion and Politics (The Collected Philosophical Papers of G. E. M. Anscombe, Vol. 3)*. Oxford: Blackwell.

Căbulea May, S. 2012. "Moral Status and the Direction of Duties," *Ethics* 123(1):113–128.

Coughlan, S. 2011. "Thousands March in Student Protest over University Fees." *BBC News*, November 9.

Cruft, R. 2013a. "Introduction." *Ethics* 123(2):195–201.

_____. 2013b. "Why Is It Disrespectful to Violate Rights?" *Proceedings of the Aristotelian Society* 113(2pt2):201–224.

Edmundson, W. A., (2004): *An Introduction to Rights.* Cambridge: Cambridge University Press.

Finnis, J. 1980. *Natural Law and Natural Rights.* Oxford: Oxford University Press.

Gewirth, A., 1982. *Human Rights: Essays on Justification and Applications.* Chicago: University of Chicago Press.

Graeber, D. 2011. *Debt: The First 5,000 Years*. Brooklyn, NY: Melville House.

Griffin, J., (2008): *On Human Rights*. New York: Oxford University Press.

Habib, A. 2014/2008. "Promises," In *The Stanford Encyclopedia of Philosophy*, edited by Edward N. Zalta. http://plato.stanford.edu/entries/promises/.

Hallward, P. 2012. "Quebec's Student Protesters Give UK Activists a Lesson." *The Guardian US*, June 1.

Hart, H. L. A. 1955. "Are There Any Natural Rights?," *Philosophical Review* 64(2): 175–191.

_____. 1982. "Legal Rights." In *Essays on Bentham: Studies in Jurisprudence and Political Theory*, edited by H. L. A. Hart. Oxford; New York: Clarendon Press.

Hedahl, M. 2013. "The Significance of a Duty's Direction." *Journal of Ethics and Social Philosophy* 7(3):1–29.

Hohfeld, W. N. 1913. "Some Fundamental Legal Conceptions as Applied in Judicial Reasoning." *Yale Law Journal* 23:16–59.

Kant, I. 1909/1797 *Metaphysik der Sitten*. In *Kants Gesammelte Schriften, ed. by the Königlich Preußische Akademie der Wissenschaften,* Vol. 6, edited by Paul Natorp. Reimer: Berlin.

Kavka, G. S. 1983. "The Toxin Puzzle." *Analysis* 43(1):33–36.

Kramer, M. H. 2008. "Rights in Legal and Political Philosophy." In *The Oxford Handbook of Law and Politics*, edited by K. E. Whittington, R. D. Kelemen, and G. A. Caldeira. Oxford; New York: Oxford University Press.

_____. 2010. "Refining the Interest Theory of Right." *American Journal of Jurisprudence* 55:31–39.

_____. 2013. "Some Doubts about Alternatives to the Interest Theory of Rights." *Ethics* 123(2):245–263.

Kramer, M. H., and H. Steiner. 2007. "Theories of Rights: Is There a Third Way?" *Oxford Journal of Legal Studies* 27(2):281–310.

Laurent, S. 2013. "Adoption et mariage homosexuel: Les faits pour comprendre." *Le Monde*, January 30.

Loa, L.-s. 2013. "Students Protest Change in University Fee Regulations." *Taipei Times*, February 22.

Long, G. 2011. "Chile Student Protests Point to Deep Discontent." *BBC News*.

Lyons, D. 1969. "Rights, Claimants and Beneficiaries." *American Philosophical Quarterly* 6(3):173–185.

Nasiru, A. A. 2013. "Ebonyi University Students Protest Increase in Fees." *Premium Times*, February 5.

Nieswandt, K. 2016. "Do Rights Exist by Convention or by Nature?." *Topoi* 35:313–325.

_____. 2018. "What Is Conventionalism about Moral Rights and Duties?" *Australasian Journal of Philosophy* [online first]:1–14.

Preda, A. 2012. "Group Rights and Group Agency." *Journal of Moral Philosophy* 9(2): 229–254.

Rawls, J. 1955. "Two Concepts of Rules," *Philosophical Review* 64(1):3–32.

_____. 1999. *A Theory of Justice.* Cambridge, MA: Belknap Press.

Raz, J. 1986. *The Morality of Freedom*. New York: Oxford University Press.

_____.1994. "Rights and Individual Well-Being." In *Ethics in the Public Domain: Essays in the Morality of Law and Politics*, edited by J. Raz. Oxford; New York: Clarendon.

_____. 2007. *Human Rights without Foundations* (University of Oxford Faculty of Law Legal Studies Research Paper Series 14).

Scanlon, T. 1990. "Promises and Practices." *Philosophy and Public Affairs* 19(3):199–226.

Simmonds, N. E. 1998. "Rights at the Cutting Edge." In *A Debate over Rights,* edited by M.H. Kramer, N. E. Simmonds, and H. Steiner. *Philosophical Enquiries.* Oxford; New York: Clarendon.

Sreenivasan, G. 2005. "Hybrid Theory of Claim Rights." *Oxford Journal of Legal Studies* 25(3):257–274.

Steiner, H. 1998. "Working Rights." In *A Debate over Rights: Philosophical Enquiries*, edited by M.H. Kramer, N. E. Simmonds, and H. Steiner. Oxford; New York:Clarendon.

_____. 2013. "Directed Duties and Inalienable Rights." *Ethics* 123(2):230–244.

Teichmann, R. 2008. *The Philosophy of Elizabeth Anscombe*. Oxford: Oxford University Press.

Than, K., M. Dunai, and M. Roddy. 2012. "Thousands of Hungarian Students Rally against Government," *Reuters, US*, December 12.

Thompson, M. 2004. "What Is It to Wrong Someone? A Puzzle about Justice." In *Reason and Value. Themes from the Moral Philosophy of Joseph Raz*, edited by R. J. Wallace, P. Petitt, S. Scheffler, and M. Smith. Oxford; New York: Clarendon.

Tongai, I. 2013. "University Head Defends Fee Hike That Sparked Protests," *University World News*, January 31.

Tylor, J. 2012. "Students on Hunger Strike to Protest Fee Hikes." *Marketplace*, May 2.

Waldron, J. 1988. *The Right to Private Property*. Oxford: Clarendon.

Wenar, L. 2011/2005. "Rights." In *The Stanford Encyclopedia of Philosophy*, edited by Edward N. Zalta, http://plato.stanford.edu/entries/rights/.

_____. 2013. "The Nature of Claim-Rights." *Ethics* 123(2):202–229.

15 On the Legal Syllogism

Luís Duarte d'Almeida*

I. Introduction

My goal in this chapter is to argue against one popular idea about the role of legal rules in legal argument: that the justification of law-applying decisions is adequately understood on the model of a deductive argument—a "legal syllogism," as it is often called—having as its "major premise" a statement of an applicable legal rule, and as a "minor premise" a statement of the relevant facts.

Before you object that this is a naïve, old-fashioned idea that nobody endorses anymore, let me be clear that my target is not what Brian Leiter has labeled "vulgar formalism." Vulgar formalism is the view that "judicial decision-making involves nothing more than mechanical deduction on the model of the syllogism."[1] This is not, as Leiter points out, "a view to which anyone today cares to subscribe."[2] Maybe no one ever really did. But Leiter goes on to say this:

> It is true enough that deductive reasoning on the model of syllogism is a characteristic feature of most well-done judicial opinions—that is, the conclusion can be

---

* Professor of Jurisprudence, University of Edinburgh. For very helpful comments and discussion, I am grateful to David Duarte, Martin Kelly, Cormac Mac Amhlaigh, Euan MacDonald, Cláudio Michelon, Pedro Múrias, David Plunkett, Fábio Shecaira, Kevin Toh, and Neil Walker; and to audiences in Edinburgh, Lisbon, Milan, and Surrey. Martin Kelly gets extra thanks for his assistance in unearthing the case I discuss in Section IV.

[1] (Leiter 2010, 111). "Mechanical" was Pound's label for the view that applying the law is purely a matter of fitting cases to rules that are already "at hand in a fixed and final form": see (Pound 1908, 607).

[2] (Leiter 2010, 111).

Dimensions of Normativity. David Plunkett, Scott J. Shapiro, and Kevin Toh.

> reconstructed as following deductively from a statement of the applicable rule of law and the statement of the facts.[3]

True enough? I don't think it is true at all. Unlike vulgar formalism, however, the view expressed in this passage is one that many authors do adopt. Some, like Leiter, seem to take it for granted. Here is Andrei Marmor, in a piece in which he proposes to "explore some structural aspects of legal syllogism":

> It is . . . the regular business of lawyers and judges to draw legal inferences. Many of those inferences look like an ordinary syllogism whereby a conclusion is derived from some premises about the normative content of the law and statements describing facts or events.[4]

Another recent endorsement comes from John Gardner:

> In a legal argument, an existing legal norm is a major premise, and a new legal norm is the conclusion. The legal arguments in everyday . . . examples [i.e., those in which a court makes its ruling by applying existing legal rules to the case in hand] are, of course, very simple. They go something like this:
>
> Tortfeasors are liable to pay full reparative damages to those whom they tortuously injure;
> Jones tortuously injured Smith to the tune of $50;
> therefore, Jones is liable to pay Smith $50 in reparative damages.[5]

Many other prominent authors have subscribed to this picture—with only minor variations—over the past decades. Kelsen appears to have been one, at least in the second edition of the *Pure Theory of Law*.[6] Hart was certainly another.[7] And Neil MacCormick and Robert Alexy stand out among those who have offered full defenses of the view that, in the words of the former,

> the legal reasoning advanced to justify legal claims or legal decisions can sometimes be entirely, and must always be in part, deductive in its essence. The thesis [is] that legal rules are properly conceptualized as hypothetical in form, prescribing that if certain circumstances (certain "operative facts") obtain, then certain normative consequences are to follow. Rules being so conceptualised, one who can establish in a given case that an instance of the relevant operative facts obtains can justifiably claim that the relevant normative consequence ought to follow, or indeed in the capacity of a judge

---

[3] (Leiter 2010, 111).
[4] (Marmor 2014, 61).
[5] (Gardner 2004, 186).
[6] See (Kelsen 1967/1960, 202, 237).
[7] See, for example, (Hart (1955, 258–262)), (Hart 2012/1961, 126–127), and (Hart 1967, 99–108).

> can justifiably decide that it does follow, and can justifiably give a legal decision giving effect to that consequence. This is a form of deductive inference, or, if you like, deductive/subsumptive reasoning: you postulate a general hypothetical rule, you establish facts in a particular case subsumable within the rule's hypothesis, and you draw the logical conclusion for the particular case from rule plus facts.[8]

This is the view I mean to reject. Some of its proponents call it "deductivism,"[9] but I will refer to it instead as "rule-deductivism," and to its defenders as "rule-deductivists." For my quarrel is not, as I will explain, with the claim per se that the justification of law-applying judicial decisions can be understood as a deductive inference. My quarrel is with what rule-deductivists believe the inference should look like, and particularly with the role they think should be assigned to legal rules.

I speak of *the* rule-deductivist view, but in fact it is far from clear what exactly the claim is—or the claims are—that these authors endorse. Their own formulations are not always transparent, and there is in the literature no received account of rule-deductivism. So I will begin, in Section II, by trying to assemble a sharper picture of what rule-deductivists hold. This will call for some charitable reconstruction: one thesis many rule-deductivists *say* they hold is plainly indefensible on logical grounds, as we will see in Section III, but there is a stronger claim we can spell out on their behalf. I then go on to argue, in Section IV, that rule-deductivism, even in its stronger version, is not a view we should accept.

This chapter is therefore primarily critical rather than constructive; though meant to stand on its own, it is also the first part of a broader project. But I will conclude by briefly sketching and motivating, in Section V, a new model of the justification of law-applying decisions—one capable of overcoming the flaws of the model of the legal syllogism.

II. Rule-Deductivism

A. The "Legal Syllogism"

We need to piece together an account of rule-deductivism, and the just-quoted passage by MacCormick is a good place to start. One point he makes is that "legal rules are properly conceptualized as hypothetical in form, prescribing that if certain circumstances (certain 'operative facts') obtain, then certain normative consequences are to follow."[10] This is a fairly orthodox claim. It is also integral to rule-deductivism. Consider the following example—from a relatively well-known essay by A. G. Guest—meant to illustrate "deductive reasoning . . . in the sense of the application of a general [legal] rule to a particular instance":

> Let us take the words of a penal statute, in this case the Representation of People Act, 1949, s. 52: "Any person shall be guilty of an offence if, at a parliamentary or local

[8] (MacCormick 1982a, 182).

[9] See (MacCormick 2005, ch. 4).

[10] See the quotation accompanying note 8 above; and see also (MacCormick 2005, 24).

> government election, he fraudulently takes out of the polling station any ballot paper." Here the legal process consists in the application of a fixed and ascertained rule to the facts of a particular case. The section of the statute constitutes the major premiss, the minor being "X (the accused) at a parliamentary or local government election fraudulently took out of a polling station a ballot paper." This, it will be seen, comprises the words of the indictment. If the minor premiss is true, the offence is made out and X will be found guilty.[11]

At first sight this looks straightforward. Guest's point is not really, of course, that the accused *will* be found guilty. He does not mean that the conclusion of the inference is a prediction. Rather, as he goes on to explain, he takes the conclusion to be a "normative" statement that the accused *ought to* be found guilty.[12] So the inference Guest describes combines, as premises, two statements of different kinds. One is meant to be a statement of a statutory rule, its form presumably to be rendered along the following lines:

> For every *x*: if *x* at a parliamentary or local government election takes out of a polling station a ballot paper, then *x* ought to be found guilty of an offence.[13]

Note also that Guest refers to the relevant rule as one that is "fixed and ascertained": it is fixed and ascertained by reference to the words of the statute. (Guest does not take much care to distinguish the rule from the "section of the statute.") That is not meant to prevent the restatement of the rule in formally clearer terms, as in the formulation above. But the example is one in which the rule being applied is the legislated rule; and the application of legislated rules, as we will also see, is something that many rule-deductivists claim to be particularly well placed to explain.

The other premise in Guest's example is a statement about the facts of some particular case. So the full inference can be displayed as follows:

(1) For every *x*: if *x* at a parliamentary or local government election takes out of a polling station a ballot paper, then *x* ought to be found guilty of an offense.
(2) The accused at a parliamentary or local government election took out of a polling station a ballot paper.
Therefore (from (1) and (2)),
(3) The accused ought to be found guilty of an offense.

---

[11] (Guest 1961, 182, footnote omitted).

[12] (Guest 1961 184–185).

[13] One occasionally finds legal rules formalised more plainly as instances of the pattern "If *p*, then *q*"; but it seems clear that we need at least the tools of predicate logic to represent the form of general norms. See (Perelman 1961, 603); (Alexy 1989/1978, 221–222); (White 1980, 741–742); (Wilson 1982, 283–284); (Brewer 1996, 943–944); and (MacCormick 2005, 68–70).

This inference, an example of what is normally called a "legal syllogism," is an instance of the following valid form:

(1) For every *x*: if *x* is *F*, then *x* ought to be *G*.
(2) *a* is *F*.
Therefore (from (1) and (2)),
(3) *a* ought to be *G*.[14]

The so-called "legal syllogism," then, is a deductively valid inference in which one premise (the "major premise") is a general statement of law, another premise (the "minor" one) a particular statement of fact, and the conclusion a particular statement of law.[15]

B. *A Model*

Rule-deductivists claim that the legal syllogism is a *model* of the justification of law-applying judicial decisions. This claim, though, needs some unpacking.

Let us start by introducing a distinction between two senses in which we can speak of the "justification" of a judicial decision. In one sense, to say that a judicial decision is justified—legally justified—is to say that it is correct according to law: it is to say that the court ought legally to have issued it, or at least that it is not the case that the court ought not legally to have issued it. Courts, however, are normally required to do more than simply issue decisions that are justified in this "objective" sense (as we may call it). Courts are normally required to *justify* their decisions: required, or at any rate expected, to give reasons—to offer arguments—showing that their decisions are indeed justified in that first, objective sense.

So there are two things we can ask of any given judicial decision. We can ask whether the decision *is* (or was) justified, issued according to law. And we can ask whether the court

---

[14] This form—sometimes called "universal *modus ponens*"—can be analyzed as a complex inference involving two deductively valid steps: (1) entails

(1′) If *a* is *F*, then *a* ought to be *G*

by universal instantiation; and (1′) and (2) together entail (3) by standard (i.e., propositional) modus ponens. See (Kalinowski 1964, 277–278); (Alexy 1980, 189); and also (Engisch 1963, 8–10).

[15] Why "so-called"? Because what rule-deductivists have in mind is not the (categorical) syllogism of traditional logic; nor does it matter that there be only three terms ("major," "middle," "minor"), each occurring exactly twice. As traditionally used by lawyers and legal theorists, the term "major premise" just stands for the legal premise, and "minor premise" for the factual one. As for "syllogism," the term is used, as Feteris (2017, 25–26) also notes, simply to mean a (deductive) argument regardless of pattern. The scheme in the text is just the simplest version of the legal syllogism; it could be refined to deal with more complex examples (e.g., rules with more intricate antecedents or consequents, including, of course, different subjects in the antecedent and the consequent): see (Wróblewski 1974, 43–44), and (Alexy 1989/1978, 222–225).

justified it, and if so whether the justification it offered was a good one—whether the decision was well justified *by* the court.

It is this second sense of "justification" that rule-deductivists have in mind when they speak of the legal syllogism as a model of the justification of law-applying decisions. They are concerned with justification in the sense of reason-giving—with "legal reasoning... purport[ing] to *show* that a decision (or a claim) *is* justifiable according to the law in force."[16]

The thought is not, of course, that judges either do or should actually *present* their arguments in the shape of a syllogism. Rule-deductivists do not hold "that it is necessary or even best to set out real legal arguments in rigorously syllogistic form."[17] What they hold is that if a law-applying judicial decision is well justified by the court—if, as Leiter puts it, the opinion is "well-done"[18]—then the court's argument can be *reconstructed* on the model of the syllogism. What does "well justified" mean? It cannot mean that the decision *is* justified in the objective sense—that is, actually correct according to law. To say that a law-applying decision is well justified is to say the argument given by the court is an argument of the right kind: an argument (a) aimed at showing that the decision is indeed legally correct; (b) whose premises are appropriately related, logically speaking, to the conclusion; and (c) which, *if* sound—if it has no false premises—succeeds in showing the decision to be legally correct. And what does it mean to say that such an argument can be *reconstructed* on the model of the syllogism? It means that the argument the court is in fact giving—however informal and enthymematic its presentation in the text of the opinion—can be fully brought out and fairly represented as an instance of that pattern.[19]

Now, rule-deductivists do not think that the legal syllogism exhausts the range of types of argument that courts could and normally do give in support of their decisions. There are many examples of well-made judicial decisions whose supporting arguments are not to be understood as legal syllogisms; rule-deductivists are concerned only with a certain class of judicial decisions. What class is that? Rule-deductivists are often unclear on that point. We need, however, to identify the relevant class—the class of the decisions that rule-deductivists take as their object of theorization—if we are to be able to assess their claim that the legal syllogism is an adequate model of the arguments made by courts in decisions of that class. I have been using the phrase "law-applying judicial decisions" to refer to the relevant class. What I mean—what I take rule-deductivists to have in mind—is the class of decisions justified on the basis of existing law that applies to the case in hand. This is not yet a fully transparent description, but it is enough to get us started.

I will argue in Section III that rule-deductivism, thus understood, is manifestly wrong: that law-applying judicial decisions are *not* aptly understood on the model of the legal syllogism. But let me first go over three disclaimers standardly offered by rule-deductivists in clarification of their views.

---

[16] (Alchourrón and Bulygin 1992, 252, emphasis added).

[17] (MacCormick 2005, 42–43).

[18] (Leiter 2010, 111).

[19] See also (Alexy 1980, 184), and (Chiassoni 1999, 157–158).

C. Discovery and Justification

The first disclaimer is that the model of the syllogism does not purport to reflect the way by which courts *reach* their decisions. The point is often stressed—since Richard Wasserstrom first cast it in these terms in the early 1960s—by appealing to a traditional distinction from the philosophy of science: rule-deductivists are concerned with the structure of justification, not with the process of discovery.[20] Here, for example, is Hart's gloss on this difference between "methods of discovery and standards of appraisal" and on its bearing on rule-deductivism:

> [I]t is important to distinguish (1) assertions made concerning the usual processes or habits of thought by which judges actually reach their decisions . . . and (3) the standards by which judicial decisions are to be appraised. The first of these concerns matters of descriptive psychology, and to the extent that assertions in this field go beyond the descriptions of examined instances, they are empirical generalizations or laws of psychology; . . . the third relates to the assessment or justification of decisions.
>
> These distinctions are important because it has sometimes been argued that since judges frequently arrive at decisions without going through any process of calculation or inference in which legal rules or precedents figure, the claim that deduction from legal rules plays any part in decision is mistaken. This argument is confused, for in general the issue is not one regarding the manner in which judges do, or should, come to their decisions; rather, it concerns the standards they respect in justifying decisions, however reached.[21]

D. Internal and External Justification

A second proviso is that the legal syllogism is not meant to be a *complete* model of the justification of law-applying judicial decisions. Recall how MacCormick presents his view: "legal reasoning advanced to justify legal claims or legal decisions," he says, "can sometimes be entirely, and must always be in part, deductive in its essence."[22] The point, then, is that the justification of law-applying judicial decisions is at least partly a matter of deduction from legal statements combined with statements of fact.

When is legal justification *wholly* "deductive in its essence"? When neither the identification of the applicable rule, nor the presence of the relevant facts, nor the classification of the particular case as one to which the rule applies, is problematic or controversial. In such "easy cases," writes David Lyons,

> the law is clear enough so that [the case] can be decided in a more or less "mechanical" way, by applying relevant rules in a logically rigorous argument. A proposition of law that decides the case is then derivable by logically deductive methodology from a

---

[20] See (Wasserstrom 1961, 22–30); and see also (Wellman 1985, 54, 65); (Alexy 1989/1978, 229); and (Atienza 2005, 4–7); and, for discussion, (Golding 1986, 124–140); (Mazzarese 1996, 105–157); (Rotolo 2001, 57–63); and (Atienza 2013, 114–116).

[21] (Hart 1967, 105).

[22] See the quotation accompanying n. 8 above.

> combination of rules of law and statements of facts about the case. The simplest model for such an argument may be termed a legal syllogism, which includes as its major premise a single rule of law, as its minor premise a statement of relevant facts, and as its conclusion the dispositive proposition of law.[23]

But rule-deductivists do not think that all cases are "easy." If there are doubts around either the identification of the applicable rule, or the description and classification of the relevant facts, or both, then, they grant, "subsumption and the drawing of a syllogistic conclusion no longer characterise the nerve of the reasoning."[24] The judge will need to offer further reasons to justify her views on what the law or the facts are; and this aspect of the justification of judicial decisions need not be, as far as rule-deductivists are concerned, "purely deductive and logical in character."[25] That is not to say, though, that the model of the legal syllogism does not capture an important aspect of the justification of the decision: it captures, rule-deductivists say, the (logically) last link, as it were, in the relevant argumentative chain.

This point is also often put in terms of a distinction, introduced by Jerzy Wróblewski, between the *internal* and the *external* justification of judicial decisions.[26] Internal justification concerns the logical validity of the inference from the relevant premises—the statement of the applicable legal rule, and the statement of the relevant facts—to the final conclusion. External justification concerns the truth of each of these premises, and therefore the soundness of the inference. What the legal syllogism purports to model, as Wróblewski and others point out, is the internal justification of law-applying decisions.[27] So while it may often be true that "[t]he Judge does not and cannot reach his decision *solely* by applying transformation rules to a conjunction of a statement of the legal rule invoked by the parties and a statement of the facts," it remains the case, rule-deductivists say, that once the judge "has decided whether the legal rule includes or excludes the present case . . . his reasoning [can] take a syllogistic form."[28]

E. *Questions of Law and Questions of Fact*

A final, closely related caveat concerns a distinction upon which the very idea of the legal syllogism seems to be predicated: that between questions of law and questions of fact. The caveat is that rule-deductivism is *not* wedded to the view that there is a strong divide between these two kinds of questions.

Consider the familiar point that "almost every rule can prove to be ambiguous or unclear in relation to some disputed or disputable context of litigation."[29] Faced with a case whose classification under the terms of the rule is doubtful, what must a judge establish? Not merely

---

[23] (Lyons 1984, 180).

[24] (Hart 2012/1961, 127).

[25] (MacCormick 1978: 36–37).

[26] See (Wróblewski 1971, 412) and (Wróblewski 1974, 39).

[27] See (Wróblewski 1974, 39); (Alexy 1989/1978, 221); (Soeteman 1995, 743–744); (Comanducci 1999, 48, 56–57); or (Bäcker 2009, 408–409).

[28] (Hart 1955, 260, emphasis in the original).

[29] (MacCormick 1978, 65–66, footnote—to Hart's *The Concept of Law*—omitted).

whether certain events took place, but whether they *count as* instances of the relevant legal predicates. That, though, is no longer a mere question of fact; as Hart puts it:

> What looks like a pure question of fact: Did he sign the document? Did they rescue a vessel? turns out in such cases (not in all cases) to be the hybrid question: Is what was done to count as signing a document, rescuing a vessel, for the purpose of this rule?[30]

The rule-deductivist account does not depend on there being a clear-cut distinction between questions of law and questions of fact. For one, the term "fact" is equivocal, and the rule-deductivist's claim is not that the minor premise of the legal syllogism must always be a description of empirical facts; there is after all no reason to think that the antecedent of the applicable rule will itself include only descriptions of empirical facts. Second, and more to the point, rule-deductivists need not deny that the external justification of the minor premise may have to involve normative judgments about whether the facts of the case in hand do count as instances of the relevant general terms "for the purpose" of the rule. For that, again, is a matter of what goes into deciding to adopt a certain premise, rather than a matter of how one's premises, once adopted, must relate logically if the court's decision is to be justified.

It is true that some authors suggest that the scheme of the legal syllogism be expanded to reflect this point about the legal classification of the facts of the case. Andrei Marmor, for example, proposes that we make room for *two* "factual" premises rather than just one: one premise describing "something that happened in the world," another asserting that such facts count as instances of the general terms featured in the antecedent of the rule.[31] Chaïm Perelman had once advanced a similar view.[32] And Robert Alexy points out that we could supplement the simpler scheme of the syllogism with as many steps as needed to address any potentially controversial classificatory issue:

(1) For every x: if x is F, then x ought to be G.
(2) For every x: if x is M_1, then x is F.
(3) For every x: if x is M_2, then x is M_1.
. . .
(4) For every x: if x is H, then x is M_n.
(5) a is H.
Therefore (from (1) to (5)),
(6) a ought to be G.[33]

Premise (1) would be the formulation of the applicable legal rule (for example, a rule as "stated" in some valid statutory provision[34]). As to premises (2) to (4), Alexy remarks, they

[30] (Hart 1955, 260).
[31] See (Marmor 2014, 83–84).
[32] (Perelman 1961, 603).
[33] (Alexy 1989/1978, 227); my notation differs slightly from Alexy's. See also (Alexy 2003, 433–434).
[34] (Alexy 1989/1978, 224).

are not necessarily derived from any positive legal rules; but they are also not descriptions of empirical facts. Rather, they can be understood as statements of whatever rules underlie the court's decision to classify the facts of the case in hand under the relevant legal predicates. Premises (2) to (4) "bridge the gap," as it were, between the statement of the legal rule in (1), and the factual description in (5).[35]

But of course, as Alexy also notes,[36] (2), (3), (4), and (5) together entail

(5′) *a* is *F*,

which together with (1) entails (6). So we might just as well say that we have here one simple syllogism with (1) as the major premise and (5′) as the minor one; and that the role of statements (2) to (5) is that of providing external justification for (5′). Alternatively, but by the same token, given that (1), (2), (3), and (4) together entail

(5″) For every *x*: if *x* is *H*, then *x* ought to be *G*,

we might say that what we have is a simple syllogism with (5″) and (5) as premises; and that premises (1) to (4) provide external justification for (5″). (Note, though, that in neither case can the full justification dispense with the statement, in (1), of the relevant "applicable norm," as Alexy calls it.[37] That is the statement that specifies the terms or predicates under which the facts of the case are to be classified.) And the same point holds with regard to Perelman's and Marmor's suggestions.[38] A judge's claim that the facts of the case satisfy the relevant legal predicates may be the product of a normative judgment; but rule-deductivists remain free to hold that once such a claim is adopted, the conclusion will follow logically under the basic scheme of the legal syllogism.

F. In Summary

With all these caveats and qualifications, is rule-deductivism starting to sound like a trivial thesis? Its endorsers would deny the charge. Rule-deductivism, they say, provides the best picture of what is involved in the requirement that judges—in accordance with their proper role—apply existing law to the case at hand. Here is how Torben Spaak puts the point:

> The primary task of judges is to *decide* cases, not to expound the law. The natural starting-point, in keeping with the separation of powers, is that the judge has, in virtue of his office, a duty to judge in accordance with the law, that is, to apply existing law rather than create new law. Accordingly, deciding a case involves (i) finding and clarifying the law, (ii) determining the facts, and (iii) applying the law to the facts.

---

[35] (Alexy 1989/1978, 229).

[36] (Alexy 1989/1978, 227 n. 41).

[37] (Alexy 1989/1978, 225).

[38] I discuss Marmor's claims in further detail in (Duarte d'Almeida 2016).

> If we assume that law is a system of norms, we may view legal decision-making as a matter of applying legal norms to facts. On this analysis, deductive justification in the form of syllogistic reasoning will play an important role in legal reasoning.[39]

The ideal of the separation of powers, of course, also loomed large behind Beccaria's original mention of the syllogism as a model of the judicial application of the law:

> Nor can the authority to interpret the laws devolve upon the criminal judges, for the same reason that they are not legislators . . . The judge should construct a perfect syllogism about every criminal case: the major premise should be the general law; the minor, the conformity or otherwise of the action with the law; and the conclusion, freedom or punishment. Whenever the judge is forced, or takes it upon himself, to construct even as few as two syllogisms, then the door is opened to uncertainty.[40]

Beccaria's wording here is too strong, even slightly nonsensical. But we need not tie rule-deductivism to so simplistic a view of the separation of powers. Some rule-deductivists do claim that legislated rules have a "single and uniquely authoritative [linguistic] formulation"[41] to be found in the words of the statute; and that the legal syllogism is *especially* well-suited to represent the application of statutory rules.[42] But one does not need to endorse these claims to agree, as all rule-deductivists do, that the model of the syllogism does aptly capture the justification of judicial decisions that apply legislated rules.

So there you have it. Rule-deductivists do not think that there is nothing more to legal reasoning or judicial decision-making than applying existing law to particular cases. They do not claim that the justification of every judicial decision issued in accordance with law stands to be represented on the model of the legal syllogism. Some cases, though, are indeed governed by existing legal rules; and rule-deductivists claim to have the best account of what an argument for applying existing rules to particular cases involves. As again MacCormick puts it:

> when particular facts of particular cases do fit uncontroversially or after non-deductive resolution of controversy into the categories stipulated in universally quantified legal rules, then the universally prescribed legal consequence has particular application in the particular case. So if a judge ought to do justice according to law . . . he ought to implement that consequence here.[43]

The court's argument in such cases, in short, is, properly reconstructed, one in which a statement of the applicable rule features as a premise that "combined with [a description of] the facts of the case, suffices to yield the ruling."[44] Or so rule-deductivists say.

---

[39] (Spaak 2003, 236–237).

[40] (Beccaria 1764, 14).

[41] (MacCormick 1978, 58).

[42] See (Alexy 1980, 186).

[43] (MacCormick 1982b, 289).

[44] (Gardner 2007, 76).

III. Rule-Deductivism and the Justification of Law-Applying Decisions

What they say, though, is not convincing—certainly not if we take them at their word.[45]

Rule-deductivists often claim to be concerned with the *application* of rules to cases, and primarily with judicial *decisions* that apply rules to cases. Wróblewski, for example, refers to the judicial decision "as an application of a general legal norm (a statute) to the concrete facts of the case," and to the legal syllogism as "a suitable way of justifying [the] judicial decision."[46] Hart is clear that what is at issue is "the reasoning involved in the *application* of legislative rules to particular cases," and that it is "the court's *decision*"—my emphases—that is "represented as the conclusion of a syllogism."[47] Gardner says that the conclusion of the inference is a judicial *ruling* that *applies* the "existing legal norm" featured as the "major premise."[48] Bäcker speaks of the "syllogistic formalisation of rule-application."[49] And MacCormick goes as far as to claim that it is the framework of the legal syllogism that allows us to make sense of "what could possibly count as applying a statute at all."[50]

But the legal syllogism cannot model this. Let us go back to the passage by A. G. Guest that I briefly discussed in Section II:

> Let us take the words of a penal statute, in this case the Representation of People Act, 1949, s. 52: "Any person shall be guilty of an offence if, at a parliamentary or local government election, he fraudulently takes out of the polling station any ballot paper." Here the legal process consists in the application of a fixed and ascertained rule to the facts of a particular case. The section of the statute constitutes the major premiss, the minor being "X (the accused) at a parliamentary or local government election fraudulently took out of a polling station a ballot paper." This, it will be seen, comprises the words of the indictment. If the minor premiss is true, the offence is made out and X will be found guilty.[51]

At first glance, I said, this seems straightforward. Not so much at second glance. Consider Guest's last sentence. "If the minor premiss is true," he says, "the offence is made out and X

---

[45] Rule-deductivism has not been without some critics. Wellman (1985, 68–80), for example, argues that the deductivist model cannot account for situations in which there are several, conflicting rules applicable to the case in hand; and that it is unwarrantedly committed to the philosophically controversial view that legal statements must be truth-apt. Neumann (1985, 19–28) argues that the reconstruction of legal arguments in the form of the syllogism does not adequately represent the structure of legal argumentation; he thinks we would do better to adopt Stephen Toulmin's schemes (and Toulmin's distinctions among "data," "claims," "warrants," and so on: see (Toulmin 2014)). And Zuleta (2005), more recently, argues that rule-deductivism is committed to an inadequate conception of the logical form of general norms. I do not mean to either endorse or reject any of these criticisms; my own discussion of rule-deductivism takes a different tack.

[46] (Wróblewski 1974, 34, 38).

[47] (Hart 1967, 99).

[48] (Gardner 2004, 186).

[49] (Bäcker 2009, 406, my translation).

[50] (MacCormick 2005, 42).

[51] (Guest 1961, 182, footnote omitted).

will be found guilty." We already know we should substitute "X *ought* to be found guilty" for Guest's "X *will* be found guilty." But it is odd that Guest should state the conclusion of the inference the way he does. Take as premises of the relevant inference the two following statements, as Guest explicitly says we should:

(1) Any person shall be guilty of an offence if, at a parliamentary or local government election, he fraudulently takes out of the polling station any ballot paper.
(2) X (the accused) at a parliamentary or local government election fraudulently took out of a polling station a ballot paper.

What follows from the conjunction of (1) and (2) is that:

(3) X shall be guilty of an offense.

This claim, however, is importantly different from what Guest says the conclusion should be:

(3*) The offence is made out and X ought to be found guilty [of an offence].

This claim—the claim in (3*)—is a conjunction; and the second conjunct bears no relation to the rest of the inference. The claim in (3), that *X* shall *be* guilty of an offense, is not the same as the claim that X ought to (or shall—it makes no difference) *be found* guilty of an offense, which is what we find in (3*). (As to the first conjunct—the claim that "the offence is made out"—it is also unclear that it does follow from (1) and (2). To say that the offense is made out is to say that X committed—*is* guilty of—the offense; and that is not obviously the same as saying that X *shall be* guilty of the offense. But let that pass.) Where then could this reference—to X's being *found* guilty of an offense—have come from?

The answer is not hard to find. Guest, too, is explicitly concerned with the *application* of statutory rules: concerned, in his own words, with "deductive reasoning . . . in the sense of the application of a general rule to a particular instance."[52] So that—the application of the relevant rule—is what the inference is aimed at justifying. But then we must keep in mind something that Guest manifestly overlooks: that the application of a legal rule is an action; it is something that someone—paradigmatically a judge or court—does.[53] What action? That will vary from case to case. In Guest's example, the relevant action would be the court's *finding* the accused guilty (and indeed proceeding to *convict* him) of the relevant offense. That is the action that counts as applying the statutory rule to the case in hand. It is, therefore, what stands to be justified by the inference. That is why Guest's conclusion, the claim in (3*), plausibly mentions X's being *found* guilty.

What Guest misses is that if his inference is to provide justification for the court's finding the accused guilty, then the conclusion would have to be something like this—a claim that the relevant action is one that the court ought to perform:

(3′) Court *C* ought to find the accused guilty of an offense.

---

[52] (Guest 1961, 182).

[53] I come back to this point in Section V.

This is the sort of claim that has to be argued *for* if one wants to justify one's application of the provision to the facts in an example such as Guest's. But that means that (3′) is also the kind of claim that would have to feature as the consequent of the relevant "major premise": otherwise the inference won't run. The major premise, then, would have to read, not as (1), but as follows:

(1′) Court C *ought to find guilty of an offense* any person who at a parliamentary or local government election fraudulently takes out of the polling station any ballot paper.

The problem is that this can no longer serve as a statement of the relevant rule—the statutory rule that the court is supposed to be applying. Why not? Remember that Guest is clear that it is "the section of the statute" (or in any case the corresponding "fixed and ascertained" rule) that features *as* the major premise of the inference. But while the formulation in (1)—Guest's own statement of the major premise—is not, at least prima facie, an implausible way of stating the content of the relevant rule, the claim in (1′) is neither equivalent to, nor entailed by, the claim in (1); and does not plausibly stand as a statement of any rule that that provision could be taken to express.

It is normally the case, of course, that courts have a duty to—under certain conditions—find guilty, and convict, and sentence, criminal wrongdoers. And it seems sensible to say, as Guest does at one point, that "in the example cited, upon proof that the accused took out of the polling station a ballot paper, the courts are commanded to apply certain sanctions to the wrongdoer."[54] That is not what I am denying. My point is simply that this is something that does not follow from the statement of the rule that the court is supposed to be applying. The action that counts as applying the rule to the case cannot be found in, or derived from, any statement of the applicable rule itself. The legal syllogism, therefore, cannot model the justification of any such action.

It is purely for the sake of convenience that I have been focusing on the passage by Guest; the error I have just tried to bring out is far from being specifically his. Take the passage by Neil MacCormick that I quoted in Section I. It included the following two sentences:

> Rules being so conceptualised [as hypothetical in form], one who can establish in a given case that an instance of the relevant operative facts obtains can justifiably claim that the relevant normative consequence ought to follow, or indeed in the capacity of a judge can justifiably decide that it does follow, and can justifiably give a legal decision giving effect to that consequence. This is a form of deductive inference . . . : you postulate a general hypothetical rule, you establish facts in a particular case subsumable within the rule's hypothesis, and you draw the logical conclusion for the particular case from rule plus facts.[55]

54 (Guest 1961, 184).

55 (MacCormick 1982a, 182).

But this is wrong on two counts. First, given a statement of some relevant rule, what someone who establishes an instance of the relevant facts can justifiably claim is that the consequence *does* follow—it follows logically, if, as MacCormick claims, the reasoning is "deductive in essence"[56]—not that it *ought* to follow. Second, and more important, it certainly does *not* follow from those two premises that a judge can justifiably *give effect* to that consequence. Giving effect to the consequence is indeed one way of applying the relevant rule; but again it is not something that can be justified on the model of the syllogism.[57]

Or take John Gardner's views on the matter; he makes the same mistake in a different way. Gardner says that a legal argument is "an argument about what to do (e.g., what ruling to make)" in which "at least some legal norms figure among the major premises."[58] He agrees, then, that a ruling—making a ruling—is an action; something a judge *does*. Gardner also says that "a legal ruling is a legally binding decision on the application of a legal rule to what lawyers call a 'case': to a situation-token rather than a situation-type."[59] To make a ruling is therefore not merely to assert that the legal rule applies to the case. To make a ruling, Gardner says, is to exercise a normative power, and thereby to bring about changes in other people's normative positions.[60]

But consider Gardner's example of a "very simple two-premise legal argument that could be made by a judge":

Rule: Any person who calls another person a liar has a duty to pay $50 to that other person.
Fact: Barnewall (a person) called Adolphus (another person) a liar.
Ruling: Thus, Barnewall has a duty to pay $50 to Adolphus.[61]

This is a valid inference. But its conclusion is not, *pace* Gardner, a ruling. The conclusion is simply a claim in law—a proposition of law. It is the proposition that Barnewall has a certain duty. It is true if the premises are both true. But propositions are not actions, and therefore they are not rulings. And while *asserting* a proposition (or *making* a claim) is, of course, an action, it is also not the sort of action that Gardner calls a ruling. Simply asserting something does not amount to the exercise of any power, and brings about no changes in anyone's normative positions.

---

56 (MacCormick 1982a, 182).

57 In *Legal Reasoning and Legal Theory*, MacCormick is more careful. He writes at one point that we would actually need "a further premise" in order to "complete the justification of the argument"; but then he says that this further premise would simply convey "what is on the face of it a seemingly obvious proposition about the judicial function"—"that there are rules of law, and that a judge's job is to apply those rules when they are relevant and applicable": see (MacCormick 1978, 32–33, 53). This, however, does not solve the problem: none of the premises (or their conjunction) in the legal syllogism implies the claim that the relevant rule is applicable to the facts of the case; the complex argument would simply not run. I return to this crucial point in Section V.

58 (Gardner 2004, 188).

59 (Gardner 2007, 73).

60 (Gardner 2007, 74).

61 (Gardner 2007, 76).

The main problem, though, is not that the ruling itself—being an action rather than a proposition (or a sentence)—does not follow logically from the conjunction of those (or any) premises. The main problem is again that the court's ruling cannot be *justified* on the basis of what is asserted in Gardner's premises. If indeed a legal argument is, as Gardner says, "an argument about what to do (e.g., what ruling to make)," then the conclusion in his example would have to be something like the claim that *the judge ought to rule that Barnewall has a duty to pay $50 to Adolphus*—which is not something that those premises entail.

What, you may ask, turns on all this? Am I not making too much of a trivial point? Could rule-deductivists not simply reply that any legal syllogism may of course be coupled with a further premise of the relevant sort? Perhaps something like this (to keep to Gardner's example):

(o) If Barnewall has a duty to pay $50 to Adolphus, then the judge ought to rule that Barnewall has a duty to pay $50 to Adolphus.

The complex inference would then validly establish the relevant proposition—which, if true, would then justify the judge's ruling. Would this not do?

No, it wouldn't. For the challenge here is not to come up with an expansion of the syllogism that would yield a valid argument for the conclusion that the judge ought to rule that Barnewall has a duty to pay to $50 to Adolphus. The challenge, if we take rule-deductivists at their word, is to come up with an argument that can plausibly be said to capture—to model—the justification of such a ruling (as a law-applying decision). As we have just seen, the legal syllogism cannot model *that*. So the question becomes this: *What* is it exactly that the legal syllogism can with minimal plausibility be said to model? In other words, how should we reinterpret the rule-deductivist's thesis that there is *something* the legal syllogism can adequately model? We need first to answer that question—and then we need to ask whether *that* reinterpreted thesis is itself defensible. For if it isn't, then no expanded version of the syllogism will succeed as a model of the justification of law-applying decisions.

IV. Rule-Deductivism and the Justification of Particular Legal Claims

I think we should charitably reinterpret rule-deductivism as the view that the legal syllogism suitably models the justification of particular legal claims—particular propositions of law—when these are put forward on the basis that a certain legal rule applies to the relevant particular case.

To see this more clearly, take Gardner's example again:

Rule: Any person who calls another person a liar has a duty to pay $50 to that other person.
Fact: Barnewall (a person) called Adolphus (another person) a liar.
Ruling: Thus, Barnewall has a duty to pay $50 to Adolphus.[62]

[62] (Gardner 2007, 76).

The conclusion of this inference is a particular legal claim—it is, more precisely, a proposition about the normative position of a particular person, Barnewall, vis-à-vis another person, under existing law. And is the sort of proposition a judge would need to put forward, and be prepared to defend, as part of some more complex argument that would justify her ruling. According to how I now propose we understand rule-deductivism, then, what the legal syllogism adequately models is the justification of claims of that sort—propositions assigning some legal normative consequence or status to some particular case—when indeed they are made and justified on the basis that there is some existing rule that applies to the relevant case. In other words: when a judge properly justifies—argues for—a claim of that sort specifically on the basis that *that* is what some existing rule as applied to the case demands or warrants, her argument to that effect can be adequately reconstructed under the scheme of the legal syllogism.[63]

Does this revised version of rule-deductivism hold up to scrutiny? It is no longer open to the sort of logical objection presented in Section III. But it fails for different reasons. Thus understood, the model of the syllogism is, I think, inadequate in even the easiest of easy cases, when there is no doubt that the relevant rule applies to the case in hand. Those are cases that the model only seems to capture well; the appearance is deceptive. But the problems with the model are more easily and effectively brought out if we look at an example of an actual judicial opinion that the rule-deductivist picture is clearly unable to capture.

A. R v Luffe

In *R v Luffe* (1807) 8 East 193, the defendant, one H. Luffe, was appealing against an order of filiation made by two Justices of the Peace judging him the father of a child conceived with a Mrs. Mary Taylor, who was married to another man. The order of filiation had been made under the statute of 6 Geo. 2. Cap. 31, § 1, which provided that:

> [I]f any single woman shall be delivered of a bastard child which shall be chargeable or likely to become chargeable to any parish [. . .], and shall, in an examination to be taken in writing, upon oath, before one or more Justices of the Peace [of that parish] charge any person with having gotten her with child; it shall and may be made lawful to and for such Justice or Justices [. . .] to issue out his or their warrant or warrants for the immediate apprehending such person so charged [unless he gives security to indemnify the parish].

It was not disputed that this statutory provision gave "jurisdiction to magistrates to take examinations for making orders of filiation in case of bastards likely to become chargeable" to a parish.[64] But the defendant argued that the provision concerned children of *single*

[63] Rule-deductivists sometimes speak, somewhat casually, of "the legal reasoning advanced to justify *legal claims or legal decisions*"—(MacCormick 1982a, 182, emphasis added)—or of arguments aimed at showing that "*a decision* (*or a claim*) is justifiable according to the law in force"—(Alchourrón and Bulygin 1992, 252, emphasis added)—as if the model of the legal syllogism were equally suited to justify both. My suggestion is that we take them to be focusing solely on "claims", understood in the way just explained.

[64] *R v Luffe* (1807) 8 East 193, at 196.

women, and that his child "being the child of a married woman, the Justices of the Peace had no jurisdiction to make an order of filiation."[65]

The Court dismissed this objection. Lord Ellenborough CJ appealed to the "general purposes of the Act"—which were (as indicated in its Recital) "to provide for the securing and indemnifying parishes and other places from the great charges frequently arising from children begotten and born out of lawful matrimony"—and argued as follows:

> [W]hen the question is whether this were a child born out of lawful matrimony, that is, out of the limits and rights belonging to that state, it is the same in substance whether it be a bastard. It is so for the general purposes of the Act. The matrimony does not cover the child if it be in other respects (according to the rule of law applicable to this subject) a bastard. And so it seems that a child born by adulterous intercourse is as much within the provision of the Act of Geo. 2, as one which is born of a single woman.[66]

There is no doubt that Lord Ellenborough CJ's view was that the provision in 6 Geo. 2. Cap. 31, § 1 was applicable to the case of the defendant. Therefore, the court concluded, the Justices of the Peace did have jurisdiction to make the order of filiation in the case of the defendant. So can that argument be modeled on the scheme of the legal syllogism?

What could the major premise be? Perhaps something like this—closely following the statutory language?

(1) For every x and every y: if x is a single woman delivered of a bastard child chargeable to a parish, and y is a man charged on oath with being the father of the child, then the Justices of the Peace of the parish have jurisdiction to make an order of filiation judging y to be the father of the child.

But then the argument could not run unless the court relied on the following statement:

(2) Mary Taylor is a single woman delivered of a bastard child chargeable to a parish, and the defendant is a man charged on oath with being the father of the child.

That was not, though, a statement on which the court based either its view that the statutory provision in 6 Geo. 2. Cap. 31 did apply to the case, or its conclusion on the point in issue. The statement in (2) was plainly false on the facts of the case, and the court did not suggest otherwise. In fact, the court made no effort to bring the case under the language of the statute. As far as the court was concerned, the relevant facts stood to be described by saying that:

(2′) Mary Taylor is a married woman delivered of a bastard child chargeable to a parish, and the defendant is a man charged on oath with being the father of the child.

---

[65] *R v Luffe* (1807) 8 East 193, at 194.

[66] *R v Luffe* (1807) 8 East 193, at 204.

It does not, of course, follow from (1) and (2′) that the Justices of the Peace have jurisdiction to make an order of filiation judging the defendant to be the father of the child. Yet that did not prevent the court from arguing that the statutory provision did apply to the facts.

The court bypassed, as it were, the supposed antecedent of the statutory rule—whether formulated as in (1) or indeed in some other way—relying instead on a different sort of consideration: the "general purposes" of the Act. What that means is that the court's argument for the claim—the particular legal claim—that the Justices of the Peace did have jurisdiction to make the order of filiation with respect to the defendant cannot be reconstructed on the model of the syllogism. So rule-deductivism is wrong.

You may think this is too quick. What could rule-deductivists say in response? I see three possible lines of defense.

B. Is Luffe *Representative?*

First, rule-deductivists could try to dismiss Lord Ellenborough CJ's remarks in *R v Luffe* as a poor example of the kind of argument with which they are concerned. Courts do not normally sidestep classificatory questions or apply statutory rules on the sole grounds that that would serve the "purposes" of the statute. Why think that the *Luffe* court was even purporting to decide in accordance with law? Isn't it more plausible to see *Luffe* as an outlier case—perhaps even a legally deviant one—and to exclude it from the class of cases that rule-deductivists aim to account for?

The fact is that *Luffe* is a perfectly representative specimen. It is true that courts do not often apply statutory rules to cases not encompassed by the language of the statute. But it does not follow that when they do, they are acting impermissibly—or that they are not applying the relevant statutory rules. Moreover, my point is conceptual, not normative. My point is that *Luffe* is an example of a court appealing to considerations of a certain sort—considerations of "purpose"—in order to justify its view that a statutory rule applies to a certain case. Whether courts were then, or are now, permitted to appeal to such considerations is, therefore, immaterial. Even in a legal system in which decisions such as *Luffe* were always impermissible, such decisions would still count, conceptually, as rule-applying decisions. They would simply be examples of illegitimate ways of applying the law. It is, after all, a contingent matter whether considerations of purpose do feature among those that can permissibly be appealed to in any given jurisdiction; and rule-deductivists are concerned with providing a general jurisprudential account of the structure of the justification of legal claims on the basis of existing legal rules, rather than an account of some jurisdiction-specific set of permissible ways of applying or appealing to such rules.

In any event, there is evidence that decisions of this sort, though comparatively rare, are generally regarded as legitimate in contemporary legal systems. Consider, for example, how another, more recent decision—the Queen's Bench Division's in *Smith v Hughes* [1960] 2 All ER—has been described in a couple of recent texts:

> A classic illustration where the scope [of criminal liability] was expanded [relative to the literal scope of the provision] is that of *Smith v Hughes* where a prostitute was charged with "soliciting *in* a street for the purpose of prostitution" [which were the exact words

of the relevant statutory provision, s. 1(1) of the Street Offences Act, 1959]. It was held that the offence was committed even where the woman was not in a street but was soliciting from a balcony *above* the street. The provision was obviously interpreted neither literally nor strictly, but according to the purpose of the Act, namely to remove the nuisance and offence of solicitation.[67] In [*Smith v Hughes*] the court did not use the plain, ordinary grammatical meaning of the words "in a street or public place". Instead, the judges looked to see what the mischief the Act was aimed at.[68]

Smith is—literally—a textbook example of a court justifying its view on the applicability of a provision to a case by turning to considerations of statutory "purpose" (or "mischief") rather than language. And *Luffe*, too, was reported at the time without any suggestion that there had been anything untoward about it; and described, rightly, as a decision on the application of the 6 Geo. 2. statutory provision:

> Upon the 18 Eliz. c. 3, which has the words "bastards begotten and born out of lawful matrimony", and the 6 Geo. II., which refers only to the case of a single woman, it was doubted whether these statutes applied if the mother was a married woman; but they were finally decided [in *R v Luffe*] to have that application.[69]

Why should we care about how the *Luffe* court, or the *Smith* court, or any doctrinal commentators, viewed these decisions? Is it not possible for at least some courts and commentators to be mistaken about what counts as law-application? Or am I implying that if a court or a lawyer refers to some particular judicial decision as a decision on the application of a rule to a case, then that decision *is* an instance of a decision on the application of a rule to a case? That is not my suggestion. But the way in which courts and lawyers refer to their own activities does constitute good pre-theoretical evidence—not irrefutable evidence, but strong evidence nonetheless—for how we as theorists should regard such activities. It is, therefore, not open to rule-deductivists to shoo away counterexamples such as *Luffe* on the sole grounds that they do not fit their account—especially given that, as I noted in Section II.A, we would be hard-pressed to find in their writings any attempt to provide a clear characterization of their own object of theorization.

In order to successfully dismiss such counterexamples, then, rule-deductivists would have to show not merely that opinions such as Lord Ellenborough CJ's in *Luffe* are not examples of what *they* take—pre-theoretically—the relevant kind of claim or decision or argument to be, but also that such a restrictive understanding of their object would actually be justified. I do not think that rule-deductivists would want, upon reflection, to make even the first of these two points. But if they did, then I do not see that they would be able to defend the second.

---

[67] (Wilson 2014, 22).

[68] (Huxley-Binns and Martin 2014, 78–79). Glanville Williams, who dedicated a whole essay to *Smith*, says that the court "dismissed the wording of the Act with unlawyerly brusqueness," but notes that "[t]he reasoning in *Smith v Hughes* was sufficiently plausible to enable the decision to have passed entirely without criticism, and moreover to be followed and extended by the courts." See (Williams 1981, 74, 79).

[69] (Theobald 1836, 416).

For although it is true that we should not just take courts and doctrinal commentators at their word no matter what, I cannot see what other considerations rule-deductivists could offer that would warrant the pre-theoretical exclusion of cases such as *Luffe* from the scope of their inquiry. Such cases may be infrequent in actual practice; but there is nothing theoretically atypical about them qua instances of decisions on the application of existing law to particular cases.

C. *A Different Major Premise?*

There is, though, a different reply that rule-deductivists—some of them, at least—might offer. I seem to be assuming, they might say, that rule-deductivism is committed to the idea that the formulation of the major premise in the legal syllogism should match, or at least track very closely, the text of the relevant statutory provision. But why assume that? Why think that formulation (1) above is the correct way of rendering the relevant rule? True, *some* rule-deductivists do take the view—as I mentioned in Section II—that legislated rules have fixed formulations to be found in the language of the relevant statute. This goes back to the point about separation of powers and about legislative authority and its role in the justification of law-applying decisions. Here, for example, is Neil MacCormick:

> That it is an essential consequence of appointment to judicial office that a judge must apply valid rules of law in exercising his jurisdiction indicates the interrelationship between adjudication and legislation—because legislation is *par excellence* the process whereby valid rules of law are made . . .
>
> I have said that "legislation is *par excellence* the process whereby valid rules of law are made"; that for two reasons. Legislation is unique as a source of law in that it yields what have been felicitously called [by Twining and Miers] "rules in fixed verbal form," rules which have a single and uniquely authoritative formulation, their formulation in the *ipsissima verba* of the legislature . . .[70]

These authors—a subset of those who endorse rule-deductivism—think that "the authoritative statement of an enacted rule remains static";[71] that "legislation presents us with more or less ready-made norms"; [72] that statutory rules are thereby "fixed and ascertained."[73] Such rule-deductivists will therefore find themselves in trouble when faced with decisions such as *Luffe*. But did I not also say in Section II that we should *not* think of rule-deductivism as being necessarily coupled with such strict and unduly reductive views on legislative authority, on the position of judges vis-à-vis lawmakers, and on the separation of powers?

---

[70] (MacCormick 1978, 57–58, footnote omitted).

[71] (Burton 2007, 43).

[72] (Spaak 2003, 237).

[73] (Guest 1961, 182). Compare also (Alexy 1980, 186), and (MacCormick 2005, 36), both of whom remark that statutory norms are typically universal norms, and suggest that when the rule being applied is a statutory rule, the relevant "universals" that must be instantiated in the particular case are those "deployed in the statute" (as MacCormick puts it).

Would it not be open to rule-deductivists, then, to point out, with regard to *Luffe*, that we should differentiate between the text of the provision, and the rule brought into existence by the valid enactment of a statute? And do courts not have to interpret statutory texts in order to grasp the rules they express? So why think that the court in *Luffe* was doing anything different? Why not say instead that what Lord Ellenborough CJ's argument reveals is that he took the provision in 6 Geo. 2. Cap. 31, § 1 to express a rule whose formulation does *not* track the statutory text *verbatim*? Which rule? Maybe one along the following lines:

(1′) For every *x* and every *y*: if *x* is a woman delivered of a bastard child chargeable to a parish, and *y* is a man charged on oath with being the father of the child, then the Justices of the Peace of the parish have jurisdiction to make an order of filiation judging *y* to be the father of the child.

Here the formulation of the antecedent—which, apart from the suppression of the adjective "single," is the same as the antecedent of formulation (1) in Section IV.A above—is one that the particular facts of the case did instantiate: Mary Taylor was indisputably a woman. Therefore, rule-deductivists might say, *R v Luffe* can be brought under the model of the syllogism after all. All we need is to take the court to have relied on a rule such as (1′), based on some suitable interpretation of the relevant statutory provision.

The problem for this reply is that that was plainly not what the *Luffe* court was doing. The point of the *Luffe* challenge is not that the court did not justify its law-applying decision on the basis of a rule—understood, along rule-deductivist lines, as a universal conditional—that closely tracked the language of the statute. The point of the challenge is that the court did not justify its law-applying decision on the basis of any rule *at all*.

The *Luffe* court was concerned with one specific question: the question of whether the provision in 6 Geo. 2. Cap. 31, § 1 applied *to the case in hand*. Now, in order to both form and justify its view on that matter, the court had no need to identify the full range of cases to which that provision would also apply. That, however, is what rule-deductivists would have to say the court had to be doing. For rule-deductivists presuppose that in order to reach a decision on the applicability of a provision to a particular case, a judge needs to ask herself what the conditions are that would have to be met by *any* case to which the provision applies. That is precisely what the major premise of the legal syllogism is supposed to specify. All Lord Ellenborough CJ claimed, however, was that the provision in 6 Geo. 2. Cap. 31, § 1 applied to the particular case in hand—a case in which the defendant had been charged with conceiving a child with a woman married to someone else. Why should that require him to articulate—let alone rely on as a premise in his argument—a universal conditional spelling out the common properties of the cases to which that provision applies? Indeed, why think that a judge would even be *capable* of answering such a question if she tried?

It is not simply that courts do not, and cannot reasonably be expected to, offer watertight descriptions of the properties that will have to be met by any case to which the relevant statutory provision applies. They cannot even be reasonably expected to offer watertight descriptions of the relevant properties *of the case in hand*—the properties by virtue of which the relevant provision applies to it. So even if rule-deductivists were to further qualify their views by claiming that the major premise of the legal syllogism does not really have to be a statement of *the* relevant applicable rule—provided it is a statement of *a* rule implied by the statement of *the* applicable rule—theirs would remain an inadequate model of the relevant kind of argument.

Rule-deductivists might be tempted to object that I am overlooking a basic point about law-applying decisions: their universalizability. How can I suggest that Lord Ellenborough CJ's decision that the provision applied to the case in hand did not bind him to any view about that provision's applicability to any other cases? Is it not a requirement of formal justice that like cases be treated alike? Does that not imply that Lord Ellenborough CJ must have been committed to at least the view that *all* cases that are similar in all relevant respects to the case before him are cases to which the provision in 6 Geo. 2. Cap. 31, § 1 applies? And does that not involve a commitment to the corresponding universal conditional?[74]

That may be so, but it misses my point. I did not say that Lord Ellenborough CJ's decision was adopted on non-universalizable grounds. I did not deny that his decision—on whether the provision in 6 Geo. 2. Cap. 31, § 1 applied to the case in hand—committed him, rationally, to the claim that every other case that is similar in all relevant respects to the case in hand is one to which that same provision would apply. My point is that his decision did not commit him to any precise and definitive view on *what exactly those relevant respects* were.[75] (What would the correct universal formulation be? That *every* case of a man charged with being the father of a child conceived with a woman married to another man was one to which the provision applies? Would this not be overinclusive? And how would we know? Some other formulation then?)

The court did not commit itself to any such universal. That is simply not how courts support their views on the application of statutory rules to particular cases.[76] MacCormick writes that "one justifies particular implementations of the legal consequence [specified in a legal rule] by showing that the relevant operative facts do obtain in a particular case in hand."[77] This is, I think, exactly wrong. One does not show—or argue—that *the* relevant operative facts—MacCormick means fact-types, not tokens—obtain in a particular case. What one argues is that the facts—the fact-tokens—that obtain in a particular case are relevant. This is not to say that we have a good jurisprudential understanding of what such arguments look like. Whatever they look like, though, it is not the legal syllogism.

D. *A Different Minor Premise?*

There is, I suppose, a third reply that some rule-deductivists might offer to try to defuse the *Luffe* challenge. Rule-deductivists might choose to insist that there really is a major premise

[74] On the formal justice requirement that every judicial decision be justified by reference to a universal norm, see (Alexy 1989/1978, 222) and (MacCormick 2005, 75).

[75] This is the same point that underlies the reconstruction of analogical arguments in law: see (Duarte d'Almeida and Michelon 2017).

[76] And even when they *do* offer general statements of what they take the applicable law or "rule" to be, such statements are not properly construed as universal conditionals on which such courts rely as premises. Evidence for this? The disclaimers that judges occasionally offer about what *they* themselves take such statements to mean, and more generally the way in which courts routinely refer to, and treat, similar general statements as made by *other* courts in previous decisions.

[77] (MacCormick 1982b, 287).

in Lord Ellenborough CJ's argument, and that it actually does track the authoritative language of the statutory rule with its explicit reference to single women:

(1) For every *x* and every *y*: if *x* is a single woman delivered of a bastard child chargeable to a parish, and *y* is a man charged on oath with being the father of the child, then the Justices of the Peace of the parish have jurisdiction to make an order of filiation judging *y* to be the father of the child.

But they could maintain that the court did endorse, however implicitly, a minor premise of the relevant kind:

(2) Mary Taylor is a single woman delivered of a bastard child chargeable to a parish, and H. Luffe is a man charged on oath with being the father of the child.

The point would not be that the *Luffe* court took this to be established as a matter of fact; Mary Taylor was not in fact single. But given that the court nevertheless held the view that the statutory rule did apply to the case of Mary Taylor, it must have adopted the view that she *counted as* a single woman for the purpose of the rule. *Luffe*, then, rule-deductivists could point out, was just one of those cases in which the adoption by the judge of the minor premise is the product of some normatively driven classificatory decision. But the model of the syllogism is perfectly capable—as we saw in Section II.E—of accommodating cases like that. We should therefore take the *Luffe* court to have been committed to something along the lines of

(2″) For every *x*: if *x* is a married woman delivered of a bastard child chargeable to a parish, then *x* is a single woman delivered of a bastard child chargeable to a parish,

which, together with the (factually true[78]) claim that

(2′) Mary Taylor is a married woman delivered of a bastard child chargeable to a parish, and the defendant is a man charged on oath with being the father of the child,

deductively entails the claim in (2). Therefore, the rule-deductivist might say, the decision in *Luffe* can be reconstructed on the model of the syllogism after all.

The problem with this reply is that it is question-begging. It has no support in the decision itself. Lord Ellenborough CJ made *no* attempt, as I pointed out, to bring the facts of the case under the classificatory terms of the provision. It is, of course, how the argument would have to look like, and how we would have to interpret it, if the model of the syllogism were, as rule-deductivists claim, a good one. But whether rule-deductivists are right is precisely what is at issue.

E. *In Summary*

What lessons should we glean from our discussion? There are two ways of interpreting the rule-deductivist view. On one reading, discussed in Section III, rule-deductivists hold that

[78] I am disregarding the possibility of "bastard" being a thick term.

the legal syllogism provides us with a suitable model of the justification of law-applying decisions. On another reading, discussed in this section, what rule-deductivists hold is that the legal syllogism provides us with a suitable model of the justification of particular legal claims made on the basis that some existing legal rule applies to the relevant case. We saw that neither position is tenable.

Our discussion has therefore brought out that we need jurisprudential accounts of *both* those issues as a well as a clearer understanding of the relations between the two. It has also begun, I hope, to provide insight into some crucial distinctions that the rule-deductivist model either obscures or overlooks. It is beyond the scope of this chapter, as I said in Section I, to address all of the many questions that these topics give rise to. Still, to conclude, I will offer a sketch—no more—of an alternative model of the justification of law-applying decisions, and a few programmatic thoughts on the work that lies ahead.

V. What Should an Alternative Model Look Like?

I want to pick up and briefly expand on some remarks I made in Section III on what it means to say that a court applied a statutory rule in a certain case. "Applying a rule" is a phrase that is often loosely used. Courts are just as likely to say they are applying a statutory rule as to say they are applying a statutory *provision*—an article or section, for example—or even several related provisions at once. Rule-deductivists, too—although they would probably maintain they are concerned with the application of statutory rules rather than provisions—are not always consistent in how they use their terms, as some of the quotes above illustrate. And I myself have not taken much care so far to emphasize the distinction. But now—as the discussion in Section IV will have made apparent—we need to be clearer. Unlike rule-deductivists, however, I think we should take courts more seriously. In order to make sense of the justification of law-applying decisions, our focus should be, I believe, on statutory provisions rather than rules.

Applying a provision to a case is only one of two related notions that need clarification if we are to bring out the structure of the justification of law-applying decisions. The other is the notion of *a provision's applying* to a case. Both are familiar notions, notions we normally use when talking about the law and judicial decisions. It is not easy, however, to explain exactly what each involves—and how they are related.

Maybe we can start by noticing some immediately apparent differences between the two notions. To say that a given statutory provision *applies—is applicable—to* a case is, ostensibly, to say something about a relation between the provision and the relevant case. To say that a court *applied* a provision to a case, by contrast, is, as I pointed out in Section III, to say something about what the court *does*. When we say that a court applied a statutory provision, part of what we mean is that the judge issued a certain decision. To issue a decision is to *rule* on an issue, and to rule on an issue is to perform a certain action: it is, for example, to *convict* a criminal defendant, to *instruct* one party to pay damages to the other, to *allow* the submission of additional evidence, and so on. Unless and until a judge has actually ruled on some issue before her, she has not applied any statute or provision. But when we say that the judge applied a certain provision, we also mean that the judge took and presented her decision as justified by reference to the relevant provision: that she believed her ruling to be in some sense warranted by—inter alia—the provision. That is what the judge will try to show in the part of her opinion in which she justifies—lays down the reasons for—her decision. Applying a statutory provision, then, involves two things: (a) the performance, by the court, of an action that (b) the court justifies by reference to the provision. What exactly does this justificatory link look like? What does it mean to justify an action "by reference" to a statutory provision? That is one of the things we need to clarify.

As to how the two notions relate to each other, it seems plausible to say that when a judge faces a case to which a certain provision *applies*—when there is a statutory provision that is applicable to the case in hand—then the judge ought *to apply* the provision to the case. That means that the judge ought to perform *whatever action* counts as the action involved in applying the provision to the case in hand. This begins to capture, I think, one central feature of the role of a judge. It also suggests the following simple point, with which rule-deductivists would, I believe, agree: in order to justify her decision—the decision she actually issues—by reference to any given statutory provision, a judge will need to claim both (a) that the case in hand is one to which the provision applies, and (b) that the issuance of that decision is the action that counts as applying the provision in the case in hand.

I say rule-deductivists would agree—at least they should agree—because I think these two aspects of the justification of law-applying decisions are also what they are attempting to capture, whether or not they fully realize it. For them, as we know, to say that *a provision applies*—is *applicable—to* a case is to say that the case satisfies the antecedent of the rule that the provision expresses. We saw in Section IV that this account cannot make sense of decisions such as *R v Luffe*, and one point I then made was that Lord Ellenborough CJ's judgment that the case in hand was one to which the relevant provision applied was not justified by reference to anything even remotely like a wholly worked-out criterion for determining the full range of cases to which that provision applied. That is not a quirk of the *Luffe* judgment. It is a perfectly general feature of law-applying judicial decisions; *Luffe* just happens to be the type of case in which this feature becomes apparent. In cases in which the application of statutory provisions is at issue, what the court needs to tackle is the question of whether the relevant provision is applicable in the case in hand. "Is this statutory provision applicable in *this* case?"—*that* is the question, not "*When* is this statutory provision applicable?"

If this is correct, we want our model of the justification of law-applying decisions to reflect it. And that means, I think, that we need to sever the ties forged by rule-deductivists between the justification of the claim that a statutory provision applies to a case, and the claim that the case satisfies the antecedent of the rule (or any rule) that the provision supposedly expresses.

Here then is one first attempt at reconstructing the structure of the justification of law-applying decisions. The point I just made—that when a judge is tasked with deciding a case and there is a valid statutory provision that applies to that case, the judge ought to decide the case by applying the provision—can be put in relatively more precise terms as follows:

> For every judge J, every case C, every provision P, and every action ϕ, if (a) J is tasked with deciding C, (b) P applies to C, and (c) ϕ-ing is what counts as applying P in C, then J ought to ϕ.[79]

[79] Straying from convention for the sake of presentational clarity, I use capital letters as variables.

My suggestion is that we model the justification of law-applying decisions as an argument that takes a conditional such as the one above as a premise, and whose remaining premises are simply the individual statements needed to instantiate its antecedent. Here is the structure of the inference (with small case letters used as individual constants):

(1) For every judge *J*, every case *C*, every provision *P*, and every action ϕ, if (a) *J* is tasked with deciding *C*, (b) *P* applies to *C*, and (c) ϕ-ing is the action that counts as applying *P* to *C*, then *J* ought to ϕ.
(2) Judge *j* is tasked with deciding case *c*.
(3) Provision *p* applies to case *c*.
(4) ϕ-ing is the action that counts as applying provision *p* to case *c*.
Therefore (from (1)–(4)),
(5) *j* ought to ϕ.

There are two general points to highlight about this scheme. The first is that it is still, of course, the scheme of a deductively valid inference. As I said in Section I, my objection to rule-deductivism has nothing to do with the fact that its endorsers propose to represent the justification of law-applying decisions in the form of a deductive argument; it has to do with the fact that they think that the argument should incorporate, as a premise, a statement *of* the rule that the court is supposedly applying.

Indeed, the scheme makes clear—and this is the second, more important point—that premise (3) is a second-order statement about some statutory provision and its relation to a case. Premise (3) mentions, rather than states, the relevant provision (or any rule that the provision is taken to express). What premise (3) states is that the provision applies to the case in hand. Rule-deductivists, by contrast, seem to want to cash out in first-order terms the second-order idea that a statutory rule applies to a case. But how could that be right? If the justification of the court's decision—the justification of the court's *applying* a provision to the case in hand—turned, as rule-deductivists claim, on the fact that the case satisfies the antecedent of the corresponding statutory rule, then what we would need as a premise in the argument would be the second-order statement *that the antecedent of the rule is satisfied* by the case—not a statement *of* the relevant rule together with a statement *of* facts that satisfy its antecedent. Conversely, an argument that featured a first-order statement *of* the relevant rule as a premise, and combined it, as in the rule-deductivists' legal syllogism, with a description of facts that satisfy the antecedent of the rule, could not itself justify the second-order claim that the rule applies to the facts. The rule-deductivist's legal syllogism, in other words, is incapable of justifying a statement such as (3).

What of the justification of a particular first-order claim in law on the basis that there is some provision that applies to the facts of the case in hand? The same thought applies. For convenience, take the *Luffe* case yet again. It seems plausible to say that the court justified the relevant first-order claim—the claim that the Justices of the Peace had jurisdiction to make an order of filiation regarding the defendant—on the basis of the second-order claim that the provision in 6 Geo. 2. Cap. 31, § 1 applied to the case of the defendant. But then what that suggests is that we reconstruct the relevant argument along the following lines:

(i) If the provision in 6 Geo. 2. Cap. 31, § 1 applies to the case of the defendant, then the Justices of the Peace of the parish have jurisdiction to make an order of filiation judging the defendant to be the father of the child.
(ii) The provision in 6 Geo. 2. Cap. 31, § 1 applies to the case of the defendant.
Therefore (from (i) and (ii)),
(iii) The Justices of the Peace of the parish have jurisdiction to make an order of filiation judging the defendant to be the father of the child.

Here too the point is that the relevant premise—premise (ii)—is an applicability claim: a second-order claim about the applicability of the provision to the case in hand, rather than a first-order statement of any rule that the provision is taken to express.

VI. Conclusion

Let me finish by stressing that the schemes just offered are meant as only a first attempt at clarifying the structure of the relevant inferences. My primary goal in this chapter has been to take issue with the rule-deductivist model of the legal syllogism. That task is completed. But there is much work still to be done on these issues, and it is likely that my proposed schemes will have to be refined as a result. For one, the mere adoption of these schemes leaves open the question of how best to understand and justify statements that a provision applies to a certain case. The very notion of a *case*, indeed, is far from easy to explain—it is probably multiply ambiguous—and stands in need of clarification. We also need a better account of the notion of a legal rule, and of how rules relate to legal provisions and applicability claims. And we need an account of both the meaning and the form of general statements of legal "rules" of the sort that lawyers commonly offer, given that we have reason to resist understanding such statements as universal conditionals. This chapter's connection to the driving theme of this volume is therefore less direct than that of other pieces here included. It tries to clear some ground for future work on a range of metatheoretical topics; but the exploration of these matters I must leave for another occasion.

References

Alchourrón, Carlos E., and Eugenio Bulygin. 1992. "Limits of Logic and Legal Reasoning," reprinted in Bulygin, *Essays in Legal Philosophy*. Oxford: Oxford University Press, 2015.

Alexy, Robert. 1980. "Die logische Analyse juristischer Entscheidungen." In *Argumentation und Recht*, edited by W. Hassemer, A. Kaufmann, and U. Neumann. Wiesbaden: Franz Steiner.

_____. 1989/1978. *A Theory of Legal Argumentation: The Theory of Rational Discourse as Theory of Legal Justification*, R. Adler and N. MacCormick trans. Oxford: Oxford University Press.

_____. 2003. "On Balancing and Subsumption. A Structural Comparison." *Ratio Juris* 16:433–449.

Atienza, Manuel. 2005. *Las Razones del Derecho: Teorías de la Argumentación Jurídica*. Mexico: UNAM.

______. 2013. *Curso de Argumentación Jurídica*. Madrid: Trotta.

Bäcker, Carsten. 2009. "Der Syllogismus als Grundstruktur des juristischen Begründens?" *Rechtstheorie* 40:404–424.

Beccaria, Cesare. 1764. "On Crimes and Punishments." In *On Crimes and Punishments and Other Writings*, R. Davies; edited by R. Bellamy and translated by R. Davies. Cambridge: Cambridge University Press.

Brewer, Scott. 1996. "Exemplary Reasoning: Semantics, Pragmatics, and the Rational Force of Legal Argument by Analogy." *Harvard Law Review* 109:923–1028.

Burton, Steven J. 2007. *An Introduction to Law and Legal Reasoning*, 3rd ed. New York: Aspen.

Chiassoni, Pierluigi. 1999. *La Giurisprudenza Civile: Metodi d'Interpretazione e Tecniche Argomentative*. Milan: Giuffrè.

Comanducci, Paolo. 1999. "Il Ragionamento Giudiziale: Lineamenti di un Modello." In *Interpretazione e Diritto Giudiziale I: Regole, Metodi, Modelli*, edited by M. Bessone. Torino: Giappichelli.

Duarte d'Almeida, Luís. 2016. "Book Review [of Andrei Marmor's *The Language of Law*]." *Ethics* 126:845–850.

Duarte d'Almeida, Luís, and Cláudio Michelon. 2017. "The Structure of Arguments by Analogy in Law." *Argumentation* 31:359–393.

Engisch, Karl. 1963. *Logische Studien zur Gesetzesanwendung*, 3rd ed. Heidelberg: Carl Winter.

Feteris, Eveline. 2017. *Fundamentals of Legal Argumentation: A Survey of Theories on the Justification of Judicial Decisions*. 2nd ed. Dordrecht: Springer.

Gardner, John. 2004. "The Legality of Law." Reprinted in Gardner. *Law as a Leap of Faith: Essays on Law in General.* Oxford: Oxford University Press, 2012.

______. 2007. "Some Types of Law." Reprinted in Gardner. *Law as a Leap of Faith: Essays on Law in General.* Oxford: Oxford University Press, 2012.

Golding, Martin P. 1986. "A Note on Discovery and Justification in Science and Law." *Nomos* 28:124–140.

Guest, A. G. 1961. "Logic in the Law." In *Oxford Essays in Jurisprudence*, edited by A. G. Guest. Oxford: Oxford University Press.

Hart, H. L. A. 1955. "Theory and Definition in Jurisprudence." *Proceedings of the Aristotelian Society: Supplementary Volumes* 29:239–264.

______. 1967. "Problems of the Philosophy of Law." Reprinted in Hart, *Essays in Jurisprudence and Philosophy*. Oxford: Clarendon Press, 1983.

______. 2012/1961. *The Concept of Law*, 3rd ed. Oxford: Oxford University Press.

Huxley-Binns, Rebecca, and Jacqueline Martin. 2014. *Unlocking the English Legal System*, 4th ed. London and New York: Routledge.

Kalinowski, George. 1964. "Le Syllogisme d'Application du Droit." *Archives de Philosophie du Droit* 9:273–285.

Kelsen, Hans. 1967/1960. *Pure Theory of Law*, M. Knight trans. Berkeley: University of California Press.

Leiter, Brian. 2010. "Legal Formalism and Legal Realism: What Is the Issue?" *Legal Theory* 16: 11–133.

Lyons, David. 1984. "Justification and Judicial Responsibility." *California Law Review* 72:178–199.

MacCormick, Neil. 1978. *Legal Reasoning and Legal Theory*. Oxford: Clarendon Press.

_____. 1982a. "Legal Deduction, Legal Predicates, and Expert Systems." *International Journal for the Semiotics of Law* 5:181–202.

_____. 1982b. "The Nature of Legal Reasoning: A Brief Reply to Dr. Wilson." *Legal Studies* 2:286–290 at 289.

_____. 2005. *Rhetoric and the Rule of Law: A Theory of Legal Reasoning*. Oxford: Oxford University Press.

Marmor, Andrei. 2014. *The Language of Law*. Oxford: Oxford University Press.

Mazzarese, Tecla. 1996. *Forme di Razionalità delle Decisioni Giudiziali*. Torino: Giappichelli.

Neumann, Ulfrid. 1985. *Juristische Argumentationslehre*. Darmstadt: Wissenschaftliche Buchgesellschaft.

Perelman, Chaïm. 1961. "La Distinction du Fait et du Droit du Point de Vue du Logicien." *Dialectica* 15:601–610.

Pound, Roscoe. 1908. "Mechanical Jurisprudence." *Columbia Law Review* 8:605–623.

Rotolo, Antonino. 2001. *Identità e Somiglianza: Saggio sul Pensiero Analogico in Diritto*. Bologna: Clueb.

Soeteman, Arend. 1995. "Formal Aspects of Legal Reasoning." *Argumentation* 9:731–746.

Spaak, Torben. 2003. "Principled and Pragmatic Theories of Legal Reasoning." In *Festskrift till Åke Frändberg*, edited by A. Fogelklou and T. Spaak. Uppsala: Iustus Forlag.

Theobald, William. 1836. *A Practical Treatise on the Poor Laws, as Altered by the Poor Law Amendment Act, and Other Recent Statutes*. London: Stevens & Sons.

Toulmin, Stephen E. 2014. *The Uses of Argument*, updated ed. Cambridge: Cambridge University Press.

Wasserstrom, Richard A. 1961. *The Judicial Decision: Towards a Theory of Legal Justification*. Stanford, CA: Stanford University Press.

Wellman, Vincent A. 1985. "Practical Reasoning and Judicial Justification: Towards an Adequate Theory." *University of Colorado Law Review* 57:45–115.

White, Patricia D. 1980. "Some Observations on MacCormick's *Legal Reasoning and Legal Theory*." *Michigan Law Review* 78:737–742.

Williams, Glanville. 1981. "Statute Interpretation, Prostitution and the Rule of Law." In *Crime, Proof and Punishment: Essays in Memory of Sir Rupert Cross*, edited by C. F. H. Tapper. London: Butterworths.

Wilson, Alida. 1982. "The Nature of Legal Reasoning." *Legal Studies* 2:269–285.

Wilson, William. 2014. *Criminal Law*, 5th ed. Harlow: Pearson.

Wróblewski, Jerzy. 1971. "Legal Decision and Its Justification." *Logique et Analyse* 14:409–419.

_____. 1974. "Legal Syllogism and Rationality of Judicial Decision." *Rechtstheorie* 5:33–46.

Zuleta, Hugo. 2005. "La Fundamentación de las Sentencias Judiciales: Una Crítica a la Teoría Deductivista." *Isonomía* 23:59–95.

16 Dworkin's Literary Analogy

Sam Shpall*

FOR DECADES RONALD Dworkin defended the view that legal interpretation is constructive. Dworkin and his commentators provide many glosses on this idea, but here is the canonical formulation: legal interpretation is an attempt *to best fit and justify the law*.[1]

Dworkin argued for this thesis in various ways. Most famously, he claimed that it is necessary for explaining the prevalence of "theoretical disagreements"—disagreements rooted in divergent conceptions of what facts ultimately ground legal content. Dworkin's expositors and critics have devoted a huge amount of attention to this argument. This chapter explores a related but separable set of ideas that have been less systematically interrogated. They are crystalized in an intriguing analogical argument, where Dworkin endorses a version of constructive interpretation about literature, and asserts a deep connection between literature and the law.

My concern here is to question this literary analogy. The main sentiment animating me is confusion about the substance of constructive interpretation, in both the legal and the literary case. My motivating thought is that confusion arises because the theory is underspecified. Dworkin has a general interpretive framework, but it conceals an ambiguity between rival specifications. These accounts cannot be equally defensible and so must be distinguished and evaluated independently. My approach is to isolate constructive interpretation as a thesis

* For especially helpful comments and encouragement I'm grateful to Brian Hedden, George Letsas, Paisley Livingston, Taylor Markey, Dan Marshall, Shyam Nair, Dalia Nassar, David Plunkett, Connie Rosati, Wojciech Sadurski, Geoffrey Sayre-McCord, Michael Sevel, Scott Shapiro, Michael Smith, Nic Southwood, Kevin Toh, Kevin Walton, and Caroline West.

[1] (Dworkin especially 1986 and 2011); (Marmor 2011, 98); (Shapiro 2011, 293).

Dimensions of Normativity. David Plunkett, Scott J. Shapiro, and Kevin Toh.

about literature, and to attempt to understand and evaluate it on its own terms—via an opinionated take on various central debates in the philosophy of art. The critical perspective that emerges has a dual purpose: it expresses a vision of literary interpretation that illuminates Dworkin's own, while also allowing a fresh perspective on the import of his literary analogy for the philosophy of law.[2]

The framing device of this chapter is my conviction that fit and justification appear to be different things. In Section I, I argue that we regularly distinguish them in commonsense understandings of literary criticism, and that we are right to do so. If fit and justification are distinct values, then the claim that interpretation aims at maximizing them necessarily underdetermines an interpretive theory.

A few possible models of the interaction between fit and justification are salient. I evaluate their plausibility in Sections II and III. The general aim of these arguments is to raise doubts about how justification could play a central role in literary interpretation, and indeed to suggest that justification of the kind Dworkin has in mind may in fact play no role at all.

The later Dworkin and some of his commentators dismiss my motivating conviction, denying that fit and justification are distinct. I consider this objection in Section IV. I grant that there may be some forms of interdependence, but deny that this undermines my arguments, and emphasize how much more than this observation is needed if we hope to vindicate constructive interpretation as Dworkin understands it.

Skepticism about Dworkin's theory of literary interpretation does not necessarily motivate skepticism about his theory of legal interpretation. We can reject the evidential claim at the heart of the literary analogy. In Section V, I argue that it is more instructive to explore the differences between these interpretive practices than their similarities. Dworkin was wrong about the evidential force of his analogy. But he was right that the comparison of legal and literary interpretation is interesting and may deepen our understanding of the law.

One point about methodology is worth emphasizing. Dworkin's thinking about interpretation evolved. He originally applied the theory of constructive interpretation to literature and social practices, and suggested that it might be extended to conversation and historical analysis.[3] Eventually, however, his view came to encompass a novel theory of concepts, which holds that almost any concept can "function interpretively" in certain contexts—and thus that even answers to questions about whether a man is bald will, in some circumstances, necessarily involve constructive interpretation.[4]

My project is more circumscribed than other possible attempts at evaluating Dworkin's thinking about interpretation. I will not analyze his ambitious claims about the theory of concepts.[5] I will not engage with the background assumption that a theory of interpretation should apply to the arts generally, rather than being tailored to specific media or genres.[6] I do not assume, as Dworkin and others do, that a theory of art interpretation should apply

---

[2] The most prominent treatment of the analogy from the literary side is the perplexing exchange between Dworkin (1982, 1983) and Stanley Fish (1982, 1984). For an excellent recent discussion see (Stecker 2003, ch. 7).

[3] (Dworkin 1986, 53).

[4] (Dworkin 2011, 164),

[5] (Plunkett and Sundell 2013).

[6] For skepticism about "global" theories see (Gaut 1993).

straightforwardly to the "interpretations" of performers.[7] I am interested in a narrower set of questions. I focus on the interpretation of literature, and especially the highly developed practice of interpreting narrative fictions such as novels and plays, which Dworkin consistently presents as his favored analogy.[8] Since Dworkin's commitments in this more restricted domain are still not entirely clear, it seems worth pursuing the more modest set of questions I have identified.

I. Fit and Justification in Literary Criticism

I will now argue that a distinction between fit and justification is routinely observed in literary criticism. If I'm right, then a theory that understands literary interpretation as an attempt to maximize fit and justification needs to answer a structural question about how these desiderata interact. The following sections elaborate and evaluate the most natural answers to this question. Collectively they also outline the central contours of a view about literary interpretation that I find attractive, and that is not constructive.

Dworkin appears to appreciate the importance of this distinction when he introduces his interpretive theory:

> [C]reative interpretation is not conversational but *constructive.* Interpretation of works of art and social practices . . . is indeed essentially concerned with purpose not cause. But the purposes in play are not (fundamentally) those of some author but of the interpreter. Roughly, constructive interpretation is a matter of imposing purpose on an object or practice in order to make of it the best possible example of the form or genre of which it is taken to belong. It does not follow, even from that rough account, that an interpreter can make of a practice or work of art anything he would have wanted it to be . . . the history or shape of a practice or object constrains the available interpretations of it. . . . Creative interpretation, on the constructive view, is a matter of interaction between purpose and object.[9]

In this famous passage Dworkin claims that constructive interpretation aims to make its object the "best possible example of the form" that it can be. He begins to outline its virtues, pointing to the "interaction between purpose and object." A natural reading has him distinguishing between, as a first approximation, *making the work artistically good* and *matching the content of the work.* The difference explains why the interpreter cannot make the work anything he might have wanted it to be.[10]

---

[7] (Dworkin 1986 and 2011) and (Raz 2009). As we will see, I think of interpretations as sets of propositions. Performances are not sets of propositions. So performances are not identical to interpretations, though they characteristically express them.

[8] I will employ examples from well-known narrative feature films, mostly because they are especially resonant. Literary examples can be easily substituted. But it is worth noting that these films essentially involve literary works, namely their screenplays.

[9] (Dworkin 1986, 52).

[10] To begin to appreciate the difficulty of reconciling Dworkin's various aims and extracting his settled view, see Dworkin (1983, 167), where he affirms that interpretations can be wrong in virtue of making a shambles of a novel, while also denying that a novel can act as its own constraint upon an interpretation. See also (1983: 170): "It is true that these two departments of interpretive convictions [that is, fit and justification] are

Dworkin further specifies the interacting virtues of interpretation with his well-known discussion of the chain novel: they are the virtues of "fit" and "justification."[11] Unfortunately, we get little clarity about the content of these notions.[12] Providing a characterization of what Dworkin means by fit, in particular, is a major interpretive problem. Nonetheless, I believe the general outlines of his interpretive virtues to be intelligible, and widely employed or presupposed in discussions of literature. So I will do my best to extract potential theories of literary interpretation from the underlying framework just introduced.

I understand a literary interpretation as a set of *interpretive claims*. An interpretive claim is a proposition about the work in question of a particular kind. Not all propositions about a literary work are interpretive claims. For example, the proposition that standard copies of *Infinite Jest* weigh around five pounds is not an interpretive claim. I will not give an account of when propositions about a work count as interpretive claims. I will trust that for the most part we know an interpretive claim when we see one.[13]

To make discussion simpler, we can think of fit and justification as scalar properties of interpretive claims. Speaking in this way is harmless, because the properties of interpretations are a function of the properties of the interpretive claims that make them up. It is helpful, because it is sometimes easier to analyze examples of individual interpretive claims.[14]

For an interpretive claim to fit its object is for it to correspond with the object's meaning or content.[15] Some claims have explanatory power in accounting for a work's meaning. Others do great violence to its meaning, in ways that ordinary interpreters easily recognize. Fitting interpretations illuminate the meaning that the work does have, and do not impute characteristics to the work that it does not have. As I will understand it, then, fit is a correspondence between the meaning of the work and the meaning attributed to it by the interpretation.

---

not wholly insulated from one another; my claim is rather that they are, for each person, sufficiently insulated to give friction and therefore sense to anyone's interpretive analysis." The latter formulation appears to anticipate (and reject) strong formulations of the No Separation View (Section IV below). For an early criticism of this passage see (Finnis 2011, 282).

11 See (Dworkin 1986, 230–231). This discussion raises complications, because the "interpretations" of a chain novelist—a joint creator of a multiply authored work—are governed by different norms than the interpretations of a literary critic. For now I will leave this issue to the side, since Dworkin thinks that the same desiderata apply in all literary interpretation (see (Dworkin 1986, 228) and (Shapiro 2011, 295)). I return to questions of authorship in more detail in Section V.

12 Stecker (2003, 172–173) rightly notes that while Dworkin needs a distinction between fit and justification in order to avoid claiming that interpretation is unconstrained, his conception of fit remains cloudy, and at times seems to be swallowed up by justification. See also Raz (1986), who worries that on Dworkin's view the Constitution might end up best interpreted as *Hamlet*; and the helpful discussion at Marmor (1992, 70, 82–84).

13 As will become clear, I reject the relatively popular view that only nonobvious claims are genuinely interpretive (see (Marmor 1992, 22), among others). One reason: the conjunction of independently obvious claims can be nonobvious, so the distinction is unstable (Makinson 1965). Another reason: if P is an interpretive claim, then not-P should be counted one as well, and obviousness does not transmit across negation. For a slightly different take see (Barnes 1988, especially ch. 2). My main arguments do not rest on this point.

14 An important part of a complete theory of interpretation is an account of how the properties of individual interpretive claims are aggregated, or mapped on to the properties of larger interpretations. For instance, the fittingness of explanatorily fundamental claims will be especially important.

15 I use the notions of meaning and content interchangeably, and assume nothing about whether a form-content distinction is viable or illuminating.

Importantly, I do not assume that the meaning of a literary work is exhausted by its semantic content.[16]

This characterization is vague and abstract. I will have something to say about why this is desirable in a moment. First, however, I hope to demonstrate with concrete examples that something like this concept of fit is systematically employed in everyday literary interpretation, and that the concept is much more theoretically innocuous than some would let on. Consider:

The *Karamazov* Set

1. Father Zosima's body decomposes.
2. Alyosha is the novel's hero.
3. Ivan's "literary thievery" remark is affectionate.
4. "I most respectfully return him the ticket" is an organizing principle.[17]
5. *The Brothers Karamazov* is polyphonic.[18]
6. Dostoevsky's grief is apparent throughout.[19]
7. *The Brothers Karamazov* has even more demons than *Demons*.[20]
8. The novel anticipates features of Freudian psychology.

The *Hamlet* Set

1. Hamlet is a pool man from Mars.
2. Claudius is Vladimir Putin.
3. Hamlet delays only because he's lazy.
4. Ophelia doesn't mind the "nunnery" speech.
5. Hamlet's soliloquies can be safely ignored.
6. *Hamlet's* characters hear each other's asides.
7. Hamlet both sees and does not see the ghost.[21]
8. In *Hamlet* Shakespeare interrogates Freud's theories.[22]

---

[16] See (Gaut 1993, 597–558 and 2010, 181–183), who argues that interpretation is about giving the meaning of a work, provided we understand meaning broadly to include, for example, traditionally non-semantic features of syntax, pragmatics, history, explanation, and so on. See also (Raz 2009, 250): "Meaning and interpretation are reciprocal notions." Contrast Fish (1983, 105), who takes Dworkin to task for "saying that there is something about an Agatha Christie novel that renders inappropriate certain interpretations . . . that at some level the novel is available in uninterpreted shape. . . ."

[17] Ivan's rejection of God, suffering, and human life, as expressed to Alyosha.

[18] (Bakhtin 1986, ch. 1). This is controversial (see (Ponomareff 1986)), in part because critics have competing definitions of polyphony. Bakhtin himself gave several.

[19] The writer's son died in 1878, during the book's conception. He was not yet three years old, and his name was Alyosha.

[20] (Pevear 1994).

[21] This claim might be true, if we had good grounds for thinking that the law of noncontradiction does not govern the world of *Hamlet*. It is important to appreciate that fictional worlds can contain impossible truths (Byrne 1993), but this does not seem to be one of those worlds.

[22] Nearby claims may well be true: that Shakespeare was interrogating aspects of human psychology that later came to be explored in a distinctive way by Freud; or, as in *Karamazov* 8, that *Hamlet* anticipates features of Freud's theories.

Though I think that all the members of The *Karamazov* Set fit well, and that all the members of The *Hamlet* set fit poorly, you needn't agree about each case to see my point. Examples like this abound, and motivate my claim that in interpreting literary works we often immediately distinguish between claims that fit and those that do not.

As Dworkin notes, the criterion of fit requires interpretive constraint: interpreters cannot interpret a work by inventing a new one. But it would be a mistake to think that pursuing fitting interpretations renders critical activity uncreative. Interpreters display insight and ingenuity when they systematize the content of complex works. They may even succeed in uncovering meanings that the work's creator could not have articulated. This relates to a crucial point of clarification about how I understand interpretive fit.

Imagine that the content of a work were fixed by some subset of its creator's mental states (e.g., some set of creatively relevant intentions).[23] Then it would follow from my account that an interpretive claim would fit in virtue of matching the content of those mental states. However, it is by no means clear that the contents of literary works are so determined. Some believe, instead, that the meaning of a work is fixed by facts about what a postulated (non-actual) author could be hypothesized to have fictionally intended. Others claim that work content is determined by what the actual author "could" have intended.[24] Others appeal to the dispositions of an ideal reader.[25] Still others claim that there is no single criterion of meaning determination, and some of them believe that the relevant criteria are medium or genre dependent.[26] I have offered a relatively neutral account of fit because I do not want to assume the truth of any of these controversial theories.[27]

Consider now the criterion of justification. For an interpretive claim to justify its object is for it to figure in an explanation of its value properties.[28] This means that interpretive claims justify a work indirectly. Whereas a claim fits in virtue of correspondence to the work's content, it justifies in virtue of grounding an explanation of the work's artistic value.

For example, the claim that *The Brothers Karamazov* anticipates features of Freudian theory might explain the sense in which the novel contains profound and original insights about the psychic dynamics of family relationships. If such insights are artistically valuable, then this interpretive claim serves to justify the work by explaining the attribution of these positive values to it. On the other hand, the claim that Hamlet's soliloquies can be safely

---

[23] Among the most influential "actual intentionalists" are (Hirsch 1967); (Knapp and Michaels 1982); (Barnes 1988); (Carroll 2001); (Iseminger 1992); and (Livingston 2005).

[24] Some important examples are (Tolhurst 1979); (Walton 1979); (Nehamas 1981); (Robinson 1985); (Nathan 1992); (Currie 1993); (Levinson 2002). "Hypothetical intentionalism" is a big tent. As Davies (2006, 237) observes, it is compatible with versions of death of the author postmodernism, as well as many more traditional approaches.

[25] (Eco 1990).

[26] (Walton 1970); (Gaut 1993 and 2010). Gaut is an interesting case of a mild constructivist who rejects stark drawings of the interpretation-evaluation distinction. I suspect he would grant, however, that fit and justification appear distinguishable, given his broad sympathy for "detectivist" models, which construe work meaning as independent of interpreter opinion.

[27] For an excellent discussion of a range of positions about the relation between intentions and work meaning see (Livingston 2005, ch. 6). Dworkin consistently obscures matters by proceeding as if something like actual intentionalism is the only available theory on which interpretation is about understanding work meaning.

[28] The relevant value properties are typically aesthetic or artistic. I ignore debates about that distinction here.

ignored cannot plausibly be used in an explanation of *Hamlet's* artistic values. If we ignore the soliloquies, we miss out on beautiful language, creative explorations of mental life, thematic richness, and more. So this interpretive claim justifies *Hamlet* poorly: it figures only in unflattering explanations of the work's value properties. To amend Dworkin's classic formulation, the interpretation fails monumentally in making the play the best work of art that it can plausibly be.

My examples so far concern great artworks. It follows from the fact of artistic greatness that fitting interpretations are highly justifying. For this reason bad or mediocre works are sometimes more useful in demonstrating that there is a distinction between fit and justification. We will see this point in the next section, when I consider an amusing dispute about the films of Ed Wood. But first I will motivate the distinction with two more examples, which I've chosen because they are culturally salient, and because they vividly demonstrate why separating fit and justification is not just sensible and commonplace, but also intellectually important.

The two films I will briefly discuss are *Fight Club* and *Zero Dark Thirty*. Both raise large interpretive questions, but I will try to isolate one central question from each. A big interpretive question about *Fight Club* is: Does the film endorse cathartic violence as an appropriate response to the alienation of young men in modern consumerist societies? A big interpretive question about *Zero Dark Thirty* is: Does the film endorse "enhanced interrogation" as an effective means to securing actionable intelligence about terrorist plots?

These questions can and must be refined in any convincing interpretive analysis of the films. To deepen our appreciation of *Fight Club*, we need to develop views about the film's lack of narrative transparency, its point of view and surprising editing choices, the role of certain characters, and so on.[29] To deepen our appreciation of *Zero Dark Thirty*, we need to defend claims about the causal story that we take to be presented by the film, about its departures from the actual historical record, and so on.[30]

Interpreters can agree that *Fight Club* endorses violence, in which case they agree on the fittingness of a fundamental interpretive claim, while disagreeing about the implications of this truth for the film's value properties. For example, one interpreter may think that this endorsement makes the film juvenile and corrupt, while another thinks that it makes the film refreshingly provocative. Both these interpreters disagree with anyone who thinks that the film does not endorse violence.

Similarly, interpreters can agree that *Zero Dark Thirty* endorses the effectiveness of enhanced interrogations, but disagree about the implications of this truth for the value of the film. For example, one interpreter may think that this endorsement makes the film misleading and sadistic, while another interpreter thinks that it makes the film realistic and morally sophisticated. Both disagree with anyone who thinks the film does not endorse the effectiveness of enhanced interrogation.[31]

---

[29] See (Wilson and Shpall 2011).

[30] See (Cole 2013).

[31] For simplicity I have assumed a moderate connection between ethical and artistic value, such that a morally odious property constitutes a pro tanto artistic deficit (see (Gaut 1998)). But some interpreters reject this "ethicism." So we have another importantly distinguishable source of disagreement: we could agree that *Fight*

These examples show that interpreters can have the same views about what interpretations fit a work, but opposing views about what justifies it. They also show that interpreters can have different views about what interpretations fit a work, but the same views about what justifies it. And they begin to show why attending to this distinction is essential for avoiding forms of confusion that often plague discourse about the arts. For instance, they show why it can be important to determine whether *Zero Dark Thirty* endorses the effectiveness of enhanced interrogations before arguing about its overall value as a film.

If you agree that it is reasonable to distinguish between fit and justification, then you probably agree that constructive interpretation is more of a framework than a fully articulated theory. It locates two aims of literary interpretation, but says nothing about how these aims are to be integrated, reconciled, or weighed against one another when they conflict.[32] In short, it gives us little guidance about how to determine the overall plausibility of an interpretation.[33] To understand the actual commitments of Dworkin's theory we need to impose some added structure. That is what I turn to now.

II. The Threshold View

Two specifications of the interaction of fit and justification are especially salient. The first I call the Threshold View. The second I call the Tie-Breaking View.[34] In this section I argue against the Threshold View as a theory of literary interpretation.

According to the Threshold View, the good literary interpreter balances fit and justification in the following way. She sets a threshold of adequate fit, which individual interpretations may or may not reach. The interpretations that exceed this threshold are "candidates." The interpreter then endorses the candidate interpretation that best justifies the work.[35]

Of course, since there are many possible fit thresholds, this view is itself quite vague. In the limiting case—the case in which the fit threshold is maximal, i.e., the case in which no candidates fit less well than any others—it is identical to the Tie-Breaking View. I will consider a version of the Threshold View that accords justification a more significant role. In

Club endorses violence, and agree that this makes it juvenile, but disagree about whether its being juvenile detracts from its artistic value.

[32] In arguing that the distinction between fit and justification is common, useful, and important, I have not committed myself to the view that there is no entanglement between these notions. It may turn out that *some* elements of justification are imported into judgments of fit—as, for instance, some norms of rationality may play a content-determining role in conversational interpretation. That this form of entanglement cannot suffice for Dworkin's purposes is one of the main ideas of Section V.

[33] This echoes a long-standing worry about Dworkin's view. See Finnis (2011, 292).

[34] See (Raz 1995, 223) for the idea that these two views are prima facie legitimate interpretations of Dworkin's theory of law. See (Greenberg 2011, 64) for the claim that it is common, but misguided, to attribute the Threshold View to him.

[35] Dworkin (1986, 233) appears to suggest this interpretation, as do his claims that only some interpretations meet a "reasonable threshold requirement of fit," and that various interpretations might have sufficient fit to be "eligible" (e.g., 1986, 284, 358, 387). Marmor (1992, 72) interprets Dworkin (1986, 66) as claiming that, at one stage of interpretation, fit is a threshold requirement. Marmor's interpretation may be constructive. I am unsure how to read the passage in question.

saying why I believe it to be implausible as a theory of the structure of literary interpretation, I will cite various considerations. But the best way to interpret these scattered reflections is as related ways of making the point that the Threshold View distorts the well-developed practice of literary interpretation.

First, consider one striking consequence of the Threshold View. The view implies that many of our big interpretive battles about literary works will bottom out in disputes about abstract aesthetic propositions that only incidentally concern the work in question. Such interpretive disagreements will ultimately concern questions about, for example, the relative artistic value of coherence and originality in literature. If you prioritize coherence, and I prioritize originality, then we will likely disagree about which interpretation best justifies a novel such as *My Brilliant Friend*.[36] But questions about the relative value of coherence and originality only incidentally concern particular pieces of literature. Thus debates about how to interpret a literary work will often have as their ultimate or most essential subject matter something besides the work we take ourselves to be interpreting.[37]

My contention is not merely that this theoretical division of labor is confusing, but that it fails to capture the contours of the critical enterprise. Interpretive battles about literary works turn on specific claims about the works themselves, not on general claims in the theory of value. This is of course compatible with thinking that great critics often blend interpretation with evaluation. In discussing *My Brilliant Friend* we may want to know about its meaning and its value—and a critic may offer sophisticated interpretive claims in the course of arguing that Ferrante is a genius. Still, we distinguish between the critic's interpretations and the way she employs them in grounding her estimation of Ferrante's achievements.

Second, the Threshold View has seemingly absurd consequences about how we should regard interpretations that most of us find clearly out of bounds. The best explanation of these intuitions is that most of us regard maximizing the value of an artwork as, at best, minimally related to interpreting it.

A well-known example of skepticism about interpretations that try to maximize artistic value is Noel Carroll's critique of J. Hoberman, particularly concerning the comical case of Ed Wood's film *Plan 9 from Outer Space*. According to Hoberman, this film should be seen as transgressing various Hollywood norms concerning editing continuity, narrative linearity, and so on. And indeed, when so interpreted it gains tremendously in value, since without this assumption the movie is paradigm schlock—a perennial candidate for the title of "worst film ever made." Carroll observes that the interpretation is nonetheless ludicrous. Among other things, transgression is an intentional concept, and all the evidence indicates that Ed Wood was not interested in it.[38]

In our lingo, Carroll argues that the transgression-hypothesis fits the movie less well than the schlock-hypothesis; he maintains that this disqualifies the transgression-hypothesis from

---

[36] In fact these may not be genuine artistic values at all. See (Vermazen 1991) on originality.

[37] Some readers might dismiss this argument as purely taxonomical. But taxonomy matters. It would be needlessly confusing to stop distinguishing between these sorts of disputes. Indeed, as I just argued in discussing *Zero Dark Thirty*, we should attend to such distinctions more often.

[38] (Carroll 1992). The example generalizes. Fascist propaganda and misogynist pornography, for instance, would be much more artistically valuable if "interpreted" as satire.

serious consideration; and then he accounts for this lack of fit with an actual intentionalist model of literary content. It is important to emphasize that this argument does not depend on Carroll's actual intentionalism. Many who do not agree with Carroll about the import of authors' actual intentions also regard this verdict about Hoberman's claims as obviously correct.[39]

Of course, the defender of the Threshold View can respond to this case by saying that Hoberman's interpretation does not fit well enough to exceed the threshold, i.e., attain candidacy. But she cannot rest with this response.[40] As examples become more compelling they come correspondingly closer to the Tie-Breaking View. What's required is a case of an interpretation that seems on balance superior to another, even though it fits less well. But it is natural to worry about any such case that an argument of the following form may be offered as an objection to it.

"You claim that your interpretation is superior to mine because it fits well enough, and results in an artistically preferable work. It follows that you acknowledge that my interpretation fits better. Suppose that, knowing this, I come to endorse your interpretation. I thereby commit to *remaking* the work. But this would make me into a creator, rather than an interpreter. I am not in that business. This shows that instead of arguing against my interpretation you have merely changed the subject."

The defender of the Threshold View can respond by saying that we have made a systematic mistake in distinguishing the projects of creation and interpretation so starkly.[41] There are several intimations of this idea in *Law's Empire*—for instance, in the discussions of courtesy (Dworkin 1986, 47–48) and the chain novelist (Dworkin 1986, 227–232). But we need a powerful argument for upending the distinction between creation and interpretation; the burden is on opponents of the distinction to unsettle it. And it is worth remembering that we observe an analogous distinction in many other interpretive contexts—from the interpretation of conversational contributions, to the interpretation of human behavior and psychology, to the interpretation of historical events, to the interpretation of philosophical works.

I conclude this section by noting that the above arguments also raise troubles for a nearby picture, which some find more prima facie attractive than the Threshold View. According to

---

[39] Levinson (1992, 298) gives a better way to characterize Hoberman's perspective on the Ed Wood films: it is not an interpretation, but a "practical recommendation for dealing with shlock most enjoyably." Stephen Davies (2006) endorses a kind of "value maximizing" theory that might appear facially similar to the Threshold View. But Davies claims that his theory is extensionally equivalent to hypothetical intentionalism, and he explicitly rejects the idea that maximizing aesthetic value can compensate for fit deficits (245): "The reading that makes the work artistically superior should not be favoured unless it is at least as consistent as its main rivals are with the work's content."

[40] See (Finnis 2011, 293), who complains that if this is Dworkin's view, it is empty until he specifies an adequacy threshold for fit.

[41] Some literary and film theorists accept interpretive "constructivism" of a more general sort—the idea that interpretations construct, rather than discover or track, work meaning. See (Bordwell 1989), and the important criticisms of Gaut (2010, 164–180) and Stecker (2003). Note that constructivism need not involve *evaluative* construction, as is seemingly licensed by the Threshold View. For instance, one might think that work meaning changes with historical and intellectual progress, and thus that interpreters construct (some) new meanings from developments in human knowledge. The view faces important difficulties, but here I just observe that it does not entail anything about the role of justification.

this view, we should dispense with the idea that there is any adequate threshold of fit. Both fit and justification always matter, which means that better fit is always a reason to favor an interpretation. The best interpretation is the one that maximizes the sum of fit and justification. Call this the Two Values View.[42]

I cannot discuss the Two Values View about literary interpretation at length, but I will outline a dialectical strategy for approaching it that seems to me sensible.

The central question for the Two Values View is whether it can avoid the implausible consequences of the Threshold View. These implausible consequences are a direct result of placing justification at the heart of good interpretive practice. So there are two relevant possibilities: either the Two Values View makes justification more central to the interpretive enterprise or it makes it less central.[43] If the former, the arguments of this section apply with yet more force.[44] If the latter, it will be more profitable to evaluate the Tie-Breaking View, which unlike the Two Values View makes clear predictions. If I am right that even the Tie-Breaking View represents a suspicious conception of literary interpretation, then further consideration of the Two Values View may be unnecessary.

III. The Tie-Breaking View

According to the Tie-Breaking View, interpretations become candidates not by exceeding some threshold of fit, but rather by winning in the fit competition. The criterion of justification is then applied to the candidate interpretations—applied, that is, only when there is a tie in fit.[45]

Is the Tie-Breaking View a plausible theory of literary interpretation? I am skeptical. I will now introduce an example of a putative interpretive tie in order to frame the perceived attractions of the Tie-Breaking View, and as a way of substantiating the suggestion that when claims about justification seem to be invoked in literary criticism, it is likely against a background of perceived ties in fit. The example I have in mind is the classic debate about Henry

---

[42] (Dworkin 1986, 246) and (Finnis 2011, 293). Thanks to Geoffrey Sayre-McCord, Brian Hedden, and Kevin Walton for discussion.

[43] Actually there is a third. The relative value of fit and justification might *vary*—depending on context, or on the aims of the individual interpreter. A version of context relativity is suggested by many of Dworkin's claims (e.g., concerning the variable importance of certainty and predictability (1986, 367). Interpreter relativity raises many complex issues that I cannot discuss adequately, though I approach them in a preliminary way below in discussing the Project Asymmetry. For our purposes I may simply note that Dworkin must reject interpreter relativity, given his insistence that there are uniquely correct answers in hard cases (1986, 412).

[44] For example, there can be no avoiding the *Plan 9* worry by claiming that it involves an implausibly low fit threshold.

[45] Stecker (2003, 171) thinks of Dworkin's theory of law in this way. Jerrold Levinson seems to endorse this view about literary interpretation, though with hedged enthusiasm (1992, 292): "if we can . . . make the author out to have created a cleverer or more striking or more imaginative piece, without violating the image of his work as an artist that is underpinned by the total available textual and contextual evidence, we should perhaps do so." He calls this a "principle of critical charity," expressing an idea I return to below in more detail. See also Raz 2009, 258), who claims "an interpretation which shows the work's meaning as dealing with what is more important is, *pro tanto*, a better interpretation . . . ,"

James's *The Turn of the Screw*, which I will assume represents the best sort of case for the relevance of justification in literary interpretation.

Suppose that the competing interpretations of *Screw* are what I will call Ghost Story and Hysteria. According to Ghost Story, the novel is a ghost story, the governess is sane and reliable, and her desperate attempts to protect her dear charges are noble, though doomed. According to Hysteria, there are no ghosts, the governess is mad and unreliable, and her psychology and conduct are devastating indictments of Victorian morality.[46] Perhaps, as is sometimes thought, Hysteria fits as well as Ghost Story, but also makes *Screw* more complex and unconventional.

I want to make two main points about this conception of literary interpretation. The first is dialectical: the Tie-Breaking View assigns justification only a marginal role, which makes it puzzling as an interpretation of Dworkin's ideas. The second is substantive: there is little reason to endorse the Tie-Breaking View over an alternative which eliminates justification from the enterprise of literary interpretation altogether.

The first point is not very controversial. According to the Tie-Breaking View, justification is relevant only when there are ties in interpretive fit. But this is an odd clarification of the literary analogy, given its stated role. We know that Dworkin's ultimate ambition is to vindicate an antipositivist account of legal interpretation and legal content in which justification, in the form of a theory of political morality, deeply infuses the legitimate exercise of judicial authority. Adjudication *essentially involves political morality*, in both easy and hard cases. Since his literary analogy purports to motivate this theory, Dworkin must think that justification plays a more fundamental role in literary interpretation than the Tie-Breaking View suggests.[47]

My second and more controversial point is that there is no reason to endorse the Tie-Breaking View over what I will call the Pure Fit View of literary interpretation, which holds that the success of literary interpretations is exhaustively determined by their fit. I will support this claim by giving an error-theoretic explanation for why we may be attracted to the Tie-Breaking View. My explanation is that it seems to express a plausible principle of charity. I will try to show that there is a better version of this principle, and that it instead supports the Pure Fit View. I stress that this argument is not essential for my general critique of Dworkin, though its success would of course make this critique stronger.

The Tie-Breaking View can be seen as extending a common idea about communication: interpreters must attempt to make their interlocutors intelligible and rational.[48] Perhaps literary interpreters should, similarly, maximize the contribution of the object of interpretation. This proposal seems generous and attractively modest. Other things equal, we should plump for the interpretation that makes an artwork better.

---

[46] See (Bromwich 2011) for a recent statement of the latter view. Slaughter (1970) describes Edmund Wilson's influential vacillations. Gaut (2010, 157) believes that James clearly intended Ghost Story, but that Hysteria is nonetheless a plausible interpretation.

[47] Notice that we might reject the literary analogy in part because we think interpretive ties are more common in the law.

[48] For example, by assuming some common standards of consistency, as in (Davidson 2006, 234). See (Marmor 1992, 58–60) for skepticism about connections between a Davidsonian principle of charity and constructive interpretation.

Furthermore, a like principle of charity can seem plausible across a wide range of interpretive contexts. If Kim says something that is equally interpretable as expressing A or B, and interpreting Kim as having expressed A commits her to having made a racist joke, then we often regard it as permissible or even obligatory to plump for interpretation B. Likewise, if Hart's argument can be equally well interpreted as having form A or form B, and interpreting it as having form A makes the argument less powerful, then many of us find it permissible or even obligatory to plump for interpretation B.

I accept these appearances. But they can be accommodated by an extra-interpretive principle of charity that does not support the Tie-Breaking View.

We are often interested in coming to a final interpretive verdict—a verdict that resolves an important lingering indeterminacy. For example, in interpreting a philosophical argument for the purpose of writing a critical response, we sometimes make our task manageable by fixing on a determinate object, even when the argument's content as it is stated remains ambiguous. When we have practical interests in resolving indeterminacy, we also frequently have interests in fixing on the best candidate interpretation: for instance, we may think kindness requires giving Kim all reasonable benefit of the doubt before attributing racist sentiments, and we may think philosophical progress requires coming to terms with the strongest argument Hart can be taken to have given. But endorsing this methodology need not commit us to the view that the interpretations we proceed with are superior to their competitors *as interpretations*. There is another nearby view: that the interpretations are genuinely tied on the merits, and that our practice of plumping does not express commitment to interpretive superiority at all, but rather to the effective satisfaction of our practical interests.

I think that our inclination to accept the Tie-Breaking View can be explained away in this manner. Justification may play a tie-breaking role in something, but not in interpretation proper. If it is indeterminate whether Hart's argument has form A or B, then an interpretation that makes it determinately B is flawed. Still, adopting the determinate B interpretation can be best for the purpose of writing a response that advances a particular debate. Since we often interpret works with aims such as this, the extra-interpretive principle of charity seems to describe some significant features of our practice without blending interpretation with evaluation. Moreover, it offers a sensible story about why justification plays the role it does.[49] While it is strictly speaking external to the interpretive enterprise, justification can be important in allowing us to promote further related interests.[50]

I cannot hope to establish the controversial Pure Fit View of literary interpretation here, but I conclude this section by sketching one reason for thinking it attractive.

---

[49] A common thought (e.g., (Gaut 1993, 599), (Davies 2006, 241)) is that we approach artworks with the aim of *appreciation*—and thus that interpretation is inevitably evaluative, at least in the sense that interpretations that render the work more valuable are pro tanto better. I do not find this argument compelling. The best way to appreciate something is to first understand its nature.

[50] Here is another error-theoretic argument for the same conclusion. Though we sometimes seem to be guided by justification in choosing between interpretations, we are actually employing a "Great Author Heuristic": assuming that greater justification is *evidence* of better fit. The heuristic is often warranted by antecedent reasons for confidence in the work's goodness or the author's proficiency. We are not guided in this way when interpreting bad or mediocre works. Thanks to Nic Southwood and Dan Marshall for discussion.

For the purpose of illustration I have presented the debate about *Screw* as the kind that might motivate the Tie-Breaking View. It is a paradigm case of a persistent interpretive disagreement, one whose intractability is, we might have thought, grounded in the more or less equal fittingness of rival interpretations. However, this diagnosis is at the end of the day suspicious. Some plausible interpretations of *Screw* claim that we needn't choose between Ghost Story and Hysteria—and thus imply that they are not rivals after all. Critics who endorse this view should, and typically do, reject the claim that Ghost Story is a true interpretation, and also reject the claim that Hysteria is a true interpretation. The novella is in their view indeterminate, and there is no reason to impose artificial determinacy upon it.[51] If this is the right response to genuine literary indeterminacy, as I believe it is, then such cases cannot motivate the Tie-Breaking View.

I will have more to say about the importance of literary indeterminacy in Section V. For now, I hope that the preceding argument begins to motivate a viable alternative to the Tie-Breaking View of literary interpretation, and contributes to my cumulative argument for skepticism about assigning justification a prominent role in this practice.

IV. The No Separation View

My arguments thus far have employed the distinction between fit and justification that I've argued is a default presupposition in commonsense literary interpretation. But the later Dworkin explicitly rejects the separation of these notions. Many influential commentators think he is right to do so. I will now address the natural worry that my arguments thus far have traded on a distinction that has already been properly repudiated.

In responding to the criticisms of Joseph Raz (2004, 286), which in some ways anticipate my own, Dworkin is "anxious to correct" one misinterpretation of the relationship between his two dimensions of interpretation:

> [Raz] apparently subscribes to the opinion that I think that the two dimensions of interpretation I distinguish—the degree to which an interpretation "fits" the data and the degree to which it confers "value" on the data—are independent, and that the second dimension comes into play only when two interpretations are "tied" in the first dimension. Though I did once introduce the distinction in that way, I took care to say that this account of the relation was a heuristic construction, and that a full analysis would show the two dimensions interdependent and neither prior to the other.[52]

[51] See (Leithauser 2012): "But "The Turn of the Screw" is greater than either of these interpretations. Its profoundest pleasure lies in the beautifully fussed over way in which James refuses to come down on either side." The same point could be made without the appeal to James's intentions.

[52] (Dworkin 2004, 381–382). This is not entirely fair to Raz, given passages like those cited in my section on the Threshold View, e.g., (Dworkin 1983, 272).

Other commentators express similar ideas, though some appear to endorse a claim about the priority of justification that Dworkin disavows, at least in the previous passage. For example, Mark Greenberg (2004, 197) claims that

> On the best understanding, fit is merely one aspect of justification, there is no threshold of fit, and how much fit matters relative to other aspects of justification is a substantive question of political morality.

David Plunkett and Tim Sundell (2013, 279) agree that fit is, for Dworkin, merely one aspect of justification. Finally, Dworkin (2006, 311) claims that Greenberg has accurately represented his views about the interaction of the dimensions of fit and justification in legal interpretation:

> As I have tried to explain elsewhere, these dimensions are best understood as each drawn from a political value. I said in *Law's Empire* and elsewhere that the crude "threshold" account of the interaction of the two dimensions was meant only to illustrate the difference between them.

These passages are hard to interpret. First, Dworkin fails to distinguish between the Threshold View and the Tie-Breaking View. More important, the passages suggest various non-identical theses: that fit is an aspect of justification, that fit and justification are interdependent, that neither fit nor justification is prior to the other, that political morality determines how much fit matters, and that there is indeed a difference between fit and justification. I will extract what I see as the two most central thoughts.

I first discuss the idea that fit is an aspect of justification, which I will refer to as the Pure Justification View. This idea cannot, on its own, suffice as a response to my organizing worry. The Pure Justification View faces the same worry, spelled out in slightly different terms.

Consider this question: Is the Pure Justification View a distinctive position? Dworkin and others evidently believe that it is. I do not see how they are entitled to this answer. According to the Pure Justification View, fit is an aspect of justification, but not the only aspect. So we might ask: How do the different aspects of justification interact in the determination of interpretive validity? There are three salient models compatible with a "difference" between the fit-aspect and the other aspects: the Threshold, Two Values, and Tie-Breaking Views. The ambiguity in Dworkin's framework is simply reframed in terms of aspects of justification.[53]

Let me illustrate with an example from recent legal theory. In his interesting discussion of stare decisis, Scott Hershovitz (2008, 114) argues that courts are not required to blindly follow past verdicts, but rather to recognize that what they have done in the past has an impact on what they ought to do now. As such, stare decisis is the judicial practice of engaging with history, and acting with integrity in the light of this history: overruling precedent, for

[53] I can put this argument in another way, by appealing to the widely recognized distinction between pro tanto (or contributory) normative notions, and all-things-considered (or decisive) ones (Shpall, 2014). To say that fit is one, but only one, aspect of justification is to say that fitting well is pro tanto justifying. But when we evaluate interpretations, we evaluate them for all-things-considered plausibility. On the Pure Justification View, this means we evaluate them for all-things-considered justifiability. So we can reasonably ask what contribution fit makes to overall justifiability. This is our guiding question framed in different words.

example, is at times an important part of the practice of stare decisis. The actual practice of engaging with precedent is thus, according to Hershovitz, a model application of Dworkin's position. The judicial aspiration to act with integrity—to embody a political value—is the best explanation of the shape of this practice.

Suppose that Hershovitz has accurately described the practice of stare decisis. Still, his discussion prompts a natural question. What, we might ask, does the Dworkinian claim about the relative importance of fit in proper judicial practice? How, for example, do prior decisions constrain legitimate judicial decision-making? It can't be that anything goes; precedent has some binding force.[54] In the last paragraph of his article, Hershovitz is forthright about the answer: "This essay has not addressed the conditions under which a court ought to overturn one of its precedents."[55]

My claim is that even if fit is only an aspect of justification—even if, for example, several justificatory elements combine to form the overarching judicial virtue of integrity—we do not have a plausibly articulated theory of interpretation until we know more about the proper interaction of these different elements. But then we have motivated, rather than neutralized, my project of investigating possible theses about their interaction.

This brings us to the second main idea I want to explore, which is the idea that fit and justification are interdependent. I will call this the No Separation View. It is the best interpretation of the underlying theme of the passages cited above. When Dworkin claims that both fit and justification are "drawn from a political value," and when Greenberg claims that how much fit matters is a "substantive question of political morality," I interpret them as claiming that it is impossible to separate an interpreter's intuitions about fit from the justificatory structure that she accepts. For that reason the distinction between fit and justification is, they believe, artificial and unsustainable.

Dworkin defends a view of this kind about literary interpretation.[56] And philosophers of art have long been interested in related questions. So we can fortunately return to the main thread of our discussion, and ask whether the No Separation View is a plausible generalization about literary critical practice. I will discuss some examples in the hopes of clarifying the proposal. And I'll argue that while we should accept some entanglement between fit and justification, we should also insist that they can and should be distinguished.

There are reasonable debates about the role of Ivan's "poem" about The Grand Inquisitor in the overall architecture of *The Brothers Karamazov.* Some critics take it to express one of the book's organizing principles (e.g., Rozanov 1972). Others believe that focus on this parable has wrongly overshadowed other important features of the novel, and has led to mistakes about its themes.[57] Now one way to express the content of these disagreements may

---

[54] Bear in mind that precedent is relevant to fit, but not wholly determinative of it. (A prior holding might cut in one direction while the Constitution cuts in another.) The argument in the text is just an exemplification of my puzzle about the structure of constructive interpretation, and not an attempt to show anything in particular about stare decisis.

[55] (Hershovitz 2008, 118). For a similarly agnostic conclusion about the implications of Dworkin's theory, see the fascinating discussion of the Fugitive Slave Law and the Emancipation Proclamation in (Levinson 2007).

[56] See especially (Dworkin 2011, ch. 7]. See also (Moore 1996) for the view that all interpretation aims at maximizing the value that justifies treating the object as a "text."

[57] For example, it may have led critics to identify Ivan with the Inquisitor, and Alyosha with Christ, which is a misleading oversimplification.

be to characterize them as disagreements about fit that are ultimately rooted in disagreements about justification. In other words, the competing views about the role of Ivan's poem are ultimately grounded in competing views about the value of the novel. Interpreters disagree about the role of the poem because they disagree about whether its centrality would make the novel better or worse. Or, even better: the interpretive dispute is rooted in a disagreement about the value of literature itself.[58]

Conceptualizing interpretive disagreement in this way is not plausible, however. For it seems plain that interpreters can disagree about the role of "The Grand Inquisitor" while agreeing about what would make the novel better. Likewise, they may disagree about the role of Ivan's story while agreeing about the value of literature. Yet the No Separation View is a necessity claim: necessarily, fit judgments are inseparable from justifications. The example indicates, on the contrary, that any inseparability is contingent.[59]

Now consider the interpretive claim that Hamlet is not a pool man from Mars. This claim fits *Hamlet* unassailably. But it would not appear to depend on contentious theories about the value of *Hamlet* or the value of literature. Many people know that Hamlet is not a pool man from Mars, and they do not have, even implicitly, any developed conceptions of literary value.[60] The fittingness of this interpretive claim depends not on what makes the play (or literature) valuable, but on the public nature of language, commonly understood rules of generation for fictional truths (Walton 1993, Chapter 4), and other conventions of the dramatic genre.

Of course, some evaluative beliefs might be presupposed by anyone who holds the views I'm alluding to about language, principles of generation, and genre conventions. For example, I may be assuming that special reasons are required for subverting the manifest communicative intentions of speakers and writers, and that absent such special reasons we are not entitled to do this, whether we are interpreting dramas or utterances. But this belief does not amount to much of a view about what justifies a work, or literature as a whole: it implies nothing about, for instance, the relative importance of style or coherence or originality or moral outlook. So we should not conclude that a general theory of literary value gets presupposed whenever we make interpretive claims.[61]

Dworkin is particularly motivated by the idea that the methodologies of different schools of literary interpretation are outgrowths of their theories of literary value (see especially

---

[58] Dworkin's view is typically formulated in this latter way, making the ultimate disagreement a highly abstract and general one (as I lamented in discussing the Threshold View). This parallels his claim that legal interpreters disagree in virtue of divergent political moralities. I will problematize this analogy in a moment.

[59] The example does locate an interesting difficulty for all theories of literary interpretation. Such theories must specify how to aggregate and weigh fit claims, and it is not immediately obvious how to do this. Suppose that the Organizing Principle interpretation of Ivan's poem makes better sense of some of the novel's features, and the Wrongly Emphasized interpretation makes better sense of others. Then we have a real question about how to choose between them: the question of what fit-features matter more and why.

[60] Some readers might remain unconvinced that "obvious" claims about a work's content can be interpretive. They might consider the claim that Hamlet is not a pool man from Mars, offered in response to an interpreter who sincerely claims that he is; or the claim that *Plan 9* is not transgressive.

[61] For an interesting comparison see (Greenberg 2004), who argues that value facts are among the determinants of legal content, while denying that morality must be the relevant value.

1986, 60 and 2011, 135). Though I have tried to show why Dworkin's ambitious claims about the necessary connections between interpretation and evaluation are implausible on their face, I think he was onto something in observing this connection.

Consider a character we'll call the Formalist, who thinks that the mental states of an author cannot be relevant to the aesthetic value of her work. She may think, as a consequence, that biographically informed criticism is bunk.[62] This shows that at least some interpretive methodologies, such as the anti-biographical one, do import substantive and controversial principles of aesthetic value.

While interesting, the insight also reveals a fundamental ambiguity plaguing Dworkin's treatment of the interpretation of literature. Dworkin consistently slides between two different characterizations of his thesis. The first, which is clearly expressed in the canonical presentation of the theory (1986, 52) and elsewhere, claims that constructive interpretation is the attempt to make *a work* the best that it can be. The second, clearly expressed in the idea about critical schools now being considered, claims that constructive interpretation is the attempt to make *the practice of literature* the best that it can be.

The latter formulation is better for the literary analogy, in one sense. It parallels the claim Dworkin aims to establish, which is that legal interpretation is an attempt to make *the law*—i.e., the body of political acts in a jurisdiction—the best that it can be. A common worry is that legal interpretation often seems to have a much more circumscribed object, such as a particular statute or holding. But notice that whatever we think about Dworkin's story, it at least has the following virtue: individual laws in a jurisdiction are related to one another not merely because they are instances of a single practice, but also because they are governed by important coherence requirements (e.g., as would apply to sub-plans of an overall plan (Shapiro 2011). It is the normative interdependence of laws in a jurisdiction that makes it at least prima facie sensible to speak of "the law" as the proper object of legal interpretation.

But the parallel characterization of literary interpretation is not sensible. Nothing similar can be said about the relationship of individual literary works to the overall social practice of literary production.[63] Two novels may have inconsistent contents and contrary aims, yet be unproblematic instances of a single literary genre. So it is mysterious why we would take an interpreter of *Screw* to be actually engaged in a project whose object is literature as a whole, even if it is not mysterious why we would take an interpreter of affirmative action policies to be actually engaged in a project whose object is the legal system as a whole. And it is natural to diagnose Dworkin's shifty characterizations as a relic of this awkwardness.

For the sake of argument we can grant that interpretive methodologies presuppose theories about the value of literature, and do so necessarily. It is a huge further step to show that deploying such methodologies in interpretation is, necessarily, an attempt to maximize the value of the practice.[64] It might more plausibly be said that interpretation aims to make

---

[62] See (Wimsatt and Beardsley 1954). As I noted above, Dworkin's (2011, 130) diagnosis of the influence of the "intentional fallacy" is not persuasive.

[63] Marmor (1992, 44) may be making a similar point when he asks: "is a theory *about* literary criticism an interpretation of literature?"

[64] Suppose that the interpretive methodology of any given interlocutor presupposes a theory about the value of conversation. In interpreting my utterance on a particular occasion, does Trish aim to make *the practice of conversation* the best that it can be? Besides its obvious weirdness, the suggestion would seem to imply that Trish

an individual work the best that it can be. As the reader knows, I have critiqued more precise versions of this thesis at great length.

The earlier arguments of this section suggest that the interdependence of fit and justification is not as deep as Dworkin thinks: first, because interpretive disagreement is compatible with evaluative agreement; second, because some interpretations seem evaluatively laden only in the minimal sense that, say, conversational interpretation is. The considerations just given suggest that, whatever one thinks of my earlier arguments, Dworkin's strongest argument for the No Separation View about literature trades on an unmotivated and implausible claim about the object of literary interpretation. I conclude that the motivating worry of this paper has not been neutralized. There is a distinction between fit and justification in literary interpretation, and a theory that presents them both as governing values must specify how they interact.

V. Three Asymmetries

What are the consequences of my arguments for our evaluation of Dworkin's theory of legal interpretation? This depends on the plausibility of his literary analogy. I have throughout this chapter intimated that the analogy is flawed. In this final section, I explore this suspicion in more detail, identifying several important differences between the practices of legal and literary interpretation, differences that we can trace to significant asymmetries between the natures of their objects. The comparison of interpretation in law and literature is illuminating, but not for the reasons Dworkin supposed.[65]

I present three asymmetries. They are not exhaustive. I cannot trace all their implications. I hope that identifying these asymmetries will help to vindicate the interest of comparing law and literature, but I leave a final evaluation of their implications for the debate about legal positivism, the debate that was Dworkin's ultimate target, to more competent philosophers of law.

---

might appropriately interpret my utterance by sewing my lips shut, assuming my antagonistic declarations tend to stifle the free flow of ideas.

[65] Dworkin motivates the analogy by arguing that both social practices such as law, and artistic practices such as literature, involve the creation of entities that are meant to be distinct from their creators (see (Dworkin 1986, 50) and (Shapiro 2011, 293)). There are two problems with this thought. First, it makes implausibly strong assumptions about the necessary character of these objects. It may get something right: novelists may be like lawmakers, and unlike speakers, in *often* intending their works to be "autonomous," or independent of their creators (further) intentions or pronouncements (for an interesting discussion see (Nathan 2005). But the notion of distinctness employed here is elusive, and it is unclear how the point is compatible with Dworkin's rejection of intentionalism (Stoljar 1998). Second, even if it is true that novels and statutes are distinct from their creators in a way that utterances are not, it is unclear how this fact alone would motivate the strong evidential claim of the literary analogy. There are many ways in which law and literature are similar, and many ways in which they are dissimilar. Noting that they are similar in one way settles nothing. See (Raz 1986, 1011) and (Marmor 2011, 102) for helpful discussion.

A. *The Determination Asymmetry*

Legal interpretation and literary interpretation both involve the resolution of indeterminacies in content. In deciding whether campaign contributions are among the forms of expression protected by the First Amendment, American judges might resolve a disputed and unclear question about what is the law of their country. Similarly, in offering interpretations of *The Metamorphosis*, literary critics might give accounts of that work's meaning that take a definitive stand about some of its many uncertain features.

However, there are important differences between the nature and purpose of interpretive resolutions in these domains. One way to begin seeing this is to notice that a central function of authoritative legal interpretation is to issue in a determinate final verdict, a verdict that resolves relevant indeterminacies in the law that have been recognized as problematic by other interpreters. The analogous purpose is not so central in literary interpretation, where the resolution of key indeterminacies is often unnecessary, undesirable, or irrelevant to a legitimate interpretive project, and where individual interpreters have great latitude to decide which indeterminacies of content they think a fruitful interpretation should settle.

This is the Determination Asymmetry. We can provide support for it by thinking about the sources of these interpretive practices, and the aims that they embody.

In general, the aims of interpretive practices are connected to the purposes or values of the objects of interpretation. We have legal interpreters because they advance the purposes of the law.[66] One purpose of the law is to guide conduct. Judges help to advance this purpose by resolving developed and trenchant interpretive disputes among citizens about the content of the law. This is an important part of their institutional function in many legal systems, a function that requires them to end contentious debates by making the law more precise.[67]

Now compare the practice of literary interpreters, which I am suggesting is plausibly connected to the purposes and values of literature. Of course there are huge unresolved debates about these purposes and values. But consider the view that literary interpreters are, like judges, normally tasked with resolving already well-circumscribed indeterminacies in content. Here are three reasons to be skeptical about it.

First, whereas this view about judges is explicable in terms of how it allows the law to better perform its conduct-guiding function, such an explanation is not available in the literary case, since the guidance of conduct is at most one marginal part of the purpose and value of literature. The same point applies, with yet more force, to other commonly accepted purposes of the law—such as fairly distributing the costs of accidents, peacefully resolving interpersonal disputes, or facilitating the efficient exchange of goods and services.

---

[66] I am thinking of judges as the paradigm legal interpreters. Admittedly professors, journalists, and others also interpret the law. But usually we do so in order to evaluate the authoritative interpretations of judges and other legal officials. So I assume that our interpretations are no less concerned with the resolution of legal indeterminacies, even though we acknowledge that in many cases they are unlikely to directly effect such resolutions in the manner of judicial opinions.

[67] Often they do so by striking down laws on the grounds that they are vague or overbroad, forcing legislatures to redraw statutes more helpfully. This supports my contention that legal indeterminacy is generally to be avoided.

Second, one of the distinctive contributions of literature is its openness—or, to indulge a genre-bending turn of phrase, a potential for penumbral emanations. It follows that systematically closing the meanings of works when we interpret them would undermine a main source of literary value.[68] For example, the power of metaphor is connected to its indeterminacy, and it is a familiar fact that many determinate resolutions of metaphorical meaning are overly reductive and stultifying—a point that applies not just to individual metaphors, but also to the interpretation of the thematic and symbolic content of whole literary works.[69] It is hard to see an interpretation of *The Metamorphosis* that reduces it to Kafka's supposed Father Complex as especially illuminating. In other words, some resolving interpretations of that novel's indeterminacy are less compelling than interpretations that preserve a broad range of metaphorical meanings.

Third, even when literary interpretation does focus on the resolution of disputed content, this aim is subservient to the guiding aim of literary interpretation generally, that of understanding the work. This explains why some resolutions of indeterminacy are interpretively fruitful while some are not. If *The Turn of the Screw* is most plausibly interpreted as ambiguous, then definitive resolutions are misguided.

Granted, not all resolutions of indeterminacy in legal interpretation would be fruitful. Judges sometimes do what they can to refrain from settling contentious issues that they think will be better settled by future judges who have more relevant information. The Determination Asymmetry is compatible with this insight. For it remains true that authoritative legal interpretations aim at resolving an externally well-defined question or sets of questions about legal content—usually for the purpose of making the law a more precise, effective, and fair guide to action—and that it is unusual for such interpretations to fail to settle the central issues about the law's content that prompted the relevant legal proceedings.[70] Indeed, even apart from the existence of fairly well-established canons of construction (which help judges make determinations in ambiguous cases), it is widely recognized that broader policy considerations can furnish interpreters with legitimate reasons for settling uncertain matters of law—though the nature and extent of this mechanism is much disputed. By contrast, canonical literary interpretations may explore new and ill-defined questions about a work's content, or well-defined questions by complicating them and making the recognized indeterminacies even more pronounced.

[68] Does a similar argument tell in favor of the Threshold View? Some appear to think so. Gaut (2010, 157, 184–188) claims that the Relativity of Truth interpretation of *Rashomon* fits less well than the Moral Degradation interpretation, and gives persuasive arguments to this effect. Nonetheless, he thinks the Relativity of Truth interpretation is "reasonable." This could mean different things. My own view is that if an interpretation fits less well than a competitor, this suffices to show that it is inferior qua interpretation. Still, it may get many things right interpretively, and be illuminating and worthwhile. It may even be a valuable creative work in its own right, in addition to being a valuable (though flawed) interpretation.

[69] There are deep problems in understanding metaphorical meaning. For a good survey of approaches in contemporary philosophy of language see (Reimer and Camp 2006).

[70] Statutory ambiguity is not the only source of indeterminacy in common law systems. Consider issues about the scope of precedent—for instance, about whether the "actual malice" doctrine of *New York Times v. Sullivan* applies to bloggers. Thanks to Taylor Markey for discussion.

I have not suggested that literary interpretation aims at indeterminacy.[71] Nor have I claimed that legal interpretation invariably makes the law more determinate.[72] Still, there is an important difference between the role of determinate verdicts in legal and literary interpretation. When the United States Supreme Court engaged in statutory interpretation in *Church of the Holy Trinity v. United States*, for example, their main goal was to figure out whether The Church of the Holy Trinity was liable.[73] They did not have the option of refusing to answer this question. But the interpreter of *Hamlet* does not face the same pressure. She will probably offer some resolutions of its disputed content, insofar as she plans to make her interpretation worth anyone's time. But she may rest content with the claim that there is no fact of the matter about why Hamlet delays, and she has tremendous freedom in deciding what features of *Hamlet*'s content she wants to explore and resolve.

The Determination Asymmetry gives us some evidence that a constructive theory of interpretation better describes legal than literary practice. Legal interpreters need to make certain determinations that their literary counterparts need not. These determinations often have moral significance. This makes some appeals to justification seem inevitable in judicial decision-making.

Some suggest that legal positivists agree with their opponents about this, and that the disagreement is solely one of description. Positivists emphasize the importance of distinguishing between reasoning that aims to determine what the law is prior to adjudication (legal interpretation), and reasoning about how to modify the law in a determinate holding (which involves appeal to moral or policy considerations). Antipositivists resist distinguishing between these modes of judicial reasoning, claiming that they are both aspects of interpretation. It is natural to wonder whether such a dispute about the title "interpretation" is worthwhile (see Stecker 2003, 163). I will say something more about this after presenting the second asymmetry.

B. The Creation Asymmetry

Most legal systems are characterized by radical multiple authorship. Most works of literature are not. This is the Creation Asymmetry.

Cases of joint creation are familiar in art. For example, a team of filmmakers is usually responsible for each feature film. Such artworks raise special issues about interpretation. For example, they frame particularly difficult questions for intentionalist theories.[74]

---

[71] In fact, my claims are compatible with a fully determinate model of literary interpretation. Suppose *The Metamorphosis* has (simplifying immensely) the content (Father Complex and Gnostic Parable). Then it does not have the content (only Father Complex). Perhaps what I have been calling indeterminacy is actually something more like depth, which is often erroneously thought to involve the "truth of competing interpretations." The main point remains: this kind of depth or openness is routinely a feature in literature, but ordinarily a gigantic bug in law.

[72] Sometimes judges overrule past precedent, and in doing so unsettle established matters of law.

[73] 143 U.S. 457 (1892). This case may be one in which fit and justification pull in opposite directions.

[74] See (Gaut 2010, 154) for an excellent discussion of the ways feature films often result from "non-meshing subplans." For parallel questions about legislative intentions see (Waldron 1995).

But joint creation is not the norm in literary practice. Dworkin was right that the chain novel is his closest analogy to legal interpretation. However, it is odd to take the chain novel as particularly illustrative. The chain novelist is an author and, if she is also a literary interpreter, she is an interpreter of an obviously nonstandard sort.

The Creation Asymmetry is confirmed by the awkwardness we addressed above in stating Dworkin's literary analogy. What is the object of constructive interpretation? In literature it is plausibly the individual work. In law, however, constructive interpretation is supposed to be directed at the legal system, rather than an individual statute or decision. The explanation of this difference should invoke the partially creative role of the legal interpreter. Her job is to resolve disputes about the legal content at issue, and since her resolutions are authoritative, they generate new law. But new laws are governed by coherence constraints relating them to the other laws of the legal system. So she must attend to the impact of her decision on the system as a whole.[75]

Multiply authored works are governed by norms that do not apply to individually authored works. Such norms apply to the production of works, and also to their interpretation. For example, even if a director has final cut privileges, she should seek to maximize agreement about the film's final version with her editors and screenwriters, to the extent that this is compatible with her own artistic convictions. Likewise it seems that if a work's authors are relatively isolated from one another—as in some chain novels, or *The Thousand and One Nights*, or the Bible or other religious texts—this has major implications for how we should proceed in interpretation. It may be, for instance, a mistake to attempt to impose too much coherence on such works.

The comparisons here are rich. To pursue one: a legal system is like the *Nights* in that multiple authors contribute to its composition over an extended period of time. However, there are many versions of the *Nights*, and no fact of the matter about whether some stories count as part of it, for the simple reason that there is no clearly demarcated criterion for inclusion in the work. The boundaries of legal systems are (one hopes) better defined, and there is more pressure toward consistency.

Legal interpretation by officials is related to their participation in the creation of a jointly authored work, and will inherit the normative requirements of this sort of enterprise. This distinguishes it from literary interpretation. It may seem to support thinking of legal interpretation as constructive. If judges are institutionally obligated to create, and if (as everyone in practice agrees) moral and policy considerations are relevant to this form of creation, then adjudication seems inherently justificatory. So it might be claimed that positivists are wrong to insist on a distinction between legal interpretation, on the one hand, and judicial reasoning about how to make new law, on the other.

I find this thought unpersuasive. Judges sometimes admit that they are making new law in hard cases.[76] This might be what they are tasked to do. But it is creative, and it is worth being forthright about that. For one thing, there are degrees of creative freedom, and we may feel

[75] Again, individual literary works stand in a different relation to their genres (i.e., instantiation) than individual laws stand in to legal systems (i.e., partial constitution). Coherence norms among laws obtain because of these facts about the metaphysics of legal systems.

[76] See (Finnis 2011, 294).

it democratically important to set boundaries. We might, for example, be less comfortable with some Threshold Views of judging than with the Tie-Breaking View.[77] That we are often uncomfortable is suggested by the tendency of American judges to cloak their creativity in the guise of "balls and strikes" jurisprudence.[78]

C. *The Project Asymmetry*

Alternative interpretive methodologies in literary criticism are frequently consistent and complementary. By contrast, alternative interpretive methodologies in the law are typically inconsistent and antagonistic. This is the Project Asymmetry.

There are distinct interpretive projects in literature, and more than one is legitimate. For example, some interpreters are interested in what an author meant to convey by a certain work, and for this reason do a great deal of biographical research. Other interpreters are interested in how an author was shaped by her cultural environment, and use historical analysis to deepen our appreciation of influences on the work's composition. Others are interested in what meanings a work displays on its own, and they set aside all information about its author and history. Others are concerned to understand broader ideological developments, and they analyze literary works as emblematic expressions of Marxism, feminism, or psychoanalytic theory. In some cases, interpreters make theoretical claims about the exclusive validity of their preferred methodology. But in many cases they do not, and they need not. Projects that deepen our understanding of literary works in all of these ways can be valuable.[79]

An obvious reason to endorse this pluralist view about the interpretation of literature is that great literary works—the works that most commonly receive interpretive attention—are extremely fertile.[80] Seldom does a single interpretation capture the totality of a great work's meanings. Given the futility of individual attempts to say everything worth saying about *The Brothers Karamazov*, it is natural for interpreters of that novel to engage in distinct kinds of projects, and for critics to regard distinct methods of approach with a spirit of tolerance and appreciation.

But a parallel claim about legal interpretive methodologies is not plausible. Justice Scalia disagreed with Dworkin about what legal interpretation requires, and their disagreement issued in inconsistent verdicts about particular cases. This is no surprise. As I have observed, the interpretive questions that judges resolve are not especially similar to interpretive questions about the meaning of a novel. Additionally, the resolutions of judges create new law, and the stakes are too high to let interpretive flowers bloom.

---

[77] See (Scalia 1997, 22): "It is simply not compatible with democratic theory that laws mean whatever they ought to mean, and that unelected judges decide what that is."

[78] See (Dworkin 1996).

[79] Notice that theories of interpretation underdetermine methodologies. A pluralist about literary meaning who accepts speaker meaning, utterance meaning, and historical meaning as relevant might employ any of the methodologies mentioned in the text.

[80] In law there is nothing like this (rough but clear) correlation between the merit of a work and the amount of interpretive attention it receives. My conception of these interpretive practices explains why. Literary interpreters usually focus on great works because these are the works that are most worth understanding. Legal interpreters, by contrast, focus on laws about which there are developed disputes of practical importance.

The Project Asymmetry does little to support constructive interpretation about the law, since it implies nothing about which interpretive methodology is legitimate. It may, however, suggest one insight about a common source of perplexity in interpreting Dworkin himself. Different legal systems assign different projects to judges.[81] The aims of legal interpretation, and the norms that govern it, are thus in some ways system-dependent. So it would be puzzling to assume that there should be a globally applicable theory of legal interpretation—let alone a single overarching theory of interpretation more broadly conceived.[82] It seems to me that notwithstanding some of Dworkin's ambitions, the most fruitful and interesting interpretation of him takes his central aim to be relatively narrow. In particular, constructive interpretation is probably best investigated as a thesis about the appropriate conduct of judges in legal systems such as that of the United States.

VI. Conclusion

The asymmetries just presented are only the tip of the iceberg. Yet they support my contention that Dworkin's favored analogy is flawed. The implications are, as I have tried to emphasize, unclear.

Constructive interpretation is a controversial thesis about any domain. I am dubious about its application in the literary case. So it may be that the disanalogies I have begun to trace are in fact grist for Dworkin's antipositivist mill. But my suggestive remarks cannot be taken as an ultimate determination about their import for legal philosophy.

In closing, I should emphasize a related but larger point. This essay has not presented a theory about the nature of legal interpretation or adjudication. I have attempted some conceptual regimentation, articulating possible views about the interaction between fit and justification. And I have advanced various theses about literary interpretation, considering throughout their similarities to views of legal interpretation that have been proposed. I have said nothing definitive, however, about whether I support a "moral reading" of the United States Constitution, about whether this would amount to a denial of legal positivism, and so on.

Agnosticism looks better on philosophers than it does on judges. I can come to one determinate verdict, however, which is that this is a fitting place to end our story.

References

Bahktin, Mikhail. 1986. *Problems of Dostoevsky's Poetics*. Minneapolis: University of Minnesota Press.

Barnes, Annette. 1988. *On Interpretation: A Critical Analysis*. New York: Blackwell.

---

[81] They also assign different roles to different judges and officials, whose decisions and powers are related to one another by an interconnected and hierarchical system of norms. In this respect the practice may resemble Talmudic or Biblical interpretation more than it resembles the interpretation of art.

[82] See (Calabresi 1980, 561), and Shapiro's (2011, ch. 12) reflections on the "economy of trust" embedded in any particular legal system.

Bordwell, David. 1989. *Making Meaning*. Cambridge: Harvard University Press.

Bromwich, David. 2011. Preface to *The Turn of the Screw*. London: Penguin Classics.

Byrne, Alex. 1993. "Truth in Fiction: The Story Continued." *Australasian Journal of Philosophy* 71(1):24–35.

Calabresi, Guido. 1980 "An Exchange: About Law and Economics: A Letter to Ronald Dworkin". Faculty Scholarship Series. Paper 1994. http://digitalcommons.law.yale.edu/fss_papers/1994

Carroll, Noel. 1992. "Art, Intention, and Conversation." In *Philosophy of Literature: Contemporary and Classic Readings*, edited by Eileen John and Dominic McIver Lopes. Oxford: Blackwell.

_____. 2001. *Beyond Aesthetics*. Cambridge: Cambridge University Press.

Coll, Steve. 2013. "'Disturbing' and 'Misleading'." *The New York Review of Books*.

Currie, Gregory. 1993. "Interpretation and Objectivity." *Mind* 102: 413–428.

Davidson, Donald. 2006. "A Coherence Theory of Truth and Knowledge." In *The Essential Davidson*, edited by Ernie Lepore and Kirk Ludwig. Oxford: Clarendon Press.

Davies, Stephen 2006. "Authors' Intentions, Literary Interpretation, and Literary Value." *British Journal of Aesthetics* 46(3):223–247.

Dworkin, Ronald. 1982. 'Law as Interpretation.' *Critical Inquiry* 9:179.

_____. 1983. "My Reply to Stanley Fish (and Walter Benn Michaels): Please Don't Talk about Objectivity Any More." In *The Politics of Interpretation*, edited by W.J.T. Mitchell. Chicago: University of Chicago Press.

_____. 1986. *Law's Empire*. London: Fontana Press.

_____. 1996. "The Moral Reading of the Constitution." *New York Review of Books*.

_____. 2004. "Ronald Dworkin Replies." In *Dworkin and his Critics*, edited by Justine Burley. Malden: Blackwell.

_____. 2006. "Response." In *Exploring Law's Empire*, edited by Scott Hershovitz. Oxford: Oxford University Press.

_____. 2011. *Justice for Hedgehogs*. Cambridge, MA: Harvard University Press.

Eco, Umberto. 1990. *The Limits of Interpretation*. Bloomington: Indian University Press.

Finnis, John. 2011. *Natural Law and Natural Rights*. Oxford University Press.

Fish, Stanley. 1982. "Working on the Chain Gang: Interpretation in the Law and in Literary Criticism Stanley Fish Critical Inquiry," *The Politics of Interpretation* 9 (1):201–216.

_____. 1983. "Wrong Again." *Texas Law Review* 62: 299, 301–02, 309.

Gaut, Berys. 1993. "Interpreting the Arts: The Patchwork Theory." *The Journal of Aesthetics and Art Criticism* 51(4):597–609.

_____. 1998. "The Ethical Criticism of Art." In *Aesthetics and Ethics: Essays at the Intersection*, edited by Jerrold Levinson. Cambridge: Cambridge University Press. pp. 182–203.

_____. 2010. *A Philosophy of Cinematic Art*. Cambridge: Cambridge University Press.

Greenberg, Mark 2004. "How Facts Make Law." *Legal Theory* 10: 157–198.

_____. 2011. "The Standard Picture and Its Discontents." *Oxford Studies in the Philosophy of Law* 1.

Hershovitz, Scott. 2008. "Integrity and *Stare Decisis*." In *Exploring Law's Empire*, edited by Scott Hershovitz. Oxford: Oxford University Press.

Hirsch, E. D. 1967. *Validity in Interpretation*. New Haven, CT: Yale University Press.

Iseminger, Gary. 1992. "An Intentional Demonstration?" In *Interpretation, Intention, and Truth*, edited by G. Iseminger. Philadelphia: Temple University Press.

Knapp, Steven, and Walter Benn Michaels. [1982]. "Against Theory." *Critical Inquiry* 8:723–742.
Leithauser, Brad. 2012. "Ever Scarier: On 'The Turn of the Screw.'" *The New Yorker*.
Levinson, Jerrold. 1992. "Intention and Interpretation." In *Philosophy of Literature: Contemporary and Classic Readings*, edited by Eileen John and Dominic McIver Lopes. Malden, MA: Blackwell.
_____. 2002. "Hypothetical Intentionalism: Statement, Objections, and Replies." In *Is There a Single Right Interpretation?*, edited by M. Krausz. University Park: Pennsylvania State University Press.
Levinson, Sanford. 2007. "Hercules, Abraham Lincoln, the United States Constitution, and the Problem of Slavery." In *Ronald Dworkin*, edited by Arthur Ripstein. Cambridge: Cambridge University Press.
Livingston, Paisley. 2005. *Art and Intention*. Oxford: Clarendon Press.
Makinson, D. C. 1965. "The Paradox of the Preface." *Analysis* 25 (6): 205–207
Marmor, Andrei. 1992. *Interpretation and Legal Theory*. Oxford: Clarendon Press.
_____. 2011. *Philosophy of Law*. Princeton, NJ: Princeton University Press.
Moore, Michael S. 1996. "Interpreting Interpretation." In *Law and Interpretation: Essays in Legal Philosophy*, edited by Andrei Marmor. Oxford: Clarendon Press.
Nathan, Daniel O. 1992. "Irony, Metaphor, and the Problem of Intention." In *Interpretation, Intention, and Truth,* edited by G. Iseminger. Philadelphia: Temple University Press.
_____. 2005. "A Paradox in Intentionalism." *British Journal of Aesthetics* 45(1):32–48.
Nehamas, Alexander. 1981. "The Postulated Author: Critical Monism as a Regulative Ideal." In *Philosophy of Literature: Contemporary and Classic Readings*, edited by Eileen John and Dominic McIver Lopes. Oxford: Blackwell.
Pevear, Richard. 1994. Forward to *Demons*, by Fyodor Dostoevsky. Malden, MA: Vintage Classics.
Plunkett, David, and Tim Sundell. 2013. "Dworkin's Interpretivism and the Pragmatics of Legal Disputes." *Legal Theory* 19:242–281.
Ponomareff, Constanstin. 1986. "Bakhtin and Dostoevsky." *University of Toronto Quarterly* 55(3):310–311.
Raz, Joseph. 1986. "A New Link in the Chain." *California Law Review* 74:1103–1119.
_____. 1995. *Ethics in the Public Domain*. Oxford: Oxford University Press.
_____. 2004. "Speaking with One Voice: On Dworkinian Integrity and Coherence." In *Dworkin and His Critics*, edited by Justine Burley. Malden, MA: Blackwell.
_____. 2009. *Between Authority and Interpretation*. Oxford: Oxford University Press.
Reimer, Marga, and Elisabeth Camp. 2006. "Metaphor." In *The Oxford Handbook of Philosophy of Language*, edited by Ernest Lepore and Barry C. Smith. Oxford: Oxford University Press.
Robinson, Jenefer. 1985. "Style and Personality in the Literary Work." *Philosophical Review* 94:227–247.
Rozanov, Vasily. 1972. *Dostoevsky and the Legend of the Grand Inquisitor.* Ithaca: Cornell University Press.
Scalia, Antonin. 1997. *A Matter of Interpretation*. Princeton, NJ: Princeton University Press.
Shapiro, Scott. 2011. *Legality*. Cambridge, MA: Harvard University Press.
Shpall, Sam. 2014 "Moral and Rational Commitment." *Philosophy and Phenomenological Research* 88(1):146–172.
Slaughter, M. 1970. "Edmund Wilson and *The Turn of the Screw*." In *Twentieth Century Interpretations of The Turn of the Screw and Other Tales,* edited by Jane P. Tompkins. Englewood Cliffs, N.J.: Prentice-Hall.

Stecker, Robert. 2003. *Interpretation and Construction: Art, Speech, and the Law*. Malden: Blackwell.

Stoljar, Natalie. 1998. "Counterfactuals in Interpretation: The Case against Intentionalism." *The Adelaide Law Review* 20(1):29–48.

Tolhurst, William. 1979. "On What a Text Is and How It Means." *British Journal of Aesthetics* 19:3–14.

Vermazen, Bruce. 1991. "The Aesthetic Value of Originality." *Midwest Studies in Philosophy* 16:266–279.

Waldron, Jeremy. 1995. "Legislators' Intentions and Unintentional Legislation." In *Law and Interpretation: Essays in Legal Philosophy*, edited by Andrei Marmor. Oxford: Clarendon Press.

Walton, Kendall. 1970. "Categories of Art." *Philosophical Review* 79 (3):334–367.

_____. 1979. "Style and the Products of the Processes of Art." In *The Concept of Style*, edited by B. Lang. University Park: Pennsylvania State University Press.

_____. 1993. *Mimesis as Make-Believe*. Cambridge, MA: Harvard University Press.

Wilson, George, and Sam Shpall. 2011. "Unraveling the Twists of *Fight Club*." In *Philosophers on Film: Fight* Club, edited by Thomas Wartenburg. Abingdon: Routledge.

Wimsatt, W. K., and Monroe Beardsley. 1954. "The Intentional Fallacy." In *The Verbal Icon: Studies in the Meaning of Poetry*. Lexington: University of Kentucky Press.

17 Constitutional Realism

Connie S. Rosati*

CONSTITUTIONAL DISCOURSE IS an important part of everyday talk in countries with a rich constitutional tradition like our own. Just consider the debates that followed the Supreme Court's decisions striking down portions of the Defense of Marriage Act, declaring a First Amendment speech right for corporations, or upholding the Affordable Care Act.[1] Participants in these debates argue, often heatedly, about whether cases were correctly or

* In thinking about the issues explored in this essay over many years, I have benefited from exchanges with Larry Alexander, Rainer Baubock, Paul Bloomfield, Sarah Buss, Victor Caston, John Drennan, Gerald Dworkin, Claire Finkelstein, Ruth Gavison, Amy Gutmann, Jeff King, David Lyons, Frank Michelman, Richard Moran, Josh Ober, Sarah Raskoff, David Sobel, Barry Strauss, André du Toit, David Velleman, and Daniel Weinstock. I have also benefitted from presenting very early versions of some of the material in this essay to members of the philosophy department at the University of Southern California, to faculty at the schools of law of the University of San Diego and the University of California, Davis, and to GALA participants at the University of California, Berkeley, School of Law. Versions of this chapter were presented at the 2015 Foundations of Normativity workshop at the University of Edinburgh, the 2015 workshop on metaethics and philosophy of law at Yale Law School, and the 2016 Analytic Legal Philosophy Conference at the University of Virginia Law School. Many thanks to my commentators, Guy Fletcher at Edinburgh and John Gardner at Yale, and to those in attendance at all three gatherings for helpful questions and comments, and to Larry Solum and David Plunkett for written comments. Early research on constitutional interpretation that ultimately led to this chapter was supported by a Laurance S. Rockefeller Fellowship at the University Center for Human Values, Princeton University. Thanks to the Center and to Amy Gutmann, its then Director, for creating an ideal work environment.

[1] Obergefell v. Hodges, 576 U.S. ___ (2015); United States v. Windsor, 570 U.S. 744 (2013); Citizens United v. FEC, 558 U.S. 310 (2010); National Federation of Independent Businesses v. Sebelius, 567 U.S. 519 (2012).

Dimensions of Normativity. David Plunkett, Scott J. Shapiro, and Kevin Toh.

incorrectly decided, whether the Court followed or abandoned constitutional principles or precedent, whether the Court properly exercised or exceeded its authority.

Attention to the content and dynamic of these exchanges suggests that constitutional discourse bears the realist earmarks of normative discourse more generally. Our constitutional claims seem to *describe* something objective, to be about some *fact* of the matter, to express (purported) *truths* about particular constitutional questions. Those who debate the morality of affirmative action programs, for instance, generally talk as if there were a correct answer from the standpoint of morality; their moral judgments seem to express true or false propositions, to concern facts about what morality requires, forbids, or permits. In similar fashion, those who debate the constitutionality of a particular affirmative action program generally talk as if there were a correct answer from the standpoint of constitutional law.[2] Their statements about what a constitution requires, forbids, or permits—what I'll call *constitutional judgments*—seem to express true or false propositions, to concern facts about what is constitutionally required, forbidden, or permitted.[3]

To describe these earmarks as realist is merely to note that they are features that constitutional discourse, like other normative discourse, shares in common with discourse that we ordinarily take to concern matters of fact and treat as about some part of reality. They are features that any metaethical or metalegal theory must account for, whether or not it does so by vindicating the descriptive appearance of the discourse. As those familiar with debates in metaethics are well aware, expressivists who subscribe to a quasi-realist program attempt to capture the realist earmarks of normative discourse by explaining our normative judgments as expressing complex conative states, such as acceptance of systems of norms or plans, and by adopting deflationary notions of truth, facts, and properties.[4] To say that constitutional discourse bears the realist earmarks of moral and other normative discourse is thus not to prejudge the question of whether our best account of that discourse will be descriptivist. Nor it is to prejudge the question of whether there are constitutional facts. Recognizing the realist earmarks of constitutional discourse is compatible not only with an expressivist account of that discourse, but also with an error theory or legal fictionalist theory, according to which our constitutional discourse is descriptivist, but involves presupposition failure, as there are no constitutional facts or properties. The critical point for now is that these features must be accounted for somehow.

---

[2] Consider the debate surrounding Grutter v. Bollinger, 539 U.S. 306 (2003) (upholding the University of Michigan Law School's admissions program on the grounds that diversity is a compelling interest and the program was narrowly tailored to advance that interest). My discussion is restricted to political constitutions and so does not pertain, for instance, to the constitutions of clubs or other religious or secular organizations. Throughout this chapter, I will talk interchangeably about constitutions and constitutional law. My interest will lie with constitutions and constitutional law as such, that is, with a certain type of normative regulation, though constitutional discourse will typically revolve around some particular system of constitutional law. Any such system may be taken to include not only the set of norms that make up a specific constitution but also those judicially developed doctrines that interpret and implement that constitution. See (Fallon 1997). I take no position herein on exactly which materials count as a part of constitutional law.

[3] More precisely, these are what I will call *first-order constitutional judgments*.

[4] See, e.g., (Blackburn 1984 and 1993). See also (Gibbard 1990 and 2003).

The past 40 years have witnessed a proliferation of theories about constitutional interpretation.[5] Yet constitutional theorists have largely not examined our constitutional judgments or considered the nature of the constitutional facts (if any) that these judgments seem to be about.[6] As a consequence, theories of constitutional interpretation have been developed without attending to the truth conditions of the very judgments they are meant to guide.[7] Proponents of these theories seem mostly to assume that constitutional judgments can be true or false, constitutional cases can be correctly or incorrectly decided, focusing their attention instead on defending what they take to be the proper interpretive or decisional norms.[8] Thus, theorists tell us, constitutional decision-makers must follow original meaning, or original interpretive methods, or seek the outcome supported by common law reasoning, or a "coherentist constructivist" outcome, or the outcome mandated by a "moral reading" of the Constitution.[9] Much attention has been paid in formulating theories of constitutional interpretation to common forms of constitutional argument.[10] Partly for this reason, it has been common to think that the choice of a theory turns merely on whether it supports judgments faithful to text, history, precedent, and tradition, or to think, more skeptically, that the choice must be "inherently value laden," a decision to favor some contested values over others.[11]

---

[5] By a theory of constitutional interpretation, I mean a theory about what determines what the law is on constitutional questions. Prominent theories include originalism, textualism, process-based theories, interpretivist theories, coherentist theories, and common-law theories. For examples of each type of theory, see (Bork 1990), (Scalia 1997), (Alexander and Sherwin 2008, 129–232), (Barnett 2004), (Balkin 2011), (Ely 1980), (Dworkin 1986), (Fallon 1987), and (Strauss 1997 and 2010).

[6] For a qualified exception to these claim, see (Dworkin 1977 and 1986). Dworkin defended the idea that there are right answers to questions of law, and so some true statements of law.

[7] Of course, those who offer theories of constitutional interpretation presumably think that the norms they propose do enable us to arrive at true statements of constitutional law. An originalist, for instance, presumably thinks that the truth conditions for constitutional judgments consist in whether those judgments follow the original meaning of the relevant constitutional provisions.

[8] Of course, some writers have advanced skeptical theses about the law, but they have generally done so without being terribly clear about just what they mean to reject when they reject the existence of correct legal answers. They have not made clear, for example, whether they mean to embrace an error theory or a noncognitivist view of legal discourse. For helpful discussion of skeptical or anti-objectivist theses about law, see (Coleman and Leiter 1993). For related discussion, see (Rosati 2004). A few contemporary theorists have suggested not that there aren't correct legal answers, but that justices ought not always to decide constitutional cases in accordance with their best judgments of what the law really is. Instead, they ought to formulate workable doctrine to guide other courts, or they ought to decide cases as minimally as possible so as to permit democratic processes to work or so as to leave room for more local experimentation and fact-finding. See (Fallon 1997); (Dorf 1998); and (Sunstein 1996 and 1999). But notice that even those who think justices ought to restrain their decision-making for one or more of these reasons seem to suppose that there may be correct legal answers.

[9] On following original meaning, on one or another understanding of what that means, see, e.g., (Bork 1990); (Scalia 1997); (Barnett 2004); (Alexander and Sherwin 2008); and (Balkin 2011); on following original interpretive methods, see (McGinnis and Rappaport 2007 and 2009); on following common law methods, see (Strauss 1997 and 2010); on coherentist constructivism, see (Fallon 1987); and on reading the Constitution morally, see (Dworkin 1996).

[10] For discussion of these, see (Bobbitt 1982) and (Fallon 1987). But see (Moore 1985 and 2002).

[11] On the latter point, see, for example, (Fallon 1999). More precisely, the choice would amount to a decision to favor some contested values over others or some interpretation of those contested values over others. The debate between Antonin Scalia and Laurence Tribe and Ronald Dworkin, two of the commentators on Scalia's

My aim in this essay is to take seriously the realist earmarks of constitutional discourse and to offer a preliminary account of the content of constitutional judgments and of the nature of the constitutional facts they seem to concern.[12] The account I offer is *descriptivist* about constitutional judgments, in that it identifies their content with propositions that represent how things are in the world in a certain respect. While allowing that there may be some legal indeterminacy, it is *realist* in that it holds that some of these propositions are true (and that there are constitutional facts) in a nondeflationary sense.[13] A descriptivist account of constitutional judgments, like other descriptivist metaethical and metalegal semantics, has the advantage of avoiding long-standing problems for expressivist theories.[14] In particular, it avoids the Frege-Geach problem, which concerns how to understand the meaning of normative sentences when used in unasserted contexts. According to expressivists, normative sentences express the speaker's attitudes. The atomic sentence "The constitution requires R" would thus express, say, the speaker's acceptance of a system of norms (or plans) that requires R. But the speaker is typically not expressing the attitudes that figure in expressivist semantics when that sentence is embedded in an interrogative ("Does the constitution require R?") or an attitude report ("A believes that the constitution requires R"), or when it occurs in disjunctions, negations, and conditionals. Although expressivists have offered sophisticated responses to the Frege-Geach problem, it is controversial whether any expressivist response can succeed. More directly, whatever the merits of expressivism when it comes to, say, moral statements, we would need compelling reasons, which I believe we currently lack, to embrace expressivism over descriptivism when it comes to constitutional judgments and legal statements more generally.[15] We would need, among other things, reason to think that the latter sorts of statements are normative in the same way that moral statements are normative.[16]

As regards realism, we have reason to adopt an error theory (or a form of fictionalism) only insofar as we have compelling reasons to doubt the existence of constitutional facts. Whatever the merits of error theories with respect to moral facts, I do not believe that compelling reasons have yet been offered for doubting that there are facts about what a constitution requires, forbids, or permits.[17] To the contrary, there are clear cases of facts about what a constitution requires, forbids, or permits, such as the fact that the U.S. Constitution requires that the president be at least 35 years old. Whether there are constitutional facts in "hard

---

Tanner Lectures, seems to exemplify the former point. See (Scalia 1997). Undoubtedly, there is some truth in each of these ideas.

[12] I am not aware of a fully developed second-order constitutional theory of the sort I begin to develop in this chapter, though the distinction between levels of theory is sometimes implicitly acknowledged. See, e.g., (Scalia 1989, 862), (Bork 1990, 143), and (Dworkin 1977 and 1986). But see (Finlay and Plunkett 2018).

[13] In my view, realism in metaethics is best understood along the lines suggested by (Copp 2007a, 7). Understood in this way, realism does not require mind-independence. See also Rosati (2018).

[14] I thus here share the rationale offered by (Finlay and Plunkett 2018) and others for offering a descriptivist account of legal statements.

[15] But for an alterative view of legal statements, see (Toh 2005).

[16] For one view about how the normativity of legal statements differs from that of moral statements, see (Copp 1995, 22–26).

[17] See the extensive literature on legal realism and critical legal studies for alleged reasons to doubt the existence of legal facts.

cases" is obviously more controversial, but even here, we as yet lack compelling reasons to doubt that there are.

All of this having been said, it is, of course, open to someone who favors an expressivist semantics to reframe my account in expressivist terms (or to offer his or her preferred expressivist semantics). And it is open to someone who favors an error theory to adopt my descriptivist semantics, while rejecting the existence of constitutional facts.

The theory that I shall offer is a kind of second-order (or metalegal) constitutional theory, whereas theories of interpretation concern issues of normative or first-order constitutional theory.[18] An account of constitutional judgments and facts will, in the first instance, help us to understand what is at issue between those who make conflicting judgments. But such an account is ultimately critical to our efforts to develop compelling first-order theories. By identifying the truth conditions for constitutional judgments, it will place us in a better position to determine appropriate interpretive norms.[19] It may also have implications for the

[18] As I understand it, the distinction between first- and second-order constitutional theories is akin to the distinction between normative and metaethical theories in moral philosophy. Second-order constitutional theories are theories about a particular kind of normative system. They offer accounts of constitutional facts and judgments and accounts of the nature and function of constitutions. First-order constitutional theories are normative theories about how to interpret constitutions and about how judges ought to adjudicate constitutional cases. First-order theories of the latter sort include an account of how various interpretive norms and norms for judicial comportment ought to influence constitutional decision-making. Interpretive norms will include norms for dealing with precedent, as even originalists recognize. See (Bork 1990, 157). Justice Scalia likewise acknowledges that "almost every originalist would adulterate [originalism] with the doctrine of *stare decisis.*" (Scalia 1989, 861). By *norms for judicial comportment,* I mean norms that speak to such questions as these: whether judges should aim to produce workable doctrine or (alternatively) restrained and "minimalist" opinions, as opposed to insisting on what each thinks is the correct rendering of the law; whether judges ought in their written opinions to present a united front that masks at least certain disagreements, or write what may be highly fractured opinions; and what tone judges ought to strike in writing opinions. Fallon treats questions of judicial comportment as distinct from questions of constitutional meaning. See (Fallon 1997). He argues that the Supreme Court's role is not solely to identify the "meaning" of the Constitution, but to "implement" it through the development of doctrine, and so justices ought to "subordinate their personal views about how the Constitution would best be implemented and . . . accept doctrinal structures that they regard as less optimal." (Fallon 1997, 59). Sunstein has argued that the current Supreme Court generally is—and ought to be—"minimalist," deciding only what must be decided to resolve the case before it satisfactorily, thereby leaving room for experimentation, fact-finding, and democratic resolution of problems. See (Sunstein 1999). I have more sympathy with the position of Wechsler (1959), which stresses the importance of principled adjudication and reasoned explanation of judicial decisions. For discussion of historical shifts in norms of opinion writing, see (Post 2001). A full constitutional theory will include both first- and second-order theories, but it may include components beyond these two. For instance, it may include what Dworkin has called a *theory of jurisdiction,* which will explain "why and when judges, rather than other groups or institutions, should make the decisions required by the theory of controversy [the theory describing the standards judges should use for deciding hard cases]." See (Dworkin 1977, viii). Theorists use different labels for the components of a theory of constitutional law. For example, David Lyons uses the label *theory of constitutional interpretation* for a theory that determines how to interpret or understand the Constitution, and he uses the label *theory of constitutional adjudication* roughly as I do. See (Lyons 1986, 76). And Bork distinguishes between his originalist theory of adjudication (which he treats as a theory of what the constitution means), and his theory of precedent. See (Bork 1990, 157).

[19] In suggesting that a second-order constitutional theory has implications for proper interpretive norms, my view differs from the position defended by Fallon (1999). Fallon argues that the choice between interpretive theories is "inherently value-laden," and must be based to some extent on considerations external to a constitutional

appropriate content of a constitution. An adequate theory of constitutional judgments and constitutional facts should thus have not only explanatory but normative import.

I focus on constitutional judgments and facts because the nature of the United States Constitution and its place in the US legal system raises distinctive questions about interpretation and adjudication. Constitutional law is, in the United States, entrenched, foundational law that places constraints on statutory and common law. The tradition of judicial review in the United States raises rule of law and separation of powers concerns, and it must be squared with both the substantive rights protections of the Constitution and its provision for democratic governance.[20] For these reasons, constitutional scholars tend to offer accounts of constitutional interpretation that treat it independently of more general questions about legal interpretation, though some have likened constitutional interpretation to common law decision-making, and others, to statutory interpretation.[21] Of course, whether these features of constitutional law have the result that a theory of constitutional judgments would differ from a theory of legal judgments more generally is an open question. Even if not, an account of constitutional judgments, of judgments that concern foundational law, may have implications for how we should understand legal statements and legal facts more generally, though I will not be able to explore in any detail possible implications herein.[22] Throughout this essay, I use examples from United States constitutional law and advert to features of the US Constitution. Nevertheless, the account I offer should, perhaps with at least some modifications, generalize to other constitutions, and so I mean for my account to be fully general.

I shall argue, roughly, that constitutional judgments express propositions about (and constitutional facts are facts about) what a specific constitution requires, forbids, or permits when it is interpreted in accordance with norms that are appropriate given the function of a constitution. I argue that we should accept this account because of its explanatory value.

---

text. He contends that the prevailing criteria appealed to by those who propose competing theories of constitutional interpretation are the values of the rule of law, political democracy, and individual rights. Although Fallon is right when he claims that our written constitution cannot by itself determine which theory of constitutional interpretation is correct and that external considerations, perhaps including appeal to substantive values, must play a role, Fallon doesn't consider the possibility that the nature of constitutional facts may help to determine which theory is correct. I believe we should not be too quick to conclude that the choice between, say, originalism and Dworkinianism, must be a choice between substantive values or between competing interpretations of "contestable" values. Nor should we be too quick to conclude, along with originalists, that if judges do not follow originalist principles, they will merely be smuggling in their own favored moral values, e.g., Millian or Rawlsian. We need first to explore fully the extent to which constraints deriving from second-order theory may determine a correct first-order theory. If constitutions as such favor particular interpretive norms, then even if those norms include some moral norms, the interpreter who employs them in adjudicating constitutional questions can hardly be charged with simply importing her favored moral views. For related discussion, see (Rosati 2015).

[20] See (Bork 1990) (arguing that an adequate theory of constitutional interpretation must properly resolve the "Madisonian Dilemma" of reconciling individual liberty with democracy).

[21] See, respectively, (Strauss 1997 and 2010) and (Scalia 1997) (distinguishing constitutional interpretation from common law interpretation, though likening the former to statutory interpretation).

[22] For a recent account of legal statements, see (Finlay and Plunkett 2018), and see Greenberg (2014), for an account of law and a corresponding account of legal interpretation.

It allows us to explain disagreement. It allows us to account for the objectivity and normativity of constitutional judgments. It also allows us to explain why first-order constitutional theorizing tends to take the shape that it does and why extant first-order theories are deficient. I shall say a bit toward the end about how this account might support certain general norms to guide constitutional reflection, but I leave for another time the challenge of exploring more fully any normative implications.

I. Preliminaries

Constitutional judgments concern constitutions, and we will need a working analysis of what a constitution is. In this essay, I shall assume the following analysis to be roughly correct: a constitution is a system of norms—which may include foundational principles, in addition to structural and procedural rules—that operates as supreme within a legal system and that constitutes a nation's governing bodies, guides governmental operations, and fixes the relationship of a government to its citizens. The norms that a constitution comprises are often canonically formulated and sometimes entrenched, as is the case with the US Constitution, but they needn't be, and so these features do not figure in the analysis of a constitution.

Like other normative systems, constitutional law regulates, and it regulates by means of judgments about what a constitution requires, forbids, or permits, such as the judgment that the US Constitution permits the states to impose enhanced criminal penalties for hate crimes or the judgment that it prohibits the states from outlawing abortion. Constitutional judgments are presumably true when they correctly report what a constitution requires, forbids, or permits—when they are correct about the constitutional facts. But what is the content of these judgments and the nature of the facts they are about?

I shall proceed by considering the kinds of judgments that we ordinarily make about constitutions and what we treat as truisms in our talk about constitutions and constitutional law, and on the basis of an account of these judgments, offer an account of the nature of constitutional facts. This strategy assumes, of course, that there is some relationship between our constitutional judgments and what we treat as truistic and the nature of the facts our judgments concern. Although this assumption is not uncontroversial, I take it that we have no real alternative to proceeding on the assumption that our judgments are generally responsive to genuine features of the world and so provide rough, though defeasible, clues as to the nature of what those judgments are about. We follow roughly the same strategy in our efforts to understand the nature of other normative facts, such as moral facts or facts about personal good. We come to understand the nature of facts in a particular normative domain by studying the judgments we are inclined to make in that domain, along with the claims we treat as truistic and the cases we regard as paradigmatic.[23] We work to understand the nature of facts about welfare, for example, by studying the judgments that we are inclined to make about what is good for someone, the claims that we treat as truistic about welfare, and the cases that strike us as paradigmatic instances of someone realizing or failing to realize her

[23] For ideas along these lines, see (Railton 1990), (Smith 1994), and (Rosati 2006).

good. The assumption on which my approach rests is, I believe, especially reasonable in the case of judgments that concern systems of our own devising, such as games and institutions.

Our truisms about constitutional law, which I here largely adapt from Joseph Raz, include the following.[24] First, there can be good and bad constitutions. Second, we cannot discover the content of a country's constitution merely by determining what that content ought to be rationally, practically, or morally. Third, two people who disagree about the moral defensibility of a constitution and constitutional law can agree about what the law is. And finally—a truism Raz does not list—disagreement can intelligibly exist regarding what a constitution requires, forbids, or permits. As I will explain, the account of constitutional judgments and facts that I offer is consistent with these truisms.

An inquiry into the content of constitutional judgments and the nature of constitutional facts is of a piece with inquiry into normative judgments and facts more generally, yet it must be sensitive to peculiar features of constitutional law, which our truisms reflect. Any specific body of constitutional law is a system of positive law, and as positive law, its content is a product of exigency and custom, of opposing political forces, and of limited knowledge and rationality. Constitutional provisions may conform to moral requirements, but like conventional moral codes, constitutions can, and often do, deviate from morality. The standard example, of course, is provided by the slave clauses of the US Constitution.[25]

Partly as a consequence of these features, constitutional judgments differ from moral judgments in at least two respects. First, constitutional judgments have what we might call a limited "subject matter jurisdiction," in that they do not cover anything close to the range of matters covered by moral judgments or judgments of practical rationality more generally. Moreover, they have a limited "personal jurisdiction," in that the scope of their authority over persons and institutions is far narrower than the scope of moral judgments or judgments of practical rationality: not everyone is bound by our constitution, and our constitutional judgments do not suppose that they are. In contrast, moral judgments and judgments of practical rationality apply to any arbitrary, relevantly situated individual, group, or institution.

Constitutional judgments are a species of normative judgment, but just what makes normative judgments "normative" has been a matter of serious debate in metaethics and in metanormative theory more generally.[26] As has been widely observed, normative judgments

[24] See (Raz 1998). Raz treats these truisms as features of our understanding of law's nature.

[25] Constitution of the United States of America, Art. I Sec. 9 and Art. IV, Sec. 2.

[26] Accounts of normativity (of what makes normative judgments normative) seem to fall into two categories. Views in the first category understand the normativity of some normative judgments in terms of their implication of other normative judgments. See, e.g., (Frankena 1942). Frankena's criticisms of Moore suggest that what makes a normative judgment normative is that it implies an ought judgment—e.g., "X is good" implies "A ought to bring X into existence." See also (Smith 1994, 95). Smith suggests that normativity is constituted by the existence of normative reasons. And see (Copp 1995, 10, and ch. 2 generally). Copp argues that the normative aspect of normative claims is that they express propositions that imply nontrivially that a relevant standard is, depending upon the type of normative claim, either current or justified. See also (Copp 2007b). Views in the second category attempt to get out of the "circle of normative judgment" by identifying normativity, not with the implication of a normative judgment, but with the expression of a (possibly complex) attitude or emotion. See, e.g., (Gibbard 1990, 9, 21, and 33). Gibbard (1990) maintains that the normativity of normative judgments consists in an element of endorsement. Some discussions of normativity center not on the question of what makes normative judgments normative but on the authority of normative claims. See (Korsgaard

function in practical ways, to guide and assess actions and attitudes. Normative judgments have a seemingly necessary connection to motivation and a kind of automatic expressive and recommending force, or what Allan Gibbard has described as an "element of endorsement," which partly explains how they function to guide feelings and actions.[27] A person who judges that she ought to Φ, for example, is reliably motivated to Φ (at least to some degree, and perhaps insofar as she is rational), and a person who tells someone to Φ expresses her approval of his Φing. It is controversial whether the connection between normative judgment and motivation is necessary, as motivational internalism maintains, or contingent, as motivational externalism maintains.[28] It is also controversial whether the expressive and recommending force of normative judgments is a feature of the semantics or of the pragmatics of those judgments.[29]

As J. L. Mackie observed normative judgments make a claim to objectivity or justification.[30] As to what makes normative judgments normative, philosophers differ. Some maintain that the normativity of normative judgments consists in their giving reasons for action and attitude or in their entailing propositions about what relevantly situated agents ought to do or feel, whereas some have maintained that it consists in the element of endorsement.[31] The claim to objectivity that normative judgments make and the reasons and obligations they provide may not be uniform across normative domains. For instance, it is frequently said that moral judgments claim overriding authority and, when true, afford categorical reasons for action, whereas aesthetic judgments and judgments of personal good do not.[32]

1996). Korsgaard describes the "normative question" as the question of why we really ought to do what morality says we ought. Since my undertaking does not require us to settle the question of what makes normative judgments normative, I shall simply assume that normative judgments typically exhibit the features specified by the main competing accounts.

[27] See (Gibbard 1990, 6–7, 10).

[28] To assume that normative judgments have a seemingly conceptual connection to motivation is not to assume the truth of what Darwall has called *judgment internalism*. Judgment internalism posits a necessary connection between motivation and (sincere) normative judgment, whereas *existence internalism* posits a necessary connection between motivation and something's having a certain normative status (e.g., a consideration's being a reason). See (Darwall 1986). See also (Brink 1989, 40), for a related distinction between *agent internalism* and *appraiser internalism*. See also (Smith 1994), and (Svavarsdottir 1999). Even if (sincere) normative judgments do not, as a conceptual matter, have a connection to motivation, they regularly have such force and function to guide attitude and action. An adequate account of normative judgments should therefore help to explain why judgment internalism might at least seem to be true.

[29] For the view that it is a pragmatic feature of normative statements, see (Finlay 2014). See also (Finlay and Plunkett 2018).

[30] See (Mackie 1977, ch. 1). And see, e.g., (Gibbard 1990, Part III). To assume that normative judgments make a claim to objectivity is not, then, to assume the truth of either normative realism or cognitivism. Normative judgments may not be able to make good on their claim to objectivity, as error theorists such as Mackie allege. And as noncognitivists or expressivists might insist, the claim to objectivity that normative judgments make can be captured without positing the existence of (robust) normative facts.

[31] See, e.g., (Raz 2010, 5) and (Schroeder 2007, 81); Frankena (1942); and (Gibbard 1990, 10), respectively. Frankena made use of the idea that normative judgments entail propositions about what agents ought to do to great effect in arguing that, contrary to G. E. Moore's claims, good cannot be simple, non-natural, and normative. Darwall (2003) has picked up on this idea in criticizing Moore and in developing his own analysis of welfare (2004). For a brief, critical discussion, see (Rosati 2003).

[32] For a discussion of the claims made by moral judgments, see (Railton 1992 and 1993).

In what follows, I draw distinctions among a number of kinds of judgments one might make about constitutions to make clearer the kind of judgment I have in mind in talking about constitutional judgments. I then offer an account of the content of these judgments, explaining how they exhibit the various features of normative judgments.

II. Constitutional Judgments

Let us begin by distinguishing between two kinds of critical judgment one might make about a constitution. The first of these offers an "external" critique. It brings to bear an independent standard of normative assessment, criticizing a particular constitution as, for instance, morally deficient. The second criticizes a constitution for its defects *as a constitution*. One might plausibly maintain that constitutions have a function, which can be understood in terms of what a constitution theoretically accomplishes such that people would rationally seek to add or include a constitution within a system of law. One can understand the function of a constitution, that is, by considering what a legal system with a constitution theoretically achieves that a legal system without one would not. It is plausible to think that all constitutions, just as such, have one or more functions and that constitutions of different types may have functions in addition to those they have in virtue of being constitutions. For instance, constitutions as such may function to make possible a stable and well-functioning government, by specifying the structure and powers of government, the process of succession, the procedures for constitutional change, and so on. Some constitutions may, in addition, function to make possible a system of government that is maximally rights protective. One might then criticize a particular constitution for including provisions that conflict with its functions or effectuate them poorly or for failing to include provisions that further those functions, so that it does less well at being the sort of thing that it is. For ease of discussion, I shall from here on talk as if constitutions have a single function. I shall not take a position as to what the function of a constitution is, but further development of my account would provide a systematic treatment of the nature of constitutions and what they are supposed to do.

This second sort of criticism of constitutions as defective—what we might call "internal" criticism—involves a type of constitutional judgment different from the one that will chiefly concern me. We need to distinguish, then, between two kinds of constitutional judgments. *First-order constitutional judgments* concern what a particular constitution requires, forbids, or permits; they include judgments that prescribe how a pending case would be correctly decided and judgments that evaluate a past case as correctly or incorrectly decided. We have already seen a number of examples of these judgments. Another would be the judgment that our constitution prohibits execution of those with intellectual disabilities.[33] *Second-order constitutional judgments* evaluate proposed or existing constitutional provisions as appropriate or inappropriate for inclusion in a constitution, not morally, practically, or rationally, but based on what a constitution is supposed to be and do. Examples would be the judgments that a flag-burning amendment or an amendment banning abortion are either appropriate or inappropriate for inclusion in a constitution.

[33] See Atkins v. Virginia, 536 U.S. 304 (2002).

My interest lies with first-order constitutional judgments, but with a specific class of these judgments. So a few additional clarifications are in order. First, our constitutional talk is complex, both because of differences in the perspectives of theoreticians and practitioners and because of the structure of the court system in the United States. Practitioners may be more interested in predicting the outcomes of cases—in how courts are likely to decide constitutional questions—and so their judgments may often concern such predictions, or relatedly, they may simply state the law as it currently stands as given by court decisions and legal doctrine. Theoreticians, in contrast, may attend less to what courts are likely to do and more to what they ought to do, if they are to interpret the law correctly. My interest lies with these theoretical constitutional judgments.[34]

Second, judgments as to whether a constitutional case was correctly decided vary depending upon which court was deciding the case. Lower courts are constrained in their constitutional decision-making to adhere to the decisions of the Supreme Court. A case might be correctly decided in a district court based on decisions of the Court that the Court would overrule, if it considered the issue again. My interest lies with what we might call "final" constitutional judgments—judgments about what the law at a time finally is.

Third, even as regards decisions by the Supreme Court, the Court constrains its own decision-making based on such considerations as separation of powers. The practice of the Supreme Court, with various qualifications, is, for example, to decide cases, when possible, without reaching constitutional questions, and to treat constitutional challenges to statutes as "facial" challenges only when they cannot be satisfactorily resolved as "as-applied" challenges. (One point at issue between the majority and dissenting opinions in *Citizens United v. FEC* concerned whether the Court really needed to treat the legal challenge as facial (as the majority opinion contended) or whether it could resolve the case by treating it as an "as-applied" challenge (as Justice Stevens's dissent contended.))[35] It is therefore important to distinguish between two quite different claims as to whether a case was "correctly decided." In one sense, a case was correctly decided when it was decided taking account not only of the law but of institutional restraints on the Court, as developed in its own doctrine—norms that would be part of a full theory of adjudication. In a different sense, though, a case was correctly decided when it was decided just on the basis of the *substantive* law. My focus is on first-order constitutional judgments of the latter kind.

Finally, H. L. A. Hart famously distinguished between *internal* and *external* statements of law.[36] Internal statements of law are those made by persons who accept the law and use it as a guide to conduct, criticism, and so on. External statements of law are those that might be made by an observer of the system, someone who knows the rules but does not take up the "internal point of view" with respect to them. We might, then, distinguish between internal and external first-order constitutional judgments. Although, in my view, these statements do not differ in their semantics, the former typically operate practically in a way that the latter may not. My interest herein lies principally with internal first-order constitutional judgments

[34] Thanks to Larry Solum for emphasizing the differences between these perspectives.

[35] Citizens United v. FEC, 558 U.S. 310 (2010).

[36] (Hart 1961/1994, 89).

as concerns the substantive law, and more precisely, with first-order constitutional judgments that are internal, theoretical, and final.

Although I shall focus principally on this class of first-order judgments, we must be attentive to the full range of claims that we make about constitutions and, moreover, to the complex combinations our judgments can take. It is possible to hold a moral view that is contrary to a particular constitution, for instance, while also holding that the constitution nevertheless in some sense deals with the matter appropriately. One can morally favor a more egalitarian society, for example, while favoring principles permitting less egalitarian outcomes as better suited for constitutionalization, given the existence of sharp yet reasonable disagreement regarding principles of distributive justice.[37] It is also possible, as a matter of first-order judgment, to approve of the decision in a particular case, while disapproving of the underlying constitutional provisions on second-order grounds. One can approve of the Court's decision in the Michigan affirmative action case, while making the second-order judgment that a norm of color-blindness is more fitting for a constitution than a norm permitting some consideration of race.

A. First-Order Constitutional Judgments

First-order constitutional judgments take a variety of forms. Some explicitly include the language of permissions, requirements, and prohibitions, as in the judgments that the Constitution permits capital punishment or prohibits the taking of property without just compensation. Others simply describe legislative enactments, judicial decisions, or executive actions as in accord with or contrary to the Constitution, as in the judgment that it was not unconstitutional for Congress to insert the words "under God" into the Pledge of Allegiance. Constitutional judgments commonly appear in either commentary on the decisions of courts or prescriptions to courts (as found, for example, in briefs of the parties, in amicus curiae briefs, or in scholarly articles), as in the judgments that *Obergefell v. Hodges* was correctly decided or that the Supreme Court ought to overturn *Roe v. Wade*.[38] I take it that any first-order constitutional judgment of the class that is of interest herein can be recast using explicitly normative language. For ease of discussion, I shall focus on statements of the form "X is constitutionally required [forbidden, permitted] in L," where L refers to the particular system of law in which a constitution figures.

Constitutional discourse, as we have seen, typically involves debate about how to decide a pending case correctly or about whether a past case was correctly decided and, more generally, about what a particular constitution really prescribes. But how are we to understand the disagreement manifested, for example, in the continuing debate about *Roe v. Wade*? When the pro-*Roe* forces insist that *Roe* was "correctly decided," that our constitution does support a limited right to abortion, and the anti-*Roe* forces insist that *Roe* was "wrongly decided," that our constitution supports no such right, what is their disagreement about?

---

[37] This is, I take it, one point captured in Rawls's notion of an overlapping consensus. (See Rawls 1993).

[38] Obergefell v. Hodges, 576 U.S. ____ (2015); Roe v. Wade, 410 U.S. 113 (1973); Planned Parenthood v. Casey, 505 U.S. 833 (1992).

Because of how a system of law works, some constitutional judgments are authoritative, namely, those made by relevant officeholders, and authoritative judgments are enforced by designated government officials, so they have characteristic effects. A clue to the semantic content of constitutional judgments might come, then, from a consideration of the effects of constitutional judgments, when they are authoritative and enforced. Consider claims about the existence and scope of fundamental rights, which seem to preoccupy advocates of competing approaches to constitutional interpretation. The effect of constitutional judgments about fundamental rights, when authoritative and enforced, is to distribute the benefits of liberty and the burdens of constitutional change. Such judgments indicate who will enjoy a freedom or protection and who must do the difficult work of constitutional amendment if a contrary view is to prevail. For example, the constitutional judgment of *Roe v. Wade* and its progeny allocates to women the (limited) right to elect abortion free of undue state interference, while imposing on opponents of abortion the difficult work of bringing about a constitutional amendment, or of seeking restriction of abortion within existing constitutional limits through direct or indirect political or legal action.[39] Constitutional judgments may also, depending on the content of a constitution, have the effect of allocating economic goods by recognizing economic rights.[40]

Sometimes constitutional judgments allocate not liberty or economic benefits but power, where power is understood as the capacity to make and enforce, through the apparatus of the government, legally authoritative decisions. Judgments under our commerce clause, for instance, most directly concern the relative powers of state and federal governments rather than individual liberty or economic benefit. Of course, the interests of individuals are implicated in the question of whether more local control over a matter will prevail. But the direct effect of the judgments is on the conduct of governing bodies.

Combining these cases, we might say that constitutional judgments concern the distribution of benefits (in liberty, economic goods, or power) and the burdens of constitutional change.[41] Call the distribution that a constitutional judgment effects when authoritative and

[39] Of course, in a federalist system such as ours, the effect is more complex. A constitutional judgment can recognize a federal constitutional right, thereby limiting the ability of either state or federal governments to pass restrictive legislation. Or it can deny a federal constitutional right, thereby denying only a federal guarantee of liberty rather than liberty itself, since state constitutional or statutory law may recognize rights that the federal constitution does not. Compare Plessy v. Ferguson, 163 U.S. 537 (1896), which upheld the doctrine of separate but equal, and Ferguson v. Gies, 82 Mich. 358 (1890), in which the Michigan Supreme Court ruled—six years before *Plessy*—that State Act No. 130 of 1885 precluded separation in public places or conveyances based on race. Thanks to Anthony Rosati for the reference to this case. Compare also Bowers v. Hardwick, 478 U.S. 186 (1986), which denied the existence of a constitutionally protected right to engage in homosexual sodomy, and Powell v. State, 270 Ga. 327 (1998), in which the Georgia State Supreme Court held that the very statute at issue in *Bowers* violated the state constitution's right to privacy. Since *Plessy* and *Bowers* were ultimately overturned, these cases perhaps more precisely illustrate not the divergence between rights protected by state constitutions and by the federal constitution as correctly interpreted, but between state constitutions and the federal constitution as it has sometimes been interpreted.

[40] Thanks to Holly Smith on this point.

[41] The importance of the distribution of political burdens is reflected in the Supreme Court's Seattle-Hunter doctrine, which treats as an equal protection violation the imposition of unique political burdens on issues of special interest to minorities. See Hunter v. Erickson, 393 U.S. 385 (1969) (holding in violation of Fourteenth Amendment an amendment to the Akron city charter requiring that fair housing ordinances be put to

enforced a "BBD," for "benefits and burdens of change distribution." That constitutional judgments, when authoritative and enforced, effect BBDs should be unsurprising, of course, since a constitution's provisions themselves effect such distributions.

Return now to the question of what is at issue between those who utter conflicting constitutional judgments. Each side makes a claim to the effect that a particular outcome is correct as a matter of existing constitutional law, so their disagreement is about the constitutional facts. Assume that each side is knowledgeable about and agreed as to what constitutes the existing "constitutional materials"—relevant texts and court decisions, for instance. But to get from these materials to the content of the law, requires employing various interpretive norms, norms about the how to understand the linguistic content of these materials, about how to weight various sources, about how to reconcile conflicting considerations, and so on. In disagreeing about the constitutional facts, those who make conflicting constitutional judgments would seem to disagree about appropriate interpretive norms or their implications.[42] Each side to the dispute supposes that certain norms are appropriate to follow in interpreting or construing a constitution, *given the sort of thing a constitution is*, that is, given a certain view of the *function* of a constitution. Each side presupposes a particular system of interpretive norms for a constitution that, together with extant legal materials, effects a particular BBD, and so each side reaches a different judgment.

In light of the forgoing considerations, we might understand the semantic content of first-order constitutional judgments as follows. A judgment of the form, "X is constitutionally required [forbidden, permitted] in L" semantically expresses the proposition that constitutional materials in L, interpreted in accordance with norms appropriate to a constitution's function, effect a BBD such that X is required [forbidden, permitted]. By norms "appropriate" to a constitution's function, we should understand norms that best further or facilitate the fulfillment of this function.

citywide vote before they could take effect, whereas ordinances regulating real estate on bases other than race required only approval of the City Counsel, because it singled out and placed a unique political burden on legislation of special interest to minorities); Washington v. Seattle School District No. 1, 458 U.S. 457 (1982) (holding in violation of Fourteenth Amendment a facially neutral anti-busing initiative, which barred only school busing plans designed to achieve racial integration, because it singled out and imposed unique political burdens on an issue of special concern to minorities). See also Romer v. Evans, 116 S. Ct. 1620, 1628 (1996) ("A law declaring that in general it shall be more difficult for one group of citizens than for all others to seek aid from the government is itself a denial of equal protection of the laws in the most literal sense."). Arguably these equal protection issues are just a special case of the problem of appropriate allocation of political burdens. One might point out that law as a whole effects distributions of benefits and power and the burdens of change, but the burdens imposed may be less onerous than the burdens constitutionalization imposes and do not serve precisely the same function. Nevertheless, the fact that law has a related effect is, I would conjecture, important to understanding the normativity of law in general and thus to arriving at a unified account of the normativity of law that can encompass constitutional law. Law in general may be normative for attitudes toward allocations of liberty, power, and burdens of political change as effected in one or another way (e.g., majority vote, constitutionalization, etc.).

[42] I will return to this point in the next section. See (Dworkin 1986). One might wonder whether this is enough to explain the heat we often find in constitutional debates. Of course, part of the explanation of the intensity of constitutional debates, as well as of the connection between constitutional judgment and motivation, is undoubtedly that constitutional questions sometimes implicate matters of broader normative concern about morality and individual welfare.

This account of the semantics of constitutional judgments vindicates the descriptive appearance of constitutional discourse. Constitutional judgments understood in this way seem to concern some fact of the matter and to express (purported) truths about particular constitutional questions. The account thus captures the claim to objectivity or justification characteristic of normative judgments. But normative judgments, as noted earlier, are commonly thought to have additional features. They also function in practical ways; they are used to guide and assess actions and attitudes. They have a seemingly necessary connection to motivation and a kind of expressive and recommending force. How are we to account for the use of constitutional judgments to guide and assess actions and attitudes? How, if at all, are they motivating and expressive of attitudes?

Given that constitutional judgments concern BBDs, we can understand them as normative for an attitude of acceptance of BBDs and for corresponding political and legal action. If this is correct, then constitutional judgments, must in some sense, express acceptance of and recommend (or discommend) the BBD those judgments would effect, were they authoritative and enforced. Even if we disagree with a constitutional judgment on moral, political, or second-order constitutional grounds, insofar as we sincerely make the judgment, we must, in effect, accept (and recommend) how, if authoritative and enforced, it would grant benefits to some and place burdens on others.

Constitutional judgments recommend BBDs, I have suggested, but it is important to be clear about the scope of the recommendation. A constitutional judgment favoring the decision in *Roe v. Wade*, for example, does not recommend abortion itself. Rather, it in some way recommends the BBD effected by *Roe*. We need to be clear, though, about the precise sense in which it recommends this distribution, if we are to see how constitutional judgments might have the recommending force characteristic of normative judgments.

There are two main possibilities. First, constitutional judgments might express acceptance of the resulting BBD just in itself. Thus, the speaker who says that *Roe* was correctly decided accepts the resulting BBD granting a qualified liberty to those seeking abortion and imposing on those who wish to alter this liberty the burden of seeking either a constitutional amendment or restrictions on abortion within existing constitutional bounds.

Although this first approach may be correct as concerns second-order constitutional judgments, it fails as a way of understanding the expressive and recommending force of first-order constitutional judgments. The latter judgments pertain to a specific constitution with its specific norms and provisions, which cannot be ignored if a judgment is to be about that constitution. Bearing in mind this obvious constraint, it seems that one can espouse a constitutional judgment, without expressing acceptance of the resulting BBD in itself. One can, for instance, think *Roe* was correctly decided, while rejecting the BBD the Court's judgment effected in that case, because one rejects the BBD effected in the *Constitution*, which one believes the Court's judgment correctly tracks. One might think a particular constitution's BBDs are mistaken—morally, rationally, prudentially, or constitutionally.[43]

These considerations suggest a second possibility. One might express acceptance of the BBD not in itself but as correct about the law. We might say then, as a first approximation,

[43] That is to say, as a matter of second-order constitutional judgment about the appropriateness of a provision as part of a constitution.

that constitutional judgments expresses acceptance of the BBDs they would effect as correct given the BBDs a constitution itself effects, at least when properly understood. First-order constitutional judgments thus express an attitude of acceptance and a recommendation. But notice that in contrast to other normative judgments, first-order constitutional judgments express a qualified attitude of acceptance. Because they express an attitude of acceptance, constitutional judgments will ordinarily be motivating. A person can sincerely avow a first-order constitutional judgment at odds with her own moral views. What's more, she can be motivated to see that the former judgment is upheld even though at odds with her moral views. Consider the views of those who oppose abortion but accept *Roe* on constitutional grounds.

The connection between constitutional judgments and motivation is not necessary. Neither it, nor the expressive and recommending force of such judgments, is a part of their semantic content. At the same time, it is not merely contingent. Rather it is internal to a certain standpoint. Consider for a moment the connection between moral judgment and motivation. Debates between internalists and externalists about moral motivation commonly focus on examples of amoralists or sociopaths, people who, it appears, can sincerely utter moral judgments while remaining utterly unmoved by them.[44] Such examples would seem to suggest, at least, that moral judgments are not motivating for any arbitrary person—not for people who cannot understand those judgments or for those who otherwise lack relevant emotional capacities.[45] But granting only this much leaves open the nature of the connection between normative judgment and motivation. The connection might depend on idiosyncratic desires, or it might depend on more fundamental features we share in virtue of our common human (biological) nature or, alternatively, in virtue of our agency.[46]

Like moral judgments, constitutional judgments are not motivating for just any arbitrary person—not for those who cannot understand them, for instance, or who lack any inclination to forgo their own interests for the sake of cooperation with others. How then might such judgments have something more than an accidental connection to motivation, and what might that connection be? How might it be true with respect to these judgments, that is, that a person who judges something constitutionally required, say, will feel some motivation to support or act in favor of it?

First-order constitutional judgments are motivating but not simply because of their connection to desires we may happen to have as particular individuals who occupy particular vantage points: rather, I want to suggest, they motivate us and express acceptance and recommendation insofar as we take up a certain vantage point in contemplating constitutional questions. Call this vantage point the "standpoint of the constitutional citizen": the standpoint of the citizen who accepts constitutional order and the rule of law. In taking up this vantage point, we step back from our particular moral, prudential, and political views and

[44] See, e.g., (Smith 1994, 60–71); (Brink 1997); (Copp 1997); and (Smith 1997).

[45] For this reason, it is common to characterize internalism in terms of a connection between moral judgment and motivation that holds *insofar as we are rational*.

[46] Certain contemporary naturalists can perhaps be understood as appealing to shared, human characteristics. See, e.g., (Brink 1989); (Railton 1986). David Velleman has defended a view of practical reason that he describes as intermediate between externalism and internalism and that connects the motivating power of reasons to motives constitutive of agency. See (Velleman 1996).

take up something like Hart's internal point of view with respect to the law.[47] From this vantage point, we see a constitution as creating reasons and obligations, and we are motivated by our constitutional judgments. The claim, then, is that first-order constitutional judgments are motivating for us, and those judgments carry expressive and recommending force insofar as we approximate to the standpoint of the constitutional citizen in reflecting on constitutional questions.

B. *Summary and Elaboration*

First-order constitutional judgments concern whether a particular BBD is supported by application to existing legal materials of interpretive norms appropriate given the function of a constitution. A judgment of the form, "X is constitutionally required [forbidden permitted] in L" semantically expresses the proposition that constitutional materials in L, interpreted in accordance with norms appropriate to a constitution's function, effect a BBD that requires [forbids, permits] X. Such judgments express the speaker's acceptance and they have motivational force, and thereby guide attitude and action, by engaging persons insofar as they take up or approximate to the standpoint of the constitutional citizen. Constitutional judgments are normative for an attitude of acceptance of BBDs as a matter of what comports with a particular constitution, and they are normative for action with regard to changing (or supporting) how a constitution currently distributes benefits and the burdens of change. Where an individual, say, judges a constitutional question as correctly decided but disapproves of the BBD a constitution effects, she will feel at least some motivation to take steps to alter that arrangement or to support others who do, while recognizing that, at least as a matter of law, she rightly bears this burden. Where she judges a matter incorrectly decided, she will feel at least some motivation to take steps, or to support the efforts of others to take steps, to rectify the error—for instance, to have a decision overturned or to limit it. A person will be motivated in these ways, that is, insofar as she takes up the standpoint of constitutional citizen. A constitutional judgment does not merely recommend an outcome and elicit attitude and action, but makes a claim to justification: namely, that a BBD is supported by correct application to existing legal materials of norms appropriate to a constitution. Insofar as what a judgment claims is correct, it affords, for those who accept the system, reasons for attitude and action, and may imply obligations on the part of relevant government officials.

Understanding constitutional judgments in this way fits with our truisms about constitutional law. Existing legal materials, which constrain what first-order constitutional judgments one can plausibly make, may themselves effect morally objectionable BBDs, so constitutions can be morally bad. Since existing legal materials constrain plausible constitutional judgments, one cannot discover the content of a constitution just by determining what it ought to be morally, rationally, or prudentially. Since two persons can agree as to which interpretive norms are appropriate and what application of those norms to existing constitutional materials implies, they can agree about what the law is, while disagreeing in their other normative assessments of it. And since people can disagree as to the function of a constitution, or as to which interpretive norms are appropriate given the function of a constitution,

[47] (Hart 1961/1994, 89–91).

or as to what those interpretive norms support when applied to existing legal materials, they can disagree in their first-order judgments.

Understanding constitutional judgments in this way enables us to account for the full range of judgments that we make about constitutions. An individual might simultaneously judge that (a) the constitution permits abortion, (b) abortion is morally wrong, and (c) the constitution correctly (or incorrectly) allocates benefits and the burdens of change with respect to abortion as a matter of appropriate constitutionalization. That is to say, her first-order constitutional judgments may diverge from her second-order constitutional judgments, as well as from her moral and prudential judgments.

III. Constitutional Facts

First-order constitutional judgments are true when the propositions they express are true. Take the judgment that *Roe v. Wade* was wrongly decided. On my proposal, the sentence, "The constitution does not permit abortion," is true just in case interpretive norms appropriate to a constitution's function, when applied to relevant authoritative constitutional materials, support the conclusion that the constitution does not permit abortion. If the account herein of the propositions constitutional judgments semantically express is correct, then we should understand the facts that first-order constitutional judgments concern as facts about what follows when interpretative norms that are appropriate given the function of a constitution are applied to relevant constitutional materials.

We might accordingly understand constitutional facts as follows, letting C stand for a particular constitution and M_C for materials relevant to a particular constitution and constitutional issue, such as constitutional text and precedent:

> X is constitutionally required [permitted, forbidden] by C if and only if and because interpretive norms that are appropriate given the function of C, when applied to authoritative constitutional materials M_C, effect a BBD that entails or supports X.

Constitutional facts, we might alternatively say, are facts about the instantiation of the properties of *being constitutionally required, permitted*, and *forbidden*; and we might analyze these properties as follows:

> *Being constitutionally required* [*permitted, forbidden*] by C is being entailed or supported by the BBD that results when interpretive norms that are appropriate to C are applied to authoritative constitutional materials M_C.[48]

---

[48] Compare Dworkin's (1977, 5) account of legal judgments: "A proposition of law may be asserted as true if it is more consistent with the theory of law that best justifies settled law than the contrary proposition of law. It may be denied as false if it is less consistent with that theory than the contrary." His account applies to legal judgments within a jurisdiction that follows the "rights thesis." It isn't entirely clear whether, when Dworkin describes the truth conditions for propositions of law, he also means to be telling us what judgments of law say. If he does, then, of course, there will be a problem about how to explain disagreements between Dworkinians and those who reject Dworkin's approach to adjudication (or his view of right answers in law). My account,

A few points of clarification about these proposals. First, as noted earlier, what it means for norms to be "appropriate" to a constitution is that they best further or facilitate the fulfillment of its function. Second, the phrase "entail or support X" is meant to allow for the possibility that although some conclusions may be entailed by application of interpretive norms to constitutional materials, other conclusions may be supported by more coherentist reasoning that achieves a kind of reflective equilibrium. Third, the proposal assumes that we have or could formulate reductive analyses of being "permitted," "required," or "forbidden," at least when these terms are qualified by the term "constitutionally." Without attempting here to offer formal analyses, we might say roughly the following. For X to be required by application of norms appropriate to a constitution to relevant materials is for X to be entailed or supported by application of those norms and for ~X to be excluded by them. For X to be forbidden by application of those norms is for those norms to exclude X. And for X to be permitted by application of those norms is for X to be neither required nor forbidden. Finally, the proposal assumes that we have a clear notion of authoritative constitutional materials, and so it assumes we have some independent test of the existence of constitutional materials. I will not try to say anything here about what such a test might be, since it raises larger questions about the nature and existence of law that we do not need to settle for present purposes.[49]

To accept this account of the nature of facts about what a constitution requires, forbids, or permits is to accept a form of *constitutional realism*, where the term "realism" is understood in its metaethical sense, rather than in the sense legal scholars have in mind when they talk about "legal realism." For constitutional realism is the opposite of a skeptical position about constitutional law.[50]

IV. Implications

At the outset, I suggested that a second-order theory of the sort sketched here will have both explanatory and normative import. It should, for example, explain disagreement.[51] And by identifying the truth conditions for constitutional judgments, it should bear on our efforts to determine appropriate interpretive norms and the proper content of a constitution. Let me here comment briefly on the explanatory power of the account and then speculate as

---

unlike Dworkin's account of the truth conditions for propositions of law, makes no direct appeal to moral justification. Any moral norms that may bear on the truth or falsity of a constitutional claim do so, I believe, either because a specific constitution includes moral provisions or because they are appropriate to a constitution's function.

[49] For example, it raises questions about whether there is such a thing as a rule of recognition. See (Hart 1961/1994).

[50] I suggested at the outset that an account of constitutional judgments and facts may be suggestive for how to understand legal statements and facts more generally. Just as constitutions may have a function, law may have a function (what it is supposed to do), and different areas of law may have distinct functions. Legal statements and facts might be understood accordingly in terms of the interpretative norms appropriate to these functions.

[51] In addition, I believe a second-order theory should explain such things as the supporting role of scholarly work and commentary when judicial arguments fail to provide an adequate rationale for a court's decisions. See (Post 2001, 1275) and generally, on historical changes in citation of law review articles in judicial opinions.

to a few highly general implications of the foregoing account with respect to appropriate interpretive norms.

A. Explanatory Implications

The account I have offered of constitutional judgments and facts allows us to explain disagreement about constitutional issues. As noted earlier, when parties argue about a constitutional issue, they are disagreeing about the constitutional facts, and so disagreeing about the function of a constitution, or about which interpretive norms are appropriate given the function of a constitution, or about what those norms imply for a given constitutional question.

The account also allows us to explain why debates among constitutional theorists take the shape that they do, why they seem to talk past one another, and why extant first-order constitutional theories are inadequate. Constitutional theorists advocate radically different approaches to constitutional adjudication. As noted earlier, theorists tell us, among other things, that constitutional decision-makers must follow original meaning, or original interpretive methods, or follow a method of common law reasoning, or aim for "coherentist constructivist" outcomes, or engage in a "moral reading" of the Constitution. A plausible explanation of why they advocate such different interpretive norms is that they differ in their views as to the nature and function of a constitution or (as seems most often the case) they have no fully developed view about it and, hence, they differ as to which interpretive norms are appropriate. This disagreement shows up in misleading disputes as to whether our constitution is a "living document" or something more akin to a contract or statute.[52] The inadequacy of extant constitutional theories might plausibly be explained by theorists' failure to grasp the truth conditions for constitutional judgments, and so their failure directly and effectively to confront the tasks they must face in constructing their theories.

B. Appropriate Interpretive Norms

If the account of constitutional judgments and facts that I have offered is correct, then those who wish to develop theories of constitutional adjudication must confront two central tasks. The first is to defend a view about the function of a constitution, and in particular, of the sort of constitution that the theory of adjudication concerns. The second is to defend certain interpretive norms as appropriate to constitutions as thus conceived.[53] Only insofar as a theory accurately captures the function of a constitution and shows certain interpretive norms to be appropriate to a constitution will that theory be capable of adequately guiding constitutional decision-making.

---

[52] Compare, e.g., (Strauss 2010) and (Scalia 1997).

[53] Of course, a great deal has been written about constitutions, and various functions have been attributed to them. But writers seem to frame their remarks in terms of specific constitutions, usually the U.S. Constitution. I have not been able to discover what I would consider to be a fully general analysis of constitutions as a type of normative structure. Partly as a consequence, those who offer theories of constitutional interpretation have not made the sort of effort I envision to connect interpretive norms to what a constitution is.

The second task will involve finding both norms that are appropriate to *any* constitution, given the function(s) constitutions have in common, and norms appropriate to the functions of a particular constitution. Some interpretive norms will be appropriate given the function of a constitution whatever it might turn out to be. Here are two such norms. First, since constitutional judgments make claims about what comports with a particular constitution, they are bound, as already noted, and as theorists from Bork to Dworkin maintain, by existing legal materials. A constitutional judgment must be such that one can rationally claim that enforcement of that judgment has the result of preserving continuity of the law. Constitutional judgments must, accordingly, be supported by an interpretive norm that we might call the *principle of continuity*, which requires a proper connection between past and present constitutional judgments.[54] This is, of course, on the assumption that it is plausible to believe that prior cases were decided correctly. Governmental action that cannot reasonably be seen as following the contours of the BBDs staked out in a constitution cannot be viewed as supported by constitutional materials together with appropriate interpretive norms. This explains the importance of norms such as stare decisis, as well as the importance of preserving a plausible distinction between constitutional adjudication and constitutional change.[55]

Second, since constitutional questions turn not only on extant constitutional materials and interpretive norms, but also on non-constitutional facts, another norm appropriate to the function of a constitution is a *principle of fact-sensitivity*. A theory of constitutional adjudication will fail to produce judgments that correctly track the constitutional facts if they are contrary to well-established non-constitutional facts or depend on ill-supported factual claims. They will involve incorrect application of constitutional norms and so fail to follow the BBDs a constitution effects.

Of course, the principles of continuity and fact-sensitivity have been presented at a high level of generality. It would obviously take more work to transform these principles into clear, interpretive norms. It would be a complex matter, for instance, to spell out the more specific interpretive norms that the principle of fact-sensitivity supports.[56] In our efforts to uncover these more specific norms, we should bear in mind that the principle of fact-sensitivity may have as a corollary that adjudication must allow for the impact of moral learning. A constitution may fall short of morality in all sorts of ways. But the norms advanced by a theory of adjudication must permit constitutional judgments to reflect moral learning consistently with existing constitutional materials, at least by reflecting nonmoral factual learning.[57] This

[54] The principle of continuity should not be confused with originalism. Much more argument would be needed to support an originalist understanding of the principle.

[55] My view, I conjecture, explains why the decisions overturning *Lochner* era cases did not amount to amendment of the Constitution outside of Article V, contra Bruce Ackerman's arguments. See (Ackerman 1991). The view that they did presupposes that the *Lochner* era cases were correctly decided. They were not, and so judicial decisions overturning *Lochner* did not amount to constitutional amendment. This is not yet to deny that amendment can ever take place outside of the Article V procedures.

[56] In a full theory of constitutional adjudication, that principle may sometimes call for so-called "provisional adjudication," so as to permit the experimentation needed to uncover information that can lead to the formulation of more adequate constitutional doctrine. See (Dorf 1998).

[57] I discuss this idea more fully in defending a "moral learning" approach to the Constitution in Rosati (2015).

is, I believe, one element of truth in the cliché that our constitution must be understood as a "living document."

The foregoing considerations suggest further that some norms or provisions may be inappropriate for constitutionalization. Provisions, for instance, that impede the influence of moral learning, or more generally, the influence of nonmoral learning, will be problematic, as will those that tend to generate conflict with other provisions, thereby making it difficult for constitutional judgments to be both well informed and continuous with past judgments.[58] As a general matter, the normativity of constitutions favors consistent provisions that allow for the influence of moral and nonmoral learning. Constitutions that contain unfavored provisions can be adjudged to that degree defective, in that they do less well than they might at being the sort of thing that they are.

V. Conclusion

The account I have offered of constitutional judgments is descriptivist, but we can imagine expressivist alternatives. One might, in Gibbardian fashion propose that to say that X is constitutionally permitted (and so on) is to express one's acceptance of a system of interpretive norms for a constitution that permits X. We can also imagine being forced to an error theory, if there were no fact of the matter about the function of a constitution or about which interpretive norms are appropriate given a constitution's function or about what appropriate interpretive norms entail. I have already explained why I favor a descriptivist and realist approach.

According to the form of constitutional realism I have sketched, constitutional judgments are about certain facts, and constitutional facts are facts about what follows from application to relevant constitutional materials of norms that are appropriate given the function of a constitution. This view enables us to account for our constitutional discourse and disagreement. And by providing us with an understanding of the truth conditions for first-order constitutional judgments, it also enables us to see the kind of inquiry we must undertake in our efforts to construct and defend theories of constitutional interpretation.

I have said just a bit to illustrate how the account might help us to uncover both appropriate interpretive norms and provisions apt for constitutionalization. If this brief speculative portion of this essay is correct, then my account may partly explain the (I believe incorrect) tendency to think that the normativity of constitutions is just a matter of their moral authority. Although I cannot be sure of this, I am inclined to believe that any plausible view about the function of a constitution will rationally favor for constitutionalization norms more likely to fit with fundamental moral principles, whether or not a constitution's function is itself peculiarly moral. For this reason, although constitutions may fall short of what morality would require, where they are not deeply and pervasively deficient as constitutions they nevertheless can make a claim on persons that ordinary rule-governed activities do not make and that resemble the claims of morality.

---

[58] I have in mind provisions such as those in our original constitution preventing Congress from eliminating slavery before the year 1808. See Constitution of the United States, Art. I, Sec. 9, and Art. V.

References

Ackerman, Bruce. 1991. *We the People: Foundations.* Cambridge, MA: Harvard University Press.

Alexander, Larry, and Emily Sherwin. 2008. *Demystifying Legal Reasoning.* Cambridge: Cambridge University Press.

Atkins v. Virginia, 536 U.S. 304 (2002).

Balkin, Jack M. 2011. *Living Originalism.* Cambridge, MA: Harvard University Press.

Barnett, Randy. 2004. *Restoring the Lost Constitution.* Princeton, NJ: Princeton University Press.

Blackburn, Simon. 1984. *Spreading the Word.* Oxford: Clarendon Press.

_____. 1993. *Essays in Quasi-realism.* Oxford: Oxford University Press.

Bobbitt, Philip. 1982. *Constitutional Fate.* New York: Oxford University Press.

Bork, Robert H. 1990. *The Tempting of America: the Political Seduction of the Law.* New York: Simon & Schuster.

Bowers v. Hardwick, 478 U.S. 186 (1986).

Brink, David O. 1989. *Moral Realism and the Foundations of Ethics.* Cambridge: Cambridge University Press.

_____. 1997. "Moral Motivation." *Ethics* 108: 4–32.

Citizens United v. FEC, 558 U.S. 310 (2010).

Coleman, Jules, and Brian Leiter. 1993. "Determinacy, Objectivity, and Authority," 142 *University of Pennsylvania Law Review* 142: 549–637, reprinted in *Law and Interpretation: Essays in Legal Philosophy, edited by* Andrei Marmor (Oxford: Oxford University Press, 1995), pp. 203–278.

Constitution of the United States of America.

Copp, David. 1995. *Morality, Normativity, and Society.* New York: Oxford.

_____. 1997. "Belief, Reason, and Motivation: Michael Smith's *The Moral Problem.*" *Ethics* 10: 33–54.

_____. 2007a. "Introduction." *Morality in a Natural World.* Cambridge: Cambridge University Press, pp 1–30.

_____. 2007b. "Moral Naturalism and Three Grades of Normativity." In *Morality in a Natural World.* Cambridge: Cambridge University Press, pp. 249–283.

Darwall, Stephen L. 1986. *Impartial Reason.* Ithaca, NY: Cornell University Press.

_____. 2003. "How Should Ethics Relate to (the Rest of) Philosophy?: Moore's Legacy." *Southern Journal of Philosophy* 41 (Supplement): 1–20.

_____. 2004. *Welfare and Rational Care.* Princeton, NJ: Princeton University Press.

Dorf, Michael C. 1998. "Foreword: The Limits of Socratic Deliberation." *Harvard Law Review* 112: 4–83.

Dworkin, Ronald. 1977. *Taking Rights Seriously.* Cambridge, MA: Harvard University Press.

_____. 1986. *Law's Empire.* Cambridge, MA: Harvard University Press.

_____. 1996. "The Moral Reading of the Constitution." In *Freedom's Law.* Cambridge, MA: Harvard University Press, pp. 1–38.

Ely, John Hart. 1980. *Democracy and Distrust: A Theory of Judicial Review.* Cambridge, MA: Harvard University Press.

Fallon, Jr., Richard H. 1987. "A Constructivist Coherence Theory of Constitutional Interpretation." *Harvard Law Review* 100: 1189–1286.

_____. 1997. "Foreword: Implementing the Constitution." *Harvard Law Review* 111: 54–152.

_____. 1999. "How to Choose a Constitutional Theory," *California Law Review* 87: 535–579.

Ferguson v. Gies, 82 Mich. 358 (1890).

Finlay, Stephen. 2014. *Confusion of Tongues: A Theory of Normative Language.* Oxford: Oxford University Press.

Finlay, Stephen, and David Plunkett. 2018. "Quasi-expressivism about Statements of Law: A Hartian Theory." In *Oxford Studies in Philosophy of Law*, Vol. 3., edited by John Gardner, Leslie Green, and Brian Leiter. Oxford: Oxford University Press, pp. 49–86.

Frankena, William K. 1942. "Obligation and Value in the Ethics of G.E. Moore." In *The Philosophy of G.E. Moore*, edited by Paul Arthur Schilpp. La Salle, IL: Open Court, pp. 93–110.

Gibbard, Allan. 1990. *Wise Choices, Apt Feelings: A Theory of Normative Discourse.* Cambridge, MA: Harvard University Press.

_____. 2003. *Thinking How to Live.* Cambridge, MA: Harvard University Press.

Greenberg, Mark. 2014. "The Moral Impact Theory of Law." *Yale Law Journal* 123: 1288–1342.

Grutter v. Bollinger, 539 U.S. 306 (2003).

Hart, H. L. A. 1961/1994. *The Concept of Law*, 2nd ed. Oxford: Clarendon Press.

Hunter v. Erickson, 393 U.S. 385 (1969).

Korsgaard, Christine. 1996. *The Sources of Normativity.* Cambridge: Cambridge University Press.

Lyons, David. 1986. "Constitutional Interpretation and Original Meaning." *Social Philosophy & Policy* 4: 75–101.

Mackie, J. L. 1977. *Ethics: Inventing Right and Wrong.* New York: Viking-Penguin.

McGinnis, John O. and Michael B. Rappaport. 2007. "Original Interpretive Principles as the Core of Originalism." *Constitutional Commentary* 24: 371–382.

_____. 2009. "Original Methods Originalism: A New Theory of Interpretation and the Case against Construction." *Northwestern Law Review* 103: 751–802.

Moore, Michael. 1985. "A Natural Law Theory of Interpretation." *Southern California Law Review* 58: 279–398.

_____. 2002. "Legal Reality: A Naturalist Approach to Legal Ontology," *Law and Philosophy* 21: 619–705.

National Federation of Independent Businesses v. Sebelius, 567 U.S.519 (2012).

Obergefell v. Hodges, 576 U.S. ____ (2015).

Planned Parenthood v. Casey, 505 U.S. 833 (1992).

Plessy v. Ferguson, 163 U.S. 537 (1896).

Post, Robert. 2001. "The Supreme Court Opinion as Institutional Practice: Dissent, Legal Scholarship, and Decision-making in the Taft Court," *Minnesota Law Review* 85: 1267–1390.

Powell v. State, 270 Ga. 327 (1998).

Railton, Peter. 1986. "Moral Realism." *Philosophical Review* 95: 163–207.

_____. 1990. "Naturalism and Prescriptivity," *Social Philosophy & Policy* 7: 151–174.

_____. 1992. "Some Questions about the Justification of Morality." *Philosophical Perspectives* 6: 27–53.

_____. 1993. "What the Noncognitivist Helps Us to See the Naturalist Must Help Us to Explain." and "Reply to David Wiggins." In *Reality, Representation, and Projection*, edited by John Haldane and Crispin Wright. New York: Oxford University Press, pp. 279–300 and 315–328.

Rawls, John. 1993. *Political Liberalism.* New York: Columbia University Press.

Raz, Joseph. 1998. "On the Authority and Interpretation of Constitutions: Some Preliminaries." In *Constitutionalism*, edited by Larry Alexander. Cambridge: Cambridge University Press.

_____. 2010. "Reason, Reasons, and Normativity." *Oxford Studies in Metaethics*, Vol. 5. Oxford: Oxford University Press, pp. 5–23.

Roe v. Wade, 410 U.S. 113 (1973).

Romer v. Evans, 116 S. Ct. 1620 (1996).

Rosati, Connie S. 2004. "Some Puzzles about the Objectivity of Law." *Law and Philosophy* 23: 273–323.

_____. 2003. "Ethics, Philosophy, and Moore's Legacy," *Southern Journal of Philosophy* 41, Supplement: 21–29

_____. 2006. "Personal Good," In *Metaethics after Moore*, edited by Terry Horgan and Mark Timmons. Oxford: Oxford University Press, 2006, pp. 107–132.

_____. 2015. "The Moral Reading of Constitutions." In *The Legacy of Ronald Dworkin,* edited by Wil Waluchow and Stefan Sciaraffa. New York: Oxford University Press, pp. 323–352.

_____. 2018. "Mind Dependence." In *Routledge Handbook of Metaethics,* edited by Tristram McPherson and David Plunkett. New York: Routledge, pp. 355–370.

Scalia, Antonin, et. al. 1989. "Originalism: The Lesser Evil." *Cincinnati Law Review* 57: 849–865.

_____. 1997. *A Matter of Interpretation: Federal Courts and the Law.* Princeton, NJ: Princeton University Press.

Schroeder, Mark. 2007. *Slaves of the Passions.* New York: Oxford University Press, 2007.

Smith, Michael. 1994. *The Moral Problem.* Oxford: Basil Blackwell.

_____. 1997. "In Defense of *The Moral Problem*: A Reply to Brink, Copp, and Sayre-McCord." *Ethics* 108: 84–119.

Strauss, David A. 1997. "Common Law Constitutional Interpretation." University of Chicago Law Review 63: 877–935.

_____. 2010. *The Living Constitution.* Oxford. Oxford University Press.

Sunstein, Cass R. 1996. "Foreword: Leaving Things Undecided," *Harvard Law Review* 110: 6–101.

_____. 1999. *One Case at a Time: Judicial Minimalism on the Supreme Court.* Cambridge, MA: Harvard University Press.

Svavarsdottir, Sigrun. 1999. "Moral Cognitivism and Motivation." *Philosophical Review* 108: 161–219.

Toh, Kevin. 2005. "Hart's Expressivism and His Benthamite Project." *Legal Theory* 11: 75–123.

United States v. Windsor, 570 U.S. 744 (2013).

Velleman, J. David. 1996. "The Possibility of Practical Reason." *Ethics* 106: 694–726.

Washington v. Seattle School District No. 1, 458 U.S. 457 (1982).

Wechsler, Herbert. 1959. "Toward Neutral Principles of Constitutional Law," *Harvard Law Review* 73: 1–35.

Index

Dimensions of Normativity. David Plunkett, Scott J. Shapiro, and Kevin Toh.

Printed in the USA/Agawam, MA
November 6, 2019

742060.001